Prentice Hall
LITERATURE
Timeless Voices, Timeless Themes

Formal Assessment

THE AMERICAN EXPERIENCE

Prentice
Hall

Upper Saddle River, New Jersey
Glenview, Illinois
Needham, Massachusetts

Grateful acknowledgment is made to the following for copyrighted material:

Bantam Books
From ARCTIC DREAMS by Barry Lopez. Copyright © 1986 by Barry Holstun Lopez.

Bilingual Press/Editorial Bilingüe
"We Live by What We See at Night" from Trumpets from The Islands of Their Eviction by Martín Espada. Copyright © 1987 by Bilingual Press/Editorial Bilingüe.

Harcourt, Inc.
From A GOOD MAN IS HARD TO FIND by Flannery O'Connor. Copyright © 1953, 1954, © 1955 by Flannery O-Connor, renewed 1981, 1982, 1983 by Regina O'Connor.

HarperCollins Publishers, Inc.
From BLACK BOY by Richard Wright.

The Modern Library
From "Sophistication" from WINESBURG, OHIO, by Sherwood Anderson. Copyright © 1995 by Modern Library.

Penguin Putnam, Inc.
From "Flight" by John Steinbeck from THE PORTABLE STEINBECK, revised, selected and introduced by Pascal Covici, Jr. Copyright © 1971 Viking Penguin, Inc.

The Sun Dial Press
From "The Luck of Roaring Camp" by Bret Harte from SELECTED STORIES OF BRET HARTE. Copyright © 1947 by The Sun Dial Press.

Note: Every effort has been made to locate the copyright owner of material reprinted in this book. Omissions brought to our attention will be corrected in subsequent printings.

ISBN 0-13-058380-4

1 2 3 4 5 6 7 8 9 10   05 04 03 02 01

CONTENTS

UNIT 1: BEGINNINGS (TO 1750)

UNIT 2: A NATION IS BORN (1750–1800)

"The Earth on Turtle's Back" (Onondaga), **"When Grizzlies Walked Upright"** (Modoc), **from** *The Navajo Origin Legend* (Navajo), **from** *The Iroquois Constitution*

Selection Test

Critical Reading

On the line, write the letter of the one best answer.

____ 1. Which of the following is a true statement about a myth?
    a. Myths are usually about everyday people and their daily lives.
    b. All myths attempt to explain the origin of earthly life.
    c. Myths often feature immortal beings.
    d. Myths rarely convey cultural values.

____ 2. "The Earth on Turtle's Back" explains the origin of
    a. the sky.
    b. the sea.
    c. the earth.
    d. the turtle.

____ 3. "The Earth on Turtle's Back" shows the importance the Onondaga placed on
    a. rain.
    b. dreams.
    c. strength in battle.
    d. old age.

____ 4. Which of these sayings expresses a cultural value clearly suggested by "The Earth on Turtle's Back"?
    a. Might makes right.
    b. If you don't succeed, try, try again.
    c. There's no place like home.
    d. The meek shall inherit the earth.

____ 5. The events in "The Earth on Turtle's Back" have the strongest resemblance to the biblical account of
    a. the Garden of Eden.
    b. the Flood.
    c. the building of the pyramids.
    d. the Ten Commandments.

____ 6. In "When Grizzlies Walked Upright," the daughter places herself in a dangerous position because she is
    a. shy.
    b. self-sacrificing.
    c. self-destructive.
    d. curious.

____ 7. In punishing the grizzlies, the Chief of the Sky Spirits shows
    a. compassion.
    b. human qualities.
    c. godlike wisdom.
    d. fairness and objectivity.

____ 8. "When Grizzlies Walked Upright" explains the origins of
   a. human beings.
   b. the earth.
   c. snow.
   d. ice.

____ 9. Recalling what you read about the Modoc in the background before the selections, you can conclude that Mount Shasta probably is
   a. on the East Coast.
   b. in the South.
   c. in the Midwest.
   d. on the West Coast.

____ 10. Another title for this excerpt from *The Navajo Origin Legend* might be
   a. *It Was the Wind That Gave Them Life.*
   b. *Where the Wind Comes From.*
   c. *How the Navajo Used Corn.*
   d. *The Cycle of Nature.*

____ 11. The selection from *The Navajo Origin Legend* shows the origin of
   a. buckskin.
   b. corn.
   c. marriage.
   d. funerals.

____ 12. In the ceremony described in *The Navajo Origin Legend*, the ears of corn are carefully laid out with their heads to the west and their tips to the east. The arrangement of the corn reflects the importance the Navajo placed on
   a. the phases of the moon.
   b. desert mirages.
   c. the prevailing west wind.
   d. the rising and setting sun.

____ 13. What was the main purpose of the Iroquois Constitution?
   a. to explain Iroquois customs
   b. to propose a moral guide
   c. to establish a form of government
   d. to record important events

____ 14. According to the Iroquois Constitution, what must outsiders do in order to become part of the Iroquois Confederation?
   a. accept and obey the Iroquois Constitution
   b. join one of the five Iroquois tribes
   c. make a pledge to the confederate lords
   d. attend a meeting of the confederate council

____ 15. In the Iroquois Constitution, what does the Tree of the Great Peace represent?
   a. strength in battle
   b. the lords' council
   c. the constitution itself
   d. the confederacy of the Five Nations

____ 16. From the opening address required of the confederate lords, it can be assumed that the Iroquois placed a high value on
   a. wealth.
   b. good health.
   c. courage in battle.
   d. the natural world.

Vocabulary and Grammar

On the line, write the letter of the one best answer.

____ 17. Where is a surgeon most likely to perform *ablutions*?
   a. at a sink before the operation
   b. at the operating table during the operation
   c. in the waiting room while talking with the patient's relatives
   d. at his desk in his office

____ 18. Which of the following people behaves with *deliberation*?
   a. a reckless daredevil
   b. a thoughtful judge
   c. an impulsive shopper
   d. a tactless chatterer

____ 19. Which of these sentences is a compound sentence?
   a. At last, with one great effort, he uprooted the tree and placed it on its side.
   b. He swam down and down, far beneath the surface, but could not reach the bottom.
   c. The Duck dove first, and then the Beaver tried.
   d. They brought the Muskrat over to the Great Turtle and placed her paw against his back.

____ 20. Which choice below combines these two sentences into a compound sentence?

   The Sky Chief expected a child. He found a grown woman.

   a. The Sky Chief expected a child, but he found a grown woman.
   b. Although the Sky Chief expected a child, he found a grown woman.
   c. Until he found a grown woman, the Sky Chief expected a child.
   d. The Sky Chief expected a child but found a grown woman.

Essay Questions

21. Virtually all civilizations have produced origin myths to explain natural phenomena. Today we continue to seek explanations for the mysteries of nature, often turning to science and technology for answers. Why do you think human beings in all times and places seek explanations for events beyond human control? What do such explanations, scientific or mythical, offer? Write an essay in which you present your views.

22. The Iroquois Constitution is a highly regarded document that probably influenced American leaders when they drafted the United States Constitution. Write an essay in which you propose reasons why the founding fathers might have been influenced by the Iroquois Constitution. In your essay, discuss the purpose of the Iroquois Constitution and the principles on which it is based.

23. Write an essay in which you compare and contrast "The Earth on Turtle's Back," "When Grizzlies Walked Upright," and the excerpt from *The Navajo Origin Legend*. Discuss what each myth reveals about the customs, attitudes, and beliefs of the tribe that created it, and then compare and contrast the customs, attitudes, and beliefs of the three tribes.

"A Journey Through Texas" from *The Journey of Alvar Núñez Cabeza de Vaca*
by Alvar Núñez Cabeza de Vaca
"Boulders Taller Than the Great Tower of Seville" by García López de Cárdenas

Selection Test

Critical Reading

On the line, write the letter of the one best answer.

_____ 1. For which of these reasons did most of the European explorers of the Americas record their experiences?
    a. They were great scholars.
    b. Writing was a way to pass the time during long expeditions.
    c. They wanted to report their experiences to those at home.
    d. They wanted to sell their stories as published works.

_____ 2. How did explorers usually seek to impress readers of their narratives?
    a. by emphasizing the ease of their travels
    b. by describing their day-to-day experiences
    c. by using vivid poetic language
    d. by stressing the difficulties they faced and the discoveries they made

_____ 3. What is the main reason that readers need to be careful in assessing the accuracy of exploration narratives?
    a. What the explorers saw was usually very difficult for them to describe.
    b. The explorers wrote down their experiences years after they took place.
    c. The narratives are very old.
    d. The explorers saw the events through their own perspectives.

_____ 4. In "A Journey Through Texas," what body of water do Cabeza de Vaca and his party encounter?
    a. the Gulf of Mexico   c. the Pacific Ocean
    b. the Atlantic Ocean   d. the Mississippi River

_____ 5. Why are the people "of the cows" not raising maize when the Spanish arrive?
    a. They have given up maize in favor of new crops introduced by the Europeans.
    b. It has not rained for two years, and they have given up planting maize until it rains again.
    c. They have heard of Spanish appropriations and do not want the Spaniards to take their maize.
    d. They have no need of maize because of the abundance of wild crops.

_____ 6. Why do the natives in "A Journey Through Texas" send women with advance messages that the Spanish are coming?
    a. Only women can travel safely among enemy groups.
    b. The women are the only ones available for the journey.
    c. The Spanish fear the men will attack them and demand that only women go.
    d. The women know the terrain better than do the men.

_____ 7. Why are the Spaniards overjoyed to learn that the native peoples they will meet have permanent houses and evidently have ample food stocks?
    a. They will be able to learn more about how the Indians live.
    b. They will be able to secure provisions for their journey.

c. They will be able to bring food to the ill natives they have left behind.

d. They will be able to stay indefinitely in the houses.

___ 8. According to Cabeza de Vaca, why do some of the natives request that the Spanish ask Heaven to send down rain?

a. They feel the Spanish have a special relationship with the heavenly powers.

b. They are desperate for rain and will seek help from any source.

c. They believe that the Spanish secretly have the knowledge to create rain.

d. They are attempting to flatter the Spanish.

___ 9. According to Cabeza de Vaca, why do the native peoples greet the explorers with great ceremonies?

a. To the natives, the Spanish seem like heavenly beings and command great respect.

b. The natives are accustomed to greeting all visitors with lavish ceremonies.

c. The natives place great stock in complicated rituals.

d. The natives hope to make the Spanish allies against their enemies.

___ 10. Which word in this sentence signals a reason: "They replied that they were afraid of losing the crops, since for two successive years it had not rained"?

a. that

b. since

c. for

d. successive

___ 11. Which of the choices below list signal words in the following passage: "One night I went away to sleep out in the field apart from them; but they soon came to where I was, and remained awake all night in great alarm"?

a. one night, out in the field, all night

b. one night, soon, all night, in great alarm

c. one night, but, soon, in great alarm

d. one night, but, soon, all night

___ 12. Which aspect of Cabeza de Vaca's account do you think is the least likely to be factually accurate?

a. the detail about the drought

b. the description of the natives' cooking methods

c. the personal fears he reveals

d. the impression he gives of the natives' awe for the Spanish

___ 13. What was the main purpose of the López de Cárdenas expedition?

a. to explore a river that the natives described to the Spanish

b. to make contact with additional groups of native peoples

c. to explore a geographical wonder

d. to colonize a new area

___ 14. What is the main reason that López de Cárdenas includes such detailed descriptions of the roughness of the terrain?

a. He feels that his ability to overcome the rough terrain will impress those to whom he is reporting.

b. The difficulty of crossing the terrain is totally unexpected.

c. The rough terrain directly affects the purpose of his expedition.

d. He has never encountered such rough terrain before.

___ 15. What relationship does the signal word *as* indicate in this passage: "They returned about four o'clock in the afternoon, *as* they could not reach the bottom"?

a. time

b. reason

c. contrast

d. direction

Vocabulary and Grammar

On the line, write the letter of the one best answer.

_____ 16. What is the meaning of the word root -*mort*-?
    a. death
    b. life
    c. build
    d. strength

_____ 17. Which word below best completes the following sentence?

       I _____ the chief to provide us with guides to show us the best way through the canyon.

    a. dispatched
    b. entreated
    c. subsisted
    d. feigned

_____ 18. Which word below is most nearly the same in meaning as *traversed*?
    a. upset
    b. contacted
    c. reached
    d. crossed

_____ 19. Which sentence below includes a verb in the past perfect tense?
    a. They replied that they were afraid of losing the crops, since for two successive years it had not rained.
    b. They said we should travel up the river toward the north.
    c. As Don Pedro de Tovar had no other commission, he returned from Tusayán and gave his report to the general.
    d. When he reached Tusayán, he was well received and lodged by the natives.

_____ 20. Which of the suggestions below would result in the best use of verb tenses in the following sentence?

       When they marched for twenty days they arrived at gorges of the river.

    a. Substitute *had marched* for *marched* and *had arrived* for *arrived*.
    b. Just substitute *had arrived* for *arrived*.
    c. Just substitute *had marched* for *marched*.
    d. Make no changes in verb tense.

Essay Questions

21. What personal characteristics do you think an explorer must have? Did the Spanish explorers you read about have these characteristics? Write an essay in which you explain what you feel makes a successful explorer and whether you think the Spanish explorers meet your profile. Be sure to include examples from the narratives to support your evaluations.

22. Write an essay comparing and contrasting the two exploration narratives. Which do you feel is the more accurate work in terms of presenting factual information? Which displays more curiosity about the newly encountered terrain and peoples? Which reveals more of the private feelings of the explorer? Be sure to cite details from the selections when you answer these questions.

23. The Spanish depended on the natives they met for the success of their expeditions. Write an essay in which you list the ways the natives helped the Spanish and analyze the relationship between the two groups. Grounding your ideas in details from the selections, make a judgment on how the Spanish treated the natives they encountered, and speculate about how the natives would be treated in the future.

from *The Interesting Narrative of the Life of Olaudah Equiano*
by Olaudah Equiano

Selection Test

Critical Reading

On the line, write the letter of the one best answer.

_____ 1. What experience does this portion of Equiano's slave narrative describe?
a. the loss of African cultural traditions
b. the fight to abolish slavery
c. the observations of a slave merchant
d. the horrors slaves faced on transatlantic voyages

_____ 2. What attitude toward slavery does the narrative most strongly convey?
a. outrage
b. understanding
c. tolerance
d. indifference

_____ 3. Why does Equiano feel that the hardships, some of which he cannot even bear to relate, are "inseparable" from the slave trade?
a. Sailing in those days meant perilous hardships for all who sailed.
b. Because captives will always resist bondage, slave traders will always institute harsh measures to control the slaves.
c. The slave traders know only harsh measures and no other way.
d. Because slavery is a form of commercial enterprise, those who engage in it are invariably greedy and cruel.

_____ 4. What was Equiano's main purpose in writing *The Interesting Narrative*?
a. to entertain readers with dramatic episodes in his life
b. to sway public opinion about slavery
c. to contrast life in Africa and life in Barbados
d. to provide detailed information on 18th-century sea travel

_____ 5. Much of the power of this selection stems from the fact that it is
a. filled with highly poetic imagery and figures of speech.
b. similar in style to an African folk tale.
c. a logical, well-reasoned argument.
d. a personal narrative.

_____ 6. Which of these details expresses the most objective viewpoint?
a. Equiano got seasick when he was on the ship.
b. Looking through the quadrant made Equiano think the world was magic.
c. The cries of slaves saddened Equiano.
d. The flying fish amazed Equiano as they flew across the ship.

_____ 7. The narrator was placed on the deck of the ship because
a. there was no room for him below deck.
b. he was being punished, and the wind and rain were fierce.
c. his captors feared he might die below deck.
d. conditions below deck were unpleasant.

from The Interesting Narrative of the Life of Olaudah Equiano **7**

_____ 8. What happens to the captives who try to get the extra fish the slave traders caught?
   a. They share the fish with the other captives.
   b. They devour the fish instantly.
   c. They are caught and flogged.
   d. They are allowed to cook and eat the fish for supper.

_____ 9. Why are the slaves so frightened on learning they must leave the ship?
   a. They fear they will drown as they leave.
   b. They fear someone will buy them.
   c. They fear someone will not buy them.
   d. They fear they will be eaten.

_____ 10. Which detail most clearly shows that not every sailor on the slave ship was always cruel to the slaves?
   a. the crew's preventing additional suicides after some captives jump overboard
   b. the mariner's giving Equiano the quadrant to look through
   c. the sailors' tossing the extra fish back into the sea
   d. the sailors' treatment of those captives who tried to get the extra fish

_____ 11. Which detail would probably not be important enough to include in a summary of the first paragraph of the selection?
   a. The crowded conditions made the ship unbearable.
   b. Most of the captives were kept below deck.
   c. The captives' chains chaffed their skin.
   d. Disease was rampant aboard the ship.

_____ 12. Often did I think many of the inhabitants of the deep much more happy than myself. I envied them the freedom they enjoyed.

   In this passage, "inhabitants of the deep" refers to
   a. fish and other sea creatures.
   b. the slaves who were below deck.
   c. the slaves who had jumped overboard.
   d. the children who had fallen into the necessary tubs.

_____ 13. Which passage most clearly highlights the cultural differences between the African slaves and those who enslaved them?
   a. "The closeness of the place, and the heat of the climate, . . . almost suffocated us."
   b. "Those of us that were the most active, were in a moment put down under the deck."
   c. "Many a time we were near suffocation from the want of fresh air, which we were often without for whole days together."
   d. "We thought by this, we should be eaten by these ugly men."

_____ 14. If you were summarizing the selection, which statement would you use to express the main idea of the last section?
   a. The traders were overjoyed at reaching Barbados.
   b. The captives were afraid that they would be eaten.
   c. The ship landed, and the captives were sold into slavery.
   d. Old slaves joined the newcomers from Africa to tell them about their fate.

_____ 15. Based on the interests Equiano shows in this selection, if freed from slavery, he would most likely become
   a. an abolitionist or a sailor.
   b. a merchant or a planter.
   c. a professor or an abolitionist.
   d. a slave owner or a slave trader.

Vocabulary and Grammar

On the line, write the letter of the one best answer.

____ 16. What is the meaning of the root -vid-?
  a. to die
  b. to hunt for
  c. to see
  d. to find

____ 17. Which word is closest in meaning to *copious*?
  a. scarce
  b. plentiful
  c. scattered
  d. duplicated

____ 18. Which word is most nearly opposite in meaning to *pacify*?
  a. enrage
  b. appease
  c. ignore
  d. subdue

____ 19. Which sentence below uses a verb in the passive voice?
  a. At last, we came in sight of the island of Barbados.
  b. We were conducted immediately to the merchant's yard.
  c. We were not many days in the merchant's custody.
  d. The buyers rush at once into the yard.

____ 20. Which statement could not describe a sentence containing a verb in the passive voice?
  a. The subject performs the action.
  b. The action is performed on the subject.
  c. The performer of the action is not known.
  d. The performer of the action is not important.

Essay Questions

21. Imagine being enslaved under the harsh conditions described by Equiano. Write a version of the narrative from your own point of view. Based on the information in Equiano's narrative, summarize the shipboard conditions, and then express what you think would be your own reactions.

22. Slave narratives were valuable tools in abolitionists' hands. Based on the details in this selection, explain why Equiano's narrative would have been helpful in the fight to abolish slavery. Cite details from the selection and the effects you think they would have on readers. Also consider how abolitionists might have used some of the details in their arguments against slavery.

23. As the biographical sketch preceding the selection suggests, Olaudah Equiano was truly a remarkable man. Write an essay in which you describe his personality, attitudes, and skills and attributes based on clues in the selection. Cite his own remarks and other details, and then consider the conclusions you can draw about him.

"Diamond Island: Alcatraz" by Darryl Babe Wilson

Critical Reading

On the line, write the letter of the one best answer.

____ 1. Who is the narrator in "Diamond Island: Alcatraz"?
   a. a US army officer
   b. a Native American grandson
   c. a Native American grandfather
   d. a historian

____ 2. Who first recorded the name "Alcatraz"?
   a. a Spanish explorer in the 1700s
   b. a Spanish explorer in the 1800s
   c. an Indian guide in the 1700s
   d. an Indian scribe in the 1400s

____ 3. The Native American name for Alcatraz is *Allisti Ti-Tanin-miji*, (Rock Rainbown) because
   a. it is filled with diamonds.
   b. rainbows always form around the island's peek.
   c. the truth radiated like colored lights from within.
   d. it always rained and made the current surrounding the island violent.

____ 4. How does the author of "Diamond Island: Alcatraz" describe the "old people" he sometimes talks with today?
   a. Mr. Miserable   c. pure savage
   b. domesticated   d. old warriors

____ 5. When was grandfather born?
   a. between 1850 and 1870
   b. in 1775
   c. in 1889
   d. between 1900 and 1920

____ 6. What is the "diamond" located on the island, according to grandfather?
   a. a diamond-shaped rock inscribed with the names of tribal elders
   b. a sparkling, shining piece of jewelry
   c. a thought or a truth
   d. the story of how his people escaped from the island

____ 7 What does the episode with the radio tell the reader about grandfather's character?
   a. He was rich and could squander money.
   b. He was unconcerned with material things.
   c. He was wasteful and careless.
   d. He loved music.

____ 8. What does the sentence reveal about grandfather or his people?

   Grandfather has been within the earth for many snows now.

   a. Grandfather died in winter.
   b. The Indians begin their New Year in winter.
   c. The Indians keep track of time according to the position of the moon.
   d. The Indians keep track of time according to the natural cycle of the seasons.

Vocabulary

____ 9. The word *autonomous* means
   a. cut off from contact with others.
   b. part of a democracy.
   c. gaining momentum.
   d. independent.

____ 10. Which word most nearly describes the meaning of *redolence*?
   a. aroma
   b. blossoming
   c. transcendence
   d. laziness

Essay Questions

11. Passing down stories such as "Diamond Island: Alcatraz" from one generation to the next is one way for Native Americans to "survive as a distinct and autonomous people." Why does Wilson believe that this oral tradition is so important? In an essay explain how Daryle Babe Wilson hopes that the newer generations of Native Americans will be able to preserve their heritage. How does he contribute to the preservation of Native American history?

12. Consider the many details used to emphasize grandfather's age in "Diamond Island: Alcatraz." Write an essay explaining the importance in the text of things that are "old." What details reinforce the sense of age? How do the references to age add significance to grandfather's story as well as to the author's sense of duty in writing down that story?

13. The importance of memory is a key theme of "Diamond Island: Alcatraz." The author suggests that history books often ignore or misrepresent what really happened in the past. How does grandfather's story conflict with the "American propaganda" surrounding the history of Alcatraz? What is the meaning of "history," and what is the importance of memory in maintaining cultural traditions and customs? Besides examples from the text, cite examples of how your life, or the life of someone you know, would be different without a knowledge of the past.

Part Test, Unit 1, Part 1: Meeting of Cultures

Critical Reading

The questions below are based on the following selection.

This passage is from "The journal of Madam KNIGHT" from the book The PRIVATE JOURNAL *kept by Madam KNIGHT on a Journey from Boston to New York in the year 1704. Sarah Kemble Knight was thirty-eight years old when she made this fascinating, dangerous trip along the Eastern coast to help a relative settle an estate. In addition to being an astute businesswoman, Knight was also the reading teacher of Benjamin Franklin.*

Their Diversions in this part of the Country are on Lecture days and Target days mostly: on the former there is Riding from town to town. And on training days The Youth divert themselves by Shooting at the Target, as they call it, (but it very much resembles a pillory,) where he that hits nearest the white has some yards of Red Ribbon presented him which being tied to his hattband, the two ends streaming down his back, he is carried away in Triumph, with great applause, as the winners of the Olympiack Games. They generally marry very young, the males oftener as I am told under twenty than above; they generally make public weddings, and have a way something singular (as they say) in some of them. Just before joining hands the Bridegroom quits the place, who is soon followed by the Bridesmen, and as it were dragged back to duty—being the reverse to the former practice among us, to steal his Bride.

There are great plenty of Oysters all along by the sea side, as far as I Rode in the Colony, and those very good. And they Generally lived very well and comfortably in their families.

On the line, write the letter of the one best answer.

_____   1. Which one of the following is the best summary of the second paragraph?
    a. Families lived comfortably near the coast, where oysters were abundant.
    b. The seaside was home to plenty of oysters.
    c. Families lived well throughout the colonies.
    d. People in families were especially prosperous.

_____   2. Knight's sense of humor emerges in her description of
    a. wedding ceremony customs.
    b. the age at which men are generally married.
    c. the availability of oysters.
    d. the Target days.

_____   3. Which statement contains signal words that help a reader determine the order of events in Knight's account?
    a. "Their Diversions in this part of the Country are on Lecture days and Target days mostly."
    b. "Just before joining hands the Bridegroom quits the place. . . ."
    c. "There are great plenty of Oysters all along by the sea side, as far as I Rode in the Colony, and those very good."
    d. "They generally marry very young. . . ."

_____   4. On the basis of this excerpt from her journal, which of the following best characterizes Madam Knight?
    a. critical
    b. sentimental
    c. fun-loving
    d. observant

_____ 5. Which is the best description of Knight's tone?
    a. sarcastic   c. conversational
    b. religious   d. indifferent

_____ 6. How do people observe "Lecture days"?
    a. bowling   c. riding from town to town
    b. shooting at the Target   d. dancing

_____ 7. What is the reward for shooting the target "nearest the white"?
    a. a new hatband   c. money
    b. a trophy   d. a red ribbon

_____ 8. Which is the *least* likely audience that Knight intended for her journal?
    a. herself   c. the people of New York
    b. the people of Boston   d. the people she met on her journey

_____ 9. In contrast to a historian's account of events, an individual's journal
    a. offers insight into the life of the writer.
    b. is a reliable record of facts.
    c. contains mediocre writing.
    d. is almost always written for publication.

_____ 10. Which one of the following reading strategies would be *least* helpful in trying to understand the second sentence in this selection?
    a. using signal words to determine relationships
    b. breaking down long sentences
    c. summarizing
    d. rereading

Vocabulary and Grammar

Each question below consists of a related pair of words in CAPITAL LETTERS, followed by four other pairs of words. Choose the pair that best expresses a relationship similar to that expressed in the capitalized words.

_____ 11. AFFLICTION : CURE ::
    a. hospitalize : patient
    b. question : answer
    c. sterile : antiseptic
    d. conflict : skirmish

_____ 12. INDICATION : CLUE ::
    a. famous : cautious
    b. concern : sympathy
    c. driver : passenger
    d. investigator : interview

_____ 13. AVARICE : GENEROSITY ::
    a. clamor : tumult
    b. study : learn
    c. tranquillity : agitation
    d. spoke : wheel

_____ 14. ABUNDANCE : SCARCITY ::
    a. relieved : concerned
    b. hiker : trespasser
    c. success : failure
    d. intensity : endurance

_____ 15. FEIGNED : GENUINE ::
   a. admirable : loathsome
   b. copious : plentiful
   c. agriculture : harvest
   d. decent : diplomatic

On the line, write the letter of the one best answer.

_____ 16. Which sentence contains the passive voice?
   a. I envied them the freedom they enjoyed.
   b. I expected every hour to share the fate of my companions.
   c. We were conducted immediately to the merchant's yard.
   d. They put us in separate parcels.

_____ 17. Which sentence contains both an action verb and a linking verb?
   a. They call the island _Colba_.
   b. The melody of the birds was so exquisite that one was never willing to part from the spot, and the flocks of parrots obscured the heavens.
   c. Going round one of these lakes, I saw a snake, which we killed, and I have kept the skin for your Highnesses.
   d. The diversity in the appearance of the feathered tribe from those of our country is extremely curious.

_____ 18. Which is an example of a compound sentence?
   a. After having dispatched a meal, I went ashore.
   b. She dove down and swam and swam.
   c. He carried her home with him, and his wife brought her up with their family of cubs.
   d. A thousand different sorts of trees and their fruit met us with a wonderfully delicious odor.

_____ 19. Which sentence contains a verb in the past perfect tense?
   a. They entreated us not to be angry any longer, because, even if it was their death, they would take us where we chose.
   b. He told us how he had found permanent houses.
   c. We prayed to God our Lord to assist us, and the sick began to get well.
   d. All over the country, where it was known, they became so afraid that it seemed as if the mere sight of us would kill them.

_____ 20. The past perfect tense shows
   a. a past action or condition that began before another past action ended.
   b. an action or condition that began and ended at a given time in the past.
   c. an action or condition that has not ended.
   d. a past action or condition that ended before another past action began.

Essay Questions

21. Journals are a valuable writing form. Write an essay to persuade a reader that he or she should keep a journal. Make reference to passages in the journals of Columbus or Núñez Cabeza de Vaca as you discuss how a journal can be both interesting and important to succeeding generations of readers.

22. Throughout history, myths and legends have provided people with explanations for events and situations that were beyond their understanding or control. Write an essay in which you explain how "The Navajo Origin Legend" or "The Earth on Turtle's Back" serves this function. Describe how each event or situation is explained in the work. Then discuss how successfully you think the selection fulfills its purpose.

23. Most constitutions are written in a straightforward, factual manner. What makes the Iroquois Constitution unlike other constitutions with which you may be familiar? Answer that question in an essay in which you argue for or against the proposition: "The Iroquois Constitution has literary as well as historical value."

24. Because of a writer's involvement with people and events, firsthand historical accounts are apt to be highly subjective. Write an essay in which you examine the ways in which Christopher Columbus, Alvar Núñez Cabeza de Vaca, or Olaudah Equiano display subjectivity in recording history.

25. Religion was an integral part of the way of life of Native American peoples. Using examples from selections by Onondaga, Modoc, Navajo, and Iroquois writers, write an essay in which you analyze how religious beliefs helped shape the way early Native Americans understood (and behaved in) the world.

from *Journal of the First Voyage to America* by Christopher Columbus

Selection Test

Critical Reading

On the line, write the letter of the one best answer.

____ 1. What is the main reason that Columbus kept this journal?
    a. to pinpoint exact locations for future mapmakers
    b. to describe the expedition to his patrons
    c. to convince Ferdinand and Isabella that he had found Asia
    d. to convince others of the validity of Spain's claims in the New World

____ 2. Columbus's journal helped his readers share his experiences by
    a. comparing his findings with familiar sights in Spain.
    b. estimating the value of each object he came across.
    c. embellishing his prose with highly poetic imagery and figurative language.
    d. identifying by name the places he had actually visited.

____ 3. What was the first thing Columbus did after going ashore?
    a. He set out to explore the country.
    b. He attempted to find the inhabitants.
    c. He searched through the abandoned houses.
    d. He set fire to the native dwellings.

____ 4. According to the journal, how did Columbus gain the confidence of the island's natives?
    a. by overpowering them with weapons
    b. by showing respect for their homes and belongings
    c. by asking their advice about where to find gold
    d. by seeking to meet with their leader

____ 5. Which of these passages most clearly shows that Columbus was writing for an audience he sought to impress?
    a. "We had no doubt that the people had fled in terror at our approach, as the house was completely furnished."
    b. "A thousand different sorts of trees, with their fruit were to be met with, and of a wonderfully delicious odor."
    c. "While we were in search of some good water we came upon a village of the natives about half a league from the place where the ships lay."
    d. "It is my wish to fill all the water casks of the ships at this place, which being executed, I shall depart immediately."

____ 6. Why does Columbus take specimens of plants he comes across?
    a. He may need them on his return voyage.
    b. He wants to bring unknown plants back to Europe in order to judge their value.
    c. He is bent on robbing the natives of anything of value.
    d. He needs them as proof that he visited the lands he is describing.

_____ 7. Why does Columbus go to special pains to mention gold in the last part of
the excerpt?
a. He receives definite information on stores of gold on the island.
b. He knows that his patrons are interested only in gold.
c. The acquiring of riches is one of the main aims of his voyage.
d. The natives he encounters have great stores of gold.

_____ 8. Which of these reasons does *not* help explain why journals can be unreliable?
a. The writer may be writing to persuade an audience.
b. The writer's impressions color the telling of events.
c. It is a record of personal reactions.
d. It provides details that can only be supplied by an eyewitness.

_____ 9. What conclusion can be drawn from Columbus's determination to take ten quintals
of aloe back with him?
a. He was determined to find valuable items of any kind.
b. Aloe was treasured in Europe.
c. His ships were too small to hold much cargo.
d. Aloe is delightfully fragrant.

_____ 10. What best describes Columbus's purpose for writing?
a. to amuse his friends and family with his stories
b. to persuade Queen Isabella and King Ferdinand that his exploration was worth
the money
c. to pay homage to the Pope
d. to convince the natives that he was friendly

_____ 11. Which adjectives best describe Columbus's attitude as revealed in the journal?
a. cruel and tyrannical
b. bored and greedy
c. informative and acquisitive
d. disappointed and unemotional

_____ 12. Why did Columbus give the natives hawk's bells and glass beads?
a. because the natives demanded payment for their services
b. because he wanted to flatter them before he tried to conquer them
c. to get information about the gold
d. to show them that he was friendly and wouldn't hurt them

_____ 13. When Columbus visits Guisay, what is his intent?
a. to deliver letters from the King and Queen and to receive an answer
b. to demand gold and other treasures
c. to buy herbs and spices
d. to bring back a large snakeskin

_____ 14. Columbus comments on the shipping activity in other ports he plans to visit. Why do
you think he mentions it?
a. He wants to go on an exploration with people on those ships.
b. He hopes to meet up with some old friends.
c. He is making it clear that this area of the world is an important place to explore.
d. He is trying to show that there is too much activity there already, and he should
stop his exploration.

_____ 15. What impression of the Americas does Columbus seem to be trying to convey?
   a. that the Americas are fully inhabited and shouldn't be further explored
   b. that the Americas are a fertile land, ready to be explored
   c. that the Americas should only be appreciated for their beauty
   d. that the natives of the Americas are hostile and should be left alone

Vocabulary and Grammar

On the line, write the letter of the one best answer.

_____ 16. Identify the sentence in which a linking verb is used.
   a. Columbus arrived at the cape of the island at 10 o'clock.
   b. At one of the lakes, he saw a snake.
   c. The scenery looked very green, like Andalusia in spring.
   d. Afterward Columbus set sail for another large island.

_____ 17. What is the meaning of the root -flict-?
   a. to bend   c. to argue
   b. to strike   d. to separate

_____ 18. Which word is closest in meaning to exquisite?
   a. difficult   c. fine
   b. complicated   d. good

_____ 19. Which word is most nearly opposite in meaning to abundance?
   a. scarcity   c. necessary
   b. plenty   d. moderation

_____ 20. Which of these parts of speech might immediately follow an action verb in a sentence?
   a. a noun that renames the subject of the sentence
   b. a pronoun that renames the subject of the sentence
   c. an adjective that describes the subject of the sentence
   d. an adverb describing the action verb

Essay Questions

21. Columbus never recognized that he had failed to reach his destination of Asia. What do you think his response would have been had he known? Write an essay in which you describe what you think Columbus's feelings would have been.

22. How different do you think Columbus's journal would have been if he had written it only for personal use and not for an audience of royal patrons? In a brief essay, consider the way in which the journal would have been different had it been strictly a private record. Discuss general differences as well as specific differences in the selection you just read, and explain the reasons for the differences.

23. The record tells us that subsequent interaction between Europeans and Native Americans was not a happy episode in the history of human affairs. Write an essay in which you describe the first interaction between Europeans and Native Americans, based on this journal excerpt. Then speculate about the different view a native might have taken of the same experiences that Columbus describes. Finally, consider if there are any indications in the journal that future relations between Europeans and natives would not continue on the same footing as Columbus describes.

from _The General History of Virginia_ by John Smith
from _Of Plymouth Plantation_ by William Bradford

Selection Test

Critical Reading

On the line, write the letter of the one best answer.

_____ 1. In the excerpt from _The General History of Virginia_, John Smith hopes to encourage other English men and women to come to the New World by showing them
a. the joys and difficulties of the voyage.
b. the means by which the settlers overcame hardships.
c. the customs of the Native Americans.
d. the beauty of the New World.

_____ 2. Which of these conditions does Smith show to be a major cause of the Jamestown settlers' difficulties?
a. The Native Americans refused to sell them food.
b. Trade between England and the New World was slow.
c. The voyage from England took much longer than expected.
d. The settlers were under constant attack from Native Americans.

_____ 3. Through his language, Smith conveys the idea that the new President is
a. energetic.
b. brave.
c. tyrannical.
d. weak.

_____ 4. Which adjective best describes Smith's impression of the Native Americans?
a. childlike
b. uncivilized
c. devout
d. benevolent

_____ 5. According to Smith's account, why do his captors spare his life after slaying his men?
a. They are in awe of his apparent power.
b. They need his help to defend their tribe.
c. They want him to join their tribe.
d. They fear retaliation.

_____ 6. Why do you think that Smith wrote much of the selection in the third person?
a. to make the account seem more objective
b. so that he could reveal other people's thoughts and experiences
c. to show Christian humility
d. to avoid boasting about his exploits

_____ 7. In which of these passages does Smith most clearly use subjective language?
a. "Some, no better than they should be, had plotted with the President."
b. "But when they departed, there remained neither tavern, beer house, nor place of relief."
c. "We were all ignorant and supposing to make our passage in two months."
d. "So to Jamestown with twelve guides Powhatan sent him."

____ 8. If *The General History of Virginia* had been written by another settler, the most likely difference would be
   a. the attitude expressed toward Native Americans.
   b. the explanation of the food shortage.
   c. the portrayal of Smith's personality and role.
   d. the description of the settlement after the sailors' departure.

____ 9. Read this sentence:

> Then finding the Captain, as is said, that used the savage that was his guide as his shield (three of them being slain and divers others so galled), all the rest would not come near him."

If you were breaking down the sentence and underlining only essential information, which of these portions would you underline?
   a. Then finding the Captain, as is said
   b. three of them being slain
   c. divers others so galled
   d. all the rest would not come near him

____ 10. Which description best conveys Bradford's attitude in this selection from *Of Plymouth Plantation*?
   a. despair at the endless suffering of his people
   b. faith in the workings of Divine Providence
   c. tolerance for the weaknesses of others
   d. suspicion of all those who are not Pilgrims

____ 11. In the selection from *Of Plymouth Plantation*, to what does the subheading "The Starving Time" refer?
   a. the period the Pilgrims spent in Holland before journeying to America
   b. the Pilgrims' transatlantic crossing
   c. the days spent sailing from Cape Cod to Hudson's River, seeking a landing site
   d. the Pilgrim's first winter in the New World, especially January and February

____ 12. In calling Squanto "a special instrument sent of God," Bradford demonstrates his personal conviction that
   a. Squanto will become a convert to Christianity.
   b. the Pilgrims would have survived without Squanto.
   c. it is important to forgive one's enemies.
   d. the Pilgrims had God on their side.

____ 13. In Bradford's account, the settlers' attitude toward the Native Americans changes from
   a. respectful to disparaging.   c. indifferent to cautious.
   b. friendly to antagonistic.   d. suspicious to appreciative.

____ 14. The incidents Bradford describes are most strongly connected with Americans' celebration of
   a. Labor Day.   c. Christmas Day.
   b. Thanksgiving Day.   d. Independence Day (July 4th).

____ 15. Break down the sentences in the following passage:

> "And of these, in the time of most distress, there was but six or seven sound persons who to their great commendations, be it spoken, spared no pains night or day, but with abundance of toil and hazard of their own health, fetched them wood, made them fires, dressed them meat, made their beds, washed their loathsome clothes, clothed and unclothed them."

Which of the following statements best expresses the passage's main idea?
a. Six or seven people risked their own health to tend the sick.
b. Six or seven people should receive great commendations.
c. Six or seven people worked very hard and risked their health.
d. Six or seven people washed the clothes of the sick.

____ 16. Which of the following were Bradford's chief purposes in writing *Of Plymouth Plantation*?

I. to record the Pilgrims' experiences in the New World

II. to encourage other Europeans to come to the New World

III. to express faith in the workings of Divine Providence

IV. to publish an interesting account and raise money for the Pilgrims

a. I and II
b. II and III
c. I and III
d. I, III, and IV

Vocabulary and Grammar

On the line, write the letter of the one best answer.

____ 17. Which word is most nearly the same in meaning as *reluctant*?
a. sundry
b. loath
c. pilfer
d. palisades

____ 18. Which word is most nearly opposite in meaning to *mollified*?
a. ignored
b. calmed
c. soothed
d. aggravated

____ 19. Which sentence contains an error in its use of possessive noun forms?
a. The twelve guide's weapons did not impress Captain Smith.
b. Most of the people did not accept the President's decision.
c. The grain had been in the ship's hold for twenty-six weeks.
d. The head of the tribe was Pocahontas's father.

____ 20. Which sentence contains no errors in its use of possessive noun forms?
a. All the colonists' fears seemed to be coming true.
b. In three month's time, half of the company died.
c. The natives' met with the settlers.
c. Among their gifts to the natives were childrens' toys.

Essay Questions

21. Because of the writer's involvement in the experiences he or she reports, firsthand historical accounts are likely to be more subjective than secondhand accounts by historians. Write an essay in which you examine the ways in which John Smith displays his subjectivity in recounting events in the selection from *The General History of Virginia*.

22. Firsthand historical accounts from colonial America can provide a valuable record of the lives of the early settlers. Write an essay in which you discuss the value of Bradford's account in *Of Plymouth Plantation*. Be sure to cite details from the selection to support your general observations and conclusions.

23. At one point in his narrative, John Smith makes the claim that "everything of worth is found full of difficulties." Write an essay in which you explain what you think Smith means by this statement. Then go on to explain how the statement applies to both the Jamestown colonists and the Pilgrims. Finally, offer your own opinion about Smith's idea, and explain why you feel as you do.

from *The Right Stuff* by Tom Wolfe

Critical Reading

On the line, write the letter of the one best answer.

_____ 1. What happens to Glenn's ship as it burns up most of its fuel?
   a. It begins to glide along smoothly and slowly.
   b. It becomes very light and begins to flex.
   c. It begins to lose altitude.
   d. It becomes weightless and begins to float in space.

_____ 2. When does Glenn feel as though he has passed "through the gate"?
   a. when the door of his capsule is shut and he knows there is no turning back
   b. when the rocket engines are lit and the ship begins liftoff
   c. when the capsule is thrown free of the rocket shaft and settles into orbit
   d. when he safely returns to earth

_____ 3. Why does Glenn "barely notice" the g-forces pushing upon him during liftoff?
   a. The g-forces were not very strong.
   b. He had experienced the same g-forces many times during training.
   c. He is too nervous worrying about the vibrations of the ship.
   d. He is concentrating too hard on making sure all the needles and switches are in the right place.

_____ 4. What is the "code of the fighter jock" that Glenn is hesitant to break during the mission?
   a. to describe everything he sees over the radio
   b. to never give in to emotion
   c. to spin the capsule like a jet fighter
   d. to maintain radio silence

_____ 5. Who are Shepard and Grissom?
   a. astronauts who preceded Glenn into space
   b. flight instructors who trained Glenn
   c. fellow astronauts whom Glenn was chosen over to conduct the mission
   d. Glenn's dogs, which he thinks about to remain calm

_____ 6. Why does Wolfe's account of Glenn's mission include such detailed descriptions of Glenn's personal reactions?
   a. Wolfe bases his narrative on interviews with Glenn.
   b. Wolfe wants to give the reader the sense of participating in the space flight.
   c. Glenn's personal reactions are so much different than those of other astronauts who have flown into space.
   d. Wolfe had gone into space himself and knew what it was really like to fly in a rocket ship.

_____ 7. What does Wolfe imply through the constant comparisons of Glenn's experiences in flight with his training on the centrifuge?
   a. that Glenn performed better in space than in training
   b. that Glenn should have paid more attention to his training in order to deal more effectively with the reality of space
   c. that Glenn had undergone exhaustive and effective training in preparation for the space mission
   d. that the training had poorly prepared Glenn for the problems he would face in space

Vocabulary

____ 8. An instructor who constantly harasses the astronauts by feeding emergency messages into a flight simulator could be described as
    a. malevolent.
    b. benevolent.
    c. beneficent.
    d. maladroit.

____ 9. Choose the word that best completes the following sentence:
At one point in Glenn's ride, the vibrations of the rocket became so loud that they _____ the roar of the engines.
    a. obliterated
    b. silenced
    c. anticipated
    d. perforated

____ 10. The word *jettisoned* means
    a. launched into space.
    b. blotted out or destroyed.
    c. whipped back and forth in a violent motion.
    d. thrown overboard to lighten the weight of a ship.

Essay Questions

11. Very few people have ever been chosen to journey into space. Recalling Glenn's experience, write an essay describing what "the right stuff" is that astronauts need to perform their missions. Choose details from the passage to illustrate the traits you mention.

12. Wolfe strives to portray Glenn's actions and perceptions as though we were reading Glenn's thoughts. Write an essay explaining the difference between this approach and a more objective, outside perspective. How would the text be different if written according to a more objective approach? Which approach do you think is more effective and/or interesting?

13. The exploration of space has often been compared with the exploration of new lands on Earth. Write an essay speculating about mankind's need to explore. What do you think compels Glenn to make his journey into space? Compare the experiences of the astronauts to those of earlier explorers. Make a judgment on how you feel space exploration has improved life on Earth. What do you think Glenn's answer would be?

Name _____ Date _____

Part Test, Unit 1, Part 2: Focus on Literary Forms—Narrative Accounts

Critical Reading

The questions below are based on the following selection.

The following excerpt is taken from The Narrative of the Expedition of Coronado *by Pedro de Casteñada. General Coronado and his men—including the writer Casteñada—set off to find the fabled Native American city of Quivira, in the southwestern plains. Their guide—a plains Indian named Turk who is cooperating with the Spanish in exchange for their promise of freedom—has intentionally led them far off course into central Texas, where they encounter natives they call the Teyas. Tiguex was a region situated in present-day New Mexico.*

. . . The guides ran away during the first few days and Diego Lopez had to return to the army for guides, bringing orders for the army to return to Tiguex to find food and wait there for the general. The Teyas, as before, willingly furnished him with new guides. The army waited for its messengers and spent a fortnight here, preparing jerked beef to take with them. It was estimated that during this fortnight they killed 500 bulls. The number of these that were there without any cows was something incredible. Many fellows were lost at this time who went out hunting and did not get back to the army for two or three days, wandering about the country as if they were crazy, in one direction or another, not knowing how to get back where they started from, although this ravine extended in either direction so that they could find it. Every night they took account of who was missing, fired guns and blew trumpets and beat drums and built great fires, but yet some of them went off so far and wandered about so much that all this did not give them any help, although it helped others. . . . It is worth noting that the country there is so level that at midday, after one has wandered about in one direction and another in pursuit of game, the only thing to do is to stay near the game quietly until sunset, so as to see where it goes down, and even then they have to be men who are practiced to do it. Those who are not, had to trust themselves to others.

The general followed his guides until he reached Quivira, which took forty-eight days' marching, on account of the great detour they had made toward Florida. He was received peacefully on account of the guides whom he had. They asked the Turk why he had lied and had guided them so far out of their way. He said that his country was in that direction and that, besides this, the people at Cicuye had asked him to lead them off on to the plains and lose them, so that the horses would die when their provisions gave out, and they would be so weak if they ever returned that they would be killed without any trouble, and thus they could take revenge for what had been done to them. . . .

On the line, write the letter of the one best answer.

____ 1. While camped at the ravine waiting for orders, the soldiers
   a. defend themselves against the Teyas.
   b. strike a bargain with Coronado.
   c. return to Tiguex for food and wait there for the general.
   d. kill buffalo and prepare the meat for the coming days.

____ 2. Why did so many soldiers get lost in the plains?
   a. They were under a kind of magic spell.
   b. The land was hilly and mazelike.
   c. The land was flat and devoid of natural landmarks.
   d. They were suffering from heat exhaustion.

_____ 3. This selection is an example of
   a. recent historical scholarship
   b. a firsthand account of historical events.
   c. a fictionalized account of historical events.
   d. a secondhand account of historical events.

_____ 4. Breaking down sentences is a useful strategy for understanding
   a. figurative language.
   b. complex sentences.
   c. sentences containing one or more challenging vocabulary words.
   d. plain language.

_____ 5. Why did Coronado's soldiers build great fires?
   a. to warn away enemies
   b. to guide missing soldiers back to camp
   c. to frighten buffalo
   d. to cheer themselves up

_____ 6. Why was it especially disorienting to hunt game on the southwestern plains at midday?
   a. It was unbearably hot.
   b. Horses became confused and alarmed.
   c. There was no way to tell direction.
   d. The ravines dried up.

_____ 7. Most historical narratives are
   a. intended for an audience of scholars.
   b. intended for an audience of just the writer.
   c. intended for a general audience.
   d. not intended for publication.

_____ 8. The first step in breaking down a long or confusing sentence is
   a. to identify the speaker.
   b. to figure out the subject.
   c. to determine what the sentence is saying about the subject.
   d. to rearrange the parts of the sentence.

_____ 9. Who was responsible for the army's journey taking forty-eight days?
   a. Turk
   b. General Coronado
   c. Diego Lopez
   d. the Teyas

_____ 10. The attitude of the people at Cicuye toward Coronado might best be described as _____.
   a. hostile
   b. diplomatic
   c. receptive
   d. cautious

Vocabulary and Grammar

On the line, write the letter of the one best answer.

_____ 11. The best synonym for *mollified* is _____.
   a. imperiled
   b. soothed
   c. worshiped
   d. wounded

_____ 12. Which word could be substituted for *sundry* without changing the meaning of the sentence?

> We wished mightily for *sundry* items we had left behind in England.

   a. various
   b. tawdry
   c. expensive
   d. useful

_____ 13. Which of the following might represent *recompense* for doing a good deed?
   a. volunteer work
   b. a heartfelt thank-you
   c. an angry look
   d. a business transaction

_____ 14. Which sentence contains an error involving a possessive noun?
   a. Such actions have ever since the world's beginning been subject to such accidents.
   b. He showed Rawhunt, Powhatan's trusty servant, two demiculverins and a millstone.
   c. Pocahontas was the kings' dearest daughter.
   d. They thought themselves happy to get out of those dangers before night overtook them, as by God's good providence they did.

_____ 15. Which contains the correct form of a plural possessive noun?
   a. four or five week's time
   b. four or five weeks' time
   c. four or five weeks time
   d. four or five's weeks time

Essay Questions

16. First-person accounts of life in "the new world" have provided several generations of Americans with vivid portraits of early European settlers' lives. Choose one of the two journal excerpts you read in Part 2 and write an essay in which you describe the experiences of those settlers as presented by John Smith or William Bradford. What was life like for the first residents of Jamestown or Plymouth Plantation?

17. John Smith and William Bradford were very different personalities, yet both had what it took to survive in the American wilderness. In an essay, describe the personal qualities you feel were necessary to survive and prosper in such perilous conditions. Use the actions and attitudes of Smith and Bradford to illustrate your points.

18. Many accounts of life in seventeenth-century America, including Smith's *General History of Virginia* and Bradford's *Of Plymouth Plantation*, offer glimpses of the European settlers' views of the Native Americans they encountered. Write an essay in which you discuss the attitudes toward Native Americans expressed in these two works. How do Smith and Bradford differ in their approach to Native American relations? Support your ideas with details from the selections.

"To My Dear and Loving Husband" by Anne Bradstreet

"Huswifery" by Edward Taylor

Selection Test

Critical Reading

On the line, write the letter of the one best answer.

_____ 1. The speaker of "To My Dear and Loving Husband" addresses
   a. her husband.
   b. herself.
   c. the Puritan leadership council.
   d. the Lord.

_____ 2. The central idea of "To My Dear and Loving Husband" is that
   a. other women cannot possibly be as happy as the speaker.
   b. the speaker loves her husband more than she loves God.
   c. heaven will repay the speaker's loving husband with eternal life.
   d. the love the speaker shares with her husband is deep and lasting.

_____ 3. Since his love is too great for her to repay, the speaker wishes that
   a. her husband acquire mines of gold.
   b. her husband experience the riches of the East.
   c. the heavens reward her husband.
   d. she could learn to love her husband as much as he loves her.

_____ 4. What chief emotions does the speaker in Bradstreet's poem express?
   a. respect and admiration for her husband
   b. concern and anxiety about the permanence of her marriage
   c. love for and happiness with her husband
   d. fear of death

_____ 5. The lines "If ever two were one, then surely we./If ever man were lov'd by wife, then thee" illustrate the Puritan Plain Style because they
   a. rhyme.
   b. make references to everyday objects.
   c. use simple, common words.
   d. focus on the love between a man and a woman.

_____ 6. Which statement below is the best paraphrase of the following lines?

   If ever wife was happy in a man,
   Compare with me ye women if you can.

   a. If ever a wife brought happiness to her man, then I do.
   b. Compared to all other wives, I am the best.
   c. If another woman were married to my husband, she would not be as happy.
   d. No woman could be happier with her husband than I am.

_____ 7. The speaker in "Huswifery" addresses
   a. a housewife.
   b. housework.
   c. a spinning wheel, a loom, and the fabric produced on them.
   d. the Lord.

_____ 8. Around what task or tasks does "Huswifery" center?
    a. spinning and weaving
    b. getting dressed
    c. all the tasks of housekeeping
    d. dyeing cloth

_____ 9. The central idea of "Huswifery" expresses the speaker's desire to
    a. become godlike.
    b. have beautiful clothes.
    c. receive God's grace.
    d. find a heavenly reward here on earth.

_____ 10. In "Huswifery," what is Taylor's most likely reason for using vivid and elaborate images not typical of the Puritan Plain Style?
    a. He wants his poetry to reflect his elegant lifestyle.
    b. He wants his words to shine with God's glory.
    c. He believes that poets should dazzle their audiences.
    d. He wants to be different from other writers of his time and place.

_____ 11. In his first stanza, Taylor develops his elaborate metaphor by
    a. creating an image of God as an eternal spool of thread.
    b. comparing parts of his being with parts of a spinning wheel.
    c. addressing his spinning wheel as if it could supply him with God's glory.
    d. drawing parallels between God and a spinning wheel.

_____ 12. When the speaker says "Then clothe therewith mine understanding, will, / Affections, judgment, conscience, memory / My words, and actions," he is
    a. asking God to guide his thoughts, words, and deeds.
    b. requesting that God hide him from the rest of the world.
    c. confessing that he does not always follow God's rules.
    d. reminding God that he needs help understanding his own faith.

_____ 13. What does the apparel at the end of "Huswifery" stand for?
    a. the poet's soul
    b. Paradise
    c. the poet's body
    d. God's grace

_____ 14. To paraphrase either poem, which would you do first?
    a. Rewrite the poem in your own words.
    b. Read the information in the footnotes.
    c. Find the subject of each sentence.
    d. Analyze the metaphors in the poem.

_____ 15. Which of these details is the best example of the references to everyday objects typical of the Puritan Plain Style?
    a. the whole mines of gold "To My Dear and Loving Husband"
    b. the riches of the East in "To My Dear and Loving Husband"
    c. the Lord's ordinances in "Huswifery"
    d. the spinning wheel in "Huswifery"

Vocabulary and Grammar

On the line, write the letter of the one best answer.

_____ 16. What kind of increase does the word *manifold* describe?
    a. a modest increase   c. a large increase
    b. a gradual increase   d. a tiny increase

_____ 17. Which word below is closest in meaning to *recompense*?
   a. payment
   b. leisure
   c. praise
   d. rethink

_____ 18. Which word below is most nearly opposite in meaning to *persevere*?
   a. labor
   b. dawdle
   c. continue
   d. join

_____ 19. Which line below contains an example of direct address?
   a. "If ever two were one, then surely we"
   b. "Thy holy word my distaff make for me"
   c. "And make Thy holy spirit, Lord, wind quills"
   d. "My words, and actions, that their shine may fill"

_____ 20. Which of the following sentences is correctly punctuated?
   a. Cousin did you listen to the sermon?
   b. Thank you, dear wife, for such a lovely thought.
   c. Did someone ask, Edwin Taylor, to read his poem "Huswifery"?
   d. Please read the poem again brother.

Essay Questions

21. The attitudes and beliefs of the Puritans are reflected in both the form and content of their writings. Write an essay in which you discuss the ways in which Puritan ideas are expressed in "To My Dear and Loving Husband." Citing details, explore not only the content of Bradstreet's poem, but also its form and the style in which it is written.

22. In his poetry, Edward Taylor often used conceits: elaborate and unusual comparisons between two startlingly different things. Write an essay in which you analyze Taylor's use of the conceit in "Huswifery." Discuss the overall comparison that he makes as well as the point-by-point comparisons that he provides. Also evaluate the effectiveness of the conceit. Do you find the comparison too startling, or does he make it "work" for you?

23. The two poems are products of a particular age. However, even though the concerns of the poems are distinctly Puritan, one could make the argument that the ideas expressed are universal. Might the poems—and the Puritan Plain Style—still be relevant today? Write an essay in which you explore this idea.

from *Sinners in the Hands of an Angry God* by Jonathan Edwards

Selection Test

Critical Reading

On the line, write the letter of the one best answer.

_____ 1. As a preacher, Edwards uses his sermon to
   a. raise money for his church.
   b. frighten his congregation into seizing the opportunity of salvation.
   c. persuade his congregation to have faith in God.
   d. rouse his congregation to revolt against England.

_____ 2. What is the central message of the sermon?
   a. There is no hope for salvation.
   b. The only hope for salvation is in good deeds.
   c. The only hope for salvation is through Christian rebirth.
   d. Sinners can save their souls through constant prayer.

_____ 3. Edwards's vivid descriptions of Hell are meant to
   a. frighten his audience.
   b. amuse his audience.
   c. fascinate his audience.
   d. make his audience feel superior.

_____ 4. Which of these people or forces does the sermon indicate is the most powerful?
   a. Hell
   b. God
   c. the congregations as a whole
   d. preachers like Edwards

_____ 5. Edwards assumes that the members of his congregation believe that they are
   a. righteous.
   b. aristocratic.
   c. sinful.
   d. immortal.

_____ 6. What contrasting images does Edwards use to describe God's wrath?
   a. heat and cold
   b. sunlight and rain
   c. darkness and light
   d. fire and water

_____ 7. Edwards uses the phrase "dead in sin" to describe
   a. people who have died while in the midst of evil activities.
   b. those who have not yet experienced the grace of conversion.
   c. those whose sins have caused their deaths.
   d. people who are not religious and never attend church.

_____ 8. Edwards compares each of his listeners to "a spider, or some loathsome insect [held] over the fire" in order to stress a human being's
   a. powerlessness in comparison to God.
   b. unimportance in God's plan.
   c. ugliness in God's eyes.
   d. courage in the face of God's wrath.

_____ 9. Toward the end of the sermon, Edwards's tone shifts from
   a. sorrowful to joyous.
   b. joyous to resentful.
   c. frightening to hopeful.
   d. sympathetic to bitter.

_____ 10. According to the final paragraphs, sinners may be able to obtain
   a. salvation.
   b. retribution.
   c. Edwards's forgiveness.
   d. consolation.

_____ 11. To which chief emotion does Edwards appeal in the following passage of the sermon?

   > How awful is it to be left behind at such a day! To see so many others feasting,
   > while you are pining and perishing.

   a. grief
   b. envy
   c. sympathy
   d. joy

_____ 12. One popular method of persuasion is the bandwagon technique, which suggests that a person should do something because everyone else is doing it. Which of these passages best illustrates that technique?
   a. "This is the case of every one of you that are out of Christ."
   b. "Those that are gone from being in the like circumstances with you, see that it was so with them; for destruction came suddenly upon most of them."
   c. "Many are daily coming from the east, west, north and south; many that were very lately in the same miserable condition that you are in, are now in a happy state."
   d. "Therefore let everyone that is out of Christ now awake and fly from the wrath to come."

_____ 13. The use of a biblical quotation at the end of the sermon strengthens Edwards's argument by
   a. associating it with an authority respected by his audience.
   b. appealing to the audience's love of poetry.
   c. changing the tone of the sermon.
   d. emphasizing Edwards's point about God's mercy.

_____ 14. Based on the context clues, what does gulf most likely mean in this passage:

   > If God should let you go, you would immediately sink and swiftly descend and
   > plunge into the bottomless gulf.

   a. gasoline or oil
   b. wide gap
   c. shallow water
   d. cloud

_____ 15. Based on the context clues, what does _exquisite_ most likely mean in this passage?

   > There will be no end to this exquisite horrible misery.

   a. very beautiful
   b. mildly attractive
   c. necessary
   d. sharp; intense

Vocabulary and Grammar

On the line, write the letter of the one best answer.

____ 16. What does the prefix *omni-* mean?
- a. all; everywhere
- b. high; atop; above
- c. knowing; wise
- d. powerful

____ 17. Which word is closest in meaning to the word *ineffable*?
- a. inadequate
- b. incomprehensible
- c. inexpressible
- d. inexact

____ 18. Which word is most nearly opposite in meaning to the word *dolorous*?
- a. overjoyed
- b. mournful
- c. generous
- d. contented

____ 19. Which sentence uses a comparative or superlative adjective correctly?
- a. Of all the sermons I've read, Jonathan Edwards's is the more dramatic.
- b. He shows Hell to be more awfuller than I ever pictured it before.
- c. People who deliver the sermon now usually invest it with a great deal of emotion, but Edwards originally gave it in a more calm voice.
- d. Perhaps his quiet tones made the delivery more effective.

____ 20. Identify the set of adjectives below in which the comparative and superlative forms are not correct.
- a. holy, holier, holiest
- b. merciful, mercifuller, mercifullest
- c. pure, purer, purest
- d. miserable, more miserable, most miserable

Essay Questions

21. As you read in the biographical sketch before the selection, Edwards was eventually dismissed from his position because of his views. Using examples from his text, write an essay in which you explain why his congregation may have decided to find a new minister.

22. Edwards uses a variety of persuasive techniques that contribute to the effectiveness of his sermon. Write an essay in which you discuss these persuasive techniques, including his use of repetition and his appeals to emotions and authority. Also explain why Edwards's sermon would probably have been less effective if he had not used these techniques.

23. Edwards had a clear strategy in mind when he wrote this sermon. In your opinion, was his method the best and most effective way to achieve his aim? Write an essay in which you summarize Edwards's goal and how he went about achieving it. Then consider whether there may have been a better way of communicating to his congregation.

Name _____ Date _____

Part Test, Unit 1, Part 3: The Emerging American Identity—
The Puritan Influence

Critical Reading

The questions below are based on the following selection.

In this excerpt from The Wonders of the Invisible World, *Cotton Mather reports on the testimony of Martha Carrier at the Salem witchcraft trials in August 1692. Mather viewed the outbreak of witchcraft as a last-ditch effort by the devil to reclaim the souls of those who had once written their names in his book. Mather used Roman numerals to separate sections of testimony.*

III. Benjamin Abbot gave his testimony that last March was a twelvemonth this Carrier was very angry with him upon laying out some land near her husband's. Her expressions in this anger were that she would stick as close to Abbot as the bark stuck to the tree, and that he should repent of it afore seven years came to an end, so as Doctor Prescot should never cure him. These words were heard by others besides Abbot himself, who also heard her say she would hold his nose as close to the grindstone as ever it was held since his name was Abbot. Presently after this, he was taken with a swelling in his foot, and then with a pain in his side, and exceedingly tormented. It bred into a sore, which was lanced by Doctor Prescot, and several gallons of corruption ran out of it. For six weeks it continued very bad, and then another sore bred in the groin, which was also lanced by Doctor Prescot. Another sore then bred in his groin, which was likewise cut, and put him to very great misery. He was brought unto death's door and so remained until Carrier was taken and carried away by the constable, from which very day he began to mend and so grew better every day and is well ever since.

Sarah Abbot also, his wife, testified that her husband was not only all this while afflicted in his body, but also that strange, extraordinary, and unaccountable calamities befell his cattle, their death being such as they could guess at no natural reason for.

IV. Allin Toothaker testified that Richard, the son of Martha Carrier, having some difference with him, pulled him down by the hair of the head. When he rose again he was going to strike at Richard Carrier but fell down flat on his back to the ground and had not power to stir hand or foot until he told Carrier he yielded, and then he saw the shape of Martha Carrier go off his breast.

On the line, write the letter of the one best answer.

_____ 1. Which one of the following is not a good paraphrase of the second paragraph?
   a. Sarah Abbot testifies that her husband's cattle were stricken with weird ailments.
   b. Sarah Abbot testifies about her husband's cattle.
   c. Abbot's wife swears that livestock fell ill and died for no apparent reason.
   d. Abbot's cattle suffer unexplainable sickness, according to his wife.

_____ 2. Benjamin Abbot claims that Martha Carrier cast a spell on him
   a. after moving away.
   b. after he had worked some land near her husband's.
   c. before he developed a bad cough.
   d. when he testified against her.

_____ 3. According to Abbot's testimony, how long was Carrier angry with him?
   a. one year   c. three weeks
   b. eight months   d. over a year

_____ 4. Which one of the following elements is not characteristic of the Puritan Plain Style?
   a. metaphors   c. short words
   b. direct statements   d. references to everyday objects

____ 5. In describing the curse that he says Carrier placed on him, Abbot lists all but which of the following symptoms?
   a. headache
   b. swelling in the foot
   c. pain in the side
   d. sores

____ 6. Abbot's symptoms did not disappear until
   a. Dr. Prescot lanced the sores.
   b. Abbot took pills prescribed by Dr. Prescot.
   c. Martha Carrier was arrested.
   d. Abbot applied ointment to the sores.

____ 7. What detail in Abbot's description of his physical ailments is clearly exaggerated?
   a. a swelling in his foot
   b. another sore bred in the groin
   c. a pain in his side
   d. a sore excreting "several gallons of corruption"

____ 8. The Puritans believed that poetry
   a. was the work of the devil.
   b. was the only appropriate outlet for emotions.
   c. should serve God by clearly expressing only useful or religious ideas.
   d. should celebrate the beauty of the natural world.

____ 9. Using context clues can help you determine that the word *expressions* in the selection's second sentence means _____.
   a. facial movements
   b. words
   c. emotions
   d. greetings

____ 10. Which one of the following is not an accurate interpretation of the selection's final sentence?
   a. Martha Carrier was involved in her son's attack on Allin Toothaker.
   b. Martha and Richard Carrier are often mistaken for one another.
   c. Martha Carrier helped her son immobilize Allin Toothaker.
   d. Richard Carrier benefited from his mother's supernatural powers when he assaulted Allin Toothaker.

Vocabulary and Grammar

On the line, write the letter of the one best answer.

____ 11. In the following sentence, the best antonym for the italicized word is _____.

   In the face of incredible hardships, the settlers did their best to *persevere*.

   a. discontinue
   b. keep on
   c. begin
   d. persist

____ 12. When Jonathan Edwards speaks of the *ineffable* torment sinners will undergo, he means that their suffering will be _____.
   a. mundane
   b. inexpressible
   c. private
   d. languorous

_____ 13. Which phrase contains a modifier that is not in the positive form?
   a. higher judgment
   b. mighty authority
   c. constantly changing
   d. undoubtedly suffering

_____ 14. The comparative form of the adjective *hopeless* is _____.
   a. hopelesser
   b. most hopeless
   c. least hopeless
   d. more hopeless

_____ 15. Which contains the correct superlative form of the adverb *directly*?
   a. She expressed her love for her husband *directest* through poetry.
   b. She expressed her love for her husband *more direct* through poetry.
   c. She *more directly* expressed her love for her husband through poetry.
   d. She *most directly* expressed her love for her husband through poetry.

Essay Questions

16. Choose a selection from this part of Unit One and write an essay in which you explain how the work expresses the author's recognition of both a physical and a spiritual world. Use references to the text to support your explanation.

17. In an essay, explain how the title "Huswifery," meaning "housekeeping," contributes to the messages and meanings of Taylor's poem. Discuss whether you think the title is appropriate, and why.

18. Puritan literature in America includes religiously inspired poetry, histories, journals, and sermons. In an essay, discuss possible reasons why this early American literature was limited to these genres. In your essay, consider the Puritan authors' purposes and intended audiences, as well as the historical events that prompted the writing.

Name _____ Date _____

from *The Autobiography* and from *Poor Richard's Almanack*
by Benjamin Franklin

Selection Test

Critical Reading

On the line, write the letter of the one best answer.

_____ 1. How does Franklin begin his project to achieve moral perfection?
   a. He imitates engraved copies.
   b. He buys a speckled ax.
   c. He compiles thirteen virtues.
   d. He avoids trifling conversation.

_____ 2. Which virtue is most difficult for Franklin to master?
   a. industry   c. sincerity
   b. order   d. temperance

_____ 3. Why does Franklin devote a week to each of the virtues?
   a. He thinks if he can strengthen one virtue through strict attention, he can retain that strength when he works on the rest.
   b. He is afraid he cannot concentrate on more than one virtue at a time.
   c. He feels that total mastery of one virtue will bring more happiness than incomplete mastery of all virtues.
   d. The teachings of Pythagoras and Socrates state that one week is all that is necessary to master a new moral habit.

_____ 4. When Franklin first devised his project to attain moral perfection, he thought it would be difficult but possible to become perfect. What quality does this suggest that Franklin possessed?
   a. self-confidence   c. sincerity
   b. pessimism   d. common sense

_____ 5. The list of virtues that Franklin draws up suggests that he was
   a. distracted and preoccupied.
   b. logical and orderly.
   c. impulsive and unpredictable.
   d. cynical and mistrustful.

_____ 6. Which of these statements best summarizes Franklin's philosophy at the end of the selection?
   a. Anything less than perfection is not acceptable.
   b. Happiness comes from the consistent application of virtue.
   c. It doesn't matter how hard you try; only results matter.
   d. A life with disorder is an unhappy one.

_____ 7. Which of these sentences most likely came from an autobiography?
   a. "I hope, therefore, that some of my descendants may follow the example and reap the benefit."
   b. "Philadelphia was a city at the heart of America's independence."
   c. "Benjamin Franklin also contributed to public service."
   d. "Almost everyone secretly desires to attain perfection in some field."

© Prentice-Hall, Inc.

____ 8. In comparison to other books about Franklin, *The Autobiography* probably gives you the best insight into
    a. the moral values of the time.
    b. Franklin's inventions.
    c. Franklin's descendants.
    d. Franklin's personality.

____ 9. This work is classified as an autobiography because Franklin is
    a. a famous person.
    b. a famous person who is no longer living.
    c. the subject of the work.
    d. the subject and author of the work.

____ 10. Which of the following statements expresses an opinion?
    a. Franklin wrote an autobiography.
    b. Franklin was a great American.
    c. Franklin writes that he tried to live his life using thirteen virtues.
    d. Franklin admits that he never completely achieved perfection.

____ 11. Which passage needs the most interpretation in order to understand the author's meaning?
    a. "Different writers included more or fewer ideas under the same name."
    b. "I made a little book, in which I allotted a page for each of the virtues."
    c. "A benevolent man should allow a few faults in himself, to keep his friends in countenance."
    d. "I hope, therefore, that some of my descendants may follow the example and reap the benefit."

____ 12. Which of the following details gives the most information about the times in which Franklin lived?
    a. Franklin's desire for perfection
    b. the story of the speckled ax
    c. the references to Socrates and Pythagoras
    d. Franklin's desire to help his descendants

____ 13. What view of human nature is suggested by Franklin's aphorism "Three may keep a secret if two of them are dead"?
    a. Human beings like to gossip.
    b. People are naturally evil.
    c. All people are trustworthy.
    d. The secrets of the dead are impossible to discover.

____ 14. "Early to bed, early to rise, makes a man healthy, wealthy, and wise" is most closely related to which of these other aphorisms?
    a. "Fools make feasts, and wise men eat them."
    b. "If your head is wax, don't walk in the sun."
    c. "Dost thou love life? Then do not squander time; for that's the stuff life is made of."
    d. "Keep thy shop, and thy shop will keep thee."

Vocabulary and Grammar

On the line, write the letter of the one best answer.

_____ 15. When Franklin called his project *arduous*, he meant it would be
   a. very difficult to do.
   b. easily done.
   c. very expensive.
   d. best done by a group.

_____ 16. When Franklin spoke of the *felicity* of his life, he referred to
   a. outrageous events.
   b. frustrated feelings.
   c. happy times.
   d. fatiguing work.

_____ 17. Identify the objective case pronoun in this passage: "Order, too, with regard to places for things, papers, etc., I found extremely difficult to acquire. I had not been early accustomed to it."
   a. the first *I*   c. *it*
   b. the second *I*   d. *too*

_____ 18. Which of these statements contains an objective pronoun?
   a. What good shall I do this day?
   b. Contrary habits must be broken, and good ones acquired.
   c. They never reached the excellence of those copies.
   d. Like him, we all have a garden to weed.

_____ 19. Which of these sentences contains a subjective pronoun?
   a. I enjoyed reading about Benjamin Franklin.
   b. Franklin's autobiography was interesting to us.
   c. Franklin wrote it in part for his descendants.
   d. Franklin wanted them to benefit from his experiences.

_____ 20. According to his aphorisms, which might Franklin think is an activity that *squanders* time?
   a. surfing the 'Net
   b. reading an encyclopedia
   c. exercising
   d. studying

Essay Questions

21. *The Autobiography* was written by Franklin himself. Imagine you have read an account of Franklin's attempt to attain perfection written by an impartial reporter. Write an essay that compares and contrasts the versions written by Franklin and the reporter. Consider how each version would use facts and opinions.

22. Near the end of the selection, Franklin writes that a perfect character might be envied and hated. Write an essay in which you either support or reject this statement. Give reasons for your opinion. Support your position by drawing on the experiences Franklin had as he tried to attain the thirteen virtues.

23. Some people consider leisure time important to a person's good health, both mental and physical. The aphorism "Dost thou love life? Then do not squander time, for that's the stuff life is made of" seems to conflict with that view. Write an essay agreeing or disagreeing with the aphorism. Your essay should take into account your interpretation of the aphorism as well as the value you place on leisure time.

The Declaration of Independence by Thomas Jefferson
from *The Crisis, Number 1*, by Thomas Paine

Selection Test

Critical Reading

On the line, write the letter of the one best answer.

_____ 1. What general observation does Paine express in the statement, "What we obtain too cheap, we esteem too lightly"?
   a. When something is hard to do, the achievement will be less rewarding.
   b. If you gain something too easily, it will not seem that important to you.
   c. Those who are wealthy can afford to be choosy.
   d. When your cause is just, there is no reason not to pursue it to the end.

_____ 2. When Paine compares America's relationship with England to the bondage of slavery, to what emotion is he appealing?
   a. anger   b. joy   c. happiness   d. hope

_____ 3. Paine's primary purpose in saying that "a common murderer, a highwayman, or a housebreaker, has as good a pretense" as the king is to
   a. show how the common criminal is persecuted by the king's representatives.
   b. emphasize the notion of democracy.
   c. stress the lawlessness of the king's actions.
   d. appeal to his audience's fear of crime.

_____ 4. Identify one reason Paine gives for supporting the fight for liberty.
   a. faith that God will reward the weak and powerless
   b. responsibility to ensure that all people are treated equally
   c. shame that the colonies have been afraid to break away from Britain
   d. duty to provide a better life for one's family

_____ 5. To what situation is Paine referring when he says, "For though the flame of liberty may sometimes cease to shine, the coal can never expire"?
   a. a fuel shortage
   b. America's oppression under British rule
   c. a temporary truce with the British
   d. Britain's unfair taxation of the colonies

_____ 6. What is the main point of Paine's essay?
   a. The time for armed struggle is over.
   b. Colonists who support Britain are weak and cowardly.
   c. The king of Britain is a fool.
   d. The colonists must endure.

_____ 7. With what does Paine compare America's war against the British?
   a. murder   c. a man defending his property
   b. all the treasures of the world   d. a thief breaking into his house

_____ 8. When Paine says the colonists must "throw not the burden of the day upon Providence, but `show your faith by your works," he means they must
   a. honor God's law by avoiding armed conflict at all costs.
   b. violate God's law against fighting if necessary.
   c. fight for their own freedom instead of relying on God's good will.
   d. ask Britain for a peaceful settlement to their dispute.

_____ 9. Paine uses "summer soldier" and "sunshine patriot" to refer to
   a. those who support the Revolution only when it is convenient.
   b. revolutionary soldiers who keep their spirits up.
   c. agricultural workers who have joined the revolutionary army.
   d. Tories.

_____ 10. Which of the following passages from *The Crisis, Number 1*, introduces an anecdote meant to persuade the audience?
   a. "I have as little superstition in me as any man living."
   b. "[A] noted one, who kept a tavern at Amboy, was standing at his door, with as pretty a child in his hand."
   c. "The far and the near, the home counties and the back, the rich and the poor, will suffer or rejoice alike."
   d. "'Tis the business of little minds to shrink."

_____ 11. From Jefferson's statement that governments are instituted to secure basic human rights, the argument logically follows that
   a. Any form of government that suppresses people's freedoms should be overthrown.
   b. monarchy is a bad form of government because rulers are not elected.
   c. the rights of men should be supported over those of women.
   d. all forms of government destroy human rights and thus should be abandoned.

_____ 12. One of Jefferson's main complaints against the king is that he has
   a. prohibited British citizens from communicating with the American colonists.
   b. created chaos by refusing to pass or administer just laws.
   c. failed to protect the colonies from invasion by other countries.
   d. tried to starve the American people by cutting off their trade routes.

_____ 13. From the Declaration of Independence, what can be inferred about Jefferson's general attitude toward revolution?
   a. All cases of injustice vindicate a revolution.
   b. People often revolt as their first course of action.
   c. Revolution is a method of last resort.
   d. Revolution is a very poor way of dealing with conflict.

_____ 14. Jefferson uses the charged word *tyrant* to characterize the king of Britain. To what emotion does this word appeal?
   a. sorrow   c. anger
   b. envy   d. pride

_____ 15. Which of the following statements most appeals to the emotions of horror and disgust?
   a. "He is at this time transporting large armies . . . to complete the works of death, desolation, and tyranny, already begun."
   b. "He has abdicated government here, by declaring us out of his protection and waging war against us."
   c. "He has dissolved representative houses repeatedly. . . ."
   d. "He has called together legislative bodies . . . for the sole purpose of fatiguing them into compliance with his measures."

_____ 16. Jefferson's list of self-evident truths is effective because it
   a. helps his audience understand the truths.
   b. creates a connection between these truths and the colonists' attempts at reconciliation with Britain.
   c. draws his readers' attention to his personal opinions about humanity.
   d. imparts a sense of reasonableness to the beginning of his argument.

Vocabulary and Grammar

On the line, write the letter of the one best answer.

____ 17. How does parallelism affect the meaning of this sentence: "Such has been the patient sufferance of these colonies; and such is now the necessity which constrains them to alter their former systems of government"?
   a. It emphasizes the colonists' patience in dealing with their hardships.
   b. It stresses the cause-and-effect relationship between the colonists' suffering and their desire to break with Britain.
   c. It implies that the colonists do not really wish to break with Britain but neverthe-less feel that they must.
   d. It stresses the universal significance of declaring independence.

____ 18. Which of these sentences contains examples of parallelism?
   a. "He has plundered our seas, ravaged our coasts, burned our towns, and destroyed the lives of our people."
   b. "In every stage of these oppressions we have petitioned for redress in the most humble terms."
   c. "He has kept among us in times of peace standing armies without the consent of our legislatures."
   d. "He has abdicated government here, by declaring us out of his protection and waging war against us."

____ 19. According to the Declaration of Independence, the colonists have suffered oppression at the hands of the British and in return have begged for
   a. magnanimity.   c. usurpations.
   b. redress.   d. perfidy.

____ 20. What does Jefferson mean when he says that the British are "deaf to the voice of . . . consanguinity"?
   a. They do not follow the teaching of religion.
   b. They take no account of their kinship with the colonists.
   c. They enjoy being tyrannical.
   d. They are too busy to listen to the colonists.

Essay Questions

21. On July 8, 1776, the Declaration of Independence was read to a crowd of people standing outside the Pennsylvania State House in Philadelphia. Imagine that you are an ordinary American man or woman in the crowd. What would your reaction be? Write an essay de-scribing your feelings about the Declaration. Give reasons for those feelings.

22. Although *The Crisis, Number 1*, was written in response to a specific situation, Paine's ar-gument has more general applications. Write an essay in which you explore the general applications of Paine's message and discuss how the existence of more universal applica-tions contribute to the value of Paine's essay as a work of literature.

23. When writing a persuasive essay or speech, writers often use parallelism to emphasize im-portant ideas, create rhythm, and make their writing more forceful and direct. Write an essay in which you examine Jefferson's use of parallelism in the Declaration of Indepen-dence and analyze how it contributes to the document's effectiveness.

"To His Excellency, General Washington" and **"An Hymn to the Evening"**
by Phillis Wheatley

Selection Test

Critical Reading

On the line, write the letter of the one best answer.

_____ 1. In "To His Excellency, General Washington," Wheatley refers to George Washington as
    a. Britannia.
    b. the American army.
    c. Columbia.
    d. the great chief.

_____ 2. At the beginning of "To His Excellency, General Washington," Wheatley portrays the United States as a goddess filled with
    a. pride.
    b. anxiety.
    c. anger.
    d. hatred.

_____ 3. In "An Hymn to the Evening," the "sable curtains" refer to
    a. winter.
    b. the west wind.
    c. darkness.
    d. thunder.

_____ 4. In "To His Excellency, General Washington," what human characteristics does Wheatley attribute to Great Britain?
    a. innocence and ignorance
    b. pride and vanity
    c. foolishness and greed
    d. malice and spite

_____ 5. In "To His Excellency, General Washington," what does Wheatley hope to show by describing Americans as a "heaven-defended race"?
    a. All other nations are immoral.
    b. America is protected by God.
    c. Religion cannot be separated from government.
    d. General Washington is an agent of destiny.

_____ 6. In "To His Excellency, General Washington," what does Wheatley imply about how others view America when she writes, "Fix'd are the eyes of nations on the scales, / For in their hopes Columbia's arm prevails"?
    a. America's fate is of little interest to the rest of the world.
    b. America has a great deal in common with the rest of the world.
    c. America's fight for freedom is a model for the rest of the world.
    d. America must win its war with Britain to justify independence.

_____ 7. In "An Hymn to the Evening," Wheatley portrays night as a time of
    a. renewal.
    b. terror.
    c. virtue.
    d. death.

_____ 8. In "An Hymn to the Evening," Wheatley describes daytime by using images from
   a. city life.
   b. the shipping industry.
   c. the Revolutionary War.
   d. nature.

_____ 9. In "To His Excellency, General Washington," Wheatley's use of personification is in part designed to
   a. distance the reader from the events described.
   b. make the poem more musical.
   c. help the reader recognize the beauty and strength of America.
   d. show her delight in acquiring and possessing inanimate objects.

_____ 10. In which of these instances does Wheatley use personification in "To His Excellency, General Washington"?
   a. when she says that America's armies know Washington from "fields of fight"
   b. when she compares night to a veil
   c. when she wishes that Washington could have "a crown, a mansion, and a throne that shine"
   d. when she describes England as a goddess who "droops" her "pensive head"

_____ 11. Which of these quotations from "An Hymn to the Evening" illustrates personification?
   a. "But the west glories in the deepest red."
   b. "And through the air their mingled music floats."
   c. "So may our breasts with every virtue glow."
   d. "Majestic grandeur!"

_____ 12. Which of the following rewritten versions clarifies this line from "To His Excellency, General Washington": "When Gallic powers Columbia's fury found"?
   a. When the French became more powerful than America's fury
   b. When the French encountered the fury of America
   c. When an angry Washington met with French government representatives
   d. When America discovered the fury and power of France

_____ 13. Which of the following rewritten versions clarifies this line from "To His Excellency, General Washington": "While round increase the rising hills of dead"?
   a. While all around the number of war dead increases
   b. While the war dead killed in the hills rise and go to heaven
   c. While more vegetation on nearby hills is destroyed by warfare
   d. While the hills of dead bodies become increasingly round in shape

_____ 14. Which of the following rewritten versions clarifies this line from "An Hymn to the Evening": "Soft purl the streams"?
   a. The streams ripple or murmur softly.
   b. The water softener ripples or murmurs in the streams.
   c. The water softly knits the streams together.
   d. The streams contain soft-looking water bubbles that resemble opaque white jewels.

Vocabulary and Grammar

On the line, write the letter of the one best answer.

_____ 15. A *propitious* act is one that is
   a. favorable.   c. possessive.
   b. outrageous.   d. criminal.

____ 16. Which word could substitute for *placid* in the line "Let placid slumbers soothe each weary mind"?
  a. terrifying
  b. turbulent
  c. tranquil
  d. tired

____ 17. A *scepter* closely resembles a
  a. vase or glass.
  b. rod or staff.
  c. star or planet.
  d. god or goddess.

____ 18. In the line "Unnumber'd charms and recent graces rise," the word *rise* is a
  a. singular subject.
  b. plural subject.
  c. singular verb.
  d. plural verb.

____ 19. In the lines "The birds renew their notes, / And through the air their mingled music floats," the subject of *floats* is
  a. birds.
  b. notes.
  c. air.
  d. music.

____ 20. In the lines "From the zephyr's wing, / Exhales the incense of the blooming spring," the subject of *exhales* is
  a. wing.
  b. incense.
  c. spring.
  d. zephyr's.

Essay Questions

21. Although the title "An Hymn to the Evening" leads you to believe that the poem will be about the evening, about two-thirds of the poem is devoted to daytime. Based on the poem, do you think Wheatley preferred the day or the night? Write an essay in which you use details and descriptions from the poem to support your opinion.

22. Based on "To His Excellency, General Washington," do you think Wheatley was very patriotic? Answer this question in an essay that uses details and impressions from the poem to support your evaluation.

23. In an essay, discuss the use of General Washington as a symbol in the poem "To His Excellency, General Washington." Considering that Washington is not mentioned until line 23, is the subject of this poem something or someone other than Washington? Who or what else could be the inspiration of the poem and the subject of Wheatley's praise?

from *Letter From Birmingham City Jail* by Dr. Martin Luther King, Jr.

Selection Test

Critical Reading

On the line, write the letter of the one best answer.

_____ 1. Which of the following acts of the police does King condemn in his letter?
  a. beating protesters with sticks
  b. pushing and cursing women and girls, slapping and kicking old men and boys
  c. firing tear gas into crowds
  d. ignoring attacks by whites on blacks

_____ 2. According to King, who said "My feet is tired, but my soul is rested"?
  a. a seventy-two-year-old woman who refused to ride segregated buses
  b. a twenty-four-year-old man who faced down jeering mobs with courage and purpose
  c. a young high school student who willingly went to jail for conscience's sake
  d. a lunch counter patron who dared to take a seat right at the counter

_____ 3. On what basis does King support the idea that "the goal of America is freedom"?
  a. America is the land of opportunity for the poor.
  b. Blacks in America have always been free.
  c. Hope is stronger than despair.
  d. America was founded on ideals of freedom that must eventually be applied to all people without exception.

_____ 4. What philosophy is King referring to with the term *integrationist*?
  a. All groups and races should freely mix everywhere in society.
  b. Blacks should have schools as good as those of whites.
  c. The belief that equality of the races is guaranteed by the Bible.
  d. The poor should have the same access to education as the rich.

_____ 5. Which system of values does King invoke in lauding the "willingness to suffer" of the people he calls the "real heroes" of the South?
  a. Libertarian
  b. Islamic
  c. Judeo-Christian
  d. African

_____ 6. What is the "evil system" that King accuses the Birmingham police department of helping to preserve?
  a. communism
  b. segregation
  c. school busing
  d. slavery

_____ 7. Why does King beg God's forgiveness if he has been "patient with anything less than brotherhood"?
  a. because he considers it a moral imperative to stand up to injustice without delay
  b. because he is sorry for the pain caused to whites by his push for racial brotherhood
  c. because he knows the right time has not yet come for racial brotherhood
  d. because he believes the time has come to fight by any means for justice

Vocabulary

On the line, write the letter of the one best answer.

_____ 8. Choose the word that best completes the following sentence: What else is there to do when you are alone for days in the dull _____ of a narrow jail cell other than write long letters, think strange thoughts, and pray long prayers?
   a. stability
   b. neutrality
   c. monotony
   d. humiliation

_____ 9. Which phrase is most nearly the same in meaning to *profundity*?
   a. intellectual depth
   b. righteous anger
   c. sacred heritage
   d. inhuman provocation

_____ 10. The word *vitality* means
   a. the reason for an action.
   b. the ability to compel or force.
   c. the right to life and liberty.
   d. the power to endure or survive.

Essay Questions

11. King was a well-known advocate of nonviolent protest. As he puts it in his letter, "it is wrong to use immoral means to attain moral ends." Write an essay explaining what this code meant for King in practice (use examples from the text). Do you agree with King's opinion that it is never permissible to use immoral means to achieve a moral end?

12. Despite his writings on liberty, Thomas Jefferson was a slave owner. Write an essay describing how someone could proclaim liberty and justice for all, yet still own slaves. How does that fact compromise the image of Jefferson in your mind? King surely knew about Jefferson's past. Explain why, for King, Jefferson's words may have outweighed his personal behavior.

13. In the conclusion to his letter, King hopes that "the dark clouds of racial prejudice will soon pass away and the deep fog of misunderstanding will be lifted from our fear-drenched communities" and that then "love and brotherhood will shine over our great nation." More than thirty years have passed since King was assassinated. Write an essay describing King's vision of a fully integrated society. Go on to analyze how much of that vision has been realized in the present day. Speculate on what still needs to be done to fulfill King's legacy. How much time do you think it will take to achieve racial harmony in this country, if, indeed, it can be achieved?

Part Test, Unit 2, Part 1: Voices for Freedom

Critical Reading

The questions below are based on the following selection.

This excerpt is from an early section of Benjamin Franklin's Autobiography. *In the final sentence, the word discovered means "revealed."*

My Brother had in 1720 or 21, begun to print a Newspaper. . . . Being still a Boy, and suspecting that my Brother would object to printing any Thing of mine in his Paper if he knew it to be mine, I contrived to disguise my Hand, and writing an anonymous Paper, I put it in at Night under the Door of the Printing House. It was found in the Morning and communicated to his Writing friends when they called in as usual. They read it, commented on it in my Hearing, and I had the exquisite Pleasure of finding it met with their Approbation, and that in their different Guesses at the Author none were named but men of some Character among us for Learning and Ingenuity.

  I suppose now that I was rather lucky in my Judges: And that perhaps they were not really so very good ones as I then esteemed them. Encouraged, however, by this, I wrote and conveyed in the same Way to the Press several more papers, which were equally approved, and I kept my Secret till my small Fund of Sense for such Performances was pretty well exhausted, and then I discovered it; when I began to be considered a little more by my Brother's Acquaintance, and in a manner that did not quite please him, as he thought, probably with reason, that it tended to make me too vain. . . .

On the line, write the letter of the one best answer.

____ 1. Benjamin Franklin
        a. signed his name to the articles he wrote for his brother's newspaper.
        b. printed several stories his brother wrote for his newspaper.
        c. signed a false name to the articles he wrote for his brother's newspaper.
        d. signed no name to the articles he wrote for his brother's newspaper.

____ 2. Why might Franklin's brother "object to printing any Thing of mine in his Paper if he knew it to be mine"?
        a. He dislikes Franklin, despite their kinship.
        b. He disagrees with Franklin's political views.
        c. He never prints unsolicited articles.
        d. He deems Franklin too young to be an adequate writer.

____ 3. What conclusion can you draw about Franklin based on the following passage from *The Autobiography*?

        I made a little book, in which I allotted a page for each of the virtues. I ruled each page with red ink, so as to have seven columns, one for each day of the week, marking each column with a letter for the day. I crossed these columns with thirteen red lines, marking the beginning of each line with the first letter of one of the virtues. . . .

        a. Franklin was organized in his approach to his project.
        b. Franklin was afraid of forgetting the virtues.
        c. Was concerned that his book did not have enough space.
        d. Franklin carried his book with him wherever he went.

____ 4. This selection presents events
        a. in a positive light.
        b. as the author's brother saw them.
        c. as historical fact.
        d. as Benjamin Franklin saw them.

_____ 5. What causes Franklin to cease his deception?
      a. He tires of misleading the editors.
      b. The printer recognizes Franklin's handwriting.
      c. The lie is detected by a learned editor.
      d. He wants to embarrass his brother.

_____ 6. What is the best characterization of Franklin's attitude toward his brother during this period, as it is revealed in the selection?
      a. fond
      b. hostile
      c. competitive
      d. casual

_____ 7. An autobiography has most in common with which of the following literary forms?
      a. a poem
      b. a historical narrative
      c. a short story
      d. a journal

_____ 8. In _The Autobiography_, what does Franklin mean when he says, "In truth, I found myself incorrigible with respect to _Order_. . . ."
      a. Franklin didn't care about achieving _Order_.
      b. _Order_ was the hardest virtue for Franklin to achieve.
      c. Franklin felt the need to tell the truth about _Order_.
      d. _Order_ was the simplest virtue for Franklin to achieve.

_____ 9. What can you infer about the author from this selection?
      a. He was wracked by guilt about his duplicity.
      b. He was an orphan.
      c. He was an ambitious young man.
      d. He despised his brother.

_____ 10. Which of the following words is most likely to produce an emotional response in a reader?
      a. judiciary   c. liberty
      b. reason   d. anonymous

Vocabulary and Grammar

On the line, write the letter of the one best answer.

_____ 11. Which word is closest in meaning to that of the italicized word in the following sentence?

      The colonists overcame many obstacles in their _arduous_ journey toward liberty.

      a. difficult   c. lengthy
      b. exciting   d. determined

_____ 12. Which of the following roots means "faith" or "trust"?
      a. -_vigil_-   c. -_ped_-
      b. -_spir_-   d. -_fid_-

_____ 13. Which of the following pairs of words expresses a relationship similar to that expressed in REDRESS : INJUSTICE?
      a. laughter : felicity
      b. flight : pursuit
      c. punishment : crime
      d. vigilance : watchfulness

____ 14. Which of the words below is an *antonym* for the italicized word in the following sentence?

> General Washington had nothing but *propitious* comments about Phillis Wheatley's poetry.

a. impious
b. unfavorable
c. inappropriate
d. unspoken

____ 15. The colonists refused to _____ to the _____ of their rights by the British crown.
a. surrender, unalienable
b. acquiesce, usurpations
c. defend, disposition
d. bow, felicity

____ 16. Which one of the following sentences contains an error in subject-verb agreement?
a. The soldier, who was separated from his comrades, is in great danger.
b. Thomas Paine's fiery words still inspires Americans.
c. Phillis Wheatley calls on one of the Muses for inspiration.
d. The time for action, not words, has arrived.

____ 17. The passage is an example of which of the following?

> He has constrained our fellow citizens . . . to bear arms against their country, to become the executioners of their friends and brethren, or to fall themselves by their hands.

a. parallelism
b. persuasive writing
c. subjective case
d. plural subject-verb agreement

____ 18. Which one of the following sentences does *not* contain a plural subject and plural verb?
a. They seek the work of war.
b. The refluent surges beat the sounding shore.
c. Columbia's scenes of glorious toils I write.
d. Nations gaze at scenes before unknown!

____ 19. The pronoun *it* is in which case in the sentence?

> Though many members of Congress contributed to *it*, the Declaration of Independence owes its literary greatness to Thomas Jefferson.

a. subjective
b. objective
c. nominative
d. possessive

____ 20. Which word or phrase below correctly completes the parallel structure of the following sentence?

> With noble intent, with firm resolution, and _____, we prepare to fight for freedom.

a. with our fellow soldiers
b. believing strongly
c. with unshakable faith
d. keeping our heads high

Essay Questions

21. The excerpt from *The Autobiography* that you read in Unit 2 explores the goals and principles that shaped Benjamin Franklin's character. Write an essay in which you explore Franklin's character. What type of person was he? What was important to him? How might his personal code of conduct have helped prepare him for his important role in American history? Use details from the selection to support your conclusions.

22. As revolutionary fervor swelled, many colonial writers publicly disagreed with Thomas Jefferson's assertion "Delay is preferable to error." Choose a selection from Part 1 of Unit 2—such as Franklin's *Autobiography* or Paine's *Crisis, Number 1*—and write an essay in which you discuss whether you believe the author of the work would have agreed or disagreed with Jefferson's statement. Support your opinion with examples from the text.

23. The American Revolution had a tremendous impact on the literature of the colonial period. Write an essay in which you discuss the ways in which the literature of the colonial period was shaped by the Revolution. Cite evidence from the selections in Part 1 of Unit 2 to support your conclusions.

24. At the signing of the Declaration of Independence, Benjamin Franklin said, "We must all hang together, or assuredly we will all hang separately." Think about the importance of unity in a time of national crisis. In an essay, discuss this topic in relation to the Revolutionary era in America. Support your thoughts with references to the attitudes expressed in *The Crisis, Number 1* and "To His Excellency, General Washington."

25. The eighteenth century has often been called the Age of Reason. Think about how writers such as Franklin, Jefferson, Paine, and Wheatley apply logical reasoning and precise thought in their work. Choose one selection from Part 1 of Unit 2 and write an essay in which you explain how it embodies—or relates to—the idea of an age of reason.

"Speech in the Virginia Convention" by Patrick Henry
"Speech in the Convention" by Benjamin Franklin

Selection Test

Critical Reading

On the line, write the letter of the one best answer.

_____ 1. The main purpose of Henry's speech is to
   a. convince the colonists that Britain will not fight.
   b. maintain peace in America at all costs.
   c. persuade the colonists to enter into war against Britain.
   d. persuade his audience that Henry would make a good president.

_____ 2. Around what major idea does Henry organize his speech?
   a. The times demand patriotism.
   b. There is no longer any possibility of peace.
   c. The colonists desire their freedom.
   d. War has already broken out.

_____ 3. What is the "storm" that Henry predicts is approaching?
   a. an argument during the Convention
   b. a hurricane from the south
   c. the wrath of God
   d. the war with Britain

_____ 4. When Henry says that his listeners should "Suffer not yourselves to be betrayed with a kiss," what is he implying?
   a. The colonies should not trust the promises and gentle words of the British.
   b. Nothing will persuade Britain to enter into war.
   c. Britain will soon treat the colonies with more respect.
   d. The colonies should seek a truce with Britain.

_____ 5. Which of these remarks uses logical arguments to appeal to reason?
   a. "Are we disposed to be of the number of those who having eyes see not, and having ears hear not the things which so nearly concern their temporal salvation?"
   b. "There is no retreat but in submission and slavery!"
   c. "The next gale that sweeps from the north will bring to our ears the clash of resounding arms!"
   d. "I ask gentlemen, sir, what means this martial array, if its purpose be not to force us to submission?"

_____ 6. Which technique of speeches does Henry use in the sentence "Is this the part of wise men, engaged in a great and arduous struggle for liberty?"
   a. repetition
   b. parallelism
   c. rhetorical question
   d. restatement

_____ 7. In which of these statements does Henry use parallelism?
   a. "Mr. President, it is natural to man to indulge in the illusions of hope."
   b. "We have petitioned; we have remonstrated; we have supplicated."
   c. "Is it that insidious smile with which our petition has been lately received?"
   d. "Our brethren are already in the field! Why stand we here idle?"

____ 8. Henry uses a rational argument to convince his readers that
     a. chains and slavery will be the result of continued inaction by the colonies.
     b. the war is inevitable and the colonies must fight.
     c. the past conduct of the British government proves that England has no intention of granting the colonies' petitions.
     d. death would be better than a forced loss of colonial liberty.

____ 9. Why does Henry make use of a biblical quotation in his speech?
     a. to appeal to reason
     b. to prove his devotion to God
     c. to appeal to his audience's faith
     d. to show he has read the Bible

____ 10. In which of these sentences does Henry appeal to emotions in order to persuade his audience that the time for action is at hand?
     a. "But different men often see the same subject in different lights."
     b. "Is life so dear, or peace so sweet, as to be purchased at the price of chains and slavery?"
     c. "And in proportion to the magnitude of the subject ought to be the freedom of the debate."
     d. "I know of no way of judging the future but by the past."

____ 11. What is the main point of Benjamin Franklin's speech in the Convention?
     a. The Constitution is too weak to be approved by the Convention.
     b. His doubts about the Constitution are too strong to allow him to support it, but he hopes others will.
     c. The Convention should support the Constitution because they have shown infallibility in the past.
     d. The Convention should support the Constitution because it is as good as it is likely to be.

____ 12. Which technique of speeches does Franklin use in this passage?

     From such an assembly can a perfect production be expected?

     a. restatement   c. rhetorical question
     b. repetition   d. parallelism

____ 13. From Franklin's words in this speech, what can you infer about his opinion of monarchy as a form of government?
     a. It is a form of despotism.
     b. It can be a beneficial form of government if it is well administered.
     c. It ought to be the form of government adopted by the new United States.
     d. It is invariably inferior to any form of democracy.

____ 14. What point is Franklin making when he quotes the French Lady who says, "But I meet with nobody but myself that is always in the right?"
     a. French people tend to think they are perfect.
     b. It is best to live alone and meet with few people.
     c. Attitudes like this lead to religious disputes.
     d. Some people think that they possess all truth.

____ 15. Why does Franklin want the delegates to the Convention to support the Constitution strongly despite any personal reservations about it?
     a. to inspire public confidence in their leadership
     b. because he believes it is perfect
     c. because that means it will be administered well
     d. because it is a product of their joint wisdom

Vocabulary and Grammar

On the line, write the letter of the one best answer.

____ 16. When Franklin hopes the Convention will "act heartily for the sake of our *posterity*," he means for the sake of
    a. immediate advantages.
    b. political leaders.
    c. fellow delegates.
    d. succeeding generations.

____ 17. Which of these statements contains a double negative?
    a. He was less well prepared than he should have been.
    b. She hadn't heard no bell ring.
    c. There is no better speaker than she.
    d. The people listening hardly understood what he implied.

____ 18. Which of these statements comes closest to Franklin's meaning when he says, "I am not sure that it is not the best"?
    a. "I am absolutely sure it is the best."
    b. "It may be the best."
    c. "I am not sure it is the best."
    d. "It may not be the best."

____ 19. When Franklin doubts his own *infallibility* regarding his opinion of the Constitution, he is saying that
    a. he could be wrong about it.
    b. he is unsure what his descendants will think about it.
    c. he cannot make up his mind about it.
    d. he feels compelled to vote against it.

____ 20. Which pair of words best completes this statement about Franklin?

Franklin would probably agree that ___ is not ___ to people who live under it.

    a. unanimity, manifest
    b. subjugation, arduous
    c. despotism, salutary
    d. posterity, insidious

Essay Questions

21. Write an essay in which you examine the blend of emotional and logical appeals that Patrick Henry uses in his "Speech in the Virginia Convention" and discuss how his use of these persuasive techniques contributes to the effectiveness of the speech.

22. What is Benjamin Franklin's opinion of the Constitution? How does he reconcile this opinion with his call for the Convention delegates to give it their unanimous support? Answer these questions in an essay that supports general statements with quotations and other details from Franklin's speech.

23. When delivering a speech, a skilled orator will use a variety of oratorical devices to emphasize important points. Write an essay in which you discuss Patrick Henry's use of oratorical devices such as rhetorical questions, repetition, restatement, and parallelism in his "Speech in the Virginia Convention." In your essay, consider whether his use of these devices is effective.

"Inaugural Address" by John F. Kennedy

Selection Test

Critical Reading

On the line, write the letter of the one best answer.

_____ 1. What is the "balance of terror" that Kennedy says has prevented "mankind's final war"?
    a. The build-up of troops on both sides of the Iron Curtain in Europe.
    b. The ability of the United States or its adversaries to place men into space.
    c. The ability of either the United States or its adversaries to destroy the world with atomic weapons.
    d. The economic burden of building up weapons, which threatens to overwhelm the world's economies.

_____ 2. Why does Kennedy emphasize United States commitment to maintaining a strong military?
    a. He is warning other nations that the United States is prepared for any sort of military challenge.
    b. He believes that a strong military contributes to the economic well-being of the nation.
    c. He is trying to scare Russia into rejecting communism.
    d. He is suggesting that the United States is prepared to attack its adversaries.

_____ 3. Which phrase best sums up Kennedy's speech?
    a. Americans must pay more taxes in support of a stronger military.
    b. Americans must sacrifice their well-being to beat back attacks by the enemies of freedom.
    c. Americans need to volunteer more in order to promote freedom around the globe.
    d. Americans must counter adversaries by staying strong, promoting freedom around the world, and sacrificing for the common good.

_____ 4. How does Kennedy characterize his inauguration as president?
    a. a celebration of freedom
    b. a victory for the Democratic party
    c. a declaration of war on poverty
    d. a day for putting the past behind

_____ 5. What four things does Kennedy call the "common enemies of man"?
    a. anger, greed, jealousy, and hate
    b. death, disease, poverty, and hunger
    c. tyranny, poverty, disease, and war
    d. slavery, famine, pestilence, and communism

_____ 6. According to Kennedy, what "revolutionary belief" is still at issue throughout the world?
    a. The right to freedom extends from God, not from the generosity of the state.
    b. The United States is destined to lead the world into a new era of freedom and prosperity.
    c. All people have the right to bear arms in defense of their freedom.
    d. Democracy is a better system of government than communism.

_____ 7. In the statement, what does Kennedy equate with the success of liberty?

"If a free society cannot help the many who are poor, it cannot save the few who are rich."

a. the rights of the rich to a fair taxation plan
b. the rights of the poor to unemployment compensation
c. increasing the wealth of the rich
d. helping people overcome poverty

Vocabulary

On the line, write the letter of the one best answer.

_____ 8. Which phrase has most nearly the same meaning as *tyranny*?
a. unequal voting rights
b. oppressive and unjust governance
c. inescapable poverty
d. a successful and prosperous society

_____ 9. Which word best completes the following sentence?

We dare not forget today that we are the _____ of that first revolution.

a. progenitors
b. heirs
c. forebears
d. kin

_____ 10. The word *eradicate* means
a. to defeat in war.
b. to criticize strongly.
c. to wipe out completely.
d. to make radical changes.

Essay Questions

11. In inaugural addresses, presidents usually outline a general course of action for the country's future. Write an essay summarizing the key goals Kennedy outlines for America. Name at least two pledges that he makes in the name of the United States and assess whether those pledges have since been carried out.

12. One of the most famous phrases in American oratory is Kennedy's "Ask not what your country can do for you, ask what you can do for your country." Write an essay describing how this idea fits into the context of Kennedy's speech. Go on to argue whether this formula works as a guiding principle in today's America. Using examples from your own life, describe the practical results of trying to live up to Kennedy's vision.

13. Kennedy places much emphasis on a free society's ability to raise people out of poverty. Write an essay arguing for or against the idea that freedom is necessary for the accumulation of wealth in a society. Cite examples from Kennedy's speech in support of your ideas or, conversely, as a view that runs counter to yours.

Name _____   Date _____

Part Test, Unit 2, Part 2: Focus on Literary Forms—Speeches

Critical Reading

The questions below are based on the following selection.

This excerpt is taken from Thomas Jefferson's "First Inaugural Address," which he delivered to Congress on March 4, 1801.

. . . Let us then, fellow-citizens, unite with one heart and one mind; let us restore to social intercourse that harmony and affection without which liberty, and even life itself, are but dreary things. And let us reflect that having banished from our land that religious intolerance under which mankind so long bled and suffered, we have yet gained little if we countenance a political intolerance as despotic, as wicked, and capable of as bitter and bloody persecutions. During the throes and convulsions of the ancient world, during the agonizing spasms of infuriated man, seeking through blood and slaughter his long-lost liberty, it was not wonderful that the agitation of the billows should reach even this distant and peaceful shore; that this should be more felt and feared by some and less by others; and should divide opinions as to measures of safety. But every difference of opinion is not a difference of principle. We have called by different names brethren of the same principle. We are all republicans; we are all federalists. If there be any among us who would wish to dissolve this Union, or to change its republican form, let them stand undisturbed as monuments of the safety with which error of opinion may be tolerated, where reason is left free to combat it. I know, indeed, that some honest men have feared that a republican government cannot be strong; that this Government is not strong enough. But would the honest patriot, in the full tide of successful experiment, abandon a government which has so far kept us free and firm, on the theoretic and visionary fear that this Government, the world's best hope, may by possibility want energy to preserve itself? I trust not. I believe this, on the contrary, the strongest government on earth. I believe it the only one where every man, at the call of the law would fly to the standard of the law; would meet invasions of the public order as his own personal concern. Sometimes it is said that man cannot be trusted with the government of himself. Can he, then, be trusted with the government of others? Or have we found angels in the form of kings to govern him? Let history answer this question. . . .

On the line, write the letter of the one best answer.

_____ 1. According to Jefferson, mankind has "bled and suffered" under
        a. political intolerance.
        b. the standard of the law.
        c. religious intolerance.
        d. banishment.

_____ 2. How does Jefferson propose to deal with dissent?
        a. tolerate it
        b. punish its perpetrators
        c. ignore it
        d. celebrate it

_____ 3. In the first sentence, which rhetorical technique does Jefferson employ?
        a. rhetorical question
        b. repetition
        c. restatement
        d. parallelism

___ 4. Which of the following words or phrases is most likely intended to stir the emotions of Jefferson's audience?
   a. a difference of principle
   b. error of opinion
   c. a republican government
   d. the world's best hope

___ 5. What or whom does Jefferson describe as "free and firm"?
   a. federalists   c. Americans
   b. republicans   d. public servants

___ 6. Which of the following best describes Jefferson's beliefs about Americans' ability to govern themselves, as stated in this speech?
   a. Constitutional monarchies are the best form of government.
   b. People can be trusted to govern themselves.
   c. Ancient history reveals whether people can govern themselves.
   d. People cannot be trusted to govern themselves.

___ 7. Jefferson's rhetorical question about "the honest patriot" abandoning the government is intended
   a. to perplex the audience.
   b. appease the audience.
   c. to go unanswered.
   d. to provoke and challenge the audience.

___ 8. "But every difference of opinion is not a difference of principle." With this statement Jefferson affirms the idea of
   a. quarrelsome debate   c. patriotic fervor
   b. unanimous agreement   d. reasoned debate

___ 9. What does Jefferson assert about the strength of the American government?
   a. It is stronger than any other government.
   b. It lacks energy to preserve its own strength.
   c. It is nearly as strong as older, more established governments around the world.
   d. It is a monument of safety.

___ 10. Which of the following sentences supports Jefferson's assertion about the strength of the American government?
   a. "I believe it the only one where every man, at the call of the law would fly to the standard of the law; would meet invasions of the public order as his own personal concern."
   b. "Let history answer this question."
   c. "We are all republicans."
   d. "Sometimes it is said that man cannot be trusted with the government of himself."

Vocabulary and Grammar

Each question below consists of a related pair of words in CAPITAL LETTERS, followed by four other pairs of words. Choose the pair that best expresses a relationship similar to that expressed in the capitalized words.

___ 11. UNANIMITY : DISCORD ::
   a. infallibility : perfection
   b. harmony : strife
   c. fear : cowardice
   d. animosity : hatred

_____ 12. TYRANT : DICTATORSHIP ::
       a. celebrity : posterity
       b. stoic : danger
       c. president : republic
       d. doctor : patient

On the line, write the letter of the one best answer.

_____ 13. Which word below is the best antonym for the italicized word in the sentence?

       Benjamin Franklin convinced convention members of the *manifest* need to support the Constitution.

       a. compelling
       b. mysterious
       c. obscure
       d. apparent

_____ 14. Something intended for *posterity* is meant for the benefit of
       a. its creators.
       b. future generations.
       c. every citizen.
       d. elderly citizens.

_____ 15. Which sentence contains an error involving a double negative?
       a. No one told them they couldn't vote in the election.
       b. The dictator didn't say nothing about the need for personal freedom.
       c. People living in a democracy never expect their rights not to be protected.
       d. Hardly any dictatorship is free from corruption.

Essay Questions

16. Benjamin Franklin felt that it was not as important to produce a "perfect" Constitution as it was to produce one that the members of the Constitutional Convention could all support. How does Franklin make this point in his "Speech in the Convention"? Why does he say it is crucial to the success of the young nation that convention members keep any negative opinions about the Constitution to themselves? Write an essay in which you explore the answers to these questions, using details from Franklin's speech to support your points.

17. In his "Speech in the Virginia Convention," Patrick Henry presents what might be viewed as a practical, rather than idealistic, reason to overcome objections to war with Great Britain. In an essay, present and evaluate the main thrust of Henry's argument. Do you feel Henry presents an effective, persuasive case for war? Why or why not?

18. In developing a persuasive speech, an effective orator must answer possible objections to its argument. Write an essay in which you analyze how Patrick Henry answers possible objections to the argument in his "Speech in the Virginia Convention." Cite details from the selection to support your points.

Name _____ Date _____

"Letter to Her Daughter from the New White House" by Abigail Adams
from *Letters from an American Farmer* by Michel-Guillaume Jean de Crèvecoeur

Selection Test

Critical Reading

On the line, write the letter of the one best answer.

____ 1. What main point does Abigail Adams's description of Washington stress?
   a. her reluctance to move there
   b. the city's isolation and unfinished state
   c. the romance of her primitive surroundings
   d. the city's beauty and impressive design

____ 2. What can be inferred about Adams's attitude toward Washington from her statement "We have, indeed, come into a *new country*"?
   a. She sees little room for improvement in Washington.
   b. She considers Washington to be unpleasant.
   c. She thinks that Washington is undeveloped.
   d. She looks on the new capital as the perfect symbol of a new nation.

____ 3. Why do you think Adams asks her daughter not to tell others the letter's revelations about the new capital?
   a. She believes only family members should have to listen to her complaints.
   b. She fears people would be appalled if they knew the true state of the capital.
   c. She realizes that her complaints stem solely from her own personal unhappiness.
   d. She recognizes that the President's wife has a duty not to complain in public.

____ 4. Which of these lines best reflects Adams's sense of humor and general good nature about her situation in the White House?
   a. "The fires we are obliged to keep to secure us from daily agues is another very cheering comfort."
   b. "We have, indeed, come into a new country."
   c. "Can you believe that wood is not to be had because people cannot be found to cut and cart it?"
   d. "Woods are all you see from Baltimore until you reach *the city*, which is only so in name."

____ 5. Adams seems to think that compared with the people who designed and constructed Washington and the White House, the inhabitants of New England are
   a. more inefficient organizers and poorer overseers.
   b. thriftier spenders and more sensible budgeters.
   c. better planners and harder workers.
   d. more disciplined thinkers and sterner masters.

____ 6. Which sentence reflects most clearly that Adams's letter is a private one?
   a. "He has had recourse to coals; but we cannot get grates made and set."
   b. "Here and there is a small cot, without a glass window, interspersed amongst the forest. . . ."
   c. "Yesterday I returned fifteen visits—but such a place as Georgetown appears— why, our Milton is beautiful."
   d. "It is a beautiful spot, capable of every improvement."

_____ 7. Why do you think it is so hard to get wood for the White House fires?
   a. It is hard to find woodcutters because the area is so underpopulated.
   b. It is hard to find woodcutters because everyone in town is a politician.
   c. The staff is afraid that burning wood will turn the White House black.
   d. The distance to the forests is so great.

_____ 8. Which of these details is a fact supporting Adams's opinion that the new White House is built "upon a grand and superb scale"?
   a. It is "an establishment very well proportioned to the President's salary."
   b. "The river, which runs up to Alexandria, is in full view of my window."
   c. "To assist us in this great castle, and render less attendance necessary, bells are wholly wanting."
   d. It requires "about thirty servants to attend and keep the apartments in proper order, and perform the ordinary business of the house."

_____ 9. What can you infer about Adams's character from the tone and details of her letter?
   a. Wealth and power do not impress her.
   b. She is very loyal to her family and friends.
   c. Comfort is extremely important to her.
   d. She is one to make the best of any situation, no matter how bad.

_____ 10. Which statement best sums up Adams's final opinion of the White House and Washington, D.C., in general?
   a. Its scale is too large for it ever to be run with efficiency.
   b. It has the potential, as yet unfulfilled, to be both beautiful and comfortable.
   c. It is poorly planned and poorly constructed, making it uncomfortable and unpleasant.
   d. It is a lovely place that everyone in the country can be proud of.

_____ 11. The title _Letters from an American Farmer_ suggests that Crèvecoeur's writing is
   a. informal and intimate.   c. logical and objective.
   b. personal but formal.   d. complex and ornate.

_____ 12. Crèvecoeur's facts about the harshness of everyday European life support his opinion that people can feel little loyalty to a nation that
   a. fails to enable its citizens to live decently.
   b. has recently lost a war.
   c. does not contain citizens from different ethnic and religious backgrounds.
   d. rewards those who own substantial property.

_____ 13. What point does Crèvecoeur make by comparing people to plants?
   a. People have no control over their own lives.
   b. Like plants, people die if they are not fed and watered.
   c. To thrive, people need to be nurtured by their country.
   d. People who do not have solid ethnic roots cannot be successful.

_____ 14. Crèvecoeur argues that American laws are indulgent, protective, and great. What fact does he use to back up this opinion?
   a. American law protects people from their own misdeeds.
   b. All Americans are allowed to vote.
   c. The law rewards those who work hard with land and freedom.
   d. The government of America is based on the desires of its people.

_____ 15. Why is this sentence typical of the style of an epistle: "I could point out to you a family whose grandfather was an Englishman, whose wife was Dutch, whose son married a French woman, and whose present four sons have now four wives of different nations"?
   a. It uses exaggeration.   c. It contains specific details.
   b. It backs up its point with evidence. d. It addresses its reader personally.

_____ 16. When Crèvecoeur argues that "Here the rewards of his industry follow with equal steps the progress of his labor," he is appealing to a belief in
   a. human equality.   c. the goodness of human nature.
   b. the importance of technology.   d. logical cause and effect.

Vocabulary and Grammar

On the line, write the letter of the one best answer.

_____ 17. When Adams says that she engaged someone "to _extricate_ us out of our difficulty," she means that she hired someone
   a. to set them free from their difficulty.
   b. to counsel them about their difficulty.
   c. to take their minds off their difficulty.
   d. to prove to them that they had no difficulty.

_____ 18. Why does Crèvecoeur use semicolons in the following passage?

> The laws, the indulgent laws, protect them as they arrive, stamping on them the symbol of adoption; they receive ample rewards for their labors; these accumulated rewards procure them lands; those lands confer on them the title of freemen, and to that title every benefit is affixed which men can possibly require.

   a. The passage is a series of items that already contains commas.
   b. The independent clauses have a close relation to one another.
   c. The semicolons reinforce the use of conjunctions.
   d. The independent clauses present contrasting ideas.

_____ 19. Where could you correctly use semicolons in the following passage?

> According to Crèvecoeur, many Europeans suffer from poverty, hunger, and war. He defines an American as someone who, giving up old ways, takes on new ones and becomes part of a new race.

   a. after _who_   b. after _ways_   c. after _war_   d. after _war_ and _ways_

_____ 20. Which word pair best completes the following sentence?

> According to Crèvecoeur, Europeans can escape ___ by coming to America, working hard, and being rewarded by ample ___.

   a. penury—asylum   c. agues—asylum
   b. penury—subsistence   d. asylum—subsistence

Essay Questions

21. Abigail Adams's letter makes us aware of the dramatic contrasts between the appearance of Washington in Adams's time and its appearance today. Write an essay discussing these contrasts, using details from Adams's letter to develop your discussion.

22. Write an essay in which you explain how Abigail Adams's letter provides a clear sense of the undeveloped state of the nation in general at the time the letter was written.

23. Write an essay in which you summarize Crèvecoeur's definition of an American and then explain whether, in your opinion, his definition can still be applied to Americans today.

from *Roots* by Alex Haley

Selection Test

Critical Reading

On the line, write the letter of the one best answer.

_____ 1. When did Haley first hear the story of Kunta?
   a. as a college student, on a trip to Africa
   b. as a high school student, from his grandfather
   c. as a college student, from a Harvard professor
   d. as a child, from his grandmother

_____ 2. What was Kunta doing when he was kidnapped into slavery?
   a. fishing for supper
   b. building a hut
   c. chopping wood
   d. sleeping

_____ 3. When Haley takes the babies handed to him by the villagers, he is not yet aware that the ceremony he is participating in is called
   a. Kamby Bolongo [the teaching of the babes].
   b. the pressing of the flesh.
   c. the laying on of hands.
   d. the meeting of the minds.

_____ 4. What does the ceremony with the babies signify to the villagers?
   a. Haley must choose one of the village women as a mate.
   b. The villagers accept Haley as one of their people.
   c. Haley has become a "godfather" to the village's children.
   d. To be recognized as one of their people, Haley must accept one of the children as his own.

_____ 5. Why was Haley greeted by shouting crowds as he arrived at the second village?
   a. The people were welcoming home a long lost relative.
   b. The people were excited to meet an American writer.
   c. The people had never seen a black man from America before.
   d. The people were expecting gifts of candy and money.

_____ 6. What is the "staggering awareness" Haley comes to as he is leaving the village?
   a. that the *griot* was really his great grandfather
   b. that he had been accepted as one of the villagers
   c. how phenomenally lucky he was to find his ancestor's clan
   d. how much of his grandmother's story was known by the *griot*

_____ 7. What is Haley's purpose in deciding to write a book about his ancestors?
   a. to record his personal story in the hopes of writing a bestseller
   b. to provide a corrected history of the capture and treatment of the African people who were brought to America as slaves
   c. to complete the project begun by his grandmother, who had always longed to know the complete story of her father, Kunta Kinte
   d. to provide a symbolic saga of the struggle for freedom waged by the enslaved ancestors of all people of African descent in America

_____ 8. What does Haley describe as "mankind's greatest flaw"?
   a. the incredible record of atrocities committed by men against fellowmen
   b. the long history of slavery perpetuated on African peoples since before Columbus
   c. the lack of an adequate response to disease and starvation in Africa and around the world
   d. the waging of war anywhere in the world

Vocabulary

On the line, write the letter of the one best answer.

_____ 9. Which phrase is nearest in meaning to *crux*?
   a. heart of the matter
   b. book learning
   c. profound knowledge
   d. mere trifle

_____ 10. Choose the word that best completes the following sentence: I could see this village's people thronging the road ahead; they were weaving, amid their _____ of crying out something.
   a. surfeit
   b. cacophony
   c. intensity
   d. fanfare

Essay Questions

11. Despite his family connection to the African villagers, Haley clearly comes from a much different background and culture. Write an essay elaborating on the differences between Haley and the villagers. What details demonstrate their differences? Go on to analyze their relationship in terms of what brings them together.

12. In the 1970's, *Roots* sparked an enormous interest among all Americans for tracing family histories. Write an essay speculating on why it was so important to Haley to trace his family's origins. Speculate on what would have happened to Haley's book if he had not been successful in finding his ancestor's clan. Go on to explain the importance or unimportance of roots to your own family.

13. At the end of this excerpt from *Roots*, the author asserts that all people of African descent without exception are from the seeds of someone like Kunta Kinte. Write an essay explaining what Haley means by such a statement. Make a judgment on how you feel African Americans have been treated since the end of slavery. Cite specific examples of progress, and the lack of progress, made by African Americans in the twentieth century. Speculate on what it means to be an African American today.

Part Test, Unit 2, Part 3: The Emerging American Identity— Defining an American

Critical Reading

The questions below are based on the following selection.

The following excerpt is from Letters From an American Farmer *by Michel-Guillaume Jean de Crèvecoeur.*

I wish I could be acquainted with the feelings and thoughts which must agitate the heart and present themselves to the mind of an enlightened Englishman, when he first lands on this continent. He must greatly rejoice that he lived at a time to see this fair country discovered and settled; he must necessarily feel a share of national pride, when he views the chain of settlements which embellishes these extended shores. When he says to himself, this is the work of my countrymen, who, when convulsed by factions, afflicted by a variety of miseries and wants, restless and impatient, took refuge here. They brought along with them their national genius, to which they principally owe what liberty they enjoy, and what substance they possess. Here he sees the industry of his native country displayed in a new manner, and traces in their works the embryos of all the arts, sciences, and ingenuity which flourish in Europe. Here he beholds fair cities, substantial villages, extensive fields, an immense country filled with decent houses, good roads, orchards, meadows, and bridges, where an hundred years ago all was wild, woody, and uncultivated! What a train of pleasing ideas this fair spectacle must suggest; it is a prospect which must inspire a good citizen with the most heartfelt pleasure. The difficulty consists in the manner of viewing so extensive a scene. He is arrived on a new continent; a modern society offers itself to his contemplation, different from what he had hitherto seen. It is not composed, as in Europe, of great lords who possess everything, and of a herd of people who have nothing. Here are no aristocratical families, no courts, no kings, no bishops, no ecclesiastical dominion, no invisible power giving to a few a very visible one; no great manufacturers employing thousands, no great refinements of luxury. The rich and the poor are not so far removed from each other as they are in Europe. Some few towns excepted, we are all tillers of the earth, from Nova Scotia to West Florida. We are a people of cultivators, scattered over an immense territory, communicating with each other by means of good roads and navigable rivers, united by the silken bands of mild government, all respecting the laws, without dreading their power, because they are equitable. . . .

On the line, write the letter of the one best answer.

_____ 1. Who does the author say were "convulsed by factions" in the past?
    a. British emigrants who settled in America
    b. Americans
    c. Native Americans
    d. European emigrants who settled in England

_____ 2. According to the author, why might the heart of an "enlightened Englishman" be agitated upon arriving in America?
    a. He might feel envious of America's success because it was settled by expatriate British men and women.
    b. He might feel confused by the "chain of settlements" lining the shores.
    c. He might be moved with pride at the thought that America's prosperity is attributable to British settlers who "took refuge here."
    d. He might feel homesickness.

____ 3. Epistles like this one are
   a. edited letters intended for scholars.
   b. private letters.
   c. posthumous letters.
   d. public letters intended for general publication.

____ 4. Which phrase derives from fact rather than opinion?
   a. the chain of settlements
   b. the silken bands of mild government
   c. their national genius
   d. this fair country

____ 5. According to Crèvecoeur, where are there "no aristocratic families, no courts, no kings, no bishops, . . . no great refinements of luxury"?
   a. America   c. Europe
   b. England   d. France

____ 6. Why does the author value life in America over life in Europe?
   a. Life is more luxurious in America.
   b. American citizens enjoy greater social and political equality.
   c. American culture is far superior to European culture.
   d. The roads and rivers of America are easily traveled.

____ 7. This selection is an example of
   a. a persuasive essay.
   b. a private letter.
   c. an aphorism.
   d. a public letter.

____ 8. Which is the best explanation of the difference between facts and opinions?
   a. Opinions are fueled by emotion, whereas facts are concerned with data.
   b. Facts exist independently in the real world, whereas opinions originate with people.
   c. Facts are statements that can be proved, whereas opinions are personal beliefs that cannot be proved.
   d. Opinions are personal ideas, whereas facts are objective ideas.

____ 9. Which adjective best describes Crèvecoeur's overall attitude toward America?
   a. critical   c. pleasant
   b. enthusiastic   d. intellectual

____ 10. Of what is the following sentence an example?

   "We are a people of cultivators."

   a. an epistle   c. an aphorism
   b. a fact   d. an opinion

Vocabulary and Grammar

The questions below consist of a related pair of words in CAPITAL LETTERS followed by four other pairs of words. Choose the pair that best expresses a relationship similar to that expressed in the capitalized words.

____ 11. DESPOTIC : TYRANT ::
   a. controlling : cruel
   b. generous : philanthropist
   c. queen : regal
   d. evil : despicable

_____ 12. EXTRICATE : MAZE ::
a. obscure : mask
b. alleviate : penury
c. freedom : liberty
d. release : prison

On the line, write the letter of the one best answer.

_____ 13. Complete the following sentence, using the comparative form of *little*.

Abigail Adams said little good about the new White House, and _____ about the surrounding countryside.

a. least
b. little
c. less
d. lesser

_____ 14. In which sentence is the semicolon used incorrectly?
a. In the city there are buildings enough, if they were compact and finished, to ac-commodate Congress and those attached to it; but as they are, and scattered as they are, I see no great comfort for them.
b. This is so great an inconvenience; that I know now what to do, or how to do.
c. Formerly they were not numbered in any civil lists of their country, except in those of the poor; here they rank as citizens.
d. The American is a new man who acts upon new principles; he must therefore en-tertain new ideas, and form new opinions.

_____ 15. Which of the sentences below shows the best use of a semicolon?
a. It is a very handsome room now, when completed however; it will be beautiful.
b. It is a very handsome room now; when completed, however, it will be beautiful.
c. It is a very handsome room now, when completed; however, it will be beautiful.
d. It is a very handsome room now; but when it is completed, it will be beautiful.

Essay Questions

16. In their literary work, many writers focus on the daily life that surrounds them. Twentieth-century readers can get a clear glimpse of daily life in eighteenth-century America from "Letter to Her Daughter From the New White House" and "Letters From an American Farmer." Write an essay in which you use details from these two literary works to describe life in America during the late eighteenth century.

17. During the second half of the nineteenth century, America emerged as an independent country and began to establish its own national character. Write an essay in which you discuss how the emergence of the American national character is reflected in one or more of the selections in Unit 2, Part 3. Cite evidence from the texts to support your points.

18. Some critics have commented that Michel-Guillaume Jean de Crèvecoeur's portrayal of America is overly idealized and his definition of an American too simplistic. Write an essay in which you react to these claims. Support your point of view with examples from the text.

"The Devil and Tom Walker" by Washington Irving

Selection Test

Critical Reading

On the line, write the letter of the one best answer.

_____ 1. The opening descriptions of the forest suggest that what Tom will find there will be
   a. treacherous and malignant.
   b. fortunate and useful.
   c. hot-tempered and vengeful.
   d. dull and depressing.

_____ 2. Which of these details most clearly suggest that the figure Tom meets is the Devil?
   a. His voice is hoarse and growling, and his hair is black.
   b. His eyes are red, and he is covered with soot.
   c. He is powerfully built and is holding an ax.
   d. He wears rude, half-Indian garb and is sitting on a tree stump.

_____ 3. What is the "one condition which need not be mentioned, being generally understood in all cases where the Devil grants favors"?
   a. the Devil's promising to make Tom rich
   b. the Devil's guiding all Tom's thoughts
   c. Tom's giving his soul to the Devil
   d. Tom's promising to become a usurer

_____ 4. What is the significance of Tom's finding most of the tall trees in the forest each "marked with the name of some great man of the colony"?
   a. The townspeople carved great men's names on trees.
   b. Landowners carved their names on trees on their property.
   c. The men had carved their own names on the trees to ensure their fame.
   d. Carved onto the trees in the Devil's forest are the names of those who made a deal with him.

_____ 5. What seems to be Tom's prime motivation in agreeing to the Devil's terms?
   a. the desire to spite his wife
   b. gratitude for the Devil's involvement in his wife's disappearance
   c. the desire to win the respect of the community
   d. greed

_____ 6. A main lesson of this story is that
   a. greed and mean-spiritedness lead to misery.
   b. husbands and wives should love each other.
   c. prayer can erase all past sins.
   d. great wealth can never produce happiness.

_____ 7. The story implies that God expresses His disapproval of humans' sins by
   a. ignoring their prayers.
   b. making them poor.
   c. causing natural disasters.
   d. giving them nightmares.

Unit 3: A Growing Nation (1800–1870)

_____ 8. In what way is Tom Walker a one-dimensional character?
   a. He has no personality traits.
   b. He uses other people for his own gain.
   c. He does not fear the Devil.
   d. He symbolizes human greed and miserliness.

_____ 9. Tom's wife is a stereotype of
   a. a Puritan homemaker.
   b. a woman of mystery.
   c. a nagging, shrewish wife.
   d. a town gossip.

_____ 10. It can be inferred from the story that New England Puritans of Tom Walker's day
   believed in
   a. many gods.
   b. witches and spirits.
   c. tolerance of all religious faiths.
   d. reincarnation.

_____ 11. From the description of Tom's "violent" religious devotion, you can infer that
   New Englanders of the 1720s probably
   a. believed that loud and vehement prayer was the key to reaching Heaven.
   b. looked suspiciously on sudden and very public conversions.
   c. welcomed religious people of all faiths to their colony.
   d. were, like Tom, usually recent converts to openly devout Christianity.

_____ 12. Which of these statements does _not_ apply to an omniscient narrator?
   a. The narrator stands outside the story.
   b. The narrator provides the thoughts or feelings of many characters.
   c. The narrator may comment on events in the story.
   d. The narrator is a character in the story who refers to himself or herself with the
      first-person pronoun _I._

_____ 13. Which of these statements best demonstrates an omniscient narrator?
   a. Tom was walking through the forest.
   b. Tom's wife was tall and greedy.
   c. Mrs. Walker hoped that Tom would make the pact, but Tom would not agree, just
      to spite her.
   d. As Tom grew older, he began to worry about what would happen after he died.

_____ 14. With which special-interest group of Irving's day does the story suggest Irving had
   the most sympathy?
   a. abolitionists
   b. New England shipbuilders
   c. Puritans
   d. bankers

_____ 15. Which of these observations about the story stems from the use of an omniscient
   narrator?
   a. The narrator focuses on Tom's experiences.
   b. The narrator never tells us what happened to Tom's wife.
   c. The narrator makes clear the motives and desires of Tom and his wife.
   d. The narrator keeps the Devil shrouded in mystery.

Vocabulary and Grammar

On the line, write the letter of the one best answer.

_____ 16. When the Devil says "You shall extort bonds," what is the meaning of the word *extort*?
   a. to write in legal language
   b. to sell by auction
   c. to break, unlink, or untie
   d. to obtain by threat or violence

_____ 17. Which is the adjective clause in this sentence?

   His reputation for a ready-moneyed man, who would lend money out for good consideration, soon spread abroad.

   a. his reputation for a ready-moneyed man
   b. for good consideration
   c. who would lend money out for good consideration
   d. soon spread abroad

_____ 18. Which relationship best describes the italicized words in this sentence?

   He built himself, as usual, a vast house, out of *ostentation;* but left the greater part of it unfinished and unfurnished, out of *parsimony.*

   a. They are identical in meaning.
   b. They are similar in meaning.
   c. They are opposite in meaning.
   d. There is no relationship.

_____ 19. In suggesting that Tom's wife is guilty of the sin of *avarice*, the narrator is criticizing her
   a. greed.
   b. spitefulness.
   c. violence.
   d. tendency to bicker.

_____ 20. What noun or pronoun does the adjective clause in this sentence modify?

   If he really did take such a precaution, it was totally superfluous; at least so says the authentic old legend, which closes his story in the following manner.

   a. precaution
   b. it
   c. legend
   d. story

Essay Questions

21. Which tree do you think is hit by the thunderbolt falling at the end of the story? In a brief essay, state your theory and then support it with information from the selection.

22. How does the use of an omniscient narrator affect this story? Analyze the effects in an essay that supports your general statements with examples from the selection. Be sure to include examples of scenes or dialogue that might *not* have been included if the story did not have an omniscient narrator.

23. At the end of the story, all of Tom's possessions disappear or are destroyed. Why do you think this happens? Offer your theory in an essay that uses information from the story to support your ideas.

"A Psalm of Life" and **"The Tide Rises, The Tide Falls"**
by Henry Wadsworth Longfellow

Selection Test

Critical Reading

On the line, write the letter of the one best answer.

_____ 1. Which of these statements is a central message of "A Psalm of Life"?
   a. Life is the first step in a long journey.
   b. Life is not worth living without love.
   c. Life is but an empty dream.
   d. People can inspire other people's lives.

_____ 2. "A Psalm of Life" urges people to
   a. sleep.
   b. act.
   c. march to the same tune.
   d. mourn.

_____ 3. Which word best describes the attitude toward life expressed in "A Psalm of Life"?
   a. accepting
   b. depressed
   c. cynical
   d. optimistic

_____ 4. What do these lines from "A Psalm of Life" imply?

   Dust thou art, to dust returnest, / Was not spoken of the soul.

   a. The dead become the soil in which new life grows.
   b. It is a mistake to say "Dust thou art, to dust returnest" at a funeral.
   c. At a funeral, not a soul is present who doesn't respect the solemn occasion.
   d. The soul lives on, even though the body dies.

_____ 5. The four-line stanzas in "A Psalm of Life" are called _____.
   a. couplets
   b. quadruplets
   c. quatrains
   d. cinquains

_____ 6. In "A Psalm of Life," what broader meaning does the image of the "footprints on the sands of time" most likely represent?
   a. a long, hot walk
   b. deeds done while alive
   c. sins of our ancestors
   d. human efforts to stop the passage of time

_____ 7. What broader meaning might the image of the "shipwrecked brother" in "A Psalm of Life" represent?
   a. any human being in difficulty
   b. a sibling who needs your help
   c. a sailor whose ship has been severely damaged
   d. poets of the world

8. In "A Psalm of Life," what broader meaning in the context of life's journey might be conveyed by this stanza?

   > In the world's broad field of battle,
   > In the bivouac of Life,
   > Be not like dumb, driven cattle!
   > Be a hero in the strife!

   a. There is strength in numbers.
   b. Because life is a painful but temporary struggle, heroes welcome the peace of eternity.
   c. People should display some individualism in their lives.
   d. To the victor belong the spoils, or benefits, of any battle.

9. "A Psalm of Life" stresses the idea that
   a. life is very short.
   b. everyone experiences death.
   c. anyone can be a hero.
   d. experience is all important.

10. In "The Tide Rises, The Tide Falls," when does the curlew call?
    a. dawn
    b. noon
    c. twilight
    d. midnight

11. Which statement best expresses the theme of "The Tide Rises, The Tide Falls"?
    a. Life and death are beyond human control.
    b. Human life is short, but nature is eternal.
    c. Humans, like nature itself, are resilient.
    d. Human emotions have no place in the natural world.

12. Which word best describes Longfellow's attitude toward death in "The Tide Rises, The Tide Falls"?
    a. accepting
    b. welcoming
    c. frightened
    d. awestruck

13. The five-line stanzas of "The Tide Rises, The Tide Falls" are called _____.
    a. couplets
    b. quatrains
    c. pentanes
    d. cinquains

14. Which statement does *not* apply to the stanzas in "The Tide Rises, The Tide Falls"?
    a. Each stanza describes a different time of day.
    b. The stanzas have no regular pattern of rhyme.
    c. The stanzas attempt to capture the rhythm of the tide.
    d. The same final line is repeated in each stanza.

15. What broader meaning might be signified by the image of the tide in the line, "And the tide rises, the tide falls"?
    a. human pollution of natural wonders
    b. life before birth
    c. life's cyclical, enduring nature
    d. people or ideas left stranded because of human indifference

Vocabulary and Grammar

On the line, write the letter of the one best answer.

____ 16. In "A Psalm of Life," what does the phrase "the *bivouac* of Life" mean?
   a. a temporary state of existence
   b. a loud and boisterous party
   c. a sturdy, well-built house
   d. a war-torn country

____ 17. What do the waves do to the footprints in these lines?

> The little waves, with their soft, white hands, / *Efface* the footprints in the sands

   a. wipe them out
   b. dampen them
   c. surprise them
   d. etch them in permanently

____ 18. What does the line "We can make our lives *sublime*" mean?
   a. We can live longer.
   b. We should recognize what goes on below the surface of our lives.
   c. We can improve our intelligence.
   d. Our lives can be inspiring.

____ 19. What is the subject in this sentence?

> Not enjoyment, and not sorrow, / Is our destined end or way

   a. enjoyment
   b. sorrow
   c. enjoyment and sorrow (compound subject)
   d. end or way (compound subject)

____ 20. Which of the following choices most accurately describes the effect of the inverted order in these lines?

> The day returns, but nevermore / Returns the traveler to the shore

   a. Placing the subject after the verb creates an additional rhyme.
   b. Placing the subject after the verb creates a more regular rhythm.
   c. Placing the subject after the verb emphasizes the word *day*.
   d. Placing the subject after the verb imparts a more elevated tone.

Essay Questions

21. In several of his written works, Longfellow uses the image of the sea. In a brief essay, discuss how the sea can be used to represent life and death. Include general examples of how the sea might be depicted as a bringer of life or death. Also include more specific examples from "The Tide Rises, The Tide Falls."

22. Although Longfellow uses the image of footprints in the sand in both of the poems in your textbook, there are differences in the way the image is used. Discuss the footprint imagery in each poem. Then compare and contrast the use of the image in the two poems, considering not only its meaning but its effectiveness.

23. Images of death are central to both of the Longfellow poems. How is the depiction of death in each poem similar? How is it different? What feelings do you get from the imagery that Longfellow uses to convey his ideas about death? Address these questions in an essay that compares and contrasts the two poems' views of death.

Name _____ Date _____

"Thanatopsis" by William Cullen Bryant
"Old Ironsides" by Oliver Wendell Holmes
"The First Snowfall" by James Russell Lowell
from *Snowbound* by John Greenleaf Whittier

Selection Test

Critical Reading

On the line, write the letter of the one best answer.

____ 1. The title "Thanatopsis" means
   a. a vision of death.
   b. the process of decaying.
   c. a metamorphosis or transformation.
   d. a feeling of euphoria or well-being.

____ 2. According to the speaker in "Thanatopsis," what will happen to him after death?
   a. His soul will go to heaven.
   b. His spirit will cease to exist.
   c. His body will be preserved in the earth.
   d. His body will become part of nature.

____ 3. According to the views presented in "Thanatopsis," death is something to be _____.
   a. feared   b. trusted   c. escaped   d. pursued

____ 4. Bryant's line "Shall send his roots abroad, and pierce thy mold" is an example of iambic _____.
   a. trimeter   b. tetrameter   c. pentameter   d. hexameter

____ 5. "Old Ironsides" was the nickname of
   a. the *U.S.S. Constitution*, a War of 1812 battleship.
   b. the *Clermont*, an early steamship.
   c. the *Titanic*, a famous luxury liner.
   d. Oliver Wendell Holmes.

____ 6. Which of these qualities does Holmes's poem attribute to "Old Ironsides"?
   a. ruthlessness   b. heroism   c. holiness   d. modesty

____ 7. Which of these statements best expresses the author's view in "Old Ironsides"?
   a. A remarkable national relic should be saved.
   b. Old ships are architectural treasures.
   c. Ships are the foundation of a country's defense.
   d. Older things are built better than newer things.

____ 8. Which choice below is the best summary of the following lines?

> Her deck, once red with heroes' blood,
> Where knelt the vanquished foe,
> When winds were hurrying o'er the flood,
> And waves were white below,
> No more shall feel the victor's tread,
> Or know the conquered knee—

   a. The defeated have knelt on the ship's deck when it was red with heroes' blood.
   b. The ship will never again experience battle victories and defeats.
   c. The ship once sped across the water and was surrounded by white waves.
   d. The ship, which once knew victories, shall now know only defeats.

____ 9. The central theme of "The First Snowfall" comments on
   a. the isolation of New England winters.
   b. the permanence of human sorrow.
   c. the sadness and spiritual recovery from loss.
   d. the touching innocence of children.

____ 10. "The mound in sweet Auburn" in "The First Snowfall" is
   a. the pile of snow that has fallen on the highway.
   b. the stiff rails softened to swan's-down.
   c. the grave of Mabel's sister.
   d. the place where Mabel is buried.

____ 11. How does Lowell set the scene in "The First Snowfall"?
   a. with a dialogue between the poet and his wife
   b. with a persuasive appeal to trust God
   c. with a narrative of his daughter's death
   d. with an extended description of a snowfall

____ 12. Which choice below best summarizes these lines from "The First Snowfall"?

   I stood and watched by the window
   The noiseless work of the sky,
   And the sudden flurries of snowbirds.
   Like brown leaves whirling by.

   a. I watched the sky through the window.
   b. I watched the snow fall.
   c. I stood and watched by the window as the sky did its work and let the snow flurry down like birds or brown leaves whirling by.
   d. I watched the leaves whirl.

____ 13. The central contrast in the selection from *Snowbound* is between
   a. the cold, harsh weather and the warmth of the speaker's family life.
   b. the sun and the moon.
   c. a brutal December and a warm October.
   d. the solitude of the speaker's farm and the bustle of city life.

____ 14. The family in *Snowbound*
   a. was not prepared for the sudden snowfall.
   b. feared the isolation of being snowed in.
   c. suffered in the cold weather of the winter storm.
   d. enjoyed the solitude brought by the snowfall.

____ 15. Which choice below best summarizes these lines from *Snowbound*?

   A tunnel walled and overlaid
   With dazzling crystal: we had read
   Of rare Aladdin's wondrous cave,
   And to our own his name we gave. . . .

   a. The boys used crystals to build a tunnel in the snow.
   b. The boys recalled their readings as they built a walled tunnel.
   c. The boys built a tunnel overlaid with dazzling crystal and, having read of Aladdin's wondrous cave, gave their own tunnel the same name, calling it Aladdin's cave.
   d. The boys built a tunnel in the snow and named it after Aladdin's cave.

____ 16. Which of the following lines is *not* written in iambic tetrameter?
   a. Her deck, once red with heroes' blood
   b. Where knelt the vanquished foe
   c. The sun that brief December day
   d. The moon above the eastern wood

____ 17. Which of these lines most varies the regular iambic meter?
   a. Yet not to thine eternal resting place
   b. Should sink beneath the wave
   c. In the full strength of years, matron and maid
   d. We reached the barn with merry din

Vocabulary and Grammar

On the line, write the letter of the one best answer.

____ 18. Which word below could replace the italicized word in the phrase "*thoughtful* quietness"?
   a. pensive   c. ominous
   b. gloaming   d. querulous

____ 19. Which words best describe a respected father figure?
   a. ominous gloaming   c. venerable patriarch
   b. querulous patriarch   d. venerable sepulcher

____ 20. In which line below does a present participle modify a noun?
   a. Ay, tear her tattered ensign down!
   b. Yet not to thine eternal resting place
   c. The lightning and the gale!
   d. The snow had begun in the gloaming

Essay Questions

21. Oliver Wendell Holmes helped convince the public to rally to save the ship called *Old Ironsides* from destruction. If Holmes had written an editorial instead of a poem, do you think it would have had the same effect on the public? Why or why not? Answer these questions in a brief essay. To support your opinion, cite specific examples from the poem, and consider the emotional responses that the examples produce.

22. The poetry of William Cullen Bryant is known for its detailed descriptions of nature. Does "Thanatopsis" fit that pattern? Respond to this question in an essay in which you explore the view of nature presented in the poem and consider the amount of detail with which nature is described. Be sure to support your opinions with details from the poem.

23. Poets often use images from nature to provoke an emotional response. Describe how nature images in at least two of the poems provoke different emotions. Consider the emotions the speaker or narrator attempts to convey and the emotional response in the reader.

Name _____ Date _____

"Crossing the Great Divide" by Meriwether Lewis
"The Most Sublime Spectacle on Earth" by John Wesley Powell

Selection Test

Critical Reading

On the line, write the letter of the one best answer.

_____ 1. The selection from Lewis's journal focuses on
   a. the reasons Lewis and Clark are making their journey across the continent.
   b. the danger, beauty, and excitement of crossing the Great Divide.
   c. the excitement of viewing the Grand Canyon for the first time.
   d. Clark's return with Charbono and the expedition's relations with local tribes.

_____ 2. Lewis most likely sent Shields to hunt because
   a. food had to be replenished since it could not be easily preserved on the journey.
   b. the expedition needed a certain type of food to offer its Native American guests.
   c. Shields had nothing to do, and Lewis wanted to keep him busy.
   d. Lewis himself was unskilled at hunting.

_____ 3. From where was the expedition obtaining the horses described in the selection?
   a. from Captain Clark's party
   b. from President Thomas Jefferson
   c. from Shields, who hunted down the wild mustangs and rounded them up for
      the expedition
   d. from the Indians

_____ 4. "We now formed our camp just below the junction of the forks on the Lard. side in
   a level smooth bottom covered with a fine turf of greensward" is an example of
   a. persuasive writing.   c. descriptive writing.
   b. fictional writing.   d. biographical writing.

_____ 5. According to the remark, "We now formed our camp just below the junction of the
   forks," the camp is probably
   a. upstream, before the junction.
   b. downstream, after the junction.
   c. at the top of a cliff, beside the junction.
   d. underground, beneath the junction.

_____ 6. Lewis and Clark met with the Indians near the river in order to _____.
   a. talk   c. fish
   b. trade   d. fight

_____ 7. Why did Lewis and Clark communicate with the Indians through Labuish,
   Charbono, and Sah-ca-ga-we-ah?
   a. Labuish, Charbono, and Sah-ca-ga-we-ah were the heads of the tribes with whom
      Lewis and Clark were meeting.
   b. Labuish, Charbono, and Sah-ca-ga-we-ah were able to speak officially for the
      United States government, but Lewis and Clark could not.
   c. Lewis and Clark did not speak the other Indians' language, and Labuish,
      Charbono, and Sah-ca-ga-we-ah did.
   d. At the time, proper diplomacy dictated that a representative of the United States
      government speak through a third party at all formal negotiations.

____ 8. Based on the details in Lewis's journals, you can conclude that the preferred method of travel for the Lewis and Clark expedition was
  a. on horseback.   c. in a wagon train.
  b. by water.   d. on foot.

____ 9. What chief emotion does the Grand Canyon inspire in Powell?
  a. fear   b. envy   c. optimism   d. awe

____ 10. Based on the details in "The Most Sublime Spectacle on Earth," the erosion in the Grand Canyon seems to be caused primarily by _____.
  a. water   b. wind   c. ice   d. heat

____ 11. According to Powell's descriptions, what is the most striking visual feature of the Grand Canyon's walls?
  a. texture   b. color   c. erosion   d. age

____ 12. Powell writes:

> Pluck up Mt. Washington by the roots to the level of the sea and drop it headfirst into the Grand Canyon, and the dam will not force its waters over the walls. Pluck up the Blue Ridge and hurl it into the Grand Canyon, and it will not fill it.

How does this passage help the reader appreciate the Grand Canyon?
  a. It helps the reader picture the location of the Grand Canyon.
  b. It helps the reader picture the colors of the Grand Canyon.
  c. It helps the reader picture the size of the Grand Canyon.
  d. It helps the reader picture how Powell cleared a path for future explorers.

____ 13. Powell describes the walls of the Grand Canyon as follows:

> The black gneiss below, the variegated quartzite, and the green or alcove sandstone form the foundation for the mighty red wall. The banded sandstone entablature is crowned by the tower limestone.

This description leads you to visualize the wall from
  a. left to right.   b. near to far.   c. top to bottom.   d. bottom to top.

____ 14. What are the sources of most of the "music" that Powell describes in "The Most Sublime Spectacle on Earth"?
  a. animals and falling rocks   c. rivers and creeks
  b. clouds and wind   d. campers singing

____ 15. What does Powell imply about the Grand Canyon when he writes that "language and illustration combined must fail" to capture it?
  a. The only way to appreciate the Grand Canyon is to be there.
  b. Artists who seek to paint or draw the Grand Canyon should work independently and not attempt to illustrate a writer's words.
  c. Early American writers and artists who traveled in the West were often not as skilled in their craft as the writers and artists in the East.
  d. Powell himself lacked the skills needed to describe or paint the canyon.

____ 16. Which passage best illustrates descriptive writing?
  a. "This morning I arose very early and dispatched Drewyer and the Indian down the river."
  b. "The heavens constitute a portion of the facade and mount into a vast dome from wall to wall, spanning the Grand Canyon with empyrean blue."
  c. "The wonders of the Grand Canyon cannot be adequately represented in symbols of speech, nor by speech itself."
  d. "It is a region more difficult to traverse than the Alps or the Himalayas."

Vocabulary and Grammar

On the line, write the letter of the one best answer.

_____ 17. Which statement is false?
   a. The words *multifarious* and *multitudinous* both contain a prefix meaning "many" or "much."
   b. The words *multifarious* and *multitudinous* are both adjectives.
   c. The words *multifarious* and *multitudinous* both imply a large number.
   d. The words *multifarious* and *multitudinous* both imply diversity.

_____ 18. Which statement is most likely true about a labyrinth?
   a. It is easy to pass through, with no lines or planes of demarcation.
   b. The exit is conspicuous.
   c. Finding your way through it can be sublime and exhilarating.
   d. It is one smooth surface that has never been excavated.

_____ 19. Which statement below is true about the following passage?

   a vast assemblage of self-willed clouds, faring here and there, intent upon purposes hidden in their own breasts

   a. It contains no participial phrases used as adjectives.
   b. It contains just one participial phrase used as an adjective.
   c. It contains two participial phrases used as adjectives.
   d. It contains three participial phrases used as adjectives.

_____ 20. What noun does the participial phrase in this sentence modify?

   The Grand Canyon of the Colorado is a canyon composed of many canyons.

   a. Grand Canyon   c. canyon
   b. Colorado   d. canyons

Essay Questions

21. In addition to exploring the territory gained in the Louisiana Purchase, Lewis and Clark were to establish friendly relations with the Native Americans they met along the way. Briefly explain why this was important. Include at least two reasons presented in the selection.

22. As Powell, Lewis, and Clark explored new territories, they encountered many adventures as well as discomforts and dangers. Do you think Powell or Lewis would look forward to another journey? Write an essay describing some of the positive and negative experiences the explorers encountered. Use examples from the text to predict whether or not they would choose to make another exploration under similar conditions.

23. John Wesley Powell was a trained geologist, at one point a geology professor at a university. A geologist is a scientist who studies the earth's surface and a variety of things and actions upon it, including soils, rocks, caves, bodies of water, and erosion of the earth's surface. Write an essay explaining how geology seems to have influenced Powell's writing. Use details from the selection to support your evaluation.

"Seeing" from *Pilgrim at Tinker Creek* by Annie Dillard

Selection Test

Critical Reading

On the line, write the letter of the one best answer.

_____ 1. What is the "green ray" that the author hopes to see someday?
   a. a rare kind of bird distinguished by a long, green tail feather
   b. a streak of light that rises for a few seconds from a setting sun
   c. an effect of lightning that occurs in the forest only during a fog
   d. a type of lizard that lives inside tree stumps

_____ 2. What does the flight of the red-winged blackbirds symbolize for the author?
   a. nature's ability to reveal as well as to conceal
   b. the coming of autumn
   c. nature's astounding variety
   d. the power of wind to affect flight

_____ 3. What does the author compare nature to?
   a. a Polaroid photograph   c. a colorful kaleidoscope
   b. a papier-mâché sculpture   d. a line drawing for children

_____ 4. What are the "free gifts" the author gave away as a child?
   a. pennies left on the sidewalk or at the base of a tree
   b. hugs and kisses for her relatives and neighbors
   c. drawings of goldfish and animals
   d. rows of flowers she planted in the front yard

_____ 5. What lesson does the author learn from the horse drawings her relatives make?
   a. To love something you must be able to describe it.
   b. People who work on horse farms are good artists.
   c. To know something exceedingly well, you must love it.
   d. The author is a poor artist.

_____ 6. Which fact does the author most closely connect with the image of "streaks of clearness in a fog"?
   a. Each cubic meter of intergalactic space contains only one atom.
   b. The most visible part of Halley's Comet is its tail, not its body.
   c. Eyes account for less than 1 percent of the weight of the head.
   d. Only 30 percent of all sunlight reaches the human brain.

_____ 7. In what city did the author grow up?
   a. Chicago   c. New York
   b. Pittsburgh   d. San Diego

_____ 8. What does the author mean by "the artificial obvious"?
   a. the ability to block out what you expect to see and concentrate on what you want to see
   b. the almost imperceptible traces of humankind in the wilderness
   c. the telephone and electric wires society has strung throughout much of the wilderness
   d. the ability to perceive the beautiful aspects of nature even in the city

Vocabulary

On the line, write the letter of the one best answer.

_____ 9. Which phrase is nearest in meaning to *rueful*?
      a. feeling or showing guilt
      b. trembling or quivering all over
      c. feeling or showing sorrow or regret
      d. attentive to small or unimportant details

_____ 10. A person who focuses on *minutiae* tries to understand
      a. small or relatively unimportant details.
      b. the slow passage of time.
      c. the ability of animals to hide in the forest.
      d. the ability of birds to fly from a tree without making a sound.

Essay Questions

11. For Dillard the sights and sounds of nature are abundant gifts that people too often over-look in daily life. Using details from the story, write an essay describing some of the gifts she came to appreciate during her year alone at Tinker Creek. Go on to describe some gift you may have received from nature. How did you come to notice it?

12. Dillard lived alone for a year in a cabin on Tinker Creek in order to get closer to nature. Write an essay describing the qualities a person needs to do such a thing. Could you live alone in nature as long as Dillard did? What aspects of nature make the prospect inviting? Which ones make it forbidding?

13. According to Dillard, to see the hidden gifts of nature you need to "keep your eyes open." Additionally, she implies that to live without a connection to nature means to lose some-thing meaningful and essential in human existence. Write an essay describing Dillard's at-titude toward nature. Do you agree or disagree with her point of view? Go on to argue whether the same ways of "seeing" can be applied profitably to man-made forms of enter-tainment. Argue for or against the idea that the man-made world holds less significance than the natural one.

Part Test, Unit 3, Part 1: Fireside and Campfire

Critical Reading

The questions below are based on the following poem.

The Village Blacksmith

Henry Wadsworth Longfellow

Under a spreading chestnut tree
    The village smithy stands;
The smith, a mighty man is he,
    With large and sinewy hands;
[5] And the muscles of his brawny arms
    Are strong as iron bands.

His hair is crisp and black and long;
    His face is like the tan;
His brow is wet with honest sweat, —
[10]   He earns whate'er he can;
And looks the whole world in the face,
    For he owes not any man.

Week in, week out, from morn till night,
    You can hear his bellows blow;
[15] You can hear him swing his heavy sledge,
    With measured beat and slow,
Like sexton ringing the village bell,
    When the evening sun is low.

And children, coming home from school,
[20]   Look in at the open door;
They love to see the flaming forge,
    And hear the bellows roar,
And catch the burning sparks that fly
    Like chaff from a threshing floor.

[25] He goes on Sunday to the church,
    And sits among his boys;
He hears the parson pray and preach,
    He hears his daughter's voice,
Singing in the village choir,
[30]   And it makes his heart rejoice.

It sounds to him like her mother's voice,
    Singing in Paradise!
He needs must think of her once more,
    How in her grave she lies;
[35] And with his hard, rough hand he wipes
    A tear out of his eyes.

Toiling, rejoicing, sorrowing,
    Onward through life he goes;
Each morning sees some task begin,

© Prentice-Hall, Inc.

[40]   Each evening sees it close;
    Something attempted, something done,
      Has earned a night's repose.

    Thanks, thanks to thee, my worthy friend,
      For the lesson thou hast taught!
[45] Thus at the flaming forge of life
      Our fortunes must be wrought;
    Thus on its sounding anvil shaped
      Each burning deed and thought!

On the line, write the letter of the one best answer.

_____ 1. The speaker admires the smith for his
    a. physical strength.   c. honest labor.
    b. beautiful family.   d. good job.

_____ 2. The image of the "flaming forge" is associated with
    a. the exhaustion of hard labor.
    b. the life experiences that shape and form us.
    c. love for deceased family members.
    d. the threshing floor.

_____ 3. Why doesn't the smith's wife attend church with him?
    a. She is ill at home.   c. She is too exhausted.
    b. She is a nonbeliever.   d. She has died.

_____ 4. Which of the following statements are true of every stanza of the poem?

    I.   Every stanza develops a separate idea.
    II.   Every stanza contains six lines.
    III.   Every stanza contains three sentences.
    IV.   Every stanza has the same basic meter.

    a. I, II, and IV   c. I, III, and IV
    b. II and IV   d. all of the above

_____ 5. The meter of this poem can best be described as
    a. iambic tetrameter.
    b. alternating lines of iambic tetrameter and iambic trimeter.
    c. iambic trimeter.
    d. alternating lines of iambic pentameter and iambic trimeter.

_____ 6. Which is the best summary of lines 13–18?
    a. The smith's sledge is heavy, and the sexton rings the bell in the evening.
    b. Week in and week out, you can hear the sledge ring like a bell.
    c. Day after day, the smith works the bellows and steadily swings his sledge.
    d. All day long in the village, you can hear blowing bellows, swinging sledges, and ringing bells.

_____ 7. From this poem you can infer that smiths in the nineteenth century were generally regarded as
    a. good businessmen.
    b. productive members of village society.
    c. people who were fond of children.
    d. strong and good-looking.

_____ 8. Lines 19–24 contain images that convey
    a. sights, smells, and sounds.
    b. smells, tastes, and physical sensations.
    c. sounds, smells, and tastes.
    d. sights, sounds, and physical sensations.

_____ 9. The smith's heart rejoices when his daughter sings because
    a. her voice is so beautiful.
    b. she sounds just like her mother.
    c. he is so proud of her singing ability.
    d. she has the lead in the village choir.

_____ 10. What is the "lesson" to which the speaker refers in the final stanza?
    a. the example of the smith's honest and simple life
    b. the idea that we must complete a task each day
    c. the benefits of family life
    d. the idea that our fortunes are shaped for us by fate

Vocabulary and Grammar

On the line, write the letter of the one best answer.

_____ 11. After he made his deal with the Devil, Tom Walker lived a lifestyle characterized by _____.
    a. ostentation   c. privation
    b. generosity   d. demarcation

_____ 12. Which of the words below could be substituted for the italicized word without changing the meaning of the following sentence?

    Walker approached his negotiations with the Devil with great *circumspection*.

    a. circularity   c. vision
    b. caution   d. judgment

_____ 13. Which of the following words is unrelated to money?
    a. patriarch   c. avarice
    b. parsimony   d. userer

_____ 14. Which sentence contains an example of a past participle used as an adjective?
    a. Ay, tear her tattered ensign down!
    b. This morning I arose very early and dispatched Drewyer and the Indian down the river.
    c. We invite the attention of our countrymen to a new design.
    d. We now formed our camp just below the junction of the forks on the Lard.

_____ 15. Which of the italicized words in the following sentence is an example of a present participle used as an adjective?

    She *glides* into his *darker musings* with a mild and *healing* sympathy.

    a. glides   c. musing
    b. darker   d. healing

_____ 16. Which of the following statements is true?
    a. The word *principal* is always an adjective.
    b. The word *principle* is always a noun.
    c. The word *principle* can be a noun or an adjective.
    d. The word *principal* is an antonym for the word *precept*.

_____ 17. Which of the following sentences does *not* contain an adjective clause?
   a. It had been one of the strongholds of the Indians during their wars with the first colonists.
   b. It was a dreary memento of the fierce struggle that had taken place in this last foothold of the Indian warriors.
   c. On the bark of the tree was scored the name of Deacon Peabody, an eminent man, who had waxed wealthy by driving shrewd bargains with the Indians.
   d. He had a shock of coarse black hair, that stood out from his head in all directions, and bore an ax on his shoulder.

_____ 18. Which of the following is not a common reason for writers to use inverted word order?
   a. to split an infinitive   c. to form a rhyme
   b. to achieve emphasis   d. to maintain a certain rhythm

_____ 19. Which of the following sentences contains a participial phrase?
   a. Here we unloaded our canoes and arranged our baggage on shore.
   b. How the flakes were folding it gently, as did robins the babes in the wood.
   c. The valley had a level smooth bottom covered with a fine turf of greensward.
   d. They are united only in a common love of truth, and love of its work.

_____ 20. Which of the words below best completes the following sentence?

   To the young boys, the sight of a world magically transformed by snow was _____.

   a. ominous   c. conspicuous
   b. sublime   d. pensive

Essay Questions

21. The way people face death reveals a good deal about their character. In several selections in Part 1 of Unit 3, characters or narrators of poems confront death—either as an abstraction or in its most concrete form. In an essay, analyze the view of death presented in one of the poems in this section. Use references from the text to support your points.

22. Setting is an important part of many of the selections in this part of Unit 3. At times, setting contributes to the shaping of events and the conveying of a theme. Choose a selection from Part 1 in which setting plays a particularly important role. Write an essay in which you analyze the effect of the setting on the scene or overall work. Use references to the text.

23. Choose one of the selections from Part 1 of Unit 3—such as "The Tide Rises, The Tide Falls" or "The First Snowfall"—in which a writer uses an image from nature to convey a theme. Then write an essay in which you discuss how the poet reveals both the literal and symbolic aspects of nature in the work.

24. Nature can inspire, awe, or comfort us. Choose a selection from Part 1 of Unit 3 and write an essay in which you describe how the work reflects a specific attitude toward nature. Cite examples from the text to support your points.

25. In 1831 the French writer and statesman Alexis de Tocqueville asserted, "America has produced very few writers of distinction." Did you find anything distinctive or noteworthy in the style or content of the writers whose work appears in Part 1 of Unit 3? Why or why not? Write an essay in which you support or refute de Tocqueville's claim. Use texts from one or more writers from Part 1 of Unit 3 to support your argument.

Name _____ Date _____

"The Fall of the House of Usher" and "The Raven" by Edgar Allan Poe

Selection Test

Critical Reading

On the line, write the letter of the one best answer.

____ 1. Which of these words best describes the single effect created by the opening description of the house in "The Fall of the House of Usher"?
   a. sadness
   b. terror
   c. wariness
   d. curiosity

____ 2. The letter that the narrator receives hints that Roderick Usher will be
   a. dull and depressed.
   b. suspicious and cruel.
   c. cautious and glum.
   d. nervous and passionate.

____ 3. After the narrator arrives, Roderick reveals that his present state stems largely from
   a. the stormy weather.
   b. the darkness of the autumn season.
   c. the fatal disease afflicting his beloved sister.
   d. the financial burden of maintaining the old family mansion.

____ 4. In contrast to Roderick Usher, the narrator presents himself as someone who values
   a. reason.
   b. money.
   c. nature.
   d. a juicy horror tale.

____ 5. Which passage most underscores the single effect of "The Fall of the House of Usher"?
   a. "There was an iciness, a sinking, a sickening of the heart—an unredeemed dreariness of thought which no goading of the imagination could torture into aught of the sublime."
   b. "Although, as boys, we had been even intimate associates, yet I really knew little of my friend."
   c. "Beyond this indication of extensive decay, however, the fabric gave little token of instability."
   d. "It had been used, apparently, in remote feudal times, for the worst purposes of a donjon-keep, and, in later days, as a place of deposit for powder."

____ 6. Which choice below presents the core meaning of the following sentence?

   One of the phantasmagoric conceptions of my friend, partaking not so rigidly of the spirit of abstraction, may be shadowed forth, although feebly, in words.

   a. The phantasmagoric conceptions partake not so rigidly.
   b. One of the phantasmagoric conceptions of my friend may be shadowed.
   c. The spirit of abstraction may be shadowed forth in words.
   d. One of the phantasmagoric conceptions of my friend may be shadowed forth in words.

____ 7. Which statement expresses a central theme of "The Fall of the House of Usher"?
   a. Too much contact with the world leads to a distortion of reality.
   b. Isolation of the mind leads to death of the body.
   c. A person cut off from the world can fall prey to irrational fears and mental illness.
   d. The mind cannot affect the body in any way.

© Prentice-Hall, Inc.

____ 8. Which detail early in "The Fall of the House of Usher" most clearly foreshadows, or hints at, the story's ending?
  a. the narrator's memories of Roderick as a boy
  b. the narrator's fear of the tarn
  c. the narrator's concern for Roderick and his sister
  d. the lofty, high-windowed room

____ 9. Why does the narrator "start" when Roderick Usher mentions "the gradual yet certain condensation of an atmosphere . . . about the waters and the walls" of the House of Usher?
  a. The narrator himself felt such an atmosphere when he approached the estate.
  b. Usher's idea is so incredible that it frightens the narrator.
  c. It gives the narrator his first inkling of his friend's instability.
  d. Usher is predicting the destruction of the house in a terrifying way.

____ 10. To what might the title "The Fall of the House of Usher" refer?

  I. the physical collapse of the Usher mansion at the end of the story

  II. the extinction of the Usher family with the demise of Roderick

  III. the fall from grace or good fortune that overtakes the Usher family

  IV. the season in which the story takes place

  a. definitely I and II and possibly III and IV
  b. possibly I and III but definitely not II or IV
  c. possibly II and III but definitely not I or IV
  d. possibly I and IV but definitely not II and III

____ 11. What does the speaker in "The Raven" feel when he first thinks that Lenore may be at his door?
  a. joy and passion   c. relief and pleasure
  b. terror and hope   d. confusion and melancholy

____ 12. When the speaker describes Lenore as "nameless *here* for evermore," what does he mean?
  a. He cannot remember Lenore's name.
  b. No one will speak Lenore's name because the angels took her.
  c. Lenore is never mentioned in the speaker's chamber because she deserted him.
  d. Lenore is so special that she is nameless in the speaker's heart.

____ 13. Which of these lines most contributes the eerie, hypnotic single effect of "The Raven"?
  a. "And the silken, sad, uncertain rustling of each purple curtain / Thrilled me— filled me with fantastic terrors never felt before"
  b. "For we cannot help agreeing that no sublunary being / Ever yet was blessed with seeing bird above his chamber door"
  c. "'Prophet!' said I, 'thing of evil!—prophet still, if bird or devil!'"
  d. "'Be that word our sign of parting, bird or fiend!' I shrieked, upstarting— / 'Get thee back into the tempest and the Night's Plutonian shore!'"

____ 14. Which of these statements expresses a central theme of "The Raven"?
  a. Loss of love causes a person to become bitter.
  b. Belief in superstition can be dangerous.
  c. Grief can cause hallucinations.
  d. Isolation can lead to madness.

____ 15. Which choice below presents the core meaning of the following sentence?
  But the Raven, sitting lonely on the placid bust, spoke only / That one word, as if his soul in that one word he did outpour.

a. But the Raven sitting lonely that one word did outpour.
b. The raven on the placid bust his soul in that one word he did outpour.
c. The raven spoke only that one word.
d. His soul in that one word he did outpour.

Vocabulary and Grammar

On the line, write the letter of the one best answer.

_____ 16. The words "not the least *obeisance* made he" stress the raven's
a. black plumage reflecting no light.
b. strange, ungainly walk.
c. inability or refusal to say more than one word.
d. refusal to behave respectfully.

_____ 17. Which word below is closest in meaning to the word *craven*?
a. dark
b. cowardly
c. calm
d. specious

_____ 18. The phrase "*equivocal appellation* of the 'House of Usher'" refers to the fact that
a. the final destiny of the House of Usher is doubtful.
b. good and evil are equally mixed within the House of Usher.
c. Roderick and Madeline often speak their family name in a booming tone.
d. the title "House of Usher" seems to include both the estate and the family.

_____ 19. Which words in this phrase are coordinate adjectives?

And the silken, sad, uncertain rustling of each purple curtain

a. *silken* and *sad* only
b. *sad* and *uncertain* only
c. *silken*, *sad*, and *uncertain* only
d. *silken*, *sad*, *uncertain*, and *purple*

_____ 20. Which sentence is *not* correctly punctuated?
a. "The Raven" is a famous, narrative poem by Edgar Allan Poe.
b. The melodious, mesmerizing lines have been memorized by many.
c. Poe's poem is about a big, black, eerie bird that can say only one word.
d. That word is used by the poem's sad, lonely, and neurotic speaker.

Essay Questions

21. Suppose you had an encounter with Poe's raven. How would you feel? How would you react? How would your response to the raven compare and contrast to that of the speaker in "The Raven"? Write an essay that answers these questions.

22. Some critics believe that the point Poe is making in "The Fall of the House of Usher" is that when creative artists like Roderick Usher completely turn away from the external world and are drawn into the internal world of their imagination, they destroy their ability to create and may eventually destroy themselves. Do you agree or disagree with this interpretation? Write an essay that states your position and supports it with examples from the story.

23. The narrator of "The Fall of the House of Usher" describes one of Usher's paintings this way:

> A small picture presented the interior of an immensely long and rectangular vault or tunnel, with low walls, smooth, white and without interruption or device. . . . [T]his excavation lay at an exceeding depth below the surface of the earth. No outlet was observed in any portion of its vast extent, and no . . . artificial source of light was discernible; yet a flood of intense rays rolled throughout, and bathed the whole in a ghastly and inappropriate splendor.

How might this painting relate to the characters and themes of the story? Answer this question using examples from the story to support your interpretation.

Name _____ Date _____

Selection Test

Critical Reading

On the line, write the letter of the one best answer.

_____ 1. Before donning the black veil, what sort of minister was Mr. Hooper?
   a. outstanding   c. frightening
   b. good   d. despised

_____ 2. What is the likeliest reason that the townspeople react so strongly to the veil?
   a. They are hiding secrets in their own souls.
   b. They are unusually emotional.
   c. They are terrified of the black crape.
   d. They fear that the minister has gone mad.

_____ 3. How does Mr. Hooper react when Elizabeth leaves him?
   a. He begs her to stay but refuses to remove his veil.
   b. He agrees to remove his veil if only she will stay.
   c. He begs her to wear a veil too.
   d. He becomes ill and depressed.

_____ 4. Over what group does the veiled minister seem to have the most power?
   a. the children of the village   c. his congregation
   b. other clergymen in the area   d. souls in agony for sinning

_____ 5. Why do you think Hawthorne is ambiguous about the minister's reason for wearing the veil?
   a. to build suspense
   b. to convey a sense of romance
   c. to emphasize the elusiveness of truth
   d. to suggest the Puritans' sense of mystery

_____ 6. Which statement expresses a central theme of the story?
   a. People are attracted by unsolved mysteries.
   b. People with faith can overcome any hardship.
   c. People are often unwilling to face the truth about themselves.
   d. People who sin should not be forgiven.

_____ 7. "The Minister's Black Veil" is a parable, which means that characters, events, and details of setting
   a. are described in realistic detail.   c. are usually historical in nature.
   b. are gloomy and sometimes terrifying.   d. are simplified to teach a moral lesson.

_____ 8. What does the village physician most likely represent in the story?
   a. wealth   c. logic and reason
   b. religious superstition   d. human emotion

_____ 9. What message about human nature is most strongly conveyed by Elizabeth's nursing of Mr. Hooper on his deathbed?
   a. Love for someone endures despite what that person does.
   b. Curiosity leads people to do odd things.
   c. Loyalty always leads to learning the truth.
   d. Hard work is seldom rewarded in this life.

___ 10. What message might be conveyed by the veiled minister at the wedding?
   a. Weddings are joyful, hopeful occasions.
   b. Brides and grooms need to be reminded that they will eventually die.
   c. Secrets between people can destroy trust and love.
   d. The marriage relationship is very difficult.

___ 11. What does the black veil most likely represent in the parable?
   a. secret love   c. modesty
   b. secret sin   d. violence

___ 12. Based on this story, how would you describe Hawthorne's view of human nature?
   a. naive   c. idealistic
   b. pessimistic   d. uncaring

___ 13. From this story, what can you infer about Hawthorne's attitude toward his Puritan ancestors?
   a. He considered them hypocritical.
   b. He admired their fortitude.
   c. He disapproved of their immorality.
   d. He envied their piety.

___ 14. What can you infer about Hawthorne's message from the following passage?

> The next day, the whole village of Milford talked of little else than Parson Hooper's black veil. That, and the mystery concealed behind it, supplied a topic of discussion between acquaintances meeting in the street, and good women gossiping at their open windows. It was the first item of news that the tavernkeeper told his guests. The children babbled of it on their way to school.

   a. Hawthorne thinks that most human beings are respectful of people's differences.
   b. Hawthorne thinks it's important for people to talk about what is happening in their community.
   c. Hawthorne thinks most human beings gossip too much.
   d. Hawthorne thinks children are the worst gossipers.

___ 15. Based on the rest of the story, what can you infer about the meaning of the following passage.

> "When the friend shows his inmost heart to his friend; the lover to his best beloved; when man does not vainly shrink from the eye of his Creator, loathsomely treasuring up the secret of his sin; then deem me a monster, for the symbol beneath which I have lived and die! I look around me, and lo! on every visage a Black Veil."

   a. It is sometimes good to hide secrets from other people.
   b. Love is not something to be valued.
   c. It is human nature to follow our hearts.
   d. Each person hides his or her darkest secrets from others for fear of what others will think.

Vocabulary and Grammar

On the line, write the letter of the one best answer.

___ 16. Which word most likely identifies what the minister's veil symbolically meant to conceal?
   a. iniquity   c. waggery
   b. vagary   d. obstinacy

_____ 17. Why is the narrator surprised that the *impertinent* people in the congregation fail to ask Mr. Hooper the reason for the veil?
  a. They command a great deal of respect.
  b. They would be likely to ask questions that might be considered disrespectful.
  c. They are afraid of speaking for fear of appearing disrespectful.
  d. They are interested in appearing intelligent.

_____ 18. Which event in the story would best be described as *indecorous*?
  a. the handsome couple getting married
  b. the people rushing out of the church in a confused way
  c. Elizabeth nursing Mr. Hooper
  d. sinners asking for Mr. Hooper when seeking consolation

_____ 19. In which sentence does Hawthorne use a participial phrase to vary his sentence openers?

> The cause of so much amazement may appear sufficiently slight. Mr. Hooper, a gentlemanly person, of about thirty, though still a bachelor, was dressed with due clerical neatness, as if a careful wife had starched his band, and brushed the weekly dust from his Sunday's garb. There was but one thing remarkable in his appearance. Swathed about his forehead, and hanging down over his face, so low as to be shaken by his breath, Mr. Hooper had on a black veil.

  a. the first sentence   c. the third sentence
  b. the second sentence   d. the fourth sentence

_____ 20. How does Hawthorne vary his sentence openers in this passage?

> The sexton stood in the porch of Milford meetinghouse, pulling busily at the bell rope. The old people of the village came stopping along the street. Children, with bright faces, tripped merrily beside their parents, or mimicked a graver gait, in the conscious dignity of their Sunday clothes. Spruce bachelors looked sidelong at the pretty maidens, and fancied that the Sabbath sunshine made them prettier than on weekdays. When the throng had mostly streamed into the porch, the sexton began to toll the bell.

  a. After several sentences in standard subject-verb order, he opens one with a prepositional phrase.
  b. After several sentences in standard subject-verb order, he opens one with an adverb.
  c. After several sentences in standard subject-verb order, he opens one with a subordinate clause.
  d. After several sentences in standard subject-verb order, he uses inverted order, in which the verb precedes the subject.

Essay Questions

21. Do you think Mr. Hooper's veil is a form of confession? Is he making a statement? Might it be both? Write an essay describing the conclusion you reach about the significance of the veil. Support your solution with examples from the story.

22. What are the characteristics of the Puritans and their religion as portrayed by Hawthorne in this story? Do you think he has a negative or positive opinion of them? What do you think is his opinion of Mr. Hooper? Write an essay answering these questions.

23. In the story, a lady of the village says, "How strange . . . that a simple black veil, such as any woman might wear on her bonnet, should become such a terrible thing on Mr. Hooper's face!" Write an essay exploring what this statement means in relation to objects and their symbolic power.

from *Moby-Dick* by Herman Melville

Selection Test

Critical Reading

On the line, write the letter of the one best answer.

____ 1. The name of the whaling ship that Ahab captains is the _____.
    a. *Pequod*   c. *Tashtego*
    b. *Quarter-Deck*   d. *Nantucket*

____ 2. The white whale against whom Ahab seeks vengeance
    a. never appears.
    b. treats the ship's crew indifferently when he finally appears.
    c. caused Ahab to lose his leg in a previous encounter.
    d. is never seen by anyone but Ahab.

____ 3. Which of these choices lists characters from *Moby-Dick* in descending rank?
    a. Ahab—Queequeg—Flask—Starbuck
    b. Ahab—Starbuck—Stubb—Ishmael
    c. Ishmael—Ahab—Starbuck—Daggoo
    d. Starbuck—Moby-Dick—Stubb—Flask

____ 4. Ahab persuades his crew members to chase the white whale by appealing mainly to their ____.
    a. patriotism   c. greed
    b. hunger   d. loyalty

____ 5. Ahab's rambling monologues show that he is _____.
    a. practical   c. vulnerable
    b. uneducated   d. single-minded

____ 6. What does Stubb mean when he says of Ahab, "The chick that's in him pecks the shell. 'Twill soon be out"?
    a. Ahab's vengeance is dangerous and the crew will soon tell him so.
    b. Something is bothering Ahab and it will soon drive him to action.
    c. Ahab's crew is growing angry and may mutiny soon.
    d. Starbuck is opposing Ahab and will have to be restrained.

____ 7. What is the chief significance of Ahab's being drowned by his own harpoon line?
    a. It stresses his inexperience as a sailor.
    b. It stresses the idea that obsession and vengefulness are self-destructive.
    c. It stresses the idea that manmade objects are more powerful than nature.
    d. It stresses Ahab's defiance.

____ 8. One of the central themes conveyed in this selection is that
    a. only the strongest survive.
    b. revenge is justifiable.
    c. whaling is indefensible.
    d. human understanding is limited.

____ 9. The selection portrays nature as
    a. sympathetic and soothing.   c. majestic and elusive.
    b. violent but tamable.   d. foolish and vengeful.

Unit 3: A Growing Nation (1800–1870)

_____ 10. Which detail in the following passage is most clearly a symbol?

> A sky hawk that tauntingly had followed the main-truck downwards from its natural home among the stars, . . . this bird now chanced to intercept its broad fluttering wing between the hammer and the wood: and simultaneously feeling that ethereal thrill, the submerged savage beneath, in his deathgrasp, kept his hammer frozen there: and so the bird of heaven, with archangelic shrieks, and his imperial beak thrust upwards, and his whole captive form folded in the flag of Ahab, went down with his ship.

a. the sky hawk
b. the stars

c. the broad fluttering wing
d. the ethereal thrill

_____ 11. Which detail listed in the choices below most clearly suggests that Ahab's footprints are a symbol in the following passage?

> Soon his steady, ivory stride was heard, as to and fro he paced his old rounds, upon planks so familiar to his tread, that they were all over dented, like geological stones, with the peculiar mark of his walk. Did you fixedly gaze, too, upon that ribbed and dented brow; there also, you would see still stranger footprints—the footprints of his one unsleeping, ever-pacing thought.

a. the familiarity of the planks
b. the fact that the planks were dented
c. Ahab's ribbed and dented brow
d. the comparison relating them to "the footprints of his one unsleeping, ever-pacing thought"

_____ 12. Which of these aspects of nature does the white whale *not* symbolize?

a. destructiveness
b. immortality

c. spiritual comfort
d. beauty

_____ 13. To Ahab's mind, Moby-Dick symbolizes a wall that

a. keeps the ship from its business of whaling.
b. protects Ahab from his own inner thoughts and desires.
c. must be broken through to reach the truth behind it.
d. has grown up between Ahab and his crew.

_____ 14. What behavior of Ahab most clearly symbolizes the restlessness and obsessive nature of his thoughts?

a. his pacing up and down on deck
b. his offering mugs of grog to the crew
c. his nailing a coin to the mast
d. his being hoisted up the mast in a basket

_____ 15. What does the sea probably symbolize in this final sentence from the selection?

> Then all collapsed, and the great shroud of the sea rolled on as it had rolled five thousand years ago.

a. humanity's power over nature
b. nature's power over humanity
c. the goodness of nature
d. the changeability of nature

Vocabulary and Grammar

On the line, write the letter of the one best answer.

____ 16. Which of these professions most requires a person to be *prescient*?
    a. meteorologist   c. whaler
    b. dog catcher   d. fortuneteller

____ 17. Which word has a meaning most nearly opposite that of *maledictions*?
    a. blessings   c. curses
    b. lies   d. pleas

____ 18. Which pair of words expresses a relationship most like the relationship of the words in capital letters?

      STUBBORNLY : AHAB ::

    a. pertinaciously : Starbuck
    b. inscrutably : Moby-Dick
    c. humorously : Tashtego
    d. presciently : the crew

____ 19. Which of these sentences illustrates correct agreement with collective nouns?
    a. The class were dismissed when the bell rang.
    b. The club are holding an election on Thursday, March 29.
    c. The crew sail for months without making port.
    d. The choir take their seats beginning around 7 P.M.

____ 20. Which of these sentences illustrates correct agreement with collective nouns?
    a. The class holds different opinions on the subject.
    b. The club enjoys talking to one another.
    c. This crew is the finest that ever sailed a whaling ship.
    d. The choir sings different parts depending on whether they are alto, soprano, tenor, and bass.

Essay Questions

21. Examine Ahab in his role as captain of the whaling ship. In what ways does he seem to be a good captain? In what ways is he a bad one? Answer these questions in an essay in which you support your opinions with details from the selection.

22. At one point Ishmael, the narrator, states, "For with little external to constrain us, the innermost necessities in our being, these still drive us on." Write an essay that shows how this statement applies to one or more characters in this selection.

23. At one point in the selection, the members of the crew gather to hear Ahab describe his goal and persuade everyone else to join him. Why do you think Melville felt that such a scene was necessary? What are some things that the scene accomplishes? Address these questions in an essay.

"Where *Is* Here?" by Joyce Carol Oates

Selection Test

Critical Reading

On the line, write the letter of the one best answer.

_____ 1. Which part of the house do the parents *not* allow the stranger to see?
  a. the son's bedroom
  b. the master bedroom
  c. the kitchen
  d. the basement

_____ 2. Who lets the stranger into the house?
  a. he comes in uninvited   c. the son
  b. the father   d. the mother

_____ 3. What does Oates suggest by having the stranger twice touch something "as if testing materiality"?
  a. The nature of material things is transitory.
  b. The stranger does not believe the house to be real.
  c. The stranger has come back from the dead.
  d. The stranger has the ability to see through walls.

_____ 4. Which part of the house does the stranger remember as one of his "happy places"?
  a. the swings in the backyard
  b. the window seat in the living room
  c. the upstairs bedroom
  d. the basement

_____ 5. What significance does the stranger's recollection of the living room as "dark by day, dark by night" have for the story?
  a. It reinforces the sense of dread that accompanies the stranger as he explores the house.
  b. It suggests that the stranger's family suffered from a disease that made them unusually sensitive to bright light.
  c. It suggests that the stranger's family was too poor to pay for electricity when he was young.
  d. It symbolizes the stranger's evil nature in comparison with the good nature of the father and mother.

_____ 6. What geometric figure does the stranger draw for the son to represent infinity?
  a. squares inside a circle
  b. a rectangle surrounding a bunch of circles
  c. circles inside one another
  d. triangles inside a square

_____ 7. What does the stranger suggest when he says to the father regarding the father's children, "You love them—of course, . . . otherwise it would all come to an end"?
  a. The stranger intends to kill the children if given the chance.
  b. The father does not really love his children.
  c. The father will soon do something to hurt his children.
  d. The stranger's own family came to a bad end.

Vocabulary

On the line, write the letter of the one best answer.

____ 8. Which word best completes the sentence?

Father, reserved by nature, but genial and even _____ when taken unaware, spoke amiably.

a. avaricious
b. precarious
c. gregarious
d. preposterous

____ 9. Something done *covertly* is
a. covered in dirt.
b. done in secrecy.
c. conveyed by electricity.
d. done openly.

____ 10. An *avuncular* handshake is one which is?
a. disturbing and unnatural
b. stodgy and reserved
c. happy and indulgent
d. nervous and morose

Essay Questions

11. Write an essay describing the mood of the story. What details of setting and character does Oates use to set the mood? Evaluate how well the details work and how successfully the author maintains the mood.

12. The stranger in "Where *Is* Here?" is mysterious and vaguely threatening. Write an essay analyzing the details by which Oates emphasizes those traits. How does the stranger make the other characters uncomfortable? Speculate on what the stranger's behavior and personality tell the reader about his "true" nature. Why do you think he came back to see his old house? What did he hope to find?

13. The mystery and ambiguity of "Where *Is* Here?" leave much room for interpretation. Write an essay analyzing the devices by which Oates builds uncertainty into the story. Choose one detail and give it a concrete meaning. How does your "added" information affect the interpretation of the story?

Part Test, Unit 3, Part 2: Shadows of the Imagination

Critical Reading

The questions below are based on the following selection.

This excerpt is from the short story "Dr. Heidegger's Experiment" by Nathaniel Hawthorne.

While he spoke, Dr. Heidegger had been filling the four champagne glasses with the water of the Fountain of Youth. It was apparently impregnated with an effervescent gas, for little bubbles were continually ascending from the depths of the glasses and bursting in silvery spray at the surface. As the liquor diffused a pleasant perfume, the old people doubted not that it possessed cordial and comfortable properties; and though utter skeptics as to its rejuvenescent power, they were inclined to swallow it at once. But Dr. Heidegger besought them to stay a moment.

"Before you drink, my respectable old friends," said he, "it would be well that, with the experience of a lifetime to direct you, you should draw up a few general rules for your guidance, in passing a second time through the perils of youth. Think what a sin and a shame it would be if, with your peculiar advantages, you should not become patterns of virtue and wisdom to all the young people of the age!"

The doctor's four venerable friends made him no answer, except by a feeble and tremulous laugh; so very ridiculous was the idea that, knowing how closely repentance treads behind the steps of error, they should ever go astray again.

"Drink, then," said the doctor, bowing. "I rejoice that I have so well selected the subjects of my experiment."

With palsied hands, they raised the glasses to their lips. The liquor, if it really possessed such virtues as Dr. Heidegger imputed to it, could not have been bestowed on four human beings who needed it more woefully. They looked as if they had never known what youth or pleasure was, but had been the offspring of Nature's dotage, and always the gray, decrepit, sapless, miserable creatures who now sat stooping round the doctor's table, without life enough in their souls or bodies to be animated even by the prospect of growing young again. They drank off the water and replaced their glasses on the table. . . . They gazed at one another and fancied that some magic power had really begun to smooth away the deep and sad inscriptions which Father Time had been so long engraving on their brows. The Widow Wycherly adjusted her cap, for she felt almost like a woman again.

"Give us more of this wondrous water!" cried they, eagerly. "We are younger—but we are still too old! Quick—give us more!"

"Patience, patience!" quoth Dr. Heidegger, who sat watching the experiment with philosophic coolness. "You have been a long time growing old. Surely you might be content to grow young in half an hour! But the water is at your service."

On the line, write the letter of the one best answer.

_____ 1. Why are the elderly people "inclined to swallow" the water "at once"?
   a. They are eager to leave the office.
   b. They are inclined to do whatever the doctor says.
   c. They are impatient to regain their youth.
   d. They are in a hurry to go home.

_____ 2. What does Dr. Heidegger mean by referring to his subjects' potential "peculiar advantages"?
   a. They are unusual people.
   b. They would experience youth for the second time.
   c. They are smarter than other people.
   d. They have established "a few general rules" by which to live.

_____ 3. Why does Dr. Heidegger caution the four elderly people to draw up rules?
   a. He fears they will want more water than he has.
   b. He doesn't want one to have an unfair advantage over the others.
   c. He fears they will revert to old behaviors and waste the gift.
   d. He wants them to approach the experiment in an orderly fashion.

_____ 4. In order to better understand the selection's third paragraph, where is the most logical place to break down its long sentence?
   a. after the semicolon
   b. after the word _repentance_
   c. after the word _friends_
   d. before the word _they_

_____ 5. The four people who drink the doctor's water are symbols for _____ .
   a. medical science   c. age
   b. youth   d. nature

_____ 6. What does the water symbolize?
   a. knowledge   c. refreshment
   b. eternal youth   d. medicine

_____ 7. The most likely allegorical meaning of the entire story concerns _____ .
   a. religious faith   c. friendship
   b. virtue   d. youth and age

_____ 8. To judge Hawthorne's message, you would
   a. ask yourself what points the author was making, and then decide whether you agree or disagree.
   b. look for the presence of a single effect in the story.
   c. analyze the elements of the author's style.
   d. break down long sentences to help you develop a concise summary of the key details and events of the work.

_____ 9. In an allegory, events, characters, and details of setting
   a. have only literal meaning.
   b. are relatively unimportant.
   c. are expressed in figurative language.
   d. have symbolic meaning.

_____ 10. Dr. Heidegger suggests that the experiment could benefit
   a. the four friends' future.
   b. young people.
   c. the cause of science.
   d. the doctor's reputation.

Vocabulary and Grammar

On the line, write the letter of the one best answer.

_____ 11. Which of the phrases below could be substituted for the italicized words in the following sentence without changing the meaning?

In discussing his friend's family estate, the narrator refers to the _equivocal appellation_ of the House of Usher.

   a. impressive appearance
   b. crumbling state
   c. ambiguous title
   d. eerie setting

____ 12. The narrator is summoned to Roderick Usher's home by an importunate plea for help. The best synonym for *importunate* is _____.
   a. desperate
   b. insistent
   c. unexpected
   d. irrational

____ 13. Two or more coordinate adjectives modify
   a. two or more nouns.
   b. the same noun to different degrees.
   c. the same noun to an equal degree.
   d. gerunds or gerund phrases.

____ 14. Which includes all the coordinate adjectives in the following sentence?

   The windows were long, narrow, and pointed, and at so vast a distance from the black oaken floor as to be altogether innaccessible from within.

   a. long, narrow
   b. long, narrow, pointed
   c. so, vast
   d. black, oaken

____ 15. Which sentence contains a collective noun?
   a. The entire ship's company were assembled.
   b. There are men from whom warm words are small indignity.
   c. The mariners began to gaze curiously at each other.
   d. Our poor hearts throb and our poor brains beat too much for that.

Essay Questions

16. Romanticism was a nineteenth-century literary and artistic movement that placed a premium on imagination, fantasy, emotion, nature, and individuality. The Romantic writers had a deep interest in mystery and the supernatural. Write an essay in which you discuss how this interest is reflected in American literature of the early nineteenth century. Develop your discussion by citing evidence from the selections in Part 2 of Unit 3.

17. The poet Richard Wilbur once commented, "'The Fall of the House of Usher' is a journey into the depths of self." How does Wilbur's statement relate to Poe's psychological portrait of Roderick Usher? How does the character of Usher reveal the darker side of the self? Write an essay in which you answer these questions in light of Wilbur's statement. In your essay, analyze the character of Roderick Usher and the changes he undergoes. Use specific references to the story to support your points.

18. Authors use foreshadowing to increase suspense in a story. In a thoughtful essay, discuss how the author of one of the works in Part 2 of Unit 3 effectively utilized the technique of foreshadowing. Give examples from the work.

from *Nature*, from *Self-Reliance*, "The Snowstorm,"
and "Concord Hymn" by Ralph Waldo Emerson

Selection Test

Critical Reading

On the line, write the letter of the one best answer.

____ 1. With which statement would you expect Transcendentalists to agree?
   a. There is no fundamental reality beyond the physical world.
   b. Human beings have less potential when they act independently.
   c. There is a spiritual relationship between humanity and nature.
   d. People should strive so that their natural souls do not become part of an oversoul.

____ 2. "Concord Hymn" was written to celebrate
   a. music and poetry.
   b. a monument to the Revolution.
   c. Massachusetts.
   d. the end of the Civil War.

____ 3. The traveler on the sled in "The Snowstorm" must
   a. hurry to miss the beginning of the storm.
   b. put on extra clothes.
   c. stop because he cannot continue traveling.
   d. rescue people trapped in town.

____ 4. Readers challenge a writer's text when they
   a. refuse to read.
   b. lend the text to others.
   c. question the writer's opinions.
   d. proofread articles to make them more accurate.

____ 5. Which statements about Transcendentalism are accurate?

   I. Transcendentalism was an intellectual movement.

   II. Transcendentalism was a largely European movement.

   III. Transcendentalists were interested in the human spirit.

   IV. Transcendentalists thought that an exploration of nature
   helped people understand universal truths.

   a. I and II only
   b. II and III only
   c. I, II, III, and IV
   d. I, III, and IV only

____ 6. How might a reader challenge the following text from *Self-Reliance*?

   Trust thyself: every heart vibrates to that iron string.

   a. The reader might reflect on personal experience to judge the statement.
   b. The reader might show that the word *thyself* is archaic, or outdated.
   c. The reader might defend the statement because it is written by a famous American philosopher.
   d. The reader might research the facts on how the heart functions.

____ 7. Which view of nature does Emerson take?
     a. Nature is indifferent to human suffering.
     b. Nature must be studied and dissected.
     c. Urban dwellers have little conception of the cruelty of nature.
     d. Nature can inspire the human spirit.

____ 8. Which of these quotations reflects a key idea of Transcendentalism?
     a. "Nothing is at last sacred but the integrity of your own mind."
     b. "The virtue in most request is conformity."
     c. "With consistency a great soul has simply nothing to do."
     d. "To be great is to be misunderstood."

____ 9. Which of these statements best characterizes the central idea of *Self-Reliance*?
     a. Meekness is the virtue that fosters self-awareness.
     b. Rely on your own instincts.
     c. Social customs serve a valuable purpose.
     d. Cruelty may be necessary to achieve philosophical goals.

____ 10. Emerson's romanticism is most clearly displayed in his
     a. careful descriptions of nature.
     b. exaggerated sense of loneliness.
     c. logically constructed arguments.
     d. reliance on emotional truth.

____ 11. In *Nature*, what does Emerson mean by describing nature as both comic and melancholy?
     a. Our view of nature depends on the season of the year.
     b. Nature mirrors an individual's moods.
     c. A skillful writer can personify nature in various ways.
     d. Nature can be two-faced or devious.

____ 12. In *Nature*, Emerson writes, "Yet it is certain that the power to produce this delight does not reside in nature, but in man, or in a harmony of both." What philosophy does this statement support?
     a. materialism   c. feminism
     b. Transcendentalism   d. creationism

____ 13. In *Self-Reliance*, Emerson writes that society "loves not realities and creators, but names and customs." Which of these adjectives best reflects Emerson's attitude in that statement?
     a. disapproving   c. encouraging
     b. accepting   d. forgiving

____ 14. Why does Emerson allude to individuals such as Socrates, Jesus, and Galileo in *Self-Reliance*?
     a. to suggest that they agreed with his philosophy
     b. to encourage readers to learn about historical figures
     c. to inspire readers through the example of their struggles
     d. to question their contribution to society

____ 15. Which of these statements could be used to challenge the text of a written work?
     a. The author presents a thorough analysis of the subject.
     b. The author constructs a rational defense of the position.
     c. The author cites excellent research.
     d. The author expresses opinions as if they were facts.

Vocabulary and Grammar

On the line, write the letter of the one best answer.

____ 16. Which pair of words expresses a relationship that is most similar to the relationship of these words in capital letters?

SUN : RADIANT ::

a. warm : hot
b. glowing : moon
c. star : small
d. perfume : fragrant

____ 17. Writers vary sentence lengths primarily to
a. increase the pleasure they take in writing.
b. sustain reader interest.
c. cut down on time spent in keyboarding.
d. maintain a steady, monotonous rhythm.

____ 18. Which word below is most nearly *opposite* in meaning from the italicized word in this statement?

He has an *aversion* to joining the team.

a. plan
b. liking
c. distaste
d. hope

____ 19. Which sentence below would best sustain reader interest just after this sentence?

Standing on the bare ground—my head bathed by the blithe air and uplifted into infinite space—all mean egotism vanishes.

a. I become a transparent eyeball.
b. Becoming a transparent eyeball, I am the lover of uncontained and immortal beauty.
c. The currents of the Universal Being circulate through me, and I am part and parcel of God.
d. In the tranquil landscape, and especially in the distant line of the horizon, man beholds somewhat as beautiful as his own nature.

____ 20. Which word below can be substituted for the italicized word in this statement?

Modern philosophers theorize that there may be order in *chaos*.

a. disorder
b. nature
c. pain
d. self-reliance

Essay Questions

21. Write an essay in which you describe two examples from Emerson's essay *Nature* that suggest a relationship between the human spirit and nature.

22. In "Concord Hymn" Emerson writes, "Here once the embattled farmers stood, / And fired the shot heard round the world." In *Nature* he writes, "The name of the nearest friend sounds then foreign and accidental: to be brothers, to be acquaintances, master or servant, is then a trifle and a disturbance." Explain the meanings of these passages, and then consider how each of them supports or does not support the Transcendentalists' ideal of an oversoul.

23. Two principal ideas of Transcendentalism are the importance of the individual and the concept of the oversoul flowing from the relationship between the natural world and the human spirit. Do you think that these two beliefs support or conflict with each other? Use examples from Emerson's writings to support your evaluation.

from *Walden* and from *Civil Disobedience*
by Henry David Thoreau

Selection Test

Critical Reading

On the line, write the letter of the one best answer.

_____ 1. Which of these statements best reflects Thoreau's philosophy as expressed in *Walden*?
   a. Human beings are creatures of great complexity.
   b. Building a cabin in the woods is practical and inexpensive.
   c. Wealth is desirable, but spiritual happiness is also important.
   d. Living a simple life close to nature lets a person concentrate on important things.

_____ 2. According to *Walden*, people thought Thoreau was a real-estate broker because
   a. he sold farmhouses in Massachusetts.
   b. he believed every person had the right to own real estate.
   c. he built his own place on Walden Pond.
   d. he visited all the farms in a twelve-mile radius of where he lived.

_____ 3. What does Thoreau mean in the following sentence?

   I do not wish to be any more busy with my hands than is necessary. My head is hands and feet.

   a. He doesn't like working very hard.
   b. He views thinking as an important part of his work.
   c. He prefers a desk job to manual labor.
   d. His partial paralysis makes walking impossible and also makes it difficult to work with his hands.

_____ 4. What aspect of his philosophy does Thoreau express in the following statement?

   If a man does not keep pace with his companions, perhaps it is because he hears a different drummer.

   a. love of nature   c. lack of materialism
   b. individualism   d. emphasis on simplicity

_____ 5. What is Thoreau's main point about time in the paragraph beginning "Time is but the stream I go a-fishing in"?
   a. Time is shallow, but eternity remains.
   b. Time is elusive; we cannot pin it down.
   c. To succeed in life, you must harness time and make it work for you.
   d. Time is of the essence.

_____ 6. One aspect of Thoreau's style is to
   a. begin a paragraph with a specific event and build to a general truth.
   b. avoid repetition of words or ideas.
   c. follow each long sentence with a short, punchy sentence.
   d. ask a series of rhetorical questions.

_____ 7. How does Thoreau's style reinforce his theme of living with deliberation?
   a. by relying on unusually difficult words
   b. by instructing the reader to pay attention

c. by imitating a scientific report

d. by repeating his main ideas

_____ 8. What does Thoreau hope to convey with the description of the path his feet had worn to the pondside within a week?

a. Establishing habits makes daily living easier.

b. Human beings fall into dull routines all too readily.

c. Living far away from friends is good discipline.

d. Everyone should march to the same tune.

_____ 9. What message does Thoreau hope to convey with his anecdote of the strong and beautiful bug in the conclusion of *Walden*?

a. Life can be beautiful, but it can also be dangerous.

b. Not all bugs are ugly.

c. Something that appears lifeless can give rise to new life.

d. Carpenters live simple lives close to nature.

_____ 10. *Walden*'s closing image of the morning star leaves readers feeling _____.

a. inspired   c. exhausted

b. hopeless   d. argumentative

_____ 11. What is the central idea of *Civil Disobedience*?

a. People must overthrow the government.

b. Trade and commerce should be strictly regulated.

c. The fewer people who run the government, the better.

d. Citizens should be willing to act on their opinions.

_____ 12. In *Civil Disobedience*, how does Thoreau support his view that the government is abused by powerful individuals?

a. He compares American and foreign governments.

b. He analyzes the structure of America's government.

c. He cites the examples of an unpopular war.

d. He alludes to several corrupt Massachusetts politicians.

_____ 13. Thoreau's view of the war with Mexico is best described as _____.

a. patriotic   c. critical

b. indifferent   d. practical

_____ 14. Which word best describes Thoreau's style in *Civil Disobedience*?

a. objective   c. scholarly

b. repetitive   d. casual

_____ 15. Based on *Civil Disobedience*, what can you infer about Thoreau's political philosophy?

a. He relies on government leaders for moral guidance.

b. He feels it is America's destiny to spread to the Pacific Ocean.

c. He stresses that we must all work together to accomplish great deeds.

d. He believes that people are politically responsible for themselves.

_____ 16. How does *Civil Disobedience* reflect ideas of Transcendentalism?

a. It stresses the individual's ability to judge the actions of government.

b. It proposes looking at nature as a way to govern harmoniously.

c. It implies that democratic governments, too, have an Over-Soul and are more spiritually attuned to people's needs than any one individual can ever be.

d. It stresses that warfare is sometimes the only means by which oppression can be cast off and society changed.

Vocabulary and Grammar

On the line, write the letter of the one best answer.

____ 17. What does Thoreau mean when he describes the fences as *dilapidated*?
- a. They are under construction.
- b. They need to be repaired.
- c. There are many fences.
- d. The fences are very high.

____ 18. Which of these sentences contains an infinitive or an infinitive phrase used as a noun?
- a. Thoreau went to the woods.
- b. Thoreau wanted to live deliberately.
- c. By simplifying his life, Thoreau concentrated on important ideas.
- d. To simply his life, Thoreau concentrated on important ideas.

____ 19. Which of these sentences contains an infinitive or an infinitive phrase used as an adverb?
- a. Thoreau wrote to share his experiences.
- b. He wanted to live a life stripped to the barest necessities.
- c. Thoreau's philosophies are very similar to those of Emerson.
- d. Each spring, he collected seeds to plant in his garden.

____ 20. Which word below can substitute for the italicized word in this sentence?

Thoreau thinks people spend too much time on *superfluous* concerns.

- a. upper-class
- b. unnatural
- c. unnecessary
- d. important

Essay Questions

21. Based on *Walden*, what would you say that living in the woods taught Thoreau about the human spirit and the natural world? Answer this question in a short essay, and support your evaluation with details from the selection.

22. Choose one of these statements from *Walden* or *Civil Disobedience*, and in an essay explain what it means and how it helps to express Thoreau's philosophy. Also indicate whether or not you agree with the statement, and explain why.

> Sell your clothes and keep your thoughts.

> If a man does not keep pace with his companions, perhaps it is because he hears a different drummer. Let him step to the music which he hears, however measured or far away.

> Let every man make known what kind of government would command his respect, and that will be one step toward obtaining it.

23. In both *Civil Disobedience* and *Walden*, Thoreau urges people to act. How would Thoreau define taking action? Does action imply physical activity? When does Thoreau think people should take action? What action does he think they should take? Using examples from the selection, write a short essay responding to these questions.

Part Test, Unit 3, Part 3: The Emerging American Identity—
The Human Spirit and the Natural World

Critical Reading

The questions below are based on the following poem.

The Rhodora: On Being Asked, Whence Is the Flower?

Ralph Waldo Emerson

In May, when sea winds pierced our solitudes,
I found the fresh Rhodora in the woods,
Spreading its leafless blooms in a damp nook,
To please the desert and the sluggish brook.
[5] The purple petals, fallen in the pool,
Made the black water with their beauty gay;
Here might the red-bird come his plumes to cool,
And court the flower that cheapens his array.
Rhodora! if the sages ask thee why
[10] This charm is wasted on the earth and sky,
Tell them, dear, that if eyes were made for seeing,
Then Beauty is its own excuse for being:
Why thou wert there, O rival of the rose!
I never thought to ask, I never knew:
[15] But, in my simple ignorance, suppose
The self-same Power that brought me there brought you.

On the line, write the letter of the one best answer.

_____ 1. Where does the speaker find the rhodora?
　　　　　a. near the sea
　　　　　b. in a damp nook in the woods
　　　　　c. near a rock
　　　　　d. in the desert

_____ 2. What larger concept does the rhodora represent?
　　　　　a. God
　　　　　b. color
　　　　　c. nature and beauty
　　　　　d. life and death

_____ 3. Which line best exemplifies the Transcendentalists' belief that fundamental reality is
　　　　beyond the reach of a person's limited senses?
　　　　　a. "I found the fresh Rhodora in the woods"
　　　　　b. "I never thought to ask, I never knew"
　　　　　c. "This charm is wasted on the earth and sky"
　　　　　d. "The self-same Power that brought me there brought you"

_____ 4. In challenging a text, a reader must
　　　　　a. question an author's assertions and reasoning.
　　　　　b. refuse to believe what he or she reads.
　　　　　c. agree with what an author asserts.
　　　　　d. break down sentences into parts.

_____ 5. According to the speaker, what question might the sages ask the rhodora?
   a. How do you have the power to change the color of black water?
   b. Why is your charm wasted on the earth and sky?
   c. Do you wish to cheapen the array of colorful birds?
   d. What is Beauty?

_____ 6. What is unexpected about the speaker's reference to his "simple ignorance" in line 15?
   a. The speaker seems wiser than the sages.
   b. The speaker's ignorance causes him acute embarrassment.
   c. The rhodora and the speaker seem equally beautiful to God.
   d. The speaker is surprised at the power of God.

_____ 7. Which word best describes Emerson's tone in this poem?
   a. comic
   b. lofty
   c. didactic
   d. somber

_____ 8. To whom or what might the word _our_ in line 1 refer?
   a. Emerson and the speaker
   b. the speaker and his wife
   c. Emerson and other Transcendentalists
   d. the speaker and the rhodora

_____ 9. In what way might the red-bird "court the flower" in line 8?
   a. by pollinating the flower
   b. by cooling his plumes
   c. by swimming in the water
   d. by spreading its blooms

_____ 10. If the poem were going to be divided into two sections, which line would be the most likely beginning of the second section?
   a. line 10   c. line 9
   b. line 5   d. line 14

Vocabulary and Grammar

On the line, write the letter of the one best answer.

_____ 11. According to the philosophy of Ralph Waldo Emerson, _____ will remember those who are not afraid to be misunderstood.
   a. suffrage
   b. posterity
   c. magnanimity
   d. chaos

_____ 12. Henry David Thoreau believed that what some people call improvements are _superfluous_, or _____.
   a. unnecessary
   b. extraordinary
   c. inferior
   d. essential

_____ 13. Which sentence does _not_ contain an infinitive?
   a. I had begun to sort my seeds.
   b. To be generous, I sold him the farm for just what I gave for it.
   c. The nearest I came to actual possession was when I bought the Hollowell Place.
   d. I could afford only to let it alone.

_____ 14. Which illustrates the use of sentences of varying lengths to emphasize and clarify an idea?

    a. Trust in your unique abilities. Don't be afraid to be misunderstood. It is better to be a nonconformist.

    b. Trust in your unique abilities without the fear of being misunderstood. Be a non-conformist.

    c. Trust in your unique abilities whenenver possible. Don't be afraind that someone might misunderstand what you say or do. It is far better to be a nonconformist if that option is open to you.

    d. Be a nonconformist. Trust in your abilities. Don't be consistent.

_____ 15. Which sentence contains an infinitive phrase used as a subject?

    a. To build an architecture of snow is the job of the snowstorm.

    b. On every fence, tree, and house, the architect of snow scurries to work.

    c. A snowstorm uses the wind both to shape and to smooth.

    d. When the snowstorm ceases, it is the sun's privilege to spotlight the dazzling creation.

Essay Questions

16. When Thoreau lived at Walden Pond, the United States was in the early stages of being transformed into an industrial nation, and most of the country's land remained uncultivated. Write an essay in which you examine the details of Thoreau's experiment, and then discuss the difficulties Thoreau might have had if he had tried to conduct his experiment today.

17. Choose one of the Emerson poems and one of the Emerson prose pieces from this part of Unit 3. In an essay, compare and contrast the ideas about nature that Emerson expresses in each work.

18. Identify the central ideas that Henry David Thoreau puts forth in the excerpt from "Civil Disobedience." Then write a persuasive essay in which you explain and then refute the American Romantics' ideas.

Unit 3: A Growing Nation (1800–1870)

Emily Dickinson's Poetry

Selection Test

Critical Reading

On the line, write the letter of the one best answer.

____ 1. In "I heard a Fly buzz—when I died—," why is there a stillness in the room?
a. The people in the room have stopped talking in order to listen to the fly.
b. The people in the room are waiting for the speaker to make her will.
c. The people in the room are waiting for the speaker's final moment.
d. The storm outdoors has momentarily ceased its "heaves."

____ 2. In the following stanza from "I heard a Fly buzz—when I died—," which words create slant rhyme?

> I heard a Fly buzz—when I died—
> The Stillness in the Room
> Was like the Stillness in the Air—
> Between the Heaves of Storm—

a. *Air* and *Storm*   c. *died* and *Room*
b. *Room* and *Storm*   d. *died* and *Air*

____ 3. Which of the following images is the central image in "Because I could not stop for Death—"?
a. a carriage ride   c. children playing
b. the horses' heads   d. the setting sun

____ 4. In "Because I could not stop for Death—," Death is personified as
a. a polite gentleman.   c. a weary gravedigger.
b. a rough and harried carriage driver.   d. a well-informed tour guide.

____ 5. In "My life closed twice before its close—," the three closings mentioned in the title refer to
a. the deaths of three loved ones in the speaker's family.
b. three great disappointments in the speaker's life.
c. two great disappointments followed by the speaker's death.
d. the parting of two loved ones followed by the speaker's death.

____ 6. Which of these statements best expresses the central message of "My life closed twice before its close—"?
a. Our lives are divided into three parts, and death is the last one.
b. Parting is heavenly when you are glad to be rid of someone but hellish when you know you will miss the person.
c. Parting may be the closest we come in life to understanding death.
d. Death is followed by immortality.

____ 7. In "The Soul selects her own Society—," the soul is compared to
a. a nation of people who do not like to travel to other nations.
b. an emperor who rides in chariots and pauses outside a gate.
c. a man who is very choosy about his friends.
d. a woman who stays in her house no matter who comes to visit her.

____ 8. What is the chief effect of the slant rhyme in this final stanza from "The Soul selects her own Society—"?

> I've known her—from an ample nation—
> Choose One—
> Then—close the Valves of her attention—
> Like Stone—

 a. It creates a harmony that stresses how well the speaker knows the soul.
 b. It creates a disharmony that suggests strife in the ample nation.
 c. It creates a disharmony that echoes the unsociable actions of the soul.
 d. It captures the sound of the running water that the valves imply.

____ 9. Which of these sentences best summarizes "There's a certain Slant of light"?
 a. An afternoon church service depresses the speaker.
 b. The speaker expresses a wish to die.
 c. A winter day reminds the speaker of her mortality.
 d. The speaker is too depressed to go outside.

____ 10. To which senses do the images in the stanza appeal?

> There's a certain Slant of light,
> Winter Afternoons—
> That oppresses, like the Heft
> Of Cathedral Tunes—

 a. sight, sound, and touch
 b. sight, sound, and smell
 c. sight, smell, and taste
 d. sound, smell, and touch

____ 11. Which statement best paraphrases the central comparison in "There is a solitude of space"?
 a. Compared to the solitude of death, the solitude of space and sea are like society.
 b. Compared to the solitude of a soul admitted to itself, the solitude of space, sea, and death are like society.
 c. Compared to the solitude of space, sea, and death, living in society is a more restrictive form of solitude.
 d. Compared to the solitude of space and sea, the solitude of death is more profound.

____ 12. "The Brain—is wider than the Sky—" compares the physical size of the brain to that of the sky and the sea. What point is Dickinson making when she uses these images?
 a. The brain is blue, like the sky and the sea.
 b. The brain is infinitely large in understanding.
 c. The brain is an empty space.
 d. The human brain is physically larger than any other animal's.

____ 13. In these lines from "Water, is taught by thirst," which words provide slant rhyme?

> Water, is taught by thirst.
> Land—by the Oceans passed.
> Transport—by throe—
> Peace—by its battles told—
> Love, by Memorial Mold—
> Birds, by the Snow.

 a. *thirst* and *passed*
 b. *throe* and *told*
 c. *told* and *Mold*
 d. *throe* and *Snow*

____ 14. In "Water, is taught by thirst," the final image of the birds being taught by the snow most likely refers to

a. birds finding water to drink by melting the snow.

b. hawks and other birds of prey following tracks of small animals in the snow.

c. birds suffering when it snows because it is hard for them to find food.

d. birds learning to take bird baths in the snow.

_____ 15. Which of the following poems focuses most strongly on a lesson that can be learned from nature?

a. "There is a solitude of space"   c. "My life closed twice before its close—"

b. "Because I could not stop for Death—"   d. "There's a certain Slant of light"

Vocabulary and Grammar

On the line, write the letter of the one best answer.

_____ 16. Which word below is the best replacement for *surmised* in the lines "I first *surmised* the Horses Heads / Were toward Eternity—"?

a. guessed   c. taught

b. screamed   d. whispered

_____ 17. Where would you most likely see a *cornice*?

a. on a tulle gown   c. on a carriage

b. on a building   d. on a gravestone

_____ 18. In the final line of "There is a solitude of space," why is Dickinson's use of the phrase "finite infinity" unusual?

a. It is redundant, since *infinity* is by definition a *finite* thing.

b. It is contradictory, since *infinity* is by definition not a *finite* thing.

c. It is ungrammatical, since *finite* cannot normally be used as an adjective.

d. It is phonetically playful, since all of the vowel sounds in the first word are repeated in the second word.

_____ 19. Which of these sentences uses a gerund as a predicate nominative?

a. Anna goes horseback riding every morning.

b. Sometimes waiting can seem intolerable.

c. Jarvis preferred to learn by listening.

d. It was losing that made Antoine angry.

_____ 20. How is the gerund used in the following sentence?

Rushing through the hall, Meena feared being late to class.

a. as the subject of the sentence   c. as a predicate nominative

b. as the direct object of a verb   d. as the object of a preposition

Essay Questions

21. Choose an image that you remember from one of Dickinson's poems, such as the carriage ride in "Because I could not stop for Death—" or the slant of light in "There's a certain Slant of Light." Write an essay explaining how the image helps Dickinson communicate her meaning.

22. Consider the three Dickinson poems in your text that focus most on the subject of death: "I heard a Fly buzz—when I died—," "Because I could not stop for Death—," and "My life closed twice before its close—." Do you think Dickinson feared death? Why or why not? Write an essay explaining your answer.

23. Write an essay exploring the identity of the teachers and the lessons being taught in "Water, is taught by thirst." First, identify and compare the "teachers" in the poem. Then analyze the relationship between each teacher and the lesson taught, and determine what makes the relationships analogous to each other. Finally, discuss what you feel is the central message of the poem.

Walt Whitman's Poetry

Selection Test

Critical Reading

On the line, write the letter of the one best answer.

_____ 1. When Whitman states, in the preface to the 1855 edition of *Leaves of Grass*, that "The United States themselves are essentially the greatest poem," he supports his opinion by citing
   a. the vitality and diversity of Americans.
   b. the rhythmic speech patterns of Americans.
   c. American respect for literary traditions.
   d. his own popularity as a poet.

_____ 2. Based on the following passage from the preface to the 1855 edition of *Leaves of Grass*, what can you infer about Whitman's attitude toward the past?

> America does not repel the past or what it has produced under its forms or amid other politics or the idea of castes or the old religions . . . accepts the lesson with calmness . . . is not so impatient as has been supposed that the slough still sticks to opinions and manners and literature while the life which served its requirements has passed into the new life of the new forms.

   a. Whitman does not think Americans have anything to learn from the past.
   b. Whitman thinks Americans should study the past for its own sake.
   c. Whitman wishes Americans would follow past traditions more carefully.
   d. Whitman is pleased Americans learn from the past while making a new way of life.

_____ 3. Structurally speaking, what makes "Song of Myself" a typical Whitman poem?
   a. its complex meter
   b. its use of regular stanzas
   c. its use of lines of fixed lengths
   d. its use of the natural cadences of human speech

_____ 4. In "Song of Myself," when the speaker says "I, now thirty-seven years old in perfect health begin, / Hoping to cease not till death," what do you think he is beginning?
   a. communicating with nature   c. reading poetry
   b. a family   d. writing poetry

_____ 5. What can you infer about the poet's attitude from these lines in "Song of Myself"?

> These are really the thoughts of all men in all ages and lands, they are not original with me, / If they are not yours as much as mine they are nothing, or next to nothing. . . .

   a. Whitman is pleased to acknowledge that he borrowed ideas in "Song of Myself" from another poet.
   b. Whitman believes that his observations are, in some sense, universally shared.
   c. Whitman believes that he can predict what people who read his poetry in the future will think.
   d. Whitman thinks that his poetry is worthless if readers disagree with him.

_____ 6. The phrase "barbaric yawp" in "Song of Myself" is an example of Whitman's
   a. pessimism.   c. informality.
   b. love of nature.   d. British roots as a poet.

Unit 3: A Growing Nation (1800–1870)

____ 7. Which of the following elements prevents "Song of Myself" from becoming an exercise in ego and selfishness?
   a. the title
   b. the exuberant, optimistic tone
   c. the poem's linking of the individual self to a universal self
   d. the diction, or word choice

____ 8. Based on the details in "Song of Myself" and "I Hear America Singing," what can you infer about Whitman's attitude toward other people?
   a. He feels affectionate toward other people.
   b. He does not like to be around people.
   c. He is bossy and likes to control the people around him.
   d. He thinks that most people are very foolish.

____ 9. "The singing" the speaker hears in "I Hear America Singing" is
   a. the language of different ethnic groups in the American melting pot.
   b. the songs from foreign lands brought to America by immigrants.
   c. the poetry of Whitman and other American poets.
   d. the individuality of Americans in different walks of life.

____ 10. In "When I Heard the Learn'd Astronomer," the speaker moves from
   a. optimism to pessimism.
   b. the world of intellect to the world of wonder.
   c. Transcendentalism to mysticism.
   d. certitude to doubt.

____ 11. The central comparison in "A Noiseless Patient Spider" is between
   a. the spider and the speaker's soul.
   b. the spider and the filament.
   c. the spider's promontory and the speaker's isolated location.
   d. the spider's filament and the soul's gossamer thread.

____ 12. Free verse is especially suited to "A Noiseless Patient Spider" because it reflects
   a. the spider's noiselessness.
   b. the spider's patience.
   c. the spider's activity of launching forth filament.
   d. the isolation of the spider and the soul.

____ 13. From the details in "A Noiseless Patient Spider," you can infer that Whitman admires the spider for its ability to
   a. use its body to explore its surroundings.
   b. quietly and patiently capture the insects it will eat.
   c. create beautiful silken web patterns.
   d. move from place to place without being noticed.

____ 14. What situation in "By the Bivouac's Fitful Flame" prompts the thoughts of life, death, and people far away?
   a. encountering the darkness of the woods
   b. recognizing the familiarity of the terrain
   c. being in the midst of war
   d. being mesmerized by the fitful flame

____ 15. Which of the following was *not* a prime reason why Whitman chose to write in free verse?
   a. to express his individuality
   b. to celebrate democracy
   c. to convey a sense of freedom
   d. to imitate earlier poets he admired

_____ 16. Based on his poetry, what can you infer about Whitman's attitude toward nature?

        I. He admires nature.

        II. He learns from nature.

        III. He considers himself to be part of nature.

        IV. He likes to spend time outdoors.

    a. I and II only   c. I, III, and IV only

    b. II and III only   d. I, II, III, and IV

Vocabulary and Grammar

On the line, write the letter of the one best answer.

_____ 17. What does the speaker in "Song of Myself" mean when he says that he holds "creeds and schools in *abeyance*"?

    a. He goes to school regularly.

    b. He has temporarily let go of philosophies he learned in school.

    c. He detests creeds and schools.

    d. He thinks that Americans of all creeds should spend more time in school.

_____ 18. Focusing on the word *effuse*, what do you think the speaker in "Song of Myself" means when he says "I *effuse* my flesh in eddies, and drift it in lacy jags"?

    a. I pour out my thoughts like the flow of water in a river or stream.

    b. I bruise myself on whirlpools and bump along the rocks in the stream.

    c. I soothe myself in a whirlpool and then daydream that I'm in billows of lace.

    d. My soul escapes my body when I drown and drifts and decays after death.

_____ 19. Which line below would best follow this line from "I Hear America Singing"?

    The delicious singing of the mother, or of the young wife at work, or of the girl sewing or washing. . . .

    a. singing what belongs to them and to no one else

    b. singing what belongs to him or her and to no one else

    c. singing what belongs to him and to no one else

    d. singing what belongs to her and to no one else

_____ 20. Who seems to be stealthily watching the speaker in these lines from "By the Bivouac's Fitful Flame"?

    Like a phantom far or near an occasional figure moving,
    The shrubs and trees, (as I lift my eyes they seem to be stealthily watching me,)
    While wind in procession thoughts, O tender and wondrous thoughts. . . .

    a. the enemy   c. the shrubs and trees

    b. a phantom or an occasional figure   d. the speaker's eyes

Essay Questions

21. Suppose Whitman had written "I Hear America Singing" in the 1990's. How would the poem be different? Write an essay describing the differences.

22. Use the information in "Song of Myself" to infer Whitman's attitude toward death. Then write an essay explaining his attitude. Be sure to cite examples of language and details that point to the general attitude you describe.

23. How does Whitman's poetry reflect his feelings about democracy? Address this question in an essay that cites examples from at least two of Whitman's poems in your texts. Include in your discussion not only the content of the poems but also their structure or form.

"I, Too" by Langston Hughes
"To Walt Whitman" by Angela de Hoyos

Selection Test

Critical Reading

On the line, write the letter of the one best answer.

_____ 1. In "To Walt Whitman," what kind of guitar does the speaker offer the famous poet?
    a. a twelve-stringed guitar
    b. a golden guitar
    c. a miniature guitar
    d. a chicana guitar

_____ 2. How does the speaker in "To Walt Whitman" identify her people?
    a. as Native Amerindian
    b. as Native American
    c. as American Indian
    d. as Latin American

_____ 3. What are the consequences of being an African American for the speaker of "I, Too"?
    a. He is indifferent to discrimination.
    b. He must eat his meals in the kitchen.
    c. He must work harder than other men.
    d. He is not allowed to speak his mind in public.

_____ 4. In the lines from "I, Too," whom does the speaker mean by "they"?

    They'll see how beautiful I am/And be ashamed

    a. white ministers who support discrimination while preaching the word of God
    b. African Americans who implore the speaker not to speak out too strongly
    c. the white-dominated society that discriminates against African Americans
    d. poets like Walt Whitman who have ignored the African American experience

_____ 5. Which word best describes the attitude of the speaker toward the famous poet in "To Walt Whitman"?
    a. respectful
    b. angry
    c. hostile
    d. embarrassed

_____ 6. In "I, Too" what does the speaker imply with the statement?

    I, too, am America

    a. that America is a land where all people are treated equally before the law
    b. that he came to America in order to enjoy freedom and opportunity
    c. that his parents were born in America
    d. that America is a land of many people, all of whom deserve recognition as full and equal citizens

_____ 7. What is it that the speaker in "To Walt Whitman" cannot find in Whitman's poetry?
   a. an open road
   b. her native people
   c. democratic principles
   d. a spirit of brotherhood

_____ 8. Which word best describes the mood of "I, Too"?
   a. lighthearted
   b. fearful
   c. determined
   d. careful

_____ 9. Why does the speaker in "To Walt Whitman" address the famous poet as "my brother"?
   a. Whitman was a great friend to her people.
   b. She is Whitman's ancestor.
   c. She identifies with Whitman as a poet.
   d. *Brother* is a Spanish form of address that does not imply kinship.

_____ 10. Why does the speaker in "I, Too" mention how "beautiful" he is?
   a. He takes pride in his race.
   b. He is muscular and strong.
   c. He is young.
   d. He is egoistic and self-satisfied.

Essay Questions

11. Write an essay comparing de Hoyos's poem with Hughes's poem. Comment on the differences or similarities in theme, style, and choice of words. What effect does the length of each poem have on the reader?

12. To de Hoyos and Hughes, Whitman the "poet democratic" was not democratic enough, having ignored the experiences of certain peoples in his poetry. Write an essay examining the role and responsibilities of a poet. What "goals" do de Hoyos and Hughes hope to achieve with their poetry? Under what circumstances, if any, should a poet, or any artist, be held responsible for representing the experience of others?

13. Both "I, Too" and "To Walt Whitman" exemplify the ways in which the American experience has become more diverse. Choose one of the two poems and write an essay speculating on what the word *diversity* means for that poet. What concrete experiences may have led the poet to write that poem? Then discuss what effect increasing diversity has for the American experience. Is there something about being an American that transcends differences in race? Would the poet you chose agree or disagree with your opinion?

Unit 3: A Growing Nation (1800–1870)

© Prentice-Hall, Inc.

I, Too/To Walt Whitman **115**

Name _____ Date _____

Part Test, Unit 3, Part 4: Focus on Literary Forms—Poetry

Critical Reading

The questions below are based on the following poem by Emily Dickinson.

> Wild Nights—Wild Nights!
> Were I with thee
> Wild Nights should be
> Our luxury!
>
> [5] Futile—the Winds—
> To a heart in port—
> Done with the Compass—
> Done with the Chart!
>
> Rowing in Eden—
> [10] Ah, the Sea!
> Might I but moor—Tonight—
> In Thee!
>
> *—Emily Dickinson*

On the line, write the letter of the one best answer.

_____ 1. According to the first stanza, what situation does not allow the speaker to experience "luxury"?
   a. "Wild Nights"
   b. conflict with her lover
   c. separation from her lover
   d. lack of money

_____ 2. In line 6, what is meant by "a heart in port"?
   a. someone who has found love
   b. someone who loves boats
   c. someone who loves a person on shore
   d. someone who does not wish to venture outside

_____ 3. How many lines of the poem have the same exact rhyme?
   a. two   c. four
   b. three   d. five

_____ 4. Which lines from the poem are an example of slant rhyme?
   a. lines 5 and 6   c. lines 5 and 7
   b. lines 6 and 8   d. lines 10 and 12

_____ 5. What is the subject of the second stanza?
   a. a sailing ship
   b. a found love
   c. a calm sea
   d. a lost love

_____ 6. In line 5, what are futile winds?
   a. a weak desire to remain in one place
   b. a powerful desire to find a different person to love
   c. no desire to find a different person to love
   d. a strong desire to drift through life

____ 7. What is Dickinson's attitude toward her subject?
    a. indifferent   c. distrustful
    b. joyful   d. passionate

____ 8. With only this poem as a reference, what can be said about Dickinson's style?
    a. Dickinson uses regular meter and rhyme.
    b. Dickinson uses stanzas of varying numbers of lines.
    c. Dickinson uses onomatopoeia.
    d. Dickinson uses irregular meter and rhyme.

____ 9. Which is not a true statement?
    a. The poem contains exact rhymes.
    b. The poem is written in free verse.
    c. The poem has stanzas.
    d. The poem contains slant rhymes.

____ 10. In line 9, what does Dickinson's speaker mean by the image "Rowing in Eden"?
    a. a life without difficulties
    b. smooth sailing
    c. being in love
    d. searching for someone to love

Vocabulary and Grammar

On the line, write the letter of the one best answer.

____ 11. Emily Dickinson speaks of the soul as being infinite, or _____.
    a. having definite limits
    b. having profound goodness
    c. having no limits
    d. having an abundance of love

____ 12. The lecture of the astronomer oppresses, or _____, Walt Whitman.
    a. weighs heavily upon
    b. brings joy to
    c. provides scientific proof to
    d. operates upon

____ 13. Although Walt Whitman received some praise for his poetry during his lifetime, other praise for his poetry was held in abeyance, or _____, until after his death.
    a. kept in a journal
    b. detained by a court order
    c. temporarily stopped
    d. spoken of in private

____ 14. Which line contains a gerund?
    a. And breaths were gathering firm
    b. Parting is all we know of heaven.
    c. With Blue—uncertain stumbling Buzz—
    d. We passed the Setting Sun—

____ 15. Which sentence contains both a pronoun and its antecedent?
    a. Emily Dickinson wrote poetry in seclusion during much of her life.
    b. As she grew older, she became more of a recluse, not even venturing from her house and garden.
    c. Despite her solitude, she wrote exceptional poetry.
    d. Emily Dickinson's sister Lavinia discovered packets of Emily's poetry in dresser drawers.

Essay Questions

16. Though writers often write about similar subjects, each has his or her own distinctive style. Write an essay in which you compare the styles of Emily Dickinson and Walt Whitman. Use specific examples from the poems in Part 4 to support your points.

17. Choose one poem by Dickinson or Whitman that concerns some form of nature as well as human beings. In an essay, analyze the poem and explain the view of the natural and human worlds that the poet expresses in the work.

18. Through its use of words, images, and sound, poetry can provide us with new ways of thinking about ordinary events, feelings, and momentous occasions. In short, poetry helps us to understand about life. In an essay, describe how either Dickinson or Whitman writes poetry that reflects the experience of living. Using examples from the poems of the poet you select, explain how the poet's ideas are universal and applicable to life in general as well as to the life of an individual.

"An Episode of War" by Stephen Crane
"Willie Has Gone to the War," words by George Cooper,
music by Stephen Foster

Selection Test

Critical Reading

On the line, write the letter of the one best answer.

_____ 1. "Willie Has Gone to War" is primarily about
   a. a brook.
   b. a young lieutenant who has been injured.
   c. a young woman who misses her beloved young man.
   d. a young soldier who has died.

_____ 2. "An Episode of War" is the story of
   a. a young soldier named Willie.
   b. how a lieutenant lost his arm.
   c. the Battle at Gettysburg.
   d. the conflict between a soldier and a doctor.

_____ 3. Which statement best explains why "An Episode of War" may be viewed as a natural-
   istic story?
   a. It takes place outdoors.
   b. In this tale an ordinary man's life is shaped by a force he cannot control, but he
      endures this life-changing event with strength and dignity.
   c. It shows the harsh realities of everyday life rather than an optimistic view of the
      world.
   d. It shows the sentimental side of war.

_____ 4. In "An Episode of War," Crane seldom directly reveals the lieutenant's thoughts or
   feelings. He may have chosen to do this to show
   a. that a good soldier has no feelings.
   b. how fascinated the lieutenant has become with the war.
   c. that the lieutenant likes to observe events around him.
   d. how his injury has stunned or shocked the lieutenant.

_____ 5. One way in which Cooper helps listeners identify with the woman in "Willie Has
   Gone to the War" is by
   a. revealing poignant feelings that listeners will have experienced as well.
   b. describing a beautiful place that is special to this woman.
   c. likening her to a bird pining for its mate.
   d. talking about war.

_____ 6. As you read "An Episode of War," thinking about the grave injuries inflicted during
   the Civil War makes you
   a. better able to envision the setting.
   b. more likely to think the lieutenant is going to have complications with his wound.
   c. better able to laugh at the humorous parts.
   d. more likely to notice details about the lieutenant's wife, mother, and sisters.

_____ 7. The fact that the lieutenant can now "see many things which as a participant in the fight were unknown to him" helps to emphasize that
  a. his injury has transformed his role in the war and his perspective on the world around him.
  b. that war is a waste.
  c. that wounded men are often treated as "non-people."
  d. that the complex machinery of war is an "aggregation of wheels, levers, and motors."

_____ 8. By describing a battery of men engaged in battle as an "aggregation of wheels, levers, motors," with "a beautiful unity," what does Crane emphasize about the wounded lieutenant?
  a. He is alone.
  b. He is an outsider now who has no place in the machinery of war.
  c. He has become more observant.
  d. He is witnessing something noble and patriotic.

_____ 9. If you make predictions about the fate of the lieutenant's arm in "An Episode of War," you must
  a. believe that the story will end happily.
  b. recognize the story's witty tone.
  c. consider the medical situation in its historical context.
  d. assume the doctor is telling the truth.

_____ 10. In "An Episode of War," details such as the rubber blanket, neat squares of coffee, breast-work, puffs of white smoke in the woods, and even an ashen looking man smoking a corncob pipe all serve to heighten the _____ of the story.
  a. naturalism
  b. sentimentalism
  c. romanticism
  d. realism

_____ 11. _Realism_ is the name given to a literary movement that
  a. was the foundation for Romanticism.
  b. focused on showing that people's lives are often shaped by forces they can't understand or control.
  c. focused on ordinary people faced with the harsh realities of everyday life.
  d. grew out of Naturalism.

_____ 12. In "Willie Has Gone to the War," the young woman loves the glade because
  a. that's where she last saw her love.
  b. it's so beautiful.
  c. it is untouched by the war.
  d. it is where she and Willie plan to build their home.

_____ 13. In "An Episode of War," why do you suppose Crane chose not to depict the amputation procedure?
  a. It was too gruesome.
  b. He couldn't find out what such an experience was like.
  c. He didn't want to shock his readers.
  d. He wanted to focus the story on the lieutenant's changing perspective on life.

_____ 14. To better understand the lieutenant's battlefield experiences in "An Episode of War," you must consider your knowledge of
  a. the 1990 Persian Gulf War.
  b. the terrible conditions facing injured Civil War soldiers.
  c. the lieutenant's military training.
  d. the lieutenant's relationship with his soldiers.

Vocabulary and Grammar

On the line, write the letter of the one best answer.

____ 15. "An Episode of War" focuses on a wounded ____, rather than on an *aggregation* of wounded soldiers.
   a. individual
   b. platoon
   c. congregation
   d. army

____ 16. The lieutenant looks *disdainfully*, or ____ toward the woods.
   a. scornfully
   b. harshly
   c. sympathetically
   d. considerately

____ 17. When the lieutenant leaves the front line, he sees a scene that looks just ____ a historical painting.
   a. as if   c. as though
   b. like   d. as

____ 18. The officer who bandages the lieutenant's wound makes the lieutenant feel ____ he doesn't know how to be properly wounded.
   a. like   c. just like
   b. as if   d. as

____ 19. The lieutenant stood looking at the distant forest, ____ contemplating how it was that a bullet could emerge from those woods and strike a man, forever changing his life.
   a. like   c. as if
   b. kind of   d. as

____ 20. By making the emotions and thoughts of the soldier ____, Crane emphasizes both his dignity and stupefaction.
   a. continuously disdainful
   b. an aggregation of vivid impressions
   c. precipitous
   d. nearly inscrutable

Essay Questions

21. How do "An Episode of War" and "Willie Has Gone to the War" move readers to identify with their main characters? Choose either selection and answer the question in a short essay supported with examples from the text.

22. Do you think "Willie Has Gone to the War" is a song of hope, despair, or some other sentiment? In a short essay, state what you believe to be the main sentiment expressed by this song. Use lyrics from the song to support your opinion.

23. "An Episode of War" is characteristic of two literary movements that were popular at the time Crane was writing: Realism and Naturalism. In an essay, define Realism as a literary movement. Then use details from "An Episode of War" to show the ways in which the story can be seen as a product of this movement.

Unit 4: Division, Reconciliation, and Expansion (1850–1914)

Name _____ Date _____

Selection Test

Critical Reading

On the line, write the letter of the one best answer.

_____ 1. "Swing Low, Sweet Chariot" is about the
   a. importance of community.
   b. need for equality.
   c. desire for freedom.
   d. uncertainty of religious faith.

_____ 2. In what literary element of a spiritual will you most likely find its key ideas?
   a. refrain
   b. opening line
   c. solo lyrics
   d. title

_____ 3. How does the sound of the repetition of the word *home* in "Swing Low, Sweet Chariot" convey the mood of the spiritual?
   a. It lulls the listener into a sense of contentment.
   b. It reminds the listener that the singer is at home.
   c. It tells the listener of the hominess of plantation life.
   d. It builds on the listener's feelings about home to emphasize the message of longing.

_____ 4. In "Swing Low, Sweet Chariot," what is home a metaphor for?
   a. the South
   b. Africa
   c. Heaven
   d. Jordan

_____ 5. In "Swing Low, Sweet Chariot," the singer hopes to
   a. live at the plantation forever.
   b. be released from hardship.
   c. swim in the Jordan River.
   d. be returned to Africa.

_____ 6. Which of the following phrases is part of the refrain of "Swing Low, Sweet Chariot"?
   a. "If you get there before I do"
   b. "A band of angels coming after me"
   c. "Tell all my friends I'm coming too"
   d. "Coming for to carry me home"

_____ 7. What is the most important function of the refrain in "Swing Low, Sweet Chariot"?
   a. The refrain introduces a biblical context for the spiritual.
   b. The refrain separates the soloist and chorus.
   c. The refrain reinforces the idea of deliverance.
   d. The refrain ends the spiritual on a happy tone.

8. What mood is suggested by listening to the rhythm and repetition of "Swing Low, Sweet Chariot"?
    a. longing, patience, and hope
    b. rebellion
    c. secrecy
    d. fear and resignation

9. What makes "Go Down, Moses" typical of spirituals?
    a. quotations from Moses
    b. lack of a refrain or chorus
    c. warnings of rebellion
    d. references to biblical figures

10. Moses is an appropriate figure for a spiritual because he
    a. received the Ten Commandments.
    b. owned slaves in Egypt.
    c. brought plagues to Egypt.
    d. led his people to freedom.

11. The spiritual is most closely related to which of the following literary traditions?
    a. call-and-response
    b. narrative poetry
    c. autobiography
    d. sermon

12. Enslaved African Americans identified with the ancient Israelites in Egypt because both groups
    a. shared religious convictions.
    b. composed religious songs.
    c. suffered oppression.
    d. liked to travel.

13. Enslaved African Americans experienced which of the following circumstances described in "Go Down, Moses"?
    I. oppression
    II. having lived in Egypt
    III. captivity
    IV. resisting an unjust authority with force

    a. I and II   c. I and III
    b. III and IV   d. I and IV

14. From the point of view of the slaveholder, what made spirituals most dangerous?
    a. They were insulting to white people.
    b. They carried hidden messages.
    c. They rejected organized Christianity.
    d. They kept alive African musical traditions.

15. How does listening to a repeated phrase such as "Let my people go" in "Go Down, Moses" help convey the spiritual's mood and message?
    a. The repetition dulls listeners' ears to key messages of the spiritual.
    b. The phrase reminds listeners that the slaves' plight is similar to that of the Israelites.
    c. The phrase is a demand and helps convey a mood of determination.
    d. The repetition of such phrases could be decoded to reveal hidden messages.

_____ 16. In a spiritual, the part sung by the chorus seldom changed because the chorus
    a. was an African tradition.
    b. sang the refrain.
    c. played the role of the Lord.
    d. let everyone take part.

Vocabulary and Grammar

On the line, write the letter of the one best answer.

_____ 17. In "Swing Low, Sweet Chariot," the singer uses direct address. What effect does directly addressing the "sweet chariot" have?
    a. It intensifies the urgency of the singer's plea.
    b. It makes the chariot seem unattainable.
    c. It indicates that the chariot must come down from Heaven.
    d. It lets listeners know that the chariot isn't real.

_____ 18. Which of the following phrases includes an example of direct address?
    a. "Thus saith the Lord,"
    b. "Go down, Moses,"
    c. "bold Moses said"
    d. "Tell old Pharaoh"

_____ 19. Choose the word closest in meaning to the underlined word in the following line from "Go Down, Moses."

    If not I'll smite your first-born dead.

    a. order   c. shoot
    b. strike   d. strangle

_____ 20. Choose the word that could best substitute for the underlined word in the following line from "Go Down, Moses".

    Oppressed so hard they could not stand.

    a. starved   c. exhausted
    b. rewarded   d. abused

Essay Questions

21. Which of the two spirituals, "Swing Low, Sweet Chariot" or "Go Down, Moses," do you think would have been considered more "dangerous" by a slave owner who paid careful attention to the words of the spirituals? Use examples from each of the spirituals to support your ideas.

22. "Swing Low, Sweet Chariot" and "Go Down, Moses" are both about the hope for release from hardship. However, the spirituals express very different views in regard to _when_ release might come about. In an essay, identify for each spiritual when release is expected and how this affects the overall mood of each spiritual.

23. Make a case for the Moses of "Go Down, Moses" as a symbol for the activities of the abolitionist Harriet Tubman. Use what you have learned about her to interpret the spiritual in this light.

from *My Bondage and My Freedom* by Frederick Douglass

Selection Test

Critical Reading

On the line, write the letter of the one best answer.

_____ 1. Which of the following statements best expresses Douglass's attitude toward slavery?
    a. Under the care of a decent master, slavery can be a tolerable situation.
    b. What makes slavery evil is how comfortable it becomes.
    c. Slavery is only possible for children to endure.
    d. Slavery goes against the nature of both slaves and slaveholders.

_____ 2. Douglass believes that Mrs. Auld was not suited to be a slaveholder because she lacked the necessary _____.
    a. physical strength
    b. cruelty
    c. intelligence
    d. humanity

_____ 3. One of the most successful strategies Douglass used for learning to read was
    a. having Mrs. Auld teach him.
    b. memorizing books read by Mrs. Auld.
    c. buying books from Mr. Knight on Thames street.
    d. getting his young white playmates to teach him in exchange for biscuits.

_____ 4. Which of the following sentences best describes the attitudes of Douglass's white playmates?
    a. The opinions of the children reflect those of their parents.
    b. The white children hate Frederick.
    c. The children believe slavery is inherently wrong.
    d. The children are afraid they will become slaves, too.

_____ 5. In what way are Douglass's efforts to educate himself paradoxical?
    a. The more he learns, the more unhappy he becomes.
    b. Even as he accumulates more facts, he is more uncertain of his principles.
    c. The faster he reads, the more books he enjoys.
    d. Forbidden to read as a child, he grows up to be an important writer.

_____ 6. *My Bondage and My Freedom* reveals that in the South of its time slaves and women were both
    a. enemies of slavery.
    b. against Christian teaching.
    c. emotional rather than reasonable.
    d. subject to white male authority.

_____ 7. What additional information would be most appropriate to Douglass's autobiography?
    a. Mrs. Auld's feelings about her husband
    b. a description of Douglass's views about Baltimore during the 1830s
    c. the bookseller's rationale for allowing Douglass to purchase a schoolbook
    d. what Mrs. Auld would have done if she had known of Douglass's unhappiness

Unit 4: Division, Reconciliation, and Expansion (1850–1914)

____ 8. If your reading purpose is to learn from a slave about his life, what overall conclusion can you draw about Frederick Douglass from this excerpt?

> My feelings were not the result of any marked cruelty in the treatment I received; they sprung from the consideration of my being a slave at all. It was *slavery*—not its mere *incidents*—that I hated.

    a. Douglass was not treated badly by his owners.
    b. Douglass did not object to the day-to-day aspects of his life as a slave.
    c. Douglass thought slavery often inspired slaveholders to commit acts of cruelty.
    d. Douglass was a proud man who believed himself entitled to freedom.

____ 9. What does Douglass mean by saying "Conscience cannot stand much violence"?
    a. Conscience and violence often work together.
    b. Most people have no conscience.
    c. Compromise one belief and the conscience is easily broken down.
    d. Anyone with a strong conscience hates violence.

____ 10. What is the most important message of *My Bondage and My Freedom*?
    a. Slavery harms both master and slave.
    b. A little learning is a dangerous thing.
    c. Human nature cannot be changed.
    d. Knowledge makes slaves better workers.

____ 11. Why is it helpful to set a purpose for reading?
    a. It helps you understand concepts such as slavery.
    b. You can debate the author's purpose for writing.
    c. It helps you focus on ideas and information as you read.
    d. You can learn about the writer's personal experiences and attitudes.

____ 12. What might you have learned had this account been written by Master Hugh?
    a. Douglass's thoughts and feelings about Mrs. Auld
    b. why Master Hugh believed that educating slaves was a bad thing to do
    c. how Douglass learned to read and write
    d. what caused Mrs. Auld to realize that she should stop trying to educate Douglass

____ 13. How do you know that Douglass is writing about his childhood from the point of view of an adult?
    a. He cannot imagine any view other than his own.
    b. He uses a very simple vocabulary.
    c. He idealizes his memories of his childhood with the Aulds.
    d. He interprets his childhood experiences with an adult's insight.

____ 14. Which of the following details would help you achieve your reading purpose of understanding slavery from a slave's point of view?
    a. Mrs. Auld often gave bread to the hungry.
    b. Little Tommy loved Mrs. Auld.
    c. Frederick had to sneak reading lessons from his white friends.
    d. Frederick's friends studied from the *Columbian Orator*.

Vocabulary and Grammar

On the line, write the letter of the one best answer.

____ 15. The word most opposite in meaning to *congenial* is ____.
    a. friendly   c. thickened
    b. hostile   d. thinned

___ 16. When Douglass first entered the family of Master Hugh, there was ____ sorrow ____ suffering for which Mrs. Auld had not a tear.
    a. either, or
    b. whether, or
    c. neither, nor
    d. not only, but (also)

___ 17. The word most nearly opposite in meaning to *stringency* is ____.
    a. strictness
    b. leniency
    c. harshness
    d. charity

___ 18. ____ had slavery made a victim of Douglass, ____ of Mrs. Auld.
    a. Not only, but also
    b. Just as, so
    c. Whether, or
    d. Neither, nor

___ 19. Because she was so ____ when he first arrived there, Douglass says that Mrs. Auld was a model of affection and tenderness.
    a. depraved
    b. benevolent
    c. stringent
    d. affected

___ 20. Correlative conjunctions are used to connect ____.
    a. words and word groups that are grammatically different
    b. nouns and adjectives
    c. similar kinds of words and word groups that are grammatically alike
    d. items in a series

Essay Questions

21. Mrs. Auld's character changed dramatically after her husband persuaded her not to teach young Frederick to read and write. Write a comparison-contrast essay in which you describe the character of Mrs. Auld before and after this turning point. Use incidents and examples from the text to show the changes in her.

22. Douglass says that

Nature has done almost nothing to prepare men and women to be either slaves or slaveholders. Nothing but rigid training, long persisted in, can perfect the character of the one or the other. One cannot easily forget to love freedom; and it is as hard to cease to respect that natural love in our fellow creatures.

Write an essay in which you argue for or against this statement. Use examples from Douglass's autobiography to support your position.

23. To explain Mrs. Auld's change in behavior towards him, Douglass says

Conscience cannot stand much violence. Once thoroughly broken down, who is he that can repair the damage? . . . It must stand entire, or it does not stand at all.

Write an essay in which you support this explanation for Mrs. Auld's behavior or present an alternative explanation.

"An Occurrence at Owl Creek Bridge" by Ambrose Bierce

Selection Test

Critical Reading

On the line, write the letter of the one best answer.

_____ 1. Which of the following quotations from this story reveals an objective point of view?
    a. "He was a captain."
    b. "He closed his eyes in order to fix his last thoughts upon his wife and children."
    c. "His whole body was racked and wrenched with an insupportable anguish!"
    d. "He had not known that he lived in so wild a region."

_____ 2. Why does the author describe how Peyton Farquhar reacts to the sound of his watch?
    a. to show that Farquhar's sense perceptions had become very distorted
    b. to illustrate the cruelty of the Union soldiers
    c. to explain why Farquhar had come to the bridge
    d. to draw a parallel between Farquhar and his executioners

_____ 3. In order to understand the relationship between the three distinct parts of the story, the reader must clarify
    a. how a civilian like Farquhar became a military prisoner.
    b. shifts in the geographical setting.
    c. the sequence of events.
    d. the story's several conflicting attitudes about the Civil War.

_____ 4. Which of the following contributes most to the feeling of suspense in "An Occurrence at Owl Creek Bridge"?
    a. the vivid descriptions of the physical setting
    b. the unexpected sequence in which the events are related
    c. the emotionless description of the procedures used to prepare for the hanging
    d. the sympathetic depiction of Peyton Farquhar's personality

_____ 5. Bierce encourages the reader to sympathize with Peyton Farquhar by
    a. distorting the passage of time.
    b. portraying the executioners as cruel.
    c. including details about Farquhar's family.
    d. implying that Farquhar is innocent.

_____ 6. When Peyton Farquhar suggests sabotage, the Federal scout suggests that the bridge can be burned down. What does this say about the scout's character?
    a. He is an honest and straightforward man.
    b. He is an arsonist at heart.
    c. He is not above setting up Farquhar.
    d. He dislikes his commandant.

_____ 7. What points of view does Bierce use in this story?
    a. objective as well as first person
    b. objective and third-person limited
    c. first person and third person
    d. only third-person limited

_____ 8. Why does Peyton Farquhar fall through the bridge at the beginning of Part III?
   a. He has escaped.
   b. The bridge collapses.
   c. He has been hanged.
   d. One of the soldiers has freed him.

_____ 9. What is the main function of the flashback in this story?
   a. to describe the effects of the war on women and children
   b. to provide insight into the treacherous nature of the Union soldiers
   c. to generate sympathy for the Southern cause
   d. to explain why Peyton Farquhar is being hanged

_____ 10. Which message is Bierce trying to convey in this story?
   a. People often get themselves into trouble by taking foolish risks.
   b. Whatever can go wrong, probably will.
   c. Soldiers must follow orders regardless of their personal feelings.
   d. War makes men cruel and indifferent to human life.

_____ 11. Which event happens first in the true sequence of events?
   a. Farquhar stands on the Oak Creek bridge with his neck "in the hemp."
   b. Farquhar's wife brings the soldier water.
   c. The rope breaks, causing Farquhar to fall into the water.
   d. Farquhar runs to greet his wife with open arms.

_____ 12. Which of the following excerpts provides a clue that certain events occur in Peyton Farquhar's imagination rather than in reality?
   a. " . . . he had frequented camps enough to know the dread significance of that deliberate, drawing, aspirated chant . . . "
   b. "The trees upon the bank were giant garden plants; he noted a definite order in their arrangement, inhaled the fragrance of their blooms."
   c. "Suddenly he heard a sharp report and something struck the water smartly within a few inches of his head, spattering his face with spray."
   d. "At last he found a road which led him in what he knew to be the right direction."

_____ 13. Why is the narrator surprised to find Petyon Farquhar about to hanged?
   a. Farquhar looks kindly and is a gentleman.
   b. Hanging has been outlawed in Alabama.
   c. Farquhar is already dead.
   d. Only gentleman are hanged in Alabama.

_____ 14. Which of the following excerpts shows a limited third-person point of view?
   a. "Peyton Farquhar was a well-to-do planter, of an old and highly respected Alabama family."
   b. "The company faced the bridge, staring stonily, motionless."
   c. "The power of thought was restored; he knew that the rope had broken and he had fallen into the stream."
   d. "The man's hands were behind his back, the wrists bound with a cord."

Vocabulary and Grammar

On the line, write the letter of the one best answer.

_____ 15. What are the meanings of the italicized words in the following sentence? "In the code of military _etiquette_, silence and fixity are forms of _deference_."
   a. training, soldiering
   b. manners, disrespect
   c. hangings, bravery
   d. behavior, courtesy

____ 16. When Peyton Farquhar swings through "unthinkable arcs of *oscillation*," he swings
      a. through thick fog.
      b. like a pendulum.
      c. with a vertical motion.
      d. with wrenching pain.

____ 17. In which of the following does the semicolon appropriately link two independent
    clauses?
      a. Bierce was a Civil War veteran; and he was a newspaper man.
      b. Bierce's life before the Civil War left him bitter; his service during the war left him
        cynical.
      c. Although his bitterness showed in his work; Bierce became a popular writer.
      d. Bierce worked for a newspaper; but he probably died in Mexico.

____ 18. Which word is closest in meaning to the italicized word in the phrase ". . . will be
    summarily hanged"?
      a. quietly
      b. promptly
      c. justifiably
      d. brutally

____ 19. Compound sentences can be formed by joining two closely related independent
    clauses with a ____.
      a. colon
      b. comma
      c. semicolon
      d. slash

____ 20. What is the main reason for connecting independent clauses with a semicolon?
      a. to emphasize the close connection between the clauses
      b. to eliminate descriptions
      c. to show that the clauses are separate
      d. to indicate a pause in the action

Essay Questions

21. Do you think Bierce agreed that "all is fair in love and war"? Answer this question in a short essay, using examples from "An Occurrence at Owl Creek Bridge" to support your position.

22. In "An Occurrence at Owl Creek Bridge," the reader is surprised to learn that the man with whom Farquhar discusses Owl Creek bridge is not a Confederate soldier but a Federal, or Union, scout. What is the true signficance of their brief conversation, and how does the incident set the tone for the rest of the story? In an essay, relate this flash-back to the events of the story and explore how this initial deception might be said to foreshadow the story's ending.

23. Ambrose Bierce uses both a flashback and different points of view to tell "An Occurrence at Owl Creek Bridge." Imagine that Bierce had written the story in the true sequence of events and from an objective point of view. Do you think the story would have been as ef-fective? State your opinion in a brief essay, supporting your opinion with examples from the story.

"The Gettysburg Address" and
"Second Inaugural Address" by Abraham Lincoln
"Letter to His Son" by Robert E. Lee

Selection Test

Critical Reading

On the line, write the letter of the one best answer.

_____ 1. In "The Gettysburg Address" Lincoln explains that the stated purpose for meeting on this battlefield is to _____.
   a. dedicate the nation to the Southern cause
   b. dedicate themselves to revenging the Gettysburg dead
   c. dedicate a portion of the field as a final resting place for fallen soldiers
   d. dedicate themselves to God

_____ 2. Lincoln's main purpose in "The Gettysburg Address" is to _____.
   a. argue why the Union will win the war
   b. explain the importance of the war and inspire people to support the Union
   c. seek money for the families of those who died
   d. identify the soldiers who died in battle

_____ 3. What idea is Lincoln expressing in the following passage from "The Gettysburg Address?

> But, in a larger sense, we cannot dedicate—we cannot consecrate—we cannot hallow—this ground. The brave men, living and dead, who struggled here, have consecrated it, far above our poor power to add or detract.

   a. This ground is made sacred by the memory of those who fought here, rather than by anything we might say or do.
   b. We shouldn't consecrate this ground.
   c. The men who fought here already had a ceremony to dedicate this ground.
   d. We should not be proud of what happened here.

_____ 4. Considering the diction of "The Gettysburg Address," describe Lincoln's view of himself and his audience.
   a. powerless and defeated
   b. humble and dedicated
   c. cowardly and fearful
   d. noble and proud

_____ 5. The main idea of Lee's "Letter to His Son" could be expressed best as
   a. belief that the integrity of the Union must be preserved at all costs.
   b. determination that the South will not be subdued.
   c. despair over a Union that can only be maintained by force.
   d. an argument in favor of secession.

_____ 6. In his letter, Lee reflects an attitude toward impending events that is
   a. fatalistic about the prospects of war.
   b. confident in the South's military strength.
   c. hateful toward the North.
   d. opposed to the principles of the Constitution.

© Prentice-Hall, Inc.

Unit 4: Division, Reconciliation, and Expansion (1850–1914)

_____ 7. One of Lee's main reasons for opposing secession is his
      a. pride as a Virginian.
      b. belief in the importance of the Union.
      c. commitment to states' rights.
      d. position as an officer in the army.

_____ 8. Lee's letter seeks to persuade by
      a. appealing to emotion.
      b. invoking the authority of great writers.
      c. making an irrational argument.
      d. analyzing events within historical context.

_____ 9. Prior knowledge in which of the following areas would best help you understand the ideas Lee expresses in his letter?
      a. the principles of the United States Constitution
      b. Lee's military experience
      c. the economy of the pre-Civil War South
      d. the relationship between Lee and his son

_____ 10. Lincoln's references to birth at the beginning and the end of "The Gettysburg Address" suggest that he
      a. recognizes the need for humor at a sad time.
      b. is concerned with population losses due to battlefield casualties.
      c. is aware of the nation's short history.
      d. wishes to relate complex ideas to a common experience.

_____ 11. Lincoln's diction in "Second Inaugural Address" suggests which purpose?
      a. to give comfort to the widows and orphans
      b. to share his personal sorrow with a friend
      c. to explore his thoughts in a private journal
      d. to impress a national audience with the importance of his message

_____ 12. Lee's diction in "A Letter to His Son" is somewhat informal because he is
      a. delivering a public speech.
      b. writing to his son.
      c. discussing a trivial subject.
      d. speaking in code to avoid suspicion.

_____ 13. From what you know of the causes of the Civil War, by what "acts of the North" might southerners, including Lee, have been aggrieved?
      a. the Union's policy regarding which states shall be slaveholding states
      b. the Union's policy regulating how much slaves should cost
      c. Lincoln's Emancipation Proclamation
      d. the Union's granting to African Americans the right to vote

_____ 14. From what you know of United States history, which document was Lincoln quoting when he said in "The Gettysburg Address" that the nation was dedicated to the proposition "that all men are created equal"?
      a. the Emancipation Proclamation
      b. the Declaration of Independence
      c. the Equal Rights Amendment
      d. the Missouri Compromise

_____ 15. In "Second Inaugural Address," how does Lincoln explain the Civil War?
      a. Insurgents sought to destroy the Union.
      b. One party wanted to make war, and the other did not.
      c. The North was aggrieved by the acts of the South.
      d. God is punishing the United States for allowing slavery.

Vocabulary and Grammar

On the line, write the letter of the one best answer.

____ 16. The word or phrase closest in meaning to *malice* is ____.
   a. good will
   b. cup
   c. spite
   d. hurt feelings

____ 17. The underscored words in the following passage from Lincoln's "Second Inaugural Address" are an example of which of the following?

> Neither party expected for the war, the magnitude, or the duration, which it has already attained. Neither anticipated that the *cause* of the conflict might cease with, or even before, the conflict itself should cease.

   a. correlative conjunctions
   b. predicate pronouns
   c. objects of the preposition
   d. parallel structure

____ 18. When Lincoln referred to war as a *scourge* he ____ war.
   a. deprecated
   b. consecrated
   c. redressed
   d. hallowed

____ 19. When Lincoln suggests that the living ought to dedicate themselves to the task of seeing "that government of the people, by the people, for the people, shall not perish from the earth," he is using which grammatical device to emphasize his ideas?
   a. loaded language
   b. sensory details
   c. parallel structure
   d. modifiers

____ 20. The word most opposite in meaning to *insurgents* is ____.
   a. rebels
   b. spies
   c. patriots
   d. soldiers

Essay Questions

21. Both Lincoln and Lee placed a great deal of importance on preserving the Union. Write an essay in which you discuss either Lincoln or Lee's ideas about the Union. Use examples from the text of Lincoln's speeches or Lee's letter to support your points.

22. Lincoln chooses details and language in "The Second Inaugural Address" to accomplish a specific purpose. Write an essay explaining what you believe that purpose to be. Support your conclusion with details and diction from speech.

23. Lincoln's speeches convey a great deal about his beliefs and his character in general. Likewise, Lee's letter reveals a good deal about the nature of its author. Choose either Lincoln or Lee as your subject. Then write an essay in which you describe the man's character, using details from his writing to support your impressions.

Part Test, Unit 4, Part 1: A Nation Divided

Critical Reading

The questions below are based on the following selection from Chapter IX of *The Red Badge of Courage* by Stephen Crane.

The protagonist Henry Fleming, called "the youth" by the narrator, has left the sanctuary of the woods and is running toward the battlefield. He encounters the dead and the dying, the tattered soldier, and then Jim, the tall soldier who had befriended him.

"Jim–Jim—Jim——"

The tall soldier opened his lips and spoke. He made a gesture. "Leave me be—don't tech me—leave me be—"

There was another silence while he waited.

Suddenly, his form stiffened and straightened. Then it was shaken by a prolonged ague. He stared into space. To the two watchers (Henry and the tattered soldier) there was a curious and profound dignity in the firm lines of his awful face.

He was invaded by a creeping strangeness that slowly enveloped him. For a moment the tremor of his legs caused him to dance a sort of hideous hornpipe. His arms beat wildly about his head in expression of implike enthusiasm.

His tall figure stretched itself to its full height. There was a slight rending sound. Then it began to swing forward, slow and straight, in the manner of a falling tree. A swift muscular contortion made the left shoulder strike the ground first.

The body seemed to bounce a little way from the earth. . . .

The youth had watched, spellbound, this ceremony at the place of meeting. His face had been twisted into an expression of every agony he had imagined for his friend.

He now sprang to his feet and, going closer, gazed upon the pastelike face. The mouth was open and the teeth showed in a laugh.

As the flap of the blue jacket fell away from the body, he could see that the side looked as if it had been chewed by wolves.

The youth turned, with sudden, livid rage, toward the battlefield. He shook his fist. . . .

The red sun was pasted in the sky like a wafer.

On the line, write the letter of the one best answer.

_____ 1. Prior to reading this excerpt from a Stephen Crane novel set in the Civil War, it would be helpful to the reader to
   a. study medicine.   c. study Civil War history.
   b. write a novel.   d. read other books by Stephen Crane.

_____ 2. From this excerpt, Henry's first experience with the death of a friend, the reader learns that Henry
   a. wanted to run from this encounter with death.
   b. held Jim's hand while watching him die.
   c. tried to protect the tattered soldier from watching Jim.
   d. was in awe of and then enraged by Jim's death.

_____ 3. Which line from the excerpt points to the Naturalism of Crane's novel?
   a. To the two watchers there was a curious and profound dignity in the lines of his awful face.
   b. As the flap of the blue jacket fell away, he could see that the side looked as if it had been chewed by wolves.
   c. Then it began to swing forward, slow and straight, in the manner of a falling tree.
   d. The red sun was pasted in the sky like a wafer.

____ 4. How does an image from nature echo what is going on in this passage?
   a. It rains, showing Henry's grief.
   b. The sun shines, showing they will win the war.
   c. The body bounces against the hard earth.
   d. The red sun mirrors Henry's hatred of war.

____ 5. Why does the author refer to his characters as "the tattered soldier," "the tall soldier," and "the youth"?
   a. to help the reader experience the characters as universal
   b. to keep the reader from getting confused by the characters' names
   c. to stereotype the characters
   d. to distance the reader from the characters

____ 6. Which would be an appropriate purpose for reading this selection?
   a. to find out about Civil War combat
   b. to learn what death might be like
   c. to identify the causes of the Civil War
   d. to learn to write good dialogue

____ 7. If the following items were arranged in chronological order, which would be last?
   a. The youth gazes upon the face of the tall soldier.
   b. The tall soldier falls to the ground.
   c. The tall soldier begins to speak.
   d. The legs of the tall soldier begin to shake with a tremor.

____ 8. Judging by the following passage, how would you characterize the diction of the novel?

   The tall soldier opened his lips and spoke. He made a gesture. "Leave me be—
   don't tech me—leave me be—"

   a. formal and abstract   c. informal and concrete
   b. informal and abstract   d. formal and concrete

____ 9. If *The Red Badge of Courage* were the autobiography of Henry Fleming, which would be true?
   a. Henry Fleming would describe the events as he experienced them.
   b. Henry Fleming would not be in the story.
   c. Stephen Crane would have been in the war.
   d. The story would focus on Jim's experiences.

____ 10. The phrase "this ceremony at the place of meeting" is used by Crane to
   a. dignify the scene of Jim's death.
   b. explain the cause of Jim's approaching death.
   c. define the red badge of courage.
   d. utter a philippic.

Vocabulary and Grammar

Questions 11–15 consist of a related pair of words in CAPITAL LETTERS followed by four lettered pairs of words. Choose the pair that best expresses a relationship similar to that of the pair in capital letters.

____ 11. BENEFACTOR : GIFT ::
   a. speaker : speech
   b. officer : army
   c. pilot : driver
   d. trumpet : orchestra

____ 12. AGGREGATION : ASSEMBLAGE ::
   a. segregation : laws
   b. annoyance : irritation
   c. aggravation : alleviation
   d. congregation : indoors

____ 13. ANARCHY : GOVERNMENT ::
   a. monarchy : England
   b. empty : full
   c. executive : judicial
   d. chaos : cosmos

____ 14. SANCTIFY : CONSECRATE ::
   a. deprecate : devalue
   b. curse : rejoice
   c. sing : whistle
   d. bake : stir

____ 15. WRITE : SPEECH ::
   a. gardener : garden
   b. upholstery : couch
   c. compose : symphony
   d. construct : demolish

On the line, write the letter of the one best answer.

____ 16. Did Stephen Crane write "An Episode of War" _____ it had happened to him personally?
   a. like   c. though
   b. as if   d. as

____ 17. Which passage is an example of parallelism?
   a. "government of the people, by the people, for the people, shall not perish from the earth."
   b. "All knew that this interest was, somehow, the cause of the war."
   c. "to do all which may achieve and cherish a just and lasting peace, among ourselves, and with all nations."
   d. "We have come to dedicate a portion of that field, as a final resting place for those who here gave their lives. . . ."

____ 18. Which sentence correctly uses the word *like*?
   a. The sky over the battlefield became gray like it might snow any minute.
   b. The charge came swiftly like the lieutenant said it would.
   c. He jerked in the saddle like he had been struck by something.
   d. He stared toward the woods like a disinterested spectator.

____ 19. Which sentence using direct address is incorrect?
   a. As you know, Susan, Frederick Douglass was a great orator.
   b. Samantha, did you read *My Bondage and My Freedom*?
   c. When he was twenty-one, Frederick Douglass escaped to Massachusetts, Michael.
   d. Douglass spoke out Jim against slavery and for civil rights.

____ 20. Which sentence uses correlative conjunctions?
   a. Either short story by Ambrose Bierce is worth reading.
   b. Bierce fought in the Civil War and later wrote a newspaper column.
   c. "An Occurrence at Owl Creek Bridge" is not only mysterious but also dramatic.
   d. At age seventy-one, Ambrose Bierce traveled to Mexico and was never heard from again.

Essay Questions

21. Using the traditional spirituals in this part as examples, write an essay in which you discuss why enslaved Africans developed and sang spirituals.

22. An autobiography generally reveals many of its writer's attitudes and beliefs. Write an essay discussing what the excerpt from *My Bondage and My Freedom* reveals about Frederick Douglass's attitudes and beliefs. Use examples from the text to support your points.

23. Write an essay in which you explain in what ways "An Episode of War" would be different if it had been written as an autobiography by the lieutenant. Demonstrate each difference you mention by rewriting a brief passage from the story in an autobiographical fashion.

24. Diction, or the writer's choice of words, must be appropriate to the subject, audience, occasion, and literary form. Write an essay in which you describe the diction of "The Gettysburg Address" and evaluate its appropriateness to the subject, audience, occasion, and literary form.

25. "An Occurrence at Owl Creek Bridge" focuses mainly on Peyton Farquhar's view of the situation, creating sympathy for his thoughts and feelings. Write an essay justifying the actions of the Federal scout, using your knowledge of the Civil War and inferences drawn from the story to develop *his* thoughts and feelings.

Name _____ Date _____

from Civil War Diaries, Journals, and Letters

Selection Test

Critical Reading

On the line, write the letter of the one best answer.

_____ 1. Which is the main impression created by the passage from *Mary Chesnut's Civil War*?
      a. Life must go on, even during war.
      b. War is frightening but exciting.
      c. All good men must defend the North.
      d. The South should not have seceded.

_____ 2. Which excerpt from "Recollections of a Private" presents a fact?
      a. "I was taught my facings . . ."
      b. "I thought the drillmaster needlessly fussy . . ."
      c. "The musket . . . seemed heavier . . . than it had looked to be . . ."
      d. "no wisdom was equal to a drillmaster's . . ."

_____ 3. In "Reaction to the Emancipation Proclamation," how did the people of Washington, D.C., react to the news of the Proclamation?
      a. with fear
      b. with suspense
      c. with excitement
      d. with disgust

_____ 4. A fact is different from an opinion because a fact _____.
      a. is a statement
      b. can be false
      c. can be proved
      d. is a personal judgment

_____ 5. Sojourner Truth experienced difficulty in riding streetcars because she was _____.
      a. African American
      b. female
      c. elderly
      d. stubborn

_____ 6. In "A Confederate Account of the Battle of Gettysburg," the statement "a small but gallant band of heroes daring to attempt what could not be done by flesh and blood" implies _____.
      a. the writer thinks horses would have been more helpful
      b. the Confederate army was sure of an easy victory
      c. the morale of the Third North Carolina and the Second Maryland was high
      d. the task facing the Confederate troops was immense

_____ 7. Which of the following excerpts most clearly reflects the style of a journal?
      a. "The convention has adjourned."
      b. "Why did that green goose Anderson go into Fort Sumter?"
      c. "Fort Sumter had surrendered."
      d. "The Herald says that this show of war outside of the bar is intended for Texas."

_____ 8. What might be assumed about a letter that is not assumed about a journal?
      a. that the intended reader knows background information about the writer
      b. that no one except the writer will read the work
      c. that the writer intends the work to be published eventually
      d. that the work contains only opinions

_____ 9. In "Recollections of a Private," the author's experiences in the army lead him eventually to accept that _____.
   a. the appearance of army uniforms is important
   b. promotion in the ranks is unfair
   c. repetition in drilling is calming
   d. opinions are best kept to oneself in the army

_____ 10. Which statement is an opinion?
   a. Then came General Ewell's order to assume the offensive.
   b. We were exposed to enfilading fire.
   c. Its nerve and spirit were undiminished.
   d. The enemy did not make a countercharge.

_____ 11. What in her journal tells you that Chesnut dislikes war?
   a. her subjective descriptions of events and people
   b. her direct statements of opinion
   c. her excitement about watching the firing on Fort Sumter
   d. her use of quotations

_____ 12. Which phrase in the following statement expresses an opinion?

   Mr. Hinton, to whom I handed the paper, read it with great force and clearness.

   a. Mr. Hinton
   b. to whom I handed the paper
   c. read it
   d. read it with great force and clearness

_____ 13. In "Recollections of a Private," enlisted man Goss probably first looked upon enlisting in the war as
   a. a serious and terrifying endeavor.
   b. an opportunity to take part in military drills.
   c. a patriotic adventure with opportunities for travel and promotion.
   d. a chance to see Washington, D.C.

_____ 14. In "Reaction to the Emancipation Proclamation," Reverend Henry M. Turner believes the issuance of President Lincoln's Emancipation Proclamation is
   a. a high point of the nation's history.
   b. a political move to increase Lincoln's popularity.
   c. important only to African Americans.
   d. important only to people in the Union.

_____ 15. A journal is most like what other literary form?
   a. novel   c. short story
   b. diary   d. biography

Vocabulary and Grammar

On the line, write the letter of the one best answer.

_____ 16. Which of the following actions might a soldier perform if the soldier behaved _audaciously_?
   a. drill procedures over and over again
   b. rush shooting into an enemy line
   c. refuse to wear a poorly tailored uniform
   d. get wounded during heavy fire

from Civil War Diaries, Journals, and Letters **139**

_____ 17. Which of the following actions is characteristic of an *obstinate* person?
   a. reacts calmly
   b. refuses to surrender
   c. curses aloud
   d. fights boldly

_____ 18. In discussing the case tried before Justice Thompson, why is "Justice Thompson" capitalized?
   a. It contains a first and last name.
   b. It contains a title used before a last name.
   c. It is a particular place (building).
   d. It is a particular court.

_____ 19. Colonel Chesnut is described as a man who is characterized by *serenity*. This type of man would be most likely to _____.
   a. speak softly and calmly
   b. speak audaciously
   c. partake in foreboding silence
   d. shout imprecations

_____ 20. The Confederates named battles after the nearest settlement, whereas the Union army named them after the nearest body of water. If Jackson had referred to the battle by its Confederate name in his letter, he would have written it as _____.
   a. the battle of manasses
   b. the Battle of manasses
   c. the battle of Manasses
   d. the Battle of Manasses

Essay Questions

21. Each of these Civil War diaries, journals, or letters recounts at least one conflict related to the Civil War. These include external conflicts, such as military battles, as well as internal conflicts that take place within those who may not actually be engaged in battle but are still "at war." Describe the internal and external conflicts revealed in at least two of the selections you have read.

22. The styles of personal writing in "Recollections of a Private" by Warren Lee Goss and in "A Confederate Account of the Battle of Gettysburg" by Randolph McKim are very different. Describe the similarities and differences in the writing styles, supporting your explanation with details from the two works.

23. Compare and contrast two of the characters you learned about in the selections. For example, you may choose to compare a Union soldier with a Confederate soldier or a white northerner with an African American northerner. Explain the characteristics and concerns they share, and explain how their lives are different. Use details from the selection to support your explanation.

"Gulf War Journal" from ***A Woman at War*** by Molly Moore

Selection Test

Critical Reading

On the line, write the letter of the one best answer.

_____ 1. Which one factor contributes most of all to Moore's feelings of unease as the war begins?
   a. not knowing what will happen next
   b. her concern for the historical buildings of Dhahran
   c. her inability to contact the newspaper offices
   d. the sight of Iraqi fighter planes flying overhead

_____ 2. Where is the Joint Information Bureau (JIB) located?
   a. in the hotel's ballroom
   b. on the hotel's roof
   c. in the hotel's basement
   d. by the hotel's swimming pool

_____ 3. What does Moore take as evidence that there is no real information to be learned at the JIB?
   a. Other reporters were setting up their equipment slowly.
   b. The general in charge of press briefings had not arrived yet.
   c. Her colleague from the *Washington Post* had already filed the first pool report.
   d. Another reporter tries to interview her about her reactions.

_____ 4. Why is the hotel a prime target?
   a. The Iraqis want to cut off the supply of information by killing all the journalists.
   b. The hotel is located next to the most active military airfield in Saudi Arabia.
   c. Four American generals are staying at the hotel.
   d. The hotel is a secret headquarters of American intelligence agents.

_____ 5. Why doesn't Moore have a gas mask to put on while in the bomb shelter?
   a. It was ordered but never arrived.
   b. She left it in her hotel room.
   c. Another reporter stole it.
   d. A hotel employee accidentally crushed it in an elevator.

_____ 6. Why does the short-wave radio report that is received in the bomb shelter soothe Moore's nerves?
   a. It extended the information vacuum.
   b. It reported that Iraqi forces were not yet counterattacking.
   c. It reported that the hotel was no longer in danger.
   d. It meant that the reporters could leave the bomb shelter.

_____ 7. Judging from Moore's account, what one factor would you say most strongly motivates the journalists in their pursuit of information about the war?
   a. a burning desire to learn the truth
   b. the fierce competition to be first with the news
   c. a reckless disregard for personal safety
   d. excellent pay for a hazardous assignment

Unit 4: Division, Reconciliation, and Expansion (1850–1914)

_____ 8. Why do the hotel employees call the roof of the hotel "Little Hollywood"?
   a. A movie was being filmed there just before the war began.
   b. Only the most elite correspondents were allowed on the roof to send reports.
   c. The correspondents showed films there during the evenings.
   d. The roof was covered with satellite dishes, cameras, and talk-show sets.

_____ 9. What activity helps Moore overcome her panic?
   a. Actually gathering and reporting details about what is happening.
   b. Smoking a cigarette with the public affairs officer.
   c. Answering questions posed by another correspondent.
   d. Activating the generator in order to use the telephone.

_____ 10. How does the British pilot describe the bombing raid he just returned from?
   a. as a necessary task completed successfully
   b. as the most exciting thing he had ever done
   c. as the scariest thing he had ever done
   d. like a child's game

Essay Questions

11. "Gulf War Journal" presents a personal account of the hours just before and after the beginning of the Persian Gulf War. Write an essay judging whether such an account provides a "better" picture of the war than an objective, factual news report would. In your essay, explore the answers to the following questions: In what ways does the personal approach make the war more accessible? Which questions does it fail to answer? Which portions of Moore's account could be used in an objective news story as well?

12. Wars are mainly conducted by professional soldiers who use their access to secret intelligence reports to create an element of surprise. Write an essay evaluating the role of journalists during wartime. Argue for or against the idea that a journalist is entitled to have access to information and ethically bound to report that information, regardless of the wishes of the military or government. Use examples from the text and current events to support your position.

13. The speed of communication has brought the horrors of war into people's very living rooms. Write an essay arguing for or against the idea that such instant information helps people to fully comprehend the devastation war can bring. Analyze how contemporary media practices might affect the perception of war by ordinary Americans. Would any factors besides the reach of the media make war today seem more or less horrific than ever?

Part Test, Unit 4, Part 2: Focus on Literary Forms— Diaries, Journals, and Letters

Critical Reading

The questions below are based on the following excerpt from *Tamsen Donner: A Woman's Journey* by Ruth Whitman.

> In the spring of 1846, a group of eighty-two pioneers set out from Independence, Missouri, with hopes of settling in California. Though they could not know it at the time, the infamous Donner party of settlers was to go down in history. Plagued by bad luck and poor planning, thirty-five of its members would die in blizzards on the Sierra Nevada, just one hundred miles outside California's Sacramento Valley. The following letter was written by party member Tamsen Donner.

May 11, 1846, Independence, Missouri

My dear sister,

    I commenced writing to you some months ago but the letter was laid aside to be finished the next day and was never touched. A nice piece of pink letter paper was taken out & <u>now has got so much soiled that it cannot be written upon & now in the midst of preparation for starting across the mountains I am seated on the grass in the midst of the tent</u> to say a few words to my dearest only sister. One would suppose that I loved her but little or I should not have neglected her so long.

    My three daughters are around me, one at my side trying to sew, Georgeanna fixing herself in an old India rubber cap & Eliza Poor knocking on my paper asking ever so many questions. They often talk to me of Aunty Poor.

    I can give you no idea of the hurry of this place. It is supposed there be 7000 waggons start from this place this season. We go to California to the bay of San Francisco. It is a four months trip. We have three waggons furnished with food & clothing drawn by three yoke of oxen each. We take cows along and milk them & have some butter though not as much as we would like. I am willing to go and have no doubt it will be an advantage to our children and to us. I came here last evening and start tomorrow morning on the long journey.

> Farewell my sister, you shall hear from
> me as soon as I have an opportunity
> Love to Mr. Poor the children &
> all friends   Farewell
>
>   T. E. Donner

On the line, write the letter of the one best answer.

_____ 1. Where was the Donner Party headed as it left Independence, Missouri?
    a. Las Vegas
    b. San Francisco Bay
    c. Sacramento
    d. Reno

_____ 2. What can be inferred from the following statement?

    It is supposed there be 7000 waggons start from this place this season.

    a. The location is an isolated one.
    b. People try to avoid the place if possible.
    c. The location is an extremely busy one.
    d. There is no one nearby.

_____ 3. Which of the following is an opinion?
  a. "I can give you no idea of the hurry of this place."
  b. "It is a four months trip."
  c. "My three daughters are around me"
  d. "We have three wagons furnished with food"

_____ 4. When in the Donner journey was this letter written?
  a. while crossing the mountains
  b. while in San Francisco
  c. near the end of the journey
  d. at the beginning of the journey

_____ 5. Who is the intended audience for this letter?
  a. the generations to follow
  b. Tamsen's friends
  c. Tamsen's only sister
  d. Tamsen's daughters

_____ 6. The underscored part of the excerpt contains
  a. facts only.   c. opinions only.
  b. facts and opinions.   d. neither facts nor opinions.

_____ 7. What characteristics of Tamsen Donner's writing identify it as a personal letter?
  a. its informality
  b. its logical organization
  c. its formal diction
  d. its step-by-step explanation of the facts

_____ 8. The author's attitude is _____.
  a. cautiously hopeful   c. resigned
  b. frightened   d. inquisitive

_____ 9. What can be inferred from the following excerpt?

  We go to California to the bay of San Francisco. It is a four months trip.

  a. Sight-seeing along the route will slow the travel.
  b. The group will depart in mid-summer.
  c. Travel was difficult and slow.
  d. Some of the travelers were ill.

_____ 10. Why does Tamsen say that people might think she does not love her sister?
  a. She is moving to California.
  b. She hasn't written sooner.
  c. She is leaving her home.
  d. She is not writing on good stationery.

Vocabulary and Grammar

Each question below consist of a related pair of words in CAPITAL LETTERS, followed by four other pairs of words. Choose the pair that best expresses a relationship similar to that expressed in the capitalized words.

_____ 11. HOSTILE : CONGENIAL ::
  a. awkward : successful
  b. emotional : frenetic
  c. trite : original
  d. aural : audible

_____ 12. CAPITULATE : SURRENDER ::
   a. propel : tow
   b. captivate : annoy
   c. navigate : steer
   d. enforce : defer

_____ 13. IMPRECATION : WITCH ::
   a. iris : flower
   b. salt : pepper
   c. speech : novel
   d. sentence : judge

On the line, write the letter of the one best answer.

_____ 14. Which sentence is correct in its use of proper nouns?
   a. The reverend Henry M. Turner describes how he tried to obtain a newspaper that announced the Emancipation Proclamation.
   b. A crowd of people gathered outside the office of the *Evening Star* Newspaper.
   c. The Reverend Turner read of the Emancipation Proclamation in the *Evening Star*.
   d. The proclamation was greeted with joy by people parading past the white house on Pennsylvania Avenue.

_____ 15. Which sentence is *incorrect* in its use of proper nouns?
   a. Union and Confederate troops fought a grueling battle near the town of Gettysburg, Pennsylvania.
   b. The Confederate troops attacked a union position on Culp's Hill.
   c. Many Confederate soldiers were killed during the three-day battle.
   d. After absorbing tremendous losses, the Confederate troops were forced to abandon their positions near Culp's Hill.

Essay Questions

16. A primary concern of the literature of the Civil War period is the human response to tragedy. Write an essay in which you discuss how the journal of Mary Chesnut reflects this theme. Cite examples from the text to support your points.

17. When people write about events as they occur, they often use simple and direct prose rather than the grander language of historical documents. Write an essay discussing how the styles of Warren Lee Goss and Randolph McKim are appropriate to their immediate involvement in the events.

18. The diaries, journals, and letters in this part reflect many different attitudes concerning the war. In an essay, compare and contrast the attitudes toward war expressed in two selections from Part 2. How do each of these voices add to your understanding of the Civil War?

Unit 4: Division, Reconciliation, and Expansion (1850–1914)

"The Boys' Ambition" from *Life on the Mississippi* and
"The Notorious Jumping Frog of Calaveras County" by Mark Twain

Selection Test

Critical Reading

On the line, write the letter of the one best answer.

_____ 1. Which of the following best describes Jim Smiley?
  a. bored and annoyed
  b. suspicious and aggressive
  c. clever and competitive
  d. gentle and tranquil

_____ 2. When the apprentice engineer is able to "cut out every boy in the village," he is able to
  a. beat any boy in the village in a fight.
  b. take a girl away from any boy in the village.
  c. ignore any boy in the village.
  d. outrun any boy in the village.

_____ 3. For the author as a boy, the Mississippi River was above all
  a. a wonder of nature.
  b. a pathway to adventure.
  c. a means of escape from Hannibal.
  d. an opportunity to get rich.

_____ 4. Base your answer on the following excerpt:

  "[Smiley's dog] would grab the other dog . . . and hang on till they threw up the
  sponge."

  In this sentence, the words "throwed up the sponge" mean that the people watching
  the dog fight would
  a. admit that they had lost the bet.
  b. bet more money on Smiley's dog.
  c. grab Smiley's dog and tie it up.
  d. try to help the other dog beat Smiley's dog.

_____ 5. The reader is led to believe that Andrew Jackson, the fighting dog, lost his last fight
  because of
  a. his own stupidity.
  b. the other dog's superior strength.
  c. a thrown sponge.
  d. a broken spirit after being tricked.

_____ 6. What makes the steamboat such a source of fascination for the boys?
  a. It is a marvel of modern technology.
  b. It is accessible only to the rich and powerful.
  c. It is a connection to the world outside Hannibal.
  d. It is connected with stories of shady dealings.

____ 7. Which of the following does Mark Twain use to add humor to this story?
   a. unexpected plot shifts
   b. misunderstandings between characters
   c. colorful names for characters
   d. all of the above

____ 8. Twain uses exaggeration in "The Boys' Ambition" primarily to
   a. make the townspeople look ridiculous.
   b. emphasize the boys' feelings about steamboating.
   c. contrast Hannibal with St. Louis.
   d. make the story entertaining.

____ 9. Who describes Smiley to the reader?
   a. Smiley
   b. the narrator
   c. Simon Wheeler
   d. the stranger

____ 10. In the sentence "By and by one of our boys went away," the expression "by and by" means
   a. after he said 'good-bye'.
   b. some time later.
   c. after purchasing his contract.
   d. mysteriously.

____ 11. Why did Smiley act indifferently when the stranger asked him about Dan'l Webster?
   a. Smiley was hoping to convince the stranger to bet on how well Dan'l could jump.
   b. Smiley was busy trying to teach Dan'l to jump, and the stranger interrupted.
   c. Dan'l looked like he had something wrong with him, and Smiley was worried.
   d. Simon Wheeler had cheated on a bet, and Smiley was angry.

____ 12. When Jim Smiley brought Dan'l Webster downtown and "lay for a bet," Twain means that Jim Smiley would
   a. talk for a while.
   b. put money on the frog.
   c. lie down and sleep.
   d. wait for someone to make a bet with him.

____ 13. Why does the author describe the arrival of the steamboat in such great detail?
   a. to emphasize the importance of the event
   b. to educate his readers about steamboats
   c. to display his expertise about steamboats
   d. to give the story a flavor of scientific objectivity

____ 14. Which of the following sayings best describes the author's attitude toward the boy who becomes an apprentice engineer?
   a. Everything comes to him who waits.
   b. Pride goes before a fall.
   c. Justice is blind.
   d. A rolling stone gathers no moss.

____ 15. One aspect of "The Notorious Jumping Frog of Calaveras County" that makes the story humorous is the fact that
   a. Simon Wheeler does not recognize how ridiculous his tale is.
   b. the narrator believes everything that Simon Wheeler tells him.
   c. Smiley refuses to believe that the frog-jumping contest was fair.
   d. the stranger thinks that he can actually fool Smiley.

Vocabulary and Grammar

On the line, write the letter of the one best answer.

_____ 16. What is the probable result of a "*monotonous* narrative"?
     a. Listeners will be educated.
     b. Listeners will be bored.
     c. Listeners will either strongly agree or disagree with the speaker.
     d. Listeners will be inspired to fight for the speaker's cause.

_____ 17. Who is best described as *garrulous* in "The Notorious Jumping Frog of Calaveras County"?
     a. the narrator
     b. Simon Wheeler
     c. Jim Smiley
     d. the stranger

_____ 18. The double negatives used in Twain's "The Notorious Jumping Frog of Calaveras County" are used to convey
     a. ignorance.
     b. humor.
     c. an emphatic negative.
     d. regional dialect.

_____ 19. The drayman's "prodigious voice" in "The Boys' Ambition" makes him well suited to
     a. alert the town.
     b. drive a dray.
     c. be an apprentice engineer.
     d. pilot the river.

_____ 20. What is the meaning of the phrase "hadn't no" in "he hadn't no idea"?
     a. had
     b. had any
     c. had no
     d. had not no

Essay Questions

21. Who is the main character of "The Notorious Jumping Frog of Calaveras County": the jumping frog Dan'l Webster or the storyteller Simon Wheeler? Write an essay stating your opinion. Support your argument with your definition of a main character and its role in a story, and describe how your choice of main character functions in Twain's tale. Use examples from the work to strengthen your essay.

22. Exaggeration, embellishment, and regional dialect are all techniques that can make a story humorous. Write a brief essay about how these techniques lend humor to one or both of these Twain selections. Support your points about the effectiveness of each humorous technique, using examples from the story or stories.

23. One central idea of "The Boys' Ambition" is that the unknown often has a much greater appeal than the familiar. Write a brief essay about the appeal of the unknown. Use examples from both "The Boys' Ambition" and your own life to support your essay.

Name _____ Date _____

"The Outcasts of Poker Flat" by Bret Harte

Selection Test

Critical Reading

On the line, write the letter of the one best answer.

_____ 1. The description of the campsite is given to
   a complete the story.
   b. show how well the author writes.
   c. help the reader visualize the region.
   d. contrast Poker Flat with Sandy Bar.

_____ 2. Which of the following best describes the feelings that the four outcasts have about one another immediately after they are driven out of Poker Flat?
   a interest and concern
   b. hostility and indifference
   c. fear and suspicion
   d. kindness and affection

_____ 3. What important plot development is brought on by Uncle Billy's stealing of the mules?
   a. It strands the rest of the travelers.
   b. It establishes Uncle Billy as a thief and "outcast."
   c. It causes the rest of the group to distrust Uncle Billy.
   d. It removes Uncle Billy from the cast of characters.

_____ 4. What is the main message of "The Outcasts of Poker Flat"?
   a. Living a life of crime is not always wrong.
   b. People who commit crimes will ultimately be punished by society.
   c. People's attitudes about criminals change when they learn why criminals turn to a life of crime.
   d. Punishment without justice is as bad as the crime.

_____ 5. Which is the most likely reason the author includes the character of the Duchess in "The Outcasts of Poker Flat"?
   a. to provide a romantic interest for Mr. Oakhurst
   b. to represent women as part of the group of outcasts
   c. to provide a reason for the group to stop halfway to Sandy Bar
   d. to compare and contrast with the character of Piney

_____ 6. The fact that Mother Shipton refers to Piney as "the child" suggests that she
   a. cares for Piney and wants to help her.
   b. wants to become Piney's legal mother.
   c. disapproves of Piney's marriage.
   d. thinks Piney is behaving selfishly.

_____ 7. Which motto best describes Uncle Billy's actions?
   a. Every man for himself.
   b. All for one and one for all.
   c. A bird in the hand is worth two in the bush.
   d. Don't put off until tomorrow what you can do today.

© Prentice-Hall, Inc.

_____ 8. Which excerpt gives the reader a sense of the regional aspects of the story?
   a. "Two or three men, conversing earnestly together, ceased as he approached, and exchanged significant glances."
   b. "Mr. Oakhurst received his sentence with philosophic calmness, none the less coolly that he was aware of the hesitation of his judges."
   c. "He bestirred himself in dusting his black clothes, washing his hands and face, and other acts characteristic of his studiously neat habits, and for a moment forgot his annoyance."
   d. "But at the head of the gulch, on one of the largest pine trees, they found the deuce of clubs pinned to the bark with a bowie knife."

_____ 9. Which word best characterizes the author's attitude toward the outcasts in "The Outcasts of Poker Flat"?
   a. resentment   c. sympathy
   b. superiority   d. condemnation

_____ 10. The statement "it was only in such easily established standards of evil that Poker Flat ventured to sit in judgment" tells the reader that Poker Flat
   a. had recently hired a sheriff.
   b. was usually lax in law enforcement.
   c. is an example of a model community.
   d. did not tolerate injustice.

_____ 11. Which of the following words best describe Mr. Oakhurst's character?
   a. intelligent and reserved   c. shy and cautious
   b. warm and enthusiastic   d. cruel and cunning

_____ 12. Which question would be most helpful to ask after learning that Mother Shipton has died?
   a. Why was her character considered expendable?
   b. Was she "redeemed" after this unselfish act?
   c. Will her death cause any characters to change their plan of action?
   d. Will her rations be given only to Piney or shared with the group?

_____ 13. What is the most important effect that Tom Simson and Piney Woods have on the outcasts?
   a. They encourage the outcasts to develop a more realistic and practical attitude about their situation.
   b. They convince the outcasts that it is possible for them to return to Poker Flat.
   c. They motivate the outcasts to become devoutly religious and to ask for forgiveness for past mistakes.
   d. They bring out the best in each of the outcasts.

_____ 14. Harte tells the reader that before Mr. Oakhurst parted from the group with Tom Simson, "He turned suddenly, and kissed the Duchess, leaving her pallid face aflame and her trembling limbs rigid with amazement." What can the reader infer from this scene?
   a. The Duchess did not enjoy being kissed.
   b. Mr. Oakhurst had already decided not to return to the camp.
   c. The Duchess was angry at Mr. Oakhurst for ridiculing her.
   d. The Duchess believed that Mr. Oakhurst planned to marry her.

_____ 15. Which element of the story shows most clearly that "The Outcasts of Poker Flat" is an example of regional literature?
   a. the point of view from which the story is told
   b. the dialect of the narrator
   c. the circumstances under which the outcasts become stranded
   d. the time of year in which the story is set

Vocabulary and Grammar

On the line, write the letter of the one best answer.

____ 16. Which term is closest to the meaning of the italicized word in this excerpt?

[T]he lovers . . . sang with great earnestness and *vociferation*.

a. loudness   c. interpretation
b. sincerity   d. melodic accuracy

____ 17. Which word is the coordinating conjunction in this sentence?

They slept all that day and the next, nor did they waken when voices and footsteps broke the silence of the camp.

a. all   c. nor
b. when   d. of

____ 18. Uncle Billy is described as a *bellicose* person who is given to using *anathemas*. Which best describes this character?

a. a mean man given to drinking
b. an ornery man given to cursing
c. a thief given to lying
d. a drunk given to abusing medication

____ 19. Which excerpt from the selection was made by someone with a *querulous* attitude?
a. "Tommy, you're a good little man."
b. "Just you go out there and cuss, and see."
c. "There's one chance in a hundred to save her yet."
d. "You are not going, too?"

____ 20. Which word is the coordinating conjunction in this excerpt?

But Mr. Oakhurst knew that scarcely half the journey to Sandy Bar was accomplished, and the party were not equipped or provisioned for delay.

a. to   c. not
b. and   d. for

Essay Questions

21. A two, or the "deuce," is the lowest ranked card in poker. Why does Mr. Oakhurst choose that card on which to write his eulogy? How is its use in keeping with his character? Write an essay that answers these questions, and use details from the selection to support your statements.

22. Some readers are surprised to learn that Mr. Oakhurst commits suicide at the end of the selection. Did this action seem within or outside of the character's prior behavior? Take a position in your essay, and support it with details about Mr. Oakhurst and other examples from the story.

23. Harte says that Mr. Oakhurst was the strongest yet the weakest outcast of Poker Flat. Do you disagree or agree with this statement? Write an essay stating your position, and use details from the selection to explain it. Give examples of Mr. Oakhurst's actions if you agree, and if you disagree, tell who you think were the strongest and weakest members of the group. (You may cite two different characters, if you wish.) Again, support your explanation with several details from the selection.

"Heading West" by Miriam Davis Colt
"I Will Fight No More Forever" by Chief Joseph

Selection Test

Critical Reading

On the line, write the letter of the one best answer.

_____ 1. Which word best characterizes Miriam Colt's tone in the following passage?

our "noble lords" complained of the great weight of the wagons

   a. respect
   b. sarcasm
   c. impatience
   d. pity

_____ 2. Why might it be dangerous for Miriam Colt's husband to let the Georgians know that he is a Free States man?
   a. Georgia is a slave state, and the Georgians are against anyone who opposes slavery.
   b. The Colts do not want to get friendly with the Georgians.
   c. The Georgians are well known for stealing from rich easterners.
   d. The Georgians oppose bringing the Vegetarian Company to the western territories.

_____ 3. Why does this sentence at the beginning of Miriam Colt's diary turn out to be ironic?

We can have, I think, good faith to believe, that our directors will fulfill on their part:

   a. The directors did not build the mills they promised they would.
   b. The site of the new city is covered with tents.
   c. The families who left the settlement made it impossible for the directors to fulfill their part.
   d. The directors did not send an escort to welcome the Colts and other settlers into the new city.

_____ 4. Which passage from "Heading West" best conveys a tone of apprehension?
   a. "The women and children, who slept in their wagons last night, got a good drenching from the heavy shower."
   b. " . . . we wonder if we shall be neighbors to each other in the great 'Octagon City.'"
   c. "I said to myself—'Is that what I have got to come to?'"
   d. "Found ourselves in this miserable hotel before we knew it."

_____ 5. What does Miriam Colt mean by this passage?

Have visited Mother very hard, for, in all probability, it is the last visit we shall have until we meet where parting never comes. . . .

   a. It is very difficult to communicate with her mother, and so the Colts won't be visiting her anymore.
   b. The Colts are visiting her mother frequently because after they leave on their journey they probably won't see her again before she dies.
   c. This is the Colts' last visit with her mother before they leave for Kansas and send for her to live join them.
   d. It's hard to visit her mother because she never wants them to leave.

6. Which of the following responses to this passage from "Heading West" would probably be the most helpful to a reader?

> One mile from the city, and Dr. Thorn has broke his wagon tongue; it must be sent
> back to Kansas City to be mended.

a. wondering why a mechanic couldn't just come out to fix the wagon
b. trying to picture what a wagon with a tongue would look like
c. remembering the feeling of frustration when the car broke down on a vacation
d. guessing about what kind of doctor Dr. Thorn is

7. What do the situations in "Heading West" and "I Will Fight No More Forever" share
that make them likely to evoke strong responses in the reader?
a. They are life-changing.   c. They picture Native Americans.
b. They involve violence.   d. They are terrifying.

8. What is the tone of Chief Joseph's speech "I Will Fight No More Forever"?
a. down but not out   c. wrathful and angry
b. zealous and promising   d. mournful and conceding

9. Which of the following is the most compelling reason for Chief Joseph's decision to
"fight no more"?
a. his previous conversation with General Howard
b. the futility of fighting and the suffering of his people
c. the deaths of several of his chiefs
d. the cruel weather

10. When Chief Joseph says "It is the young men who say yes and no," he means
a. it is not up to the young men to make the decision about fighting.
b. the young men understand the situation.
c. all the power rests in the hands of the young men.
d. the young men lack the experience and decisiveness to lead.

11. Words such as *sad, sick, cold,* and *tired* establish what element of Chief Joseph's
speech?
a. paradox   c. tone
b. personification   d. rhythm

12. Which most clearly expresses the meaning of Chief Joseph's phrase "From where the
sun now stands"?
a. from this time on   c. today
b. in this exact place   d. while there is still light

13. Chief Joseph's speech, addressed to his chiefs, is using which approach to elicit a
response?
a. the tradition of the Nez Percé tribe
b. a carefully argued position
c. strong emotional appeal
d. his authority as the tribe's leader

14. "I Will Fight No More Forever" possesses historical value because it
a. is the only Native American text that we have.
b. parallels General Howard's account.
c. details Native American rituals.
d. provides some insight into the mind and heart of a key Native American chief.

15. Feeling sorrow and pity as you read the words of Chief Joseph is an example of
a. the tone of the speech.   c. the emotion of the speech.
b. a response to the speech.   d. the historical value of the speech.

Vocabulary and Grammar

On the line, write the letter of the one best answer.

_____ 16. Which of the following quotations from "Heading West" is an example of a sentence fragment that is missing a subject?
    a. "A hot summer day."
    b. "Look around, and see the grounds. . . ."
    c. "At nightfall came to a log cabin at the edge of the wood. . . ."
    d. "In a large tent here is a cook stove. . . ."

_____ 17. Which quotation from "Heading West" is best characterized by the word *genial*?
    a. "The town looks new, but the hue is dingy."
    b. "as we leave the smoking embers of our camp-fire this morning."
    c. " . . . what a beautiful country is spread out before us!"
    d. "We ladies, or rather, 'emigrant women,' . . . around the camp-fire."

_____ 18. Why do the settlers in "Heading West" feel *nonplussed* to find that the Secretary of the company was out walking in the rain with his wife on the evening they arrive at the settlement?
    a. The Secretary's treatment of his wife is cause for anger among the settlers.
    b. The settlers have everything they want and don't need to talk to him.
    c. The settlers don't like the Secretary's wife and are relieved she isn't there to greet them.
    d. The Secretary's behavior is strange, and the settlers don't know what to make of it.

_____ 19. What word best suggests the actions of the directors of the Vegetarian Company regarding the money they have received from the members to build mills?
    a. terra firma   c. depredations
    b. profusion   d. emigrants

_____ 20. Which of these quotations from "Heading West" is a sentence fragment missing its verb?
    a. " A hot summer day."
    b. "Dined on the prairie, and gathered flowers . . . "
    c. "Here too came in the Santa Fe and Indian trade . . ."
    d. "Bade our friends good bye, in Potsdam, this morning at the early hour of two o'clock."

Essay Questions

21. Chief Joseph's speech of surrender, reported by newspapers all across the country, made a tremendous impression on Americans. Why do you think people were so moved by Chief Joseph's words? Write an essay discussing people's reactions to the speech and the reasons for it.

22. Settlers ventured into the American West in the hope of making a better life for themselves and their families. The personal costs and dangers of such an undertaking could be great. Write an essay describing the costs and dangers of moving west for Miriam Colt and her family. Cite examples from the selection to support your observations.

23. As Chief of the Nez Percé tribe, Chief Joseph had a deep attachment to and love for his people. Write an essay in which you discuss how Chief Joseph's message and choice of words in "I Will Fight No More Forever" conveys his feelings for his people. Develop your discussion by citing evidence from the selection.

Name _____   Date _____

"**To Build a Fire**" by Jack London

Selection Test

Critical Reading

On the line, write the letter of the one best answer.

_____ 1. In "To Build a Fire," there is an external conflict between
   a. the beauty of nature and the cruelty of nature.
   b. society and the individual.
   c. human beings and nature.
   d. instinct and civilization.

_____ 2. Which of the following character flaws brings about the man's tragic end?
   a. cowardice   b. carelessness   c. overconfidence   d. greed

_____ 3. Toward the end of "To Build a Fire," the man has an internal conflict between his
   a. body and his will.
   b. short-term goals and his long-term goals.
   c. conscience and his needs.
   d. animal nature and his spiritual nature.

_____ 4. Which of the following themes is expressed by the contrasting ways in which the dog
and the man cope with the cold?
   a. Animals are naturally superior to humans.
   b. Animals are unable to have or express emotions.
   c. Humans need to be as well attuned to nature as animals in order to survive in it.
   d. Humans are so closely tied to civilization that they cannot return to nature.

_____ 5. Until the story's end, the man's attitude toward the advice provided by the old-timer
of Sulphur Creek was one of
   a. respect.   b. curiosity.   c. confusion.   d. ridicule.

_____ 6. Which passage from the beginning of the story gives the strongest clue to the attitude that contributes to the man's death?
   a. "It was a steep bank, and he paused for breath at the top, excusing the act to
      himself by looking at his watch."
   b. "He was used to the lack of sun. It had been days since he had seen the sun, and
      he knew that a few more days must pass before that cheerful orb, due south,
      would just peep above the skyline and dip immediately from view."
   c. "The man flung a look back along the way he had come."
   d. "He was a newcomer in the land, a *chechaquo*, and this was his first winter."

_____ 7. Which example best reflects the main external conflict of the story?
   a. the encounter between the old timer and the man
   b. the hostility between the man and the dog
   c. the opposing emotions of the man near the end of the story
   d. the conflict of the man's animal nature and his spiritual nature

_____ 8. Which of the following details reflects the story's central theme most clearly?
   a. The fire was put out by an avalanche of snow from the branches that the man
      had inadvertently agitated.
   b. Even though it was high noon, there was no sun in the sky.
   c. At precisely the expected time, the man arrived at the forks of the creek.
   d. While attempting to build a fire, the man burned his hands.

_____ 9. What is the central idea of "To Build a Fire"?
   a. People choose their own destinies.
   b. Nature is more powerful than humans.
   c. In nature humans live by instinct.
   d. Heed the advice of the experienced.

_____ 10. Which internal conflict does the man experience toward the end of the story?
   a. terror versus faith   c. sorrow versus stoicism
   b. reality versus hope   d. regret versus rage

_____ 11. In "To Build a Fire," London's attitude toward the Alaskan wilderness can best be described as
   a. nostalgic.   c. apprehensive.
   b. respectful.   d. affectionate.

_____ 12. During the course of the story, the man changes from
   a. being haughty to being helpless.
   b. being rational to being spiritual.
   c. being heartless to being caring.
   d. being courageous to being fearful.

_____ 13. Which of the following clues is most likely to lead a reader to predict that the man will make it to camp?
   a. "For the moment, the cold of space was outwitted."
   b. "He had forgotten to build a fire and thaw out."
   c. "He was pleased at the speed he had made. If he kept it up, he would certainly be with the boys by six."
   d. "Once in a while the thought reiterated itself that it was very cold and that he had never experienced such cold."

_____ 14. Which of following is the correct way to predict while reading a story?
   a. Don't try to correct your first prediction, but just read on quickly to the end of the story.
   b. Start making predictions about the end of the story about halfway through it.
   c. Check your predictions as you read, and revise them if necessary.
   d. Avoid using your own experience when making predictions about your reading.

Vocabulary and Grammar

On the line, write the letter of the one best answer.

_____ 15. Choose the correct vocabulary word to complete the sentence.

   If the man had been more given to _____ thoughts from the beginning, he might have survived.

   a. unwonted   c. conjectural
   b. peremptory   d. none of the above

_____ 16. Which of the following quotations contains an adverb clause explaining _under what circumstances_?
   a. "When all was ready, the man reached in his pocket for a second piece of birch bark."
   b. "If he had only had a trail mate he would have been in no danger now."
   c. "As he looked apathetically about him, his eyes chanced on the dog. . . ."
   d. "He could not pick and choose, for he had to lift the fuel between the heels of his hands."

_____ 17. What does the adverb clause in the following quotation tell?

His theory of running until he reached camp and the boys had one flaw in it.

a. when
b. where

c. under what circumstances
d. to what extent

_____ 18. What best explains this ironic quotation from the story?

and the moccasin strings were like rods of steel all twisted and knotted as by some conflagration.

a. The moccasin laces are so twisted and frozen that they are like steel rods contorted by a hot, destructive fire.
b. The soft moccasin laces are now frozen and hard like steel.
c. The man is trying to do the right thing by taking off his moccasins, but he can't.
d. The tied laces are as tangled as if they had been blown around in a high wind.

_____ 19. Which of the following quotations from "To Build a Fire" does NOT contain an adverb clause?
a. "But before he could cut the strings, it happened."
b. "Since the freezing point is thirty-two above zero, it meant that one hundred and seven degrees of frost obtained."
c. "As he sat and regained his breath, he noted that he was feeling quite warm and comfortable."
d. "It experienced a vague but menacing apprehension that subdued it and made it slink along at the man's heels. . . ."

_____ 20. Which word best suggests the way the man treats the dog in the story?
a. unwonted
b. conjectural

c. peremptorily
d. none of the above

Essay Questions

21. The man in "To Build a Fire" has taken on a great challenge by choosing to work in a very remote and cold place. If you had to choose a great physical challenge of some type, what would you choose to do? Write an essay describing what your own challenge would be like. What do you think you might gain from such an experience? How would you use the experience of the man in the story to help you survive your challenge?

22. Sometimes an author will include a minor character who has virtues that the protagonist lacks. In Jack London's "To Build a Fire," that minor character is a dog. The dog consistently displays more innate common sense and wisdom than the man. Write an essay in which you compare and contrast the dog's and the man's attitudes toward the dangerously cold journey they are taking. Include at least three specific actions of the dog that show its instincts, under the circumstances, to be superior to the man's judgment.

23. To maintain suspense, authors may provide clues that lead readers to predict the outcome but also give readers details that make them uncertain about the outcome. In some cases, the outcome may be predictable, but how the ending works out keeps readers in suspense. When you first read "To Build a Fire," were you uncertain about the outcome, or did you know what would happen, but not how? What clues made you respond to the story the way you did? Write an essay relating your thought and prediction process as you read "To Build a Fire." Use examples from the selection where necessary.

Unit 4: Division, Reconciliation, and Expansion (1850–1914)

from *Lonesome Dove* by Larry McMurtry

Selection Test

Critical Reading

On the line, write the letter of the one best answer.

_____ 1. Which word best describes Augustus's attitude toward the cattle drive?
    a. scornful
    b. wistful
    c. happy-go-lucky
    d. fearful

_____ 2. What image of the cattle does the narrative portray?
    a. dirty as pigs
    b. wild as antelope
    c. tender as butter
    d. mild as pigeons

_____ 3. Why, despite the hard conditions, does Newt have no intention of complaining about the difficulties of the cattle drive?
    a. He was afraid that Call would fire him.
    b. He had been looking forward to it for too long.
    c. He was afraid Augustus would whip him.
    d. He was afraid the other cowboys would question his toughness.

_____ 4. Of what use are the bandanas the cowboys carry?
    a. They hide the cowboys' faces from Native Americans.
    b. They can be used to filter dirt out of water.
    c. They help keep the cowboys from breathing trail dust.
    d. They can be used in the place of bandages to bind up a wound.

_____ 5. What does the title *Lonesome Dove* refer to?
    a. Call's nickname
    b. a saloon in Montana
    c. a lost calf
    d. a town in Texas

_____ 6. The word *aggrieved* means
    a. made mad.
    b. saddened.
    c. offended.
    d. strangled.

_____ 7. What does the following excerpt suggest about Augustus?

> It was only when he [Call] met Deets that he realized Augustus hadn't followed. He was still sitting on old Malaria, back on the little hill, watching the sunset and the cattle herd.

    a. Augustus is afraid of driving the cattle all the way to Montana.
    b. Augustus tends to avoid hard work.
    c. Augustus is angry at Call for organizing the cattle drive.
    d. Augustus has a contemplative side and tries to enjoy every moment of life.

____ 8. What is Augustus used to doing during the afternoon instead of driving cattle?
  a. sitting on his porch
  b. playing poker in a saloon
  c. fixing dinner for his wife
  d. sleeping

____ 9. When Augustus says, "I hope this is hard enough for you, Call. I hope this makes you happy," he implies that
  a. Call needs to challenge himself in order to be happy.
  b. Call is forcing the cowboys to make a dangerous trip unnecessarily.
  c. Call has accomplished very little in his life before the cattle drive.
  d. Call does not really care about the money he could make on the cattle.

____ 10. Riding at the back of the herd is undesirable because
  a. debris falling off the wagons makes the horses stumble.
  b. the cowboys at the back of the herd always have to eat last.
  c. the cowboys have to catch up to the herd.
  d. the dust kicked up by the herd makes it hard to breathe.

Essay Questions

11. One of the things that makes life, and literature, interesting is the mixing of personalities. Using details from the passage, write an essay comparing and contrasting the personalities of Call and Augustus. Explain why they were drawn to each other and how each character is or is not suited to carrying out the hard task of the cattle drive.

12. Like most works of literature, *Lonesome Dove* carries several levels of meaning. Write an essay briefly outlining the plot of this passage. In your essay, speculate on the "hidden" meanings of the cattle drive, and explain how the cattle drive is used as a metaphor.

13. The cowboy is one of America's most romantic and enduring images. Write an essay describing the real life of a cowboy. Base it upon the passage from *Lonesome Dove*. In your essay, compare that image to other cultural images of cowboys that you are familiar with (such as those from films, television, or books). As though you were casting a movie, describe the qualities needed in a "mythic" cowboy and then the ones necessary in a "real" cowboy. Make a judgment about how the mythic image of a cowboy has helped or hindered the development of American society.

Part Test, Unit 4, Part 3: Forging New Frontiers

Critical Reading

The questions below are based on the following selection.

This excerpt is from "The Luck of Roaring Camp," a short story by Bret Harte in which a baby has been born to the only woman in the mining town of Roaring Camp. When the mother dies, the baby is left to the care of the gruff miners, who are transformed by this tiny infant.

By the time he was a month old, the necessity of giving him a name became apparent. He had generally been known as "the Kid," "Stumpy's boy," "the Cayote" (an allusion to his vocal powers) and even by Kentuck's endearing diminutive of "the [durned] little cuss." But these were felt to be vague and unsatisfactory, and were at last dismissed under another influence. Gamblers and adventurers are generally superstitious, and Oakhurst one day declared that the baby had brought "the luck" to Roaring Camp. It was certain that of late they had been successful. "Luck" was the name agreed upon, with the prefix of Tommy for greater convenience. No allusion was made to the mother, and the father was unknown. "It's better," said the philosophical Oakhurst, "to take a fresh deal all round. Call him Luck, and start him fair." A day was accordingly set apart for the christening. What was meant by this ceremony the reader may imagine, who has already gathered some idea of the reckless irreverence of Roaring Camp. The master of ceremonies was one "Boston," a noted wag, and the occasion seemed to promise the greatest facetiousness. This ingenious satirist had spent two days in preparing a burlesque of the church service, with pointed local allusions. The choir was properly trained, and Sandy Tipton was to stand [as the] godfather. But after the procession had marched to the grove with music and banners, and the child had been deposited before a mock altar, Stumpy stepped before the expectant crowd. "It ain't my style to spoil fun, boys," said the little man, stoutly, eyeing the faces around him, "but it strikes me that this thing ain't exactly on the squar [sic]. It's playing it pretty low down on this yer baby to ring in fun on him that he ain't goin' to understand. And ef [sic] there's going to be any god-fathers round, I'd like to see who's got any better rights than me." A silence followed Stumpy's speech. To the credit of all humorists be it said that the first man to acknowledge its justice was the satirist, thus stopped of his fun. "But," said Stumpy, quickly, following up his advantage, "we're here for a christening, and we'll have it. I proclaim you Thomas Luck, according to the laws of the United States and the State of California. . . ."

On the line, write the letter of the one best answer.

_____ 1. What characteristics make this story an example of Regionalism?
    a. It could take place in any time and place.
    b. It could only take place in a mining camp among gamblers and rough miners.
    c. It could take place in the fashionable city of Boston.
    d. It could take place in Europe.

_____ 2. Besides Regionalism, which other characteristic of the story is exhibited in the following passage?

He had generally been known as "the Kid," "Stumpy's boy," "the Cayote" (an allusion to his vocal powers) and even by Kentuck's endearing diminutive of "the [durned] little cuss."

    a. humor
    b. surrealism
    c. pathetic fallacy
    d. tragedy

_____ 3. The conflict in this excerpt is to be found in
   a. what to do with the mother's body.
   b. how to find the father.
   c. what to name the infant.
   d. what to feed the infant.

_____ 4. When does Oakhurst add significantly to Harte's use of cultural detail in the story?
   a. when he makes reference to the infant's mother
   b. when he tells the men to make the infant a fresh deal
   c. when he plans to speak at the christening
   d. when he rides off into the sunset

_____ 5. What is the motive for Stumpy's interrupting the spoof of the christening?
   a. He feels responsible for the baby and doesn't want the infant to be the object of fun.
   b. He wanted to give the satirical speech before everyone in the town.
   c. He doesn't want the choir to sing.
   d. He doesn't think it is right without a member of the clergy.

_____ 6. Judging by this excerpt and what you know of irony, what do you predict will happen?
   a. Thomas Luck will grow up to be a gambler.
   b. Thomas Luck will grow up to be a miner.
   c. Thomas Luck will turn out to be unlucky.
   d. Thomas Luck will bring heartbreak to the town.

_____ 7. Which is not an example of regional dialect?
   a. "'It's better . . . to take a fresh deal all round. Call him Luck and start him fair.'"
   b. "'It's playing it pretty low down on this yer baby to ring in fun on him'"
   c. "'it strikes me that this thing ain't exactly on the square'"
   d. "'But,' said Stumpy, quickly, following up his advantage, 'we're here for a christening'"

_____ 8. What is the key descriptive term Harte uses for the characters in the story?
   a. melancholy
   b. glamorous
   c. sensitive
   d. superstitious

_____ 9. What is the significance of the name of the baby's birth place, Roaring Camp?
   a. Lions live there.
   b. There is a roaring river nearby.
   c. It is a loud, noisy place where babies are not usually found.
   d. It must be so quiet they named it Roaring as a joke.

_____ 10. What evidence is there already that the infant has had a positive influence on the men?
   a. They didn't fight over the name.
   b. They planned a mock christening.
   c. They were willing to stop the mock christening.
   d. They did not speak of the mother and father.

Vocabulary and Grammar

On the line, write the letter of the one best answer.

_____ 11. What kind of feeling is a *transient* feeling?
   a. fleeting   c. deep
   b. prolonged   d. excruciating

____ 12. Someone who believes in *monotheism* believes
     a. in nothing.   c. man is a god.
     b. in many different gods.   d. in one god.

____ 13. A *belligerent* person is most likely to create
     a. a beautiful garden.
     b. a chorus.
     c. an argument.
     d. a remedy for illness.

____ 14. Choose the correct word to complete the sentence:

     The student guessed, or _____, that Mr. Oakhurst would be a survivor among the outcasts of Poker Flat.

     a. stated   c. indicated
     b. conjectured   d. argued

____ 15. Which sentence is an example of a correct use of the compound predicate?
     a. The morning was bitterly cold and there was no one traveling on the path, which was covered with new snow.
     b. The man, who didn't care about the cold, took no precautions; instead, he went off on his way.
     c. The man looked about, felt his cold cheeks and nose, and decided to keep going.
     d. Acting strangely, the dog understood this was no day for travel.

____ 16. Which sentence does *not* contain an adverb clause?
     a. A man spotted a wounded cowboy who lay in the street.
     b. Because the cowboy was mortally wounded, he lay in the street.
     c. The cowboy started to speak because he wanted to save others from his fate.
     d. Before the man could return, the cowboy died.

____ 17. Which is a sentence fragment?
     a. Listen to the steamboat whistle.
     b. Feeling cranky, he decided against going to the dock.
     c. Running fast through the town.
     d. The dock was crammed with people waiting to board the steamboat.

____ 18. Which sentence contains a coordinating conjunction?
     a. The Colt family loaded their wagon, and then they headed west.
     b. The wagon was loaded with many trunks of various kinds.
     c. The journey, which took a long time, necessitated the fording of rivers.
     d. At journey's end, the Colts were tired and disappointed.

____ 19. Which is *not* a sentence fragment?
     a. Winds howled.
     b. Snow, without letting up for a long time.
     c. Trapped in the mountains because of the deep snow.
     d. An outcast sacrificing food for others.

____ 20. Which sentence contains a double negative?
     a. Simon Wheeler hardly stopped to take a breath once he started talking.
     b. Jim Smiley had a frog that couldn't scarcely be outjumped by any other frog.
     c. Hardly a day went by without the frog's demonstrating great jumping ability.
     d. Almost nothing could keep that frog from outleaping every other frog.

Essay Questions

21. Write an essay that defines and describes the American cowboy to an audience that is not familiar with the American West. Cite one or more of the following works to support your observations: "The Outcasts of Poker Flat," "Pecos Bill Becomes a Coyote," "The Legend of Gregorio Cortez," and "The Streets of Laredo."

22. An account of an event by someone who experienced it is quite different from an account of the same event written by an outsider. In an essay, describe the advantages and disadvantages of a first-hand account by analyzing "Heading West." What can you learn from "Heading West" that you might not learn from a story about Colt's journey written by a someone who did not make the same trip? What are some disadvantages of reading a first-hand account? Support your opinions with examples from the text.

23. Regionalism, which focused on capturing the distinctive qualities of the people and environment of a particular region, was an important literary movement in the second half of the nineteenth century. Choose the works of at least two different authors featured in Part 3 that you feel exhibit characteristics of Regionalism. Using examples from the texts, write an essay in which you illustrate how the literary works exemplify the movement.

24. Critics have noted that Jack London's "To Build a Fire" contains most of the elements of classical tragedy—specifically, that the unnamed hero in London's story has a "tragic flaw" in his personality; that he is treated sympathetically by the author; that he struggles against forces he cannot control; that his fight against destiny is valiant but futile; that he accepts his fate with dignity. Write an essay in which you explain how each of these elements of classical tragedy is illustrated in "To Build a Fire."

25. Henry James in his work *The Art of Fiction* claims that fiction should have "truth of detail" and "the air of reality." Choose a fictional selection from Part 3, and write an essay explaining how the work meets these two of James's criteria. Do "truth of detail" and "the air of reality" contribute to your enjoyment of the story? Cite examples from the work to support your points.

© Prentice-Hall, Inc.

"The Story of an Hour" by Kate Chopin

Selection Test

Critical Reading

On the line, write the letter of the one best answer.

____ 1. Readers in Kate Chopin's time must have found "The Story of an Hour" particularly shocking because of the contrast between Mrs. Mallard's response to her husband's death and
   a. the response that society would consider appropriate.
   b. the love that Mr. Mallard feels for his wife.
   c. her response to the discovery that he is actually alive.
   d. her professions of affection for her husband.

____ 2. When Mrs. Mallard reflects that, "It was only yesterday she had thought with a shudder that life might be long," she becomes aware of the irony that she
   a. had worried about a life that she now knows will be short.
   b. has not been punished for such unacceptable thoughts.
   c. now desired something she has previously feared.
   d. had not valued her husband properly until she lost him.

____ 3. Mrs. Mallard's reflection that she had recently wished for a short life soon has additional irony for the reader because
   a. the reader knows that she still wants her life to be short.
   b. she gets what she wanted after she stopped wanting it.
   c. the reader sees her as a less worthy person than her husband.
   d. she has too much intensity of feeling to wish for a short life.

____ 4. Why does Mrs. Mallard refuse her sister Josephine's offer to keep her company?
   a. Mrs. Mallard does not want to upset her sister.
   b. Mrs. Mallard prefers not to display emotion to others.
   c. Mrs. Mallard needs privacy to confront her true feelings.
   d. Mrs. Mallard wants Josephine to keep Richard company.

____ 5. When Mrs. Mallard looked out the window as she reacted to the news of her husband's death, she saw "patches of blue sky showing here and there through the clouds" and "the tops of trees that were all aquiver with the new spring life." These images are most probably intended to
   a. point out the irony of nature's indifference to human affairs.
   b. evoke a flavor of the beautiful Louisiana countryside.
   c. suggest Mrs. Mallard's intense feeling for nature.
   d. symbolize Mrs. Mallard's promise of new life.

____ 6. How does Mrs. Mallard "hear the story" of her husband's death?
   a. with a paralyzed inability to accept its meaning
   b. with sudden, wild weeping
   c. with a shriek of joy and relief
   d. with a sigh and a dull stare in her eyes

_____ 7. What is the meaning of the following passage from the story?

> A kind intention or a cruel intention made the act seem no less a crime as she looked upon it in that brief moment of illumination.

a. Mrs. Mallard finally realizes that her husband had been cruel to her when she thought he was being kind.

b. She hadn't known until now whether her husband's intention had been cruel or kind.

c. She now understands that imposing your own will on someone is a crime, no matter whether the intention is cruel or kind.

d. She suddenly understands that her self-assertion is a crime, whether her intention was cruel or kind.

_____ 8. Under which type of irony would you classify Josephine's fear that her sister will "make herself ill" by grieving alone in her room?

a. situational   b. dramatic   c. verbal   d. none of the above

_____ 9. In "The Story of an Hour," Kate Chopin is primarily concerned with the

a. sacrilege of rejoicing at someone's death.

b. importance of confirming reports of tragic events.

c. difficulty of distinguishing between illusion and reality.

d. individual's right to self-expression.

_____ 10. After the initial storm of tears, Mrs. Mallard's response to the news of her husband's death is motivated largely by a wave of

a. self-assertion.   b. anger.   c. self-pity.   d. vengeance.

_____ 11. Which of the following excerpts from "The Story of an Hour" best illustrates the author's use of irony?

a. "She wept at once, with sudden, wild abandonment, in her sister's arms."

b. "She was young, with a fair, calm face, whose lines bespoke repression and even a certain strength."

c. "And yet she had loved him—sometimes. Often she had not. What did it matter!"

d. "'Louise, open the door! I beg; open the door—you will make yourself ill.'"

_____ 12. Kate Chopin's "The Story of an Hour" is a powerful illustration of the

a. cruel irony of fate.   c. emptiness of marriage.

b. tragedy of thwarted love.   d. injustice of life.

_____ 13. Why is Richards so concerned about "bearing the sad message" to Mrs. Mallard himself?

a. He wants to keep less sensitive and careful friends from doing it.

b. He doesn't trust Josephine to get the message right.

c. He wants to see her reaction when she first hears the news.

d. He knows she won't believe the story unless he confirms it.

_____ 14. What is the best reason for considering the title "The Story of an Hour" ironic?

a. The events in the story take much longer than an hour.

b. It is really a story about people.

c. The title is deceptively undramatic compared to the events.

d. The words suggest the opposite of their usual meaning.

_____ 15. What word best characterizes this statement about Louise's feeling for her husband?

> And yet she had loved him—sometimes.

a. joyful   b. sorrowful   c. ironic   d. insincere

© Prentice-Hall, Inc.

Unit 4: Division, Reconciliation, and Expansion (1850–1914)

Vocabulary and Grammar

On the line, write the letter of the one best answer.

_____ 16. Which of the following sentences contains an appositive phrase?
   a. Louise's sister Josephine tried to comfort her.
   b. Her fair, calm face bore lines that reflected repression and even a certain strength.
   c. Her husband's friend Richards had learned of the tragedy at the newspaper office.
   d. One strong impulse ruled her, an overwhelming feeling of self-assertion.

_____ 17. Which vocabulary word best suggests Mrs. Mallard's emotional state regarding her marriage before she hears of her husband's death?
   a. elusive
   b. repression
   c. tumultuously
   d. importunities

_____ 18. What was the result of Josephine's *importunities* outside her sister's door?
   a. They gave support to Mrs. Mallard's feelings of self-assertion.
   b. They made Mrs. Mallard impatient and annoyed with her.
   c. They persuaded Mrs. Mallard to leave her room.
   d. They led her to overhear Mrs. Mallard weeping.

_____ 19 Which sentence below is correctly punctuated?
   a. He stood framed in the doorway—her husband, Brently Mallard.
   b. He stood framed in the doorway, her husband Brently Mallard.
   c. He stood framed in the doorway her husband Brently Mallard.
   d. He stood framed in the doorway her husband—Brently Mallard.

_____ 20. When Kate Chopin refers to the feeling stealing over Louise Mallard as *elusive*, she means the feeling is
   a. terrifying to face.
   b. painful to imagine.
   c. necessary to escape.
   d. difficult to grasp.

Essay Questions

21. Do you admire Mrs. Mallard for daring to take joy in this revelation of freedom, or do you condemn her for reacting with such callousness to her husband's death? Explain your answer in an essay, and cite details from the selection to support it.

22. How might Josephine and Richards have reacted if they had learned about Mrs. Mallard's true feelings regarding her husband's death? Imagine their reactions and write an essay describing and explaining them. Cite examples from the selection to explain what you know about each character, as well as the attitudes of the period. Use these examples to support your conclusions.

23. The Victorian world in which Kate Chopin lived and wrote was one of strong social restraints. The rules and expectations of marriage, the exaltation of romantic love, and the dominance of the husband over the wife prevented many Victorian women from viewing their circumstances honestly. Do you think Mrs. Mallard is a victim of Victorian attitudes toward marriage? Why or why not? Write an essay in which you give your opinion of Mrs. Mallard and her circumstances. Support your argument with evidence from Mrs. Mallard's thoughts in the aftermath of her husband's presumed death.

Name _____ Date _____

"**April Showers**" by Edith Wharton

Selection Test

Critical Reading

On the line, write the letter of the one best answer.

____ 1. What is a story's exposition?
   a. the introduction of the characters, setting, and situation
   b. the central struggle between the main characters
   c. the rising action
   d. the falling action

____ 2. Even though it is never expressly stated, the story gives the impression that "April Showers" is
   a. a very good novel but not ready for publication.
   b. Theodora's first novel.
   c. about a character just like Theodora herself.
   d. a book everyone in Theodora's town would enjoy reading.

____ 3. By choosing the pen name Gladys Glyn, Theodora was
   a. trying to keep people from finding out her real identity.
   b. taking the name of a relative who had died.
   c. trying to appear modest.
   d. emulating Kathleen Kyd.

____ 4. Which of the following statements best describes Mrs. Dace?
   a. She is impatient with Theodora.
   b. She suffers from a chronic illness.
   c. She is not very interested in her children.
   d. She likes to eat breakfast in bed.

____ 5. What happens at the story's climax?
   a. Theodora sends her manuscript in to the *Home Circle*.
   b. Theodora's novel is accepted for publication.
   c. Theodora finds that the story printed in the *Home Circle* is not hers.
   d. Theodora walks home with her father.

____ 6. Wharton shows readers only one line from Theodora's novel, but that line shows that the novel is
   a. extremely romantic.
   b. written for children.
   c. full of spelling errors.
   d. badly written.

____ 7. After Theodora sends off her manuscript to the *Home Circle*, the readers share with her a sense of _____.
   a. antagonism
   b. anticipation
   c. contrition
   d. commiseration

© Prentice-Hall, Inc.

_____ 8. The resolution of the conflict of the story happens when
    a. Theodora receives a letter from the *Home Circle*.
    b. Miss Brill asks for Theodora's autograph.
    c. Theodora finds out why her story wasn't published.
    d. Theodora meets her father at the station.

_____ 9. Who or what is Kathleen Kyd?
    a. a pen name for Frances G. Wollop
    b. Theodora's pen name
    c. a local busybody
    d. Theodora's mother

_____ 10. When she finds out that her novel is to be published in *Home Circle*, the thing Theodora enjoys most is
    a. the knowledge that she would finally make some money.
    b. proving to her father that she was worth something.
    c. her newfound local fame.
    d. the publishers' calling her "Madam."

_____ 11. What does Theodora do when she believes that the *Home Circle* printed the wrong story?
    a. She drops everything and goes to Boston.
    b. She argues with her father.
    c. She forgets to give her sister cod-liver oil.
    d. She sets out to find Kathleen Kyd.

_____ 12. The denouement in this story creates for the reader a feeling of _____.
    a. curiosity   c. confusion
    b. empathy   d. shock

_____ 13. Edith Wharton probably intended readers to react to the events of the story in much the same way that _____ did.
    a. Dr. Dace   c. Mrs. Dace
    b. Miss Brill   d. Theodora

_____ 14. Anticipating her father's reaction when she returned home from Boston fills Theodora with _____.
    a. eagerness
    b. excitement
    c. dread
    d. amusement

Vocabulary and Grammar

On the line, write the letter of the one best answer.

_____ 15. A gerund is a form of a
    a. noun used as a verb.
    b. verb used as a noun.
    c. verb used as a clause.
    d. prepositional phrase.

_____ 16. Which of the following sentences contains a gerund phrase?
    a. Theodora went running down the stairs.
    b. Her father had walked to the train station to meet her.
    c. Remembering his own sad walk home was what made Dr. Dace go to meet Theodora.
    d. Theodora and her father slowly walked home together.

____ 17. Instead of being angry with Theodora at the end of the story, her father tells her something that shows his ____.
   a. antagonism
   b. manuscript
   c. commiseration
   d. contrition

____ 18. Knowing she has worried her mother and disappointed her father fills Theodora with ____.
   a. antagonism
   b. contrition
   c. commiseration
   d. admonition

____ 19. In the following sentence, how does the underlined gerund function?

   Writing was the only thing that made Theodora feel special.

   a. subject
   b. direct object
   c. subject complement
   d. object of a preposition

____ 20. When Theodora reads Kathleen Kyd's name under the title "April Showers," she feels great ____ toward the other author.
   a. antagonism
   b. contrition
   c. commiseration
   d. ambivalence

Essay Questions

21. There is an old saying that "April showers bring May flowers." Roughly translated, this means that you have to experience some pain to grow or to appreciate pleasure. Write an essay explaining how this saying applies to Edith Wharton's story. What pain is presented in the story? What growth or appreciation of pleasure do you see? Use evidence from the story to support your answers.

22. The events of a story make up its plot, which can be divided into the following parts: exposition, conflict, rising action, climax, resolution, and denouement. Write an essay discussing these plot elements in relation to the events of "April Showers." What is the general definition of each element? What events in the story correspond to each element?

23. Although writers need self-confidence to work at a difficult craft, too much self-confidence can turn into a harmful pride. Write an essay explaining how Theodora's youthful pride in "April Showers" could be considered harmful. How does her pride affect her as a writer? How does it affect those around her? Illustrate your points with examples of Theodora's prideful behavior and attitudes.

Name _____ Date _____

"Douglass" and **"We Wear the Mask"** by Paul Laurence Dunbar

Selection Test

Critical Reading

On the line, write the letter of the one best answer.

_____ 1. In "We Wear the Mask," Dunbar suggests the world sees his fellow African Americans
  a. in a harsh and honest light.
  b. only when they hide their feelings.
  c. when they are filled with "tears and sighs."
  d. as they are praying to Christ.

_____ 2. What is symbolized in these lines from "We Wear the Mask"?

  but oh the clay is vile
  Beneath our feet, and long the mile;

  a. an evil person   c. a broken promise
  b. a long, hard life   d. an act of revenge

_____ 3. In "Douglass," Dunbar wishes that Douglass had been
  a. a poet.
  b. a boat pilot.
  c. alive to guide them.
  d. sympathetic to their cause.

_____ 4. In "Douglass," Dunbar uses the image of a boat in a stormy sea mainly to symbolize the
  a. joy and excitement of African Americans immediately after slavery was abolished.
  b. parallel between nature's power and the enduring quality of African American culture.
  c. seafaring traditions of many African cultures.
  d. turmoil and hardships African Americans still faced after emancipation.

_____ 5. The speaker in "We Wear the Mask" believes that wearing the mask is
  a. evil.   c. impossible.
  b. foolish.   d. essential.

_____ 6. In "We Wear the Mask," the overall emotional tone that Dunbar uses is one of
  a. aggression.   c. hopefulness.
  b. defeat.   d. bitterness.

_____ 7. Which words are an example of a slant rhyme?
  a. *pilot* and *lieth*
  b. *thou* and *know*
  c. *tide* and *ride*
  d. *mask* and *mile*

_____ 8. Which definition most closely distinguishes a slant rhyme?
  a. The words appear within a single line.
  b. The words appear within a single sentence.
  c. The vowel sounds are similar.
  d. The beginning consonants must be the same.

_____ 9. In "We Wear the Mask," Dunbar suggests that the mask shows
   a. anger.
   b. despair.
   c. happiness.
   d. strength.

_____ 10. What is an appropriate interpretation of the following lines from "We Wear the Mask"?

   Why should the world be overwise,
   In counting all our tears and sighs?

   a. We should not think that anyone is able to guess our thoughts.
   b. Too much knowledge brings misery and hardship to the world.
   c. We must realize that we are really no wiser than anyone else.
   d. Why should we think anyone cares what we really feel?

_____ 11. According to "We Wear the Mask," why do African Americans wear the mask?
   a. to pretend that they were white
   b. to convince themselves that they had made more gains than they actually had
   c. to hide their feelings about slavery and racial violence
   d. to display their material and intellectual success

_____ 12. Which of the following presents the most appropriate interpretation of these lines from the first stanza of "Douglass"?

   Not ended then, the passionate ebb and flow,
   The awful tide that battled to and fro;
   We ride amid a tempest of dispraise.

   a. When slavery ended, African Americans began to quarrel among themselves as some individuals competed to gain power and influence over the rest of the African American community.
   b. The struggle for equality and against prejudice is not over; in fact, it's worse.
   c. The Civil War did not end when slavery was abolished but continued for several years afterward.
   d. The strength and character of African Americans were not destroyed by slavery but continued to grow in spite of it.

_____ 13. Which message is conveyed in "We Wear the Mask"?
   a. African Americans were not completely free to be themselves even after slavery was abolished.
   b. African Americans could not be truly free until they embraced the Christian faith.
   c. African Americans needed to take decisive actions to eliminate the prejudice against them.
   d. African Americans needed to rediscover their cultural heritage before they could understand themselves.

_____ 14. In "Douglass," Dunbar leaves the reader feeling
   a. that no improvements will happen soon for African Americans.
   b. that Frederick Douglass was a great speaker.
   c. afraid to travel by ocean because of tempests.
   d. the world is slowly getting more racially tolerant.

_____ 15. Which definition most closely distinguishes an internal rhyme?
   a. The rhyming words appear within a single line.
   b. The vowel sounds must be identical.
   c. The vowel sounds are similar or identical.
   d. The consonants after the vowel sounds in both words are the same.

Vocabulary and Grammar

On the line, write the letter of the one best answer.

____ 16. In "We Wear the Mask," how does a mouth with *myriad* subtleties help pay a debt to human *guile*?
    a. By saying countless small things, we can be very crafty in how we humans portray ourselves.
    b. By smiling broadly, we can give back something to the human spirit.
    c. By seeing each mouth as a human being, we can better visualize human society.
    d. When communicating in eloquent speech, one can make almost anyone believe in anything.

____ 17. In "Douglass," the line "And Honor, the strong pilot, lieth *stark*" implies that honor is
    a. floating all around us.
    b. angry and seething.
    c. cold, stiff, and dead.
    d. waiting for its soldiers.

____ 18. Which punctuation mark should be used after the interjection to indicate that the speaker *really* doesn't like the color?
    a. No—I don't like that color!
    b. No, I don't like that color!
    c. No: I don't like that color!
    d. No! I don't like that color!

____ 19. In "Douglass," the line "We ride amid a *tempest* of dispraise" gives the image of being
    a. lulled by a rocking motion.
    b. swept up by a hurricane.
    c. carried by a bubbling stream.
    d. lifted by a chilly breeze.

____ 20. Which punctuation after the interjection best expresses a calm, pensive emotion?
    a. Ah? Douglass, we have fall'n on evil days.
    b. Ah! Douglass, we have fall'n on evil days.
    c. Ah, Douglass, we have fall'n on evil days.
    d. Ah. Douglass, we have fall'n on evil days.

Essay Questions

21. Restate in an essay Dunbar's sentiments as expressed in "We Wear the Mask" to a person unfamiliar with the poem. Use details from the poem to support your interpretation of it.

22. Paul Laurence Dunbar was the son of former slaves. His father escaped to Canada but returned to the United States to fight in the Union army. Dunbar was the first African American to make a significant attempt to earn his living as a writer. Knowing this, reread one or both of the poems and write an essay explaining how you think Dunbar looked upon the position of African Americans in post-Civil War society. Use details from one or both of the poems in your essay, as well as historical facts of the era.

23. One critic has stated that Paul Laurence Dunbar's "We Wear the Mask" is a poem "about concealed racial fire." Write an essay in which you argue either for or against that viewpoint. Is Dunbar's poem about race, or is it more universal? Support your opinion with evidence from one or both of the poems, as well as facts from Dunbar's life and work.

"Luke Havergal" and **"Richard Cory"** by Edwin Arlington Robinson
"Lucinda Matlock" and **"Richard Bone"** by Edgar Lee Masters

Selection Test

Critical Reading

On the line, write the letter of the one best answer.

_____ 1. What is the speaker's main motive for talking to Luke Havergal in this poem?
   a. to comfort Luke
   b. to convince Luke to act on his feelings
   c. to chastise Luke for being overly emotional
   d. to provide Luke with hope for a brighter future

_____ 2. Which of the following best describes the tone of "Luke Havergal"?
   a. angry   c. indifferent
   b. hopeful   d. brooding

_____ 3. Which of the following most likely explains the relationship between Luke Havergal
   and the woman mentioned in the poem?
   a. The woman was Luke's lover, but she died.
   b. The woman was Luke's enemy, and she destroyed his life.
   c. The woman was a homeless vagrant whom Luke saw and pitied.
   d. The woman was a murderer who killed Luke's family.

_____ 4. Who is the speaker of "Luke Havergal"?
   a. Luke Havergal   c. a ghost
   b. a living woman   d. Edwin Arlington Robinson

_____ 5. Who is the speaker of "Richard Cory"?
   a. Richard Cory   c. a member of Richard Cory's family
   b. a person in the town   d. Edwin Arlington Robinson

_____ 6. Why did the speaker of "Richard Cory" envy Richard Cory?
   a. because he was wealthy and admirable
   b. because he had a large family
   c. because he led a happy life
   d. because he was a community leader

_____ 7. What do you think is the message of the poem "Richard Cory"?
   a. Rich people should give to the poor.
   b. Rich people want to be envied.
   c. People admire those who are wealthy.
   d. Money can't make a person happy.

_____ 8. Which of the following passages from "Richard Cory" shows that the speaker admired Richard Cory's character and manners?
   a. "He was a gentleman from sole to crown,"
   b. "But still he fluttered pulses when he said, / 'Good-morning'"
   c. " . . . and he glittered when he walked."
   d. "And he was rich—yes, richer than a king—"

© Prentice-Hall, Inc.   *Havergal/Cory/Matlock/Bone* **173**

_____ 9. Which sentence best describes Lucinda Matlock's view of life?
   a. The parties and explorations of youth are the best part of life; old age is full of pain, suffering, and loneliness.
   b. You need anger to get you through the hardships of life; the angrier you are, the more likely you are to survive to an old age.
   c. You must work hard and you may encounter sorrow, but life is basically fulfilling and rewarding.
   d. People's lives are determined by fate, and no one really cares about what you think or how you feel.

_____ 10. Lucinda Matlock criticizes the people who lived after her because they
   a. do not appreciate how hard she has worked.
   b. ridicule the things she considered important in life.
   c. let little things get them down and don't appreciate life.
   d. make no effort to learn from her life.

_____ 11. Which of the following best describes the tone of Masters's "Lucinda Matlock"?
   a. contented   c. self-righteous
   b. despairing   d. disappointed

_____ 12. Which of the following excerpts gives the best insight into the personality of Lucinda Matlock?
   a. "One time we changed partners,"
   b. "Enjoying, working, raising the twelve children,"
   c. "And by Spoon River gathering many a shell,"
   d. "Anger, discontent, and drooping hopes?"

_____ 13. Which of the following passages from "Richard Bone" shows that the speaker feels uncomfortable about chiseling deceptive epitaphs?
   a. "I did not know whether what they told me/Was true or false."
   b. "And I chiseled them whatever they wished,/All in ignorance of its truth."
   c. "I knew how near to the life/Were the epitaphs that were ordered . . . "
   d. "And made myself party to the false chronicles/Of the stones,"

_____ 14. What does this passage from "Richard Bone" suggest about the speaker's attitude?

   But still I chiseled whatever they paid me to chisel
   And made myself party to the false chronicles

   a. He is indifferent to the truth.
   b. He has been influenced to hide the truth.
   c. He prefers not to know the truth.
   d. He will chisel only true epitaphs.

Vocabulary and Grammar

On the line, write the letter of the one best answer.

_____ 15. How does the italicized noun clause function in the following line from "Richard Bone"?

   And I chiseled for them whatever they wished. . . .

   a. as a direct object   c. as a predicate nominative
   b. as an indirect object   d. as the object of a preposition

© Prentice-Hall, Inc.

____ 16. Which of the following words could be substituted for *imperially* in the following passage from "Richard Cory" without changing the meaning of the sentence?

> He was a gentleman from sole to crown,
> Clean favored, and *imperially* slim.

a. surprisingly

b. majestically

c. beautifully

d. shockingly

____ 17. Which of the following statements most accurately paraphrases the following excerpt from "Lucinda Matlock"?

> At ninety-six I had lived enough, that is all
> And passed to a sweet *repose*.

a. At age ninety-six, I moved into a nursing home.

b. At age ninety-six, I stopped working and started having fun.

c. At age ninety-six, I decided to stop working and retire.

d. At age ninety-six, I died and got a long overdue rest.

____ 18. In the following passage from "Richard Bone," what does the word *epitaph* mean?

> They would bring me the *epitaph*
> And stand around the shop while I worked

a. inscription

b. headstone

c. grave marker

d. dead body

____ 19. The italicized words in this excerpt from "Richard Bone" are a noun clause. How does this noun clause function in its sentence?

> When I first came to Spoon River
> I did not know *whether what they told me*
> *Was true or false.*

a. as a subject

b. as a direct object

c. as an indirect object

d. as a predicate nominative

____ 20. A noun clause is a subordinate clause that

I. has a subject and a verb.

II. cannot stand alone as a sentence.

III. is used as a noun in a sentence.

a. I and II

b. II and III

c. I and III

d. I, II, and III

Essay Questions

21. Choose one of the poems in this selection and write a short biographical essay on the title character. Draw conclusions about the life the character led or is leading, and support those conclusions with details from the poem. Consider the tone of the poem you choose, and use that as a clue to the kind of life the person led.

22. How would you describe Lucinda Matlock's attitude toward younger people? Write an essay describing how she comes to give the advice she does in the poem. Do you think she despises people who are younger than she, or is she motivated by a desire to ensure that they do not miss out on life? Support your conclusions with details from the poem.

23. What do you think the speaker of "Luke Havergal" wants Luke Havergal to do? Write an essay, using evidence from the poem to answer the question and support your answer.

Name _____ Date _____

Selection Test

Critical Reading

On the line, write the letter of the one best answer.

_____ 1. The description of Aunt Georgiana as having "an incessant twitching of the mouth
and eyebrows . . . resulting from isolation and monotony, and from frequent physical
suffering" reveals her character through
    a. a dialogue with another character.
    b. the narrator's observations of her physical appearance.
    c. her own thoughts and comments.
    d. Mrs. Springer's reactions.

_____ 2. Aunt Georgiana returned to Boston to
    a. settle an estate.
    b. hear the latest Wagner selections.
    c. visit Clark, her nephew.
    d. see if she should move back.

_____ 3. The selection says that Aunt Georgiana and her husband "took a homestead in Red
Willow County."[6] The "6" tells us we can find out more about Red Willow County
    a. in footnote number six.
    b. in the sixth definition under *County* in a dictionary.
    c. in the sixth map at the end of the book.
    d. by reading six paragraphs ahead.

_____ 4. As a young boy, Clark appears to have been
    a. oblivious and lazy.
    b. tough and quick-witted.
    c. studious and dull.
    d. diligent and sensitive.

_____ 5. We learn in the first paragraph that the letter announcing Aunt Georgiana's arrival
comes from Nebraska. Therefore, we assume she lives in Nebraska. We can find out
Aunt Georgiana lives on a small homestead in Red Willow County by
    a. using an atlas.
    b. reading a footnote.
    c. reviewing past sentences.
    d. reading ahead.

_____ 6. Which of the following aspects of Aunt Georgiana's life does the author appear to
value most highly?
    a. piety   c. modesty
    b. poverty   d. devotion

_____ 7. The description of the Nebraska farm creates an atmosphere of
    a. adventure and tension.
    b. desolation and hardship.
    c. boredom and apathy.
    d. productivity and vitality.

_____ 8. Which of the following factors probably contributed most to Aunt Georgiana's general bewilderment during her visit?
   a. the long and difficult journey to Boston
   b. her age, which had brought about a certain forgetfulness
   c. the contrast in settings between Boston and the Nebraska farm
   d. the suddenness of her departure from Nebraska

_____ 9. What is the central idea of "A Wagner Matinée"?
   a. the oppression of women by men
   b. the high price of foolish young love
   c. the pain of realizing what you have lost
   d. the hardships of frontier

_____ 10. What can the reader infer about Aunt Georgiana's character from the following passage?

   She questioned me absently about various changes in the city, but she was chiefly concerned that she had forgotten to leave instructions about feeding half-skimmed milk to a certain weakling calf.

   a. She tended to be absent-minded in her daily chores.
   b. She found it difficult to rely on others.
   c. She focused more on her responsibilities than on what gives her pleasure.
   d. She disliked the city and longed to be back on the farm.

_____ 11. Why does Clark come to live with Aunt Georgiana as a boy?
   a. He was orphaned when he was a young boy.
   b. His parents sent him there while they traveled in Europe.
   c. He was an apprentice farmer for his Uncle Howard.
   d. The selection does not explain.

_____ 12. Which is a reading strategy for clarifying?
   a. knowing how other characters feel about the main character
   b. knowing what tense the sentence is written in
   c. memorizing sections of text
   d. rereading a previous passage to refresh your memory

_____ 13. The tone of "A Wagner Matinée" can best be described as
   a. sympathetic.
   b. distant.
   c. accusatory.
   d. apologetic.

_____ 14. Clark's remembrances of his aunt helping him with his studies and music indicate that she
   a. stayed connected to her love of teaching and music through him.
   b. punished him for her own lack of ambition.
   c. realized his talent could be put to better use in the city.
   d. wanted to educate herself through him.

_____ 15. Which of the following passages is an example of characterization?
   a. "There they measured off their eighty acres by driving across the prairie in a wagon. . . . "
   b. "When the musicians came out and took their places, she gave a little stir of anticipation. . . . "
   c. "The world there is the flat world of the ancients. . . . "
   d. ". . . the people filed out of the hall chattering and laughing, glad to relax and find the living level again. . . . "

Vocabulary and Grammar

On the line, write the letter of the one best answer.

____ 16. Which word is closest to the italicized word in the following excerpt?

> "Well, we have come to better things than the old *Trovatore* at any rate, Aunt Georgie?" I queried, with well-meant *jocularity*.

    a. love
    b. shyness
    c. caution
    d. humor

____ 17. Clark uses the word *reverential* to describe his feelings for his aunt, meaning he
    a. fears her.
    b. respects her.
    c. ignores her.
    d. dislikes her.

____ 18. Which sentence includes a reflexive pronoun?
    a. She had resigned herself to a life without music.
    b. Myself, I could not wait to return to the East.
    c. But for Aunt Georgiana, she herself could not remember what it was like to live her own life.
    d. The farm itself was a full-time responsibility.

____ 19. The selection tells us that, before the concert, Aunt Georgiana seems *semi-somnambulant* and *inert*. The two words that best describe her state of being are
    a. *timid* and *respectful.*
    b. *sleepy* and *motionless.*
    c. *restless* and *cheerful.*
    d. *still* and *fearful.*

____ 20. Which sentence includes an intensive pronoun?
    a. The isolation built upon itself to create a lonely prison.
    b. The ladies looked among themselves to see who appeared to be the finest.
    c. We ourselves enjoyed the Wagner concert very much.
    d. He silently congratulated himself for making the correct decision.

Essay Questions

21. There are several indications that Aunt Georgiana retained her love of music throughout her time in Nebraska. In an essay, describe which details in the selection indicate that music remained alive in Aunt Georgiana's heart, even years after she left the conservatory.

22. At the end of the story, Aunt Georgiana pleads with Clark that she does not want to leave the concert. Write an essay in which you interpret the deeper meaning of her response to the end of the concert. What does leaving the concert hall symbolize for Aunt Georgiana? Support your explanation with details from the story.

23. In first-person narration, the reader learns only as much about the narrator as the narrator chooses to reveal. A person reading "A Wagner Matinée" learns a great deal more about Aunt Georgiana than about her nephew Clark. Write a descriptive essay about Clark, the narrator, based on information in the story. Although nothing is said about Clark's appearance, you can infer his personality from his thoughts, statements, and actions. Be as specific as possible, and support your observations with examples from the text.

"Cats" by Anna Quindlen

Selection Test

Critical Reading

On the line, write the letter of the one best answer.

____ 1. Which possible subtitle best fits the story in "Cats"?
   a. In the Heat of the Night
   b. A Mother's Love
   c. A Lonely Old Woman
   d. When Death Calls

____ 2. What does Quindlen sprinkle along the property line to chase away the cats?
   a. sulfuric acid
   b. coffee grinds
   c. black pepper
   d. rotten vegetables

____ 3. What does absence of the neighbor's son suggest about his true relationship with his mother?
   a. They love but do not like each other very much.
   b. They are not as close as she pretends.
   c. The son hates his mother.
   d. The mother is overly critical of her son.

____ 4. Why did the neighbor become so fond of Quindlen's son?
   a. He gave her flowers.
   b. He was nice to her cats.
   c. He reminded her of her own youth.
   d. He reminded her of her own son.

____ 5. According to the neighbor, why doesn't her son visit more often?
   a. His job in California keeps him too busy.
   b. He had a fight with his father and refuses to see him.
   c. His military assignment keeps him far away.
   d. His wife does not allow him to visit.

____ 6. Which phrase best describes the neighbor's personality?
   a. talkative and outgoing
   b. garrulous and sympathetic
   c. gruff and hard-nosed
   d. amicable and pleasant

____ 7. Who is called "Bop Bop" in the story?
   a. the neighbor's son
   b. the neighbor's favorite cat
   c. the neighbor's parakeet
   d. both the neighbor and Quindlen's son

8. Who takes care of the neighbor after she returns from the hospital?
    a. Quindlen
    b. a home health-care aide
    c. her own son
    d. another neighbor across the street

9. Who died just one month before the neighbor?
    a. Quindlen's son
    b. the neighbor's son
    c. the neighbor's husband
    d. the neighbor's favorite cat

10. Which of the following excerpts suggests that the neighbor is not telling the truth about her relationship with her son?
    a. "During the time we lived next door to her, he came home once."
    b. "I never heard her say a bad word about him."
    c. "She said it broke his heart not to see his father more."
    d. "We sent roses to the funeral home, and the son's wife sent a nice thank-you note."

Essay Questions

11. Quindlen has said that she approached her newspaper columns as "a conversation with a person that it just so happens I can't see." Using examples from the text, write an essay describing how Quindlen is able to connect with her readers. Did Quindlen succeed in this text in touching you in some way? How?

12. At the end of "Cats," Quindlen wonders what "lasting lessons" the old neighbor might have taught her son and herself. Write an essay describing what some of those lessons might be, both for Quindlen and her son. Describe an episode from your own life where you or a family member lost touch with a close friend or relative. How did that loss affect you? What did you do, or could you have done, to deal with the feelings you experienced?

13. America is often described as a country of rugged individualists. Write an essay explaining how such an attitude may contribute to feelings of isolation and loneliness in modern society. Speculate as to whether, and by what means, contemporary life makes it harder or easier to overcome feelings of loneliness and isolation.

Part Test, Unit 4, Part 4: Living in a Changing World

Critical Reading

The questions below are based on the following selection.

This excerpt is from the opening paragraphs of "The Sentimentality of William Tavener," a short story by Willa Cather.

It takes a strong woman to make any sort of success of living in the West, and Hester undoubtedly was that. When people spoke of William Tavener as the most prosperous farmer in McPherson County, they usually added that his wife was a "good manager." She was an executive woman, quick of tongue and something of an imperatrix. The only reason her husband did not consult her about his business was that she did not wait to be consulted.

It would have been quite impossible for one man, within the limited sphere of human action, to follow all Hester's advice, but in the end William usually acted upon some of her suggestions. When she incessantly denounced the "shiftlessness" of letting a new threshing machine stand unprotected in the open, he eventually built a shed for it. When she sniffed contemptuously at his notion of fencing a hog corral with sod walls, he made a spiritless beginning on the structure—merely to "show his temper," as she put it—but in the end he went off quietly to town and bought enough barbed wire to complete the fence. . . . Silence, indeed, was William's refuge and his strength.

William set his boys a wholesome example to respect their mother. People who knew him very well suspected that he even admired her. He was a hard man towards his neighbors, and even towards his sons; grasping, determined, and ambitious.

There was an occasional blue day about the house when William went over the store bills, but he never objected to items relating to his wife's gowns or bonnets. So it came about that many of the foolish, unnecessary little things that Hester bought for her boys, she had charged to her personal account. . . .

On the line, write the letter of the one best answer.

_____ 1. What is the speaker's tone in this story?
    a. serious
    b. somber
    c. playful
    d. foreboding

_____ 2. How could you interpret the relationship between Hester and William?
    a. cooperative
    b. warm and tender
    c. bitter and hateful
    d. competitive but loving

_____ 3. What does this sentence tell you about William's character?

> When she incessantly denounced the "shiftlessness" of letting a new threshing machine stand unprotected in the open, he eventually built a shed for it.

    a. William knows when Hester is right.
    b. William has come to ignore Hester's nagging.
    c. William enjoys annoying Hester.
    d. William only makes his own decisions.

_____ 4. Which of the following does the author add for humor?
  a. "The only reason her husband did not consult her about his business was that she did not wait to be consulted."
  b. "When she sniffed contemptuously at his notion of fencing a hog corral with sod walls, he made a spiritless beginning on the structure—merely to 'show his temper,' as she put it—but in the end he went off quietly to town and bought enough barbed wire to complete the fence."
  c. "William set his boys a wholesome example to respect their mother."
  d. "When people spoke of William Tavener as the most prosperous farmer in McPherson County, they usually added that his wife was a 'good manager.'"

_____ 5. In light of the following passage, the title of the story, "The Sentimentality of William Tavener," is an example of which type of irony?

  > He was a hard man towards his neighbors, and even towards his sons; grasping, determined, and ambitious. . . . many of the foolish, unnecessary little things that Hester bought for her boys, she had charged to her personal account.

  a. dramatic irony
  b. verbal irony
  c. situational irony
  d. an ironic detail

_____ 6. Which parent would the Tavener children most likely turn to for help?
  a. William, because he would be direct and responsive
  b. William, because he understands boys better than Hester does
  c. Hester, because she is more compassionate to the children than William is
  d. Hester, because she doesn't have much to do

_____ 7. Who was responsible for the Tavener's financial success?
  a. William Tavener, because he owned the farm
  b. William Tavener, because he bought pigs
  c. Hester Tavener, because she was a good manager
  d. Hester Tavener, because she had a good job

_____ 8. Hester is described as "something of an imperatrix." From what you've read about Hester, what do you think an imperatrix is?
  a. a monarch or ruler
  b. the trustee of a will
  c. a timid person
  d. an unnamed narrator

_____ 9. Who is the speaker of the story?
  a. William
  b. William's wife, Hester
  c. William and Hester's sons
  d. the author, Willa Cather

_____ 10. The following passage is an example of _____.

  > He was a hard man towards his neighbors, and even towards his sons; grasping, determined, and ambitious.

  a. humor
  b. irony
  c. rhyme
  d. characterization

Vocabulary and Grammar

On the line, write the letter of the one best answer.

____ 11. A good _____ on the tombstone of a pioneer would contain the word *courage*.
    a. repression   c. tempest
    b. epitaph   d. jocularity

____ 12. Willa Cather wrote of the _____ difficulties of pioneer life on the plains of Nebraska.
    a. elusive   c. minimal
    b. myriad   d. reverential

____ 13. The most _____ feature of Aunt Georgiana's physical state was a constant twitching of the eyebrows and mouth.
    a. salient   c. reverential
    b. stark   d. inert

____ 14. The best antonym for the italicized word in the sentence is _____.

> Just how much the music meant to Aunt Georgiana was *apparent*; its meaning showed clearly in the tears that she shed.

    a. inert   c. elusive
    b. incessant   d. stark

____ 15. Which is correctly punctuated?
    a. No! I don't want to leave the concert hall.
    b. No I don't want to leave the concert hall.
    c. No; I dont want to leave the concert hall.
    d. No: I don't want to leave the concert hall.

____ 16. Which sentence contains a noun clause used as a predicate nominative?
    a. This music is what I need the most.
    b. What the musician said was not clear.
    c. I remember what he said.
    d. A program will be given to whoever arrives.

____ 17. How is the noun clause used in the sentence?

> That you overslept is a poor excuse for tardiness.

    a. predicate nominative
    b. subject
    c. direct object
    c. object of a preposition

____ 18. Which would *not* be an appositive for the following sentence?

> Richard Cory, _____, was the envy of everyone.

    a. a fine gentleman
    b. a well-dressed man
    c. smiling proudly
    d. a man of fine manners

____ 19. Which sentence does *not* contain an example of a reflexive pronoun?
    a. People watched Richard Cory and could imagine themselves in his place.
    b. He moved himself up in their esteem without even trying.
    c. He himself would say "Good-morning" in a fine fashion.
    d. You might at first think yourself fortunate to be like him.

_____ 20. Complete the following sentence with the proper pronoun.

As Richard Cory walked by, other people compared _____ with him.

a. himself
b. themselves
c. yourselves
d. herself

Essay Questions

21. The Nebraska Willa Cather portrayed scarcely exists. Write an essay in which you compare 1920's rural life as described by Willa Cather with today's lifestyle in your own community. Would Aunt Georgiana be as deprived of the arts she loved if she lived in your community? What would make possible the availability of theater, music, and art virtually anywhere today?

22. Chose one of the women protagonists in the selections in Part 4. The works of Kate Chopin, Willa Cather, and Edgar Lee Masters all contain good examples. Write an essay in which you explain how the heroine you chose is reflective of the restrictions and stereotypes of the age. Explain how their lives might be different today. Support your answers with examples from the text.

23. The unexpected often happens in life and literature. Choose a poem or story in Part 4 that had an unexpected theme or ending. Write an essay describing the work and your reaction to it. What did you think the theme of the work would be when you began reading? How were you surprised? What were the author's intentions in writing the work this way? Support your observations with examples from the text.

24. The nature of courage is often explored in literature. From a selection in Part 4, choose one character who you think is courageous and, in an essay, discuss how that person shows courage. What circumstances require the character to display courage? How does he or she show it? What do you learn about the nature of courage from reading the story? Support your observations and conclusions with examples from the selection.

25. The theme of isolation is prevalent in post–Civil War literature. Explore the theme by choosing a character from Part 4 who experiences loneliness, isolation, or a sense of being a social outsider. Discuss the character's situation and his or her way of handling it. Use examples from the selection to support your points.

"The Love Song of J. Alfred Prufrock" by T. S. Eliot

Selection Test

Critical Reading

On the line, write the letter of the one best answer.

_____ 1. "The Love Song of J. Alfred Prufrock" is written in the form of
a. an epic poem.   c. a dramatic monologue.
b. a prose poem.   d. a dramatic dialogue.

_____ 2. The setting can best be described as
a. a fall evening in a city.
b. a summer afternoon in a city.
c. a spring morning in the country.
d. a winter night in a city.

_____ 3. What best describes the mood of the evening "spread out against the sky / Like a patient etherized upon a table"?
a. hopeful   c. romantic
b. suspenseful   d. melancholy

_____ 4. When Eliot describes "The muttering retreats / Of restless nights in one-night cheap hotels / And sawdust restaurants with oyster-shells," he is referring to love's
a. hidden dangers.
b. sometimes sordid surroundings.
c. mysterious power.
d. sometimes shameful deceits.

_____ 5. What natural association links Prufrock's observations of the yellow fog with his thoughts about there being "time yet for a hundred indecisions / . . . Before the taking of a toast and tea"?
a. the connection between fog and tea
b. the similarity between the murky fog and his indecisive thoughts
c. the relationship between the yellow color of the fog and the color of sunlight
d. the parallel between the mysterious nature of fog and the nature of love

_____ 6. In a dramatic monologue, an imaginary character addresses
a. the cast of the play.   c. fewer than three characters.
b. only one other character.   d. a silent listener.

_____ 7. What musical device does Eliot use in the following excerpt from "The Love Song of J. Alfred Prufrock"?

Before the taking of a toast and tea.

a. alliteration
b. internal rhyme
c. simile
d. narrative

_____ 8. In the following lines, what sound device lends musicality to the poem?

> Have known the evenings, mornings, afternoons, /I have measured out my life with coffee spoons.

    a. end rhyme
    b. repetition
    c. alliteration
    d. iambic pentameter

_____ 9. Which of the following quotations from the poem uses the musical device of repetition?
    a. "Is it the perfume from a dress/ That makes me so digress?"
    b. "I grow old . . . I grow old . . ./ I shall wear the bottoms of my trousers rolled."
    c. "Then how should I begin/ To spit out the butt-ends of my days and ways?"
    d. "I should have been a pair of ragged claws/ Scuttling across the floors of silent seas."

_____ 10. In a dramatic monologue, the thoughts and feelings that are expressed are those of the
    a. poet or playwright.
    b. protagonist.
    c. character who is speaking.
    d. antagonist.

_____ 11. How does Prufrock think others view him?
    a. as a fully accepted member of his social set
    b. as a menacing figure
    c. as a heroic figure
    d. as an aging, conventional person of little consequence

_____ 12. What is one of the themes of the poem?
    a. Love is the most powerful force in life.
    b. Life is an exhilarating and rewarding adventure.
    c. Love is a complicated and confusing emotion that is closely tied to one's fears and self-image.
    d. An unexamined life is not worth living.

_____ 13. Which statement best describes the attitude about human relationships expressed in the poem?
    a. People are their own best companions.
    b. People can learn from the experiences of others.
    c. True understanding between two people is impossible.
    d. Without love or friendship, life is meaningless.

_____ 14. What image is suggested by the use of repeated vowel and consonant sounds in the following line from "The Love Song of J. Alfred Prufrock"?

> By sea-girls wreathed with seaweed red and brown.

    a. blowing wind
    b. drowning
    c. aging
    d. rolling waves

Vocabulary and Grammar

On the line, write the letter of the one best answer.

____ 15. Which phrase is most nearly the same in meaning to *insidious?*
  a. subtly treacherous
  b. boldly evil
  c. obviously hostile
  d. deeply secret

____ 16. The word *digress* means to
  a. remove from political office.
  b. elaborate on an aside.
  c. exit from a room.
  d. stray from the subject.

____ 17. Which of the following words means the opposite of *obtuse?*
  a. overweight   b. insightful   c. unintelligent   d. thin

____ 18. Which of these italicized phrases is *not* an adjectival modifier?
  a. a melody *repeated in various keys*
  b. a motive *for betrayal*
  c. sing out *loud and clear*
  d. the flame *that burns so brightly*

____ 19. Which of the following italicized phrases is an example of a participial phrase?
  a. "Is it perfume *from a dress*"
  b. "I know the voices *dying with a dying fall*"
  c. "The yellow fog *that rubs its back upon the window-panes*"
  d. "There will be time *to murder and create*"

____ 20. Which of the following italicized phrases is an example of an infinitive phrase?
  a. "Is it perfume *from a dress*"
  b. "I know the voices *dying with a dying fall*"
  c. "The yellow fog *that rubs its back upon the window-panes*"
  d. "There will be time *to murder and create*"

Essay Questions

21. J. Alfred Prufrock's disillusionment with his life and his uncertainty about himself reflect life in the early decades of the twentieth century. In an essay, discuss Prufrock's personality, beliefs, and experiences. Is Prufrock a typical man of his times, or is he unusual? Why do you think Eliot chose to write about a man like Prufrock? Use specific details from the poem as evidence of your interpretation of Prufrock.

22. "The Love Song of J. Alfred Prufrock" is written in the form of a dramatic monologue. Write an essay explaining how the use of this form combined with poetic images enables the poet to present a memorable and moving portrait of Prufrock. Why is the dramatic monologue a particularly revealing form? Would a short story about Prufrock have been as effective as Eliot's dramatic monologue in verse? Support your points with details from the poem.

23. The title of a poem may provide clues to its interpretation. Sometimes the clues are obvious, sometimes not. Write an essay in which you interpret the meaning and significance of the title "The Love Song of J. Alfred Prufrock." Do you think this "love song" is about love in any sense? Is it a typical song? Present evidence from the poem to back up your interpretation.

Selection Test

Critical Reading

On the line, write the letter of the one best answer.

_____ 1. In "A Few Don'ts by an Imagiste," Ezra Pound instructs poets not to use an expression like "dim lands *of peace*" because it
   a. has no sense of freedom from time limits.
   b. is chopped into separate iambs.
   c. mixes an abstraction with the concrete.
   d. has no exact parallels in music.

_____ 2. In Pound's "The River-Merchant's Wife: A Letter," why does the young wife wish to meet her husband at Cho-fu-Sa?
   a. She is frightened of being alone.
   b. She is bored with her life at home.
   c. She misses her husband terribly.
   d. She is eager to see the goods he has bought in his travels.

_____ 3. Which idea is represented by the description of the two children in the first stanza of "The River-Merchant's Wife: A Letter"?
   a. ignorance   c. mortality
   b. innocence   d. romance

_____ 4. Which of the following senses is *not* appealed to by the following line from Ezra Pound's "The River-Merchant's Wife: A Letter"?

   I played about the front gate, pulling flowers.

   a. sight   c. taste
   b. smell   d. touch

_____ 5. Which of the following statements best communicates the meaning of "In a Station of the Metro"?
   a. Human contact in the city is as vulnerable and fleeting as a petal in a rainstorm.
   b. People rush around so fast in cities that they disappear as quickly as they appear.
   c. To a person with a very good imagination, petals on a branch can look like faces.
   d. In the darkness of a subway station, faces can suddenly look like flower petals.

_____ 6. What mood is evoked by the imagery in "In a Station of the Metro"?
   a. confusion   c. joy
   b. despair   d. wistfulness

_____ 7. William Carlos Williams wrote poetry that evokes emotions and ideas through its presentation of
   a. abstract objects.   c. simple ideas.
   b. things.   d. complex ideas.

_____ 8. The influence of Imagism in "The Red Wheelbarrow" is most clearly reflected in the
   a. emotions suggested in the poem.
   b. use of musical rhythms.
   c. simplicity of the images and language.
   d. lack of rhyme.

_____ 9. Which of the following statements best describes the image Williams creates in his poem "The Red Wheelbarrow"?
   a. The image has a single, specific meaning that the author conveys successfully.
   b. The image is open to interpretation based on the individual reader's emotional and intellectual response.
   c. The image has a meaning that can't be expressed in prose.
   d. The image closely resembles a painting.

_____ 10. What is the theme of Williams's poem, "The Great Figure"?
   a. Modern life is noisy, tense, and dangerous, as symbolized by the fire engine speeding in the rain.
   b. An ordinary detail of everyday life can have beauty, power, and significance.
   c. The number 5 has great meaning to the poet, which he successfully conveys to the reader.
   d. The poet wants the reader to think about the disaster to which the fire engine is racing in the rain.

_____ 11. Which of the senses are engaged by Williams's poem, "This Is Just to Say"?
   a. sight and hearing
   b. sight and taste
   c. sight, hearing, and taste
   d. sight, taste, and touch

_____ 12. Which detail best conveys H. D.'s spiritual feelings about the pear tree?
   a. "no flower ever parted silver/from such rare silver"
   b. "higher than my arms reach/you front us with great mass"
   c. "no flower ever opened/so staunch a white leaf"
   d. "bring summer and ripe fruits/in their purple hearts"

_____ 13. Which statement best summarizes the theme of "Pear Tree"?
   a. The pear tree is so beautiful that it hardly seems real.
   b. The blossoming pear tree symbolizes the coming of summer.
   c. The beauty of the pear tree symbolizes the enormous gap between humans and nature.
   d. The pear tree embodies both celestial and earthly beauty.

_____ 14. To which senses does the imagery in "Pear Tree" appeal most strongly?
   a. hearing and smell
   b. sight and touch
   c. sight and hearing
   d. taste and touch

_____ 15. In "Heat," the lines "O wind, rend open the heat,/cut apart the heat,/rend it to tatters" allow the reader to imagine the heat as a
   a. comforting blanket.   c. heavy curtain.
   b. delicate veil.   d. swinging door.

_____ 16. By creating an image of the wind as a plow, H. D. suggests that the wind can
   a. generate cooler temperatures.
   b. blow the heat away.
   c. break up the heat.
   d. bring the rain.

Vocabulary and Grammar

On the line, write the letter of the one best answer.

____ 17. Which of the following words is closest in meaning to the italicized word in the following sentence?

> It is better to present one Image in a lifetime than to produce *voluminous* works.

    a. plentiful
    b. large
    c. insightful
    d. precise

____ 18. Which of the following words is closest in meaning to the word *apparition*?
    a. disappearance
    b. mistiness
    c. beauty
    d. phantom

____ 19. Which of the following nouns is concrete?
    a. wheelbarrow
    b. dogma
    c. suspicion
    d. loneliness

____ 20. An abstract noun *cannot* name
    a. a quality such as value.
    b. a characteristic such as intelligence.
    c. an idea such as freedom.
    d. a particular flower.

Essay Questions

21. The poems of William Carlos Williams emphasize what he called "the here and now"—the exact moment of an experience rather than its meaning or implications. Do you think this is a simplistic way of looking at life, or do you think it has some value? Explain your ideas in an essay.

22. Imagism as a poetic movement flourished for less than a decade. In his later years, William Carlos Williams said, "We have been looking for too big, too spectacular a divergence from the old. . . . It was a natural blunder from the excess of our own feelings." Write an essay in which you express your opinion of Williams's statement. Base your essay upon his three poems in this unit—"The Red Wheelbarrow," "The Great Figure," and "This Is Just to Say"—that were written under the influence of Imagism.

23. Imagist poets tried to create vivid, precise images that produce a sudden moment of illumination. They excluded all but the essential details needed to create an emotional response. Ezra Pound's fourteen-word poem "In a Station of the Metro" is a classic work of Imagism. It began as a thirty-line poem based on Pound's observation of a group of beautiful faces as he stepped off a subway train in Paris. Write an essay in which you speculate on what Pound might have included in his original, longer description of the incident. Use the content of "In a Station of the Metro" as your point of departure.

Name _____ Date _____

Selection Test

Critical Reading

On the line, write the letter of the one best answer.

_____ 1. Why is the following passage a particularly telling characterization?

> When, as Judy's head lay against his shoulder that first night, she whispered, "I don't know what's the matter with me. Last night I thought I was in love with a man and tonight I think I'm in love with you—" it seemed to him a beautiful and romantic thing to say. It was the exquisite excitability that for the moment he controlled and owned.

   a. It reveals the basic thrust of both Judy's and Dexter's feelings.
   b. It explains why Dexter is so drawn to Judy.
   c. It shows how young both Judy and Dexter really are.
   d. It illustrates the fact that Dexter has lost touch with reality.

_____ 2. What eventual effect does Dexter's obsession with Judy and the things she represents have on his life?
   a. He works hard to become wealthy, successful, and respected.
   b. He loses his ability to experience and enjoy the passions and joys of life.
   c. He builds his life around the illusion that she will someday be his.
   d. He realizes that the aspirations he once had for himself are meaningless.

_____ 3. Judy's alternating indifference and attention to Dexter have the effect of
   a. making him feel confused about what he wants.
   b. ultimately strengthening his resolve to resist her.
   c. making her even more desirable to him.
   d. helping him learn that hard work is the best way to deaden painful feelings.

_____ 4. As a teenager, why is Dexter particularly fond of the fall?
   a. The crisp coolness of the fall inspires him with an urgency to accomplish something before the winter sets in.
   b. It is the precious time that precedes the long, cold dreariness of the Minnesota winter.
   c. It is a time that allows him to analyze and synthesize the desires that the summer raises in him.
   d. The weather is most beautiful during the fall months in the area where he lives.

_____ 5. When Dexter Green first meets Judy Jones, she is about to beat her nurse. The reader learns that Dexter believes Judy may be justified in beating the nurse. What does this tell the reader?
   a. Judy is a moral child.   c. Judy is unusually weak for a girl.
   b. Dexter is enthralled by Judy.   d. Dexter has no sense of right and wrong.

_____ 6. Upon his second encounter with Judy Jones, when she hits Mr. Hedrick with a golf ball, Dexter Green is overwhelmed by her _____.
   a. sincerity   b. intelligence   c. bad manners   d. beauty

_____ 7. Who is the most important person to Judy Jones as a young woman?
   a. her father   b. Dexter Green   c. the next man she meets   d. herself

_____ 8. Which character trait does Dexter establish when he quits his caddying job?
   a. abandoning his commitments
   b. choosing paths that will lead to success
   c. seeking unattainable goals
   d. letting his obsession with Judy control his decisions

_____ 9. Fitzgerald first reveals Dexter's reverence for the ideals of high society by
   a. describing his dreams as a teenager.
   b. commenting that Dexter reached out for the best.
   c. revealing Dexter's thoughts about the men for whom he caddies.
   d. describing his first reaction to Judy Jones.

_____ 10. Why is Judy Jones's beauty important to her character?
   a. She was such an ugly child.
   b. She uses it to get what she wants.
   c. It gives a contrast to her humbleness.
   d. It allows her to move into a higher social circle.

_____ 11. Why does Dexter Green quit seeing Irene Scheerer?
   a. Dexter decides to become engaged to Judy Jones instead.
   b. Irene's parents strongly object to Dexter, so she breaks the engagement.
   c. Irene tells Dexter she is in love with a man from New York.
   d. Dexter decides that, although pleasant, Irene is too boring for him.

_____ 12. After Judy Jones hits Mr. Hedrick with a golf ball, the reader learns "[h]er glance fell casually on each of the men—then scanned the fairway for her ball." From this, the reader can conclude that Judy Jones was
   a. ashamed that she had hit Mr. Hedrick and did not want him to look her in the eye.
   b. embarrassed about being such a bad golfer.
   c. concerned more about where her shot lay than about Mr. Hedrick.
   d. overwhelmed by Dexter Green and did not want him to figure that out.

_____ 13. Which of the following statements best describes the theme of "Winter Dreams"?
   a. Those whose lives are based on the pursuit of illusions are doomed to disappointment.
   b. A person without dreams or illusions cannot live a full life.
   c. Love that is based on physical beauty cannot be as satisfying as love based on inner character.
   d. The pursuit of material satisfaction interferes with the pursuit of emotional satisfaction.

_____ 14. Dexter Green probably becomes engaged to Irene Scheerer because of his
   a. strong love for Irene.   c. desire for stability.
   b. jealous fit over Judy Jones.   d. desire for Irene's inheritance.

_____ 15. Why does Fitzgerald choose not to provide a physical description of Dexter?
   a. Dexter's appearance is important only to the point that Judy is attracted to him.
   b. Dexter's lack of physical characteristics makes him more puzzling and enigmatic.
   c. Judy's beauty is emphasized by the lack of physical details about Dexter.
   d. The story is about Dexter's personality and his emotional and mental traits.

Vocabulary and Grammar

On the line, write the letter of the one best answer.

_____ 16. Which of the following would a "_pugilistic_ youth" be most likely to do?
   a. serenade a woman with a love song   c. start a fight with another boy
   b. be one of the best dancers at a ball d. be the richest student in his class

____ 17. Which word is closest in meaning to the italicized word in the following phrase?

> the great white bulk of the Mortimer Joneses' house, *somnolent*, gorgeous,
> drenched with the splendor of the damp moonlight

    a. drowsy   b. enormous   c. radiant   d. proud

____ 18. What image does Fitzgerald portray when he says Judy Jones was "swimming to the floating surfboard with a sinuous crawl"?
    a. Judy swims noisily.   c. Judy swims sleepily.
    b. Judy swims quickly.   d. Judy swims gracefully.

____ 19. Which of the following sentences shows the correct placement of the dash?
    a. When—a new man came to town everyone dropped out dates were automatically canceled.
    b. When a new man came to town everyone—dropped out dates were automatically canceled.
    c. When a new man came to town everyone dropped out—dates were automatically canceled.
    d. When a new man came to town everyone dropped out dates were automatically— canceled.

____ 20. In which of the following excerpts do the dashes interrupt what someone is saying?
    a. " 'The best—caddy I ever saw,' shouted Mr. Mortimer Jones over a drink that afternoon."
    b. " . . . in the way her lips twisted down at the corners when she smiled, and the— Heaven help us!—in the almost passionate quality of her eyes."
    c. "The smile again—radiant, blatantly artificial—convincing."
    d. "When he was twenty-three Mr. Hart—one of the gray-haired men who like to say 'Now there's a boy'—gave him a guest card . . ."

Essay Questions

21. In real life, people have contradictory attributes—particularly in their desires and needs— making them complete and complicated human beings. When, like real people, fictional characters possess contradictory attributes, a story is more believable and successful. Choose one of the story's main characters—Dexter Green or Judy Jones—and write an essay describing his or her attributes. How are the character's wants and needs contradictory? Would the character be as convincing without contradictory attributes?

22. A biographer of F. Scott Fitzgerald points out that in trying "to understand the failure of his own dreams," Fitzgerald explored the role that women played in his life: "Only a girl in whom were joined the superlatives of beauty and social position—or, failing these, the prestige of having a number of suitors—was worth the attention of this buccaneer." Write an essay in which you relate the biographer's statement to Fitzgerald's story "Winter Dreams." Which "superlative" attributes does Judy Jones possess? In what sense is Dexter Green a "buccaneer"? Include evidence to support your points.

23. Many of Fitzgerald's stories embody the author's fascination with and growing distrust of America's wealthy society in the 1920's. Choose two characters from "Winter Dreams"— one who seems to share the author's fascination and one who might represent the wealthy society he distrusts. Write an essay explaining how Fitzgerald's fascination and distrust are manifested in the two characters. How do the characters interact? What does this interaction show about Fitzgerald's fascination and distrust? Support your analysis with details from the story.

Name _____ Date _____

"The Turtle" from *The Grapes of Wrath* by John Steinbeck

Selection Test

Critical Reading

On the line, write the letter of the one best answer.

____ 1. After the sedan driver saw the turtle, she swerved to
a. avoid the turtle.
b. hit the turtle.
c. avoid the truck.
d. dislodge a wild oat head.

____ 2. Which of the following words best describes the setting of the story?
a. wet   c. cold
b. dry   d. urban

____ 3. What did the turtle carry across the road?
a. an ant   c. a tiddly-wink
b. a grasshopper   d. wild oat seeds

____ 4. What theme might the head of wild oats in the story represent?
a. reproduction
b. revenge
c. hardship
d. the importance of family

____ 5. When you run across an unfamiliar word in a sentence, where can you find context clues to help define it?
a. a dictionary
b. a thesaurus
c. on the previous page
d. in the text around the word

____ 6. An author's theme is rarely
a. directly stated.
b. indirectly stated.
c. within a story.
d. shown through story details.

____ 7. A theme is best described as
a. a detailed fable.
b. a game played with a small disk.
c. an insight into life.
d. a story with long sentences.

____ 8. Which of the following excerpts is related to the central theme of the story?
a. "The sun lay on the grass and warmed it . . ."
b. "The hind feet kicked his shell along, and it scraped on the grass, and on the gravel."
c. "As though they worked independently the hind legs pushed the shell against the wall."
d. "And as the turtle crawled on down the embankment, its shell dragged dirt over the seeds."

____ 9. The embankment, the road, and the truck are all ____ the turtle.
   a. themes for
   b. obstacles for
   c. ignored by
   d. avoided by

____ 10. In *The Grapes of Wrath*, the Joads encounter kind people as well as people who make their lives more difficult. Which character in the turtle story might represent people who help the Joads?
   a. the sedan driver
   b. the truck driver
   c. the ant
   d. the turtle

____ 11. In *The Grapes of Wrath*, the Joads encounter kind people as well as people who make their lives more difficult. Which character in the turtle story might represent people who make the Joads' lives more difficult?
   a. the sedan driver
   b. the truck driver
   c. the ant
   d. the turtle

____ 12. Which of the following sentences tells you the most about the turtle's demeanor?
   a. "His horny beak was partly opened, and his fierce, humorous eyes, under brows like fingernails, stared straight ahead."
   b. "As though they worked independently the hind legs pushed the shell against the wall."
   c. "But the head of wild oats was held by its stem around the front legs."
   d. "Now the going was easy, and all the legs worked, and the shell boosted along, waggling from side to side."

____ 13. From the sentence, "His front wheel struck the edge of the shell, flipped the turtle like a tiddlywink, spun it like a coin, and rolled it off the highway," you can figure out that a tiddlywink is something that ____.
   a. rolls
   b. spins
   c. flips
   d. strikes edges

____ 14. From the phrase, "and the grass heads were heavy with oat beards to catch on a dog's coat, and foxtails to tangle in a horse's fetlocks," you can figure out that a fetlock is
   a. part of a fox.
   b. part of a horse.
   c. a type of grass.
   d. a type of dog.

Vocabulary and Grammar

On the line, write the letter of the one best answer.

____ 15. The expression of similar ideas in similar grammatical form is called
   a. perpendicular structure.
   b. perpendicular themes.
   c. parallel structure.
   d. parallel themes.

_____ 16. In the following line, what are the parallel phrases?

> [A]nts and ant lions to set traps for them, grasshoppers to jump into the air . . .

    a. to set—to jump
    b. to set traps for—to jump into
    c. ants—ant lions
    d. ants—grasshoppers

_____ 17. The word *protruded* means
    a. pulled back.
    b. thrust forward.
    c. in favor of.
    d. interrupted.

_____ 18. Where would you expect to find an embankment?
    a. inside a turtle shell
    b. on a truck
    c. next to a lake
    d. under a lake

_____ 19. Which of the following is *not* an example of parallel grammatical structure?
    a. ". . . and suddenly head and legs snapped in, and the armored tail clamped in sideways."
    b. "The turtle had jerked into its shell, but now it hurried on . . ."
    c. "Pushing hind legs strained and slipped, boosting the shell along . . ."
    d. "The old humorous eyes looked ahead, and the horny beak opened a little."

_____ 20. In the word *protruded*, the prefix *pro-* means _____.
    a. against
    b. without
    c. thrust
    d. forward

Essay Questions

21. To anthropomorphize means to give human form or personality to things that are not human. Write an essay in which you show how Steinbeck anthropomorphizes the turtle. What human characteristics does he give the turtle? What effect does such humanizing have on the reader?

22. The novels and stories of John Steinbeck often have characters who face hardships. Decide whether "The Turtle" is an example of such a story. Write an essay explaining your position. How would you characterize the events of the turtle's life in the story? Does it matter that the turtle is not human? Support your position with details from the story.

23. Although this selection from *The Grapes of Wrath* is entitled "The Turtle," it might just as appropriately have been called "The Seeds." Write an essay in which you agree or disagree with this statement. What is the relationship between the turtle and seeds in the story? Include evidence to support your position.

"anyone lived in a pretty how town" and **"old age sticks"** by E. E. Cummings
"The Unknown Citizen" by W. H. Auden

Selection Test

Critical Reading

On the line, write the letter of the one best answer.

_____ 1. In the following line from "anyone lived in a pretty how town," why does Cummings alter normal word order?

(with up so floating many bells down)

a. to convey a sense of social optimism
b. to emphasize the number of church bells
c. to reflect the breakdown of social order
d. to imitate the motion of bells ringing

_____ 2. In "anyone lived in a pretty how town," Cummings begins the word "anyone" with a lowercase letter in order to
a. suggest the character's common humanity.
b. emphasize the character's deceptive nature.
c. call attention to the character.
d. show contempt for the character.

_____ 3. Why does Cummings describe the women and men in the pretty how town as being "(both little and small)"?
a. to indicate their youth
b. to emphasize their small-mindedness
c. to suggest their charm
d. to show their timidity

_____ 4. What is the theme of "anyone lived in a pretty how town"?
a. Ordinary people can achieve great things.
b. Loneliness and lack of love can kill people.
c. True humanity is squelched by conventional society.
d. Creativity triumphs over small-mindedness.

_____ 5. In "anyone lived in a pretty how town," what group is Cummings satirizing in the line, "they sowed their isn't they reaped their same"?
a. anyone and noone
b. people who live quiet, productive lives
c. people who live safe, conforming lives
d. the citizens of the pretty how town

_____ 6. Why does Cummings break up the word "growing" in the last two lines of "old age sticks"?
a. to imitate the faltering speech of old people
b. to emphasize the grumbly nature of old people
c. to preserve the sticklike shape of the poem
d. to emphasize the gradual nature of aging

_____ 7. Which statement summarizes the theme of "old age sticks"?
     a. Young people are the hope of the future.
     b. Young people and old people should work together.
     c. Age diminishes the free spirit of youth.
     d. Old people deserve respect from the young.

_____ 8. In "old age sticks," what is the group that is the subject of the last stanza doing there?
     a. They are yanking down signs.   c. They are getting old.
     b. They are dying.   d. They are sticking up signs.

_____ 9. In "The Unknown Citizen," Auden directs his satire against what he sees as too great an emphasis on
     a. independence and freedom.   c. creativity and initiative.
     b. obedience and conformity.   d. originality and eccentricity.

_____ 10. A central theme of "The Unknown Citizen" is that modern society
     a. encourages people to think on their own.
     b. rewards people for behaving morally.
     c. discourages people from acting boldly.
     d. pressures people to report on their neighbors.

_____ 11. One object of Auden's scorn in "The Unknown Citizen" is what he sees as too great an emphasis on
     a. individuals, anecdotes, and unusual ways of thinking.
     b. measurement, statistics, and standard models of behavior.
     c. feelings, emotions, and subjective attitudes toward life.
     d. details, peculiarities, and specific quirks of personality.

_____ 12. In "The Unknown Citizen," what is Auden's attitude toward the modern version or sense of the word "saint"?
     a. He condemns it because it implies someone who condones insincerity.
     b. He applauds it because it implies someone who never does anything wrong.
     c. He despises it because it implies someone who never takes risks.
     d. He approves of it because it implies someone who chooses the heroic.

_____ 13. What pair of questions does Auden call "absurd" in "The Unknown Citizen"?
     a. Was he kind? Was he happy?   c. Was he free? Was he rich?
     b. Was he rich? Was he poor?   d. Was he free? Was he happy?

_____ 14. Which line from "The Unknown Citizen" is the best example of the way Auden uses elements of structure to affect the meaning of his poem?
     a. "But satisfied his employers, Fudge Motors Inc."
     b. "A phonograph, a radio, a car and a frigidaire."
     c. "He was fully sensible to the advantages of the Installment Plan"
     d. "He was married and added five children to the population."

_____ 15. In "The Unknown Citizen," whom did the citizen serve "in everything he did"?
     a. his employers, Fudge Motors Inc.   c. public opinion
     b. the Greater Community   d. the state

_____ 16. Which quotation from "The Unknown Citizen" is the clearest example of satirical writing?
     a. "Except for the War till the day he retired / He worked in a factory and never got fired, . . ."
     b. "And his Health-card shows he was once in hospital but left it cured."
     c. "He was married and added five children to the population."
     d. "Our researchers into Public Opinion are content / That he held the proper opinions for the time of year. . . ."

Vocabulary and Grammar

On the line, write the letter of the one best answer.

____ 17 Which word best expresses the subject matter of "old age sticks"?
   a. prohibitions
   b. satire
   c. psychosis
   d. youth

____ 18. What might Social Psychology workers have been especially concerned about in their reports on the unknown citizen?
   a. his emotions and attitudes
   b. his physical fitness
   c. his productivity on the job
   d. the number of children he had

____ 19. In which passage does E. E. Cummings make the most unconventional use of parentheses?
   a. "children guessed(but only a few / and down they forgot as up they grew/autumn winter spring summer)/that noone love him more by more"
   b. "youth yanks them / down(old/age/cries No/Tres)&(pas)"
   c. "Women and men(both dong and ding)"
   d. "one day anyone died i guess / (and noone stooped to kiss his face)"

____ 20. What is the best reason for the use of parentheses in the following quotation from "The Unknown Citizen"?

> Yet he wasn't a scab or odd in his views,
> For his Union reports that he paid his dues,
> (Our report on his Union shows it was sound)
> And our Social Psychology workers found. . . .

   a. The material is relevant but interrupts the sentence.
   b. The parentheses call special attention to the extra material.
   c. The material is very closely connected to the rest of the sentence.
   d. The words are those of another speaker.

Essay Questions

21. In "The Unknown Citizen," Auden implies that the society treats the citizen as just another statistic. How do you think the citizen would feel about being treated this way? How might he want to be treated instead? Write an essay in which you answer these questions.

22. Poets, through their poems, sometimes reveal their personal concerns about the nature of society. This tells the reader something about the poet—his or her likes, dislikes, beliefs, fears, and hopes. A reader of "The Unknown Citizen" can form a reasonably accurate picture of what the poet dislikes and, by inference, what he admires. Write an essay in which you speculate on the kind of person and the kind of society that Auden respects. Support your opinion with evidence from the poem.

23. It has been said that in "anyone lived in a pretty how town," E. E. Cummings focuses on the eternal rhythms of life, the seasons of nature, and the cycle of human rituals that are universally connected with childhood, adulthood, and death. In an essay, discuss Cummings's focus. What elements in the poem support this statement about his focus?

Name _____ Date _____

"**The Far and the Near**" by Thomas Wolfe

Selection Test

Critical Reading

On the line, write the letter of the one best answer.

_____ 1. Why does the little house give the engineer such "extraordinary happiness"?
   a. The house reminds him of his own wife and family.
   b. Seeing the house introduces variety into the boring routine of his job.
   c. The vision of the house does not change despite the changes in his life.
   d. The house is the only beautiful spot on an otherwise unremarkable route.

_____ 2. Which of the following details from the story *best* illustrates the source of the engineer's later disillusionment?
   a. "To one side of the house there was a garden. . . ."
   b. "He had seen them in a thousand lights, a hundred weathers."
   c. "[H]e felt that he knew their lives completely, to every hour. . . ."
   d. "The whole place had an air of tidiness, thrift, and modest comfort."

_____ 3. What makes the engineer want to visit the cottage?
   a. He wants to see if the cottage is as beautiful as he thinks it is.
   b. He feels that its inhabitants have become part of his life.
   c. He wants to thank the women for brightening his life over the years.
   d. He thinks the visit will give a sense of closure to his career.

_____ 4. Which of the following details from the story foreshadows a climactic ending?
   a. ". . . a tidy little cottage of white boards, trimmed vividly with green blinds."
   b. "For a moment the progress of the engine could be marked by heavy bellowing puffs of smoke. . . ."
   c. "Every day for more than twenty years . . . a woman had appeared. . . ."
   d. "He felt for them . . . such tenderness as a man might feel for his own children. . . ."

_____ 5. Based on this passage, what can you predict will happen later in the story?

> But no matter what peril or tragedy he had known, the vision of the little house and the women waving to him . . . became fixed in the mind of the engineer as something beautiful and enduring, something beyond all change and ruin, and something that would always be the same, no matter what mishap, grief or error might break the iron schedule of his days.

   a. The women will always wave at the engineer.
   b. The engineer will ask the women to stop waving.
   c. Something will happen to change the engineer's vision.
   d. The engineer will get tired of watching the women wave every day.

_____ 6. Which of the following details is a clue predicting the ending of the story?
   a. "He had driven his great train, loaded with its weight of lives, across the land ten thousand times."
   b. "He had known all the grief, the joy, the peril and the labor such a man could know . . . and now . . . he had grown old."
   c. "It was all as unfamiliar, as disquieting as a city in a dream, and the perplexity of his spirit increased as he went on."
   d. "Yes, this was the house he sought, the place he had passed so many times, the destination he had longed for with such happiness."

7. Which of the following details does *not* help the reader predict the ending of the story?
   a. "Everything was as strange to him as if he had never seen this town before."
   b. "He knew at once that he had found the proper place."
   c. "Why did he now feel this sense of confusion, doubt and hopelessness?"
   d. "And instantly, with a sense of bitter loss and grief, he was sorry he had come."

8. Why is the story's ending anticlimactic?
   a. The women do not invite him into their house.
   b. The house is exactly the same as the engineer expected.
   c. The women don't understand why it is important to the engineer to visit them.
   d. The engineer isn't sure that these are the same women who were waving to him.

9. Which of the following effects do you think Wolfe is striving for by giving "The Far and the Near" this anticlimax?

   . . . suddenly he knew that he was an old man. His heart, which had been brave and confident when it looked along the familiar vista of the rails, was now sick with doubt and horror as it saw the strange and unsuspected visage of an earth which had always been within a stone's throw of him, and which he had never seen or known.

   a. laughter   b. surprise   c. shock   d. insight

10. Which of the following sentences best explains the meaning of this passage?

    . . . suddenly he knew that he was an old man. His heart, which had been brave and confident when it looked along the familiar vista of the rails, was now sick with doubt and horror as it saw the strange and unsuspected visage of an earth which had always been within a stone's throw of him, and which he had never seen or known.

    a. The women's house looked tidy from a distance, but close up, it appears to be run-down and neglected.
    b. Now that the engineer is old, his heart has become weak and sick.
    c. The world that was so near to the engineer geographically turned out to be very far from him personally.
    d. The engineer has discovered that the women are terrible and mean.

11. The engineer's expectations of the women are bound to be disappointing because
    a. they cannot be as wonderful as he has built them up to be.
    b. his expectations are based on illusions he created over twenty years.
    c. his life experience has been completely different from theirs.
    d. the women have no reason to consider the engineer friendly or trustworthy.

12. What is the theme of "The Far and the Near"?
    a. The imagination can be one of the most tragic human attributes.
    b. Travel often exposes people to the foolishness of their expectations.
    c. Unexpected gestures to strangers are bound to be misunderstood.
    d. Up close, things are rarely as perfect as they seem from afar.

13. What ultimate effect does the engineer's visit to the cottage have on him?
    a. It makes him suspicious of the people around him.
    b. It teaches him that life basically consists of a set of unrealistic illusions.
    c. It turns him into a bitter and cynical old man.
    d. It shatters his faith in the ultimate beauty and goodness of life.

14. What is the probable reason Wolfe titled this story "The Far and the Near"?
    a. What is near in some ways turns out to be far in others.
    b. The women are near the tracks, but the train travels very far.
    c. The engineer is near to the women but far from his own family.
    d. The engineer is near to other people but far from happiness.

The Far and the Near   **201**

_____ 15. How might the title "The Far and the Near" apply to the women?
   a. They are far from the engineer but near to each other.
   b. They are far from the engineer in personality but near to him in age.
   c. They feel friendly toward the faraway train but afraid of the engineer when he is near.
   d. They wave to the train because it travels from a place that is near to one that is far.

Vocabulary and Grammar

On the line, write the letter of the one best answer.

_____ 16. Which two words best express the imagery of the phrase in italics?

> But her face was harsh and pinched and meager; *the flesh sagged wearily in sallow folds.* . . .

   a. bright; clownish   b. tired; friendly   c. mean; angry   d. wrinkled; sickly

_____ 17. Which of the italicized phrases in the following passages is a nonrestrictive participial phrase?
   a. "the great train, *having halted for a breathing space at the town nearby*, was beginning to lengthen evenly into its stroke"
   b. "a cheap automobile *stalled upon the tracks*, set with the wooden figures of people paralyzed with fear"
   c. "a battered hobo *walking by the rail*, too deaf and old to hear the whistle's warning"
   d. "a form *flung past his window* with a scream"

_____ 18. Which of the following words is closest in meaning to *visage*?
   a. appearance   b. terror   c. rocks   d. opinion

_____ 19. Which of the following words could be substituted for *tempo* without changing the meaning of the excerpt?

> . . . finally nothing could be heard but the solid clacking tempo of the wheels receding into the drowsy stillness of the afternoon.

   a. rhythm   b. melody   c. tune   d. monotone

_____ 20. In the following excerpt, of what is the italicized part an example?

> . . . finally nothing could be heard but the solid clacking tempo of the wheels *receding into the drowsy stillness of the afternoon.*

   a. an anticlimax   c. a restrictive participial phrase
   b. a prediction   d. a nonrestrictive participial phrase

Essay Questions

21. In an essay, interpret the engineer's feelings and explain why he might have found the women and the house "beautiful and enduring." Use details from the story to explain why they were so important to him.

22. When the climax of a story is unexpectedly disappointing, ridiculous, or trivial, it is called an anticlimax. In an essay, discuss how the ending of "The Far and the Near" is anticlimactic; include details from the story.

23. In Wolfe's "The Far and the Near," the railroad engineer realizes, after his retirement, that he is unable to recapture the past. Write an essay in which you interpret the engineer's state of mind at the end of the story. Why does he feel "confusion, doubt and hopelessness"? What has changed for him?

"Of Modern Poetry" and **"Anecdote of the Jar"** by Wallace Stevens
"Ars Poetica" by Archibald MacLeish
"Poetry" by Marianne Moore

Selection Test

Critical Reading

On the line, write the letter of the one best answer.

_____ 1. The central theme of "Of Modern Poetry" is that a modern poem must
   a. still be written in a traditional way.
   b. reflect the people of the time.
   c. use techniques such as similes and paraphrasing.
   d. draw from the past in order to speak to the people of the present.

_____ 2. What is one theme of "Anecdote of the Jar"?
   a. Humans have interfered with nature under the guise of beautifying the world.
   b. The human ability to create can be as destructive as it is productive.
   c. The human impulse to produce order out of chaos results in a sterile, uninteresting world.
   d. Humans have the power either to enhance or to destroy the beauty of nature.

_____ 3. In "Anecdote of the Jar," which of the following might the jar most logically symbolize?
   a. the ambivalence that many people feel toward the wilderness
   b. the order that nature imposes on herself
   c. the carelessness of humans in dealing with nature
   d. the power that human civilization holds over nature

_____ 4. Which of the following excerpts is a simile?
   a. "I placed a jar in Tennessee, / And round it was, upon a hill."
   b. "we cannot understand: the bat / holding on upside down . . ."
   c. "A poem should be wordless / As the flight of birds."
   d. "A poem should not mean / But be."

_____ 5. The theme of "Ars Poetica" suggests that a poem should
   a. minimize the reader's tendency to react emotionally.
   b. strengthen the reader's intellectual grasp of life.
   c. appeal more to the senses than to the intellect.
   d. rely on lush imagery and elaborate diction.

_____ 6. Which is the best way to paraphrase the following excerpt from "Ars Poetica"?

   A poem should be equal to:
   Not true.

   a. The lines of a poem should be equal in length—not true to real life.
   b. A poem should be equal to an object or emotion—not true to it.
   c. A poem should be true for some people but false for others.
   d. A poem's subject should usually be fairly represented, but not always.

_____ 7. Which simile from MacLeish's "Ars Poetica" appeals primarily to the sense of sight?
   a. "palpable and mute / As a globed fruit"
   b. "motionless in time / As the moon climbs"
   c. "Dumb / As old medallions to the thumb"
   d. "Silent as the sleeve-worn stone"

_____ 8. What quality of poetry does the opening simile from "Ars Poetica" evoke?

> A poem should be palpable and mute
> As a globed fruit.

   a. complexity
   b. concreteness
   c. perfection
   d. lyricism

_____ 9. Which lines convey the central paradox of the poem "Ars Poetica"?
   a. "A poem should be wordless / As the flight of birds."
   b. "Dumb / As old medallions to the thumb."
   c. "A poem should be motionless in time / As the moon climbs."
   d. "A poem should not mean / But be."

_____ 10. What does Moore suggest by the line "imaginary gardens with real toads in them"?
   a. The proper subject matter of poetry is folklore.
   b. Poetry can be used in scientific study.
   c. Poems fuse the real and the imagined.
   d. Poems convey only partial truths.

_____ 11. Which word best describes the speaker's tone in "Poetry" by Moore?
   a. brisk   c. stern
   b. bitter   d. insulting

_____ 12. Which is the best way to paraphrase the following excerpt from "Poetry"?

> Reading it, however, with a perfect contempt for it, one discovers in
> it after all, a place for the genuine.

   a. Poetry is more genuine when the poet dislikes writing.
   b. Even when one reads poetry disdainfully, one can find truth in it.
   c. Only people who hate poetry can find truth in it.
   d. Poetry that shows a contempt for the reader is truthful.

_____ 13. Which is the best way to paraphrase the following excerpt from "Poetry"?

> nor is it valid / to discriminate against "business documents and / schoolbooks"

   a. Nor should you criticize factual writing.
   b. Nor should you criticize writings that teach.
   c. Nor should you criticize writings that don't rhyme.
   d. Nor should you criticize all other styles of writing.

_____ 14. The message of "Poetry" is that
   a. poets should avoid obscuring the meaning in their poems.
   b. reading poetry is a waste of a person's time.
   c. real poetry is in business documents and schoolbooks.
   d. too much poetry is about unimportant subjects.

Vocabulary and Grammar

On the line, write the letter of the one best answer.

_____ 15. Which excerpt from "Ars Poetica" uses a subject complement?
   a. "A poem should be palpable and mute"
   b. "Memory by memory the mind—"
   c. "Not true."
   d. "The leaning grasses and two lights above the sea—"

____ 16. When something is palpable, it is able to be ____.
   a. heard   c. eaten
   b. seen   d. touched

____ 17. Which line from "Of Modern Poetry" uses a subject complement?
   a. "Its past was a souvenir."
   b. "In an emotion as of two people, as of two"
   c. "And, like an insatiable actor, slowly and"
   d. "Not to the play, but to itself, expressed"

____ 18. Which of the following would an *insatiable* actor be most likely to do?
   a. choose a bit role in a play over a starring role
   b. need to rehearse lines over and over to remember them
   c. want to keep performing night after night
   d. be loud and presumptuous in his or her personal life

____ 19. Which of the following is most nearly opposite in meaning to *slovenly*?
   a. attractive   c. fast
   b. slim   d. tidy

____ 20. Sentences containing subject complements are especially effective when a writer's purpose is to
   a. describe an action.
   b. paraphrase a key idea.
   c. define something.
   d. criticize something.

Essay Questions

21. Poems are sometimes remembered for an unforgettable line or image. Marianne Moore's "Poetry," for example, contains the often quoted portrayal of good poetry: "imaginary gardens with real toads in them." Write an essay in which you identify and discuss memorable lines or images from at least one other poem in this selection. Include a discussion of Moore's "imaginary gardens" image, analyzing its effectiveness.

22. In "Ars Poetica," Archibald MacLeish writes several short couplets that give examples, ultimately supporting the idea that "A poem should not mean / But be." Which do you think is more effective in making the author's point to the audience: using examples, as in "Ars Poetica," or using a more direct approach, as in Wallace Stevens's "Of Modern Poetry"? Give details from the two poems to support your choice.

23. Wallace Stevens wrote that poetry "touches the sense of reality, it enhances the sense of reality, heightens it, intensifies it." Yet some readers feel that Stevens's poems convey a sense of *un*reality. Write an essay in which you state and support your opinion on whether Stevens's "Anecdote of the Jar" touches and enhances the reader's sense of reality. Use evidence from the poem to sustain your position.

Part Test, Unit Five, Part 1:
The Emerging American Identity—Facing Troubled Times

Critical Reading

The questions below are based on the following selection.

This excerpt is taken from the short story "Sophistication," by Sherwood Anderson, from his collection of stories about an average, Middle-American town, Winesburg, Ohio.

Pushing his way through the crowds in Main Street, young George Willard concealed himself in the stairway leading to Doctor Reefy's office and looked at the people. With feverish eyes he watched the faces drifting past under the store lights. Thoughts kept coming into his head and he did not want to think. He stamped impatiently on the wooden steps and looked sharply about. "Well, is she going to stay with him all day? Have I done all this waiting for nothing?" he muttered.

George Willard, the Ohio village boy, was fast growing into manhood and new thoughts had been coming into his mind. All that day, amid the jam of people at the Fair, he had gone about feeling lonely. He was about to leave Winesburg to go away to some city where he hoped to get work on a city newspaper and he felt grown up. The mood that had taken possession of him was a thing known to men and unknown to boys. He felt old and a little tired. Memories awoke in him. To his mind his new sense of maturity set him apart, made of him a half-tragic figure. He wanted someone to understand the feeling that had taken possession of him after his mother's death.

On the line, write the letter of the one best answer.

_____ 1. George is waiting for
a. Doctor Reefy.
b. someone he has arranged to meet.
c. a woman he knows whom he hopes may pass by.
d. a couple he knows.

_____ 2. Main Street is crowded because
a. Winesburg is a bustling city.
b. there has been some kind of accident.
c. there is a fair in town.
d. everyone is waiting for the woman to appear.

_____ 3. What conclusions can you draw about George Willard from the fact that "[t]houghts kept coming into his head and he did not want to think"?
a. He is agitated.
b. He is not well-educated.
c. He is sad and angry at the same time.
d. He is bored.

_____ 4. George's main mood in this selection is
a. sadness at the thought of his mother's death.
b. frustration that his friend has not come.
c. anger at being confined by small town life.
d. impatience to express to someone his new feelings of maturity.

_____ 5. George Willard is probably
a. thirty years old.   c. fourteen years old.
b. nineteen years old.   d. thirty-five years old.

____ 6. Which of the following quotations is an example of indirect characterization?

        I. "George Willard, the Ohio village boy, was fast growing into manhood."
        II. ". . . he had gone about feeling lonely."
        III. "To his mind, his new sense of maturity . . . made of him a half-tragic figure."
        IV. "He felt old and a little tired."

a. I   c. II, IV
b II, III, IV   d. none

____ 7. How should we interpret this remark?

    To his mind, his new sense of maturity set him apart, made of him a half-tragic figure.

a. The death of George's mother caused him to grow up quickly.
b. George has a new, more adult outlook, but he is still full of youthful self-importance.
c. The difficulties of George's situation have made him disillusioned and cynical.
d. George is a self-indulgent teenager who thinks he is an adult.

____ 8. Given what you have learned in the excerpt, which of the following choices is the best prediction of what will happen next in the story?
a. George will meet up with the woman for whom he has been waiting.
b. George will accost Doctor Reefy and demand that he release the woman.
c. George will become a very successful newspaper reporter in the city.
d. George will have a conversation with his father.

____ 9. Which of the following pairs of quotations probably gives the best clue to the story's theme?
a. "He stamped impatiently. . . ."/ "He was about to leave Winesburg to go away to some city. . . ."
b. ". . . he had gone about feeling lonely."/ "He was about to leave Winesburg to go away to some city. . . ."
c. "To his mind his new sense of maturity set him apart. . . ."/ ". . . he hoped to get work on a city newspaper. . . ."
d. "To his mind his new sense of maturity set him apart. . . ."/ "He wanted someone to understand the feeling that had taken possession of him. . . ."

____ 10. Which of the following choices best sums up the probable theme of the story?
a. Impatience will never get you anywhere.
b. Young people need someone to acknowledge that they have grown up.
c. Love conquers all difficulties.
d. Growing up leads to disillusionment.

Vocabulary and Grammar

On the line, write the letter of the one best answer.

____ 11. Choose the pair of words that best expresses a relationship similar to that of the pair in capital letters.

    TIMOROUS : SOLDIER ::

a. dangerous : acid   c. clumsy : juggler
b. persuasive : proposal   d. blazing : fire

_____ 12. Choose the pair of words that best expresses a relationship similar to that of the pair in capital letters.

SOMNOLENT : ENERGETIC ::

a. mischievous : well-behaved   c. smiling : happy
b. demolished : broken   d. chopped : sliced

_____ 13. Psychology is the study of
    a. myths.
    b. brain waves.
    c. mind and behavior.
    d. cycles of life.

_____ 14. Complete the following sentence with the best word combination.

Ezra Pound was a(n) _____ editor, and he would have scorned writers who _____ too frequently.

    a. obtuse/malingered
    b. meticulous/digressed
    c. pugilistic/protruded
    d. derivative/expatiated

_____ 15. In which of the following sentences is the dash the best choice of punctuation mark?
    a. Dexter made his fortune—by founding his own business.
    b. The title of E. E. Cummings's poem—if the poem had a title—has escaped me.
    c. Modernist poets—who can be difficult to understand—experiment with new styles.
    d. The jar—which sits on a hill in Tennessee—creates a focus of human significance in the wilderness.

_____ 16. Which of the following sentences uses parentheses incorrectly?
    a. The young man who used to caddy on the golf course became quite wealthy (if you can imagine!).
    b. The Steinbeck story "The Turtle" (see page 688) reflects the endurance of Americans during the Great Depression.
    c. The poet (most often contrasted with T. S. Eliot) is W. H. Auden.
    d. The average income of Americans soared in the 1920's, then plummeted when the Great Depression hit (see table above).

_____ 17. In which of the following sentences is the subject complement a noun?
    a. For Cummings, old age is more conservative than youth.
    b. The "unknown citizen" might be any person living in modern times.
    c. Nobody would want to be as anxious as the speaker in "Prufrock."
    d. "Forgive me / they were delicious."

_____ 18. In which of the following sentences is the subject complement an adjective?
    a. The little red wheelbarrow is glazed with rain water.
    b. Wallace Stevens was a poet who worked in insurance.
    c. An important influence on the Imagists was Chinese and Japanese poetry.
    d. Judy is the love of Dexter's life.

_____ 19. Which of these sentence contains a correctly punctuated participial phrase?
    a. Caddying at the golf course Dexter Green won the respect of men much older than himself.
    b. Judy Jones, born into the upper class, had the habit of falling in love with poor men.
    c. "Poems should not mean / but be"; poets, who try too hard to mean, may write badly.
    d. The little girl almost hitting the servant whom her mother sent out with her, is Judy Jones.

____ 20. Which is an example of parallel structure?
   a. "I have measured out my life with coffee spoons."
   b. "Forgive me / they were delicious."
   c. "It is better to present one Image in a lifetime than to produce voluminous works."
   d. "For a moment he stopped, his head held high."

Essay Questions

21. Write an essay in which you compare the main characters of three of the stories in this part. Describe the important characteristics of each character, the situation he or she confronts, and how he or she responds to it. What are the similarities and differences among their characteristics, situations, and responses?

22. Disillusionment—the death of a dream—is a prominent theme in the literature of this period. It surfaces in Fitzgerald's "Winter Dreams," Steinbeck's "The Turtle," Eliot's "The Love Song of J. Alfred Prufrock," and Wolfe's "The Far and the Near." Choose three of these works, then write an essay explaining how each embodies the theme of disillusionment.

23. The historical context in which a writer works helps to shape his or her work. The prosperous years after World War I—the Jazz Age—were filled with glittering promises and empty hearts; the Great Depression nearly sank the country's hopes and dreams under the weight of economic ruin. Write an essay in which you discuss the influence of historical background on two of the works in this part.

24. The writers associated with the Modernist movement in the arts shared the desire to capture the essence of modern life in both the form and content of their works. Choose two poems in this part that in some way capture the flavor of modern life. Then write an essay in which you compare and contrast the theme and technique of the poems. What is the writer's view of modern life? What kinds of words and images does the author use to convey that view? What is the quality of the speaker's voice in the poem (sad, lecturing, joyful, sarcastic)?

25. Poetry is a blend of sound, thought, image, and feeling. Pick three poems from this part, each one by a different author, and contrast the mixture of these ingredients in each. Does one emphasize sound, leading to surprising twists in thought? Does one demand that we give an emotional response to ideas? Back up your discussion with quotations from each poem.

Name _____ Date _____

"In Another Country" by Ernest Hemingway
"The Corn Planting" by Sherwood Anderson
"A Worn Path" by Eudora Welty

Selection Test

Critical Reading

On the line, write the letter of the one best answer.

_____ 1. When the narrator says the wounded soldiers "were all very polite and interested in what was the matter, and sat in the machines that were to make so much differ-ence," he is being _____.
    a. ironic   c. objective
    b. sympathetic   d. observant

_____ 2. Why does the narrator feel separated from the three Italian soldiers who had won medals?
    a. The narrator is afraid to die, but the other soldiers are not.
    b. The other soldiers have done brave deeds in battle, but the narrator has not.
    c. The other soldiers speak English, but the narrator can't speak Italian.
    d. The other soldiers will be returning to the war, but the narrator will not.

_____ 3. Why does the major never miss a day with the machines?
    a. Self-discipline is important to him.
    b. It is his duty as an officer to become fit for service.
    c. His injury is improving rapidly.
    d. He wants to talk with the narrator.

_____ 4. The major's attitude toward the doctor is best described as _____.
    a. amused
    b. furious
    c. indifferent
    d. determined

_____ 5. Hemingway employs a direct, unadorned style of writing in order to
    a. remove all uncertainty about what he is trying to say.
    b. allow the reader to draw his or her own conclusions.
    c. deemphasize the importance of language.
    d. reduce the story to its essentials.

_____ 6. Which of the following statements best describes the theme of "In Another Country"?
    a. Life is full of loneliness and loss.
    b. War makes all men brothers.
    c. Heroes are made, not born.
    d. For a brave man, anything is possible.

_____ 7. "The Corn Planting" is told from a first-person point of view. You can tell this is so because
    a. an outside narrator tells the story.
    b. it is told by a minor character.
    c. the narrator refers to himself as "I."
    d. the narrator is the best character to tell the story.

____ 8. A limited third-person point of view is one in which the story is told by
a. an outside narrator with only one perspective.
b. a narrator who seems to know everything about the story.
c. a narrator who is not one of the main characters in the story.
d. a narrator who refers to himself as "I."

____ 9. What can you infer about Phoenix's personality from her reactions to the obstacles she encounters along the path?
a. She is basically an optimistic and hopeful person.
b. She is resilient and takes difficulties in stride.
c. She feels more at home in the city than in the country.
d. She has an unrealistic confidence in her strength.

____ 10. Which of Phoenix's character traits come most into play in her interaction with the hunter?
a. cunning and resolve
b. bitterness and anger
c. pride and courage
d. guilt and shame

____ 11. Which of the following statements best supports the interpretation that Phoenix's grandson is still alive?
a. Phoenix makes the journey to Natchez.
b. Phoenix seems embarrassed to have forgotten the reason for her visit.
c. Phoenix describes the boy in vivid detail to the nurse.
d. The nurse gives Phoenix the medicine.

____ 12. Which detail best supports the interpretation that Phoenix's grandson is dead?
a. Phoenix expects him to be surprised by a paper windmill.
b. Phoenix takes a long time to respond to the nurse's question about him.
c. The nurse's records say he swallowed lye two to three years ago.
d. The nurse asks Phoenix whether the boy is dead.

____ 13. What point of view is used in the following passage?

"You scarecrow," she said. Her face lighted. "I ought to be shut up for good," she said with laughter. "My senses is gone. I too old. I the oldest people I ever know. Dance, old scarecrow," she said, "while I dancing with you."

a. first-person
b. first-person limited
c. third-person limited
d. third-person by a main character

____ 14. Which literary technique is most instrumental in conveying the story's ambiguity?
a. limited third-person narration
b. visual description
c. foreshadowing
d. indirect characterization

____ 15. In what way does the title "A Worn Path" clearly represent the focus of the story?
a. It symbolizes the great weariness Phoenix feels as she ages.
b. It points to the gradual wearing away of Phoenix's vitality and wits.
c. It illustrates the repetitiveness of an old person's life.
d. It emphasizes Phoenix's sense of purpose and resolve.

Vocabulary and Grammar

On the line, write the letter of the one best answer.

____ 16. Which of the following passages is punctuated correctly?
   a. "What will you do when the war is over if it is over"? he asked me.
   b. "What will you do when the war is over if it is over? he asked me."
   c. What will you do when the war is over if it is over? he asked me.
   d. "What will you do when the war is over if it is over?" he asked me.

____ 17. When the narrator of "In Another Country" says that the major did not marry his wife until he was definitely *invalided* out of the war, he means that
   a. the major did not want to marry if he were at risk of dying in the war.
   b. the major did not marry his wife until he was about to leave for the war.
   c. the major was not allowed to marry while he was still fighting in the war.
   d. the major would have preferred going to war to marrying his wife.

____ 18. Phoenix Jackson's cane is described as "limber as a buggy whip." This means that
   a. it belongs on a buggy.
   b. it is flexible.
   c. it is made of the same material as a buggy whip.
   d. Phoenix uses it on horses.

____ 19. What is the punctuation error in the following sentence?

   "Sweet gum makes the water sweet", she said.

   a. There should not be any quotation marks in the sentence.
   b. The quotation marks should go around the whole sentence.
   c. The comma should be inside the quotation marks.
   d. There should be no comma in the sentence.

____ 20. When the nurse in "A Worn Path" says that Phoenix's grandson is "an *obstinate* case," she means that
   a. the grandson is a spoiled, stubborn child.
   b. Phoenix is stubborn because she continues to make the trip.
   c. Phoenix should bring her grandson with her to see the doctor.
   d. the grandson never gets better because his throat will never heal.

Essay Questions

21. Fiction writers may reveal the nature of a character mainly through his or her involvement with other characters. Hal in "The Corn Planting" is such a character. Write an essay describing Hal's character. What can you tell about his character from his involvement in the lives of the Hutchensons? What do we know about him outside of this involvement? Support your answer with details from the story.

22. Sometimes characters who are different on the surface and live quite different lives share similar outlooks and character traits. Write an essay comparing the major in "In Another Country" to Phoenix Jackson in "A Worn Path." How are their approaches to life similar? How are they different? Use examples from the stories to make your points.

23. In stories told from a first-person point of view, the reader learns only about the narrator's experiences and thoughts. How much the reader finds out depends on how closely involved the narrator is with the events of the story. Write an essay discussing the role of the first-person narrator in "In Another Country" and in "The Corn Planting." How do the narrators of these stories differ in their involvement? Why do you think the author of each story chose to tell it using a first-person narrator? Give evidence from the stories to support your answers.

Name _____ Date _____

"**Anxiety**" by Grace Paley

Selection Test

Critical Reading

On the line, write the letter of the one best answer.

_____ 1. How does the old woman probably perceive her role in her conversation with the young father?
   a. the ramblings of an eccentric
   b. the intrusions of a busybody
   c. a selfless act of salvation
   d. the imparting of folk wisdom

_____ 2. Which word best describes the old woman's attitude toward modern life?
   a. joyful   c. apprehensive
   b. withdrawn   d. inhibited

_____ 3. When the old woman leans out of her window, she describes it as emerging into "unshadowed visibility." What does this passage suggest about the woman's life?
   a. She lives alone.
   b. She rarely leaves her apartment.
   c. She hates the sunlight.
   d. She is hard of hearing.

_____ 4. What does the old woman fear most?
   a. street traffic   c. gang violence
   b. domestic abuse   d. nuclear war

_____ 5. What does Paley emphasize by constructing the story in the form of an unpunctuated dialogue?
   a. the dominance of the old woman's viewpoint
   b. the father's need to learn from the old woman
   c. the eccentricity of the old woman's statements
   d. the hypocrisy of the father's behavior toward his daughter

_____ 6. If the central lesson of the story is "take responsibility for the world around you, especially for your children's future," which excerpt best expresses this moral?
   a. "I was angry at Rosie because she was dealing with me as though I was a figure of authority, and it's not my thing, never has been, never will be."
   b. "And they live beyond that trisection across other dangerous avenues."
   c. "That the murder of our children by these men has got to become a terror and a sorrow to you, and starting now, it had better interfere with any daily pleasure."
   d. ". . . why don't you start all over again, right from the school door, as though none of this had ever happened."

_____ 7. What does the old woman mean to suggest by comparing the little girl's future to "a film which suddenly cuts to white"?
   a. The little girl's fate is predetermined.
   b. The little girl's future promises danger and unhappiness.
   c. The little girl's life is full of potential and hope.
   d. The little girl's future is fragile and uncertain.

_____ 8. Which of the following images symbolizes the old woman's sense of apprehension?
    a. fierce fast horses
    b. roadways
    c. graceful brown mustaches
    d. teachers

_____ 9. Which of the following details suggests that the old woman is coming to the end of her own life?
    a. her lack of family
    b. moving the marigolds aside
    c. the disappearance of other older women from the tenements
    d. the dangerous street corner near her building

_____ 10. Which opposition symbolizes the old woman's scale of good versus evil?
    a. natural (good) versus manmade (evil)
    b. heaven (good) versus earth (evil)
    c. children (good) versus adults (evil)
    d. scientists (good) versus automakers (evil)

Essay Questions

11. Write an essay explaining the title of the story and its relation to the old woman's character. Choose specific details to describe the old woman's "anxiety," and make a judgment about whether she is justified in her way of thinking. What other factors that are only implied in the story might affect her emotions?

12. Despite the old woman's anxiety about the world, there are hints in the story of her hopefulness and deep love of life. Write an essay discussing these details. Does the old woman's love for life heighten or alleviate her feelings of anxiety?

13. "Anxiety" combines elements of a personal essay, which addresses problems in society in an informal manner, and a character sketch, which explores and analyzes a single personality. In an essay, explain which passages or details seem to belong to which kind of work. Point out both the global preoccupations of the protagonist and the personal quirks that the author wants to emphasize. Make a judgment as to whether the different aspects of the text interact equally, or whether one dominates the other.

Part Test, Unit Five, Part 2:
Focus on Literary Forms—The Short Story

Critical Reading

The questions below are based on the following selection.

This excerpt is taken from "Flight," a short story by John Steinbeck about a fateful twist in a young man's life.

Mama Torres had three children, . . . Emilio and Rosy, whom Mama kept fishing on the rocks below the farm when the sea was kind and when the truant officer was in some distant part of Monterey County. And there was Pepé, the tall smiling son of nineteen, a gentle affectionate boy, but very lazy. Pepé had a tall head, pointed at the top, and from its peak, coarse black hair grew down like a thatch all around. Over his smiling little eyes Mama cut a straight bang so he could see. Pepé had sharp Indian cheek bones and an eagle nose, but his mouth was as sweet and shapely as a girl's mouth, and his chin was fragile and chiseled. He was loose and gangling, all legs and feet and wrists, and he was very lazy. Mama thought him fine and brave, but she never told him so. She said, "Some lazy cow must have got into thy father's family, else how could I have a son like thee." And she said, "When I carried thee, a sneaking lazy coyote came out of the brush and looked at me one day. That must have made thee so."

Pepé smiled sheepishly and stabbed at the ground with his knife to keep the blade sharp and free from rust. It was his inheritance, that knife, his father's knife.

On the line, write the letter of the one best answer.

_____ 1. This story is told
   a. from a first-person main character point of view.
   b. from a limited third-person point of view.
   c. from a first-person minor character point of view.
   d. from an unlimited, or omniscient, third-person point of view.

_____ 2. Which of the following quotations from the selection most helps you identify with Pepé?
   a. "He was loose and gangling . . . , and he was very lazy."
   b. "Mama thought him fine and brave . . ."
   c. "Over his smiling little eyes Mama cut a straight bang . . ."
   d. "Pepé smiled sheepishly and stabbed at the ground with his knife . . ."

_____ 3. Which of the following quotations from the selection most helps you identify with Mama Torres?
   a. "Mama thought [Pepé] fine and brave, but she never told him so."
   b. "Mama Torres had three children . . ."
   c. "She said, 'Some lazy cow must have got into thy father's family, else how could I have a son like thee.'"
   d. "Over his smiling little eyes Mama cut a straight bang so he could see."

_____ 4. Steinbeck tells us that "The knife was with Pepé always, for it had been his father's knife," repeating the phrase "his father's knife." He does not explain how Pepé feels about his father, though. This sentence, and the repetition of the phrase,
   a. helps the reader predict what will happen next.
   b. helps the reader understand Pepé's father.
   c. helps the reader feel the importance of the knife to Pepé.
   d. helps the reader understand Pepé's relationship with his father.

_____ 5. Judging from this excerpt, the Torres family is probably
   a. disliked by many.   c. middle-class.
   b. poor.   d. popular with their neighbors.

_____ 6. Mama Torres addresses Pepé as "thee" probably because
   a. Steinbeck wants to show that the family belongs to a special religious group.
   b. Steinbeck wants to show that the family lives in the Western United States.
   c. Steinbeck wants to match in English the special way in which Spanish-speakers address family members.
   d. Steinbeck wants to show that the story is set in olden times.

_____ 7. Mama tells Pepé that "some lazy cow must have got into thy father's family" because
   a. she dislikes Pepé's father.
   b. she is angry with Pepé.
   c. she wants to conceal her fondness for Pepé.
   d. she wants Pepé to help her.

_____ 8. In this excerpt, the point of view is made evident by the narrator's
   a. telling us exactly what each character is thinking.
   b. telling us the story only from Mama's point of view.
   c. showing us what is important to each character.
   d. describing the personality of each character in detail.

_____ 9. The family probably makes a living by
   a. catching and growing its own food.
   b. working in the local factory.
   c. making clothing for wealthy people.
   d. working in the local store.

_____ 10. The contrast between Pepé's "eagle nose" and his "fragile and chiseled" chin draws attention to the fact that
   a. he is too lazy to help his mother.
   b. he is almost, but not yet, a man.
   c. he looks fierce, but is actually gentle.
   d. he is very handsome.

Vocabulary and Grammar

On the line, write the letter of the one best answer.

_____ 11. By walking such a long distance, despite her difficulties moving, Phoenix Jackson shows how _____ she is.
   a. obstinate   c. limber
   b. grave   d. invalided

_____ 12. The soldiers in "In Another Country" no longer fight, because they are _____.
   a. obstinate   c. limber
   b. grave   d. invalided

_____ 13. The news of Will Hutcheson's accident was _____.
   a. obstinate   c. limber
   b. grave   d. invalided

_____ 14. Which sentence is punctuated correctly?
   a. "I'm an old woman without an education", said Phoenix Jackson.
   b. "I'm an old woman without an education," said Phoenix Jackson.
   c. "I'm an old woman without an education, said Phoenix Jackson.
   d. "I'm an old woman without an education, said Phoenix Jackson."

___ 15. What is the error in the punctuation of these sentences?

"It is very difficult," he said. "I cannot resign myself".

   a. The comma should be outside the quotation marks.
   b. The first period should be a comma.
   c. The second period should be inside the quotation marks.
   d. There are no errors.

Essay Questions

16. The stories in this part deal with war, death, and human perseverance. What did you learn about people's spirit? Write an essay in which you discuss how the following characters deal with misfortune and loss: Phoenix in "A Worn Path," Will Hutchenson's parents in "The Corn Planting," and the soldiers and the major in "In Another Country." Explain what message each author delivers about the human spirit.

17. These stories present characters who face two challenges in their lives. Choose one story from this part ("In Another Country," "The Corn Planting," or "A Worn Path") and write an essay describing the two different conflicts in it. Discuss the difference between the two challenges and between the ways in which the characters meet each challenge. What message does the author convey by contrasting the two challenges?

18. Each story in this part ("In Another Country," "The Corn Planting," and "A Worn Path") uses point of view to emphasize its theme as well as tell an effective story. For each of two stories in this part, identify the point of view used, the main theme, and the story's climax. Explain in an essay how the story's climax reveals a new dimension to the theme, and show how the point of view chosen allows each author to make this climax especially effective, surprising, or mysterious.

"**Chicago**" and "**Grass**" by Carl Sandburg

Selection Test

Critical Reading

On the line, write the letter of the one best answer.

_____ 1. What is the theme of "Chicago"?
   a. People love their native cities no matter how brutal and poverty stricken they are.
   b. In its early days, Chicago had more variety and activity than any other American city.
   c. When cities get too big, they dwarf the lives of the people who live in them.
   d. Like people, cities grow up with their own personalities and have both good and bad traits.

_____ 2. Which of the following lines from "Chicago" is an example of Sandburg's use of apostrophe?
   a. "I have seen the gunman kill and go free to kill again."
   b. "And they tell me you are crooked and I answer: Yes, it is true"
   c. "I turn once more to those who sneer at this my city"
   d. "Under the smoke, dust all over his mouth, laughing with white teeth"

_____ 3. The passage below is the beginning of the poem "Chicago." What is the function of the passage?

   Hog Butcher for the World
   Tool Maker, Stacker of Wheat,
   Player with Railroads and the Nation's Freight Handler;
   Stormy, husky, brawling,
   City of the Big Shoulders:

   a. The narrator is addressing Chicago by its various nicknames.
   b. The narrator is describing Chicago to its critics.
   c. The narrator is complimenting Chicago on its accomplishments.
   d. The narrator is criticizing Chicago for its bad deeds.

_____ 4. Why does the narrator of "Chicago" say that the young man has "a terrible burden of destiny" and that he laughs "even as an ignorant fighter laughs who has never lost a battle"?
   a. The young man is destined to lead the cities of America.
   b. The young man laughs even though he is bound to lose some battles.
   c. The young man does not realize that it is his destiny never to lose a battle.
   d. The young man laughs at the terrible destiny of the other cities.

_____ 5. To which of these lines from "Chicago" would a reader respond with the sense of hearing?
   a. "I have seen your painted women under the gas lamps"
   b. "Flinging magnetic curses amid the toil of piling job on job"
   c. "here is a tall bold slugger set vivid against the little soft cities"
   d. "under his wrist is the pulse, and under his ribs the heart of the people"

_____ 6. To which of these lines from "Chicago" would a reader respond with the sense of touch?
   a. "I have seen your painted women under the gas lamps"
   b. "Flinging magnetic curses amid the toil of piling job on job"
   c. "here is a tall bold slugger set vivid against the little soft cities"
   d. "under his wrist is the pulse, and under his ribs the heart of the people"

_____ 7. The speaker in "Chicago" portrays the city as a
   a. brash, swaggering, and ignorant yet essentially good young man.
   b. cold and aloof yet cunning boy.
   c. excitable, enthusiastic, naive little child.
   d. somber, serious, determined adult.

_____ 8. In "Grass," the speaker makes the point that
   a. nature can undo the damage that is wrought by war.
   b. we should remember those who died in wars long ago.
   c. battlefields become instant burial grounds for those who are killed.
   d. the carnage of the war may not be remembered years later.

_____ 9. What is the theme of "Grass"?
   a. Nature heals the damage that war wreaks on society.
   b. People depend on time to help them forget the damage done by the war.
   c. The tragedies of humanity are insignificant in comparison to the relentless forces of nature.
   d. Nature is superior to humanity because it doesn't destroy itself.

_____ 10. To respond to the italicized words in these lines, which of the following would you use?

   And pile them high at _Gettysburg_
   And pile them high at _Ypres_ and _Verdun_.

   a. background knowledge   c. emotions
   b. senses   d. knowledge about Sandburg

_____ 11. To respond to the entire poem "Grass," which of the following would you use?

   I.   background knowledge
   II. senses
   III. emotions
   IV. knowledge about Sandburg

   a. I and IV   b. II and III   c. I and III   d. I, II, and III

_____ 12. What image is Sandburg trying to create with the following lines?

   Two years, ten years, and passengers ask the conductor:
      What place is this?
      Where are we now?

   a. a newspaper article   c. a tour group
   b. a train passing by   d. a memorial

_____ 13. Why do you think that the grass says, "Let me work"?
   a. Someone is trying to stop the grass from working.
   b. The grass is in favor of war and likes to cover bodies.
   c. The grass is ready to grow because that is what grass does.
   d. The grass wants to hide the atrocities of war.

_____ 14. Who or what is the speaker in "Grass"?
   a. the grass   b. a gravedigger   c. train passengers   d. a train conductor

_____ 15. Sandburg wrote his poem from the point of view of the grass in order to
        a. emphasize the power of nature.
        b. create a clearer image of the grass.
        c. illustrate the forgetful nature of humanity.
        d. inject a cynical element into the poem.

Vocabulary and Grammar

On the line, write the letter of the one best answer.

_____ 16. What type of sentence is this?

      I am the grass; I cover all.

        a. interrogative   b. declarative   c. imperative   d. exclamatory

_____ 17. Which of the following is an example of an interrogative sentence?
        a. "Pile the bodies high at Austerlitz and Waterloo."
        b. "Shovel them under and let me work."
        c. "What place is this?"
        d. "I am grass."

_____ 18. Which of the following is closest in meaning to _brutal_ and _wanton_ as used here?

      And they tell me you are brutal and my reply is: On the faces of women and children I have seen the marks of wanton hunger.

        a. sad   b. desperate   c. careless   d. cruel

_____ 19. In the next passage, what does _cunning_ indicate about the city of Chicago?

      Come and show me another city with lifted head singing so proud to be alive and coarse and strong and cunning.

        a. The city has a loud voice.
        b. The city survives partly because it struggles hard.
        c. The city thrives in part because of its sharp wits.
        d. The city tries to deceive other cities.

_____ 20. What type of sentence is this one from "Grass"?

      Shovel them under and let me work.

        a. interrogative   b. declarative   c. exclamatory   d. imperative

Essay Questions

21. In "Chicago," the speaker of the poem acts as a judge, arbitrating a dispute between the city and its critics. Write an essay discussing the charges of the critics against Chicago, and the speaker's verdict. Why does the speaker reach this verdict and not another one? Use details from the poem to support your answer.

22. "Chicago" describes the city by using images of violence, brutality, and suffering. In an essay, describe another image that you could use to portray this city. Explain your choice.

23. "Grass" could be understood as a reflection on the statement "Time heals all wounds." However, it could also be understood as a reflection on the pointlessness of fighting a war that may barely be remembered by future generations. In an essay, explain which interpretation you think is more appropriate. Why do you think so? Use details from the poem to support your answer.

Name _____ Date _____

"The Jilting of Granny Weatherall" by Katherine Anne Porter

Selection Test

Critical Reading

On the line, write the letter of the one best answer.

____ 1. At the beginning of the story, what disturbs Granny Weatherall most about Doctor Harry's presence?
   a. She feels that he treats her with insufficient respect.
   b. She refuses to acknowledge that she is not well.
   c. She remembers him from when he was a child.
   d. She thinks he is too young to practice medicine.

____ 2. Which of the following events came first in Granny's life?
   a. her moving in with Cornelia
   b. John's death
   c. her contracting double pneumonia
   d. George's jilting her

____ 3. John Weatherall would probably remember Ellen Weatherall as
   a. a dying, stubborn woman.
   b. feminine and fashionable.
   c. a fence builder.
   d. a grandmother.

____ 4. Which moment happens the latest in Granny Weatherall's life?
   a. Granny sends wine to Sister Borgia.
   b. Lydia asks Granny for advice about the grandchildren.
   c. Granny nurses the sick children.
   d. Granny wants to spank Cornelia for being dutiful.

____ 5. What do Granny's flashbacks reveal about her relationships with her children?
   a. Cornelia used to be her favorite child.
   b. She has always resented her children for restricting her life.
   c. She was a source of comfort to her children when they were young.
   d. She believes her children love their father more than they love her.

____ 6. What are the predominant character traits revealed by Granny's thoughts?
   a. strength and industriousness
   b. kindness and intelligence
   c. patience and indulgence
   d. confidence and compliance

____ 7. Granny Weatherall's thoughts about her old age are naturally linked to her thoughts about her children by her
   a. memories of her father's behavior.
   b. children's unwillingness to allow her to live her own life.
   c. thoughts about her work as a country nurse.
   d. children's treatment of her as if she were a child.

____ 8. Stream of consciousness is a narrative technique that presents thoughts as if they were coming directly from a character's _____.
   a. mouth   c. mind
   b. heart   d. diary

_____ 9. Which of the following details do you learn through the use of flashbacks?
   a. Granny Weatherall lives with her daughter Cornelia.
   b. Cornelia has been a good and dutiful daughter.
   c. John Weatherall died when his wife was still a young woman.
   d. Granny Weatherall does not respect Doctor Harry.

_____ 10. Which moment takes place in the story's present?
   a. Granny wants to give Cornelia the amethyst set.
   b. Granny faces the priest alone.
   c. Granny gathers the children around her as she lights the lamps.
   d. Granny dusts the bronze clock with the lion on top.

_____ 11. Why was Father Connolly in the room?
   a. to have a cup of tea
   b. to give Granny the last rites
   c. to play cards with Cornelia and Hapsy
   d. to gossip with the family

_____ 12. What is the story's theme?
   a. Death can be fought off with stubbornness and strength.
   b. Even the moment of death often provides no relief from one's memories of life's troubles.
   c. People who have suffered find relief as death approaches.
   d. Sorrows can be forgotten with the help of love and compassion.

_____ 13. Which attribute does Granny Weatherall seem to value most?
   a. being orderly
   b. being young
   c. being dutiful
   d. being argumentative

_____ 14. In what way does Granny Weatherall associate Father Connolly's presence with her jilting?
   a. Father Connolly reminds her of George, but with black eyes instead of blue.
   b. Her religious beliefs helped her recover from being jilted.
   c. She had always felt that being jilted was a sin she should have confessed.
   d. She had faced the priest alone when George didn't arrive for the wedding.

Vocabulary and Grammar

On the line, write the letter of the one best answer.

_____ 15. Which of the following could be an example of _frippery_?
   a. saving love letters
   b. buying blue silk lampshades
   c. making sure no fruit is wasted
   d. digging post holes until a fence is finished

_____ 16. An imperative sentence usually does not contain a stated_____.
   a. article   c. subject
   b. object   d. verb

_____ 17. Which of the following is an imperative sentence?
   a. "Leave a well woman alone."
   b. "She was never like this, never like this!"
   c. "What'd you say, Mother?"
   d. "I do."

____ 18. A person filled with *piety* would most likely
       a. pray a lot.
       b. enjoy raising children.
       c. be a good farmer.
       d. be jilted.

____ 19. Someone with *dyspepsia* would most likely have
       a. a headache.
       b. an upset stomach.
       c. swollen legs.
       d. shortness of breath.

____ 20. Which of the following is an imperative sentence?
       a. I should hope you would leave.
       b. I want you to leave right now.
       c. I hope to leave you.
       d. Leave now.

Essay Questions

21. Katherine Anne Porter chose to call this story "The Jilting of Granny Weatherall." Write an essay stating why you think this title was chosen to represent this fictional work. What do you think this title signifies in the story? Use events from the story to back up your opinion.

22. Benjamin Disraeli, a British statesman, is credited with the statement, "Youth is a blunder; [adult]hood a struggle; old age a regret." Do you think Granny Weatherall would agree or disagree with this statement? State your position in an essay. Support your position with details from the selection.

23. Katherine Anne Porter uses the narrative technique of stream of consciousness to present Granny's thoughts and to indicate how close she is to death. Write a brief essay discussing Porter's use of this technique. How would you describe stream of consciousness? How well does it indicate how close Granny is to death? Include details from the selection that illustrate the technique.

The Jilting of Granny Weatherall **223**

Name _____ Date _____

"Race at Morning" and **"Nobel Prize Acceptance Speech"** by William Faulkner

Critical Reading

On the line, write the letter of the one best answer.

____ 1. In "Race at Morning," after the last hunters at Hollyknowe camp finish shooting, why does Mister Ernest give up following the dogs and turn Dan north back toward camp?
  a. It's late in the day, and he wants to get back to camp before dark.
  b. He believes the hunters at Hollyknowe camp have wounded the buck.
  c. He's too exhausted to continue the hunt.
  d. He knows the chase is over and the buck is heading back to the bayou.

____ 2. In "Race at Morning," why doesn't Mister Ernest shoot the buck when he has a chance?
  a. He wants the buck to live so they can hunt it again the next November.
  b. Because the hunting season, which ended at dusk, is over.
  c. He forgot to reload his gun.
  d. He knows the narrator doesn't want the buck to be killed.

____ 3. Which of these excerpts from "Race at Morning" includes an example of dialect?
  a. "Don't you know where he's heading?"
  b. "And then we seen him again."
  c. "We heard the shots; it sounded like a war."
  d. "He had been hunting deer in these woods for about a hundred years."

____ 4. In "Race at Morning," after the hunt ends and Mister Ernest and the narrator are walking home in the dark, Mister Ernest tells the narrator to "Get on the horse. . . . We don't want to spoil him." Why does Mister Ernest say this?
  a. The narrator is walking too slowly.
  b. He is worried that Dan will become lazy if he's not ridden.
  c. He knows the narrator is tired and needs to ride.
  d. He thinks there's still a chance to catch the buck if they both ride.

____ 5. Who are the featured characters in this passage from "Race at Morning"?

> Because he had been a good feller ever since I had knowed him, which was even before that day two years ago when maw went off with the Vicksburg roadhouse feller and the next day pap didn't come home neither, and on the third one Mister Ernest rid Dan up to the door of the cabin on the river he let us live in, so pap could work his piece of land and run his fish line, too, and said, "Put that gun down and come on here and climb up behind."

  a. Mister Ernest and the narrator   c. the narrator, maw, and pap
  b. the roadhouse feller, maw, and pap   d. Dan and Mister Ernest

____ 6. In this passage from "Race at Morning," where does the action take place?

> Because he had been a good feller ever since I had knowed him, which was even before that day two years ago when maw went off with the Vicksburg roadhouse feller and the next day pap didn't come home neither, and on the third one Mister Ernest rid Dan up to the door of the cabin on the river he let us live in, so pap could work his piece of land and run his fish line, too, and said, "Put that gun down and come on here and climb up behind."

  a. in the big woods during the hunt   c. at Mister Ernest's house
  b. at the narrator's cabin on the river   d. at the hunting camp

____ 7. In this passage from "Race at Morning," what is the narrator doing?

> Because he had been a good feller ever since I had knowed him, which was even before that day two years ago when maw went off with the Vicksburg roadhouse feller and the next day pap didn't come home neither, and on the third one Mister Ernest rid Dan up to the door of the cabin on the river he let us live in, so pap could work his piece of land and run his fish line, too, and said, "Put that gun down and come on here and climb up behind."

    a. remembering the first time he met Mister Ernest
    b. explaining why he is angry with his parents
    c. telling why he likes riding Dan
    d. telling how he came to be living with Mister Ernest

____ 8. Which of the words from this sentence from "Race at Morning" are an example of the narrator's dialect?

> So I went to bed, and after a while Mister Ernest come in and I wanted to tell him again how big them horns looked. . . .

    a. went; while   b. come; them   c. him; horns   d. bed; looked

____ 9. What does the narrator in "Race at Morning" mean when he says that hunting and farming are "jest the other side of each other"?
    a. Both are risky activities.
    b. They are both outdoor activities.
    c. You can't do both at the same time.
    d. Both are necessary and equal parts of a full life.

____ 10. Using standard English, how would you write the following line from "Race at Morning"?

> Because me and Mister Ernest was going to git him.

    a. Cause me and Mister Ernest was going to get him.
    b. Because Mister Ernest and me were gonna get him.
    c. Because Mister Ernest and I were going to get him.
    d. Because I and Mister Ernest was going to get him.

____ 11. In "Race at Morning," when Mister Ernest says that *maybe* is the "best word in our language" and the one that "mankind keeps going on," he means that
    a. people want to have hope in the future.
    b. people don't want to know the future.
    c. people fear certainty.
    d. people can't count on anything.

____ 12. In his "Nobel Prize Acceptance Speech," Faulkner says that young writers today have forgotten the "problems of the human heart in conflict with itself" because they
    a. are worried about being blown up.
    b. know that readers are no longer interested in reading about these personal problems.
    c. think the topic has been written about too much.
    d. would rather write about universal truths.

____ 13. When Faulkner says in his "Nobel Prize Acceptance Speech" that until writers learn to write about the universal truths, they are writing "not of the heart but of the glands," he means they are writing about
    a. romantic topics instead of scientific subjects.
    b. medical topics.
    c. fiction instead of factual events.
    d. superficial topics rather than subjects that really matter.

____ 14. What is Faulkner's main point in his "Nobel Prize Acceptance Speech"?
      a. The writer must learn not to be afraid.
      b. The writer's most important duty is to help human beings endure and prevail.
      c. He thinks himself unworthy of the prize.
      d. He wants to use the prize money for some worthy cause.

Vocabulary and Grammar

On the line, write the letter of the one best answer.

____ 15. Which word has most nearly the same meaning as *moiling*?
      a. following   c. swirling
      b. quarreling   d. running

____ 16. The word *scrabbling* means ____.
      a. scribbling   c. struggling
      b. climbing   d. scrambling

____ 17. What is a glade?
      a. a sluggish, marshy inlet   c. an open space surrounded by woods
      b. a slender, flexible twig   d. dense woods

____ 18. The narrator ____ the buck swimming across the bayou and ____ Mister Ernest.
      a. seen; told   c. saw; telled
      b. seen; tells   d. sees; tells

____ 19. The dogs ____ all morning, and even Eagle ____ out.
      a. runned; was wear   c. ran; was wore
      b. had run; was worn   d. had ran; was worn

____ 20. When Faulkner ____ the Nobel Prize, he ____ passionately about the writer's duty to humankind.
      a. was given; spoke   c. was given; spoked
      b. was gave; spoke   d. was give; spoke

Essay Questions

21. Apart from the narrator and Mister Ernest, the most important characters in "Race at Morning" are the animals Dan, Eagle, and the buck. Although minor characters, they are developed with individual personalities and placed in situations in which they must make critical decisions. In an essay, describe the character traits of these animals and assess their importance to the plot. How fully are their personalities developed? Which of these characters is most important to the development of the story?

22. The narrator of "Race at Morning" is uneducated—he can't even write his own name—but is he intelligent? Write an essay in which you assess the narrator's intelligence. Give examples to support your conclusion. What does the narrator's use of language tell you about his intelligence? Is he simply Mister Ernest's ears, or does he help in other ways, too? Is he able to think through complex issues and arrive at valid conclusions?

23. In his "Nobel Prize Acceptance Speech," Faulkner says that writing about "the human heart in conflict with itself" is what makes writing worthwhile. Write an essay in which you explain how Faulkner investigated this conflict within the hearts of the narrator and Mister Ernest in his story "Race at Morning." What events or situations demonstrate that Mister Ernest and the narrator have internal conflicts? Does either character resolve any conflicts?

Robert Frost's Poetry

Selection Test

Critical Reading

On the line, write the letter of the one best answer.

_____ 1. For the speaker in "Birches," what does swinging on birch trees most clearly symbolize?
   a. a novel way to control and manipulate nature
   b. a temporary return to a youthful, carefree state
   c. a creative way to achieve and exercise virtue
   d. a permanent escape from the physical, material world

_____ 2. For the speaker of "Mending Wall," what does the wall itself most clearly symbolize?
   a. suspicion, mistrust, and bias
   b. safety, security, and strength
   c. family, history, and custom
   d. order, harmony, and discipline

_____ 3. For the speaker of "Mending Wall," the neighbor represents all that is
   a. wild and natural.
   b. enlightened and logical.
   c. primitive and irrational.
   d. respectful and well mannered.

_____ 4. The neighbor in "Mending Wall" tells the speaker of the poem that good fences make good neighbors. What does he mean by this?
   a. He doesn't want the speaker on his property.
   b. He doesn't want to get to know the speaker any better.
   c. He has had problems with other landowners in the past.
   d. All the other neighbors have fences on their property.

_____ 5. The buzz saw in " 'Out, Out—' " most likely symbolizes
   a. uncontrollable technology.
   b. nature in its unspoiled state.
   c. the inevitability of death.
   d. order, discipline, and hard work.

_____ 6. What do the following lines from " 'Out, Out—' " tell you about the farm family in the poem?

> They listened at his heart.
> Little—less—nothing!—and that ended it.
> No more to build on there. And they, since they
> Were not the one dead, turned to their affairs.

   a. They were not very saddened by the boy's death.
   b. They did not know how to express their sadness.
   c. They felt that death was a natural part of life.
   d. They felt that they were to blame for the boy's death.

_____ 7. A central idea of "Stopping by Woods on a Snowy Evening" is the conflict between the attractions of
   a. virtue and temptation.   c. town and country.
   b. solitude and society.   d. duty and rest.

_____ 8. For the speaker of "Acquainted With the Night," what does night itself most likely symbolize?
   a. adventure and mystery
   b. danger and peril
   c. loneliness and doubt
   d. protection and comfort

_____ 9. What is an iamb?
   a. five lines of poetry
   b. unrhymed verse
   c. one unstressed syllable followed by a stressed syllable
   d. one line of blank verse

_____ 10. What is the form of blank verse?
   a. unrhymed lines of iambic pentameter
   b. rhymed lines of iambic pentameter
   c. one unstressed syllable followed by a stressed syllable
   d. the flow of human speech

_____ 11. Reading blank verse as a group of sentences rather than a group of poetic lines allows the reader to hear
   a. how the verse captures the poet's dense imagery.
   b. each individual iamb.
   c. how the verse captures the rhythm of human speech.
   d. the unstressed beats in the poem.

_____ 12. For what reason does Robert Frost sometimes deviate from the blank-verse structure he has set up?
   a. to force the reader to hear the poem's stressed and unstressed syllables
   b. to emphasize an image, event, or idea
   c. to achieve metrical variety
   d. to make the poem easier to understand

_____ 13. One of the best ways to understand a poem written in blank verse is to
   a. pick out key words in each line.
   b. figure out its rhyme scheme.
   c. mark the stressed and unstressed syllables.
   d. read it out loud as a group of sentences.

Vocabulary and Grammar

On the line, write the letter of the one best answer.

_____ 14. A person who shows great *poise* is probably _____.
   a. confident
   b. happy
   c. nervous
   d. interesting

_____ 15. If a person's facial expression is *rueful*, that person is probably experiencing _____.
   a. confusion
   b. joy
   c. regret
   d. pity

_____ 16. Which of the following lines from "Birches" contains an infinitive?
   a. "When I see birches bend to left and right"
   b. "He always kept his poise / To the top branches, climbing carefully"
   c. "So was I once myself a swinger of birches."
   d. "And they seem not to break"

_____ 17. Which of the following lines from "Stopping by Woods on a Snowy Evening" does *not* use an infinitive as an adjective?
a. "He will not see me stopping here / To watch his woods fill up with snow."
b. "My little horse must think it queer / To stop without a farmhouse near."
c. "He gives his harness bells a shake / To ask if there is some mistake."
d. "The woods are lovely, dark, and deep, / But I have promises to keep"

_____ 18. If you describe the moon as *luminary*, you mean that it
a. gives off heat.
b. gives off light.
c. is surrounded by bright stars.
d. can be seen only at night.

_____ 19. An infinitive can function as

I.   a noun.
II. an adjective.
III. an adverb.

a. I and II
b. I and III
c. II and III
d. I, II, and III

_____ 20. What is an infinitive?
a. a verb form
b. a subject compound
c. a subject complement
d. a word root

Essay Questions

21. As you read Frost's poems, you probably noted that they are often tinged with a feeling of regret. Many of Frost's poems contain a sense of rueful longing for lost childhood or for a bygone way of life. In an essay, discuss specific examples from the poems concerning this loss of innocence, the death of childhood, the end of life, the longing for a simpler way of life, and so on. Use quotations from the poems to illustrate your points. Why do you think such themes hold such mass appeal?

22. Robert Frost is famous for having written poems that seem simple but actually operate on a number of different emotional and intellectual levels. For example, in "Mending Wall," Frost depicts two neighbors with very different attitudes toward the fence line that divides their property. One, the speaker, proclaims that "Something there is that doesn't love a wall, that wants it down." The other, the speaker's neighbor, insists that "Good fences make good neighbors." Consider the two statements, and write an essay about the merits of each point of view. In what situations might the speaker's attitude about the unimportance of boundaries and walls backfire? How might the neighbor's unyielding stance about the necessity of defined boundaries cause problems? Discuss how these statements might be said to illustrate two common American points of view.

23. Most poets are known for more than one or two poems. Robert Frost wrote perhaps the greatest number of poems that are familiar to American readers. Of them, Frost called "Stopping by Woods on a Snowy Evening" his "best bid for remembrance." The poem excels in the three parts that Frost regarded as essential: the point or idea; the details that develop it; and the technique with which it is crafted. Write an essay in which you analyze Frost's "Stopping by Woods on a Snowy Evening," exploring each of these three parts. Be as specific as possible.

"The Night the Ghost Got In" by James Thurber
from *Here Is New York* by E. B. White

Selection Test

Critical Reading

On the line, write the letter of the one best answer.

_____ 1. Writers often create humor by depicting serious events in a comic light. Which aspect of "The Night the Ghost Got In" would not be amusing without Thurber's embellishment?
   a. the unidentified sound in the house
   b. the mother breaking the neighbor's window
   c. the grandfather bounding out of bed in his nightshirt and leather jacket
   d. the behavior of the police

_____ 2. Thurber notes that his "grandfather was in the attic, in the old walnut bed which, as you will remember, once fell on my father." How does this detail contribute to the essay's humor?
   a. It helps the reader identify with the experience Thurber describes.
   b. Thurber displays his conversational style in this detail.
   c. Thurber exaggerates the importance of the bed.
   d. It emphasizes the family's tendency toward mishaps.

_____ 3. Which aspect of the interaction between Thurber's mother and Mr. Bodwell is an example of hyperbole?
   a. the narrator's mother shouting "Burglars!"
   b. Mr. Bodwell "shouting, frothing a little, shaking his fist"
   c. Mr. Bodwell being confused about where the burglars were
   d. the narrator's mother wanting to throw another shoe

_____ 4. Which of the following is one of the most humorous aspects of Thurber's story?
   a. The narrator believes there was a ghost in the house.
   b. No one seems to mind that the grandfather shot a policeman.
   c. None of those involved seems to recognize the absurdity of the situation.
   d. The police come across as such silly characters.

_____ 5. What does the cop mean to say when he tells his colleagues that the mother seems "historical"?
   a. horticultural   c. hysterical
   b. hospitable   d. hypocritical

_____ 6. Which of the following statements best summarizes the theme of "The Night the Ghost Got In"?
   a. A small misunderstanding can have extreme implications.
   b. The police are not as dependable as they are expected to be.
   c. People who seem to be out of touch with reality are often quite sane.
   d. Jumping too quickly to conclusions usually leads to trouble.

_____ 7. What is the most significant contribution of Thurber's shower to the subsequent events in the essay?
   a. The shower prevents him from hearing the footsteps clearly.
   b. His lack of clothes makes the police suspicious of him.
   c. His naked state keeps his mother from letting in the police.
   d. The towel around his waist makes his grandfather think he is a deserter.

_____ 8. Thurber uses hyperbole in presenting the actions of the police when he
    a. creates the impression that they destroy the house in their search for the burglar.
    b. relates their disappointment at finding no clues.
    c. tells how they lock the grandfather in the attic.
    d. describes their quick reaction to the creaking in the attic.

_____ 9. In "The Night the Ghost Got In," which detail is a digression that has little purpose other than comic effect?
    a. the footsteps   b. the narrator's towel   c. the shoe   d. the zither

_____ 10. What is E. B. White's meaning in this sentence about New York?

> Each area is a city within a city within a city.

    a. New York has many governmental bodies.
    b. New York has a variety of ethnic and cultural groups.
    c. New York has small neighborhoods, each of which is almost self-sufficient.
    d. New York has huge apartment buildings that residents hardly ever leave.

_____ 11. What does this excerpt from *Here Is New York* imply about the city?

> And the town has a somewhat relaxed air, and one can lie in a loincloth, gasping and remembering things.

    a. No real New Yorkers stay in the city during the summer.
    b. You don't have to dress up in New York.
    c. Sick people often come to New York.
    d. New York is hot in the summertime.

_____ 12. Which of the following excerpts from White's essay is an example of hyperbole?
    a. "The oft-quoted thumbnail sketch of New York is, of course: 'It's a wonderful place, but I'd hate to live there.'"
    b. "Let him walk two blocks from his corner and he is in a strange land and will feel uneasy till he gets back."
    c. "Manhattan has been compelled to expand skyward because of the absence of any other direction in which to grow."
    d. "To an outlander a stay in New York can be and often is a series of small embarrassments and discomforts and disappointments."

_____ 13. What informal essay characteristic does this *Here Is New York* excerpt exemplify?

> I have an idea that people from villages and small towns, people accustomed to the convenience and the friendliness of neighborhood over-the-fence living, are unaware that life in New York follows the neighborhood pattern.

    a. loose organization   c. tendency to digress
    b. expression of the author's opinion   d. clear purpose to entertain

_____ 14. Which sentence best states E. B. White's opinion about New York?
    a. It is a majestic city of which all Americans can be proud.
    b. It is one of the world's most sophisticated and charming cities.
    c. It is fascinating, complex, difficult—and there is no other city like it.
    d. It is hot, difficult, and too big, with nothing of interest to anyone except tourists.

_____ 15. Which line most strongly suggests that the *Here Is New York* excerpt is an informal essay?
    a. "But the curious thing about New York is that each large geographical unit is composed of countless small neighborhoods."
    b. "This, more than any other thing, is responsible for its physical majesty."
    c. "The city is literally a composite of tens of thousands of tiny neighborhood units."
    d. "It is a miracle that New York works at all. The whole thing is implausible."

Vocabulary and Grammar

On the line, write the letter of the one best answer.

____ 16. Which of the following excerpts from *Here Is New York* contains commas in series?
a. "I am, at the moment of writing this, living not as a neighborhood man in New York but as a transient, or vagrant, in from the country for a few days."
b. "New York is nothing like Paris; it is nothing like London; and it is not Spokane multiplied by sixty, or Detroit multiplied by four."
c. "But the city makes up for its hazards and its deficiencies by supplying its citizens with massive doses of a supplementary vitamin: the sense of belonging to something unique, cosmopolitan, mighty, and unparalleled."
d. "By rights New York should have destroyed itself long ago, from panic or fire or rioting or failure of some vital supply line in its circulatory system or from some deep labyrinthine short circuit."

____ 17. When E. B. White describes the smoke-fog from New Jersey as "leaving the high offices suspended, men groping and depressed, and the sense of world's end," he is using
a. a digression.   c. commas in series.
b. informal language.   d. conversational style.

____ 18. Choose the pair that best expresses a relationship similar to that in the pair in capital letters.

SUBTERRANEAN : SUBMARINE ::

a. buried : sunken   b. cold : damp   c. terrestrial : floating   d. dirty : clean

____ 19. Choose the pair that best expresses a relationship similar to that in the pair in capital letters.

FEAR : CLAUSTROPHOBIA ::

a. year : hour   b. disease : measles   c. anger : emotion   d. food : diet

____ 20. The word that best describes how Mrs. Thurber approached the events retold in "The Night the Ghost Got In" is _____.
a. claustrophobically   c. intuitively
b. blasphemously   d. fearfully

Essay Questions

21. Eccentric characters are one of the traditional features of humorous writing. Usually these characters act in ways that stretch the bounds of credibility without becoming completely preposterous. In Thurber's "The Night the Ghost Got In," the narrator's mother and grandfather fit this description. Write an essay in which you describe the personalities and actions of the narrator's mother and grandfather. Comment on their believability.

22. One critic said of E. B. White, "His interests are broad—nothing, it seems, that is human is alien to him. His eye and intelligence see what lies beneath the surface." In an essay, discuss how *Here Is New York* supports these points, citing specific examples from the text. What does "nothing . . . human is alien to him" imply?

23. Humor is often based on the depiction of other people's behavior. Sometimes this sort of humor is used at the expense of its subjects and is unkind. Write an essay in which you explain what determines the line between humor and unkindness and apply it to *Here Is New York* and Thurber's essay. Is there humor in these pieces that crosses the line? Use examples from the essays to support your ideas.

from *Dust Tracks on a Road* by Zora Neale Hurston

Selection Test

Critical Reading

On the line, write the letter of the one best answer.

_____ 1. This excerpt from *Dust Tracks on a Road* is mostly an account of a writer's
   a. early experiences with the outside world.
   b. escape from her humble origins.
   c. struggle against racism.
   d. literary tastes.

_____ 2. What can you infer about Hurston's attitude toward whites at the beginning of the selection?
   a. She was afraid of them.
   b. She saw whites as a way to expand her experience.
   c. She regarded them as something curious.
   d. She felt that they looked down on her.

_____ 3. Why did Hurston's grandmother find her brazenness "unthinkable"?
   a. She thought Zora's actions reflected badly on her.
   b. She thought Zora's activities were illegal.
   c. She knew Negroes who had been lynched for minor offenses.
   d. She knew that she was not as creative as her granddaughter.

_____ 4. What do the dust tracks in the title symbolize?
   a. poverty in a backwater southern community
   b. the path to a new way of life
   c. finding the way home after getting lost
   d. returning to one's roots

_____ 5. Why was a Negro school a curiosity to visitors?
   a. There was little contact between races at the time the writer describes.
   b. The educational practices differed from those in schools for whites.
   c. The children were better educated than in the schools the visitors knew.
   d. The visitors had never met Negro children before.

_____ 6. Why were the schoolchildren threatened when visitors came to observe them?
   a. The teachers would get in trouble if the children misbehaved.
   b. The visitors rewarded the teachers if the children were well-behaved.
   c. The teachers were concerned about making a good impression.
   d. The visitors wanted to observe the teachers' disciplinary techniques.

_____ 7. Why were the ladies so impressed with Hurston?
   a. She was the best-behaved child in class.
   b. Her reading ability was greater than that of her classmates.
   c. She was neater and better dressed than her classmates.
   d. She was bright and outspoken.

_____ 8. What can you infer about Hurston's taste in literature as a child?
   a. She preferred stories with a clear moral.
   b. She preferred stories about gods and goddesses.
   c. She preferred the New Testament to the Old Testament.
   d. She preferred adventure and exciting tales.

____ 9. Hurston carefully describes her reading likes and dislikes for the purpose of
   a. persuading others that reading is important.
   b. revealing her character and personality.
   c. helping children choose appropriate books.
   d. showing that she liked the same things white people did.

____ 10. Which might best explain Hurston's purpose in presenting her critical feelings about school?
   a. to confess that she was a liar
   b. to show that being educated is not dependent on loving school
   c. to reveal how inferior her school was
   d. to show how little she values education

____ 11. Which of the following was probably *not* one of Zora Neale Hurston's purposes in writing her autobiography?
   a. to portray the African American culture of her community
   b. to share the experiences of her life
   c. to show how she struggled against racism and prejudice
   d. to inspire others to get an education

____ 12. What do you think the author's purpose was for writing this sentence?

   If white people liked trashy singing like that, there must be something funny about them that I had not noticed before.

   a. to show how much contempt she had for white people
   b. to reveal a moment of doubt in her positive view of white people
   c. to explain why she disliked white people's way of worshiping
   d. to emphasize her belief that white people had bad taste in music

____ 13. Which excerpt best shows that Zora Neale Hurston wanted to present herself as an unusual child who did not fit stereotypes?
   a. "I slipped one hand behind me and switched my dress tail at them, indicating scorn."
   b. "I liked geography and reading, and I liked to play at recess time. Whoever it was invented writing and arithmetic got no thanks from me."
   c. "I had never been too keen on dressing up. It called for hard scrubbings with Octagon soap suds getting in my eyes, and none too gentle fingers scrubbing my neck and gouging in my ears."
   d. "I came to start reading the Bible through my mother. She gave me a licking one afternoon for repeating something I had overheard. . . . She locked me in her room . . . and the Bible was the only thing in there for me to read."

____ 14. Which is a possible reason Hurston might have had for emphasizing the mythology she read and loved as a child?
   a. to show the origins of her later career as a folklorist
   b. to make clear how much she liked white culture
   c. to make a case for reading stories to children
   d. to emphasize the importance of reading for education

Vocabulary and Grammar

On the line, write the letter of the one best answer.

____ 15. Which event is the best example of a *caper*?
   a. Zora's friends snickering so she could hear them when she is called to Mr. Calhoun's desk
   b. the white ladies telling Zora not to open her cylinder-shaped present until she got home

c. Zora reading the myth of Pluto and Persephone to the visitors

d. Zora hailing white travelers from her gatepost

_____ 16. It was not _____ that made Zora take such delight in the gift of pennies, but rather their beauty.

a. brazenness

b. foreknowledge

c. poverty

d. avarice

_____ 17. Usually, Zora's school had some _____ when people were going to visit, but not when the two white ladies from Minnesota came.

a. avarice

b. preparations

c. foreknowledge

d. fears

_____ 18. Which excerpt contains an example of parallelism in coordinate elements?

a. "But I knew better than to bring that up right there, so I said yes, I *loved* school."

b. "Perhaps a year before the old man died, I came to know two other white people for myself."

c. "But the books gave me more pleasure than the clothes."

d. "He put his hand on my shoulder and gave me little pats."

_____ 19. Which sentence contains an error in parallelism?

a. The author's purpose was to tell about her childhood, describe her community, and give insight into her character.

b. Zora went off to see the ladies scrubbed, clad in a gingham dress, and her hair tied by a red ribbon.

c. Zora didn't know whether Hennie, Stell, or someone else had laughed loudest.

d. The white visitors were kind and sympathetic, but curious.

_____ 20. Which sentence best uses parallelism in coordinate elements to express the meaning of the following passage?

> Zora didn't like characters to be sweet. She didn't like them being passive. She liked them active. She liked them to be dutiful.

a. Zora didn't like characters sweet and being passive, but active and dutiful.

b. Zora didn't like sweet or passive characters, nor active and dutiful ones.

c. Zora didn't like sweet, passive characters, but active, dutiful ones.

d. Zora didn't like sweet and passive characters but she liked them active and being dutiful.

Essay Questions

21. The episodes writers choose to include in an autobiography reflect their perceptions about experiences that helped mold their character. In an essay, explain what the information in this selection reveals to you about Zora Neale Hurston's character. Include details from the selection to support your conclusion.

22. Zora's encounters with white people not only show us things about her but also reveal some attitudes and feelings of these people toward African Americans. In an essay, discuss these attitudes and feelings as they are revealed in this narrative. Are they all directly stated, or must some be inferred from events? Why do you think the white women provide Zora with books and clothing? Use specific examples to make your points.

23. One critic said of *Dust Tracks on a Road* that with it "Zora had found a recipe for success—entertain but don't blame." Write an essay discussing this view of Zora's purpose. In what sense does the selection support the critic's view? In what sense does it not? Cite examples from the text to support your ideas.

"Refugee in America," "Ardella," "The Negro Speaks of Rivers," and
"Dream Variations," by Langston Hughes
"The Tropics in New York" by Claude McKay

Selection Test

Critical Reading

On the line, write the letter of the one best answer.

____ 1. Which of the following statements best describes the theme of "Refugee in America"?
   a. A refugee's life is a hard one.
   b. Everyone should experience singing and crying in order to stay healthy.
   c. Liberty means a great deal when you know what it is like to live without it.
   d. It is better to live in America than anywhere else.

____ 2. Which line from "Refugee in America" gives you a clue about who the speaker is?
   a. "On my heart-strings freedom sings"
   b. "All day everyday."
   c. "There are words like *Liberty*"
   d. "You would know why."

____ 3. In "Ardella," what would the speaker compare Ardella to "Were it not for [her] eyes"?
   a. a night without stars
   b. a sleep without dreams
   c. music without songs
   d. a song without dreams

____ 4. In "Ardella," what can you infer about the speaker's feelings for Ardella?
   a. The speaker is related to Ardella.
   b. The speaker envies Ardella.
   c. The speaker admires Ardella.
   d. The speaker doesn't know Ardella.

____ 5. In "Ardella," the speaker probably feels that Ardella is _____.
   a. quiet   c. intelligent
   b. enslaved   d. happy

____ 6. The theme of the "The Negro Speaks of Rivers" concerns the
   a. long history of the black race.
   b. human qualities of rivers.
   c. religious beliefs of blacks.
   d. travels of black explorers.

____ 7. In "The Negro Speaks of Rivers," which word best describes the speaker's attitude?
   a. arrogant
   b. humble
   c. proud
   d. self-deprecating

____ 8. In "Dream Variations," the speaker sees day as a time to _____.
   a. eat   c. dance
   b. rest   d. write

_____ 9. In "Dream Variations," which phrase best describes the "dream"?
   a. to have joyous days and restful nights
   b. to feel the warmth of the tropical sun
   c. to be dark like the night
   d. to have pleasant dreams while sleeping

_____ 10. Which line from "Dream Variations" gives you a clue about what the speaker looks like?
   a. "To fling my arms wide"
   b. "Dark like me—"
   c. "That is my dream!"
   d. "A tall, slim tree . . ."

_____ 11. With which statement would the speaker of "Dream Variations" be most likely to agree?
   a. Night is a time for dreaming.
   b. Night is a time for celebration.
   c. Night is a time for revitalization.
   d. Night is a time for variations.

_____ 12. In "The Tropics in New York," the speaker remembers the homeland's skies as being
   a. blocked by skyscrapers.
   b. forever cloudy.
   c. dusky gray.
   d. mystical blue.

_____ 13. In "The Tropics in New York," why is the fruit in the first stanza described so carefully?
   a. to help the reader visualize what the fruit looks like
   b. to tie in the themes of dewy dawns and tears
   c. to help describe a market in New York City
   d. to give the reader a sense of the tropics

_____ 14. Which line from "The Tropics in New York" tells you the speaker is not in the tropics when the poem is written?
   a. "Bananas ripe and green, and ginger-root"
   b. "Set in the window, bringing memories"
   c. "In benediction over nun-like hills."
   d. "I turned aside and bowed my head and wept."

Vocabulary and Grammar

On the line, write the letter of the one best answer.

_____ 15. Which word from "Refugee in America" is closest in meaning to the word "liberty," also used in the poem?
   a. freedom
   b. sweet
   c. everyday
   d. cry

_____ 16. In "The Negro Speaks of Rivers," Hughes describes rivers as "dusky" to call attention to their _____.
   a. darkness
   b. age
   c. mystery
   d. sadness

_____ 17. In "The Negro Speaks of Rivers," the Congo probably "lulled" the speaker to sleep with
   a. rampaging rapids.
   b. a gentle murmur.

    c. a magnificent waterfall.

    d. stillness and quiet.

____ 18. Which line from "The Negro Speaks of Rivers" is written in the present perfect tense?

    a. "My soul has grown deep like the rivers."

    b. "I bathed in the Euphrates when dawns were young."

    c. "I built my hut near the Congo and it lulled me to sleep."

    d. "I heard the singing of the Mississippi. . . ."

____ 19. Which of the following is the correct way to write ". . . fling my arms wide" in the present perfect tense?

    a. want to fling my arms wide

    b. have flung my arms wide

    c. had flung my arms wide

    d. flinging my arms wide

____ 20. Which line from "The Tropics in New York" is written in the past tense?

    a. "Cocoa in pods and alligator pears"

    b. "In benediction over nun-like hills."

    c. "And, hungry for the old, familiar ways"

    d. "I turned aside and bowed my head and wept."

Essay Questions

21. A poet's first published poem sometimes creates a powerful impression. That was true of Langston Hughes's "The Negro Speaks of Rivers," published in 1921. Black readers recognized it immediately as a great poem about their heritage. Critics in general praised it lavishly. The poem, which celebrates the black experience more movingly than any prior poem, contributes to black awareness and black pride. Write an essay in which you analyze how the poem achieves its effectiveness.

22. Although the pronoun *I* is used for the speakers, or voices, of the poems, in "Refugee in America," "The Negro Speaks of Rivers," and "The Tropics in New York" the speakers are not all the same. Write an essay comparing and contrasting the speakers in these three poems. Whom does the *I* represent in each poem? In each poem, what effect does the use of *I* have on the reader?

23. In three of the four poems by Hughes in this section, words and images of darkness appear. An example is the closing of "The Negro Speaks of Rivers":

> I've known rivers:
> Ancient, dusky rivers.
> My soul has grown deep like the rivers.

Write an essay discussing these lines and other words and images in these poems in which images of darkness appear. What meanings do these images have in the poems? What point do you think Hughes is trying to make by using them? Use details from the poems to support your answers.

"From the Dark Tower" by Countee Cullen
"A Black Man Talks of Reaping" by Arna Bontemps
"Storm Ending" by Jean Toomer

Selection Test

Critical Reading

On the line, write the letter of the one best answer.

____ 1. What does the title of "From the Dark Tower" suggest about the poem?
   a. The poem is from the heart of blacks facing inequality.
   b. The poem was written in a tall, dark tower.
   c. The reader should watch for a metaphor about a deep, dark well.
   d. The poem is about a time before electricity was widely used.

____ 2. In "From the Dark Tower," what is suggested by the line, "And wait, and tend our agonizing seeds"?
   a. relief for dry seeds from an upcoming storm
   b. a desire for a better yield from future crops
   c. hope for a better future for blacks
   d. a desire for a better way of life for all agricultural workers

____ 3. Which part of history probably most influenced "From the Dark Tower"?
   a. the American Revolution
   b. the Civil War
   c. the recent slavery of blacks
   d. the disdain for agriculturists by industrialists

____ 4. In "From the Dark Tower," which line is evidence of black pride at the time of the Harlem Renaissance writers?
   a. "Not always countenance, . . . / That lesser men should hold their brothers cheap"
   b. "Not everlastingly . . . Shall we beguile their limbs with mellow flute"
   c. "The night whose sable breast . . . is no less lovely being dark"
   d. "So in the dark we hide the heart that bleeds"

____ 5. In "From the Dark Tower," what does Cullen imply about the job situation during the 1920's for blacks as compared with whites?
   a. It is equal after a long, hard fight.
   b. It is the closest to equal it is ever going to be.
   c. It is unequal, but the situation is much improved over a few years earlier.
   d. It is unequal, but someday this will be changed.

____ 6. What is the theme of "A Black Man Talks of Reaping"?
   a. Because generations of black people were poorly rewarded for honest work, their descendants have given up on honest work.
   b. The early generations of black people made poor decisions when they planted their crops, and their descendants are suffering the results.
   c. The hard work of black slaves is not appreciated by their descendants, who do not understand the value of labor.
   d. When farmers have poor luck with their crops, it is not surprising that their children decide to seek other types of work.

_____ 7. Which of the following lines from "A Black Man Talks of Reaping" most directly describes the results of inequality?
    a. "I planted safe against this stark, lean year."
    b. ". . . my children glean in fields they have not sown, and feed on bitter fruit."
    c. ". . . wind or fowl would take the grain away."
    d. "I scattered seed enough to plant the land in rows from Canada to Mexico."

_____ 8. Who is the speaker in "A Black Man Talks of Reaping"?
    a. the human race
    b. the black people
    c. the present-day farmers
    d. the Harlem youth

_____ 9. "A Black Man Talks of Reaping" is best described as
    a. a series of brief metaphors comparing the stages of a man's life to the seasons of the agricultural year and his feelings to a farmer's tasks.
    b. a single extended metaphor comparing the black race to a family of farmers trying to survive off the land in different parts of the world.
    c. a single extended metaphor comparing the work of the black race to one man's planting and harvest for a single year.
    d. three brief metaphors comparing a man's life to a season's planting, his death to a harvest, and his children's lives to bitter fruit.

_____ 10. In "A Black Man Talks of Reaping," what does the speaker's sowing represent in Bontemps's metaphor?
    a. human effort
    b. the passage of time
    c. the nobility of farming
    d. the futility of work

_____ 11. In "A Black Man Talks of Reaping," what does reaping represent?
    a. enjoying life
    b. dying
    c. being rewarded
    d. harvesting grain

_____ 12. The theme of "Storm Ending" concerns the
    a. beauty of a rainstorm in a drought-stricken landscape.
    b. damage that follows in the wake of a fierce thunderstorm.
    c. relief to the senses after a storm has ended.
    d. visual images evoked by the sound of thunder.

_____ 13. In "Storm Ending," which word best describes Toomer's characterization of the thunder?
    a. beautiful
    b. destructive
    c. frightening
    d. invigorating

_____ 14. Which statement best describes the use of metaphor in "Storm Ending"?
    a. A brief metaphor compares the thunder to a flower, and then an extended metaphor compares it to a bell.
    b. In an extended metaphor comparing thunder to a bell, Toomer also compares it to a flower.
    c. The poem comprises several brief metaphors comparing thunder to various different kinds of flowers.
    d. In an extended metaphor comparing thunder to a flower, Toomer also compares it to a bell and a person.

Vocabulary and Grammar

On the line, write the letter of the one best answer.

____ 15. Which word is the closest in meaning to the word *increment*, as used in the following line of poetry?

> The golden *increment* of bursting fruit

a. excitement
b. increase
c. color
d. flavor

____ 16. Which word is the closest in meaning to the word *beguile*, as used in the following line of poetry?

> Shall we *beguile* their limbs with mellow flute

a. relax
b. charm
c. surround
d. drown

____ 17. Which of the following words is closest in meaning to the verb *countenance*?
a. satisfy
b. reap
c. glean
d. tolerate

____ 18. In the excerpt below, the adjective is _____, and it is _____ the word it modifies.

> I scattered seed enough to plant the land

a. seed; before
b. seed; after
c. enough; before
d. enough; after

____ 19. In the excerpt below, the adjective is _____, and it is _____ the word it modifies.

> they have not sown, and feed on bitter fruit.

a. sown; before
b. sown; after
c. bitter; before
d. bitter; after

____ 20. In the excerpt below, the adjective is _____, and it is _____ the word it modifies.

> Stretching clappers to strike our ears . . . / Full-lipped flowers / Bitten by the sun / Bleeding rain

a. full-lipped; before
b. full-lipped; after
c. flowers; before
d. flowers; after

Essay Questions

21. Sometimes it is possible to capture the mood of a poem in a single word or phrase. Choose a word or phrase that you feel describes the mood of the poem, "A Black Man Talks of Reaping." In an essay, discuss your choice and why you made it. How does your word or phrase capture the mood of the poem? Support your decision with details from the poem.

22. All three of the poems in this section make use of metaphors to convey their meaning. Select one poem and write an essay explaining how it uses metaphors. What kinds of feelings do the metaphors evoke? Use examples from the poem to clarify your points.

23. Some critics think Jean Toomer intended to write about the African American experience in his poem "Storm Ending." Write an essay agreeing or disagreeing with this view of the poem. How do you think this poem relates to the general purposes of the Harlem Renaissance writers? Support your position with specific examples.

"**i yearn**" by Ricardo Sánchez

Selection Test

Critical Reading

On the line, write the letter of the one best answer.

_____ 1. What is the significance of the particular cities the poet mentions in "i yearn"?
a. They are all in Texas.
b. They all have Spanish names.
c. They are all centers of Chicano immigration.
d. They are all places he has lived.

_____ 2. How long has the speaker been away from his homeland?
a. three months
b. almost a year
c. three years
d. ten years

_____ 3. What does the speaker describe as "hollow"?
a. life away from the barrios of his homeland
b. his relationship with his father
c. the food and customs of Anglo-Americans
d. his decision to leave his homeland

_____ 4. Which thing does the speaker *not* mention about his homeland?
a. the food
b. the people
c. the language
d. the climate

_____ 5. How does the speaker describe the typical greeting of his people?
a. joyful
b. reserved
c. warm
d. unrestrained

_____ 6. Which quality does the speaker seem to value the most in his people?
a. their ability to blend in with the local populations in the United States
b. their beautiful language
c. their great pride in themselves
d. their love of food and music

_____ 7. According to the speaker, how do Chicanos speak in a special way?
a. they always look you in the eye
b. they always touch you on the arm
c. they always smile when they talk
d. they roll their tongues when they speak

_____ 8. From whom does the speaker want to hear "qué tal, hermano"?
a. his brother
b. anyone from home
c. his family
d. his best friend

_____ 9. With which conception of "home" do you think the speaker would most agree?
- a. You can't go home again.
- b. Home is where the heart is.
- c. You should never leave home.
- d. The answers to life's problems can be found at home.

_____ 10. The lack of capital letters possibly symbolizes
- a. the poet's acknowledgment of his people's second-class status.
- b. the poet's lack of education in the English language.
- c. the poet's refusal to recognize the conventions of Anglo society.
- d. the poet's feelings of alienation in his adopted homeland.

Essay Questions

11. Write an essay identifying the central theme of "i yearn." What details led you to identify the theme you did? Compare this poem to an experience of your own, or to another poem, book, or film with which you are familiar. How was the same theme dealt with in the example you chose?

12. Songwriter Joni Mitchell once wrote, "You don't know what you've got till it's gone." In an essay, relate Mitchell's words to Sanchez's poem. What does Sanchez miss and why? Speculate as to why Sanchez would leave his home or stay away from it if he misses it so much.

13. In "i yearn," poet Ricardo Sanchez in part provides a celebration of his ethnic identity. In an essay, discuss the link in this poem between ethnicity, identity, and being away from home. How does Sanchez deal with the pressures his adopted place exerts on his ethnicity? Make a judgment about the role ethnicity has played in forming a modern American identity, and how much that American identity has helped or hindered newcomers in pursuing their lives here.

Part Test, Unit Five, Part 3: From Every Corner of the Land

Critical Reading

The questions below are based on the following selection.

This excerpt is from Richard Wright's memoir of his early life, Black Boy: A Record of Childhood and Youth.

The eighth grade days flowed in their hungry path and I grew more conscious of myself; I sat in classes, bored, wondering, dreaming. One long dry afternoon I took out my composition book and told myself that I would write a story: it was sheer idleness that led me to it. What would the story be about? It resolved itself into a plot about a villain who wanted a widow's home and I called it *The Voodoo of Hell's Half-Acre*. It was crudely atmospheric, emotional, intuitively psychological, and stemmed from pure feeling. I finished it in three days and then wondered what to do with it.

The local Negro newspaper! That's it . . . I sailed into the office and shoved my ragged composition under the nose of the man who called himself the editor.

"What is that?" he asked.

"A story," I said.

"A news story?"

"No, fiction."

"All right, I'll read it," he said.

He pushed my composition book back on his desk and looked at me curiously, sucking at his pipe.

"But I want you to read it *now*," I said.

He blinked. I had no idea how newspapers were run. I thought that one took a story to an editor and he sat down then and there and read it and said yes or no.

"I'll read this and let you know about it tomorrow," he said.

I was disappointed; I had taken time to write it and he seemed distant and uninterested.

"Give me the story," I said, reaching up for it.

He turned from me, took up the book and read ten pages or more.

On the line, write the letter of the one best answer.

_____ 1. What can you determine about the period in which Wright grew up from his reference to "[t]he local Negro newspaper"?
   a. He probably grew up after the civil rights era.
   b. He probably grew up at the height of the Black Nationalist movement.
   c. He probably grew up in the days before the Civil War.
   d. He probably grew up during the days of segregation.

_____ 2. What is Wright's purpose in this passage?
   a. To make fun of a newspaper editor
   b. To explain how he began to write and publish fiction
   c. To criticize policies of segregation
   d. To show how smart he was in the eighth grade

_____ 3. Wright achieves his purpose in this passage in which of the following ways?
   a. He shows that he wanted to become a famous writer early on.
   b. He shows that his start as a writer came of boredom and that he was aided by his ignorance of publishing.
   c. He shows us that his stubborn pursuit of his goals allowed him to achieve success.
   d. He shows us that the key to becoming a published writer is persuasive ability.

_____ 4. What is the probable meaning of Wright's metaphor of the "hungry path" in which the "eighth grade days flowed"?
   a. He was hungry all the time, like someone who had walked far.
   b. The days passed as quickly as a hungry animal eats.
   c. The times were dangerous, like a hungry animal.
   d. He craved more from his days, like a person hungry for food.

_____ 5. Judging from this passage, Wright's purpose in writing his autobiography is probably
   a. to gain the reader's sympathy for his childhood experiences.
   b. to make fun of people who take writing too seriously.
   c. to reflect on his childhood self from an adult perspective.
   d. to explain how he became famous.

_____ 6. Which of the following choices explains a way in which the passage resembles an informal essay?
   a. It is a piece of fiction.
   b. It is about the person who wrote it.
   c. It is about a past experience.
   d. It has a loose, casual style.

_____ 7. Why does the editor end up reading Wright's story on the spot?
   a. He realizes that Wright is very smart.
   b. He does not want to be unkind.
   c. Reading it is easier than getting Wright to change his assumptions.
   d. He probably realizes that he needs to fill space in the paper.

_____ 8. Why does Wright submit his story to a newspaper?
   a. It seems like the logical next step.
   b. He wants to get his name in the papers.
   c. He hopes publishing the story will get him out of class.
   d. He is impressed with his own work.

_____ 9. Which of the following choices best expresses Wright's opinion of the story he wrote in eighth grade?
   a. It was effective, because it was based on pure feeling.
   b. It was sophisticated, since it was filled with emotion and psychological insight.
   c. It was an enthusiastic effort, but lacked polish and a deep theme.
   d. It was embarrassing, because it is not as good as his later work.

_____ 10. Why does Wright start to take his story back from the editor?
   a. He has sudden second thoughts about its worth.
   b. He is hurt that the editor is not interested in the story or in him.
   c. He realizes that this gesture will help him get his way.
   d. He has second thoughts about its value.

Vocabulary and Grammar

On the line, write the letter of the one best answer.

_____ 11. RETROSPECTIVE : PREDICTION ::
   a. antique : futuristic
   b. nostalgia : ambition
   c. past : future
   d. elective : office

_____ 12. ASPIRATION : GOAL ::
   a. reminiscence : memory
   b. fondness : hate
   c. hotel : home
   d. insensitivity : pity

____ 13. Mister Ernest saw the deer running through the _____ .
  a. frippery
  b. geography
  c. glade
  d. distillery

____ 14. Granny Weatherall showed _____ toward those who liked _____ .
  a. antagonism/frippery
  b. contrition/blaspheming
  c. commiseration/reaping
  d. avarice/dyspepsia

____ 15. Theodora's _____ expression showed her _____.
  a. brutal/piety
  b. brutal/cunning
  c. rueful/contrition
  d. rueful/brazenness

____ 16. Which of the following sentences contains a gerund phrase?
  a. The rider is stopping by the woods on a snowy evening.
  b. Hunting the buck every November was a tradition in the county.
  c. Grandfather was sleeping in the attic the night the ghost got in.
  d. The police did not quite know what to make of the blaspheming grandfather.

____ 17. Which of the following sentences is an imperative sentence?
  a. Mister Ernest told him to go to school.
  b. New York is a big city!
  c. There were a hundred pennies in that roll?
  d. Don't throw shoes through the neighbors' window.

____ 18. Which of the following sentences contains an infinitive?
  a. From happiness to despair, Theresa discovers, is a short distance.
  b. "He will not see me stopping here / To watch his woods fill up with snow."
  c. Zora Neale Hurston did not wear shoes to school.
  d. Theresa's father went to the train station and met her.

____ 19. Which sentence uses commas in a series correctly?
  a. It was a cold, raw, dark November day.
  b. It was a cold raw dark, November day.
  c. It was a cold, raw, dark, November day.
  d. It was a cold, raw dark November day.

____ 20. Which of the following choices correctly uses the past and the present-perfect tenses to combine the example sentences, resulting in a sentence that makes the most sense?

> Jean Toomer is forgotten for years after his death.
>
> Jean Toomer is recognized in recent times as a central figure of the Harlem Renaissance.

  a. Although Jean Toomer *has been* forgotten for years after his death, he *was* recognized in more recent times as a central figure of the Harlem Renaissance.
  b. Although Jean Toomer *was* forgotten for years after his death, he *has been* recognized in more recent times as a central figure of the Harlem Renaissance.
  c. Although Jean Toomer *was* forgotten for years after his death, he *was* recognized in more recent times as a central figure of the Harlem Renaissance.
  d. Although Jean Toomer *has been* forgotten for years after his death, he *has been* recognized in more recent times as a central figure of the Harlem Renaissance.

Essay Questions

21. Death can be a dramatic moment in a literary work. Write an essay in which you compare and contrast the death of Granny in Katherine Anne Porter's "The Jilting of Granny Weatherall" with the death of the boy in Robert Frost's " 'Out, Out—.' " From what point of view do we see death in each of these works? What attitude toward death does each author express? What conclusions about the nature of life do these attitudes imply?

22. The images of *reaping* and of *night* reappear in a few of the poems of the Harlem Renaissance in this part. Bontemps's "A Black Man Talks of Reaping" weighs what he has sown and what his children reap. Cullen's "From the Dark Tower" begins, "We shall not always plant while others reap." Hughes writes, "Night coming tenderly / Black like me" ("Dream Variations"); Cullen writes, "The night whose sable breast relieves the stark, / White stars is no less lovely being dark" ("From the Dark Tower"). In an essay, explain why these two images are especially important to these poets, given the historical situation they faced.

23. Carl Sandburg said that there are "poets of the cloister and the quiet corner, of green fields and the earth serene in its changes." He contrasts these poets with those of "streets and struggles, of dust and combat . . . of plain folk living close to the hard earth. . . ." Write an essay in which you explain to which of these groups Sandburg, Frost, Hughes, and Toomer each belong—to "the poets of the cloister" or the poets of "streets and struggles." If you think one of these poets could be grouped in either group, explain why.

24. Some might argue that the writers in this part show an exceptional concern with the connections between past and present—with the role history or tradition plays in defining who we are today. Others might say that at least some of the writers in this part are more concerned with timeless truths—human realities that are always valid. Write an essay in which you support one of these ideas, using two works (or the works of two of the authors) in this part.

25. From Vermont to Mississippi, from the skyscrapers of New York City to the fields of the South, place plays an important role in the works of the writers in this part. Choose two authors, and explain the significance of a place in each of their works. You might consider, for instance, how living in a particular place defines a character's identity, and whether the character must "move beyond" or "settle into" this place. You might also consider whether certain places—Frost's Vermont, Hughes's "dusky rivers," or White's Manhattan—take on a special significance and come to designate more than just a geographical location.

Name _____ Date _____

"The Life You Save May Be Your Own" by Flannery O'Connor

Selection Test

Critical Reading

On the line, write the letter of the one best answer.

_____ 1. When Mr. Shiftlet meets the old woman and her daughter, the author's description
of him conveys the impression that he is most interested in the
a. chance to teach the daughter.
b. possibility of a job.
c. location of the farm.
d. car in the yard.

_____ 2. Mr. Shiftlet's statement that he has "a moral intelligence" is ironic because
a. the daughter cannot hear him speak.
b. he lacks a sense of morality in everything he does in the story.
c. neither the mother nor the daughter can understand his language.
d. he shows very little intelligence in the story.

_____ 3. Which of the following statements by the old woman is ironic?
a. " 'One that can't talk,' she continued, 'can't sass you back or use foul language.' "
b. " 'Are you married or are you single?' "
c. " 'And I wouldn't let no man have her but you because I seen you would do right.' "
d. " 'She can sweep the floor, cook, wash, feed the chickens, and hoe.' "

_____ 4. How are the old woman and Mr. Shiftlet similar?
a. Both are shrewd opportunists.
b. Both are unconcerned about Lucynell's future.
c. Both are hypocritical.
d. Both want to improve the property.

_____ 5. What does Mr. Shiftlet do to earn Mrs. Crater's trust?
a. He makes himself useful and teaches Lucynell a word.
b. He admires the sunset, and she figures that such a man must be trustworthy.
c. He expresses a liking for Lucynell.
d. He speaks of how he was raised, and Mrs. Crater respects his values.

_____ 6. What effect does the wedding have on Mr. Shiftlet?
a. He is momentarily happy.
b. He admits his mistakes.
c. He reveals more of his true nature.
d. He promises to change.

_____ 7. What is a reasonable prediction for a reader to make based on the following passage?

The old woman watched from a distance, secretly pleased. She was ravenous for
a son-in-law.

a. Mr. Shiftlet will fall in love with Lucynell.
b. The old woman will keep only the best interests of her daughter in mind.
c. The old woman will convince Mr. Shiftlet to marry her daughter.
d. The old woman will force Lucynell to learn to speak.

_____ 8. Based on the following passage, what might you predict will happen next in the story?

> "She [Lucynell] looks like and angel of Gawd," he murmured.
> "Hitchhiker," Mr. Shiftlet explained. "I can't wait. I got to make Tuscaloosa."

    a. He will leave Lucynell for good.
    b. He will pick up more hitchhikers
    c. He will meet Lucynell's mother in Tuscaloosa.
    d. He will stay with Lucynell despite his true feelings.

_____ 9. A grotesque character is
    a. a physically unattractive character.
    b. an unpleasant character.
    c. one who acts immorally or unlawfully.
    d. one who is dominated by some kind of obsession.

_____ 10. Which of the following statements made by Mr. Shiftlet reveals that he is a grotesque character?
    a. "I'd give a fortune to live where I could see me a sun do that every evening."
    b. "Nothing is like it used to be, lady. The world is almost rotten."
    c. "How you know my name ain't Aaron Sparks, lady . . .?"
    d. "Maybe the best I can tell you is, I'm a man . . ."

_____ 11. In what way is Mrs. Crater a grotesque character?
    a. in the way she is stingy with her money
    b. in the way she speaks
    c. in the way she dotes on her daughter
    d. in the way she keeps her farm

_____ 12. The climax of the story occurs when Mr. Shiftlet
    a. fixes the old car.
    b. teaches Lucynell to speak.
    c. marries Lucynell.
    d. leaves Lucynell in the diner.

_____ 13. Which of the following qualities does the hitchhiker at the end of the story represent?
    a. truthfulness
    b. evil
    c. innocence
    d. ingratitude

_____ 14. What is the story's thematic conflict?
    a. innocence versus experience
    b. belief versus action
    c. wealth versus poverty
    d. weakness versus strength

_____ 15. What lesson is the author trying to convey in this story?
    a. Actions speak louder than words.
    b. The meek shall inherit the earth.
    c. Kindness to strangers goes unrewarded.
    d. Life is a gamble.

Vocabulary and Grammar

On the line, write the letter of the one best answer.

____ 16. The old woman's home is described as *desolate* because
   a. the house is in a small clearing in a forest.
   b. the house and buildings are shabby looking.
   c. it is hard to find.
   d. it suits her and her daughter.

____ 17. The figure walking up the road *listed*, or ____.
   a. counted
   b. observed shrewdly
   c. tilted
   d. strolled

____ 18. Someone who is *morose* is ____.
   a. gloomy
   b. eager
   c. scheming
   d. seriously ill

____ 19. Which item restates the following sentence correctly in the subjunctive mood?

   The mother gazed at her daughter as if she was an angel.

   a. The mother gazed at her daughter as though she was an angel.
   b. The mother gazed at her daughter believing her to be an angel.
   c. The mother gazed at her daughter like an angel.
   d. The mother gazed at her daughter as if she were an angel.

____ 20. Which of the following sentences is in the subjunctive mood?
   a. I wish you would decide what you want for dinner.
   b. We were expecting better behavior from Mr. Shiftlet.
   c. Mrs. Crater asks that he take good care of Lucynell.
   d. If anyone knows her whereabouts, please let me know.

Essay Questions

21. All three of the characters in O'Connor's story are grotesque in some way. Think carefully about the old woman. Consider her surroundings, her appearance, and her behavior. Then, in an essay, explain how O'Connor reveals the woman as grotesque. Remember to consider anything bizarre about her that might be the result of an obsession of some sort.

22. Mr. Shiftlet's character is a dominating one. He seems to have a number of different sides. Examine this character. Is he a con man? Is he sincere? Does he realize he is occasionally nasty? Do you think he takes pleasure in fixing up the old woman's farm, or does he do it only to get her car? Did you ever find yourself almost liking him? If so, what did you like and at what point in the story? In an essay, address these questions and draw conclusions about what motivates Mr. Shiftlet.

23. "The Life You Save May Be Your Own" has a symbolic meaning as well as a literal one. From the moment Mr. Shiftlet's figure forms "a crooked cross," the story contains symbols that add depth. The human heart, the 1928 or '29 Ford, the hitchhiker—these are a few of the elements with symbolic significance. Write an essay in which you point out and interpret at least three of the symbols in this story. You may use the symbols identified here or choose others. Explain clearly your interpretation of the symbols.

"**The First Seven Years**" by Bernard Malamud

Selection Test

Critical Reading

On the line, write the letter of the one best answer.

_____ 1. Which of the following phrases is the best description of Feld's relationship with his daughter through most of the story?
a. proud and boastful of her accomplishments
b. alienated, but attempting to build a better relationship with her
c. understanding and appreciative of her uniqueness
d. loving, but disappointed by her decisions

_____ 2. Which of the following statements illustrates how a reader might identify with Miriam?
a. I, too, am devoted to my parents and look to them for guidance.
b. My parents mean well, but they really need to trust me and let me make my own decisions.
c. Once I went on a first date and had a really terrific time.
d. My greatest dream is to attend college and read the classics.

_____ 3. What happens when Max enters the shop and asks Feld to repair some shoes?
a. Sobel sees Max, grabs his coat, and storms out.
b. Max sees Miriam's picture and is immediately taken with her.
c. Feld trades the repair work for some accounting help.
d. Feld convinces Max to ask Miriam for a date.

_____ 4. Which of the following does Max represent to Feld?
a. a chance to improve his own life
b. a way to realize a dream
c. an escape from a life of hard work
d. a professional with solid values

_____ 5. How does the author characterize Max in this story?
a. unattractive, but sensitive
b. poor, but sincere
c. unattractive and uninteresting
d. intelligent and interesting

_____ 6. What can the reader infer about Miriam by the way she responds to her father's attempt to match her with Max?
a. She is resentful toward her father for trying to run her life.
b. She is willing to experience new things but makes up her own mind.
c. She is too young and idealistic to know what is good for her.
d. She is enthusiastic and appreciative of her father's concern for her.

_____ 7. What experience would help a reader identify with Feld and some of his issues with Sobel?
a. being an employee
b. being a matchmaker
c. being a shoemaker
d. being a small business owner

_____ 8. Which of the following statements best describes the relationship between Feld and Sobel?
   a. Feld depends on Sobel but does not regard him highly.
   b. Feld feels grateful for Sobel's help but is irritated by his work habits.
   c. Sobel works for Feld for very little money because of his gratitude toward Feld.
   d. Sobel relies on Feld's good nature to keep his job.

_____ 9. Why is Feld angry when he first realizes that Sobel loves Miriam?
   a. He feels deceived by Sobel.
   b. He knows Max doesn't have a chance with Miriam.
   c. He feels deceived by Miriam.
   d. He is embarrassed by his visit to Sobel's room.

_____ 10. Feld's epiphany in the story probably leads him to acknowledge that
   a. education is not as important as love.
   b. Miriam will make her own choices about her life.
   c. Sobel and Miriam are more intelligent than he realized.
   d. his dreams are based on his own insecurities.

_____ 11. At the end of the story, Feld begins to soften toward Sobel. This occurs because Feld recognizes that
   a. he needs Sobel to work for him.
   b. Sobel would be a good husband for Miriam.
   c. Sobel deeply loves his daughter.
   d. Sobel is just like him.

_____ 12. Which of the following lines from the story hints at how Feld feels following his epiphany?
   a. "The room was quiet."
   b. "Feld rose and left."
   c. "He went slowly down the stairs . . ."
   d. ". . . once outside, . . . he walked with a stronger stride."

_____ 13. Based on the information in the story, what can a reader reasonably predict about Miriam?
   a. She will probably date Max again.
   b. She will probably go to college.
   c. She will probably marry Sobel.
   d. She will probably lose interest in books.

_____ 14. What is Sobel doing at the end of the story?
   a. working out his anger by pounding on the repaired last
   b. working steadily toward the time when he can approach Miriam
   c. returning to Feld's shop because it's the only job he can get
   d. taking pity on Feld because of his poor health

_____ 15. "The First Seven Years" is primarily about
   a. difficulties in communication.
   b. misunderstandings between generations.
   c. the necessity of practical dreams.
   d. the reexamination of cherished values.

Vocabulary and Grammar

On the line, write the letter of the one best answer.

____ 16. The word *who* or *whom* is missing from the following sentence. Choose the answer that correctly identifies the missing word and states the word's function in the sentence.

> Feld hoped his daughter, _____ he so loved, would have a better life than his own.

   a. *who;* subject of *loved*
   b. *who;* object of *hoped*
   c. *whom;* subject of *hoped*
   d. *whom;* object of *loved*

____ 17. Feld wants more for Miriam than to meet *illiterate* shipping clerks, people who are
   a. not wealthy.
   b. uneducated.
   c. unable to read or write.
   d. part of the working class.

____ 18. In which of the following sentences is *who* or *whom* used correctly?
   a. Sobel was a fellow countryman whom Feld felt he could trust.
   b. Miriam, whom had a job, preferred the independence of her own income.
   c. Max was a neighbor who Feld thought to be very respectable.
   d. Feld was the sort of man whom needed to think things through.

____ 19. The assistant who replaced Sobel can be seen as *unscrupulous* because he
   a. was less skilled than Sobel.
   b. was not restrained by ideas of right and wrong.
   c. was employed only for a short time.
   d. did not speak to Feld.

____ 20. Sobel worked with *diligence*, which means he worked _____.
   a. constantly and carefully
   b. with eagerness
   c. with great skill
   d. slowly

Essay Questions

21. Feld wants his daughter to have a more comfortable life than his own. Miriam, on the other hand, doesn't seem to be complaining. She has chosen "independence," which means she has taken a job instead of committing herself to being supported by her father while she goes to college. In an essay, explain how Miriam's choice gives her independence. What does her choice provide for her that her father's plan does not? What would Feld's plan to send her to college provide for Miriam that her own plan does not? Given that Miriam's father *can* afford to send her to college, do you think she made the best decision?

22. "The First Seven Years" is told from Feld's point of view. This helps readers feel well acquainted with him. In an essay, describe the character of Feld, his hopes and dreams, and how they change. How does the story build to his epiphany? What clues does the story hold to indicate that the answer to his dreams for Miriam may be right in front of him?

23. Everyone has a different idea of what it takes to be happy and successful. In "The First Seven Years," each character has slightly different ideals and goals. In an essay, analyze what is revealed about Feld, Sobel, Max, and Miriam. Explain what each character's actions indicate about that person's notion of what it takes to be happy and successful. With whose notion do you agree most? In your essay, consider attitudes toward love, education, and wealth.

"The Brown Chest" by John Updike

Selection Test

Critical Reading

On the line, write the letter of the one best answer.

_____ 1. "The Brown Chest" is best described as a story about
   a. a family heirloom.
   b. a man's changing relationship with his son.
   c. a man's changing attitude toward his heritage.
   d. how a man deals with his mother's death.

_____ 2. At what point does the main character discover that his own drawings and report cards have been added to the chest?
   a. after sneaking past the guest bedroom in the upstairs hall
   b. just before the move to the second house
   c. after his mother's death
   d. when Morna opens the chest

_____ 3. When the main character is a boy, the chest is physically on the edges of his life—in the upstairs hall and, later, in the attic. How is this symbolic of the man's attitude?
   a. He didn't really know what was inside and didn't want to know.
   b. He was extremely curious about the chest.
   c. He often wanted to put his own belongings in the chest.
   d. He had strict instructions from his mother never to go near or open the chest.

_____ 4. Which features of the following sentence particularly help a reader break it down?

   His children, adults all, came from afar and joined him in the house, where their grandmother had at last died, and divided up the furniture—some for them to carry away, some for the local auctioneer to sell, and some for him, the only sur-vivor of that first house, with its long halls and haunted places, to keep and to as-similate to his own house, hundreds of miles away.

   a. It has ten commas.
   b. It has a dash and repeats the word *some* three times.
   c. It has a reference to another scene from earlier in the story.
   d. It has a reference to the main character's present residence.

_____ 5. What detail about the chest is mentioned four times and seems to have made a strong impression on the main character?
   a. its contents   b. its construction   c. its smell   d. its value

_____ 6. In what part of the story does this passage reveal the main character's feelings?

   The chest went down and down, into the past, and he hated the feeling of that well of time, with its sweet deep smell of things unstirring, waiting, taking on the moldy flavor of time, not moving unless somebody touched them.

   a. the first part, in the first house
   b. the second part, in the country house
   c. the period following his mother's death
   d. the end of the story, in the barn with Gordon and Morna

_____ 7. What words in the following passage contribute to the atmosphere of tediousness surrounding the men's work?

For days they lived together, eating takeout food, poisoning mice and trapping cats, moving from crowded cellar to jammed attic like sick men changing position in bed, overwhelmed by decisions, by accumulated possessions . . .

a. eating, poisoning, trapping

b. together, changing, decisions

c. crowded, overwhelmed, oppression

d. days, moving, possessions

_____ 8. What was Updike's main purpose in referring to "auburn hair" here?

Her headscarf had slipped back, exposing auburn hair glinting above the vapor of her breath, in evanescent present time.

a. He wanted to add more visual details to the scene.

b. He wanted to show how different Morna was from the family.

c. He wanted to hint that Morna, like her name, had a Celtic background.

d. By giving Morna the same color hair as that from the 1919 haircut, he ties her in with the family.

_____ 9. What would be the best strategy for breaking down this long sentence?

Delicately but fearlessly, she lifted the lid, and out swooped, with the same vivid-ness that had astonished and alarmed his nostrils as a child, the sweetish deep cedary smell, undiminished, cedar and camphor and paper and cloth, the smell of family, family without end.

a. Pay attention to details.

b. Pay attention to punctuation.

c. Look for parallel structures.

d. Look for transition words.

_____ 10. What word best identifies the atmosphere Updike creates in this passage?

A little box labelled in his mother's handwriting "Haircut July 1919" held, wrapped in tissue paper, coils of auburn hair startlingly silky to the touch.

a. ridiculing   b. disrespectful   c. grieving   d. sentimental

_____ 11. What is the significance of the main character's misreading the map and causing Gordon and himself to get lost?

a. Getting lost causes them to have a terrible argument.

b. Gordon proves his skill at navigating in heavy traffic on unfamiliar roads.

c. It makes Gordon wonder about his father's eyesight.

d. It causes the main character to realize that everyone makes mistakes; perhaps Gordon's lack of a job means he was just "temporarily lost."

_____ 12. How does the main character feel about having his mother's furniture in his barn?

a. He is comforted by remembrances of his childhood.

b. He avoids it; it seems cheap and useless.

c. He longs to get it out of the barn and put it in his own house.

d. He regrets that he doesn't have a safer place to keep it.

_____ 13. In what way does the story change when Morna is introduced?

a. The main character becomes full of bitter despair for his son's future.

b. The main character becomes confused about his attachment to his mother's belongings.

c. The atmosphere is for the first time sentimental.

d. The atmosphere becomes positive and hopeful.

_____ 14. What does the man seem to realize at the very end of the story?

a. His son is going to marry Morna.

b. He would rather keep the furniture than let Gordon take it.

c. The chest represents the history as well as the future of his family.

d. The chest just needed someone like Morna to appreciate it.

_____ 15. Once you break down a long sentence, reinforce the important ideas by
  a. copying the sentence in a notebook.
  b. paraphrasing the sentence.
  c. summarizing the sentence.
  d. removing all the unnecessary phrases and clauses.

Vocabulary and Grammar

On the line, write the letter of the one best answer.

_____ 16. The end of the story gives the impression that Gordon will be able to *assimilate* his grandmother's furniture. This means he will
  a. blend it in with what he has.
  b. replace everything he currently owns.
  c. repair and refinish the furniture.
  d. have furniture made that looks just like his grandmother's.

_____ 17. Choose the phrase that is most similar in meaning to the word *egregious*.
  a. very talkative   c. hopelessly lost
  b. remarkably bad   d. inappropriately dressed

_____ 18. The highway on which the men became lost was described as *unfathomable* because
  a. the older man remembered traveling on it as a boy.
  b. it went in the wrong direction.
  c. traffic was so heavy that they couldn't move.
  d. it was impossible to figure out.

_____ 19. Which of the following sentences begins with an adverb clause?
  a. When he lifted the lid of the chest, an amazing smell rushed out.
  b. He found the place in the chest lid where a split had occurred.
  c. The map-reading blunder righted the balance between them.
  d. And so on and so on, until he couldn't bear it and asked his son to help him carry the chest.

_____ 20. What word or phrase does the italicized adverb clause modify, and what does the clause tell about that word or phrase?

  When the roof was being repaired, the whole space was thrown open to the weather.

  a. *space*; in what condition   c. *was thrown open*; when
  b. *weather*; what   d. *open*; how much

Essay Questions

21. What attitudes toward the brown chest does the main character exhibit throughout the story? In an essay, describe the man's attitude at various points in his life, explaining why you think his attitude changes.

22. The main character's younger son, Gordon, enters the story at two points. First, he helps his father clear out his grandmother's house. Later, he comes to claim some of his grandmother's furniture. In an essay, compare and contrast the atmosphere of the story during the two scenes in which Gordon is present.

23. Recall how the main character's mother is described, and how the main character views her when he is a young boy. What feelings about this mother-son relationship does Updike create? What details generate those feelings? Then consider the man's relationship with his son. How do they act toward each other? What atmosphere does this father-son relationship create? In an essay, explain how Updike creates feelings about relationships.

"Hawthorne" by Robert Lowell
"Gold Glade" by Robert Penn Warren
"The Light Comes Brighter" by Theodore Roethke
"Traveling Through the Dark" by William Stafford
"The Adamant" by Theodore Roethke

Selection Test

Critical Reading

On the line, write the letter of the one best answer.

____ 1. Based on the poem "Hawthorne," which words best describe Hawthorne?
    a. brilliant and excitable
    b. solitary and meditative
    c. bitter and resentful
    d. innocent and happy

____ 2. Lowell's diction—*lazy, aged, stunted, dismal*, for example—in the first three stanzas of "Hawthorne"
    a. explains the impact of Hawthorne's writing.
    b. contrasts Salem with Boston.
    c. reveals Hawthorne's genius.
    d. depicts Salem as a decaying town.

____ 3. What is the theme of "Hawthorne"?
    a. Hawthorne led a lonely, unhappy life.
    b. Salem stunted Hawthorne's literary ability.
    c. Hawthorne's surroundings had a great effect on his writing.
    d. Hawthorne was a mysterious figure.

____ 4. The speaker of "Gold Glade" cherishes his memory of the glade because
    a. it represents a place of extraordinary beauty.
    b. he came upon the glade unexpectedly.
    c. no one else knows about the glade.
    d. fall is his favorite season.

____ 5. How does Warren's style in "Gold Glade" mirror the poem's theme?
    a. The simple, everyday language is appropriate for a poem about nature.
    b. The breathless tone of the first few stanzas underscores the theme of wandering and discovery.
    c. The varying rhythm and rhyme scheme reflect the recklessness of youth.
    d. The poem's mournful tone emphasizes the speaker's longing for the gold glade.

____ 6. Which is the best paraphrase of these lines from "Gold Glade"?

    Wandering, in autumn, the woods of boyhood,
    Where cedar, black, thick, rode the ridge

    a. When I was a boy, I wandered through the woods.
    b. I remember wandering through the cedar forest.
    c. On a fall day in my youth, I wandered through woods where cedars covered the ridge.
    d. A boy went to the woods in autumn and saw cedars on the ridge.

_____ 7. What is the best paraphrase of this line from "The Light Comes Brighter"?

> The ovenbird will match the vocal brook.

   a. The ovenbird will hide in the water.
   b. The ovenbird will take a swim.
   c. The ovenbirds are the color of the water.
   d. The ovenbirds will start to sing.

_____ 8. Which words best describe the speaker of "The Light Comes Brighter"?
   a. peaceful and expectant   c. knowledgeable and appreciative
   b. discouraged and unhappy   d. detached and scientific

_____ 9. Which of the following lines from "The Light Comes Brighter" is the best example of formal, poetic diction, or the least like everyday diction?
   a. "The sun cuts deep into the heavy drift"
   b. "The water stored in narrow pools escapes"
   c. "Soon field and wood will wear an April look"
   d. "The leafy mind, that long was tightly furled"

_____ 10. The subject of "The Adamant" is _____.
   a. machinery   c. truth
   b. spring   d. tools

_____ 11. What is the best paraphrase of this stanza from "The Adamant"?

> Compression cannot break
> A center so congealed;
> The tool can chip no flake:
> The core lies sealed.

   a. Nothing can penetrate the heart of a hard substance.
   b. No force can destroy an ultimate truth.
   c. Truth will always remain.
   d. In the end, the truth will be known.

_____ 12. What special circumstance creates a dilemma for the speaker of "Traveling Through the Dark"?
   a. The deer he finds is injured but still alive.
   b. The dead deer he finds has a living fawn inside it.
   c. He struck the deer accidentally.
   d. He has nowhere to deposit the deer's body.

_____ 13. What does "Traveling Through the Dark" reveal about the current relationship between humans and the natural world?
   a. Humans have a reckless disregard for nature.
   b. Humans have an inherent superiority over nature.
   c. Humans and nature have found a way to coexist.
   d. Nature has a purity that humans no longer possess.

_____ 14. Which elements of style have the greatest impact on the meaning of the following lines from "Traveling Through the Dark"?

> I thought hard for us all—my only swerving—,
> then pushed her over the edge into the river.

   a. diction and sound devices
   b. capitalization and line length
   c. punctuation and diction
   d. tone and rhythm

Vocabulary and Grammar

On the line, write the letter of the one best answer.

____ 15. For the following pair of related words, choose the lettered pair of words that best expresses a similar relationship.

        brooding : meditation

    a. singing : tenor   c. evaluating : analysis
    b. jumping : energetic   d. freezing : thaw

____ 16. Where would a traveler most likely encounter a *declivity*?
    a. at sea   c. on the plains
    b. in the desert   d. in the hills

____ 17. Which is the best synonym for *vestiges*?
    a. footprints   c. apparel
    b. photographs   d. dizziness

____ 18. The ____ of crows sounds throughout the valley.
    a. melody   c. screeches
    b. call   d. word

____ 19. All the weary ____ of the day ____ measured on the glowing clock dial.
    a. hour; is   c. hours; is
    b. hour; are   d. hours; are

____ 20. Late-night ____ on the canyon road ____ to avoid deer.
    a. driver; swerve   c. drivers; swerve
    b. driver; swerves   d. drivers; swerves

Essay Questions

21. Each of these poets writes of people, places, or experiences that triggered meditation or inspiration. Which of these poems was most meaningful to you? In a brief essay, explain how a particular poem and poet led you to inspiration or meditation. Include a description of the thinking or action the poem prompted in you.

22. In these poems, Lowell, Warren, Roethke, and Stafford all explore their sense of emerging identity. In your opinion, which poet expresses this idea most meaningfully? Write an essay in which you describe how the poet's work reflects his self-exploration.

23. A poet's style can affect the way in which readers respond to his or her poetry. Choose two poems from the selections—one whose style you most admire and one whose style you least admire. Write an essay in which you compare and contrast the two styles, and explain how the style affects your response to the poems. Support your opinion with specific examples from the poems.

Name _____ Date _____

"Average Waves in Unprotected Waters" by Anne Tyler

Selection Test

Critical Reading

On the line, write the letter of the one best answer.

_____ 1. Which of the following details builds suspense in the opening scene of the story?
   a. "She felt too slight and frail, too wispy for all she had to do today."
   b. "He hardly ever changed his expression."
   c. "She had to struggle to stuff his arms in the sleeves."
   d. "He came, dragging out every step."

_____ 2. Which words best characterize Bet?
   a. indecisive and moody
   b. insightful and creative
   c. sentimental and weak
   d. strong and enduring

_____ 3. What is ironic about Mrs. Puckett's gift of cookies to Arnold?
   a. Bet knows he will get messy if he eats them.
   b. Although they are a goodbye gift, Arnold doesn't realize it.
   c. Mrs. Puckett still treats Arnold like a child.
   d. Arnold dislikes peanut-butter cookies.

_____ 4. What does the following line foreshadow?

   Small though he was, he was strong, wiry; he was getting to be too much for her.

   a. Without proper care, Arnold will run away from home.
   b. As Arnold grows older, Bet will need others to care for him.
   c. Arnold will forget Bet once he is at the hospital.
   d. Bet will be glad when Arnold is out of the house.

_____ 5. What is the writer's purpose in describing the long train trip to Parkinsville?
   a. to reveal Arnold's behavior
   b. to allow time for flashbacks
   c. to build suspense about the trip's purpose
   d. to pose questions about Bet's life

_____ 6. Which of the following episodes from the story is an example of a flashback?
   a. dressing Arnold for the train
   b. Arnold's catnaps as a baby
   c. Arnold's laughter at the woman who sneaked onto the train
   d. the walk down the hallway of the institution

_____ 7. What effect does Bet's flashback about Arnold's father have on the reader?
   a. It explains how Bet ended up alone with Arnold.
   b. It shows that Bet's parents were right about him.
   c. It suggests the loneliness of Bet's present life.
   d. It stresses the theme of abandonment.

_____ 8. The flashback about Bet trying to learn to bodysurf shows that
    a. Bet is a person with varied interests.
    b. Arnold's disability stems from his mother's problems.
    c. Bet blames herself for Arnold's condition.
    d. Bet has always been unyielding when faced with a challenge.

_____ 9. What is Bet's attitude toward her own life?
    a. bitterness
    b. anger
    c. resignation
    d. joy

_____ 10. Why is Bet so upset that the train is late?
    a. She needs to get back to work as soon as possible.
    b. She particularly dislikes waiting in train stations.
    c. She doesn't want to think about what she has done.
    d. She is bored because she doesn't have anything to do.

_____ 11. The main conflict in the story is an
    a. external conflict between Bet and Arnold.
    b. external conflict between Bet and the institution.
    c. internal conflict within Arnold.
    d. internal conflict within Bet.

_____ 12. Which passage foreshadows Bet's leaving Arnold at the hospital?
    a. "At the train station, she bought the tickets and then a pack of Wrigley's spearmint gum."
    b. "'Listen,' she said, 'I want you to wait for me right in the driveway. I don't want you to go on away.'"
    c. "He had never slept well, not ever, not even as a baby."
    d. "She opened the door and nudged Arnold out ahead of her."

_____ 13. Which character exists only in flashback, not in the stream of the story's main events?
    a. Bet
    b. Arnold
    c. Avery
    d. Mrs. Puckett

_____ 14. Which of the following best summarizes the theme?
    a. Even a decision made out of love can be very painful.
    b. A single mother does the best she can with her resources.
    c. For a poor person, life is unfair.
    d. A child with disabilities need not be institutionalized.

Vocabulary and Grammar

On the line, write the letter of the one best answer.

_____ 15. Which word best describes the *opposite* of Bet's physical appearance?
    a. orthopedic   c. staunch
    b. stocky   d. transparent

_____ 16. Bet and Arnold walked _____ down the stairs, the suitcase banging _____ against Bet's shins.
    a. slow; heavy   c. slowly; heavy
    b. slow; heavily   d. slowly; heavily

_____ 17. Which item or object on the train ride would be *transparent*?
   a. train window
   b. stick of gum
   c. Arnold's suitcase
   d. cookie

_____ 18. In the taxi, Bet wept _____ because she felt _____ about leaving Arnold.
   a. uncontrollable; bad
   b. uncontrollable; badly
   c. uncontrollably; bad
   d. uncontrollably; badly

_____ 19. Bet looked _____ when she arrived at the station, asking _____ about the train schedule.
   a. terrible; frantic
   b. terrible; frantically
   c. terribly; frantically
   d. terribly; frantic

_____ 20. The short, _____ man wore _____ shoes.
   a. transparent; staunch
   b. staunch; orthopedic
   c. orthopedic; transparent
   d. stocky; orthopedic

Essay Questions

21. Tyler uses foreshadowing to build suspense in her story. At what point did you realize the purpose of Bet and Arnold's trip? What instances of foreshadowing served as clues? Write a brief essay in which you explain how foreshadowing helped build suspense in the story.

22. Tyler interrupts the chronology of her story with a flashback in which Bet remembers her childhood, her unhappy marriage, and her solitary years that brought her to the present moment on the train. What effect does this flashback have on the story? In a brief essay, explain what this flashback adds to the story and to your understanding of its events and characters.

23. Contemporary fiction seldom ends with a neat resolution of the problems raised. Anne Tyler's "Average Waves in Unprotected Waters" ends with Bet, the protagonist, expecting that life thereafter will be "just something on a stage, for her to sit back and watch." Write an essay in which you predict what life for Bet will be like with Arnold at Parkins State Hospital. Will she be happier? Will she remarry? Use your imagination in foretelling a new life for Bet. Also, in making your predictions, use the information you already know about Bet from the story.

from *The Names* by N. Scott Momaday
"**Mint Snowball**" by Naomi Shihab Nye
"**Suspended**" by Joy Harjo

Selection Test

Critical Reading

On the line, write the letter of the one best answer.

____ 1. The gift of a horse was an important moment in Momaday's life because he
  a. longed to travel far from home.
  b. came to view the horse as a link to his Kiowa heritage.
  c. won many races on the horse.
  d. was a skilled horseman.

____ 2. Which words best describe the young Momaday?
  a. cautious and intelligent
  b. reckless and wild
  c. frugal and timid
  d. adventurous and determined

____ 3. Which experience might best help a modern teenager relate to Momaday's experiences with Pecos?
  a. spending a weekend at a ranch
  b. watching a movie about the Southwest
  c. restoring a used car
  d. reading one of Momaday's books

____ 4. Which line from Momaday's essay is taken from an anecdote?
  a. "On the back of my horse I had a different view of the world."
  b. "Such a journey must begin in the nick of time, on the spur of the moment . . ."
  c. "When the signal was given I should then have to get up on my horse while the others were breaking away . . ."
  d. "I do not know how long Pecos lived."

____ 5. Why does Momaday believe that "it may be that in [Pecos's] last days an image of me like thought shimmered in his brain"?
  a. Momaday felt a strong bond with Pecos.
  b. Momaday saw Pecos not long before the horse died.
  c. Pecos appeared to Momaday in a vision.
  d. Pecos resented Momaday for selling him.

____ 6. Which sentence best summarizes the theme of Momaday's essay?
  a. Journeys of discovery must be made alone.
  b. Life's lessons, though difficult, are worth learning.
  c. One must persevere to succeed in life.
  d. To know one's true identity, a person must discover his or her heritage.

____ 7. What happened to the Mint Snowball recipe?
  a. Nye adapted it.
  b. Nye's grandfather stole it from her great-grandfather.
  c. Nye's mother kept a secret copy.
  d. Nye's great-grandfather sold it.

_____ 8. What is the effect of Nye's anecdote about her mother trying to re-create the recipe for the Mint Snowball?
    a. It adds an entertaining element to the essay.
    b. It introduces dramatic irony.
    c. It symbolizes Nye's sense of loss and displacement.
    d. It explains the importance of the recipe to Nye's family.

_____ 9. What does Nye mean when she states near the end of her essay that "there is something missing"?
    a. Her recipe for the Mint Snowball lacks a certain ingredient.
    b. She feels out of place in modern society.
    c. She cannot explain her feelings of discontentment.
    d. She wishes her family members were closer to one another.

_____ 10. Which would be the best strategy to help a reader relate to Nye's experience?
    a. recalling the taste or smell of a favorite food from childhood
    b. remembering an anecdote about a grandparent
    c. visiting an old-fashioned drugstore
    d. analyzing Nye's use of symbols

_____ 11. What is significant about the first time Harjo heard jazz?
    a. It was the first music she ever heard.
    b. She was a musically gifted child.
    c. Her father was a jazz musician.
    d. It opened up a new world to her.

_____ 12. A reader can best relate to Harjo's experience with jazz by recalling
    a. the moment when he or she first realized that the world is full of possibility.
    b. a lullaby from childhood.
    c. the sights and sounds of driving in a car.
    d. a childhood hero.

_____ 13. Harjo relates her anecdote about hearing the jazz trumpeter to
    a. explain her love of music.
    b. share an amusing story.
    c. make a point about self-discovery.
    d. critique a musical genre.

_____ 14. How did jazz affect Harjo's view of the world?
    a. She realized that people can be flawed.
    b. She longed to learn more about her heritage.
    c. She felt trapped by circumstance.
    d. She understood the relationship between music and art.

Vocabulary and Grammar

On the line, write the letter of the one best answer.

_____ 15. Momaday's first view of the world from horseback was _____.
    a. supple
    b. concocted
    c. flamboyant
    d. revelatory

____ 16. What is the meaning of the italicized word in the following sentence?

The Kiowas owned more horses per *capita* than any other tribe on the Great Plains.

 a. capital
 b. person
 c. farm
 d. region

____ 17. Nye relates vivid memories of the _____ her great-grandfather _____.
 a. confluence; supple
 b. elixir; replicate
 c. flamboyant; concocted
 d. elixir; concocted

____ 18. Harjo recalls the smell of aftershave that _____ her father's car.
 a. concocted
 b. permeated
 c. replicated
 d. congregated

____ 19. In which item does a bracketed word indicate a word omitted from an elliptical clause?
 a. My mother had watched my grandfather make the syrup so often she thought she could replicate [it].
 b. My mother had watched my grandfather make [the] syrup so often she thought she could replicate it.
 c. My mother had watched my grandfather make the syrup so often [that] she thought she could replicate it.
 d. My mother had watched my grandfather make the syrup so [often] she thought she could replicate it.

____ 20. Which sentence contains an elliptical clause?
 a. "It was around the time I acquired language . . ."
 b. "She wrote down what she did."
 c. "It was appropriate that I should make a long journey."
 d. "I could feel my horse under me . . ."

Essay Questions

21. The childhood experiences these writers recall happened in different places many years ago. How can you relate to their experiences? Choose the one writer whose experience you most strongly related to your own. In an essay, explain how you connected to the writer's experience and how this experience helped you understand the author's ideas.

22. Momaday, Nye, and Harjo use anecdotes in their essays to make points about larger issues. In your opinion, which anecdote most effectively conveys the writer's idea? Write an essay in which you analyze the anecdote and explain how it is an effective tool for conveying the writer's message.

23. Writers can use anecdotes to establish mood quickly. Of the anecdotes in these selections, which struck you most forcefully with its ability to set or change the mood of the essay? Write a brief essay in which you examine the effect of this anecdote on the piece's mood and overall meaning.

Name _____ Date _____

Selection Test

Critical Reading

On the line, write the letter of the one best answer.

_____ 1. "Everyday Use" is the story of
    a. a young woman's return home.
    b. a house that burns down.
    c. a new marriage.
    d. a young man meeting his inlaws.

_____ 2. Maggie looks forward to Dee's visit with
    a. anticipation and confidence.
    b. worry and fear.
    c. excitement and scorn.
    d. nervousness and awe.

_____ 3. The story is set in a
    a. poor rural area.
    b. poor city neighboorhood.
    c. wealthy country home.
    d. middle-class suburb.

_____ 4. Why is Maggie timid and insecure?
    a. She knows that her mother loves Dee more.
    b. She grew up in poverty.
    c. Her mother gives away her possessions.
    d. She was scarred by a fire.

_____ 5. Dee showed her love for her family by
    a. asking for family heirlooms.
    b. reading to them.
    c. introducing her husband to them.
    d. changing her name to reflect her African roots.

_____ 6. Why doesn't Dee bring her friends home?
    a. She does not like her family.
    b. Her friends embarrass her.
    c. She is ashamed of her poverty.
    d. She has no friends.

_____ 7. Which words best describe Wangero?
    a. generous and shy
    b. homely and shy
    c. stylish and shallow
    d. caring and respectful

_____ 8. The narrator says Dee would prefer her to have "skin like an uncooked barley pancake," meaning
    a. moist and smooth.
    b. light in color.
    c. soft and sticky.
    d. fresh smelling.

___ 9. The narrator calls Dee "Miss" Wangero to show that Dee is
    a. more important than she is.
    b. an older woman.
    c. arrogant and distant from her.
    d. a stranger to her.

___ 10. What motivates the narrator to give Maggie the quilts?
    a. Wangero does not like them.
    b. Maggie knows how to make them.
    c. Maggie is more deserving than her sister.
    d. Maggie wants them more than her sister does.

___ 11. What do the specific details in this passage reveal about Maggie?

> It was Grandma Dee and Big Dee who taught her [Maggie] how to quilt herself. She stood there with her scarred hands hidden in the folds of her skirt. She looked at her sister with something like fear but she wasn't mad at her.

    a. Maggie has no feeling for the quilts.
    b. Maggie is afraid of her sister.
    c. Maggie is a needy person who depends upon her mother and sister.
    d. Maggie accepts the hardships life has handed her.

___ 12. What do the specific details in this passage reveal about Dee (Wangero)?

> After dinner Dee (Wangero) went to the trunk at the foot of my bed and started rifling through it. . . . Out came Wangero with two quilts. . . . "Mama," Wangero said sweet as a bird. "Can I have these old quilts?"

    a. Dee is a considerate and loving daughter.
    b. Dee brashly goes after what she wants.
    c. Dee respects her mother's privacy.
    d. Dee has very fond memories of her grandmother's quilts.

___ 13. What do the specific details in this passage reveal about the narrator's relationship with each of her daughters?

> I did something I never had done before: hugged Maggie to me, then dragged her on into the room, snatched the quilts out of Miss Wangero's hands and dumped them into Maggie's lap.

    a. The narrator loves Maggie's faith and is brave enough herself to challenge Dee's bossy, spoiled behavior.
    b. The narrator pities Maggie, but respects Dee, who has left home to make something of herself.
    c. The narrator loves Dee more than Maggie.
    d. The narrator is afraid of "Miss Wangero," who bosses both Maggie and the narrator.

___ 14. Why does Dee want the churn top?
    a. Uncle Buddy whittled it.
    b. She has fond memories of churning butter.
    c. She believes the churn top is a valuable heirloom.
    d. She wants a memento from her childhood.

Vocabulary and Grammar

On the line, write the letter of the one best answer.

____ 15. The word *furtive* means ____.
     a. honest   b. sneaky   c. open   d. quiet

____ 16. The word or phrase most nearly opposite in meaning to the word *oppress* is ____.
     a. hire   b. ignore   c. free   d. enslave

____ 17. The word *doctrines* means ____.
     a. honorary degrees
     b. visiting teachers or professors
     c. meek personalities
     d. beliefs or rules that are taught

____ 18. What is lacking in the sentence fragment "Dee next"?
     I. subject
     II. verb
     III. subject and verb
     IV. a complete thought

     a. I   b. II   c. III   d. II and IV

____ 19. Which of the following groups of words from "Everyday Use" is a sentence fragment?
     I. "But she will never bring her friends."
     II. "Nervous girls who never laughed."
     III. "A dress so loud it hurts my eyes."
     IV. "She's dead."

     a. I   b. II   c. II and III   d. I and IV

____ 20. Which of the following groups of words from "Everyday Use" is a sentence fragment?
     a. "I looked at her hard."
     b. "This was Maggie's portion."
     c. "You just don't understand."
     d. "But a real smile, not scared."

Essay Questions

21. Walker uses specific details to describe the narrator, Dee, and Maggie. These details also illustrate the differences among these three characters. In an essay, analyze the physical, emotional, and intellectual differences between the narrator and her two daughters. Support your answer with descriptive details from "Everyday Use."

22. When the narrator informs Dee that the quilts were promised to Maggie, "for when she marries John Thomas," Dee exclaims, "Maggie can't appreciate these quilts! She'd probably be backward enough to put them to everyday use." In an essay, explain why you agree or disagree with Dee's statement. Use details from "Everyday Use" to support your response.

23. In an essay, analyze what motivates Dee's interest in her heritage. Compare and contrast Dee's motivations with Maggie's knowledge of specific stories and details about their heritage. How does their appreciation of their heritage differ?

from *The Woman Warrior* by Maxine Hong Kingston

Selection Test

Critical Reading

On the line, write the letter of the one best answer.

_____ 1. This selection from *The Woman Warrior* focuses mainly on the personal impressions of which character?
   a. Brave Orchid's niece
   b. Brave Orchid's daughter
   c. Brave Orchid
   d. Moon Orchid

_____ 2. What is the best description of Brave Orchid's feelings as she waits in the airport?
   a. anxious and uncomfortable
   b. annoyed and impatient
   c. happy and carefree
   d. bored and indifferent

_____ 3. What do Brave Orchid's children do as she waits for the arrival of Moon Orchid?
   a. They sit with their mother.
   b. They talk to soldiers.
   c. They wander around the airport.
   d. They sit at home.

_____ 4. What is the main reason Brave Orchid is bothered by the behavior of her children?
   a. She does not want them talking to strangers.
   b. She does not understand them, and she feels that they do not understand the seriousness of the situation.
   c. She does not want them wasting money on food and pay television.
   d. She feels they will leave the airport without her if the plane does not arrive soon.

_____ 5. Why do the young soldiers in the airport attract Brave Orchid's attention?
   a. They remind her of her husband when he was a young man.
   b. They seem fearful about going to war.
   c. Her own son is a soldier, probably fighting in Vietnam.
   d. They resemble cowboys.

_____ 6. How does background information provided about Brave Orchid's life explain why she might have strong feelings against the idea of her son and other young men going to fight in Vietnam?
   a. She has always been an anti-war activist.
   b. Since she went to so much trouble to come to America, she feels her son should remain with her.
   c. She does not believe in the war being fought in Vietnam.
   d. She fled a war-torn China, so she knows the harsh realities of war firsthand.

_____ 7. What does Brave Orchid try to keep safe, using willpower and her powers of concentration?
   a. her former village in China
   b. her son and daughter
   c. her sister's airplane and her son's ship
   d. bundles of food

8. What do Brave Orchid's thoughts and actions at the airport reveal about her feelings toward the arrival of her sister?
   a. She is dreading her sister's arrival.
   b. She is anxious for her sister's safe arrival.
   c. She does not feel a great deal of concern about her sister's arrival.
   d. She resents having to spend so much time in the airport.

9. According to Brave Orchid, how were she and other immigrants treated by customs officers at Ellis Island when they arrived in America?
   a. They were given a warm welcome.
   b. They were scrutinized and treated with disdain.
   c. They were virtually ignored.
   d. They were given a great deal of assistance.

10. According to background information, what is "the Golden Mountain"?
   a. Ellis Island
   b. China
   c. the airport
   d. America

11. Judging from the woman Brave Orchid mistakenly points out as her sister, what does Brave Orchid fail to realize?
   a. how much her sister will have aged
   b. that her sister might not come
   c. her sister's correct height
   d. her sister's hair color

12. Why is each sister so shocked by the other's appearance?
   a. They don't remember looking so much alike.
   b. Their aged appearances show how much time has gone by.
   c. They can't believe they didn't recognize each other.
   d. They look like their children.

13. Why does the narrator refer to some American and Chinese people as "ghosts"?
   a. They are memories that haunt her life.
   b. She is frightened by all people.
   c. Her memories of her life experiences are vague and unclear.
   d. The people are figments of her mother's imagination.

14. What is one main reason why this selection from *The Woman Warrior* might be considered different from traditional memoirs?
   a. It is nonfiction.
   b. It is written in the third person and focuses on the personal impressions of someone other than the writer.
   c. It is about a significant personal experience.
   d. It is written in the first person and focuses on the personal impressions of the writer.

15. What seems to be Brave Orchid's strongest attitude toward American culture?
   a. She feels alienated from and slightly distrustful of American culture.
   b. She is eager to adopt American customs as her own.
   c. She is bored with American culture and continually wishes for more excitement.
   d. She feels American culture is quite similar to the Chinese culture with which she is familiar.

____ 16. What part of this selection best illustrates the complications faced by bicultural families?
   a. Brave Orchid's memory of Ellis Island and her own immigration experience
   b. Brave Orchid's concerns about her son in Vietnam
   c. the conflict between Brave Orchid and her children
   d. the meeting between Brave Orchid and Moon Orchid

Vocabulary and Grammar

On the line, write the letter of the one best answer.

____ 17. Brave Orchid felt the soldiers waiting to go to war should be crying ____ instead of standing there calmly.
   a. inaudibly
   b. cautiously
   c. obviously
   d. hysterically

____ 18. Where should single quotation marks be placed in the following sentence?

   Brave Orchid asked, "Did you hear my children say The plane's landed early?"

   a. Brave Orchid asked, "Did you hear my children say, 'The plane's landed early?' "
   b. Brave Orchid asked, "Did you hear my children say, 'The plane's landed early'?"
   c. Brave Orchid asked, "Did you hear my children say, 'The plane's landed early?" '
   d. Brave Orchid asked, " 'Did you hear my children say, The plane's landed early?' "

____ 19. Which is the best meaning of the word *gravity* as it is used in the following line?

   Moon Orchid, who never understood the gravity of things, started smiling and laughing . .

   a. seriousness   c. humor
   b. terror   d. strangeness

____ 20. Which of the following sentences is punctuated correctly?
   a. Brave Orchid's niece said, "Did you hear me call out, Mama"?
   b. Brave Orchid said, "I know the captain will say, 'Abandon ship!'"
   c. Brave Orchid said, "The captain will say, 'Abandon ship;' or he might say Watch out for bombs.'"
   d. Moon Orchid said to her sister, "Did you say 'You are old?'"

Essay Questions

21. The subtitle of *The Woman Warrior* is *Memoirs of a Girlhood Among Ghosts.* On whose impressions and experiences does the selection focus? What are some examples of this character's impressions? What does the reader learn from these impressions? Answer these questions in an essay.

22. In an essay, describe Brave Orchid. What does she value? How does she feel about American culture? What parts of the selection clearly reveal Brave Orchid's concerns and beliefs?

23. In an essay, describe the relationship Brave Orchid has with her children. What specific places in the selection reveal Brave Orchid's feelings toward their behavior? What does Brave Orchid's attitude toward her children reveal about the conflicts faced by immigrants and their children?

Name _____ Date _____

"**Antojos**" by Julia Alvarez

Selection Test

Critical Reading

On the line, write the letter of the one best answer.

_____ 1. What are *antojos*?
    a. friends
    b. cravings
    c. fruits
    d. good deeds

_____ 2. What warning do family members give Yolanda?
    a. Do not travel north alone.
    b. Do not eat fruit at this time of year.
    c. Be prepared for bad weather.
    d. Be careful with your money.

_____ 3. Which of the following situations from "Antojos" depicts rising action?
    a. Yolanda leaves the men who fixed her tire.
    b. Yolanda and the boys pick guavas.
    c. Yolanda passes a bus on her way to the shore.
    d. Yolanda gives the boy a dollar and drops him off at the cantina.

_____ 4. In what way is Yolanda different from her aunts?
    a. She is not interested in family.
    b. She is not as educated.
    c. She is more sheltered.
    d. She is more outgoing and independent.

_____ 5. Which plot element is shown in the following passage?

> Suddenly, a short, dark man, and then a slender, light-skin man emerged
> from a footpath . . .
> Yolanda's glance fell on the machetes that hung from their belts.

    a. exposition   c. rising action
    b. climax   d. denouement

_____ 6. The woman in the village advises Yolanda to allow the little boys to pick guavas for her, and Yolanda's voice has "an edge" as she says, "But they taste so much better when you've picked them yourself." How is she feeling when she responds in this way?
    a. She feels happy that the woman is trying to protect her.
    b. She feels relieved that she will not have to pick the guavas herself.
    c. She feels annoyed because it seems as though the woman is trying to keep her from seeing her country on her own.
    d. She feels hurt because it appears that the woman does not like her.

_____ 7. Why are the children so eager to accompany Yolanda?
    a. They want to trick her.
    b. They want to ride in her car.
    c. They want guavas for themselves.
    d. They are bored.

____ 8. When the men emerge from the woods and speak to Yolanda, why is it that "she could not speak" and "her tongue felt as if it'd been stuffed in her mouth like a rag to keep her quiet"?
   a. She is tired from picking guavas.
   b. She is annoyed at being bothered.
   c. She is so relieved to see people.
   d. She is frightened.

____ 9. Why does Yolanda allow the men to believe she is American and cannot speak Spanish?
   a. Because of the fighting within her country, she feels she is safer being thought of as an outsider.
   b. She enjoys lying about her identity.
   c. She is ashamed of her heritage and plans to return to America anyway.
   d. She believes the men are American.

____ 10. How is Yolanda's behavior different from the behavior of the men who change her tire?
   a. Yolanda is rude to the men when they try to help her.
   b. The men treat Yolanda with caution while she tries to make conversation.
   c. Although Yolanda is suspicious of the men, they are not suspicious of her.
   d. Yolanda is friendlier than they are.

____ 11. How is Yolanda probably feeling when, after the men help her rather than hurt her, she offers them money?
   a. anxious
   b. guilty
   c. displeased
   d. suspicious

____ 12. What happens when Jose tries to get help?
   a. He gets lost, gives up, and goes home.
   b. Because of the troubles in the country, people are suspicious and unwilling to help him.
   c. Many people respond sympathetically and try to follow him back to the broken-down car.
   d. People refuse to help him because they do not like Yolanda.

____ 13. How might you best describe the way Jose and Yolanda are feeling at the end of the story, after their experiences?
   a. excited
   b. somber
   c. tired
   d. annoyed

____ 14. What is the main reason the story is called "Antojos"?
   a. The name reflects Yolanda's craving for guavas.
   b. The name reflects Yolanda's craving to experience her homeland authentically.
   c. The name reflects suspicion, which is a theme in the story.
   d. The name reflects Yolanda's relationship with her family.

____ 15. What is the significance of the Palmolive poster in the story?
   a. The poster is a sign of the country's decline.
   b. The woman in the poster resembles Yolanda.
   c. To Yolanda, the woman in the poster represents people in her country calling out to her.
   d. The poster is a symbol of happiness and contentment.

Vocabulary and Grammar

On the line, write the letter of the one best answer.

_____ 16. What is the best meaning of the word *dissuade* as it is used in this sentence?

When she told of her plans to go north, her aunts tried to dissuade her.

a. encourage   c. distract
b. discourage   d. upset

_____ 17. Identify the complete absolute phrase in the following sentence.

Jose clutching his dollar, they exchanged good-byes.

a. Jose clutching
b. they exchanged good-byes
c. Jose clutching his dollar
d. they exchanged

_____ 18. What is the best meaning of the word *appease* as it is used in this sentence?

Enough guavas to appease even the greediest island spirit for life!

a. satisfy
b. include
c. support
d. disappoint

_____ 19. Identify the complete absolute phrase in the following sentence:

She left them behind, her small car driving easily up the highway.

a. She left them behind, her small car driving easily
b. easily up the highway
c. She left them behind
d. her small car driving easily up the highway

_____ 20. Which of the following is the best meaning of the word *collusion* as it is used in this sentence from "Antojos"?

The men exchanged a look—it seemed to Yolanda of collusion.

a. hate
b. conspiracy
c. friendliness
d. annoyance

Essay Questions

21. In an essay, explain the function of the flashback scene in "Antojos." What happens in the scene? Why is it important to the story? What key information do readers get from this scene?

22. In an essay, explain the title "Antojos." What double meaning does it have in this story? When is the word used? What theme does it emphasize?

23. In "Antojos," the character of Yolanda meets two strangers who change her tire and a village boy who helps her pick guavas. What does Yolanda learn from these experiences? How has she grown by the end of the story? Answer these questions in an essay, supporting your response with facts from the story.

"Freeway 280" by Lorna Dee Cervantes
"Who Burns for the Perfection of Paper" by Martín Espada
"Hunger in New York City" by Simon Ortiz
"Most Satisfied by Snow" by Diana Chang
"What For" by Garrett Hongo

Selection Test

Critical Reading

On the line, write the letter of the one best answer.

_____ 1. How might you summarize the following stanza from "Freeway 280"?

Las casitas [little houses] near the gray cannery, / nestled amid wild abrazos [hugs] of climbing roses / and man-high red geraniums / are gone now. The freeway conceals it / all beneath a raised scar.

a. A freeway has been built over a neighborhood of little houses and flower gardens.
b. Flowers grow alongside a raised highway.
c. A raised scar covers a freeway and little houses.
d. Little houses, flowers, and a freeway are near the gray cannery.

_____ 2. In "Freeway 280," why does the poet include several Spanish words and phrases?
a. to name items that cannot be identified in English
b. to compare and contrast the two languages
c. to reach more readers
d. to emphasize her search for her heritage

_____ 3. In "Freeway 280," the phrase "that part of me mown under like a corpse or a loose seed" refers to the poet's
a. flowers that have been destroyed.
b. memories of the beautiful homes in her old neighborhood.
c. neglected cultural heritage.
d. lost personal possessions.

_____ 4. In "Who Burns for the Perfection of Paper," what does the speaker remember most about his printing job?
a. the money he earned
b. other employees with whom he worked
c. the routine and the pain of the job
d. the commute from school to work

_____ 5. What is the most valuable lesson the speaker of "Who Burns for the Perfection of Paper" learned from his experience making legal pads?
a. that a career in the printing business would be challenging and painful
b. that accomplishments are often the result of pain and hard work
c. that one needs to be careful to avoid injury at any job
d. that paper can be sharp and glue can sting

_____ 6. In "Who Burns for the Perfection of Paper," what do the "hidden cuts" represent?
a. the negligence of the printing plant
b. the difficulty of holding a job while attending high school
c. the sometimes painful and difficult experiences that shape every individual
d. the challenges of law school

_____ 7. In what kind of environment does the speaker in "Hunger in New York City" experience hunger?
   a. in a close-knit village of familiar faces
   b. in an unfamiliar city of concrete and automation
   c. in a natural area filled with cold spring water and dancing
   d. among family and friends

_____ 8. In "Hunger in New York City," to what kind of hunger does the poet refer?
   a. hunger for cleaner air
   b. hunger for a satisfying career
   c. hunger for healthful foods
   d. hunger for the traditional values of his heritage

_____ 9. How might you best describe the voice of "Hunger in New York City"?
   a. desperate and longing   c. peaceful and content
   b. angry   d. urgent

_____ 10. Why does the poet in "Most Satisfied by Snow" prefer snow?
   a. It does not press against the windows.
   b. It is heavier than fog.
   c. It is more attractive than fog.
   d. It is more substantial than fog.

_____ 11. How might you describe the voice of "Most Satisfied by Snow"?
   a. sarcastic   c. spare and abrupt
   b. emotional   d. peaceful and dreamlike

_____ 12. Which of the following is the best summary of the poem "Most Satisfied by Snow"?
   a. Fog presses against the windows and keeps the speaker from looking outside at the snow.
   b. Fog presses against the window, but snow has a more significant physical presence. It is not as vague. The speaker learns this lesson and flowers in self-knowledge.
   c. Fog presses against the window, and snow that fills outdoor spaces is lovely, but the speaker prefers the beauty of flowers. Flowers make her thoughts flower.
   d. The speaker looks out the window at the snow and fog, dreaming of spring and beautiful flowers.

_____ 13. What does the speaker in "What For" remember most about his father?
   a. his father's hard work and sacrifices
   b. his father's laziness
   c. his father's songs and card games
   d. his father's abilities as a doctor of pure magic

_____ 14. How might you summarize the following stanza from "What For"?

   I wanted to heal the sores that work / and war had sent to him, / let him play catch in the backyard / with me, tossing a tennis ball / past papaya trees without the shoulders / of pain shrugging back his arms.

   a. The speaker experienced a great deal of pain in his shoulders and wanted to learn from his father how to work and toss a ball despite pain.
   b. The speaker was angry with his father for spending so much time at his job. He wanted his father to quit his job and spend his days at home.
   c. The speaker felt his father was a better ballplayer than soldier, and that he should spend his days perfecting this skill.
   d. The speaker's father was exhausted and sore from hard work and war, and the speaker wanted to give his father a chance to relax and enjoy life.

____ 15. What does the speaker of "What For" value most?
   a. hard work
   b. playing by the ocean
   c. communication and time spent with family
   d. war stories

Vocabulary and Grammar

On the line, write the letter of the one best answer.

____ 16. Which of the following is the best meaning of the word *pervade* as it is used in the following lines from "Most Satisfied by Snow"?

   Spaces pervade
   us, as well

   a. injure   c. intrigue
   b. spread throughout   d. confuse

____ 17. Identify the complete participial phrase in the following sentence.

   Brushing glue up and down the stack, I felt my hands sting.

   a. I felt
   b. Brushing glue
   c. Brushing glue up and down the stack
   d. I felt my hands sting

____ 18. The boy listened closely to the priest's reading of the _____.
   a. liturgy   c. trough
   b. calligraphy   d. automation

____ 19. Which of the following is the best meaning of the word *conjure* as it is used in this sentence?

   He wanted to become a doctor of magic and conjure relief for his father.

   a. invent   c. prevent
   b. reject   d. summon

____ 20. Which word is modified by a participial phrase in the following sentence?

   I saw my father's arms shrugged back in pain.

   a. back   c. father's
   b. arms   d. pain

Essay Questions

21. In an essay, discuss attitudes toward work in the poems "Who Burns for the Perfection of Paper" by Martín Espada and "What For" by Garrett Hongo. What work experiences are being described in the poems? What do the speakers learn from these experiences?

22. In what ways do the poems "Freeway 280" by Lorna Dee Cervantes, "Hunger in New York City" by Simon Ortiz, and "What For" by Garrett Hongo address the importance of family and heritage? What message do the poems share? Answer these questions in an essay.

23. In an essay, compare and contrast the voices of at least three of the five poems you've read. What is unique about the voice in each of your chosen poems? Are the voices in the poems similar in any way? Explain why or why not.

Freeway/Perfection/Hunger/Most Satisfied/What For   **277**

Part Test, Unit 6, Part 1: Literature Confronts the Everyday

Critical Reading

The questions below are based on the following selection.

In this excerpt, from Flannery O'Connor's short story "A Good Man Is Hard to Find," a father, mother, grandmother, and two children have stopped at "Red Sammy's" roadside restaurant for lunch. One of the children, June Star, has begun to dance to a song on the jukebox.

"Ain't she cute?" Red Sam's wife said, leaning over the counter. "Would you like to come be my little girl?"

"No I certainly wouldn't," June Star said. "I wouldn't live in a broken-down place like this for a million bucks!" and she ran back to the table.

"Ain't she cute?" the woman repeated, stretching her mouth politely.

"Aren't you ashamed?" hissed the grandmother.

Red Sam came in and told his wife to quit lounging on the counter and hurry up with these people's order. His khaki trousers reached just to his hip bones and his stomach hung over them like a sack of meal swaying under his shirt. He came over and sat down at a table nearby and let out a combination sigh and yodel. "You can't win," he said. "You can't win," and he wiped his sweating red face off with a gray handkerchief. "These days you don't know who to trust," he said. "Ain't that the truth?"

"People are certainly not nice like they used to be," said the grandmother.

"Two fellers come in here last week," Red Sammy said, "driving a Chrysler. It was a old beat-up car but it was a good one and these boys looked all right to me. Said they worked at the mill and you know I let them fellers charge the gas they bought? Now why did I do that?"

"Because you're a good man!" the grandmother said at once.

"Yes'm, I suppose so," Red Sam said as if he were struck with this answer.

His wife brought the orders, carrying the five plates all at once without a tray, two in each hand and one balanced on her arm. "It isn't a soul in this green world of God's that you can trust," she said. "And I don't count nobody out of that, not nobody," she repeated, looking at Red Sammy.

"Did you read about that criminal, The Misfit, that's escaped?" asked the grandmother.

"I wouldn't be a bit surprised if he didn't attact this place right here," said the woman. "If he hears about it being here, I wouldn't be none surprised to see him. If he hears it's two cent in the cash register, I wouldn't be a tall surprised if he . . ."

"That'll do," Red Sam said. "Go bring these people their Co'-Colas," and the woman went off to get the rest of the order.

On the line, write the letter of the one best answer.

_____ 1. To whom is the grandmother's first speech addressed?
     a. June Star   c. Red Sam's wife
     b. Red Sam   d. Herself

_____ 2. Which most dramatically allows you to envision the action?
     a. "'Did you read about that criminal, The Misfit, that's escaped?' asked the grand-mother."
     b. "'Aren't you ashamed?' hissed the grandmother."
     c. "His wife brought the order, carrying the five plates all at once without a tray, two in each hand and one balanced on her arm."
     d. "'And I don't count nobody out of that, not nobody,' she repeated, looking at Red Sammy."

_____ 3. Given its context, the phrase "stretching her mouth politely" indicates that Red Sam's wife
   a. forms a smile to cover her feelings.
   b. yawns out of boredom.
   c. wipes her mouth.
   d. screams silently.

_____ 4. What does Red Sam's wife mean by saying "I don't count nobody out of that" and looking straight at her husband?
   a. She wants to make certain that he is listening to her.
   b. She means that she doesn't trust even him.
   c. She means that he shouldn't trust her.
   d. She means that he was foolish to give gas away.

_____ 5. From the author's diction, you can infer that the story is set
   a. in a rural area in the South.   c. near an eastern lake.
   b. in a wealthy southern suburb.   d. in the "Wild West."

_____ 6. In literature, a grotesque character is one who
   a. has become bizarre, perhaps through some kind of obsession.
   b. exploits other characters.
   c. makes readers feel distaste or contempt.
   d. cannot communicate effectively with other characters.

_____ 7. Thinking about why Red Sammy "let them fellers charge the gas they bought" would help a reader determine
   a. the story's atmosphere.   c. the moment of epiphany.
   b. the character's motivation.   d. the author's diction.

_____ 8. By contrasting two characters, you can often
   a. summarize a story.
   b. deepen your appreciation of an author's use of figurative language.
   c. begin to envision a story's action.
   d. begin to uncover a major conflict in a story.

_____ 9. The story Red Sam shares with the grandmother is an example of
   a. an epic.   c. a maxim.
   b. an anecdote.   d. a parable.

_____ 10. What is ironic about the grandmother's saying that people are "not nice like they used to be"?
   a. She is trying to swindle Red Sam.
   b. Red Sam and his wife have been kind to the family.
   c. The Misfit is on the loose.
   d. Red Sam's wife has been rude to the family.

Vocabulary/Grammar and Style

On the line, write the letter of the one best answer.

_____ 11. Which sentence begins with an adverb clause?
   a. It was big enough for him to lie in, but he had never dared try.
   b. In the first house he lived in, it sat up on the second floor, a big wooden chest, out of the way and yet not.
   c. The new house was smaller, with more outdoors around it.
   d. Two of the three children, the two that were married, had many responsibilities and soon left.

_____ 12. Which sentence contains an error in the use of adjectives or adverbs?
   a. A sly look came over his face.
   b. There was no answer at once and no particular expression on his face.
   c. The old woman's three mountains were black against the dark blue sky and were visited off and on by various planets and by the moon after it had left the chickens.
   d. He swung both his whole and his short arm up slow so that they indicated an expanse of sky and his figure formed a crooked cross.

_____ 13. A _desolate_ area of countryside could be described as _____.
   a. bustling
   b. cogent
   c. forlorn
   d. old-fashioned

_____ 14. _Unscrupulous_ employees would probably cause their employer to feel _____.
   a. anxious
   b. self-satisfied
   c. placid
   d. rejuvenated

_____ 15. Ice _permeated_ with mint syrup is
   a. decorated with it.
   b. spoiled by it.
   c. surrounded by it.
   d. filled with it.

_____ 16. _Furtive_ eyes create an impression of _____.
   a. sneakiness
   b. commonness
   c. glee
   d. honesty

_____ 17. Which sentence contains an error in subject-verb agreement?
   a. The light comes brighter from the east.
   b. Once more the trees assume wintry shapes as branches shed their last leaves.
   c. Truth never is undone; its shafts remains.
   d. The teeth of knitted gears turn slowly through the night.

_____ 18. Which sentence uses _who_ or _whom_ incorrectly?
   a. As for education, what was it, she asked, but books, which Sobel, who diligently read the classics, would as usual advise her on.
   b. Who he was the shoemaker for a moment had no idea.
   c. Or suppose Miriam, who harped so often on independence, blew up in anger and shouted at him for his meddling?
   d. He had to get up to open the store for the new assistant, a speechless, dark man with an irritating rasp as he worked, who he would not trust with the key.

_____ 19. Which sentence contains an error in the use of adjectives or adverbs?
   a. All this made the chest, simply in shape as it was, strange, and ancient, and almost frightening.
   b. Everything in the house that had always been in a certain place was swiftly and casually uplifted and carried out the door.
   c. The unloading, including the reloading of the righted chest, all took place by flashlight, hurriedly, under the drumming sound of rain on the flat roof.
   d. Delicately but fearlessly, she lifted the lid.

_____ 20. Which of the following is a sentence fragment?
>   a. I never had an education myself.
>   b. A dress so loud it hurts my eyes.
>   c. Out came Wangero with two quilts.
>   d. This was Maggie's portion.

Essay Questions

21. A good strategy for involving yourself in a literary work is to identify with a character. Choose a selection—such as "The First Seven Years," "Suspended," "Hunger in New York City," or "The Brown Chest"—that contains a character, narrator, or speaker who may share some of your attitudes or personality traits. In an essay, summarize what you know about this literary figure; then explain some similarities and differences between that figure and yourself.

22. An author can create a distinctive atmosphere in a work of fiction, nonfiction, poetry, or drama. Choose a selection from this part that features a particularly notable atmosphere. In an essay, describe the atmosphere the author creates and explain how it contributes to the total effect of the work.

23. Characters in literature are motivated by dreams, needs, and desires, among other impulses. Choose a selection—such as "The Life You Save May Be Your Own," "Average Waves in Unprotected Waters," or "Traveling Through the Dark"—in which a character acts in some interesting or unusual way. In an essay, speculate on (and explain) the motivation for this character's behavior.

24. Paraphrasing is a good way to deepen or solidify your understanding of especially challenging poems. Choose a poem such as "The Adamant," "Gold Glade," or "Hawthorne" and paraphrase each sentence in it.

25. Discussions of a poet's style are more concerned with the form than with the content of the verse. Choose poems by two poets from this part of Unit 6. Then write an essay in which you compare and contrast the poets' styles.

Name _____ Date _____

from *The Mortgaged Heart* by Carson McCullers
"Onomatopoeia" by William Safire
"Coyote v. Acme" by Ian Frazier

Selection Test

Critical Thinking

On the line, write the letter of the one best answer.

_____ 1. "The Mortgaged Heart" by Carson McCullers is mainly about
    a. love
    b. loneliness
    c. fear
    d. community

_____ 2. Which of the following best summarizes the main idea of "The Mortgaged Heart"?
    a. Living in a city creates profound isolation.
    b. Only people who belong to a *We* can be happy.
    c. For Americans, loneliness stems from the search for identity.
    d. Europeans and Americans search for identity in different ways.

_____ 3. What line of reasoning does McCullers present in "The Mortgaged Heart" to support her point that love is the way of overcoming loneliness?
    a. Love allows an individual to see the world in a new and accepting light.
    b. Love creates a sense of moral isolation.
    c. Only the maverick can escape loneliness.
    d. Personal love is better than having a sense of one's identity.

_____ 4. In "The Mortgaged Heart," McCullers contrasts Americans and Europeans to
    a. explain different schools of art.
    b. denounce fear of foreigners.
    c. support her idea about the nature of American loneliness.
    d. illustrate the difference between morality and immorality.

_____ 5. "The Mortgaged Heart" is an example of
    a. an expository essay.
    b. a satirical essay.
    c. a persuasive essay.
    d. an analytical essay.

_____ 6. What is the primary purpose of this opening sentence from "Onomatopoeia"?

    The word onomatopoeia was used above, and it had better be spelled right or one usage dictator and six copy editors will get zapped.

    a. to vent Safire's frustration with copy editors
    b. to make a joke
    c. to demonstrate the use of onomatopoeia
    d. to criticize a writing style

_____ 7. "Onomatopoeia" is mainly about
    a. William Safire's writing process.
    b. the definition and examples of onomatopoeia.
    c. the creation of onomatopoeia.
    d. the ways in which different writers use onomatopoeia.

____ 8. In "Onomatopoeia," the word *zap* intrigues Safire because it
   a. imitates an imaginary noise.
   b. sounds like the action of a ray gun.
   c. is a relatively new example of onomatopoeia.
   d. has many different uses.

____ 9. What type of essay is "Onomatopoeia"?
   a. analytical   c. satirical
   b. narrative   d. expository

____ 10. Frazier's main purpose in writing "Coyote v. Acme" is to
   a. criticize violence in children's programming.
   b. ridicule legal language.
   c. question the validity of product liability lawsuits.
   d. analyze the effects of cartoon viewing.

____ 11. "Coyote v. Acme" is a satirical essay because it
   a. uses irony and humor to criticize a topic.
   b. paints an amusing picture of its topic.
   c. imitates legal language to make its main point.
   d. explores different aspects of a topic.

____ 12. In "Coyote v. Acme," what is the purpose of Exhibits A–D?
   a. They summarize the different incidents involving Acme products.
   b. They support the attorney's line of reasoning.
   c. They illustrate Mr. Coyote's injuries.
   d. They analyze the seriousness of the lawsuit.

____ 13. In "Coyote v. Acme," the attorney's description of Mr. Coyote's disfigurements following the "premature detonation" of an Acme bomb is an example of _____.
   a. exposition
   b. irony
   c. narration
   d. analysis

____ 14. Which sentence is an example of the line of reasoning in "Coyote v. Acme"?
   a. "In an instant, the fuse burned down to the stem, causing the bomb to detonate."
   b. "Mr. Coyote is self-employed and thus not eligible for Workmen's Compensation."
   c. "Adjacent to the boulder was a path which Mr. Coyote's prey was known to frequent."
   d. "The sequence of collisions resulted in systemic physical damage to Mr. Coyote . . ."

Vocabulary and Grammar

On the line, write the letter of the one best answer.

____ 15. The _____ was that a bomb caused the _____ explosion.
   a. caveat; tensile
   b. aesthetic; maverick
   c. contiguous; pristine
   d. corollary; precipitate

____ 16. Springs have a _____ design.
   a. pristine
   b. contiguous
   c. tensile
   d. aesthetic

____ 17. The ____ ignored the ____.
   a. maverick; caveat
   b. caveat; maverick
   c. corollary; caveat
   d. maverick; corollary

____ 18. McCullers believes that moral isolation is unique to ____ Americans.
   a. we
   b. us
   c. they
   d. them

____ 19. In which of the following does the pronoun case match the appositive?
   a. Two characters, the Road Runner and him, raced across the television screen.
   b. Us children howled with laughter.
   c. Mother told us, Jimmy and I, to turn off the cartoon.
   d. We, Jimmy and I, protested loudly.

____ 20. Which pronoun correctly replaces the underlined words in the following sentence?

   The judge asked them, Mr. Coyote and his attorney, to stand.

   a. him
   b. he
   c. they
   d. them

Essay Questions

21. In their essays, McCullers and Frazier make definite points about their topics. What line of reasoning do they follow? Focusing on one of these writers, write an essay in which you explain the author's main point and identify the line of reasoning that supports it.

22. Essay writers choose specific essay forms to present their ideas. Of these three essays, which do you think makes its point best? Why do you think so? Write an essay of your own in which you identify the type of essay and the writer's main point, and analyze the essay's effectiveness.

23. Why does Frazier choose Wile E. Coyote for his satire? Write an essay in which you explore Frazier's use of the cartoon and draw conclusions about its satiric qualities. In your essay, translate the cartoon incidents to the real-life circumstances Frazier is criticizing.

"Straw Into Gold" by Sandra Cisneros
"For the Love of Books" by Rita Dove
"Mother Tongue" by Amy Tan

Selection Test

Critical Reading

On the line, write the letter of the one best answer.

_____ 1. Cisneros's writing was most influenced by
   a. her mother's cooking.
   b. her childhood in a Mexican neighborhood in Chicago.
   c. her travels in Europe.
   d. the Texas landscape.

_____ 2. Which of the following details best supports the message in "Straw Into Gold"?
   a. She has received an NEA grant and traveled to many places.
   b. Cisneros was closest to her brother Henry.
   c. Her first novel was based on childhood experiences.
   d. She recalls the fairy tale of the woman who spun straw into gold.

_____ 3. In writing that she left home both before her brothers did and without marrying,
   Cisneros reveals in "Straw Into Gold" that she
   a. does not value family relationships.
   b. enjoys traveling.
   c. is stubborn.
   d. has a strong sense of herself and what she wants.

_____ 4. In "Straw Into Gold," straw is a symbol for _____.
   a. hope
   b. tortillas
   c. discouragement
   d. obstacles

_____ 5. Which best summarizes the theme of "Straw Into Gold"?
   a. Being a writer is an excellent way to see the world.
   b. Latino writers face special challenges.
   c. As human beings, we are capable of doing things we thought were impossible.
   d. Parents have a great impact on their children.

_____ 6. As a child, Rita Dove felt most comfortable with books because
   a. she had always wanted to be a writer.
   b. she was painfully shy.
   c. her teacher encouraged her to read.
   d. her family moved frequently.

_____ 7. By describing her love of the story in which an outcast boy becomes a hero, what
   point is Dove making in "For the Love of Books"?
   a. Books allow readers to identify with others.
   b. Even science fiction can stir strong emotions.
   c. We should be considerate of one another's feelings.
   d. Writers find inspiration in unlikely places.

_____ 8. In "For the Love of Books," Dove describes writing a novel based on her grade-school spelling list. This detail reveals that she
   a. had a vivid imagination.
   b. was unhappy and isolated in school.
   c. decided at an early age to be a writer.
   d. was a disciplined student.

_____ 9. Given the language and style of Dove's writing in "For the Love of Books," what type of writing seems to have influenced her most?
   a. scientific articles
   b. essays
   c. fiction
   d. translations of Italian poetry

_____ 10. "For the Love of Books" is an appropriate title for Dove's essay because it
   a. explains why people love to read.
   b. describes how reading gave Dove encouragement and inspired her to pursue writing.
   c. describes the first moment that Dove discovered the power of books.
   d. lists Dove's best-loved books.

_____ 11. In "Straw Into Gold," what taboo did Cisneros break?
   a. She became a writer.
   b. She left home before her brothers and before she married.
   c. She wrote about her own personal experiences.
   d. She traveled widely and lived in Europe.

_____ 12. In "Straw Into Gold," Cisneros's mother is best described as
   a. businesslike.
   b. emotional.
   c. tough and smart.
   d. shy and moody.

_____ 13. In "Mother Tongue," Tan posing as her mother on the telephone reveals that Tan
   a. is dishonest.
   b. is controlling.
   c. feels empathy for her mother.
   d. feels embarrassed by her mother.

_____ 14. Which of the following details in "Mother Tongue" supports Tan's message?
   a. When she writes, Tan envisions her mother as her reader.
   b. Her mother reads many English language publications.
   c. Tan received better scores in math.
   d. Tan has become an accomplished writer.

_____ 15. The main idea of "Mother Tongue" is that
   a. immigrants are often misperceived.
   b. Asian American students need to be encouraged in English, as well as in mathematics.
   c. Chinese and English are vastly different languages.
   d. Tan was greatly affected by her mother's use of language.

Vocabulary and Grammar

On the line, write the letter of the one best answer.

____ 16. Cisneros was in a _____ when asked to make corn tortillas.
   a. nomadic
   b. benign
   c. quandary
   d. semantic

____ 17. Dove might have _____ her spelling words in a notebook.
   a. transcribed
   b. empirical
   c. benign
   d. semantic

____ 18. When reading analogy questions, Tan had difficulty recognizing _____ clues.
   a. nomadic
   b. empirical
   c. benign
   d. semantic

____ 19. What type or types of sentence structures are represented in the following quotation?

> The talk was going along well enough, until I remembered one major difference that made the whole talk sound wrong. My mother was in the room.

   a. complex sentences
   b. simple and compound sentences
   c. simple and complex sentences
   d. compound and complex sentences

____ 20. Which quotation contains varied sentence structure?
   a. "I guess they assumed I knew how to cook Mexican food because I was Mexican. They wanted specifically tortillas, though I'd never made a tortilla in my life."
   b. "To make matters worse, I had left before any of my six brothers had ventured away from home. I had broken a terrible taboo."
   c. "We were co-conspirators. We were pals."
   d. "Why are there few Asian Americans enrolled in creative writing programs? Why do so many Chinese students go into engineering?"

Essay Questions

21. By describing personal experiences and feelings in a reflective essay, a writer arrives at a deeper understanding. Choose one of these essays, and, in an essay of your own, explain how the author comes to understand a problem or aspect of herself more deeply through her reflections.

22. In their reflective essays, these three writers describe pivotal experiences in their development as writers. In your opinion, which writer reveals the most about herself in her essay? Write an essay of your own in which you state your opinion and support it with evidence from the original essay.

23. Tan explains that her mother's language had the greatest influence on her understanding of English. Do you agree that family members have the greatest effect on a child's intellectual development? State your opinion in an essay, and support it with evidence from at least two of the essays.

Part Test, Unit 6, Part 2: Focus on Literary Forms—Essay

Critical Reading

The questions below are based on the following selection.

This excerpt is from Barry Lopez's nonfiction book Arctic Dreams. *As it begins, Lopez has just finished recounting two anecdotes that remind him of "the long human struggle, mental and physical, to come to terms with the Far North," where he has traveled extensively to research his book.*

. . . As I traveled, I came to believe that people's desires and aspirations were as much a part of the land as the wind, solitary animals, and the bright fields of stone and tundra. And, too, that the land itself existed quite apart from these.

The physical landscape is baffling in its ability to transcend whatever we would make of it. It is as subtle in its expression as turns of the mind, and larger than our grasp; and yet it is still knowable. The mind, full of curiosity and analysis, disassembles a landscape and then re-assembles the pieces—the nod of a flower, the color of the night sky, the murmur of an ani-mal—trying to fathom its geography. At the same time the mind is trying to find its place within the land, to discover a way to dispel its own sense of estrangement. . . .

Along creek washouts, in the western Arctic especially, you might stumble upon a mammoth tusk. Or in the eastern Arctic find undisturbed the ring of stones used by a hunter 1500 years ago to hold down the edge of his skin tent. These old Dorset camps, located along the coasts where arctic people have been traveling for four millennia, are poignant with their suggestion of the timeless determination of mankind. On rare occasions a traveler might come upon the more imposing stone foundations of a large house abandoned by Thule-culture people in the twelfth century. (The cold, dry arctic air might have preserved, even down to its odor, the remains of a ringed seal killed and eaten by them 800 years ago.) More often, one comes upon the remains of a twentieth-century camp, artifacts far less engaging than a scrap of worked caribou bone, or carved wood, or skewered hide at a Dorset or Thule site. But these artifacts disintegrate just as slowly—red tins of Prince Albert brand crimp-cut tobacco, cans of Pet evaporated milk and Log Cabin maple syrup. In the most recent camps one finds used flashlight batteries in clusters like animal droppings, and a bewildering variety of spent rifle and shotgun ammunition.

You raise your eyes from these remains, from whatever century, to look away. The land as far as you can see is rung with a harmonious authority, the enduring force of its natural history, of which these camps are so much a part. But the most recent evidence is vaguely disturbing. It does not derive in any clear way from the land. Its claim to being part of the natural history of the region seems, somehow, false. . . .

On the line, write the letter of the one best answer.

_____ 1. According to the author, which is not truly "a part of the land" in the arctic region?
a. the wind
c. maple syrup cans
b. human aspirations
d. fields of stone and tundra

_____ 2. In the second paragraph, what does Lopez say about the relationship between the arctic landscape and humans' ability to understand it?
a. The landscape is greater than humans' ability to find meaning in it.
b. The landscape is equal to humans' ability to understand it.
c. The human mind is subtler than the landscape.
d. Both the landscape and the human mind try to understand geography.

____ 3. This selection does *not* contain elements and characteristics of
    a. an analytical essay.   c. a reflective essay.
    b. an expository essay.   d. a satirical essay.

____ 4. To support his ideas about the relationship between human beings and the arctic landscape, which of the following does Lopez *not* use?
    a. examples   c. facts
    b. definitions   d. reasons

____ 5. Which of the following is *not* an example or record of "human aspirations" relating to the Arctic?
    a. a ring of stones in a Dorset camp
    b. disintegrating tins of crimp-cut tobacco
    c. the color of the night sky
    d. the odor of the remains of a ringed seal

____ 6. Why might the "variety of spent rifle and shotgun ammunition" strike Lopez as bewildering?
    a. It is hard to understand the need for so many different kinds of ammunition.
    b. Ammunition is rather expensive.
    c. A wide variety of ammunition is impressive.
    d. There are no weapons visible.

____ 7. In this selection, Lopez takes apart and explains the subject of
    a. arctic weather.
    b. the habits of arctic mammoths.
    c. the connection between the arctic landscape and humans' fascination with it.
    d. the relationship between solitary arctic animals and a "sense of estrangement."

____ 8. To be an excellent reader of an essay, you should
    a. memorize the most important information in the work.
    b. identify the writer's message and decide what you think of it.
    c. argue with the writer in your mind.
    d. identify the facts.

____ 9. What are the earliest traces of human activity in the Arctic mentioned by Lopez?
    a. a mammoth tusk
    b. stone foundations of a house abandoned by Thule-culture people
    c. tobacco tins
    d. rings of stones in Dorset camps

____ 10. Why might "the most recent evidence" disturb Lopez, whereas earlier evidence of human exploration does not?
    a. He is in love with the past.
    b. The later remains are of no historical significance.
    c. He believes that pollution threatens the Arctic.
    d. Only the most recent remains contain elements that are not native to the Arctic.

Vocabulary and Grammar

The two questions below consist of a related pair of words in CAPITAL LETTERS, followed by four other pairs of words. Choose the pair that best expresses a relationship similar to that expressed in the capitalized words.

____ 11. PRISTINE : PURE ::
    a. lonely : dissatisfied   c. faction : impurity
    b. charitable : generous   d. multifaceted : bright

_____ 12. THOUGHTFUL : INSTINCTIVE ::
     a. literature : speech
     b. reflective : thoughtful
     c. nomadic : rooted
     d. nascent : emerging

On the line, write the letter of the one best answer.

_____ 13. A person in a mental *quandary* probably feels _____.
     a. uncertain
     b. dogged
     c. malevolent
     d. benevolent

_____ 14. Which sentence correctly uses pronouns with appositives?
     a. The European, secure in his family ties and rigid class loyalties, knows little of the moral loneliness that is native to us Americans.
     b. The European, secure in his family ties and rigid class loyalties, knows little of the moral loneliness that is native to our Americans.
     c. The European, secure in his family ties and rigid class loyalties, knows little of the moral loneliness that is native to we Americans.
     d. The European, secure in his family ties and rigid class loyalties, knows little of the moral loneliness that is native to your Americans.

_____ 15. In order to vary the structure of their sentences, writers would be unlikely to use
     a. compound sentences.
     b. simple sentences.
     c. complex sentences.
     d. imperative sentences.

Essay Questions

16. In a reflective essay a writer can adopt an informal tone to express a personal view of some subject. Using Rita Dove's essay "For the Love of Books" as a model, write a reflective essay about your own relationship with books or with some other object, idea, or activity that is important to you.

17. Essayists are interested in conveying their ideas to readers. Choose an essay that interests you from this part. Think about how you would evaluate the message of the writer of this essay. Then write an essay of your own in which you explain whether you believe the writer's idea is valid and why.

18. Choose your favorite essay from this unit. In a well-organized essay, analyze the literary techniques that the essayist uses to address his or her topic. First identify the kind of essay it is, and then note its specific purpose. Next, analyze the techniques used to achieve that purpose. For instance, does the author use humor or a personal, confiding style to make the point? Do any special figures of speech or images mark the essay?

"**The Rockpile**" by James Baldwin

Selection Test

Critical Reading

On the line, write the letter of the one best answer.

____ 1. Why were the boys forbidden to play on the rockpile?
   a. The other boys who played there were not nice.
   b. It was too dangerous.
   c. Their mother couldn't watch them while they played there.
   d. Their father thought it was evil.

____ 2. John is different from the boys on the rockpile because he is _____.
   a. younger
   b. less studious
   c. more timid
   d. less responsible

____ 3. What does the rockpile symbolize?
   a. carefree youth
   b. evil and danger
   c. forbidden joys
   d. blind obedience

____ 4. The episode of the boy who drowned is presented to
   a. explain why Elizabeth wouldn't let the boys play on the rockpile.
   b. convey the evils of the neighborhood.
   c. introduce important characters in the story.
   d. make the reader believe that another character will die.

____ 5. What is the most immediate effect of Roy's injury?
   a. Gabriel demands an explanation.
   b. John anticipates his father's anger.
   c. Roy lies silent on the sofa.
   d. Elizabeth begins to worry.

____ 6. Which is a cause of Elizabeth's protectiveness toward John?
   a. John is not Gabriel's child.
   b. The other children tease him.
   c. John often gets into trouble.
   d. Gabriel favors him.

____ 7. Which phrase best describes the kind of mother Elizabeth is?
   a. devoted and supportive
   b. attentive but uncaring
   c. neglectful and cold
   d. harsh but concerned

____ 8. What makes John's relationship with Gabriel different from that of the other children?
   a. He is the oldest.
   b. He looks like Gabriel.
   c. He is not Gabriel's biological son.
   d. He frequently disobeys Gabriel.

____ 9. Which word or phrase best describes the kind of father Gabriel is to John?
   a. lenient
   b. uncaring
   c. stern but loving
   d. strict and unforgiving

____ 10. Which of the following sentences demonstrates the effect of the setting on the characters?
   a. "The sun fell across them and across the fire escape with a high, benevolent indifference . . ."
   b. "In the summertime boys swam in the river, diving off the wooden dock, or wading in from the garbage-heavy bank."
   c. "Then someone screamed or shouted; boys began to run away, down the street, toward the bridge."
   d. "John stood near the window, holding the newspaper advertisement and the drawing he had done."

____ 11. In Elizabeth's view, who is responsible for Roy's accident?
   a. Elizabeth
   b. Roy
   c. John
   d. Gabriel

____ 12. What causes Gabriel to soften his hatred toward Elizabeth?
   a. John agrees to pick up his lunchbox.
   b. He remembers his love for Roy.
   c. He remembers that Elizabeth is his wife and the mother of his children.
   d. Roy stops crying.

____ 13. The theme of "The Rockpile" is best described as a tension between
   a. urban and suburban environments.
   b. father and son.
   c. anger and compassion.
   d. religion and society.

____ 14. What kind of mood is created by the phrase "bending his dark head near the toe of his father's heavy shoe"?
   a. ominous
   b. intimate
   c. playful
   d. tedious

Vocabulary and Grammar

On the line, write the letter of the one best answer.

____ 15. John was ____ in his drawing when he was suddenly ____ by the sounds of shouting from the rockpile.
   a. engrossed; arrested
   b. arrested; engrossed
   c. intriguing; engrossed
   d. intriguing; arrested

____ 16. A ____ man carried Roy over to Elizabeth.
   a. latent
   b. decorously
   c. perdition
   d. benevolent

____ 17. Although Gabriel did not make a threatening move toward John, his stance conveyed a _____ .
   a. benevolent perdition
   b. latent malevolence
   c. jubilant malevolence
   d. latent perdition

____ 18. Which sentence contains a restrictive adjective clause?
   a. "Once a boy, whose name was Richard, drowned in the river."
   b. ". . . their mother had gone into the kitchen to sip tea with Sister McCandless."
   c. ". . . he was afraid of the rockpile and of the boys who played there."
   d. "She looked back at Gabriel, who had risen . . ."

____ 19. In which item does a nonrestrictive adjective clause appear in italic type?
   a. *She looked back* at Gabriel, who had risen, . . . staring at her.
   b. *She looked back at Gabriel,* who had risen, . . . staring at her.
   c. She looked back at Gabriel, who had risen, . . . *staring at her.*
   d. She looked back at Gabriel, *who had risen,* . . . staring at her.

____ 20. Which item correctly refers to this sentence: Baldwin knew 1930's Harlem, which is the setting of "The Rockpile"?
   a. A nonrestrictive adjective clause modifies *Harlem.*
   b. A restrictive adjective clause modifies *Harlem.*
   c. A nonrestrictive adjective clause modifies *Baldwin.*
   d. A restrictive adjective clause modifies *Baldwin.*

Essay Questions

21. "The Rockpile" reveals many cause-and-effect relationships. In a brief essay, identify one cause-and-effect relationship, and explain how identifying cause and effect helps you understand the characters' attitudes and behavior.

22. How does the 1930's Harlem setting affect the characters in "The Rockpile"? Which dangers or influences are real? Which are symbolic? Write an essay in which you explain how the setting influences the characters' beliefs and behavior.

23. The conflicts that create dramatic tension in a story may arise from internal struggle within one person, struggle among humans, or struggle between humans and nature. In an essay, describe which of these categories you think best fits the conflict present in "The Rockpile." Support your conclusions with evidence from the story.

The Rockpile

Name _____ Date _____

from *Hiroshima* by John Hersey
"Losses" and "The Death of the Ball Turret Gunner" by Randall Jarrell

Selection Test

Critical Reading

On the line, write the letter of the one best answer.

_____ 1. What is the best way to describe how the people in *Hiroshima* are feeling in the days and hours preceding the atomic bomb explosion?
   a. calm
   b. uneasy
   c. riotous
   d. hopeful

_____ 2. Unaware of the threat of an atomic bomb, what do people in *Hiroshima* believe is inevitable?
   a. an end to the war
   b. a surrender
   c. a population increase
   d. an air raid

_____ 3. In *Hiroshima*, what is the main reason John Hersey provides so many details about the activities of people in Hiroshima in the hours before the bomb was dropped?
   a. to lengthen his story
   b. to give readers insight into their lives, which have been disrupted by the war
   c. to entertain readers
   d. to show how people in the community interact with one another

_____ 4. What might you infer about the theme of *Hiroshima* from the following passage?

> They still wonder why they lived when so many others died. Each of them counts many small items of chance or volition—a step taken in time, a decision to go indoors, catching one streetcar instead of the next—that spared him.

   a. The theme deals with the idea that some people are much more fortunate than others.
   b. The theme deals with the idea that people are safe only inside their homes.
   c. The theme deals with the cruel and random destruction caused by the bomb.
   d. The theme deals with the different ways in which people deal with tragedy.

_____ 5. What theme is implied in the following passage from *Hiroshima*?

> . . .but undoubtedly she also felt a generalized, community pity, to say nothing of self-pity. She had not had an easy time. Her husband, Isawa, had gone into the Army just after Myeko was born, and she heard nothing from or of him for a long time, until, on March 5, 1942, she received a seven-word telegram: "Isawa died an honorable death at Singapore."

   a. that it is dangerous to be a soldier
   b. that war cruelly and coldly destroys the lives of individuals
   c. how different people deal with self-pity
   d. that fathers should not be soldiers

_____ 6. Who are the speakers in the poem "Losses"?
   a. families of soldiers
   b. soldiers
   c. planes
   d. teachers

_____ 7. Which of the following images from *Hiroshima* is ironic?
   a. Dr. Fujii sat down cross-legged in his underwear on the spotless matting of the porch, put on his glasses, and started reading the Osaka *Asahi*.
   b. There, in the tin factory, in the first moment of the atomic age, a human being was crushed by books.
   c. Mrs. Nakamura went back to the kitchen, looked at the rice, and began watching the man next door.
   d. Mr. Tanimoto is a small man, quick to talk, laugh, and cry. He wore his black hair parted in the middle and rather long . . .

_____ 8. In *Hiroshima*, why does Hersey describe over and over the moment of the bomb's explosion, each time from a different person's perspective?
   a. to add a level of suspense to the piece
   b. so that people can understand the terror felt by individuals at that moment
   c. to show how people handle themselves under stress
   d. so that people can see which structures withstood the explosion and which did not

_____ 9. What theme can you infer from the following lines from "Losses"?

   In bombers named for girls, we burned / The cities we had learned about in school— / Till our lives wore out . . .

   a. War gives young men a chance to travel.
   b. Pilots become emotionally attached to their planes.
   c. Young men fighting in war should be educated.
   d. War is violent and cruel.

_____ 10. In "Losses," when are soldiers given medals?
   a. when they save lives   c. when they die
   b. when they last long enough   d. when they burn a city

_____ 11. In "Losses," what idea is emphasized by the line "When we died they said, 'Our casualties were low.' "?
   a. In war, every death is seen as a tragedy.
   b. War is an exciting experience.
   c. In war, death is often treated with indifference.
   d. People die because they make mistakes.

_____ 12. In "The Death of the Ball Turret Gunner," what woke the speaker when he was six miles from earth?
   a. enemy antiaircraft fire   c. the voice of his pilot
   b. the sound of a hose   d. the engine of the plane

_____ 13. In "The Death of the Ball Turret Gunner," to what does the gunner compare the ball turret in which he sits?
   a. a cloud   c. a womb
   b. a dream   d. black flak

_____ 14. In "The Death of the Ball Turret Gunner," what is thematically significant about the fact that Jarrell chose to write about a gunner rather than any other type of soldier?
   a. The gunner sat in a glass sphere beneath a World War II aircraft.
   b. The gunner's sole function was to shoot at aircraft, so he constantly confronted death.
   c. The gunner fired his gun from an upside-down position.
   d. The gunner constantly thought of his mother.

_____ 15. What is implied by this line in "The Death of the Ball Turret Gunner"? When I died they washed me out of the turret with a hose.
   a. It is difficult to remove someone from a turret.
   b. People grieved for the gunner.
   c. Treatment of the gunner's body is cold and inhuman.
   d. The gunner died nobly.

Vocabulary and Grammar

On the line, write the letter of the one best answer.

_____ 16. Which is the best meaning of *rendezvous* as used in the line ". . . for at that time the B-29s were using Lake Biwa, northeast of Hiroshima, as a rendezvous point . . ."?
   a. resting place   c. communication
   b. destruction zone   d. meeting place

_____ 17. In which pair of sentences is a transition used correctly to show the relationship between ideas?
   a. Miss Sasaki prepared her family's meals. She left for work.
   b. Miss Sasaki prepared her family's meals. However, she left for work.
   c. Miss Sasaki prepared her family's meals. Then she left for work.
   d. Miss Sasaki prepared her family's meals. Therefore, she left for work.

_____ 18. Which is the best meaning of *incessant* as used in the sentence "Mrs. Nakamura was at first annoyed as she listened to the sound of her neighbor's incessant hammering."?
   a. constant   c. violent
   b. loud   d. deliberate

_____ 19. Choose the best transition or transitional phrase to show the relationship between the ideas in these two sentences "The Reverend Mr. Tanimoto was alone. His wife had been commuting with their year-old baby to spent nights in Ushida."?
   a. for some reason   c. even though
   b. therefore   d. because

_____ 20. Which is the best meaning of *convivial* as used in the line "At fifty, he was healthy, convivial, and calm . . ."?
   a. reserved   c. bitter
   b. sociable   d. sluggish

Essay Questions

21. At the end of "Losses," Randall Jarrell writes "When we died they said, 'Our casualties were low.'" At the end of "The Death of the Ball Turret Gunner," Jarrell writes, "When I died they washed me out of the turret with a hose." In an essay, discuss the theme that these two lines have in common. What attitude toward war do both reveal?

22. In an essay, explain John Hersey's attitude toward war and the bombing of Hiroshima. What details provided in the story reveal his attitude?

23. In an essay, compare and contrast the selection from *Hiroshima*, "Losses," and "The Death of the Ball Turret Gunner." What different points of view do the three pieces present? In what ways are they thematically similar?

Unit 6: Prosperity and Protest
(1946–Present)

"Mirror" by Sylvia Plath
"In a Classroom" by Adrienne Rich
"The Explorer" by Gwendolyn Brooks
"Frederick Douglass" and **"Runagate Runagate"** by Robert Hayden

Selection Test

Critical Reading

On the line, write the letter of the one best answer.

____ 1. Who is the "I" in the poem "Mirror"?
    a. the woman   c. the lake
    b. the mirror   d. the pink room

____ 2. What does Plath reveal about herself in "Mirror"?
    a. She fears her own aging.   c. She is vain.
    b. She is cruel.   d. She rejoices in her youth.

____ 3. In "Mirror," the mirror is important because
    a. it evokes pleasant memories of the poet's childhood.
    b. it was a favorite object in the poet's room.
    c. it was given to her by her mother.
    d. it symbolizes the poet's self-reflection.

____ 4. In "Mirror," the metaphor of a mirror as a lake
    a. emphasizes the smoothness of the mirror's surface.
    b. symbolizes the woman's transformation from a young girl to an old woman.
    c. echoes the woman's tears as she looks at herself in the mirror.
    d. reinforces the objectivity with which the mirror reflects reality.

____ 5. In the poem "In a Classroom," what situation is being described?
    a. People are collecting stones.
    b. People are removing books from the classroom.
    c. People are reading and discussing poetry.
    d. People are voicing their dislike of poetry.

____ 6. In "In a Classroom," in what are students most interested?
    a. the mechanics of how poetry is written
    b. the deeper meanings behind the poetry they read
    c. doing away with poetry
    d. getting Jude interested in poetry

____ 7. From details in "In a Classroom," how might you best interpret the description of Jude's behavior?
    a. He is interested in learning how to construct a poem.
    b. He is interested in finding meaning in poetry and in his life.
    c. He is the class leader.
    d. He dislikes people in the class.

____ 8. In "The Explorer," the speaker's main goal is to
    a. talk to his neighbors.   c. find a quiet place.
    b. deal with his grief.   d. open a closed door.

9. How might you interpret the details the speaker in "The Explorer" provides about his surroundings?
   a. The apartment is dirty.
   b. The apartment house in which the speaker lives is burning.
   c. Neighbors are trying to keep the speaker out of their homes.
   d. Home is an uncomfortable place for the person in the poem.

10. What biographical information about Gwendolyn Brooks enhances a reader's understanding of theme and context in "The Explorer"?
    a. She was the first African American writer to win a Pulitzer Prize.
    b. She grew up in an inner-city neighborhood.
    c. She worked as a teacher.
    d. She was named Poet Laureate of Illinois.

11. According to "Frederick Douglass," how will Douglass be remembered?
    a. by words carved on a statue   c. by bronze statues
    b. by the lives of free people   d. by poetic tributes

12. In "Frederick Douglass," the poet expresses his hope
    a. for a time when liberty will be automatically assumed for all.
    b. for a formal tribute to the work of Frederick Douglass.
    c. that politicians will legislate freedom for all.
    d. that his freedom to hunt will continue.

13. How does knowing that Robert Hayden was an African American writing during the 1930's deepen readers' understanding of "Frederick Douglass"?
    a. They see that every problem Douglass faced had been solved by the time Hayden was born.
    b. They see that Hayden did not really know Douglass well.
    c. They understand that even many years after the efforts of Frederick Douglass, African Americans still struggled with issues of freedom and liberty.
    d. They understand that Douglass's ideas were outdated in the 1930's.

14. What kind of movement is conveyed by these lines from "Runagate Runagate"?

    . . . falls rises stumbles on from darkness into darkness / and the darkness thicketed with shapes of terror / and the hunters pursuing and the hounds pursuing . . .

    a. slow creeping   c. confident swaggering
    b. frantic running   d. clumsy shuffling

15. Who is speaking in this passage from "Runagate Runagate"?

    If you see my Pompey, 30 yrs of age, / new breeches, plain stockings, negro shoes; / . . . Catch them if you can, but it won't be easy. / They'll dart underground . . .

    a. a slave holder   c. an escaped slave
    b. Harriet Tubman   d. John Brown

16. How might knowledge of slavery and the Underground Railroad deepen a reader's understanding of the following lines from "Runagate Runagate": "No more auction block for me / no more driver's lash for me / . . . And before I'll be a slave / I'll be buried in my grave"?
    a. It might provide vivid imagery lacking in the poem.
    b. It might help readers understand the vocabulary of the selection.
    c. It indicates that the Underground Railroad was not usually effective.
    d. It explains that the "auction block" refers to the practice of selling slaves, and the "driver's lash" refers to the abuse slaves had to endure.

Vocabulary and Grammar

On the line, write the letter of the one best answer.

____ 17. Which is the best meaning of *preconceptions* as used in this passage from "Mirror"?

> I am silver and exact. I have no preconceptions. / Whatever I see I swallow immediately / Just as it is . . .

a. ideas formed beforehand
b. deep thoughts
c. negative feelings
d. angry feelings

____ 18. Which line does *not* demonstrate parallel structure?
a. There were no boundaries and there were no quiet rooms.
b. The woman greeted the mirror with tears, anger, and unhappiness.
c. People in the classroom liked reading and to study different elements of poetry.
d. Some darted underground and some plunged into quicksand.

____ 19. Which is the best meaning of *din* as used in this passage from "The Explorer"?

> Somehow to find a still spot in the noise / Was the frayed inner want, the winding, the frayed hope / Whose tatters he kept hunting through the din."

a. dim lighting
b. loud noise
c. stillness
d. tangled maze

____ 20. Which line does not demonstrate parallel structure?
a. He walked through scrambled halls, and he listened to human voices.
b. The slaves declared that they wanted no more auction blocks and no more abuse.
c. I swallow what I see, and I reflect the truth.
d. On their journey, the fugitives faced danger and there was also pain.

Essay Questions

21. In an essay, explain how the images in "Frederick Douglass" and "Runagate Runagate" enhance understanding of historical events. Then explain the theme found in both poems.

22. In the poem "The Explorer," the poet writes,

> Somehow to find a still spot in the noise / Was the frayed inner want, the winding, the frayed hope / Whose tatters he kept hunting through the din. / A satin peace somewhere. / A room of wily hush somewhere within.

In an essay, interpret this passage. What does it reveal about the subject's state of mind? What does the subject want? How does this passage relate to the poem's central message?

23. Struggle is a common theme in poetry. Sometimes the speakers or subjects of poems face struggles, either within themselves or with outside forces. What struggles are reflected in "Mirror," "In a Classroom," "The Explorer," "Frederick Douglass," and "Runagate Runagate"? With what or whom do speakers or subjects of these poems struggle? Answer these questions in an essay.

"For My Children" by Colleen McElroy
"Bidwell Ghost" by Louise Erdrich

Selection Test

Critical Reading

On the line, write the letter of the one best answer.

_____ 1. What are the tales that McElroy shares in "For My Children"?
    a. the story of her children's cultural heritage
    b. the history of St. Louis
    c. stories that her grandmother told when she was young
    d. Bible stories

_____ 2. What does the speaker of "For My Children" mean by the following passage?

    But skin of honey and beauty of ebony begins / In the land called Bilad as-Sudan.

    a. The people who live in Bilad as-Sudan have beautiful skin.
    b. The speaker has silky, beautiful skin.
    c. The speaker looks like the people who live in Bilad as-Sudan.
    d. The origin of her physical characteristics is unknown.

_____ 3. What quality makes "For My Children" a lyric poem?
    a. It tells about real events in the poet's life.
    b. Its musical stanzas express the speaker's thoughts and feelings.
    c. It makes extensive use of visual imagery.
    d. It has no regular rhyme or meter.

_____ 4. Which word best describes the feeling or emotion expressed in "For My Children"?
    a. guilt   c. regret
    b. desire   d. celebration

_____ 5. How many complete thoughts are expressed in this stanza from "For My Children"?

    The line of your cheeks recalls Ibo melodies / As surely as oboe and flute. / The sun dances a honey and cocoa duet on your faces. / I see smiles that mirror schoolboy smiles / In the land called Bilad as-Sudan; / I see the link between the Mississippi and the Congo.

    a. one   c. three
    b. two   d. four

_____ 6. In "For My Children," what does the speaker see in "profile and bust" of her children?
    a. skin of honey
    b. her ancestral heritage
    c. Ibo cheeks
    d. Watusi height

_____ 7. What link does the speaker see at the end of "For My Children"?
    a. the link between herself and her children
    b. the link between herself and St. Louis
    c. the link between the Mississippi and the Congo
    d. the link between St. Louis and Burundi

_____ 8. In "Bidwell Ghost," why does the ghost wait by the road each night?
    a. to revisit the site of a great, personal tragedy
    b. to stop passing cars
    c. to frighten passersby
    d. to see her family home

_____ 9. What happened to the Bidwell ghost's home?
    a. It fell apart due to neglect.
    b. It was sold.
    c. It was destroyed by fire.
    d. It was abandoned twenty years ago.

_____ 10. Which word best describes the overall mood of "Bidwell Ghost"?
    a. mysterious
    b. frightening
    c. joyful
    d. tragic

_____ 11. Which image from "Bidwell Ghost" best suggests nature's endurance and renewal?
    a. "The heat charred the branches / of the apple trees, / but nothing can kill that wood."
    b. "First the orchard bowed low and complained / of the unpicked fruit, / then the branches cracked apart and fell."
    c. "The windfalls sweetened to wine / beneath the ruined arms and snow."
    d. "Each spring now, in the grass, buds form on the tattered wood.

_____ 12. In "Bidwell Ghost," what effect is achieved by breaking this single sentence into a three-line stanza?

    Each night she waits by the road / in a thin white dress / embroidered with fire.

    a. The focus is placed on the ghost's thin white dress.
    b. The startling image of the Bidwell ghost is dramatized.
    c. The event of the Bidwell ghost's nightly visit is emphasized.
    d. The event of the tragic fire is introduced.

_____ 13. What feeling do the line breaks and rhythms of "Bidwell Ghost" reinforce?
    a. sorrow
    b. fear
    c. anger
    d. gentleness

_____ 14. What is the speaker's attitude toward the ghost in "Bidwell Ghost"?
    a. The speaker is frightened by the ghost.
    b. The speaker is impatient with the ghost's nightly visits.
    c. The speaker worries over the ghost as if she were a lost or lonely child.
    d. The speaker grieves over the ghost's tragedy.

Vocabulary and Grammar

On the line, write the letter of the one best answer.

_____ 15. The word _heritage_ means
    a. an extended family.
    b. something handed down from one's ancestors or the past.
    c. ancient history.
    d. the time and place where one is born.

_____ 16. Which word could be substituted for *effigies* without changing the meaning of this passage from "For My Children"?

> Where effigies of my ancestors are captured / In Beatle tunes, / And crowns never touch Bantu heads.

    a. photographs   c. melodies
    b. relatives   d. likenesses

_____ 17. Which word from "For My Children" is a synonym for *shackles*?
    a. concerns   c. chains
    b. prisons   d. huts

_____ 18. Which line contains a verb in the present perfect tense?
    a. "I have stored up tales for you, my children"
    b. "So I search for a heritage beyond St. Louis"
    c. "I cradled my knees"
    d. "The line of your cheeks recalls Ibo melodies"

_____ 19. In the line from "Bidwell Ghost," what does the present perfect verb tense indicate about the event in time?

> It has been twenty years

    a. habitual action
    b. an action completed in the past
    c. something that began in the past and continuing in the present
    d. a future action

_____ 20. Which line contains a verb in the future tense?
    a. "Each night she waits by the road"
    b. "The heat charred the branches/of the apple trees"
    c. "She will climb into your car"
    d. "The windfalls sweetened to wine"

Essay Questions

21. In the last stanza of "For My Children," the speaker says, "I see smiles that mirror school-boy smiles / In the land called Bilad as-Sudan; / I see the link between the Mississippi and the Congo." In an essay, explain what the speaker means by "the link between the Mississippi and the Congo" and what feelings she has about that link.

22. In an essay, describe a lyric poem's characteristics. Then explain why "For My Children" and "Bidwell Ghost" are examples of lyric poetry. Support your analysis with details from both poems.

23. In an essay, compare and contrast the role that heritage plays in "For My Children" and "Bidwell Ghost." Use examples from the poems to support your analysis.

"The Writer in the Family" by E. L. Doctorow

Selection Test

Critical Reading

On the line, write the letter of the one best answer.

_____ 1. What happens to the narrator's father?
   a. He moves to Arizona.
   b. He dies.
   c. He opens an electric appliance store.
   d. He contracts bronchitis.

_____ 2. What do the aunts tell the grandmother about what has happened to Jack?
   a. that he has died
   b. that he has gone on vacation
   c. that he has joined the Navy
   d. that he has moved to Arizona for his health

_____ 3. How does Aunt Frances involve Jonathan in her plan?
   a. She asks him to visit his elderly grandmother.
   b. She turns him against his mother.
   c. She asks him to write letters from Jack to the grandmother.
   d. She invites him to dinner at Larchmont.

_____ 4. Why do the aunts make key family decisions without consulting Jonathan's mother?
   a. They consider her to be an outsider.
   b. They don't want to trouble her.
   c. They know she is in mourning.
   d. They live a great distance apart.

_____ 5. Which action best reveals the true nature of Aunt Frances's character?
   a. She inquires after Harold.
   b. She weeps after reading Jonathan's first letter.
   c. She tells Jonathan that he is a talented man.
   d. She conceals Jack's death from the grandmother.

_____ 6. Jonathan can be considered a dynamic character because he
   a. does not change throughout the story.
   b. undergoes a change in his understanding of his father.
   c. causes the conflict between his mother and Aunt Frances.
   d. challenges Aunt Frances.

_____ 7. Why is there a bitter, long-standing argument between Jonathan's father's side of the family and Ruth, Jonathan's mother?
   a. Ruth holds Jack's side of the family responsible for his death.
   b. Aunt Frances and Ruth have never gotten along very well.
   c. Each side holds the other responsible for the fact that Jack did not live up to anyone's expectations.
   d. Jack's side of the family always puts on airs.

_____ 8. Which adjective best describes Jonathan's family's economic situation?
   a. well-set   c. dire
   b. comfortable   d. tight

_____ 9. Aunt Frances can be considered a static character because she
   a. is in conflict with Jonathan's mother.
   b. is a strong, dominant character.
   c. is totally unpredictable.
   d. remains unchanged throughout the story.

_____ 10. Is it correct to say that the characterization of Jonathan's mother is dynamic?
   a. yes, because she cheers up when Harold's girlfriend comes to dinner
   b. no, because her character remains for the most part angry and bitter
   c. no, because she remains optimistic throughout the course of the story
   d. yes, because her feelings toward her dead husband change

_____ 11. Which word best describes Jonathan's writing letters to his grandmother?
   a. thoughtful
   b. cruel
   c. dishonest
   d. kind

_____ 12. Which word best describes Aunt Frances's behavior when she returns Jonathan's final
   letter to him?
   a. manipulative
   b. considerate
   c. disappointing
   d. inevitable

_____ 13. What event prompts Jonathan's feelings toward his father to change?
   a. He learns that his father, too, wanted to become a writer.
   b. He connects the photo of his youthful father on his training ship with his father's
      set of Great Sea Novels.
   c. He learns of his father's belated success as a businessman.
   d. He learns of his father's many disappointments.

_____ 14. What does Jonathan's dream about his father represent?
   a. Jonathan's grief over his father's death.
   b. Jonathan's rejection of his father.
   c. Jonathan's love for his father.
   d. Jonathan's fond memories of his father.

Vocabulary and Grammar

On the line, write the letter of the one best answer.

_____ 15. _Bronchitis_ means
   a. a species of tree native to Arizona.
   b. an instrument for measuring atmospheric pressure.
   c. a disease or inflammation of the lung's passageways.
   d. a disease or inflammation of the tendons.

_____ 16. Which word or phrase could be substituted for _cronies_ without changing the meaning of the sentence?

   > And so it came about that as we mourned him at home in our stocking feet, my
   > grandmother was bragging to her cronies about her son's new life in the dry air
   > of the desert.

   a. close companions   c. relatives
   b. neighbors   d. enemies

___ 17. For Jonathan's mother, the family _____ contained a collection of unforgivable remarks.
    a. cronies
    b. portrait
    c. anthology
    d. barometer

___ 18. The death of Jonathan's father, which deeply _____ Ruth, had a great _____ upon Jonathan and Harold as well.
    a. effected; affect
    b. affected; effect
    c. affected; affect
    d. effected; effect

___ 19. Finding the set of Great Sea Novels _____ Jonathan's understanding of his father.
    a. affect
    b. effect
    c. affected
    d. effected

___ 20. How did Jonathan's letters _____ the elderly grandmother?
    a. affects
    b. effected
    c. effect
    d. affect

Essay Questions

21. In an essay, explain the purpose of Jonathan's final letter to his grandmother. Was his letter purposely cruel, as Aunt Frances says? In what spirit do you think Jonathan wrote the final letter? What do you think he hoped to express in it? Support your answer with details from the story.

22. Jonathan is a dynamic character. Describe in an essay the characteristics that make him so. Use examples from the story to illustrate how Jonathan changes, what prompts this change, and what new understanding he gains.

23. At the end of the story, Aunt Frances and Jonathan strongly disagree with each other regarding Jonathan's mother. Aunt Frances believes that Jonathan has been "poisoned" by his mother's bitter feelings. She also believes that Ruth "drove poor Jack crazy with her demands." In an essay, explain what you think of Aunt Frances's words and actions. How would you judge her point of view? Who do you think has the more accurate understanding of Ruth? Why?

"Camouflaging the Chimera" by Yusef Komunyakaa
"Ambush" by Tim O'Brien

Selection Test

Critical Reading

On the line, write the letter of the one best answer.

_____ 1. Whose experiences are described in the poem "Camouflaging the Chimera"?
  a. American soldiers in Vietnam   c. civilians who are victims of war
  b. Vietcong soldiers   d. mythological Greek soldiers

_____ 2. In "Camouflaging the Chimera," the poet's use of the first-person pronoun *we* emphasizes
  a. the way in which the soldiers, when at war, function as a unit.
  b. the friendships between the soldiers.
  c. the habits and mannerisms of the soldiers.
  d. the poet's wish to separate himself from his experiences.

_____ 3. In "Camouflaging the Chimera," what does Komunyakaa mean when he writes, "We wove/ourselves into the terrain . . ."?
  a. They became lazy and would not get up from the ground to fight.
  b. They made maps of the area so that they would never become lost.
  c. To hide, they covered themselves with mud, branches, and grass.
  d. They quietly weaved when they weren't fighting.

_____ 4. In "Camouflaging the Chimera," what do these lines suggest about the soldiers' experience? "We hugged bamboo & leaned/against a breeze off the river . . ."
  a. They hide near bamboo, leaning toward an occasional breeze.
  b. They relax behind bamboo, enjoying a river breeze.
  c. They lie resting in the shade of bamboo.
  d. They march between rows of bamboo.

_____ 5. For what have the soldiers in "Camouflaging the Chimera" been waiting?
  a. for daylight, when they will plan a new strategy
  b. for night, when they plan to leave their ambush site and attack
  c. for night, when they will rest
  d. for daylight, so they can prepare food and seek shelter

_____ 6. In the title "Camouflaging the Chimera," why does the poet associate the soldiers with a Chimera, a fire-breathing monster?
  a. Many soldiers are overheated after waiting around in the hot jungle.
  b. The soldiers look like monsters in their camouflage.
  c. The soldiers tell myths to pass the time as they wait.
  d. Soldiers on attack become a frightening and destructive force.

_____ 7. In the first paragraph of "Ambush," what effect does the use of first person have on the reader's understanding of the narrator?
  a. He appears to take his experience in Vietnam lightly and delights in talking about it.
  b. He appears to be a thoughtful man struggling with a difficult experience in his past.
  c. He appears to have a difficult relationship with his young daughter.
  d. He appears to be a bitter and untruthful man.

____ 8. In "Ambush," how does the narrator feel when he sees the enemy soldier?
    a. terrified
    b. angry
    c. excited
    d. calm

____ 9. In the scene from "Ambush" that shows the narrator holding and tossing the grenade, what does the first-person narration help readers to understand?
    a. He is uncomfortable with having to take a life as a matter of duty.
    b. He is proud to be a soldier and willing to do anything for his country.
    c. He feels killing is unpleasant but feels secure in the fact that he must do his job.
    d. He feels excited to be in such an eventful environment.

____ 10. What do these words of the narrator of "Ambush" mean? "It was not a matter of live or die. There was no real peril. Almost certainly the young man would have passed by. And it will always be that way."
    a. People will think of him as a terrible person because he killed a man.
    b. He lives with the guilt that he killed a man because he panicked.
    c. He knows he did the only thing he could.
    d. He will always remember his bravery in preventing a dangerous situation.

____ 11. Envisioning which passage from "Ambush" helps you to understand the narrator's sense of horror over the realization that he has killed a man?
    a. "The grenade bounced once and rolled across the trail. I did not hear it, but there must've been a sound, because the young man dropped his weapon. . . ."
    b. "I did not see him as the enemy; I did not ponder issues of morality or politics or moral duty. I crouched and kept my head low."
    c. "He lay at the center of the trail, his right leg bent beneath him, his one eye shut, his other eye a huge star-shaped hole."
    d. "The grenade made a popping noise—not soft but not loud either—not what I'd expected—and there was a puff of dust and smoke. . . ."

____ 12. In "Ambush," how does Kiowa respond to the narrator's reaction to the killing?
    a. He expresses sadness over the incident.
    b. He becomes angry with him for killing the man when it wasn't completely necessary.
    c. He tells him that killing is always unpleasant and that his feelings are normal.
    d. He tells him that it was a good kill, and that he should shape up and accept the fact that he is fighting a war.

____ 13. What is the main reason Kiowa and the narrator in "Ambush" do not understand each other when they discuss the killing?
    a. Kiowa does not like the narrator's second-guessing his job.
    b. Kiowa views the victim as just a casualty of war, and the narrator views the victim as a human being.
    c. Kiowa does not know why the narrator threw the grenade.
    d. It is late at night, and both the narrator and Kiowa are exhausted.

____ 14. In "Ambush," what is the significance of the scene the narrator imagines at the end of the story?
    a. It reveals the depth of his regret over taking the life of another human being.
    b. It shows how much he misses his days spent as a soldier.
    c. It reaffirms to the reader his belief in the cause for which he was fighting in Vietnam.
    d. It reveals the fact that time has helped him to move past a bad experience and go on with his life.

_____ 15. In "Ambush," what is the most important message that O'Brien wants to deliver?
   a. that killing is part of war
   b. that not everyone is meant to be a soldier
   c. that the taking of another human life is not to be regarded casually
   d. that individuals must put aside personal feelings to fight for an important cause

Vocabulary and Grammar

On the line, write the letter of the one best answer.

_____ 16. Choose the meaning of *ambush* as it is used in the sentence. The soldiers, being part of an ambush, climbed trees to spy on the enemy camp.
   a. peace-keeping mission   c. a violent attack
   b. a strategic planning session   d. a lying in wait to attack by surprise

_____ 17. Which sentence contains a noun clause acting as a direct object?
   a. The soldiers took turns keeping watch over their camp.
   b. Kiowa tried to tell the narrator about what being a soldier means.
   c. The narrator hoped that someday his daughter would read his story.
   d. Memories are what bother the narrator.

_____ 18. Choose the meaning of *ammunition* as it is used in the sentence: Before launching the attack, the soldiers gathered plenty of ammunition.
   a. strength and courage
   b. nourishment
   c. something hurled by a weapon or exploded like a weapon
   d. guns

_____ 19. Which sentence contains a noun clause acting like an object of a preposition?
   a. The soldier felt that his actions were wrong.
   b. The men painted themselves with mud from the river.
   c. VC soldiers struggled as they climbed up the hillside.
   d. Soldiers were searching for whatever they could find.

_____ 20. Choose the best meaning of *gape* as it is used in the sentence.

   All he could do was gape at the sight of the young man's body.

   a. cry hysterically   c. gasp
   b. stare open-mouthed   d. shout

Essay Questions

21. Both "Camouflaging the Chimera" and "Ambush" present images that help readers to envision the experiences of soldiers fighting in the Vietnam War. In an essay, discuss the images that help you envision the action in each. How does envisioning these images help you find meaning in them?

22. In "Ambush," what does the narrator's reaction to his killing of an enemy soldier reveal about his personality? What is he able to recognize in his victim? In what way is he different from the soldier who describes the action as "a good kill"? What does this piece convey about compromises people might have to make to be effective soldiers? Answer these questions in an essay.

23. Both "Camouflaging the Chimera" and "Ambush" emerged from the writers' experiences of fighting the Vietnam War. In an essay, explain what is similar and what is different about their experiences and what these pieces convey about war.

Name _____ Date _____

The Crucible, **Act I,** by Arthur Miller

Selection Test

Critical Reading

On the line, write the letter of the one best answer.

_____ 1. What is Reverend Parris upset about at the opening of Act I?
   a. rumors of witchcraft circulating in the community
   b. Abigail's dismissal from the Proctor household
   c. his daughter's condition and the possible connection to her inappropriate activities in the woods
   d. Tituba's influence over the children

_____ 2. From the comments of Parris in Act I, his concern for his daughter seems primarily based on his
   a. anxiety about his reputation.
   b. fear for the fate of her soul.
   c. great love for his only child.
   d. terror of the Devil.

_____ 3. In Act I, how does Reverend Parris's belief in the supernatural affect his response to his daughter's illness?
   a. He refuses to send for a doctor.
   b. He professes his faith that God will heal her.
   c. He seeks help from Reverend Hale.
   d. He believes Abigail's assertion that Betty was not bewitched.

_____ 4. What can be inferred from Act I about the attitude of Puritans toward their slaves?
   a. They saw their slaves as equals in God's sight.
   b. They saw their slaves as being only a step removed from paganism.
   c. They feared and mistrusted their slaves.
   d. They treated their slaves as valued members of the household.

_____ 5. Thomas Putnam's attitude toward Reverend Parris is one of
   a. mistrust.
   b. respect.
   c. pity.
   d. contempt.

_____ 6. This passage is from the background information at the opening of Act I. For what detail that comes out later in Act I does this information prepare you?

   > Long-held hatreds of neighbors could now be openly expressed, and vengeance taken, despite the Bible's charitable injunctions. Land-lust which had been expressed before by constant bickering over boundaries and deeds, could now be elevated to the arena of morality . . .

   a. Putnam arguing with Proctor about a piece of land to which both men lay claim
   b. Reverend Parris complaining about his salary
   c. Abigail's reluctance to tell the truth about what happened in the woods
   d. Abigail's dismissal from service in the Proctor household

_____ 7. How does Mrs. Putnam justify sending Ruth to Tituba?
   a. Tituba promised to revive Mrs. Putnam's dead children.
   b. Mrs. Putnam didn't think a little foolish "conjuring" would do any harm.
   c. Mrs. Putnam thought it might help Ruth, who seemed to be ailing.
   d. Mrs. Putnam feels she deserves to know why she has had to endure the deaths of seven children.

_____ 8. Mrs. Putnam's comments suggest that her primary motivation in hunting for witches is
    a. anger at having lost her children.
    b. compassion for the two sick girls.
    c. curiosity about the mysterious events in the woods.
    d. resentment of Reverend Parris.

_____ 9. Which phrase best describes Abigail Williams's character?
    a. impulsive and thoughtless
    b. naive and timid
    c. proud and manipulative
    d. affectionate and vulnerable

_____ 10. From Act I, it can be inferred that the Puritans associated the forest with
    a. dancing and other amusements.
    b. disorder and evil.
    c. God's presence in nature.
    d. the purity of the natural world.

_____ 11. From the scene in which the girls are alone, what can be inferred as the basis of Abigail's influence over the other girls?
    a. her beauty and cleverly crafted purity
    b. her social position as the minister's niece
    c. her charm and magnetic persuasiveness
    d. her use of her early experiences to terrorize them

_____ 12. Which word best describes John Proctor's words and actions in Act I?
    a. compassionate   c. independent
    b. devout   d. shrewd

_____ 13. Considering Tituba's state of mind when she began naming names, what can you infer about her motivation?
    a. She was afraid of Reverend Hale and thought naming names would save her from punishment.
    b. She actually saw Goody Good and Goody Osburn in the forest and wanted to tell the truth.
    c. She was confused and was talking about a dream she once had.
    d. She didn't like the women she named, and she hoped they'd be punished.

_____ 14. Why does Reverend Parris send for Reverend Hale?
    a. Parris feels the Salemites will be more accepting of an outside opinion.
    b. Hale is considered an expert in matters of witchcraft and the Devil.
    c. Hale is the most skilled medical person in the region.
    d. Parris feels utterly unprepared to deal with the issues he fears are at hand.

_____ 15. Given this piece of information from the stage directions, what can readers conclude about Tituba's behavior at the end of Act I?

> _She enters as one does who can no longer bear to be barred from the sight of her beloved, but she is also very frightened because her slave sense has warned her that, as always, trouble in this house eventually lands on her back._

    a. Tituba is so fond of Betty that she'll try anything to help her.
    b. Tituba is actually in love with Reverend Parris and confesses to keep him out of trouble.
    c. Tituba's "slave sense" is what got her and the girls into trouble in the first place.
    d. She is so sure that trouble will befall her that she plays along with Hale as he pushes her for information.

Vocabulary and Grammar

On the line, write the letter of the one best answer.

____ 16. Abigail has an "endless capacity for dissembling," which means
  a. she is a destructive person.
  b. she is very quick to get at the heart of a matter.
  c. she frequently conceals her true motives from those around her.
  d. she is able to keep track of the different stories she tells to different people.

____ 17. Someone who has a *predilection* has
  a. a decisive nature.
  b. a desire to hold an elected office.
  c. an ability to foresee events.
  d. a preexisting preference.

____ 18. Which of the following characterizes an *ingratiating* person?
  a. Nancy does odd jobs for the neighbors to earn money for college.
  b. Marla volunteers to help her teacher sort papers after school.
  c. Ned argues with his neighbor about a broken fence.
  d. When no one is looking, Sal pushes fallen leaves onto his neighbor's yard.

____ 19. Choose the sentence in which the italicized pronoun is correct.
  a. Mary Warren is bolder than *her*.
  b. Abigail fears the actions of Mercy and *she*.
  c. Parris blames and mistrusts Betty and *her*.
  d. Mr. Putnam is more eager than *them* to cry witchcraft.

____ 20. Choose the item that correctly identifies the omitted word and the case of the italicized pronoun in this incomplete construction. Although Abigail is frightened, she is more clever and confident than *they*.
  a. ". . . than they [is]."; object
  b. ". . . than they [are]."; subject
  c. ". . . than [with] they."; object
  d. ". . . than [about] they."; subject

Essay Questions

21. What kind of man is Reverend Parris? What does Miller reveal about him, both through background information and dialogue? How do Parris's nature and background affect his response to issues and situations in Act I? Answer these questions in an essay, and cite examples of Parris's actions and the motivations behind them.

22. The root of the conflict in Act I is Reverend Parris's discovery of Tituba and the girls in the woods on the night before the action in the play begins. In an essay, trace the pieces of information that are revealed about the scene in the woods. Who did what and who saw what? How and when are pieces of information revealed to the reader, and for what reasons? Finally, explain why you think Miller reveals all information about the activities in the woods through dialogue, not through background information. How and why is his method effective?

23. Miller provides extensive background information about the community of Salem as well as about its residents. What is the community like? What are the inhabitants like? How do they interact with one another? What are their beliefs? Explain how the atmosphere of Salem and the nature of its residents lend themselves to the situation that develops in Act I. How does the information Miller provides add meaning to the reading of the play? Answer these questions in an essay.

The Crucible, **Act II,** by Arthur Miller

Selection Test

Critical Reading

On the line, write the letter of the one best answer.

_____ 1. What is the setting of Act II of *The Crucible*?
   a. the following day at the home of John and Elizabeth Proctor
   b. Reverend Parris's home, about a week after the accusations of witchcraft have begun
   c. the Proctors' home, eight days after the girls have begun to accuse people
   d. the Salem meeting house, just before Abigail's trial

_____ 2. Which of the following sentences best describes the relationship between John and Elizabeth Proctor at the opening of Act II?
   a. They are warm and affectionate.
   b. They seem not to care about each other.
   c. They seem ill at ease together.
   d. They are hostile and bitter toward each other.

_____ 3. When Elizabeth says to Proctor, "The magistrate sits in your heart that judges you," she means that Proctor
   a. carries the knowledge of his own guilt.
   b. is too quick to judge himself.
   c. should speak more openly about his thoughts.
   d. knows that she loves him and forgives him.

_____ 4. Proctor's comment to Mary Warren, "It's strange work for a Christian girl to hang old women," implies that he thinks Mary's behavior is
   a. cruel.   c. cowardly.
   b. hypocritical.   d. rash.

_____ 5. Which of the following words best characterizes Mary Warren?
   a. pious   c. gullible
   b. jealous   d. vicious

_____ 6. What is Mary's motive in giving the "poppet" to Elizabeth?
   a. She wants to make friends with Elizabeth.
   b. She wants Elizabeth to see her as an innocent girl.
   c. She wants to plant evidence of witchcraft in Elizabeth's house.
   d. She wants to make peace with Elizabeth after disobeying her.

_____ 7. When Mary says that the crowd parted for Abigail like the sea for Israel, she makes
   a. a comparison to politics.   c. eventual trouble for Abigail.
   b. an allusion to the Bible.   d. a bigoted joke.

_____ 8. When Hale appears at the Proctors' door, he is described as "different now—drawn a little, and there is a quality of deference, even of guilt, about his manner now." What accounts for this change?
   a. He has seen events go beyond his expectations in Salem.
   b. He no longer believes in witchcraft but must proceed.
   c. He feels guilty that he has also felt desire for Abigail.
   d. He fears that even he may be at risk.

____ 9. Hale's interview with Proctor reveals Hale to be
  a. blinded by power.
  b. troubled but rigid.
  c. kind but foolish.
  d. tolerant and open.

____ 10. What is Proctor's attitude toward Parris?
  a. He respects Parris's devotion to God.
  b. He differs with Parris on issues of church doctrine.
  c. He believes that Parris is too interested in wealth.
  d. He thinks that Parris is too lenient in judging people.

____ 11. Why does Proctor forget the commandment forbidding adultery?
  a. He has a guilty conscience.
  b. He has never properly learned the commandments.
  c. He believes that it is an unjust commandment.
  d. He is afraid of revealing his own sin.

____ 12. When Rebecca Nurse is charged, Hale is troubled. What does he intend to point out by this allusion to the story that the Devil was once an angel?

  an hour before the Devil fell, God thought him beautiful in Heaven.

  a. that people sometimes change as they get older
  b. that even beauty is no indicator of goodness
  c. the impossibility of determining God's will
  d. the powerful skills of deception the Devil has

____ 13. In anger, Proctor calls Hale "Pontius Pilate." Proctor's intention is to
  a. imply that Hale shares pagan beliefs.
  b. charge Hale with manufacturing evidence.
  c. send Hale to the Bible for study and thought.
  d. accuse Hale of doing injustice by doing nothing.

____ 14. What is implied about human nature by the number of accusations that are brought forth?
  a. People are generally irresponsible and weak.
  b. People who do not express their feelings openly cannot be trusted.
  c. People are basically vengeful and cruel.
  d. People want to find a scapegoat when things go wrong for them.

____ 15. Proctor believes that Abigail accuses Elizabeth of witchcraft because
  a. Elizabeth treated Abigail harshly.
  b. Abigail wants to punish Proctor for rejecting her.
  c. Abigail fears that Elizabeth will denounce her for seducing Proctor.
  d. Abigail wants to distract attention from the episode in the woods.

Vocabulary and Grammar

On the line, write the letter of the one best answer.

____ 16. If one does something *avidly*, one does it
  a. eagerly.   c. quickly.
  b. shamefully.   d. reluctantly.

____ 17. If one shows *deference*, one shows
  a. ignorance.   c. respect.
  b. disregard.   d. knowledge.

____ 18. Something that is an *abomination* is
   a. deafening.
   b. inevitable.
   c. popular.
   d. disgusting.

____ 19. Introductory words in sentences should be
   a. set off by commas.
   b. punctuated as if they were separate sentences.
   c. avoided.
   d. enclosed in quotation marks.

____ 20. Which sentence is punctuated *incorrectly*?
   a. Well, one may always wonder about the appearance of evil.
   b. Yes there is a modern point to the play.
   c. No historical records exist that contain dialogue.
   d. Of course, reasonable conjecture seems fair enough.

Essay Questions

21. Abigail Williams does not appear in Act II, but she has cast a long shadow from Act I, and her importance in Act II is powerful. Write an essay in which you tell about the significance of Abigail Williams in Act II, explaining her effect on characters and actions in this part of the play.

22. In Act II, Mary Warren gives Elizabeth Proctor a doll, a "poppet," which she says is a present. The shifts in blame surrounding the doll become a major factor in the actions of Act II. How does Miller use this token to create drama? Write an essay that explains the role of the poppet in the plot. Include how it is viewed, the plot developments surrounding it, and what characters do and don't know about the real responsibility for it.

23. One pivotal character in Act II has an apparently weak character as a human being. What motivates Mary Warren throughout this part of the play? What does she want? How is it that she becomes such a focal point? Write an essay in which you assess the nature of Mary Warren as she appears in Act II, and explain how her character illustrates some of the play's concerns. Use examples from the play to support your ideas.

The Crucible, **Act III**, by Arthur Miller

Selection Test

Critical Reading

On the line, write the letter of the one best answer.

____ 1. What can the audience infer from Judge Hathorne's questioning of Martha Corey at the beginning of Act III?
a. The court is determined to uncover the truth at any cost.
b. Martha Corey's love of reading is the source of the accusations against her.
c. The court presumes that anyone accused of witchcraft is guilty.
d. Even the most respected citizens have come under suspicion.

____ 2. Hathorne's comments to Giles Corey and Francis Nurse imply that he wants to arrest them because
a. he believes they are challenging his authority.
b. they are trying to introduce improperly obtained evidence.
c. he considers them to be unprincipled and reckless.
d. they have slandered Thomas Putnam.

____ 3. Francis Nurse tells the judges that the girls are frauds. Hathorne's response is, "This is contempt, sir, contempt!" What is this an example of?
a. verbal irony
b. dramatic irony
c. sarcasm
d. foreshadowing

____ 4. What is Proctor's main purpose in bringing Mary Warren to court?
a. to strengthen her character
b. to discredit Reverend Parris
c. to save his wife from condemnation
d. to demonstrate the illegality of the court's proceedings

____ 5. During the presentation of the evidence, Proctor's behavior toward Danforth can best be described as
a. crafty.
b. defiant.
c. evasive.
d. respectful.

____ 6. Which character represents the tactic of making personal attacks on the integrity of witnesses?
a. Herrick
b. Danforth
c. Hathorne
d. Parris

____ 7. As the action proceeds, the allusion to the story of Raphael and Tobias becomes ironic because
a. the developments contradict the message of the story.
b. the story is revealed to be false.
c. the developments show that the characters have misunderstood the story.
d. certain characters twist the meaning of the story to suit their own purposes.

_____ 8. Which type of figure is represented by Ezekiel Cheever?
   a. the witness who uses the investigation as an instrument of personal vengeance
   b. the witness who suffers for his refusal to incriminate others
   c. the naive witness who harms others by cooperating in an unjust process
   d. the public figure who misuses the power of office

_____ 9. Why is Parris's charge of conspiracy effective?
   a. It gives a plausible explanation for the divisions in the parish.
   b. It appeals to Danforth's fears of subversion.
   c. It feeds Danforth's sense of his own importance.
   d. It plays on Danforth's personal antagonism to ward Giles Corey and Francis Nurse.

_____ 10. What motivates Hale's attempt to intervene on behalf of Proctor?
   a. Hale's admiration for the Proctors
   b. Hale's commitment to the truth
   c. Hale's questioning of Danforth's integrity
   d. Hale's dislike of Parris

_____ 11. What development causes Mary Warren to recant her confession and rejoin Abigail and the other girls?
   a. John Proctor's confession of his relationship with Abigail
   b. Judge Danforth's persistent questions
   c. the confusion about Elizabeth Proctor's "poppets"
   d. Abigail's pretending to be attacked by Mary's spirit

_____ 12. Why is the phrase "out of her infinite charity" in the following passage an example of verbal irony?

> MARY WARREN, _screaming at him:_ No, I love God; I go your way no more. I love God, I bless God. _Sobbing, she rushes to_ ABIGAIL. Abby, Abby, I'll never hurt you more! _They all watch, as_ ABIGAIL, _out of her infinite charity, reaches out and draws the sobbing_ MARY _to her, and then looks up to_ DANFORTH.

   a. It contradicts the audience's knowledge about Abigail's true nature.
   b. It presents a piece of information of which the audience is not aware.
   c. It emphasizes Abigail's ability to be forgiving under stress.
   d. It reveals Abigail's weakening condition.

_____ 13. Which of the following is a consequence of Mary's going back to the side of the girls?
   a. Abigail accuses Mary of being in the Devil's service.
   b. Proctor is arrested.
   c. Reverend Hale accuses Mary of being a fraud.
   d. Marshal Herrick leads Mary away to recover from her ordeal.

_____ 14. What does Proctor mean when he tells Danforth, "God damns our kind especially, and we will burn, we will burn together"?
   a. We who commit wrongs knowingly are the most guilty of all.
   b. The whole community will suffer damnation for the injustices being committed here.
   c. Danforth will suffer damnation if he condemns Proctor to death.
   d. Although women are accused of witchcraft, men are greater sinners.

_____ 15. Which of the following pairs of categories would _not_ be useful for organizing the characters in Act III?
   a. Christians and non-Christians
   b. accusers and accused
   c. believers in witchcraft and nonbelievers in witchcraft
   d. liars and truth tellers

____ 16. What character does *not* fit into one of these categories: accuser, accused, court official?
a. John Proctor
b. Mary Warren
c. Reverend Hale
d. Giles Corey

Vocabulary and Grammar

On the line, write the letter of the one best answer.

____ 17. Someone who is *confounded* is
a. secure.
b. decisive.
c. well established.
d. puzzled.

____ 18. Which of the following best describes a *prodigious* event?
a. a rain shower, one of several in a week
b. a minor fender bender, for which neither driver files an insurance claim
c. an earthquake that causes floods, landslides, and loss of life and property
d. an ancient tree falls in a huge forest, crushing several others in its fall

____ 19. Choose the item that correctly identifies and labels the subject and verb in this inverted sentence. With them is Judge Danforth, a grave man in his sixties.
a. plural subject—*them*; plural verb—*joining*
b. singular subject—*Judge Danforth*; singular verb—*joining*
c. singular subject—*Judge Danforth*; singular verb—*is*
d. singular subject—*man*; singular verb—*is*

____ 20. Choose the inverted sentence whose subject and verb agree in number.
a. Amazed at the charge is Corey and Proctor.
b. There are serious concerns in the community.
c. Here come the judge to make his ruling.
d. In the vestry waits the angry husbands.

Essay Questions

21. In an essay, identify at least three ironic statements or events in Act III. For each, describe the situation and explain why the statement or event is ironic. How does it represent something different from what readers or audience members expect or know to be true?

22. In an essay, describe Reverend Hale's role in Act III. What advice does he give to other characters, and under what circumstances? How is Hale's role different from that of all the other characters? Knowing what you know about Hale from Acts I and II, do you think his behavior is in keeping with his *previous* behavior, or contradictory to it? Explain your answer.

23. Judge Danforth is clearly a powerful and influential figure in Act III. What sort of man is he? What does he truly think of the proceedings? What does it mean when the stage directions say that he is rapidly calculating this, when told that Mary Warren admits she never saw spirits? What does it mean when Danforth acknowledges "with deep misgivings" that Mary's confession "goes to the heart of" the whole situation? What evidence is there that Danforth has at least a few thoughts about the folly of the proceedings? Why doesn't he stop the whole process? Answer these questions in an essay.

Name _____ Date _____

The Crucible, **Act IV,** by Arthur Miller

Selection Test

Critical Reading

On the line, write the letter of the one best answer.

_____ 1. The setting of Act IV is
    a. Parris's house, where the investigation began.
    b. the Salem jail, the autumn after the trial.
    c. the prison in Andover, just before the Proctors' child is due.
    d. Danforth's chambers in Boston, where he hears final appeals.

_____ 2. What can the audience infer from the brief scene involving Tituba, Sarah Good, and Herrick that opens Act IV?
    a. Tituba and Sarah Good are about to be executed for witchcraft.
    b. Tituba and Sarah Good have come to believe the accusations against them.
    c. Herrick is drinking in order to dull his anguish at the injustices being done.
    d. Herrick has come to believe in the visions described by Tituba and Sarah Good.

_____ 3. Parris hopes that Rebecca Nurse and John Proctor will confess because he believes that
    a. confession will save their souls from damnation.
    b. sparing their lives will prevent public rebellion.
    c. their confessions will confirm the justice of all the trials and executions.
    d. their confessions will strengthen the faith of doubting parishioners.

_____ 4. What idea about the law is conveyed by Danforth's determination to proceed with the executions immediately?
    a. Judges tend to be corrupted by the power of their office.
    b. To delay doing justice is to commit injustice.
    c. Laws made by human beings cannot be reconciled with divine law.
    d. Injustice may be committed in the name of the law.

_____ 5. Danforth treats Parris with contempt because
    a. he sees that Parris is motivated by fear for his own safety and reputation.
    b. he thinks that Parris was a fool to trust Abigail Williams.
    c. he sees that Parris cares more for wealth than for the spiritual welfare of his parish.
    d. he thinks that Parris values mercy over justice.

_____ 6. What is ironic about calling the confessions of witchcraft "coming to God"?
    a. The confessions are made publicly, not in prayer.
    b. The confessions are lies and therefore sins against God.
    c. The confessions confirm that sins against God have been committed.
    d. Confession saves the confessor from death, thereby postponing the confessor's "coming to God."

_____ 7. What lesson has Elizabeth Proctor learned during her three months' imprisonment?
    a. that all people carry the seeds of evil within themselves
    b. that human beings cannot be held responsible for their actions
    c. that one should not judge human frailty too harshly
    d. that there are no meaningful standards of right and wrong

____ 8. Why does Hale want Proctor to confess to witchcraft?
   a. to save Proctor from execution
   b. to save others accused of witchcraft
   c. to prevent public disorder
   d. to allow Proctors' family to keep his property

____ 9. When Proctor refuses to condemn others to save himself, his behavior contrasts most strongly with the behavior of
   a. Parris.
   b. Hathorne.
   c. Danforth.
   d. Corey.

____ 10. The climax of Act IV occurs when
   a. Parris reveals that Abigail Williams has disappeared.
   b. Elizabeth Proctor is brought into the cell.
   c. Proctor decides to confess to witchcraft.
   d. Proctor refuses to sign the confession.

____ 11. Which theme is reflected by Proctor's decision to tear up the confession?
   a. Personal honor determines the worth of one's self.
   b. Government authority can be resisted single-handedly.
   c. Forgiveness can be extended to the guilty as well as the innocent.
   d. The variability of justice is an evil in itself.

____ 12. Proctor's determination to preserve his good name speaks to the McCarthy era of the 1950's in that
   a. fear of persecution caused many to keep silent.
   b. laws were passed to prevent this kind of persecution.
   c. the Salem authorities act like communists.
   d. reputations were ruined by irresponsible accusations.

____ 13. A theme represented by Danforth's behavior is that
   a. good and evil must finally be determined by law.
   b. those in power tend to act in the interest of preserving power.
   c. the absence of evidence renders authority powerless.
   d. legal systems cannot take personal character into account.

____ 14. After Proctor is taken off to execution, Parris urges Elizabeth to go to her husband in order to
   a. comfort him in his final moments.
   b. try once more to persuade him to confess.
   c. show that she believes the death sentence is just.
   d. make a last appeal to the mercy of the judges.

____ 15. Which idea about the play is applicable today?
   a. Superstitions of colonial America are no longer an issue.
   b. Belief in the supernatural is *ipso facto* dangerous.
   c. Government is overly concerned with religious issues.
   d. Fear and suspicion can lead to perversions of justice.

Vocabulary and Grammar

On the line, write the letter of the one best answer.

____ 16. Someone who is *adamant* is
   a. condemned.
   b. regretful.
   c. numb.
   d. stubborn.

____ 17. *Retaliation* is
   a. explaining or accounting for something.
   b. returning an injury or wrong.
   c. temptation or enchantment.
   d. selling or compromising one's integrity.

____ 18. Someone who is *conciliatory* is a(n)
   a. advisor.
   b. opponent.
   c. peacemaker.
   d. scholar.

____ 19. Which sentence is grammatically *correct*?
   a. *The Crucible* raises issues about paranoia, politics, and personality.
   b. The play raised above merely historical drama by considering contemporary events.
   c. Miller's treatment of the theme had risen modern issues.
   d. Miller's own raise from a poor childhood is inspiring.

____ 20. Which sentence is grammatically *incorrect*?
   a. Perhaps it is not so amazing that the citizens raised so little objection to the persecution of neighbors.
   b. Reverend Hale in particular, whose opinion of Proctor rose each time they met, should have stopped things.
   c. If Hale had rose to object sooner, senseless tragedy might have been averted.
   d. Raising questions about the accusers' motives would have been a good place to start.

Essay Questions

21. In Act IV, we learn that Abigail has stolen money and run away, but we do not hear exactly why. Write an essay in which you assess her motives for running away, based on what you know of her from the play. Use examples from the play to support your answer.

22. The word *crucible* means "a container for melting or purifying metals" and "a severe test." Why are both meanings appropriate for Miller's play? Write an essay explaining how characters are both reduced to their essences and tested. Use examples from the play to support your ideas.

23. Trials for sorcery, heresy, and witchcraft had been going on for centuries in Europe. Inquisitions had occurred since the Middle Ages, and the judicial methods used were not far different from those in *The Crucible*. Why do you think Miller might have chosen the Salem witch trials of 1692? How does this setting serve his dramatic and thematic goals? Write an essay explaining why Salem, Massachusetts, is an appropriate setting for the themes of *The Crucible*.

Part Test, Unit 6, Part 3:
The Emerging American Identity—Social Protest

Critical Reading

The questions below are based on this poem.

We Live By What We See at Night

by Martin Espada

When the mountains of Puerto Rico

flickered in your sleep

with a moist green light,

when you saw green bamboo hillsides

before waking to East Harlem rooftops

or Texas barracks,

when you crossed the bridge

built by your grandfather

over a river glimpsed

only in interrupted dreaming,

the craving for that island birthplace

burrowed, deep

as thirty years' exile,

constant as your pulse.

This was the inheritance

of your son, born in New York:

that years before

I saw Puerto Rico,

I saw the mountains

looming above the projects,

overwhelming Brooklyn,

living by what I saw at night,

with my eyes closed.

On the line, write the letter of the one best answer.

_____ 1. What are the likely identities of *you* and *I* in the poem?
   a. *You* refers to the father, *I* to the grandfather.
   b. *You* refers to the son, *I* to his father.
   c. *You* refers to the father, *I* to his son.
   d. *You* refers to the grandfather, *I* to the father.

_____ 2. What impression do the images of Puerto Rico convey to the reader?
   a. It is a lush, beautiful place.
   b. It is a vast, lonely place.
   c. It is a pleasant, friendly, urban landscape.
   d. It is a pulsating, intense island.

_____ 3. The theme of Espada's poem involves
   a. the sensitivity of children.
   b. the importance of place.
   c. the distortions of memory.
   d. the suffocating quality of city life.

_____ 4. What are the natural stopping points in this poem?
   a. verses   c. quatrains
   b. punctuation marks   d. line endings

_____ 5. Which images in this poem embody the theme of dreams and the imagination?
   a. "East Harlem rooftops"
   b. "mountains looming above the projects"
   c. "thirty years' exile"
   d. "born in New York"

_____ 6. "We Live by What We See at Night" is a good example of
   a. a narrative poem.   c. a lyric poem.
   b. an epic poem.   d. a sonnet.

_____ 7. How does the speaker know Puerto Rico?
   a. He travels there from Texas.
   b. He grows up in Puerto Rico.
   c. He saw the island thirty years ago.
   d. He imagines the island while living in Brooklyn, New York.

_____ 8. Which is the best description of the son's "inheritance"?
   a. respect for hard work   c. wealth
   b. respect for elders   d. the gift of imagination

_____ 9. Which line shows most vividly how setting affects the speaker's father?
   a. "before waking to East Harlem rooftops"
   b. "when you crossed the bridge"
   c. "the craving for that island birthplace"
   d. "over a river glimpsed"

_____ 10. This poem comprises how many sentences?
   a. three   c. twenty-three
   b. one   d. two

Vocabulary and Grammar

The three questions below consist of a related pair of words in CAPITAL LETTERS, followed by four other pairs of words. Choose the pair that best expresses a relationship similar to that expressed in the capitalized words.

_____ 11. MALEVOLENCE : UNKINDNESS ::
   a. intriguing : boring
   b. affliction : curse
   c. benevolent : malicious
   d. jubilation : suspense

____ 12. INCESSANT : OCCASIONAL ::
a. convivial : merry
b. frigid : cool
c. rendezvous : secrecy
d. wily : sly

____ 13. SHACKLES : RESTRAIN ::
a. effigy : likeness
b. gape : expression
c. barometers : measure
d. preconceptions : prejudices

On the line, write the letter of the one best answer.

____ 14. People who behave *decorously* show
a. poor manners.
b. an unusual sense of humor.
c. a fondness for informality.
d. good taste.

____ 15. A *latent* desire is one that is ____.
a. irrelevant
b. inactive
c. inappropriate
d. ill timed

____ 16. Which of the following is an inverted sentence?
a. Down the street came the woman, Richard's mother, screaming, her face raised to the sky and tears running down her face.
b. John watched him sourly as he carefully unlocked the door and disappeared.
c. She paused for a moment to look sharply at John.
d. His eyes were struck alive, unmoving, blind with malevolence.

____ 17. Which sentence contains a noun clause?
a. He had never been west.
b. He wanted to know what I'd been dreaming.
c. My aunts had decided on their course of action without consulting us.
d. Neither the picture nor the medal was proof of anything.

____ 18. Which sentence is incorrectly punctuated?
a. Oh this man shall be remembered not with statues' rhetoric!
b. When he dared, Mr. Tanimoto raised his head and saw that the rayon man's house had collapsed.
c. So we agreed to throw out or sell anything inessential.
d. Well, I hope I don't have to do this anymore, Aunt Frances.

____ 19. Which transitional phrase shows the relationship of ideas in the passage?

> Mrs. Nakamura went back to the kitchen, looked at the rice, and began watching the man next door. At first, she was annoyed with him for making so much noise, but then she was moved almost to tears by pity. Her emotion was specifically directed toward her neighbor, tearing down his home, board by board . . .

a. Began
b. Next door
c. At first
d. Board by board

_____ 20. Which passage uses the present perfect tense and the present tense in sequence to make clear the relationship of ideas in time?

    a. And before I'll be a slave I'll be buried in my grave

    b. I have looked at it so long I think it is a part of my heart.

    c. I began this ancestral search that you children yield now in profile and bust.

    d. She told it to me in a room alone—I have no proof for it.

Essay Questions

21. To deepen your involvement with a literary work, you can evaluate the behavior of characters, basing on your own sensibility and your knowledge of what you might do in similar circumstances. Choose a selection—such as "The Writer in the Family," "Ambush," or "The Rockpile"—that describes interesting or debatable actions. In an essay, explain how you evaluate these actions. Include an explanation of the criteria you use to make your judgment.

22. Characters in literature (like individuals in real life) can be shaped by the specific time and place they inhabit. Choose a selection in which setting plays a key role. In an essay, explain how setting influences the personality or behavior of one or more characters in the work.

23. Lyric poems have the potential to be among the most intense personal expressions in all of literature. Choose one lyric poem from this part that made a particularly strong impression on you. In an essay, analyze both the form and content of this poem and explain why you find the work so arresting.

24. It can be illuminating to juxtapose two literary works and analyze them in light of each other. Choose two selections that strike you as a provocative pairing. Compare and contrast the works—stylistically as well as thematically—in a well-considered essay.

25. In literature, the theme of social protest can take many different forms. Choose a selection that you believe registers an important social protest in a particularly effective manner. In an essay, explain the nature of the protest and the reasons why the author is so successful in expressing it.

ANSWERS
Unit 1: Beginnings (to 1750)

"The Earth on Turtle's Back" (Onondaga), "When Grizzlies Walked Upright" (Modoc), from *The Navajo Origin Legend* (Navajo), from *The Iroquois Constitution*

Selection Test (p. 1)

Critical Reading/Vocabulary and Grammar

1. c 2. c 3. b 4. b 5. b 6. d 7. b 8. a 9. d 10. a 11. c 12. d 13. c 14. a 15. d 16. d 17. a 18. b 19. c 20. a

Questions are classified in these categories:
Comprehension 6(E), 10(E), 13(A), 14 (A)
Interpretation 5(C), 7(A), 9(E), 15(C)
Literary Analysis 1(A), 2(E), 8(A), 11(A)
Reading Strategy 3(E), 4(C), 12(C), 16(A)
Vocabulary 17(A), 18(E)
Grammar 19(A), 20(C)
E = Easy, A = Average, C = Challenging

Essay Questions

21. (Easy) *Guidelines for student response:* Students will probably contend that such explanations help make the world make sense to people. They may point out that human beings are naturally curious, and so are inclined to try to explain the things that happen around them. Students may also offer the view that having an explanation of a natural phenomenon gives a sense of security, and also may enable humans to harness the phenomenon for their own benefit.

22. (Average) *Guidelines for student response:* Students' essays should be based on information included in the myths. Among the similarities they highlight should be the fact that all three peoples had reverence for the natural world. The differences in the myths are based for the most part on the different environments in which the people lived.

23. (Challenging) *Guidelines for student response:* Students should point out that the Iroquois Constitution is based on respect, honesty, and a concern for the group over the individual. The founding fathers may have used the Iroquois Constitution as a model because of the way it provided a way for different groups—or states—to come together in a confederacy while retaining their individual rights and privileges.

"A Journey Through Texas" from *The Journey of Alvar Núñez Cabeza de Vaca* by Alvar Núñez Cabeza de Vaca
"Boulders Taller Than the Great Tower of Seville" by García López de Cárdenas

Selection Test (p. 4)

Critical Reading/Vocabulary and Grammar

1. c 2. d 3. d 4. a 5. b 6. a 7. b 8. a 9. a 10. b 11. d 12. d 13. a 14. c 15. b 16. a 17. b 18. d 19. a 20. c

Questions are classified in these categories:
Comprehension 4(E), 5(A), 6(E), 13(A)
Interpretation 7(E), 8(C), 9(C), 14(C)
Literary Analysis 1(A), 2(A), 3(A), 12(C)
Reading Strategy 10(E), 11(A), 15(A)
Vocabulary 16(E), 17(A), 18(A)
Grammar 19(E), 20(A)
E = Easy, A = Average, C = Challenging

Essay Questions

21. (Easy) *Guidelines for student response:* Students may mention characteristics such as bravery, resourcefulness, intelligence, curiosity, determination, self-confidence, imagination, strength, ruggedness, adaptability, and endurance. While students may contend that the Spanish exhibited most of these traits, they may feel that the Spanish lacked sensitivity to their surroundings and the people they met and/or that they lacked curiosity about certain aspects of the areas they were exploring.

22. (Average) *Guidelines for student response:* Students will likely feel that the Cabeza de Vaca narrative is more personal and the López de Cárdenas narrative is more factual and objective. They may also feel that Cabeza de Vaca displays more curiosity about the lands he crossed, while López de Cárdenas shows a more single-minded

"A Journey Through Texas" from *The Journey of Alvar Núñez Cabeza de Vaca* by Alvar Núñez Cabeza de Vaca

"Boulders Taller Than the Great Tower of Seville" by García López de Cárdenas
(continued)

interest in completing his mission. Students should cite sufficient examples to support their general statements about the selections.

23. (Challenging) *Guidelines for student response:* Students should explain that the natives provided the Spanish with guides, food, water, dwellings, and information. Students will probably contend that the Spanish, while perhaps not actively mistreating the native peoples, had ethnocentric attitudes and feelings of superiority and that they established a power relationship with the natives, ordering them to do their bidding. Students may speculate that the natives in the future would chafe under Spanish domination and that future relationships would be hostile or troubled.

from *The Interesting Narrative of The Life of Olaudah Equiano*
by Olaudah Equiano

Selection Test (p. 7)

Critical Reading/Vocabulary and Grammar

1. d 2. a 3. b 4. b 5. d 6. a 7. c 8. c 9. d 10. b 11. c 12. a 13. d 14. c 15. a 16. c 17. b 18. a 19. b 20. a

Questions are classified in these categories:
Comprehension 7(A), 8(E), 9(E)
Interpretation 3(C), 5(A), 6(A), 10(A), 12(E), 13(C), 15(C)
Literary Analysis 1(E), 2(A), 4(A)
Reading Strategy 11(C), 14(A)
Vocabulary 16(E), 17(E), 18(A)
Grammar 19(A), 20(E)
E = Easy, A = Average, C = Challenging

Essay Questions

21. (Easy) *Guidelines for student response:* While students' descriptions of their personal responses to the shipboard captivity will differ, they should be based on details contained in the narrative and their writing in total should provide an adequate summary.

22. (Average) *Guidelines for student response:* Students should cite details showing the hardships of the slaves and the shock and horror these details would most likely inspire in readers. They may also discuss how reading the selection would help humanize slaves for white readers by showing the narrator to be a sensitive, intelligent human being forced to face inhuman conditions. Among the details students may suggest that abolitionists use are those revealing the horrors of the slave crossings, the harshness of the slave traders, and the cruelties of the slave market.

23. (Challenging) *Guidelines for student response:* Students may point out that Equiano's writing shows his obvious intelligence, that his eye for detail and interest in the quadrant and flying fish show his curiosity, that his feelings for his fellow captives show his compassion, and that his condemnation of the treatment of the captives shows his sense of justice.

"Diamond Island: Alcatraz"
by Darryl Babe Wilson

Selection Test (p. 10)

Critical Reading/Vocabulary

1. b 2. a 3. c 4. c 5. a 6. c 7. b 8. d 9. d 10. a

Questions are classified in these categories:
Comprehension 2(A), 4(A), 5(E), 6(A)
Interpretation 1(A). 3(C), 7(C), 8(C)
Vocabulary 9(E), 10(A)
E = Easy, A = Average, C = Challenging

Essay Questions

11. (Easy) *Guidelines for student response:* Student's should note that as time passes, new generations of native Americans lose ties to their past. Oral tradition keeps history alive. Darryl Babe Wilson does his part to record history by writing down the story of his grandfather.

12. (Average) *Guidelines for student response:* Students should point to the repetitive use of the word *old* and adjectives that evoke age, such as *ancient, leathery,*

creased and wrinkled, etc. Students should describe a value system that prizes things with long histories and traditions over things that are new, especially when they destroy links to the past. The author's need to write is based on preserving links with the past. Students might reject the allusions to age as a rhetorical ploy.

13. (Challenging) *Guidelines for student response:* Students should point out that Wilson records his grandfather's story to provide a "proper identity" to Alcatraz and a "real" history to his people. Students should point out that the "victors" usually record only one side of history. Students might question whether a "real" history could ever be written. On a personal level, students might cite historical awareness as something that informs their character and upbringing. Conversely, students might favor abandoning the past in order to move beyond painful memories.

Part Test, Unit 1, Part 1: Meeting of Cultures (p. 12)

Critical Reading/Vocabulary and Grammar

1. a 2. a 3. b 4. d 5. c 6. c 7. d 8. d 9. a
10. a 11. b 12. b 13. c 14. c 15. a 16. c
17. b 18. c 19. b 20. d

Questions are classified in these categories:
 Comprehension 6(E), 7(E)
 Interpretation 2(A), 4(A), 5(A)
 Literary Analysis 8(C), 9(A)
 Reading Strategy 1(E), 3(E), 10(C)
 Vocabulary 11(A), 12(A), 13(A), 14(E), 15(A)
 Grammar 16(A), 17(A), 18(A), 19(C), 20(C)
 E = Easy, A = Average, C = Challenging

Essay Questions

21. (Easy) *Guidelines for student response:* Students' essays should refer to the journals in Part 1 as examples. Students should communicate an understanding of how journals give a personal perspective on history. They should explain how a journal will allow future generations to understand events from the student's lifetime.

22. (Average) *Guidelines for student response:* Students' essays should discuss how these myths have been used to answer the question of how human life began in the world. They may note the many references to nature, as well as the personhood of the creating spirit. Students may also note that both stories offer accounts of life preceding human life on earth. They should back their opinions about how well each myth fulfills its purpose with an explanation of their reasoning.

23. (Average) *Guidelines for student response:* Essays should focus on the richness of the language and imagery in the Iroquois Constitution, citing the use of symbols and ritual, as well as the extended metaphor of the tree and its roots for the confederation. Most students will support the argument that the Iroquois Constitution has value as a literary document because it reflects the richness of the Iroquois culture; it is a literary document that will influence the writing of other such documents.

24. (Average) *Guidelines for student response:* Students' essays should be organized around the evident bias in the writing of one of these authors and how that bias found expression due to the background of the writer, the purpose of the document, and the intended audience. For example, students could focus on the fact that Columbus needed to support the idea that the King and Queen of Spain had spent their money wisely in sponsoring his expedition.

25. (Challenging) *Guidelines for student response:* Students' essays should identify characteristics of faith in the Native American community. Many Native Americans see the sacred and the secular as two sides of the same coin. Their belief that there is "spirit" in all of life inspired their respect for their natural environment and fellow creatures.

from *Journal of the First Voyage to America* by Christopher Columbus

Selection Test (p. 16)

Critical Reading/Vocabulary and Grammar

1. b 2. a 3. a 4. b 5. b 6. b 7. c 8. d 9. a
10. b 11. c 12. d 13. a 14. c 15. b 16. c
17. b 18. c 19. a 20. d

from *Journal of the First Voyage to America* by Christopher Columbus
(continued)

Questions are classified in these categories:
    Comprehension 2(C), 3(E), 4 (A)
    Interpretation 6(E), 7(A), 2(C)
    Literary Analysis 1(A), 5(E), 8(C)
    Reading Strategy 10(A), 12(A), 13(A), 14(A), 15(C)
    Vocabulary 17(E), 18(A), 19(A)
    Grammar 16(A), 20(C)
    E = Easy, A = Average, C = Challenging

Essay Questions

21. (Easy) *Guidelines for student response:* Students' essays might attempt to convey the great sense of disappointment Columbus would have undoubtedly felt at not achieving his goal; or the essays might consider how Columbus might have tried to hide his disappointment and make the best of things in order to continue to paint a rosy picture for his patrons.

22. (Average) *Guidelines for student response:* Students' essays should indicate that Columbus would probably have not included as much information clearly meant to impress his royal patrons. His journal might also, if meant only for personal consumption, have betrayed a sense of doubt about the success of his voyage.

23. (Challenging) *Guidelines for student response:* Students' essays should be based on the information contained in the journal and indicate that a native might have reacted with awe, fear, hostility, or perhaps a culturally taught hospitality on first encountering the European visitors. Students may speculate that Columbus initially treated the natives well in order to make easier his acquisition of the riches he expected to find. They may feel that his mention of acquiring gold indicates that he would have no compunctions about taking what he wanted when the opportunity arose.

from *The General History of Virginia* by John Smith
from *Of Plymouth Plantation* by William Bradford

Selection Test (p. 19)

Critical Reading/Vocabulary and Grammar

1. b 2. c 3. d 4. b 5. a 6. a 7. a 8. c 9. d
10. b 11. d 12. d 13. d 14. b 15. a 16. c
17. b 18. d 19. a 20. a

Questions are classified in these categories:
    Comprehension 1(E), 2(A), 5(A), 11(E)
    Interpretation 3(E), 4(A), 10(B), 13(A), 14(C)
    Literary Analysis 6(C), 7(A), 8(C), 12(A), 16(C)
    Reading Strategy 9(E), 15(C)
    Vocabulary 17(E), 18(A)
    Grammar 19(A), 20(A)
    E = Easy, A = Average, C = Challenging

Essay Questions

21. (Easy) *Guidelines for student response:* Students' essays should discuss Smith's purpose of persuading others to support or participate in the New World settlement, examine the heroic role in which he places himself, consider his use of the third person in discussing himself and its likely persuasive effects on readers, and detail his subjective remarks about the president, the Native Americans, and others.

22. (Average) *Guidelines for student response:* Students' essays should show how the narrative presents factual information such as the geography of the coast, the reasons the Pilgrims landed at Plymouth, the types of food they ate, the way they dealt with sickness, how they interacted with one another and with the Native Americans, and how they explained what happened around them. Students may discuss and evaluate some or all of these details in conjunction with history they know from Social Studies or other outside knowledge.

23. (Challenging) *Guidelines for student response:* Students should point out that both the Pilgrims and the Jamestown settlers faced many difficulties. They may point out that Smith seems to believe that people do not appreciate things unless they are forced to struggle for them and that the Pilgrims seemed especially strengthened by their ordeal. Students'

evaluation of Smith's idea should be supported by examples and logical reasoning.

from *The Right Stuff* by Tom Wolfe

Selection Test (p. 22)

Critical Reading/Vocabulary

1. b 2. c 3. b 4. d 5. a 6. b 7. c 8. a 9. a 10. d

Questions are classified in these categories:
Comprehension 1(A), 2(C), 4(C), 5(E)
Interpretation 3(A), 6(C), 7(A)
Vocabulary 8(E), 9(A), 10(E)
E = Easy, A = Average, C = Challenging

Essay Questions

11. (Easy) *Guidelines for student response:* Students could cite a wide range of characteristics, including courage, sense of purpose, preparedness, dedication, strength, bravado, the ability to remain calm, and so on.

12. (Average) *Guidelines for student response:* Students should be able to distinguish between first-person and third-person narratives. Students might also consider subjective versus objective points of view. Students should point out the immediacy of Wolfe's narrative, which captures the emotions involved in Glenn's accomplishment, but they might also suggest that a more neutral, objective narrative would better convey the technical specifics of space flight. Students should cite at least one passage and suggest how it could be rewritten to reflect an objective, outside point of view.

13. (Challenging) *Guidelines for student response:* Students might speculate on the restlessness of the human spirit in general, or they might consider the love of exploration characteristic of Western cultures. Students should compare one or more earlier expeditions (for example, Columbus's, Magellan's, Lewis and Clark's, pioneers') with space exploration. Students might suggest that space exploration is beneficial to humankind because it brings in new information and creates technologies (such as those for freeze-drying food or monitoring physiological processes) that can also be used on Earth. Conversely, they might view space exploration as a costly waste of resources.

Part Test, Unit 1, Part 2: Focus on Literary Forms— Narrative Accounts (p. 24)

Critical Reading/Vocabulary and Grammar

1. d 2. c 3. b 4. b 5. b 6. c 7. c 8. b 9. a
10. a 11. b 12. a 13. b 14. c 15. b

Questions are classified in these categories:
Comprehension 1(A), 5(A), 9(A)
Interpretation 2(A), 6(E), 10(A)
Literary Analysis 3(C), 7(A)
Reading Strategy 4(A), 8(A)
Vocabulary 11(E), 12(C), 13(A)
Grammar 14(A), 15(A)
E = Easy, A = Average, C = Challenging

Essay Questions

16. (Easy) *Guidelines for student response:* Students' essays should focus on information about settlements as documented by Smith or Bradford. They might note details about the exploration and settling of land; interactions with people already living in the region; the hardships of sickness, hunger, and lack of shelter experienced by the settlers; and the settlers' reliance on the Native Americans for food and provisions.

17. (Average) *Guidelines for student response:* Students should discuss at least three different character traits they believe were necessary to survival in the New World; wherever possible, traits should be illustrated with examples or inferences gleaned from the journals of Smith and Bradford. Suggested character traits include good leadership qualities (Smith organizes the settlers to build houses); strong religious faith (Bradford believes that God has safeguarded their journey across the ocean); good communications skills (both Bradford and Smith build relationships with the Native Americans).

18. (Challenging) *Guidelines for student response:* Using specific examples from the texts, students should note that both Smith and Bradford express distrust of the Native Americans at first, but they eventually come to good terms with them. Both the Jamestown and Plymouth settlers are, in fact, saved from starvation by the local natives. Smith also portrays the Native Americans as violent and unpredictable

and credits his own bravery and intelligence with turning them from enemies to friends. Bradford's account, in contrast, is one of mutual respect and cooperation with the Native Americans.

"To My Dear and Loving Husband"
by Anne Bradstreet
"Huswifery" by Edward Taylor

Selection Test (p. 27)

Critical Reading/Vocabulary and Grammar
1. a 2. d 3. c 4. c 5. c 6. d 7. d 8. a 9. c
10. b 11. b 12. a 13. d 14. b 15. a 16. c
17. a 18. b 19. c 20. b

Questions are classified in these categories:
   Comprehension 1(E), 3(E), 7(E), 8(A)
   Interpretation 2(A), 4(C), 9(A), 11(A), 13(C)
   Literary Analysis 5(A), 10(C), 15(A)
   Reading Strategy 6(A), 12(C), 14(C)
   Vocabulary 16(A), 17(E), 18(A)
   Grammar 19(E), 20(E)
   E = Easy, A = Average, C = Challenging

Essay Questions
21. (Easy) *Guidelines for student response:* Students should point to the request in line 10 and paradox in line 12 as evidence for the speaker's concern with her and her husband's relationship to God and the afterlife. Students should cite details that illustrate the simple language and direct statements of Puritan Plain Style and may suggest that the simplicity and directness help mirror the Puritan world view. Students may note that the main aim of the poem is to describe a relationship of wholesomeness and righteousness inextricably tied to the love it also expresses.

22. (Average) *Guidelines for student response:* Students should identify Taylor's comparison between the process of spinning wool and weaving it into cloth and the living of a righteous life as the main conceit of the poem. They should then go on to show how the comparison is made more elaborate through more specific point-by-point comparisons. Finally, students should comment on the effectiveness of the comparison and support their opinions with examples and logical reasoning.

23. (Challenging) *Guidelines for student response:* Students may contend that the Puritan Plain Style remains an effective way to get one's ideas across. They may be of the opinion that the sentiments expressed in both poems are both sentiments that could easily be expressed by someone writing today, although some of the comparisons (the spinning wheel, for example) would, of course, be different. Students may also point out that religion is still a powerful force in many people's lives, and so these poems would have a special relevance for many readers.

from *Sinners in the Hands of an Angry God* by Jonathan Edwards

Selection Test (p. 30)

Critical Reading/Vocabulary and Grammar
1. b 2. c 3. a 4. b 5. c 6. d 7. b 8. a 9. c
10. a 11. b 12. c 13. a 14. b 15. d 16. a
17. c 18. a 19. d 20. b

Questions are classified in these categories:
   Comprehension 4(E), 6(A), 9(E), 10(A)
   Interpretation 2(A), 5(C), 7(C), 8(C)
   Literary Analysis 1(A), 3(A), 11(C), 12(C), 13(A)
   Reading Strategy 14(A), 15(E)
   Vocabulary 16(E), 17(E), 18(A)
   Grammar 19(A), 20(E)
   E = Easy, A = Average, C = Challenging

Essay Questions
21. (Easy) *Guidelines for student response:* Students should give examples of the sometimes extreme hectoring tone in the sermon and the continuous condemnation of the audience as sinners almost beyond redemption. Students will probably contend that the congregation eventually decided that Edwards at one point crossed a line and that a more moderate minister would be more appropriate.

They may suggest that to stress only the negative is not what Christianity is all about.

22. (Average) *Guidelines for student response:* Students should cite examples of appeals to the emotions of fear and envy,

   the bandwagon appeal toward the end, and Edwards's repetition of certain basic ideas, such as the wrath of God being a consuming flame. Students should point out that these persuasive techniques "work" in the sense that they make the consequences of actions stark and immediate. The absence of the persuasive techniques would drain the sermon of its effect.

23. (Challenging) *Guidelines for student response:* Students should list Edwards's basic goal—persuading his congregation to repent and be "born again"—and his techniques: evocative images, dramatic descriptions, strident condemnations, and so on. Students may offer the view that the stridency of Edwards's sermon may have been counterproductive. They may believe that appealing to the good in people might be more productive than pointing out the bad in people.

Part Test, Unit 1, Part 3: The Emerging American Identity— The Puritan Influence (p. 33)

Critical Reading/Vocabulary and Grammar

1. b 2. b 3. d 4. a 5. a 6. c 7. d 8. c 9. b 10. b 11. a 12. b 13. a 14. d 15. d

Questions are classified in these categories:
   Comprehension 2(A), 3(A), 5(E), 6(A)
   Interpretation 7(E), 10(C)
   Literary Analysis 4(A), 8(A)
   Reading Strategy 1(A), 9(C)
   Vocabulary 11(A), 12(A)
   Grammar 13(A), 14(A), 15(A)
   E = Easy, A = Average, C = Challenging

Essay Questions

16. (Easy) *Guidelines for student response:* Students should provide clear explanations of how their chosen work gives evidence of the writer's belief in the spiritual realm. Students may point out how Bradstreet directly addresses the topics of marriage and love—central aspects of her actual life in the real world—using allusion to "the heavens," prayer, and everlasting life. Taylor uses everyday household objects as a metaphor for his relationship with God. Edwards directly links behavior in this life with God's punishment or reward in the afterlife.

17. (Average) *Guidelines for student response:* Students' essays should focus on the poem through the lens of its title. After noting that *huswifery* means "housekeeping," students should point out how Taylor uses the tools of the seventeenth-century housekeeper—the spinning wheel, distaff, spool, loom, quills, cloth, etc.—as metaphors for his relationship with God. Taylor may be suggesting that the physical work and discipline of housekeeping can help one grow closer to God. Students should support their evaluation of the title's effectiveness with a well-reasoned explanation.

18. (Challenging) *Guidelines for student response:* Students should discuss at least two or three factors that contributed to limiting Puritan literature to the few given genres. Puritans often had little spare time to devote to writing lengthier works, such as novels or full-length dramas; they believed that the purpose of all literature was to edify, not to entertain, and would therefore have shunned any form of creative writing (such as romantic poetry, ballads, novels, dramas, etc.) that did not express a useful or religious idea; their commitment to build a theocracy inspired the Puritans to focus on sermons and religious poems as a means of helping to spread their religious message.

© Prentice-Hall, Inc.

Answers **331**

Unit 2: A Nation Is Born (1750–1800)

from *The Autobiography* and from *Poor Richard's Almanack*
by Benjamin Franklin

Selection Test (p. 36)

Critical Reading/Vocabulary and Grammar

1. c 2. b 3. a 4. a 5. b 6. b 7. a 8. d 9. d
10. b 11. c 12. b 13. a 14. c 15. a 16. c
17. c 18. d 19. a 20. a

Questions are classified in these categories:
Comprehension 1(E), 2(E), 3(A)
Interpretation 4(A), 5(A), 6(C)
Literary Analysis 7(C), 8(A), 9(E)
Reading Strategy 10(E), 11(A), 12(C)
Vocabulary 15(E), 16(A),
Grammar 17(E), 18(A), 19(A)
E = Easy, A = Average, C = Challenging

Essay Questions

21. (Easy) *Guidelines for student response:*
Students should realize that *The Autobiography* is written from the author's point of view and therefore may be biased, while an impartial reporter's work would probably be less biased. Phrases and sentences from the selection might be rewritten as those of an outside observer; for example, "for something, that pretended to be reason, was every now and then suggesting to me that such extreme nicety as I exacted of myself might be a kind of foppery in morals, which, if it were known, would make me ridiculous" might be rewritten as "Franklin was concerned that people would think he was foolish for trying to achieve perfection."

22. (Average) *Guidelines for student response:*
Students may respond either way as long as they support their positions with details from the selection. Students who support the statement may say that at one point Franklin felt that perfection was an admirable trait and that he would thus admire the trait in others. Students who reject the statement may point out that Franklin felt frustrated with himself for not being able to master the virtue of order and thus may feel envy for someone who did achieve the virtue.

23. (Challenging) *Guidelines for student response:* Students may take either position

as long as it is supported by their interpretation of the aphorism and other details in their essays. Some students may interpret the aphorism strictly—any activity that is not productive is squandering time. Others may interpret it more loosely—wasting time means different things to different people; what one person considers wasting time may bring fulfillment to another, and vice versa. Students' positions will also depend on the value they place on leisure time.

The Declaration of Independence
by Thomas Jefferson
from *The Crisis*, Number 1,
by Thomas Paine

Selection Test (p. 39)

Critical Reading/Vocabulary and Grammar

1. b 2. a 3. c 4. d 5. b 6. d 7. d 8. c 9. a
10. b 11. a 12. b 13. c 14. c 15. a 16. d
17. b 18. a 19. b 20. b

Questions are classified in these categories:
Comprehension 4(E), 6(A), 12(A)
Interpretation 1(A), 5(E), 7(A), 8(A), 9(C), 13(A)
Literary Analysis 10(A), 11(C), 16(C)
Reading Strategy 2(E), 3(A), 14(E), 15(C)
Vocabulary 19(A), 20(A)
Grammar 17(C), 18(E)
E = Easy, A = Average, C = Challenging

Essay Questions

21. (Easy) *Guidelines for student response:*
Students might mention one or more of the following: anger, because the document reminds them of the wrongs done by the king; fear, because the Declaration is treason and means more war; sorrow, because life will change and long-standing ties with Britain will break; uncertainty, because no one knows the outcome of events; hope, because things could get better; pride, because the colonies have taken a stand and expressed it in strong but reasonable terms; joy, because the colonies are throwing off tyranny; and patriotism, because people are taking

the first steps toward becoming an independent nation.

22. (Average) *Guidelines for student response:* Students may say Paine's essay would have raised spirits because of its expression of thanks and love for those fighting; the assurance that God will give them victory; the nobility of their cause (peace and freedom for their children); the justice of the war (a defensive war against tyranny); the rallying cry for support from everyone; and the praise of those who follow principles and stand firm in difficult times. Some students may say that the essay would not raise spirits because of its emphasis on difficult conflict with the possibility of death; on giving up a safe, peaceful course; and on the idea that the rewards are deferred to the next generation.

23. (Challenging) *Guidelines for student response:* Students should recognize that Jefferson uses parallelism quite effectively in the Declaration of Independence to help create a structured argument in favor of the separation of the colonies from Britain and to emphasize the key elements of that argument. For example, Jefferson repeatedly uses the word *that* to stress each of the rights of all people. In the heart of the Declaration, in which Jefferson lists the many ways in which the king of Great Britain has used his power over the colonists in a tyrannical way, Jefferson highlights his accusations by beginning each one with the words "He has" and a past participle.

"To His Excellency, General Washington" and "An Hymn to the Evening" by Phillis Wheatley

Selection Test (p. 42)

Critical Reading/Vocabulary and Grammar

1. d 2. b 3. c 4. c 5. b 6. c 7. a 8. d 9. c 10. d 11. a 12. b 13. a 14. a 15. a 16. c 17. b 18. d 19. d 20. b

Questions are classified in these categories:
   Comprehension 1(E), 2(C), 3(A)
   Interpretation 5(E), 6(A), 7(A), 8(E)
   Literary Analysis 4(C), 9(E), 10(A), 11(A)
   Reading Strategy 12(A), 13(A), 14(A)
   Vocabulary 15(C), 16(A), 17(A)
   Grammar 17(A), 19(A), 20(C)
   E = Easy, A = Average, C = Challenging

Essay Questions

21. (Easy) *Guidelines for student response:* Students may have logical reasons for choosing either day or night as Wheatley's preferred choice. Students who believe she liked day better may support their opinion with descriptions of the rain, spring, birds, and sunset. Students who believe she liked night better may support their opinion by pointing out that the title is dedicated to the evening and that the poem contains descriptions of sable curtains, restful sleep, and renewal from sleep, as well as the message that the tranquillity of night strengthens people for the day.

22. (Average) *Guidelines for student response:* Students will probably feel that Wheatley was very patriotic. These students may mention, among other things, Wheatley's portrayal of America as a goddess, her praise for America's champion General Washington, her picture of a fierce and faithful American army, her depiction of America as strong and "heaven-defended," and her view of America as a model for other countries.

23. (Challenging) *Guidelines for student response:* Most students will likely equate General Washington with America itself. They may compare specific details praising Columbia, an embodiment of America, with details praising Washington himself. They may point out that Wheatley portrays Americans as "heaven-defended" and Washington as someone with "virtue on his side." Students may also discuss the title, suggesting that the poem is really written to all Americans, even though it is specifically addressed to General Washington.

from *Letter From Birmingham City Jail* by Martin Luther King, Jr.

Selection Test (p. 45)

Critical Reading/Vocabulary

1. b 2. a 3. d 4. a 5. c 6. b 7. a 8. c 9. a 10. d

from *Letter From Birmingham City Jail*
by Martin Luther King, Jr.
(continued)

Questions are classified in these categories:
Comprehension 1(A), 2(E), 5(A), 6(A)
Interpretation 3(C), 4(A), 7(A)
Vocabulary 8(A), 9(A), 10(E)
E = Easy, A = Average, C = Challenging

Essay Questions

11. (Easy) *Guidelines for student response:* Students should point out King's willingness to go to jail for his beliefs; his refusal to confront authority with violence; his use of peaceful marches instead of forceful confrontation; and the actions of the "real heroes" of the South he describes. Students may or may not agree with King's approach. Some may point out ways in which African-American leaders have adhered to or distanced themselves from King's philosophy.

12. (Average) *Guidelines for student response:* Students should show some appreciation for the pressures a given society exerts on its people. Jefferson was a product of a specific time and place, when landowners in the South also owned slaves. Nevertheless, his words carry universal and timeless meaning. King believes in the eternal right to freedom as it is expressed in Jefferson's Declaration of Independence.

13. (Challenging) *Guidelines for student response:* Students should note that blacks have made great strides but have probably not come as far as King would have hoped. While much public space is integrated, there is still much lack of understanding between the races, and many places where blacks and whites are not welcome to mix. Prejudice endures and may or may not soon be overcome. Students may cite recent flash points in race relations (Rodney King incident, O. J. Simpson trial) to describe the gulf that still exists between white and black America.

Part Test, Unit 2, Part 1: Voices for Freedom (p. 47)

Critical Reading/Vocabulary and Grammar

1. d 2. d 3. a 4. d 5. a 6. c 7. d 8. b 9. c
10. c 11. a 12. d 13. c 14. b 15. b 16. b
17. a 18. c 19. b 20. c

Questions are classified in these categories:
Comprehension 1(E), 5(A)
Interpretation 2(A), 6(A), 9(C)
Literary Analysis 4(E), 7(C)
Reading Strategy 3(A), 8(A), 10 (A)
Vocabulary 11(A), 12(A), 13(C), 14(C), 15(A)
Grammar 16(A), 17(A), 18(C), 19(A), 20(A)
E = Easy, A = Average, C = Challenging

Essay Questions

21. (Easy) *Guidelines for student response:* Students should discuss Franklin's desire to lead a life that is both moral and productive. Essays should note his discipline, as evidenced by his methodical approach to ridding himself of bad habits and acquiring good ones. Franklin's sense of self-discipline and high personal standards made him well-suited to become a well-respected leader and personal role model for the new country.

22. (Average) *Guidelines for student response:* Students should support their conclusions with reasonable arguments and references to the appropriate text. Franklin's emphasis on personal perfection would probably lead him to agree with Jefferson; Franklin would probably believe that it is better to be cautious and correct than quick and prone to error. Paine, who expresses the belief that the time for delay has passed and that action is the proper response, would probably have disagreed with Jefferson.

23. (Average) *Guidelines for student response:* Essays should express the idea that literature generally mirrors the values and concerns of the culture in which it is created. The American colonists' preoccupation with liberation from Great Britain influenced much of the literature of the day, which focused on shaping the character of the fledgling nation (Franklin) and uniting the colonists in the cause of freedom (Jefferson, Paine, and Wheatley).

24. (Average) *Guidelines for student response:* Community and unity were essential to the success of the colonists' quest for liberty. Essays should refer to Paine's discussion of Tories and to the varied opinions that brought disharmony and threatened the success of the revolutionary effort. The poem also supports the necessity of unity:

Wheatley encourages colonists to be aware that the world is watching.

25. (Challenging) *Guidelines for student response:* Students' choice of selection and supporting details should reflect the belief in the intellectual ability and inherent morality of man that characterized the Age of Reason. Franklin's *Autobiography* reflects the era's faith in the perfectability of mankind. Jefferson's Declaration is clearly structured and logical in its explanation of the necessity of declaring independence and giving ordinary citizens the right to self-government. Paine's *Crisis*, while impassioned, is rooted in the ideas that the reasonable person must react when presented with injustice. The formality and classical allusions of Wheatley's poetry elevated American literature to a new level of intellectual sophistication.

"Speech in the Virginia Convention" by Patrick Henry
"Speech in the Convention" by Benjamin Franklin

Selection Test (p. 51)

Critical Reading/Vocabulary and Grammar

1. c 2. b 3. d 4. a 5. d 6. c 7. b 8. c 9. c 10. b 11. d 12. c 13. b 14. d 15. a 16. d 17. b 18. b 19. a 20. c

Questions are classified in these categories:
Comprehension 1(E), 2(A), 3(E), 11(A)
Interpretation 4(A), 13(C), 14(A), 15(C)
Literary Analysis 6(E), 7(A), 12(E)
Reading Strategy 5(A), 8(C), 9(C), 10(A)
Vocabulary 16(C), 19(A), 20(C)
Grammar 17(E), 18(A)
E = Easy, A = Average, C = Challenging

Essay Questions

21. (Easy) *Guidelines for student response:* Students who are stirred by the speech and find it effective, moving, and convincing will probably cite Henry's emotion-charged view that the stake is freedom or slavery and that liberty is worthy of great sacrifice and his more logical depiction of British actions as seemingly bent on subjugation and of the colonists as having exhausted all peaceful means of settling the conflict. Students who are less moved or

convinced by the speech may find it excessive in its expression, suspiciously one-sided and warlike, and they may wonder if it is a triumph of rhetoric over reason.

22. (Average) *Guidelines for student response:* Students should mention that Franklin has reservations about the new Constitution but is not sure if he is right about them. He urges unanimous support of the Constitution on the grounds that it may well be the best Constitution possible, given the large number of people collaborating on it, and it is better to present au-nanimous front that will make the people of the new nation more enthusiastic about accepting it.

23. (Challenging) *Guidelines for student response:* Students may include some or all of these points along with the rhetorical device, such as rhetorical question, Henry uses to stress each one. Answering those who object out of hope for peace, Henry replies that the past actions of the British leave no room for hope—nor do their present actions of a military buildup. Answering those who say other means than war should be tried, Henry replies that the colonists have been trying these means for ten years, to no avail. To those who say the colonies are too weak, Henry says that they will never be stronger than they are now and that they have a holy cause—liberty—that justifies their actions even if they are defeated.

"Inaugural Address" by John F. Kennedy

Selection Test (p. 54)

Critical Reading/Vocabulary

1. c 2. a 3. d 4. a 5. c 6. a 7. d 8. b 9. b 10. c

Questions are classified in these categories:
Comprehension 4(E), 5(C), 6(A)
Interpretation 1(C), 2(A), 3(C), 7(A)
Vocabulary 8(A), 9(A), 10(E)
E = Easy, A = Average, C = Challenging

Essay Questions

11. (Easy) *Guidelines for student response:* Among the goals students could cite are maintaining a strong military; promoting freedom abroad; promoting cooperation

"Inaugural Address" by John F. Kennedy
(continued)

with adversaries; promoting a global alliance for the betterment of all mankind; and raising people out of poverty. Students could cite the pledge to bear any burden in defense of freedom; to stay loyal to allies; to ensure freedom in states that have recently escaped tyranny; to help poor villagers around the globe; to ally for progress with neighbors to the south; and to support the United Nations. Students may point to America's active role in the world or may argue that America has done too little to advance the causes put forth by Kennedy, either at home or abroad.

12. (Average) *Guidelines for student response:* Students should describe how Kennedy's speech leads up to the phrase or, conversely, how the idea is unconnected to the rest of the speech. Students could address Kennedy's phrase in terms of current arguments for less government. Students might place positive emphasis on volunteerism, while disapproving of organized government programs. Students should be able to differentiate between allegiance to their society and to their government. Students may also stress the importance of being involved in their communities.

13. (Challenging) *Guidelines for student response:* Students may cite the present economic boom, stating that conditions exist so that anyone who works hard can get ahead; or they might state that despite the economic boom many people live in poverty, even in the United States. Students should address the question of freedom and capitalism, perhaps citing countries like Singapore, where individual rights are curtailed, but economic prosperity is rampant.

Part Test, Unit 2, Part 2: Focus on Literary Forms— Speeches (p. 56)

Critical Reading/Vocabulary and Grammar

1. c 2. a 3. d 4. d 5. c 6. b 7. b 8. d 9. a
10. a 11. b 12. c 13. c 14. b 15. b

Questions are classified in these categories:
Comprehension 1(A), 5(A), 9(E)
Interpretation 2(C), 6(C)

Literary Analysis 3(A), 7(A), 8(E)
Reading Strategy 4(A), 10(A)
Vocabulary 11(A), 12(A), 13(A), 14(A)
Grammar 15(C)
E = Easy, A = Average, C = Challenging

Essay Questions

16. (Easy) *Guidelines for student response:* Students should note Franklin's argument that no one's judgment is flawless. Since all people have "their prejudices, their passions, their errors of opinion," they will never be able to produce a "perfect" Constitution and must instead focus on seeing that it is properly administered. The people must have a good opinion of the Constitution or it will fail; therefore, the united support of the Convention is essential to its success. Any apparent dissent will hurt the United States in the eyes of other nations and its own people.

17. (Average) *Guidelines for student response:* Student essays should focus on the heart of Henry's argument: Embrace the war since evidence indicates that it is inevitable. They should elaborate on Henry's argument, using details from the text: The British have not responded to continued petitions, they gather war ships that can be meant for no country but America, and their troops are already clashing with colonists in the north. Evaluations should be well reasoned and supported.

18. (Challenging) *Guidelines for student response:* Essays should discuss Henry's technique of acknowledging each of his opponents' arguments before refuting it with a rhetorical questions; for example, "They tell us, sir, that we are weak. . . . But when shall we be stronger?" Students should detail how Henry uses past experience with the British, physical evidence of Britain's militaristic intentions, and the argument that hopes for peace are futile.

"Letter to Her Daughter from the New White House" by Abigail Adams

from *Letters from an American Farmer* by Michel-Guillaume Jean de Crèvecoeur

Selection Test (p. 59)

Critical Reading/Vocabulary and Grammar

1. b 2. c 3. d 4. a 5. c 6. c 7. a   8. d 9. d
10. b 11. a 12. a 13. c 14. c 15. d 16. d
17. a 18. b 19. c 20. b

Questions are classified in these categories:
   Comprehension 1(E), 10(A), 13(A)
   Interpretation 2(A), 3(C), 4(A), 5(C), 7(A),
      9(A), 16(C)
   Literary Analysis 6(A), 11(A), 15(E)
   Reading Strategy 8(C), 12(C), 14(A)
   Vocabulary 17(E), 20(A)
   Grammar 18(E), 19(A)
   E = Easy, A = Average, C = Challenging

Essay Questions

21. (Easy) *Guidelines for student response:*
    Students should cite details from the letter
    and compare them to such things as the
    present-day city's roads, buildings, and
    monuments; its teeming populace and hec-
    tic pace; and the modern conveniences that
    make travel and communication easier.

22. (Average) *Guidelines for student response:*
    Students should recognize that Adams'
    casual description of getting lost on the
    way to Washington and her statement that
    there is nothing between the capital and
    Baltimore but woods give a strong immedi-
    ate picture of how undeveloped the coun-
    try is. Other details add to this sense as
    the letter progresses: the capital is a city
    in name only; small cottages without glass
    windows are scattered in the forest; there
    are few humans to be seen; obtaining sim-
    ple amenities in the nation's capital is dif-
    ficult; many buildings are unfinished, the
    President's home in particular.

23. (Challenging) *Guidelines for student re-
    sponse:* Students should mention such
    points as these in their summaries:
    According to Crèvecoeur, an American is
    an immigrant or a descendant of immi-
    grants; he is melted into a new race; he
    has left his past culture behind and
    adopted a new one; he is a free and full

citizen of his new country; he will entertain new ideas and form new opinions; he
will love his new country because, unlike
his old, it rewards his labors and its laws
protect him; and he will work hard, because work is in his self-interest here.
Students who feel that the definition applies today may say that people of different backgrounds (no longer just Europeans) are still melted into a new
American people, that Americans are still
patriotic because they have freedom and a
good life here, and that Americans generally enjoy a high standard of living. Those
who disagree may feel that America's different racial and ethnic groups have not
all melted into a new people, that economic disparities have little or nothing to
do with hard work or lack of it, or that
many Western European countries now
have less poverty than America has.

from *Roots* by Alex Haley

Selection Test (p. 62)

Critical Reading/Vocabulary

1. d. 2. c 3. c 4. b 5. a 6. c 7. d 8. a 9. a
10. b

Questions are classified in these categories:
   Comprehension 1(E), 2(E), 3(C), 8(A)
   Interpretation 4(C), 5(A), 6(A), 7(C)
   Vocabulary 9(A), 10(A)
   E = Easy, A = Average, C = Challenging

Essay Questions

11. (Easy) *Guidelines for student response:*
    Students should point out one important
    detail that demonstrates the differences
    between Haley's background and culture
    and that of the villagers: Haley does not
    understand the villagers' language or cus-
    toms. Students should also address the
    vast gulf between someone brought up
    and educated in the United States and a
    villager in Africa. Nevertheless, students
    should be able to speak of the kinship and
    shared history that binds Haley to
    his distant relatives.

12. (Average) *Guidelines for student response:*
    Students should point to Haley's desire to
    know more about his family history than
    the few scraps preserved in his notebooks.

from *Roots* by Alex Haley
(continued)

Students might say that to live without knowledge of the past is crippling to a full sense of self. Students might further speculate that by recording his chronicle Haley honors the memory of his ancestors. Students should state why, or why not, they think Haley's book might have been different if he had not found his ancestor's clan. Finally, students should provide some personal details demonstrating the presence or absence of knowledge about their own families and how that makes them feel.

13. (Challenging) *Guidelines for student response:* Students should point out that Haley believes Kunta's story is shared by many people who were enslaved in Africa. Students should be able to demonstrate some knowledge of progression from the Civil War to the present day in the position of African Americans in society. Students should be able to cite someone whose experience shows positive strides, as well as someone whose experience demonstrates a lack of progress. Students might agree or disagree that life is better for African Americans today.

Part Test, Unit 2, Part 3: The Emerging American Identity—Defining an American
(p. 64)

Critical Reading/Vocabulary and Grammar

1. a 2. c 3. d 4. a 5. a 6. b 7. d 8. c 9. b
10. a 11. b 12. d 13. c 14. b 15. c

Questions are classified in these categories:
  Comprehension 1(A), 5(E)
  Interpretation 2(A), 6(C), 9(E)

Literary Analysis 3(A), 7(E)
Reading Strategy 4(C), 8(C), 10(A)
Vocabulary 11(A), 12(A)
Grammar 13(A), 14(A), 15(E)
E = Easy, A = Average, C = Challenging

Essay Questions

16. (Easy) *Guidelines for student response:* Citing evidence from both Crèvecoeur and Adams, students should conclude that most Americans lived in the countryside and depended on farming for their livelihood. They may cite details about the domestic life of the middle and upper classes from Adams's letter, such as the necessity of using servants to care for large homes; the fact that wood and coal were precious commodities, since fires were kept burning even during the summer; and the custom of social visiting.

17. (Average) *Guidelines for student response:* Essays should cite the ideas expressed by both Franklin and Crèvecoeur. Franklin's aphorisms emphasize the virtues and social values of hard work, education, practicality, discipline, etc. Crèvecoeur describes Americans as a new breed of people who work hard for their own benefit, lack the old prejudices, think freely, and adopt new principles.

18. (Challenging) *Guidelines for student response:* Most students will probably agree with the criticism, noting that Crèvecoeur does not acknowledge the existence of any need or hunger in the country, and that not every American could truly have been as prosperous, liberal, and enlightened as Crèvecoeur suggests. The essays should include support from the letter to substantiate students' point of view.

Unit 3: A Growing Nation (1800–1870)

"The Devil and Tom Walker"
by Washington Irving

Selection Test (p. 67)

Critical Reading/Vocabulary and Grammar

1. a 2. b 3. c 4. d 5. d 6. a 7. c 8. d 9. c
10. b 11. b 12. d 13. c 14. a 15. c 16. d
17. c 18. c 19. a 20. c

Questions are classified in these categories:
  Comprehension 2(A), 3(E), 5(A)
  Interpretation 1(C), 4(A), 6(A), 7(C), 8(A), 9(E)
  Literary Analysis 12(C), 13(A), 15(C)
  Reading Strategy 10(A), 11(C), 14(C)
  Vocabulary 16(E), 18(A), 19(E)
  Grammar 17(E), 20(C)
  E = Easy, A = Average, C = Challenging

Essay Questions

21. (Easy) *Guidelines for student response:* Students should realize that the tree was the one with Tom Walker's name carved on it. They should cite details that suggest that the Devil carves on the trees the names of the souls he owns and, upon death, destroys the tree by burning.

22. (Average) *Guidelines for student response:* Students may point out that the use of an omniscient narrator allows Irving to make clear the motives and desires of the different characters and also to make general comments on the morals of the characters and the times. Students should give examples that illustrate different characters' thoughts and perceptions and the narrator's general comments. Students should make clear that without an omniscient narrator, some of these important story elements would be absent; others would have to be revealed indirectly, through dialogue and action.

23. (Challenging) *Guidelines for student response:* Students will probably hypothesize that the possessions disappeared or were destroyed because the Devil took back his wealth, perhaps out of spite or to use again on another victim. Information about the Devil's craftiness should be used in the explanation.

"A Psalm of Life" and "The Tide Rises, The Tide Falls"
by Henry Wadsworth Longfellow

Selection Test (p. 70)

Critical Reading/Vocabulary and Grammar

1. d 2. b 3. d 4. d 5. c 6. b 7. a 8. c 9. c
10. c 11. b 12. a 13. d 14. b 15. c 16. a
17. a 18. d 19. d 20. b

Questions are classified in these categories:
  Comprehension 1(E), 2(E), 10(E)
  Interpretation 3(A), 4(C), 9(C), 11(C), 12(A)
  Literary Analysis 5(E), 13(E), 14(C)
  Reading Strategy 6(A), 7(A), 8(A), 15(C)
  Vocabulary 16(A), 17(E), 18(A)
  Grammar 19(A), 20(C)
  E = Easy, A = Average, C = Challenging

Essay Questions

21. (Easy) *Guidelines for student response:* Examples of the sea representing life might include the sea as a passageway for the journey of life and the sea as a provider of water and life. Examples of the sea representing death might include the sea washing out signs of life and the sea as a cause of drowning. Students should recognize the use of the sea in "The Tide Rises, The Tide Falls" as an image of the continuity of life in the face of one human death.

22. (Average) *Guidelines for student response:* Students should indicate that the footprints in the sand in both poems represent deeds or actions performed while a person is living. In "A Psalm of Life," the footprints remain after the person is gone and may inspire another person. In "The Tide Rises, the Tide Falls," the footprints are washed away, signifying that the person has died or that the person's achievements did not last. Students may suggest that the footprints in "A Psalm of Life" refer to great deeds that endure, but the footprints in "The Tide Rises, The Tide Falls" refer to the actions of daily life, which cease when the person dies.

23. (Challenging) *Guidelines for student response:* Students may say that the two viewpoints of death presented in the poems are a source of inspiration ("A Psalm of Life") and eventual acceptance ("The Tide Rises, The Tide Falls"). The presentations of death are alike in that neither viewpoint shows death as something to be feared. They are different in that, in the first poem, death is something in the future, which cannot be avoided but should not be awaited passively. Feelings evoked include inspiration, exuberance, and hope. In the second poem, death is presented as something that should be expected and that could happen soon. Feelings evoked include acceptance, a sense of solitude in the journey, and a comforting recognition that while one human being may die, nature— and life itself—go on.

"Thanatopsis" by William Cullen Bryant; **"Old Ironsides"** by Oliver Wendell Holmes; **"The First Snowfall"** by James Russell Lowell; **from Snowbound** by John Greenleaf Whittier

Selection Test (p. 73)

Critical Reading/Vocabulary and Grammar

1. a 2. d 3. b 4. c 5. a 6. b 7. a 8. b 9. c
10. c 10. c 11. d 12. b 13. a 14. d 15. d
16. a 17. c 18. a 19. c 20. b

Questions are classified in these categories:
Comprehension 1(E), 2(C), 5(E), 10(A), 13(E)
Interpretation 3(A), 6(A), 7(A), 9(A), 11(E), 14(A)
Literary Analysis 4(E), 16(A), 17(C)
Reading Strategy 8(C), 12(C), 15(A)
Vocabulary 18(A), 19(C)
Grammar 20(A)
E = Easy, A = Average, C = Challenging

Essay Questions

21. (Easy) *Guidelines for student response:* Most students will probably feel that the poem would be more influential than an editorial. Students may cite examples of Holmes's use of rhythm, rhyme, vivid descriptions, and emotional exclamations—none of which would ordinarily appear in an editorial.

22. (Average) *Guidelines for student response:* Students should discuss the role of nature as a source of comfort to the speaker and the poem's depiction of death as a part of nature. While evaluations may differ, they should recognize that "Thanatopsis" is filled with detailed descriptions of nature, such as the description of the forest, the ocean, and the skies.

23. (Challenging) *Guidelines for student response:* Student responses may discuss how "Thanatopsis" uses nature to build a sense of something larger than the individual and to give a sense of comfort and belonging; how "Old Ironsides" uses images of stormy seas to describe the trials that the ship has undergone and stress its value to the American nation; how "The First Snowfall" depicts the snowfall as a comforting blanket that envelopes and heals; or how *Snowbound* uses images of a snowstorm to convey a sense of beauty, stresses the storm as a source

of privacy and isolation, and contrasts images of the storm and cold with the warmth and security of the speaker's family life.

"Crossing the Great Divide" by Meriwether Lewis
"The Most Sublime Spectacle on Earth" by John Wesley Powell

Selection Test (p. 76)

Critical Reading/Vocabulary and Grammar

1. d 2. a 3. d 4. c 5. b 6. a 7. c 8. b 9. d
10. a 11. b 12. c 13. d 14. c 15. a 16. b
17. d 18. c 19. c 20. c

Questions are classified in these categories:
Comprehension 1(E), 6(E), 9(A)
Interpretation 2(A), 3(A), 7(E), 8(C), 10(C), 15(C)
Literary Analysis 4(E), 11(A), 14(A), 16(E)
Reading Strategy 5(A), 12(A), 13(C)
Vocabulary 17(A), 18(C)
Grammar 19(A), 20(A)
E = Easy, A = Average, C = Challenging

Essay Questions

21. (Easy) *Guidelines for student response:* Students will probably give reasons such as providing the explorers with horses; allowing the explorers to pass peacefully; establishing relations for future trade; and providing the explorers with food, water, directions, and other aid.

22. (Average) *Guidelines for student response:* Negative experiences might include physical challenges. For example, Powell writes that the Grand Canyon is more difficult to explore than the Himalayas or the Alps. Lewis describes looking for horses in case they could not continue their journey on water. Lewis speaks of having a slight breakfast and sending Shields off to hunt, reminding us that the explorers had to find fresh food along the way. Opinions on explorers' future plans may vary. Students are likely to predict that Powell would be anxious to return to the wilderness and to support their evaluation with his many expressions of wonder and his remark at the end of the selection: "If strength and courage are sufficient for the task, by a year's toil a concept of sublimity

can be obtained never again to be equaled on the hither side of Paradise." Students may also feel that Lewis would be interested in returning but should recognize that he is much more businesslike in tone and does not reveal his feelings very much in this selection.

23. (Challenging) *Guidelines for student response:* Being a geologist, Powell knew how to recognize rocks and rock formations, which probably influenced his report of the layers of rock in the Grand Canyon and how those rocks were formed. The geologist's perspective also contributed to his understanding of the erosion and other factors that created the canyon and may also have added to his sense of time, of the canyon being built over ages. Students may feel that Powell's interest in geology could have prompted him to feel more fascination with the Grand Canyon than an average viewer. They should also recognize that his writings demonstrate a gift for description as well as knowledge about the earth.

"Seeing" from *Pilgrim at Tinker Creek* by Annie Dillard

Selection Test (p. 79)

Critical Reading/Vocabulary

1. b 2. a 3. d 4. a 5. c 6. d 7. b 8. a 9. c 10. a

Questions are classified in these categories:
Comprehension 1(A), 3(A), 4(E), 7(E)
Interpretation 2(C), 5(A), 6(C), 8(C)
Vocabulary 9(A), 10(A)
E = Easy, A = Average, C = Challenging

Essay Questions

11. (Easy) *Guidelines for student response:* Students should be able to recall the episodes with the birds, the bullfrog, the fog, and so on. They should relate some experience of their own, describing it with similar detail and a sense of renewed perception.

12. (Average) *Guidelines for student response:* Students might mention attraction to solitude, self-reliance, power of observation, strength of character, and so on. Students might surmise that Dillard was not so much alone in the wilderness as she was in communion with nature. Students should speculate on their own ability to endure such a test, telling what they like about nature and what would make it hard for them to duplicate Dillard's feat.

13. (Challenging) *Guidelines for student response:* Students should reiterate Dillard's reverence for the natural world. After agreeing or disagreeing, they must relate that attitude to the products of the modern entertainment industry or industry in general. Students might argue that Dillard's powers of observation would be equally well rewarded if focused on art, or they might argue that modern society constitutes a wasteland best escaped through a return to nature.

Part Test, Unit 3, Part 1: Fireside and Campfire (p. 81)

Critical Reading/Vocabulary and Grammar

1. c 2. b 3. d 4. a 5. b 6. c 7. b 8. d 9. b 10. a 11. a 12. b 13. a 14. a 15. d 16. b 17. a 18. a 19. c 20. b

Questions are classified in these categories:
Comprehension 3(E), 9(E)
Interpretation 1(C), 10(A)
Literary Analysis 4(A), 5(C), 8(A)
Reading Strategy 2(A), 6(C), 7(A)
Vocabulary 11(A), 12(A), 13(A), 20(A)
Grammar 14(A), 15(A), 16(A), 17(C), 18(E), 19(A)
E = Easy, A = Average, C = Challenging

Essay Questions

21. (Average) *Guidelines for student response:* Students' essays should analyze the view of death presented in a "A Psalm of Life," "The Tide Rises, The Tide Falls," "Thanatopsis," or "The First Snowfall." The first Longfellow poem strives against death; the second accepts it as part of nature's endless cycles. In "Thanatopsis," Bryant presents death as a natural event not to be feared by the individual who already feels at home in nature. Lowell confronts a concrete example—the death of his own daughter—and the resulting pain that still scars his family life. Students should refer to specific examples from the text to support their points.

22. (Easy) *Guidelines for student response:* Students' essays may focus on the importance of time and place in such works as "The Devil and Tom Walker," "The Tide Rises, The Tide Falls," "Thanatopsis," and *Snowbound.* Students might discuss how the physical setting of the swamp emphasizes the evil represented by the Devil in "The Devil and Tom Walker." The sea, which is the setting of "The Tide Rises, The Tide Falls," helps convey the theme of nature's eternal cycles. The primeval forest that forms the backdrop to "Thanatopsis" lends a brooding, even mystical mood to the theme of the cyclic nature of life and death. Students who select *Snowbound* should note that the strength of the storm and the magical beauty of the snow-covered landscape underscore Whittier's theme of the power of nature.

23. (Average) *Guidelines for student response:* Students should choose one selection and analyze how images of nature are used to convey theme. For example, in "The Tide Rises, the Tide Falls," Longfellow uses images of the seashore—ocean, sand, curlew, twilight, darkness—and of animals and human beings to express his ideas about the immutability of death. In "The First Snowfall," the snow is a symbol of the healing process, which, like the snow that covers the scars of the earth, is sent by God to smooth the scars of grief. Essays should include specific references to the work(s) cited.

24. (Average) *Guidelines for student response:* Students should associate a specific view or attitude with an appopriate selection, supporting their choice with references to the text. Students should cite "The Most Sublime Spectacle on Earth" as an example of nature's ability to awe, as evidenced by Powell's acknowledgement of the insuffiency of words to describe the wonders of the Grand Canyon. When faced with death, both real and abstract, the writers of "The First Snowfall" and "Thanatopsis" found comfort and meaning in nature and

natural events. The speaker of *Snowbound* is inspired by nature's power to transform the world as we know it.

25. (Challenging) *Guidelines for student response:* Accept any well-supported, well-reasoned opinion that focuses on at least two writers whose works are found in Part 1. Most students will probably refute de Tocqueville by illuminating the literary quality or original style or content of several Part 1 selections. They might, for example, argue the merits of Washington Irving's distinctively American version of an old European legend and support their claim with references to his individual style and his imaginative characterizations. Others may point to the originality displayed by Margaret Fuller and Ralph Waldo Emerson in establishing a new voice for philosophical thought and literary criticism.

"The Fall of the House of Usher" and "The Raven" by Edgar Allan Poe

Selection Test (p. 85)

Critical Reading/Vocabulary and Grammar

1. c 2. d 3. c 4. a 5. a 6. d 7. c 8. b 9. a
10. a 11. b 12. d 13. a 14. d 15. c 16. d
17. b 18. d 19. c 20. a

Questions are classified in these categories:
Comprehension 2(A), 3(A), 8(C), 11(E)
Interpretation 4(A), 7(A), 9(C), 10(C), 12(E), 14(C)
Literary Analysis 1(E), 5(A), 13(A)
Reading Strategy 6(E), 15(A)
Vocabulary 16(A), 17(E), 18(C)
Grammar 19(E), 20(A)
E = Easy, A = Average, C = Challenging

Essay Questions

21. (Easy) *Guidelines for student response:* Students might mention feelings such as surprise, fear, dislike, curiosity, or even pleasure in their encounter with the raven. They may say that they would respond to the raven less dramatically and more scientifically than the speaker does. They might take the bird's appearance less personally. They may be less likely to see it as a supernatural messenger and may suggest that the word "Nevermore"

has no real significance and is simply the only word it learned from a former master.

22. (Average) *Guidelines for student response:* Students who agree with this interpretation should note that just about everything Usher does is unrelated to any existence outside his house or mind. They should mention such things as Usher's strange creations in all area of art, especially his abstract paintings; the painful acuteness of his senses; and his absorption in fantasy literature. Students who disagree may say that Usher represents anyone completely isolated from others, not just a creative artist. Some students may point to Usher's affluence, rather than his creativity, as the root of his problem. They may cite evidence such as his large estate, servants, and lack of gainful employment to suggest that wealth and privilege without purpose may be destructive. Some students may see in Usher a member of a doomed family whose weaknesses through several generations lead to destruction, or they may place more emphasis on supernatural causes, such as a family curse, as the root of his problems.

23. (Challenging) *Guidelines for student response:* Students may relate this description of an endless, empty yet enclosed space to the theme of the destruction of the creative mind turned away from the real world. There is nothing concrete for the light in the space to illuminate, and so it is sterile, even horrible. Students may see the painting as the image of Roderick's inner being: full of the light of imagination and ability, but without any real substance, and from which escape has become impossible. Some students may see the painting as an embodiment of the world of the House of Usher: a horrible place, essentially devoid of meaning, yet bathed in the light, as if it contained something important.

"The Minister's Black Veil"
by Nathaniel Hawthorne

Selection Test (p. 88)

Critical Reading/Vocabulary and Grammar

1. b 2. a 3. a 4. d 5. c 6. c 7. d 8. c 9. a
10. b 11. c 12. b 13. a 14. c 15. d 16. a
17. b 18. b 19. d 20. c

Questions are classified in these categories:
Comprehension 1(A), 3(E), 4(E)
Interpretation 2(C), 5(C), 6(A), 12(A), 13(C)
Literary Analysis 7(E), 8(C), 9(A), 10(C), 11(A)
Reading Strategy 14(A), 15(A)
Vocabulary 16(E), 17(A), 18(A)
Grammar 19(E), 20(E)
E = Easy, A = Average, C = Challenging

Essay Questions

21. (Easy) *Guidelines for student response:* Some students may feel that Hooper's veil is confession of general wrongfulness stemming from the belief that all human-beings are sinners in the wake of the Fall of Man (original sin in the Garden of Eden) or is a confession of more specific wrongdoing, even of some particularly ter-rible sin, the details of which Mr. Hooper is hiding. Others may feel that he is mak-ing a statement and is less concerned with confessing his own sins than with giving his congregation a terrible reminder of their own sins, or of the belief that human beings are all sinners. Some stu-dents may say that the veil can function in both ways at the same time.

22. (Average) *Guidelines for student response:* Students will probably recognize that Hawthorne's Puritans are close-knit in their small communities and that their lives center around the church, making the pastor an important figure. They are concerned with religion and sin to a great degree. Some students may mention that Hawthorne is stressing the Puritans' hypocrisy, despite their concern with reli-gion and sin. On the other hand, they may note that Hawthorne does make the Puri-tans seem human: they admire each other, they gossip, they celebrate happy events, the children make merry. Some students may feel that Hawthorne is fond of Hooper, whom he shows as a gentle soul; others may feel that he sees Hooper's veil as an extreme, even harmful gesture, and may mention his behavior toward Elizabeth as particularly extreme and cruel.

23. (Challenging) *Guidelines for student re-sponse:* Students should mention that objects need not be strange or unique in themselves to acquire symbolic power. Rather, they become symbolic because

of their particular setting, the events of which they are a part, and the people who use them. So a veil on the bonnet of a woman may be purely decorative or may symbolize ornamentation or proper dress; a veil worn by a nun or a Moslem woman may symbolize purity or piety; a veil worn by a widow may symbolize grief. When such a veil is taken out of that common context and used in a more bizarre way, it becomes a potent symbol, with power beyond the ordinary to cause an emotional reaction in all who see it.

from *Moby-Dick* by Herman Melville

Selection Test (p. 91)

Critical Reading/Vocabulary and Grammar

1. a 2. c 3. b 4. c 5. d 6. b 7. b 8. d 9. c
10. a 11. d 12. c 13. c 14. a 15. b 16. d
17. a 18. b 19. d 20. c

Questions are classified in these categories:
Comprehension 1(E), 2(E), 3(A), 4(A)
Interpretation 5(E), 6(A), 7(A), 8(C), 9(C)
Literary Analysis 12(E), 13(C), 14(C), 15(A)
Reading Strategy 10(E), 11(C)
Vocabulary 16(E), 17(A), 18(A)
Grammar 19(A), 20(A)
E = Easy, A = Average, C = Challenging

Essay Questions

21. (Easy) *Guidelines for student response:* Ahab's good points could include the leadership ability that helps him unite and motivate the crew, his apparent liking and respect for his men, his generosity with money, and his physical bravery. Bad points should include his abandonment of the business of the voyage, his obsessive personality, and, most important, his willingness to endanger the lives of his crew to fulfill his own ends.

22. (Average) *Guidelines for student response:* Students should recognize that these words apply well to Ahab. He is a ship's captain and thus at sea has a great deal of power with almost no external restraints. He also seems to lack the constraints that religious

faith or fear of physical danger might provide. Thus there is nothing to keep him from being driven by his innermost necessities—hatred and vengefulness for Moby Dick. Students may even say that without external restraints, Ahab is a victim of his inner self. They may also see in Starbuck the opposite of Ahab: the external restraints of his position on the ship—he must obey Ahab—keep him from being driven by his inner recognition that Ahab's mission is wrong.

23. (Challenging) *Guidelines for student response:* Students may say that the scene is a good way of clarifying Ahab's motivation dramatically, through his own words and actions, rather than by having Ishmael merely summarize them. Students may also say that to make the idea of the mission against Moby-Dick believable, Melville had to show the great psychological power that Ahab exerts over his crew, whom he must persuade to give up their usual business and follow him, and without whose willing help Ahab cannot hope to succeed. In addition, the scene explores Ahab's obsession in his confrontation with Starbuck, tells us about reactions of some other characters to the quest and to Ahab, and establishes the reality of Moby-Dick outside the mind of Ahab. With its high drama and ritualistic events, the scene, despite clear elements foreshadowing, catches the reader up in Ahab's passion.

"Where *Is* Here?" by Joyce Carol Oates

Selection Test (p. 94)

Critical Reading/Vocabulary

1. d 2. d 3. a 4. b 5. a 6. d 7. d 8. c 9. b
10. c

Questions are classified in these categories:
Comprehension 1(E), 2(A), 4(A), 6(A)
Interpretation 3(C), 5(C), 7(C)
Vocabulary 8(A), 9(E), 10(A)
E = Easy, A = Average, C = Challenging

Essay Questions

11. (Easy) *Guidelines for student response:* Students should emphasize the details that reinforce a sense of mystery and dread in the story, such as the winter setting, the damp chill of the evening, the

stranger's limp and the mysterious way he roots around outdoors before coming in, and the mother's unexplained "surge of feeling" and her mysterious bruise. Students might find that the details all hang together into a consistent whole, or they might find fault with some weak linkages.

12. (Average) *Guidelines for student response:* Students should point out that the stranger has no name, limps weirdly, reacts strangely to questions, barges around the house without asking, begs to see the basement, makes cryptic statements, and so on. Students might speculate that the stranger is a ghost because of the two slips of the tongue: "And so too *we* were" and "we've all been dead." Students should also point out the vagueness of material boundaries (the references to materiality, the moving door frame, the changing light after he leaves) that seem to accompany his visit, suggesting his presence as something bizarre and unnatural.

13. (Challenging) *Guidelines for student response:* Students might cite such ambiguous details as the geometric figure representing infinity, as well as the other philosophical riddles and unanswerable questions posed to the stranger as a child by his mother. Students might suggest that there probably is no one correct "meaning" to the story. Students should take one of the mysterious details, give it a cause, and then explain how their addition serves to make a concrete interpretation possible.

Part Test, Unit 3, Part 2: Shadows of the Imagination
(p. 96)

Critical Reading/Vocabulary and Grammar

1. c 2. b 3. c 4. a 5. c 6. b 7. d 8. a 9. d
10. b 11. c 12. b 13. c 14. b 15. a

Questions are classified in these categories:
Comprehension 1(C), 3(A), 19(E)
Interpretation 2(A)
Literary Analysis 5(A), 6(E), 7(A), 9(A)
Reading Strategy 4(E), 8(C)
Vocabulary 11(C), 12(A), 13(A)
Grammar 13(A), 14(A), 15(A)
E = Easy, A = Average, C = Challenging

Essay Questions

16. (Easy) *Guidelines for student response:* The students' essays should focus on the gothic or supernatural elements of the stories in this part. Citing specific references from the works, students should discuss the eerie setting, oppressive mood, and unnatural events that characterize "The House of Usher" and "The Raven"; the air of menace and mystery created by the black veil in Hawthorne's story; and the almost mystical ritual with which Captain Ahab unites the crew in search of Moby-Dick, as well as Ahab's own seemingly supernatural obsession with the whale.

17. (Average) *Guidelines for student response:* Through Usher, Poe explores the darker side of the inner self and portrays a human mind's descent into madness. Students should provide a general profile of Usher's character, noting the duality of his personality ("alternately vivacious and sullen"), his sensitivity to sensations, and his susceptibility to his surroundings. Essays should then trace the progress of Usher's condition as he succumbs to the fear and mental illness that represent the dark side of the self. Students should support their points with specific references from the text (for example, "a full consciousness on the part of Usher of the tottering of his lofty reason upon her throne")

18. (Challenging) *Guidelines for student response:* Students should cite specific details that foreshadow the ending of the selected work. Essays on "The House of Usher" should focus on details about the setting, Usher's physical and mental decline, and the lifelike quality of Lady Madeline's corpse. Essays on *Moby-Dick* should cite details of the scene on the deck (Starbuck's misgivings, the pledge to kill Moby-Dick or die trying), Ahab's goodbyes, the symbolism of the third day of the pursuit, the appearance of the sharks, and the loss of the ship's flag—all of which foreshadow the coming end of the Pequod.

from *Nature*, from *Self-Reliance*, "The Snowstorm," and "Concord Hymn" by Ralph Waldo Emerson

Selection Test (p. 99)

Critical Reading/Vocabulary and Grammar

1. c 2. b 3. c 4. c 5. d 6. a 7. d 8. a 9. b
10. d 11. b 12. b 13. a 14. c 15. d 16. d
17. b 18. b 19. a 20. a

Questions are classified in these categories:
   Comprehension 2(E), 3(A), 7(A)
   Interpretation 9(A), 10(A), 11(A), 13(A), 14(C)
   Literary Analysis 1(C), 5(A), 8(A), 12(E)
   Reading Strategy 4(E), 6(A), 15(A)
   Vocabulary 16(A), 18(A), 20(E)
   Grammar 17(A), 19(E)
   E = Easy, A = Average, C = Challenging

Essay Questions

21. (Easy) *Guidelines for student response:* Students should cite or summarize lines from *Nature* that focus on the relationship between nature and the human spirit; for example, "In the woods is perpetual youth. Within these plantations of God, a decorum and sanctity reign"; "Standing on the bare ground—my head bathed by the blithe air and uplifted into infinite space—all mean egotism vanishes. I become a transparent eyeball: I am nothing: I see all: the currents of the Universal Being circulate through me: I am part or parcel of God"; and "Nature always wears the colors of the spirit."

22. (Average) *Guidelines for student response:* "The shot heard round the world" underscores patriotism and the American struggle for liberty as a model for the world. Students who feel these quotations contradict each other may say that the quotation from Nature criticizes nationalism and hence patriotism. Students who feel that they do not contradict each other may say that both place great value on freedom and independence.

23. (Challenging) *Guidelines for student response:* Students who feel that the two beliefs have an inherent conflict may focus on the tension between the self-reliant individual and the spiritual community. Those who feel there is no real conflict may say that Emerson stresses that one must be an independent, self-reliant individual to reach the spiritual heights of the Over-Soul and that the individual is in conflict only with society on a more material plane.

from *Walden* and from *Civil Disobedience* by Henry David Thoreau

Selection Test (p. 102)

Critical Reading/Vocabulary and Grammar

1. d 2. d 3. b 4. b 5. a 6. a 7. d 8. b 9. c
10. a 11. d 12. c 13. c 14. b 15. d 16. a
17. b 18. b 19. a 20. c

Questions are classified in these categories:
   Comprehension 2(E), 5(C), 13(A)
   Interpretation 3(A), 8(A), 9(C), 10(A), 12(E)
   Literary Analysis 6(A), 7(C), 14(C)
   Reading Strategy 1(A), 4(A), 11(A), 15(A), 16(C)
   Vocabulary 17(E), 20(A)
   Grammar 18(A), 19(C)
   E = Easy, A = Average, C = Challenging

Essay Questions

21. (Easy) *Guidelines for student response:* Students should recognize that by moving to the woods, Thoreau was able to simplify his life, thereby allowing himself to concentrate on what he considered the important things involving the human spirit; he also lived closer to nature and gained a keener appreciation of its beauty and power. Among the details students may cite are the details about the poet appreciating a farm more than a farmer does; the descriptions of the Hollowell farm; the paragraph beginning "I went to the woods because I wished to live deliberately"; all the elaboration, in the next paragraph, on the idea of "Simplicity, simplicity, simplicity!"; and the details in the paragraph beginning "However mean your life is, meet it and live it."

22. (Average) *Guidelines for student response:* Students should show how these statements reflect Thoreau's philosophy: "Sell your clothes and keep your thoughts" stresses his desire to strip life to its bare essentials so that we can concentrate on important matters of the human spirit; "If a man does not keep pace with his companions, . . ." stresses the importance he places on individualism and nonconfor-

mity; "Let every man make known what kind of government would command his respect, and that will be one step toward obtaining it" again stresses the value he places on individualism and also shows his hopeful view that the government might be changed through individual effort. Some students may find Thoreau's views appealing; others may find them too impractical, optimistic, or self-centered; or they may feel that the nonconformity he values would actually make some people very unhappy. After stating whether or not they agree with Thoreau's view, students might cite examples from history, current events, and/or personal experience to support their own opinions.

23. (Challenging) *Guidelines for student response:* Students should recognize that by taking action, Thoreau does not mean that people need to be busy, but that they need to contemplate the essentials of nature and the human spirit. Students may suggest that taking action can involve expressing one's opinion, refusing to go along with the rest of society, and/or dedicating oneself to a simple life experiencing nature and the human spirit. The many references to time stress Thoreau's idea that life is precious. It seems Thoreau is urging people to take action immediately, not to wait.

Part Test, Unit 3, Part 3: The Emerging American Identity— The Human Spirit and the Natural World (p. 105)

Critical Reading/Vocabulary and Grammar

1. b 2. c 3. b 4. a 5. b 6. a 7. b 8. d 9. a
10. c 11. b 12. a 13. c 14. b 15. a

Questions are classified in these categories:
Comprehension 1(E), 2(E), 3(A)
Interpretation 9(C), 10(A)
Literary Analysis 4(A), 8(C)
Reading Strategy 5(A), 6(C), 7(A)
Vocabulary 11(A), 12(A)
Grammar 13(A), 14(C), 15(C)
E = Easy, A = Average, C = Challenging

Essay Questions

16. (Easy) *Guidelines for student response:* Students' essays may discuss how Thoreau's time at Walden was an experi-

ment tried for a short period before the author went on to try other lifestyles. His time was spent in observing nature, contemplating society, and living true to his own moral dictates. Students may speculate that it would be difficult today to claim land, even for a brief time, for homesteading on what is now Walden Pond or some other lakeside retreat. There would be authorities to deal with, building codes to meet, and environmental considerations that would prevent such an activity.

17. (Average) *Guidelines for student response:* Students' essays should compare and contrast the ideas about nature expressed in one poem and one prose piece by Emerson. For example, both the excerpt from *Nature* and "The Snowstorm" celebrate the natural world. However, in the prose work, Emerson focuses on the connection forged between the human and natural worlds. In the poem he focuses only on the beauty, wonder, and majesty of nature's forms.

18. (Challenging) *Guidelines for student response:* Students' essays should identify and explain Thoreau's central ideas—for example, that the American citizenry is more powerful than the American government—in the excerpt from "Civil Disobedience." Then they should refute these ideas in a clear, well-organized way.

Emily Dickinson's Poetry

Selection Test (p. 108)

Critical Reading/Vocabulary and Grammar

1. c 2. b 3. a 4. a 5. d 6. c 7. d 8. c 9. c
10. a 11 b 12. b 13. a 14. c 15. d 16. a
17. b 18. b 19. d 20. b

Questions are classified in these categories:
Comprehension 1(A), 5(A), 9(A),11(C)
Interpretation 4(A), 6(C), 7(A), 15(A)
Literary Analysis 2(E), 9(C), 13(E)
Reading Strategy 3(E), 10(E), 12(A), 14(C)
Vocabulary 16(E), 17(E), 18(C)
Grammar 19(A), 20(A)
E = Easy, A = Average, C = Challenging

Essay Questions

21. (Easy) *Guidelines for student response:* Students should choose an image from one of Dickinson's poems and explain

what Dickinson is trying to communicate by using this image. For example, the fly in "I heard a Fly buzz—when I died—" may illustrate the sense of awe and quiet attention with which people approach death.

22. (Average) *Guidelines for student response:* Students should recognize that Dickinson does not seem to fear death, but that she realizes it is impossible to predict what happens to a person after death. She also recognizes that death means parting with the people one is close to in life. Dickinson seems to believe in an immortal soul and to expect that immortality will accompany death. In "Because I could not stop for Death—," she speculates that after death, centuries may pass very quickly (presumably until Judgment Day). Some students may note that Dickinson seems to think that people are fundamentally alone and that the soul may in fact be more isolated in life than it is after death.

23. (Challenging) *Guidelines for student response:* Students should recognize that the teachers in the poem often seem to teach their opposites; for example, thirst teaches water, the oceans teach the land, battles teach peace, and death teaches love. The lessons are more often positive (water, peace, love), while the teachers are more often negative and involve human suffering (thirst, battles, death). Dickinson's message thus might be that we appreciate joy only after suffering, or that we need both the good and the bad in life because negative experiences or the absence of something helps define its meaning. Some students may note that love and death and birds and snow are not precisely opposites, but that love may fear death and birds clearly fear, or at least want to avoid, the coming of snow. These students may suggest that Dickinson's message is that we learn the most from the things and experiences that we most fear.

Walt Whitman's Poetry

Selection Test (p. 111)

Critical Reading/Vocabulary and Grammar

1. a 2. d 3. d 4. d 5. b 6. c 7. c 8. a 9. d
10. b 11. a 12. c 13. a 14. c 15. d 16. d
17. b 18. a 19. d 20. c

Questions are classified in these categories:
Comprehension 1(A), 9(C), 11(E), 14(E)
Interpretation 4(A), 6(E), 7(C), 10(A)
Literary Analysis 3(E), 12(C), 15(A)
Reading Strategy 2(C), 5(A), 8(A), 13(C), 16(A)
Vocabulary 17(A), 18(C)
Grammar 19(E), 20(A)
E = Easy, A = Average, C = Challenging

Essay Questions

21. (Easy) *Guidelines for student response:* Students should recognize that Whitman admired the average person, and was more likely to write about jobs that involved physical work, such as carpentry or mechanics, than about jobs that involve a lot of education, such as practicing law or medicine. They should also realize that America is bigger and includes more occupations than it did in Whitman's day. Students may wish to include some fairly recent occupations, such as computer programmer or astronaut.

22. (Average) *Guidelines for student response:* Whitman seems to feel that death is not an unhappy event but rather one that he accepts as part of nature. By observing nature, Whitman learns about death. Some students may quote lines such as the following: "The smallest sprout shows there is really no death," and "to die is different from what anyone supposed, and luckier."

23. (Challenging) *Guidelines for student response:* Whitman's poetry shows that he values diversity of ethnic background, occupation, income level, and so on. It also shows that he admires the average person. Traveling through the United States, he found Americans from all walks of life to be admirable. Whitman also does not value formal advanced education, which especially in his day was accessible to only a

few, any more than he values informal education, which people gain by observing life and nature.

"I, Too" by Langston Hughes
"To Walt Whitman"
by Angela de Hoyos

Selection Test (p. 114)

Critical Reading

1. d 2. a 3. b 4. c 5. a 6. d 7. b 8. c 9. c 10. a

Questions are classified in these categories:
Comprehension 1(A), 2(A), 3(E), 7(E)
Interpretation 4(C), 5(A), 6(C), 8(C), 9(A), 10(A)
E = Easy, A = Average, C = Challenging

Essay Questions

11. (Easy) *Guidelines for student response:* Students should point out each poem's telegraphic style and theme of speaking for an underrepresented people. Students might find de Hoyos's language more colloquial than Hughes's. Students should make a judgment about the effectiveness of the short form, perhaps comparing it compared with Whitman's often-lengthy works.

12. (Average) *Guidelines for student response:* Students might argue that poets are or are not responsible for depicting all peoples in their work. Students might note a difference between "personal" poetry, which seeks to describe the experiences of an individual speaker, and "public" poetry, which seeks to capture general moods and experiences. Students might suggest that when Whitman ventured to write of the "common man" he should have been careful to include all people. Students might argue, on the other hand, that poetry and art have no social responsibility of any kind.

13. (Challenging) *Guidelines for student response:* Students should note the policies of discrimination that affected African Americans or Native Americans. Students should point out that both poems argue for the inclusion of all peoples in American society. Students might suggest that increasing diversity has enriched the American experience, which is not dependent on race but on the ideals of freedom and opportunity. Students might suggest that the author they chose would agree with this. From personal experience, students might themselves be less optimistic that race can or has become secondary to being an American.

Part Test, Unit 3, Part 4: Focus on Literary Forms— Poetry (p. 116)

Critical Reading/Vocabulary and Grammar

1. c 2. a 3. d 4. b 5. d 6. c 7. d 8. d 9. b 10. c 11. c 12. a 13. c 14. b 15. a

Questions are classified in these categories:
Comprehension 2(C)
Interpretation 1(A)
Literary Analysis 3(C), 4(C), 6(C), 8(E), 9(A)
Reading Strategy 5(C), 7(C), 10(C)
Vocabulary 11(A), 12(E), 13(E)
Grammar 14(A), 15(A)
E = Easy, A = Average, C = Challenging

Essay Questions

16. (Easy) *Guidelines for student response:* Students' essays should compare and contrast the writing of Dickinson and Whitman. Both have written love poems of great stylistic originality. Yet whereas Dickinson used traditional forms and elements (such as stanzas and the use of occasional end rhyme and slant rhyme), Whitman was revolutionary in his use of free verse. Both poets' works are rich with figurative language.

17. (Average) *Guidelines for student response:* Students' essays should analyze the poet's presentation of the natural and human worlds in a single poem. For example, in "There's a certain Slant of light," Dickinson focuses on natural elements—light, shadows, and "the Landscape"—that have a profound emotional effect on the human speaker. These natural elements make the speaker feel oppressed and despairing in an ineffable way.

18. (Challenging) *Guidelines for student response:* Students' essays should focus on how the chosen poet presents ideas and images that are relevant to

life in general and to the life of an individual. For example, a student might say that in such poems as "Song of Myself" and "When I Heard the Learn'd Astronomer," Walt Whitman expresses the interconnectedness of all life in the former and an individual aspect of life in the latter.

Unit 4: Division, Reconciliation, and Expansion (1850–1914)

"An Episode of War" by Stephen Crane
"Willie Has Gone to the War,"
words by George Cooper, music by Stephen Foster

Selection Test (p. 119)

Critical Reading/Vocabulary and Grammar

1. c 2. b 3. b 4. d 5. a 6. b 7. a 8. b 9. c
10. d 11. c 12. a 13. d 14. b 15. a 16. a
17. b 18. b 19. c 20. d

Questions are classified in these categories:
Comprehension 1(E), 2(A), 12(E),
Interpretation 4(C), 5(C), 7(A), 8(C), 13(C)
Literary Analysis 3(C), 10(A), 11(A)
Reading Strategy 6(A), 9(E), 14(A)
Vocabulary 15(A), 16(E), 20(C)
Grammar Skill 17(A), 18(C), 19 (A)
E = Easy, A = Average, C = Challenging

Essay Questions

21. (Easy) *Guidelines for student response:* Students who address "Willie Has Gone to the War" will likely cite the heroine's universal feelings of loss, loneliness, hope, and longing. Students who address "An Episode of War" may note that the lieutenant's injury at the story's beginning makes him a sympathetic character. Accept any essay that contains a well-reasoned argument in support of the writer's opinion.

22. (Average) *Guidelines for student response:* Students may focus on the song's hope, noting that the glade is untouched by war and will bloom again in spring; its despair, pointing out that the speaker is weeping for her loved one and that "The leaves of the forest will fade"; or on other sentiments, such as love and longing. Accept any conclusion that is well supported with lyrics from the song.

23. (Challenging) *Guidelines for student response:* Students should define Realism as a literary movement whose advocates sought to depict real life as faithfully and accurately as possible by focusing on ordinary people faced with the harsh realities of everyday life. They may point out how the lieutenant was wounded while occupied with mundane duties and trace his journey through the harsh realities of the battle zone. They should also mention how Crane's use of vivid and historically accurate details heightens the story's realism.

"Swing Low, Sweet Chariot" and "Go Down, Moses" Spirituals

Selection Test (p. 122)

Critical Reading/Vocabulary and Grammar

1. c 2. a 3. d 4. c 5. b 6. d 7. c 8. a 9. d
10. d 11. a 12. c 13. c 14. b 15. c 16. b
17. a 18. b 19. b 20. d

Questions are classified in these categories:
Comprehension 1(E), 4(A), 13(C)
Interpretation 5(E), 9(E), 10(A), 12(E), 14(A)
Literary Analysis 2(A), 6(E), 7(A), 11(A), 16(C)
Reading Strategy 3(C), 8(A), 15(A)
Vocabulary 19(A), 20(C)
Grammar Skill 17(C), 18(E)
E = Easy, A = Average, C = Challenging

Essay Questions

21. (Easy) *Guidelines for student response:* Students should recognize that, in a veiled way, "Go Down, Moses" is about escaping slavery during life, whereas "Swing Low, Sweet Chariot" is about death's deliverance from hardship. The recurring refrain of "Let my people go" would have been more disturbing and worrisome to a slave owner than the references to Heaven and angels in "Swing Low, Sweet Chariot." Students may

also cite the mention of violence (smiting the first-born) in "Go Down, Moses" as part of the spiritual's undercurrent of rebellion.

22. (Average) *Guidelines for student response:* For "Swing Low, Sweet Chariot," students should indicate that the release from hardship is not expected until after death. "Swing Low, Sweet Chariot" does not, therefore, have a "rebellious" feel to it. Students may say that faith in God and Heaven are an important part of the mood of the spiritual. For "Go Down, Moses," students should recognize that the spiritual speaks of the possibility of freedom during life by its recounting the story of Moses and the enslaved Israelites' escape from slavery. The mood of "Go Down, Moses," therefore, has elements of rebellion, bravery, and determination.

23. (Challenging) *Guidelines for student response:* Students may cite the fact that Tubman was called the Moses of her people. The repeated refrain, "Go down, Moses" could refer to Tubman's repeated trips from the North back *down* to the South to guide more people to freedom. Students may also mention that Tubman's repeated risking of her own life during her journeys paralleled the risk Moses took in standing up to the Egyptian pharaoh.

from *My Bondage and My Freedom*
by Frederick Douglass

Selection Test (p. 125)

Critical Reading/Vocabulary and Grammar

1. d 2. b 3. d 4. c 5. a 6. d 7. b 8. d 9. c
10. a 11. c 12. b 13. d 14. c 15. b 16. c
17. b 18. a 19. b 20. c

Questions are classified in these categories:
   Comprehension 2(E), 3(A), 6(A)
   Interpretation 1(A), 4(A) 5(C), 9(C), 10(A)
   Literary Analysis 7(C), 12(A), 13(A)
   Reading Strategy 8(C), 11(A), 14(E)
   Vocabulary 15(E), 17(A), 19(E)
   Grammar Skill 16(C), 18(E), 20(C)
   E = Easy, A = Average, C = Challenging

Essay Questions

21. (Easy) *Guidelines for student response:* Students should provide details that show

that Mrs. Auld was a benevolent and congenial woman at the outset who, after having been persuaded not to teach Frederick to read or write, became angry and harsh in her behavior towards him whenever she suspected him of attempting to read. One example of her changed behavior is the incident of her rushing at him with fury to snatch away a book or newspaper.

22. (Average) *Guidelines for student response:* Students will probably argue in favor of this statement, since this is the position Douglass persuasively supports with incidents and examples throughout his account. Students may support their position with the example of the young white boys who, not yet trained as slaveholders, are naturally sympathetic to Douglass. Accept any answer that is well-supported with examples from the text.

23. (Challenging) *Guidelines for student response:* Some students will support this statement, noting that Mrs. Auld could not incorporate her husband's attitude without undergoing a complete transformation from benevolent to harsh, angry, and domineering. Others may explain her behavior as a twisted sort of benevolence, arguing that Mrs. Auld hoped to spare young Frederick the recognition of his horrid situation that learning might bring.

"An Occurrence at Owl Creek Bridge" by Ambrose Bierce

Selection Test (p. 128)

Critical Reading/Vocabulary and Grammar

1. a 2. a 3. c 4. b 5. c 6. c 7. b 8. c 9. d
10. d 11. b 12. b 13. a 14. c 15. d 16. b
17. b 18. b 19. c 20. a

Questions are classified in these categories:
   Comprehension 2(A), 8(C), 10(A), 12(C)
   Interpretation 4(C), 5(A), 6(E), 13(A)
   Literary Analysis 1(A), 7(A), 14(A)
   Reading Strategy 3(C), 9(E), 11(A)
   Vocabulary 15(C), 16(A), 18(E)
   Grammar Skill 17(A), 19(E), 20(A)
   E = Easy, A = Average, C = Challenging

"An Occurrence at Owl Creek Bridge"
by Ambrose Bierce
(continued)

Essay Questions

21. (Easy) *Guidelines for student response:* Students will probably feel that Bierce does *not* agree. His view of war is so grim that he clearly feels all things people do in war are neither fair nor justified.

22. (Average) *Guidelines for student response:* Students should realize that the meeting is critical to the story: the Union army would not have captured Farquhar had he not been entrapped by the Federal scout. Students can infer from its core of deception that the rest of the story contains a key deception: Farquhar thinks that he has escaped and returned home when he has actually been hanged.

23. (Challenging) *Guidelines for student response:* Some students may prefer a true sequence of events and an objective point of view, perhaps because continuity could help the reader follow the story better and make it more straightforward. Other students may prefer to keep the story as written, perhaps because the changing point of view and sequence of events help make the story interesting.

"The Gettysburg Address" and
"Second Inauguaral Address"
by Abraham Lincoln
"Letter to His Son" by Robert E. Lee

Selection Test (p. 131)

Critical Reading/Vocabulary and Grammar

1. c 2. b 3. a 4. b 5. c 6. a 7. b 8. d 9. a 10. d 11. d 12. b 13. a 14. b 15. d 16. c 17. d 18. a 19. c 20. c

Questions are classified in these categories:
Comprehension 1(A), 3(A), 6(A), 7(E)
Interpretation 2(E), 5(A), 10(A), 15(C)
Literary Analysis 4(C), 11(A), 12(E)
Reading Strategy 8(A), 9(E), 13(C), 14(C)
Vocabulary 16(E), 18(C), 20(A)
Grammar Skill 17(A), 19(E)
E = Easy, A = Average, C = Challenging

Essay Questions

21. (Easy) *Guidelines for student response:* Students should provide details to show that Lincoln and Lee both wished to preserve the Union at all costs. For example, they might include Lee's statement ". . . I can anticipate no greater calamity for the country than a dissolution of the Union" or Lincoln's attempt at Gettysburg to inspire new devotion to the Union.

22. (Average) *Guidelines for student response:* Most students will cite as Lincoln's purpose that he is trying to re-unite the North and South and "bind up the nation's wounds." Supporting details might include Lincoln's listing of the many commonalities between North and South, such as the experience of the war itself. The parallel structure Lincoln uses further emphasizes the link he has drawn between these common features.

23. (Challenging) *Guidelines for student response:* Lincoln will likely be described as a humble, idealistic, God-fearing man. Lee will likely be described as a passionate, emotional, and extremely loyal man. However, accept any characterization that is well-supported with details from the text.

Part Test, Unit 4, Part 1: A Nation Divided (p. 134)

Critical Reading/Vocabulary and Grammar

1. c 2. d 3. b 4. d 5. a 6. a 7. a 8. c 9. a 10. a 11. a 12. b 13. b 14. a 15. c 16. b 17. a 18. d 19. d 20. c

Questions are classified in these categories:
Comprehension 4(E)
Interpretation 2(A), 5(C), 10 (A)
Literary Analysis 3(A), 8(A), 9(A)
Reading Strategy 1(A), 6(A), 7(A)
Vocabulary 11(E), 12(A), 13(A), 14(E), 15(C)
Grammar 16(A), 17(E), 18(A), 19(E), 20(C)
E = Easy, A = Average, C = Challenging

Essay Questions

21. (Easy) *Guidelines for student response:* Students' essays should discuss how music helped enslaved African Americans create and preserve religious and cultural

traditions. Essays should note the use of coded lyrics enabled communication without arousing suspicion from slave owners. Examples from the spirituals should support students' essays.

22. (Average) *Guidelines for student response:* Students' essays should focus on Frederick Douglass's passion for learning and commitment to justice. Students should note his bravery and firm resolve in the face of racial prejudice, his dedication to self-improvement, and his staunch belief that all people should be free.

23. (Average) *Guidelines for student response:* Students' essays should note at least a few of the following differences: The lieutenant can explain exactly how being physically wounded felt; he can describe in detail his emotional state; he can explain why he did certain things, such as looking toward the woods so strangely; he can describe his thoughts at meeting the doctor. Rewritten passages should be in the first person, describing thoughts and feelings first-hand.

24. (Average) *Guidelines for student response:* Students' essays should note the formal and public occasion of Lincoln's address, acknowledge that the speech needed to be respectful of the dead, but also passionate in its insistence for a united country. Diction such as "under God" both confirmed listeners' commonly held religious beliefs and inspired them to greater devotion. Students should use supporting examples from the speech to document their ideas.

25. (Challenging) *Guidelines for student response:* Students' essays should recognize the scout's commitment to his cause of preserving the Union and ending slavery. This position should be supported with logical arguments about the evils of slavery and the need to end it at all costs along with reasonable inferences about the scout's character.

from Civil War Diaries, Journals, and Letters

Selection Test (p. 138)

Critical Reading/Vocabulary and Grammar

1. b 2. a 3. c 4. c 5. a 6. d 7. b 8. a 9. d
10. c 11. a 12. d 13. c 14. a 15. b 16. b
17. b 18. b 19. a 20. d

Questions are classified in these categories:
Comprehension 1(C), 3(E), 5(E), 9(E)
Interpretation 6(A), 11(A), 13(A), 14(C)
Literary Analysis 7(A), 8(C), 15(E)
Reading Strategy 2(A), 4(E), 10(A), 12(E)
Vocabulary 16(A), 17(A), 19(C)
Grammar Skill 18(E), 20(A)
E = Easy, A = Average, C = Challenging

Essay Questions

21. (Easy) *Guidelines for student response:* Mary Chesnut: The conflicts are between the Union and the Confederate at Fort Sumter and between Mary Chesnut's love of the Confederacy and her dislike of war; Warren Lee Goss: Goss is caught between his pre-war civilian life and his new role as an enlisted man; Randolph McKim: The conflict is the Battle of Gettysburg; Stonewall Jackson: The conflicts are the Battle of Bull Run and the underlying conflict between Jackson's pride in his troops and his modesty; Reverend Henry M. Turner: The conflict is between slavery and freedom; Sojourner Truth: The conflict is between Truth and those who seek to deprive her of her rights.

22. (Average) *Guidelines for student response:* Students' essays should indicate that Goss's writing is very personal and familiar, whereas McKim's account is factual and to the point. The explanation should be supported by appropriate details from the two works.

23. (Challenging) *Guidelines for student response:* Students' essays should accurately identify and describe the characters. Comparison and contrast would be structured around parallel features or characteristics and should be well supported with details from the selections.

"Gulf War Journal" from *A Woman at War* by Molly Moore

Selection Test (p. 141)

Critical Reading

1. a 2. a 3. d 4. b 5. a 6. b 7. b 8. d 9. a
10. c

Questions are classified in these categories:
Comprehension 2(A), 3(A), 4(E), 5(E), 8(E), 10(A)
Interpretation 1(C), 6(A), 7(C), 9(A)
E = Easy, A = Average, C = Challenging

Essay Questions

11. (Easy) *Guidelines for student response:* Students should be able to distinguish between objective and subjective reporting. Students might suggest that the personal approach makes the war seem more real to them, but the objective approach answers more basic questions concerning the big picture. Students should point out that the quotes Moore gathers from the pilots could easily fit into her news report about the first bombing raids.

12. (Average) *Guidelines for student response:* Students may assign to journalists the dual roles of supporter and watchdog for the government. As watchdogs, journalists should be entitled to information access but must use their judgment on when to report that data. For example, Molly Moore needs accurate information to do her job; however, broadcasting information about troop movements might endanger soldiers.

13. (Challenging) *Guidelines for student response:* Students may note that constant and instant exposure to images of war can desensitize ordinary Americans to war. The broadcast media's placement of violent news stories in the most prominent broadcast time slots emphasizes these stories, while the proliferation of "infotainment," news analysis, and journalism by politicians blurs the line between media and war participants. Students may suggest that the "news" has become like any other TV show, in which the lack of time to contemplate and digest information leaves the media consumer ultimately quite distanced from the information.

Part Test, Unit 4, Part 2: Focus on Literary Forms—Diaries, Journals, and Letters (p. 143)

Critical Reading/Vocabulary and Grammar

1. b 2. c 3. a 4. d 5. c 6. a 7. a 8. a 9. c
10. b 11. c 12. c 13. d 14. c 15. b

Questions are classified in these categories:
Comprehension 1(E), 4(A), 10(E)
Interpretation 2(A), 8(A), 9(A)
Literary Analysis 5(A), 7(E)
Reading Strategy 3(A), 6(E)
Vocabulary 11(E), 12(A), 13(E)
Grammar 14(C), 15(C)
E = Easy, A = Average, C = Challenging

Essay Questions

16. (Easy) *Guidelines for student response:* Essays should address Mary Chesnut's tone and substance in her account of the Fort Sumter battle. Students may conclude that one human response to tragedy is to hide from it behind superficial and frivolous distractions. For example, Mary's account is full of gossipy innuendo and reflects a playfulness that seems inappropriate to the surrounding events.

17. (Average) *Guidelines for student response:* Students' essays should note that both selections use simple and direct language, although the Goss piece is written more like a story, with humor and creativity as well. As both writers focus on their personal participation and neither views the surrounding events as tragic, their simple prose appropriately recounts the facts and events as these writers experienced them.

18. (Challenging) *Guidelines for student response:* Students' essays should focus on the similarities and differences between the attitudes of two writers. For example, students may choose to contrast Warren Lee Goss's light-hearted approach to the military with the far more serious attitude of Randolph McKim, who has experienced bloody defeat in battle.

"The Boys' Ambition" from *Life on the Mississippi* and "The Notorious Jumping Frog of Calaveras County" by Mark Twain

Selection Test (p. 146)

Critical Reading/Vocabulary and Grammar

1. c 2. b 3. b 4. a 5. d 6. c 7. d 8. d 9. c
10. b 11. a 12. d 13. a 14. c 15. a 16. b
17. b 18. d 19. a 20. c

Questions are classified in these categories:
Comprehension 1(E), 2(C), 9(E)
Interpretation 3(C), 5(A), 6(C), 11(A), 13(A), 14(C)
Literary Analysis 7(C), 8(A), 15(A)
Reading Strategy 4(A), 10(E), 12(A)
Vocabulary 16(A), 17(A), 19(A)
Grammar Skill 18(A), 20(C)
E = Easy, A = Average, C = Challenging

Essay Questions

21. (Easy) *Guidelines for student response:* Students should state that Simon Wheeler is the main character, as he tells the story from his unique point of view. Students should define the main character as the character around whom the story revolves or on whom it focuses. Though he is not the subject of his own narrative, he drives the action of the short story, and his interpretation and telling of the events give the story its distinctive humorous tone. Students should support their response with examples from the story, including how Wheeler's storytelling is humorous, and how the very premise of the story is derived from Wheeler's actions.

22. (Average) *Guidelines for student response:* Students should give examples of all three techniques. Examples of exaggeration include the desire to kill the apprentice engineer in "The Boys' Ambition" and Simon Wheelers's tale in "The Notorious Jumping Frog of Calaveras County." Examples of embellishment include the apprentice engineer's escape from the steamboat accident as well as several statements made by Simon Wheeler. Many examples of regional dialect can be found in the dialogue from either story.

23. (Challenging) *Guidelines for student response:* Students' essays should explain why the unknown has a much greater appeal than the familiar, and give one or more of these examples from "The Boys' Ambition": instances of the boys' dreaming of different careers as the "perfect" career; and the idea that life on the Mississippi River in a steamboat would be idyllic.

"The Outcasts of Poker Flat" by Bret Harte

Selection Test (p. 149)

Critical Reading/Vocabulary and Grammar

1. c 2. b 3. a 4. d 5. d 6. a 7. a 8. d 9. c
10. b 11. a 12. c 13. d 14. b 15. c 16. a
17. c 18. b 19. b 20. b

Questions are classified in these categories:
Comprehension 2(E), 10(A), 11(A)
Interpretation 4(C), 6(A), 7(A), 9(E), 10(A), 13(C)
Literary Analysis 1(E), 8(A), 15(A), 14(C)
Reading Strategy 3(A), 5(C), 12(A)
Vocabulary 16(E), 18(C), 19(A)
Grammar Skill 17(E), 20(E)
E = Easy, A = Average, C = Challenging

Essay Questions

21. (Easy) *Guidelines for student response:* Students should explain that Mr. Oakhurst was a gambler and that he loved poker. He saw being snowed in as a streak of bad luck that eventually led to a losing game. Therefore, it makes sense that he would use the lowest ranked card to represent himself, signifying that he knew he would lose this "hand" in the card game of life.

22. (Average) *Guidelines for student response:* Students' answers will vary, depending on the position they take. Either position can be correct, provided it is clearly articulated and supported with examples from the selection and details about the character of Mr. Oakhurst.

23. (Challenging) *Guidelines for student response:* Students' answers will vary, depending on the position they take. Students should be graded on their clarity and support of their positions. They should use details from the selection, including the leadership Mr. Oakhurst shows the party after they are left, as examples of strength, and his suicide as an example of weakness.

"Heading West"
by Miriam Davis Colt
"I Will Fight No More Forever"
by Chief Joseph

Selection Test (p. 152)

Critical Reading/Vocabulary and Grammar

1. b 2. a 3. a 4. c 5. b 6. c 7. a 8. d 9. b
10. d 11. c 12. a 13. c 14. d 15. b 16. c
17. c 18. d 19. c 20. a

Questions are classified in these categories:
Comprehension 2(A), 3(C), 9(C)
Interpretation 5(A), 10(A), 12(A), 14(E)
Literary Analysis 1(A), 4(C), 8(A), 11(E)
Reading Strategy 6(C), 7(A), 13(A), 15(E)
Vocabulary 17(A), 18(A), 19(E)
Grammar Skill 16(C), 20(E)
E = Easy, A = Average, C = Challenging

Essay Questions

21. (Easy) *Guidelines for student response:*
Students can describe how people may have
been impressed by the simple humanity of
the Chief's words, as well as the sufferings
of his people. Students should discuss how
people may have also been moved by pity
for the defeated; by the caring of a leader for
his family and people; by the realization
that these "enemies" were humans too; and
by guilt over the government's actions.

22. (Average) *Guidelines for student response:*
Students should include among the costs
to the Colts such things as selling their
farm; sending their money to the Vegetarian Company; separation from old friends
and relatives, some of whom they will
never see again; the labor of starting all
over again; and the lack of services and
amenities on the frontier. Dangers include
disease, accidents, depredations of others,
the loss of their investment, and the fear
of the unknown.

23. (Challenging) *Guidelines for student response:* Students should identify Chief
Joseph's decision to surrender as coming
from his realization that further fighting
cannot help his people. He risks appearing
less heroic in order to save what is left of
his people. The stark repetition of *dead*
conveys his feelings of loss, and the images
of his people freezing convey his sorrow.
His desire for time to look for his children

conveys his caring attitude. His weariness
with war grows from his love of his people.

"To Build a Fire" by Jack London

Selection Test (p. 155)

Critical Reading/Vocabulary and Grammar

1. c 2. c 3. a 4. c 5. d 6. a 7. b 8. a 9. b
10. b 11. b 12. a 13. c 14. c 15. c 16. b
17. d 18. a 19. d 20. c

Questions are classified in these categories:
Comprehension 2(A), 12(E)
Interpretation 4(C), 5(E), 8(C), 9(A), 11(A)
Literary Analysis 1(A), 3(A), 7(C), 10(A)
Reading Strategy 6(A), 13(A), 14(E)
Vocabulary 15(A), 18(C), 20(E)
Grammar Skill 16(A), 17(C), 19(C)
E = Easy, A = Average, C = Challenging

Essay Questions

21. (Easy) *Guidelines for student response:*
Students should describe their challenge
in as much detail as possible. They should
also mention the experience of the man,
showing why respect for the power of what
they are challenging is also important.
They might mention learning about their
challenge, welcoming advice from people
who have experienced similar challenges,
being careful and observant, and working
at keeping—and using—their heads.

22. (Average) *Guidelines for student response:*
Students should mention that the man
has no more respect for the cold than he
does for the dog; he feels he can subdue
them both simply by asserting his human
power. His attitude toward taking extra
precautions is that doing so would be a
sign of weakness; he does not confront nature with the imagination or intelligence
that successful humans muster in place of
instinct. The dog, of course, follows instincts, which are more reliable than the
thoughts of the man. The dog has no "ego";
he uses experience as a guide.

23. (Challenging) *Guidelines for student response:* Students who were uncertain for
most of the story may mention details such
as the man's generally cheerful state of
mind, his powers of keen observation, his
ability to make a fire at lunch time, etc. In
opposition to these, they should mention

the man's ignorance of the nature of the cold, his lack of imagination, his increasingly dangerous and stupid errors, and the instincts of the dog. Students who knew the outcome early in their reading should cite what provided clues. They should also mention if they knew how the end would come, and which clues helped.

from *Lonesome Dove*
by Larry McMurtry

Selection Test (p. 158)

Critical Reading

1. a 2. b 3. b 4. c 5. d 6. c 7. d 8. a 9. a 10. d

Questions are classified in these categories:
Comprehension 2(E), 4(A), 5(E), 8(A), 10(A)
Interpretation 1(A), 3(C), 7(C), 9(C)
Vocabulary 6(E)
E = Easy, A = Average, C = Challenging

Essay Questions

11. (Easy) *Guidelines for student response:* Students should contrast Gus's love of conversation, sense of drama, and personal satisfaction with Call's reserved nature, restlessness, and personal unease. Students might suggest that opposites attract, that they complement each other well, and that both types are needed to carry out the cattle drive. In fact, they must work together to complete it.

12. (Average) *Guidelines for student response:* Students should suggest that the cattle drive is a device for revealing character. The drive itself is a metaphor for the personal challenges each cowboy, but especially Call, must face in achieving happiness and a sense of self worth. Students should see the cattle drive as a means of testing the bonds of friendship and character.

13. (Challenging) *Guidelines for student response:* Students should describe the hard life of the "real" cowboy, citing the dust, thick brush, conflict with Native Americans, etc. Students should compare that with other cultural images, from John Wayne to the Lone Ranger. Students might cite other references in which cowboys are portrayed realistically. Students might suggest that the cowboy myth has been

good for America, fueling Americans' love for an active and independent lifestyle.

Part Test, Unit 4, Part 3: Forging New Frontiers (p. 160)

Critical Reading/Vocabulary and Grammar

1. b 2. a 3. c 4. b 5. a 6. c 7. d 8. d 9. c 10. c 11. a 12. d 13. c 14. b 15. c 16. a 17. c 18. d 19. a 20. b

Questions are classified in these categories:
Comprehension 10 (C)
Interpretation 5(A), 8(A), 9(A)
Literary Analysis 3(E), 4(A), 7(E)
Reading Strategy 1(E), 2(A), 6(C)
Vocabulary 11(A), 12(A), 13(E), 14(A)
Grammar 15(C), 16(C), 17(A), 18(C), 19(E), 20(A)
E = Easy, A = Average, C = Challenging

Essay Questions

21. (Easy) *Guidelines for student response:* Students' essays should discuss the phenomenon of the American cowboy as developed in literature. The essay should use at least one example from the selections. Possible examples include Bret Harte's character Oakhurst as the typical western gambler, tough but with a soft heart, out to make money off of others but generous in troubled times. The cowboy of "The Streets of Laredo" is an example of what can happen to a cowboy who goes astray. Students may also cite the characters of Pecos Bill and Gregorio Cortez. Accept any well-reasoned, well-supported portrayal.

22. (Average) *Guidelines for student response:* Advantages of reading a first-hand account can include learning exactly what happened, learning precise details of an event, and having access to the thoughts and feelings of the participants. Disadvantages can include a lack of perspective, the characterization of events due to point of view or personal feelings, and a focus on details rather than the big picture. Students should support their assertions with evidence from the text.

23. (Average) *Guidelines for student response:* Students may cite works such as "The Boys' Ambition" or "The Celebrated Jumping Frog of Calaveras County" by Mark Twain and "The Outcasts of Poker Flat" by Bret Harte. Students should explain how

the work captures the flavor of the given region through its portrayal of characters and their environment.

24. (Average) *Guidelines for student response:* Students' should document how each characteristic of a tragedy can be found in Jack London's "To Build a Fire." They should discuss the man's tragic flaw of overconfidence, which contributes to his inevitable fate of death at the hands of nature, the force he cannot control. They should show how his behavior near the end of the story supports his portrayal as a tragic figure.

25. (Average) *Guidelines for student response:* Students' essays will be organized around the two characteristics from Henry James's work: detail and reality. "The Notorious Jumping Frog of Calaveras County," "To Build a Fire," and "The Outcasts of Poker Flat" all contain examples of both. Students should show an example of each and then state how each example builds a better story.

"The Story of an Hour"
by Kate Chopin

Selection Test (p. 164)

Critical Reading/Vocabulary and Grammar

1. a 2. c 3. b 4. c 5. d 6. b 7. c 8. b 9. d
10. a 11. d 12. a 13. a 14. c 15. c 16. d
17. b 18. c 19. a 20. d

Questions are classified in these categories:
  Comprehension 4(E), 6(A), 13(A)
  Interpretation 1(E), 5(C), 7(A), 9(A), 10(C)
  Literary Analysis 8(E), 12(E), 14(C), 15(C)
  Reading Strategy 2(A), 3(A), 11(C)
  Vocabulary 17(A), 18(E), 20(A)
  Grammar Skill 16(A), 19(A)
  E = Easy, A = Average, C = Challenging

Essay Questions

21. (Easy) *Guidelines for student response:* Students who admire Mrs. Mallard should mention that she felt trapped in her marriage, that in accepting her feelings she is throwing off hypocrisy, and that her desire to face the world alone reflects

strength of character. Those who condemn her should stress that her joy is selfish, that her thoughts about weeping as she sees her husband's body seem hypocritical, that her freedom has come from the death of another human being, one she supposedly loved.

22. (Average) *Guidelines for student response:* Students should back their conclusions using details from the story and their own knowledge of prevailing Victorian attitudes. Whether they argue that Josephine would support her sister or think her wicked, they should realize that Josephine would be deeply shocked at first. Students should conclude that Richards would probably be totally uncomprehending of and scandalized by Mrs. Mallard's feelings and cite one or more of the following reasons: He is a close friend of the husband; he has the Victorian attitude that women need men to shelter them from the shocks of life; and he may believe that women don't want freedom from marriage.

23. (Challenging) *Guidelines for student response:* Students who agree that Mrs. Mallard is a victim should mention the irony that her only escape from the strictures of Victorian marriage is the death of her husband. Freedom for a married woman is simply not a choice. Those who disagree may mention that the reason she feels joy so soon after her husband's presumed death is that she did not let herself be completely victimized by marriage. In her heart, she did not buy into the prevailing attitudes. As a widow, she will probably be stronger and live a more enjoyable life than others in her position, who are true victims.

"April Showers" by Edith Wharton

Selection Test (p. 167)

Critical Reading/Vocabulary and Grammar

1. a 2. b 3. d 4. b 5. c 6. a 7. b 8. c 9. a
10. c 11. a 12. b 13. d 14. c 15. b 16. c
17. c 18. b 19. a 20. a

Questions are classified in these categories:
  Comprehension 4(A), 9(A), 11(E)

Interpretation 2(C), 3(C), 6(C), 10(E), 13(E)
Literary Analysis 1(A), 5(A), 8(C), 12(C)
Reading Strategy 7(A), 14(E)
Vocabulary 17(E), 18(A), 20(A)
Grammar 15(A), 16(A), 19(A)
E = Easy, A = Average, C = Challenging

Essay Questions

21. (Easy) *Guidelines for student response:* Students should apply the saying to the story, citing evidence for their explanation. For example, they may say that the pain of the rejection that so dampens her spirits helps Theodora to grow out of her youthful pride and selfishness. Students might also say that her pain leads to a new understanding of her father and closeness with him.

22. (Average) *Guidelines for student response:* Students should define the elements correctly and select the story events that correspond to each one. They will probably say that the exposition consists of Theodora's finishing and submitting her novel. The conflict is whether the novel will be accepted. The rising action consists of Theodora's problems with her family as she waits, the novel's acceptance (perhaps a false climax), and her continuing anticipation of its publication. The climax is the discovery that her novel has not been published. The resolution comes with the magazine's explanation of its error. The denouement is the meeting of Theodora and her father at the station and the comforting walk home.

23. (Challenging) *Guidelines for student response:* Students should use examples from the story to support the idea that Theodora's pride is harmful. For example, they might say that it has blinded her to any faults in her own writing, which makes any improvement of it impossible. They might also cite her haughty attitude toward her potential audience. They might also mention that letting everyone in town know about her novel makes the final rejection even more bitter. Theodora's pride has also led her to neglect family duties, such as sewing buttons on her brother's coat.

"Douglass" and "We Wear the Mask"
by Paul Laurence Dunbar

Selection Test (p. 170)

Critical Reading/Vocabulary and Grammar

1. b 2. b 3. c 4. d 5. d 6. d 7. b 8. c 9. c
10. d 11. c 12. b 13. a 14. a 15. a 16. a
17. c 18. d 19. b 20. c

Questions are classified in these categories:
  Comprehension 1(A), 3(E), 9(E)
  Interpretation 5(E), 6(A), 11(A), 13(A), 14(C)
  Literary Analysis 7(E), 8(A), 15(A)
  Reading Strategy 2(A), 4(C), 10(C), 12(C)
  Vocabulary 16(C), 17(A), 19(A)
  Grammar Skill 18(A), 20(A)
  E = Easy, A = Average, C = Challenging

Essay Questions

21. (Easy) *Guidelines for student response:* Students should indicate that the poem expresses the needs of African Americans who are pretending to be happy with their position instead of showing their true feelings. Students should use details from the poem to support their position, including how they wear masks that "hide" their eyes and cheeks and present a smile instead, and how the world does not see the tears and sighs of the people.

22. (Average) *Guidelines for student response:* Students' answers will vary but should indicate that Dunbar was keenly aware that despite emancipation and victory in the Civil War, the struggles of the African American community went on and, in some ways, got worse. Details from the selections that support this include his plea to Douglass for his leadership, his statement in "Douglass" that the community is still awash in a tempest, and that they have to hide their true feelings in "We Wear the Mask."

23. (Challenging) *Guidelines for student response:* Students' answers will depend on the position they choose, but they should defend their positions with citations from one or both of the selections and any other knowledge they have of Dunbar's life and other works. Most students will probably feel the poem is about concealed racial fire, although the poem may be applied more universally to any group of people

"Douglass" and "We Wear the Mask"
by Paul Laurence Dunbar
(continued)

who face discrimination. Supporting examples include the bitter tone of "We Wear the Mask," the use of the word *guile* and the statement that African Americans are in "debt," and the line "but let the world dream otherwise," which suggests the foolishness of the outside world.

"Luke Havergal" and "Richard Cory"
by Edwin Arlington Robinson
"Lucinda Matlock" and "Richard Bone" by Edgar Lee Masters

Selection Test (p. 173)

Critical Reading/Vocabulary and Grammar

1. b 2. d 3. a 4. c 5. b 6. a 7. d 8. a 9. c
10. c 11. a 12. b 13. d 14. b 15. a 16. b
17. d 18. a 19. b 20. d

Questions are classified in these categories:
  Comprehension 1(A), 3(A), 9(A), 10(A)
  Interpretation 2(A), 6(E), 7(C), 11(A)
  Literary Analysis 4(E), 5(E)
  Reading Strategy 8(A), 12(A), 13(C), 14(C)
  Vocabulary 16(A), 17(E), 19(C)
  Grammar Skill 15(C), 18(A), 20(C)
  E = Easy, A = Average, C = Challenging

Essay Questions

21. (Easy) *Guidelines for student response:* Students should choose one of the four title characters and write a biographical essay on him or her. They can imagine details not mentioned in the poem, but they should support their imaginings with details from the poem. They should also draw biographical information from the tone of the poem; for example, from the tone of the portrait painted of him in the poem, Luke Havergal can be said to lead a sad and mournful life.

22. (Average) *Guidelines for student response:* Students should recognize that Lucinda Matlock's tone is not bitter or angry, but in fact lovingly chiding of the younger generation. Students can support this statement with such details from the poem as her gentle tone, her life-loving attitude despite terrible tragedy, and her open and friendly demeanor, as portrayed by Masters.

23. (Challenging) *Guidelines for student response:* As it is unclear exactly what the speaker wants Luke Havergal to do, many interpretations are possible, provided they are supported by the text. The speaker tells Luke to go to the western gate, which might be a real gate, or a symbolic one. The speaker may want Luke to accept the death of the woman and the sadness that goes with it, or the speaker may be suggesting that Luke will have to die in order to be with the woman. The speaker seems to want Luke to take action without expecting that any happiness will come from it.

"A Wagner Matinée" by Willa Cather

Selection Test (p. 176)

Critical Reading/Vocabulary and Grammar

1. b 2. a 3. a 4. d 5. d 6. d 7. b 8. c 9. c
10. c 11. d 12. d 13. a 14. a 15. b 16. d
17. b 18. a 19. b 20. c

Questions are classified in these categories:
  Comprehension 2(E), 9(A), 11(A)
  Interpretation 4(E), 6(A), 7(A), 13(E), 14(C)
  Literary Analysis 1(A), 10(C), 15(C)
  Reading Strategy 3(A), 5(A), 8(C), 12(E)
  Vocabulary 16(A), 17(E), 19(C)
  Grammar Skill 18(A), 20(A)
  E = Easy, A = Average, C = Challenging

Essay Questions

21. (Easy) *Guidelines for student response:* Students should give some or all of the following examples of Aunt Georgiana's retaining her love of music: helping young Clark learn music, worrying that Clark may also have to sacrifice music, keeping some music books, enjoying the music of the young cow puncher, and all of her reactions during the Wagner concert.

22. (Average) *Guidelines for student response:* Students should recognize that Aunt Georgiana's reluctance to leave the concert is really a desire to cling to a time and place in her life when she was once happy: when she lived in the cultured city of Boston and taught at the Conservatory. Now that she has been reawakened to the beauty of the life and music she gave up so long ago, she is desperate not to return to her hard, bleak life in Nebraska.

23. (Challenging) *Guidelines for student response:* Students should describe Clark on the basis of the selection. They may at first feel he is shallow because he seems to be ashamed of his aunt, but they should also recognize his sensitivity; he loves his aunt and appreciates the tremendous sacrifices she has made. Students may observe that Clark callowly takes for granted that which his aunt misses so dearly and seems to want to prove his cultural superiority, but they should also realize that he comes to understand and regret the depth of the pain awakened in his aunt.

"Cats" by Anna Quindlen

Selection Test (p. 179)

Critical Reading
1. c 2. c 3. b 4. d 5. c 6. c 7. d 8. b 9. c
10. a

Questions are classified in these categories:
Comprehension 2(A), 5(A), 7(A), 8(A), 9(E)
Interpretation 1(C), 3(A), 4(E), 6(C), 10(C)
E = Easy, A = Average, C = Challenging

Essay Questions
11. (Easy) *Guidelines for student response:* Students should recognize the details in the text that are "universal" in scope, as well as the conversational tone Quindlen uses. Students should suggest that such general situations are held in common by a majority of people. Students should elaborate on their personal reactions to Quindlen's essay.

12. (Average) *Guidelines for student response:* Students should suggest that one lesson Quindlen could have learned is to always remain close to her son. The son may someday recognize the hurt a mother feels when abandoned by her family. Students should relate a personal episode describing their feelings of loss and how they overcame them.

13. (Challenging) *Guidelines for student response:* Students should recognize that while individualism can have virtues, such an ethic often keeps people from reaching out to each other in the mistaken belief that they should be able to cope by themselves. Students should rec-

ognize that our media-driven society can create alienation by forging false bonds between celebrities and real people; they should also recognize that technology can foster new community ties, such as over the Internet.

Part Test, Unit 4, Part 4: Living in a Changing World (p. 181)

Critical Reading/Vocabulary and Grammar
1. c 2. d 3. a 4. a 5. b 6. c 7. c 8. a 9. d
10. d 11. b 12. b 13. a 14. c 15. a 16. a
17. b 18. c 19. c 20. b

Questions are classified in these categories:
Comprehension 6(E), 7(E)
Interpretation 2(A), 4(A), 8(A)
Literary Analysis 1(E), 3(A), 5(C), 9(A)
Reading Strategy 10(A)
Vocabulary 11(A), 12(E), 13(A), 14(A)
Grammar 15(A), 16(A), 17(A), 18(E), 19(C), 20(E)
E = Easy, A = Average, C = Challenging

Essay Questions
21. (Easy) *Guidelines for student response:* Students should recognize that Aunt Georgiana would not be so deprived today by contrasting the limitations, as seen in the story, with what is available in many communities. Advances in transportation, communication, and technology have all helped reduce people's isolation. Television, radio, the Internet, and the growth of arts groups across the country can make theater, music, and art available virtually anywhere.

22. (Average) *Guidelines for student response:* Students should choose either Mrs. Mallard, Lucinda Matlock, or Aunt Georgiana for discussion. Students should compare the opportunities available to the character using evidence from the selections, and compare them to opportunities that would be available now. For example, Mrs. Mallard might not feel so trapped in her marriage if she were not living under Victorian constraints, Lucinda Matlock's life would have been less painful had her children been exposed to modern medicine, and Aunt Georgina could have taken advantage of improvements in technology, transporta-

tion, and education to overcome the isolation of the prairie.

23. (Average) *Guidelines for student response:* Students should choose one poem or story for examination and tell what surprised them about the text. Examples could include Richard Cory's suicide, Lucinda Matlock's upbeat tone despite tragedy and her chastising of younger people, or the irony of Mrs. Mallard's death on the heels of her great happiness in "The Story of an Hour." Students should recognize that in each case, the character's true nature is revealed as the selection proceeds. Students should give their opinions of why the writer chose to incorporate the unexpected and support their opinions with citations from the text.

24. (Challenging) *Guidelines for student response:* Students should choose one character that shows courage. Examples include Aunt Georgina going to the prairie, Frederick Douglass leading the African Americans, Dunbar's speaker in "We Wear the Mask," Lucinda Matlock and the tragedy she encounters in her life, or Mrs. Mallard preparing to ignore the custom of her time and lead a life of her own. Students should explain what circumstances force the chosen character to act courageously, how he or she shows courage, and what the character teaches them about the nature of courage.

25. (Challenging) *Guidelines for student response:* Students' essays will address the theme of isolation as the characters experienced it in post–Civil War America. Examples include the Mrs. Mallard's isolation from her true self, Aunt Geogiana's isolation in Nebraska while removed from the world of culture, the isolation of Richard Cory and Luke Havergal, and the sense of being on the fringes of society expressed by the speaker of Dunbar's poem "We Wear the Mask."

Unit 5: Disillusion, Defiance, and Discontent (1914–1946)

"The Love Song of J. Alfred Prufrock" by T. S. Eliot

Selection Test (p. 185)

Critical Reading/Vocabulary and Grammar

1. c 2. a 3. d 4. b 5. b 6. d 7. a 8. a 9. b
10. c 11. d 12. c 13. c 14. d 15. a 16. d
17. b 18. c 19. b 20. d

Questions are classified in these categories:
  Comprehension 2(E), 4(C), 5(A)
  Interpretation 3(A), 11(A), 12(A), 13(A)
  Literary Analysis 1(E), 6(E), 10(E)
  Reading Strategy 7(A), 8(C), 9(A), 14(C)
  Vocabulary 15(E), 16(E), 17(E)
  Grammar 18(A), 19(A), 20(A)
  E = Easy, A = Average, C = Challenging

Essay Questions

21. (Easy) *Guidelines for student response:* Students should present their interpretations of Prufrock supported by specific details from the poems. For example, they may say that Prufrock feels his life is meaningless when he claims to "have measured out [his] in coffee spoons." They could see self-doubt in his realization that he is not Hamlet but only a minor character. They could find despair at his approaching death in the image of the eternal Footman. Students might suggest that Eliot meant Prufrock to exemplify a typical man living in an era of uncertainty and anxiety caused by rapid social, political, and technological change.

22. (Average) *Guidelines for student response:* Students should explain how a dramatic monologue is the perfect vehicle for self-analysis and how the poetic images reveal Prufrock's personality and his response to his social environment. For example, students might mention that a monologue enables Prufrock not only to describe and comment on his external experiences but also to divulge his disconnected, half-formed but revealing thoughts and feelings. Students may mention how the poetic images both describe things and reveal Prufrock's emotional state. Evening,

for example, spread "[l]ike a patient ether-ized upon a table" alerts the reader to Prufrock's depression. Students will prob-ably point out that a short story would normally rely less on images to convey a portrait of the character.

23. (Challenging) *Guidelines for student re-sponse:* Students should interpret the meaning and significance of the title using examples from the poem to support their ideas. They might, for example, point out the irony in the words "love song" and describe how Eliot undermines the conventions of a love poem to present a portrait of lovelessness. They might also state that the poem is a song only in the sense that it is a poem. In form, it is a dramatic monologue, nothing like a conventional song.

Imagist Poets

Selection Test (p. 188)

Critical Reading/Vocabulary and Grammar
1. c 2. c 3. b 4. c 5. a 6. d 7. b 8. c 9. a
10. b 11. d 12. b 13. d 14. b 15. c 16. c
17. a 18. d 19. a 20. d

Questions are classified in these categories:
Comprehension 1(A), 2(E), 15(C)
Interpretation 3(A), 5(A), 10(C), 12(C), 13(A), 16(A)
Literary Analysis 6(A), 7(A), 8(C), 9(C)
Reading Strategy 4(A), 11(E), 14(E)
Vocabulary 17(E), 18(E)
Grammar 19(A), 20(A)
E = Easy, A = Average, C = Challenging

Essay Questions
21. (Easy) *Guidelines for student response:* Students may take either position as long as they illustrate it with examples from the poems. Students who agree that the state-ment is a simplistic way of looking at life, for example, may not feel that a red wheelbarrow and two white chickens re-flect enough of life to move the reader. Those who feel that the statement has some value may argue that such images allow the reader to consider personal meanings or implications, rather than having them imposed by the poet.

22. (Average) *Guidelines for student response:* Students may either agree or disagree with Williams's statement but should sup-port their ideas with examples from the three poems. Those who agree, for exam-ple, may state that in a poem like "The Great Figure," the fleeting impression of the fire truck with its gold figure 5 is true to life, but nothing more. It represents nothing, and so it is trivial. They may point out that such poetry might have been difficult for people used to complex subjects and elevated language to accept. Those who disagree may state that the Imagists really didn't make such a huge divergence but merely took poetry back to its roots, when poets and readers were connected by, and found significance in, moments such as a red wheelbarrow and two chickens.

23. (Challenging) *Guidelines for student re-sponse:* Students should develop Pound's vision imaginatively and display an under-standing of the image in the poem. For example, they may suggest that Pound's use of the word "apparition" means that the sight of the faces was unexpected, perhaps as the train pulled rapidly into the station. The beauty of the faces is ex-pressed in the choice of the word "petals." The "wet, black bough" may mean that Pound's original poem described a rainy day with people in dark raincoats carrying umbrellas.

"Winter Dreams" by F. Scott Fitzgerald

Selection Test (p. 191)

Critical Reading/Vocabulary and Grammar
1. a 2. b 3. c 4. c 5. b 6. d 7. d 8. d 9. a
10. b 11. a 12. c 13. a 14. c 15. d 16. c
17. a 18. d 19. c 20. a

Questions are classified in these categories:
Comprehension 2(A), 9(A), 11(E)
Interpretation 4(C), 6(E), 7(E), 13(C), 14(A)
Literary Analysis 1(C), 8(C), 10(A), 15(C)
Reading Strategy 3(A), 5(E), 12(A)
Vocabulary 16(A), 17(E), 18(A)
Grammar 19(E), 20(A)
E = Easy, A = Average, C = Challenging

"Winter Dreams" by F. Scott Fitzgerald
(continued)

Essay Questions

21. (Easy) *Guidelines for student response:* Students' essays should identify traits, supported with examples from the story, that are contradictory in nature. For example, Dexter Green shows contradictory traits in the way he carefully and meticulously plans his professional life compared with the impetuous and often destructive decisions he makes about Judy Jones.

22. (Average) *Guidelines for student response:* Students should cite the attributes of Judy Jones and Dexter Green that relate to the biographer's statement. Students will probably state that the "superlative" qualities that Judy Jones possesses are both exquisite beauty and a high social position, as well as a number of suitors. Dexter Green could be called a "buccaneer" because he is dashing and intelligent, and he is considered a "good catch" by many unmarried women and their families.

23. (Challenging) *Guidelines for student response:* Students should identify two characters and focus on how they embody Fitzgerald's fascination with and distrust of wealthy society. For example, they might identify Dexter Green as a character who is fascinated by wealthy society. Early in the story he excels at golf, a sport of the wealthy. Later he becomes infatuated with Judy Jones, who seems to embody the beauty and flair but also the callousness and coldness of wealthy society.

"The Turtle" from *The Grapes of Wrath* by John Steinbeck

Selection Test (p. 194)

Critical Reading/Vocabulary and Grammar

1. a 2. b 3. d 4. a 5. d 6. a 7. c 8. d 9. b 10. a 11. b 12. a 13. c 14. b 15. c 16. a 17. b 18. c 19. b 20. d

Questions are classified in these categories:
Comprehension 1(E), 3(A),
Interpretation 2(A), 9(E), 10(A), 11(A), 12(C)
Literary Analysis 4(C), 6(A), 7(A), 8(C)
Reading Strategy 5(A), 13(E), 14(E)
Vocabulary 17(A), 18(E), 20(C)

Grammar 15(A), 16(E), 19(C)
E = Easy, A = Average, C = Challenging

Essay Questions

21. (Easy) *Guidelines for student response:* Students should use examples from the story to show how Steinbeck humanizes the turtle. For example, Steinbeck refers to the turtle as "he" or "him" throughout, calls his front feet "hands," and speaks of his "fierce, humorous eyes." Students might also mention that focusing closely on the turtle's journey across the road makes it seem larger than life and heroic, as when the turtle hoists himself over the parapet. Students will probably agree that humanizing the turtle makes the reader care about him and identify with his struggles.

22. (Average) *Guidelines for student response:* Students may take either position as long as they support it with details from the story. Those who agree with the statement will characterize many events of the turtle's life as hardships or sufferings. They could cite such examples as scaling the embankment, having the red ant run into his shell, and being hit by the truck. Students who disagree might argue that because the turtle is an animal, the term "hardships" doesn't really apply. The turtle is just following instincts to survive in trying to make his way across the road.

23. (Challenging) *Guidelines for student response:* Students can either agree or disagree with the statement but should support their position with details from the story. Those who agree might conclude that the seeds are more important to the theme of reproduction than the turtle, who is just one of many vehicles for seeds. They might cite the first paragraph, in which the focus is on seeds and the turtle has not yet appeared, and the last few sentences, in which the "planting" of the seeds is described. Those who disagree could mention the detailed emphasis on the turtle throughout the body of the story, which leads the reader to forget the earlier focus. They may argue that without the turtle, the seeds it carries would not survive.

"anyone lived in a pretty how town" and "old age sticks" by E. E. Cummings
"The Unknown Citizen" by W. H. Auden

Selection Test (p. 197)

Critical Reading/Vocabulary and Grammar

1. d 2. a 3. b 4. c 5. c 6. b 7. c 8. c 9. b
10. c 11. b 12. c 13. d 14. c 15. b 16. d
17. a 18. a 19. b 20. a

Questions are classified in these categories:
Comprehension 8(E), 13(E), 15(A)
Interpretation 3(A), 4(A), 7(A), 10(C), 11(E), 12(A)
Literary Analysis 5(C), 9(A), 16(C)
Reading Strategy 1(A), 2(A), 6(C), 14(C)
Vocabulary 17(A), 18(A)
Grammar 19(E), 20(A)
E = Easy, A = Average, C = Challenging

Essay Questions

21. (Easy) *Guidelines for student response:* In their responses, students should interpret how the citizen might feel about being treated as a statistic. They should also suggest how he might want to be treated instead. For example, they might say he would be upset to be considered a statistic. He might wish that the government had been more actively concerned with his happiness and freedom, rather than with his conformity.

22. (Average) *Guidelines for student response:* Students should support their speculations with evidence from "The Unknown Citizen." For example, Auden dislikes a society that puts a high premium on conforming. He appears suspicious of the materialistic focus of modern life, by which people are encouraged to react to advertisements by buying things they can't really afford (the Installment Plan).

23. (Challenging) *Guidelines for student response:* Students should choose appropriate elements to support the statement. For example, the poem mixes subject matter about human rituals such as marriage and burials with repeated lines about natural cycles—"spring summer autumn winter" and "sun moon stars rain." Students might also argue that Cummings writes about faceless people (someones and everyones), instead of individual characters, to convey a sense of the universal.

"The Far and the Near" by Thomas Wolfe

Selection Test (p. 200)

Critical Reading/Vocabulary and Grammar

1. c 2. c 3. b 4. d 5. c 6. c 7. b 8. c 9. d
10. c 11. b 12. d 13. d 14. a 15. c 16. d
17. a 18. a 19. a 20. c

Questions are classified in these categories:
Comprehension 1(E), 3(A), 13(C)
Interpretation 2(C), 10(A), 12(A), 14(C), 15(A)
Literary Analysis 4(A), 8(E), 9(A), 11(C)
Reading Strategy 5(E), 6(C), 7(E)
Vocabulary 16(E), 18(A), 19(A)
Grammar 17(A), 20(A)
E = Easy, A = Average, C = Challenging

Essay Questions

21. (Easy) *Guidelines for student response:* Students should use details from the story to support their interpretation of the engineer's feelings. For example, students might say that the women always make time during their day for this one gesture. This otherwise insignificant gesture makes the engineer feel hopeful and believe that there is always some good in the world.

22. (Average) *Guidelines for student response:* In their responses, students should clearly demonstrate why the story's ending is anticlimactic. They should use details from the story to support their assertions. For example, when the engineer visits the women, he discovers that there is no particular reason why they wave—their wave is not really the brave, free gesture that he imagined it to be.

23. (Challenging) *Guidelines for student response:* Students should interpret the engineer's state of mind at the end of the story by explaining why he feels confusion, doubt, and hopelessness and what has changed. For example, students might say that the engineer feels the way he does because his perspective has completely changed. As a person with an important job, he had confidence that led him to shape what he saw from the majestic distance of his train into idealized, magical visions. Up close, from a more

"The Far and the Near" by Thomas Wolfe
(continued)

realistic perspective, the people and things he embellished in his visions are ordinary and even unpleasant.

"Of Modern Poetry" and **"Anecdote of the Jar"** by Wallace Stevens
"Ars Poetica" by Archibald MacLeish
"Poetry" by Marianne Moore

Selection Test (p. 203)

Critical Reading/Vocabulary and Grammar

1. b 2. d 3. d 4. c 5. c 6. b 7. b 8. b 9. d
10. c 11. a 12. b 13. a 14. a 15. a 16. d
17. a 18. c 19. d 20. c

Questions are classified in these categories:
   Comprehension 9(A)
   Interpretation 1(A), 2(C), 3(C), 5(C), 11(E),
      14(A)
   Literary Analysis 4(A), 7(E), 8(E), 10(C)
   Reading Strategy 6(C), 12(A), 13(A)
   Vocabulary 16(E), 18(A), 19(A)
   Grammar 15(A), 17(A), 20(A)
   E = Easy, A = Average, C = Challenging

Essay Questions

21. (Easy) *Guidelines for student response:*
   Students may choose any of the other three poems in the selection and identify lines or images that are memorable to them. For example, they might choose MacLeish's "A poem should not mean/But be" because it is such a strong and simple definition of a poem. Or students might consider the opening lines of Moore's "Poetry" significant because the poet admits to sharing readers' negative feelings about poetry. Students will probably feel that the "imaginary gardens" image is effective because it gives a vivid impression of fantasy mixed with reality, which captures what poetry is all about.

22. (Average) *Guidelines for student response:*
   Students may take either position as long as it is supported by details from the two poems. Those who feel that examples are most effective might suggest that if a poem cannot be explained, it can only be likened to something else, like a "globed fruit" or "the flight of birds." They may point out that Stevens also uses examples in liken-

ing a poem to "an insatiable actor." Students who prefer Stevens's approach may argue, for example, that his description of what a poem does or must do, such as "learn the speech of the place," makes it easier to grasp his idea of poetry.

23. (Challenging) *Guidelines for student response:* Students may take either position as long as it is supported by examples from "Anecdote of the Jar." Some students may think the poem is realistic because it is filled with realistic, concrete images. Other students may think the poem is unrealistic because the concrete image of the jar symbolizes the much broader abstraction of human civilization and because the concrete image of the Tennessee wilderness stands for the natural world in general.

Part Test, Unit 5, Part 1: The Emerging American Identity— Facing Troubled Times (p. 206)

Critical Reading/Vocabulary and Grammar

1. c 2. c 3. a 4. d 5. b 6. d 7. b 8. a 9. d
10. b 11. c 12. a 13. c 14. b 15. b 16. c
17. b 18. a 19. b 20. c

Questions are classified in these categories:
   Comprehension 1(E), 2(E), 4(A)
   Interpretation 5(A), 7(C)
   Literary Analysis 6(C), 10(A)
   Reading Strategy 3(E), 8(A), 9(A)
   Vocabulary 11(E), 12(A), 13(E), 14(C)
   Grammar 15(A), 16(A), 17(E), 18(A), 19(C),
      20(A)
   E = Easy, A = Average, C = Challenging

Essay Questions

21. (Easy) *Guidelines for student response:*
   The students' essays will focus on characterization in the works in this part. The characters should be compared on the basis of their important physical characteristics, their personalities, and the way in which they solve the problems or react to the circumstances in which they find themselves. A superior essay will focus on what is essential to each character and to the situation of each, and will show the connection between the character's personality and background on the one hand, and his or her response to the situation on the other.

22. (Average) *Guidelines for student response:* The students' essays should first define the "dream" in the work (for example: love and social class in "Winter Dreams," meaningful existence in "Prufrock," or community in "The Far and the Near"). They should then explain what truth or what force challenges that dream (social class undermines love, but love gives the lie to class in "Winter Dreams"; modern life undermines the hope for meaningful existence in "Prufrock"; the growing isolation of individuals undermines the fantasy of community in "The Far and the Near"). Students should also show by what means the truth is revealed. A superior essay will clearly contrast the "dream" and the means of disillusionment in each work. It will also consider for each story whether the reader or characters are left with hope.

23. (Average) *Guidelines for student response:* The students' essays may connect the Jazz Age with Fitzgerald's "Winter Dreams," the Great Depression with Steinbeck's story, and the disappearance of the frontier and the growth of the railroad with Wolfe's "The Far and the Near." A superior essay will show how each piece comments on as well as reflects the times in which it was written.

24. (Challenging) *Guidelines for student response:* The students' essays will focus on modernism and how it characterizes two poems in this part. The essay should address the poem's take on modern life. For instance, Eliot's "Prufrock" clearly captures the emptiness of modern life; Auden's "Unknown Citizen," its anonymity. The essay should also note the techniques used by each poet to convey his or her view of modern life (Eliot's fragmentary images, Cummings's near-nonsense language). Superior essays will show the thematic significance of the technique (e.g., Eliot's fragmented images reflect a life he believes is fragmentary; Cumming's "nonsense" helps wake us from a life that is in danger of growing sterile).

25. (Challenging) *Guidelines for student response:* Students' essays may focus on the intellectual weight of Eliot and Auden, the emphasis on image in Pound, Williams, and H. D., and the emphasis on sound in E. E. Cummings. Superior essays will show how other poetic elements work with the poet's main thrust.

"In Another Country" by Ernest Hemingway
"The Corn Planting" by Sherwood Anderson
"A Worn Path" by Eudora Welty

Selection Test (p. 210)

Critical Reading/Vocabulary and Grammar

1. a 2. b 3. a 4. c 5. b 6. a 7. c 8. a 9. b
10. a 11. a 12. b 13. c 14. a 15. d 16. d
17. a 18. b 19. c 20. d

Questions are classified in these categories:
Comprehension 2(C), 4(E), 6(C)
Interpretation 1(C), 5(A), 11(A), 12(A)
Literary Analysis 7(C), 8(A), 13(A), 14(E)
Reading Strategy 3(E), 9(E), 10(C), 15(A)
Vocabulary 17(A), 18(A), 20(E)
Grammar 16(A), 19(A)
E = Easy, A = Average, C = Challenging

Essay Questions

21. (Easy) *Guidelines for student response:* Students should describe Hal's character, using details from the story that relate to his involvement with the Hutchensons. They might mention that he appears to be a good person in befriending Will in Chicago. He appears to be very kind and caring, since he visits the Hutchensons regularly and is reluctant to give the Hutchensons the news of their son's death. Except that he was educated in Chicago and is a high school principal, we know nothing else about him.

22. (Average) *Guidelines for student response:* Students should use examples from the stories to compare Phoenix Jackson and the major. For example, both characters respond to their troubles by maintaining a hard discipline with little complaint: Phoenix regularly makes the difficult journey, and the major comes to the hospital daily and keeps his grief mostly to himself. If students believe that Phoenix's grandson is dead, then she and the major are alike in their difficulty in accepting the death of a

"In Another Country" by Ernest Hemingway
"The Corn Planting" by Sherwood Anderson
"A Worn Path" by Eudora Welty
(continued)

loved one. For differences, students could refer to their nationalities, gender, education, and circumstances.

23. (Challenging) *Guidelines for student response:* Students should use examples from the stories in discussing the role of the narrators and their involvement with the events. They may mention, for example, that the narrator of "In Another Country" plays a more direct role in the story's events, although he also tells about other characters. The first-person point of view brings the reader closer to the tragedies of war. In "The Corn Planting," much of what the narrator reports is hearsay from Hal, such as the letters from Will and his parents' reaction to them. At the end, the narrator becomes a direct observer and provides a unique perspective on the strangeness of the old couple's act.

Anxiety by Grace Paley

Selection Test (p. 213)

Critical Reading

1. c 2. c 3. b 4. d 5. a 6. c 7. d 8. b 9. c
10. a

Questions are classified in these categories:
   Comprehension 4(A), 6(C), 8(A), 9(C)
   Interpretation 1(C), 2(E), 3(C), 5(C), 7(A), 10(A)
   E = Easy, A = Average, C = Challenging

Essay Questions

11. (Easy) *Guidelines for student response:* Students should be able to link the title with the particular fears and worries of the old woman, including such details as "dreams of scientists and the bulky dreams of automakers," "dangerous street corners," nuclear war, and other images of imminent danger and death, all of them arising from the modern mechanical world. Students may judge the old woman to be justified because there really are such dangers in the world, or they might argue that she is overreacting. Among factors that may affect the old woman's feel-

ings, students should identify her own mortality, feelings of powerlessness (she yells after the father and daughter, but they already cannot hear her), and her apparent isolation.

12. (Average) *Guidelines for student response:* Students should be able to cite the following details as revealing the old woman's hopefulness and love of life: the springtime setting; the marigolds and other images of nature (horses); the fact that she cares enough to get involved with other people; her recognition of the "nice grin" she brings to the face of the father; her love for children ("lovely examples" of humankind); and her fondness for cookies, juice, and milk. Students should note the paradoxical relationship between these details and the old woman's anxiety, i.e., her love of life exacerbates her fears and worries.

13. (Challenging) *Guidelines for student response:* Students should see all of the topical material (nuclear war, dangerous streets, abusive parenting) as pertaining to the personal essay. They should identify the psychological picture of the old woman as belonging to the character sketch. Some students might suggest that the picture of urban anxiety, and not the specific topics the old woman brings up, is the real subject of the story and, thus, the two generic impulses work together in giving a picture of the modern malady of urban anxiety.

Part Test, Unit 5, Part 2: Focus on Literary Forms— The Short Story (p. 215)

Critical Reading/Vocabulary and Grammar

1. d 2. d 3. a 4. c 5. b 6. c 7. c 8. c 9. a
10. c 11. a 12. d 13. b 14. b 15. c

Questions are classified in these categories:
   Comprehension 7(A), 10(C)
   Interpretation 5(E), 6(C), 9(A)
   Literary Analysis 1(A), 8(C)
   Reading Strategy 2(A), 3(E), 4(A)
   Vocabulary 11(C), 12(A), 13(E)
   Grammar 14(A), 15(C)
   E = Easy, A = Average, C = Challenging

Essay Questions

16. (Easy) *Guidelines for student response:* The students' essays should focus on how the characters in these three stories deal with hardship and loss. Students should not only describe the conflict or hardship faced by the character and how the character meets it, but draw a lesson from the story about human courage or human limitations. Superior essays will note that each story presents two different kinds of challenges to its characters: in each, the death of a beloved is one that cannot be overcome with effort or will, but must be dealt with symbolically.

17. (Average) *Guidelines for student response:* The students' essays will deal with the different kinds of challenges faced by characters in one of the stories in this part. In each story, the characters face one challenge that calls for endurance or courage, and another—the loss of a loved one—that is unanswerable. In "In Another Country," the major and the soldiers are challenged by their physical wounds, which they face bravely; the major, though, finds his wife's death more difficult to face than his wound. In "The Corn Planting," the parents answer the news of their son's death by performing chores in the middle of the night, as if the solution to one challenge (making a living) could also meet the other (the death of a loved one). Phoenix in "A Worn Path" shows an amazing resiliency in the trek she makes into town; her reason for undertaking this challenge, though, is that she has never quite faced the challenge of accepting her grandson's death. Superior essays may conclude that the author's message in each case is ambivalent: life goes on in the face of loss, but the loss of a loved one is never really overcome.

18. (Challenging) *Guidelines for student response:* Students' essays should identify and describe each of the following for two of the stories: point of view, theme, and climax. The point of view in "In Another Country" and "The Corn Planting" is first-person; the point of view in "A Worn Path" is third-person limited. The theme in each case involves the loss of a loved one, and the climax comes at a point where we can contrast the way in which the character meets other challenges with the way in which they react to grief. Superior essays will note that, by using first-person narrators who are in some sense outsiders (in "In Another Country" and "The Corn Planting") or by using a limited third-person point of view, the author is able to distance the reader from the main character's reaction at the climax. This distancing makes the climax more surprising, and allows the reader to see the tragic or heroic (or deluded) nature of the main character's reaction.

"Chicago" and "Grass"
by Carl Sandburg

Selection Test (p. 218)

Critical Reading/Vocabulary and Grammar

1. d 2. b 3. a 4. b 5. b 6. d 7. d 8. c 9. a
10. d 11. b 12. c 13. a 14. a 15. a 16. b
17. c 18. d 19. c 20. d

Questions are classified in these categories:
   Comprehension 7(A), 8(C), 12(E)
   Interpretation 1(C), 4(A), 9(A), 13(C), 15(A)
   Literary Analysis 2(E), 3(C), 14(E)
   Reading Strategy 5(E), 6(E), 10(A), 11(A)
   Vocabulary 18(E), 19(A)
   Grammar 16(A), 17(E), 20(A)
   E = Easy, A = Average, C = Challenging

Essay Questions

21. (Easy) *Guidelines for student response:* Student essays should discuss the charges against the city and the verdict of the speaker, using examples from the poem. For example, they might point out that the speaker actually agrees with the critics that Chicago is a city of poverty and crime, yet he finds its youthful vitality, its will to work hard, and its ability to laugh at adversity admirable.

22. (Average) *Guidelines for student response:* Students should pick an image that captures other aspects of the city giving strong reasons for their choices. For example, they might choose an image of building: structures rising from the prairie created by the people—architects, businesspeople, and workers interacting as a team to make a better life for all.

"Chicago" and **"Grass"** by Carl Sandburg
(continued)

23. (Challenging) *Guidelines for student response:* Students may choose either interpretation as long as they support it with details from the poem. For example, students who understand the poem as a reflection on the statement "Time heals all wounds" may say that it stresses the fact that the physical scars of war are quickly erased by nature. Those who read the poem as an illustration of the pointlessness of war might suggest that as the physical scars of war disappear, so the reasons for fighting the war may be forgotten.

"The Jilting of Granny Weatherall"
by Katherine Anne Porter

Selection Test (p. 221)

Critical Reading/Vocabulary and Grammar

1. b 2. d 3. b 4. d 5. c 6. a 7. d 8. c 9. c
10. a 11. b 12. b 13. a 14. d 15. b 16. c
17. a 18. a 19. b 20. d

Questions are classified in these categories:
Comprehension 1(E), 2(A), 12(E)
Interpretation 4(E), 9(C), 11(C), 13(C), 14(A)
Literary Analysis 3(E), 8(E), 10(C)
Reading Strategy 5(A), 6(E), 7(A)
Vocabulary 15(A), 16(A), 17(A)
Grammar 18(A), 19(A), 20(A)
E = Easy, A = Average, C = Challenging

Essay Questions

21. (Easy) *Guidelines for student response:* Students may choose different interpretations as long as they support their opinions with events from the story. For example, they might feel that the title signifies the importance of the jilting to Granny and its continuing effect on her. Others might suggest that Granny's approaching death evokes many of the same feelings in her that her jilting did.

22. (Average) *Guidelines for student response:* Students may choose either position, as long as it is supported with details from the story. For example, students who agree might suggest that Granny committed a blunder in her youth by agreeing to marry George. She admits her adulthood

was a struggle, especially after John died. Most students will probably state that Granny Weatherall would disagree with the last part of the statement, as she does not seem to regret much in her old age, except a chance to tell George he did no lasting damage. Those who disagree might say that Granny seems too spunky to agree with such a depressing blanket indictment of life.

23. (Challenging) *Guidelines for student response:* Students should define stream of consciousness and state how well it indicates how close Granny is to death, supporting their answers with specific details. For example, they might say that stream of consciousness reflects the thoughts coming directly from a character's mind and that it creates a realistic and vivid personal view of death approaching a character. They could contrast Granny's coherence at the beginning, where she carries on a conversation with the doctor, with her growing difficulty in communicating as the story progresses. They might also say that, at first, she can distinguish between present events and memories of her past but loses this ability toward the end of the story.

"Race at Morning" and "Nobel Prize Acceptance Speech"
by William Faulkner

Selection Test (p. 224)

Critical Reading/Vocabulary and Grammar

1. d 2. a 3. b 4. c 5. a 6. b 7. d 8. b 9. d
10. c 11. a 12. a 13. d 14. b 15. c 16. d
17. c 18. d 19. b 20. a

Questions are classified in these categories:
Comprehension 1(E), 2(A), 12(E)
Interpretation 4(E), 9(C), 11(C), 13(C), 14(A)
Literary Analysis 3(E), 8(E), 10(C)
Reading Strategy 5(A), 6(E), 7(A)
Vocabulary 15(A), 16(A), 17(A)
Grammar 18(A), 19(A), 20(A)
E = Easy, A = Average, C = Challenging

Essay Questions

21. (Easy) *Guidelines for student response:* Students should describe the character traits of Dan, Eagle, and the buck. For example, they might describe Dan as an in-

telligent and powerful horse; Eagle as a smart, experienced, and determined lead dog; and the buck as an intelligent, brave, and wily deer, knowing just how to elude the hunters following its trail and the many who are arrayed along its path. Students may conclude that all these characters are reasonably well developed as minor characters. They will probably say that the buck is the most important of these characters because without it the hunt could not occur.

22. (Average) *Guidelines for student response:* Students' essays should assess the intelligence of the narrator and provide examples to support their conclusions. Students might point out that although the narrator's use of language indicates a lack of formal education, he demonstrates high intelligence in evaluating events and analyzing issues, as in his realization that the 351 days spent working and the 14 days spent hunting each year are not different or of unequal value but opposite sides of the same thing.

23. (Challenging) *Guidelines for student response:* Students should identify events or situations in which Mister Ernest and the narrator are struggling with internal conflicts. Mister Ernest, for example, demonstrates an internal conflict over the values of hunting when he pursues the buck all day only to pass up the opportunity to shoot the deer when he has the chance. In his explanation that hunting and farming are not two different things but "jest the other side of each other," the narrator reveals that he is working to resolve an internal conflict over the values of work relative to the need for recreation.

Robert Frost's Poetry

Selection Test (p. 227)

Critical Reading/Vocabulary and Grammar

1. b 2. a 3. c 4. b 5. a 6. c 7. d 8. c 9. c
10. a 11. c 12. b 13. d 14. a 15. c 16. d
17. d 18. b 19. d 20. a

Questions are classified in these categories:
   Comprehension 2(E), 7(A), 8(A)
   Interpretation 1(A), 3(C), 4(C), 5(C), 6(C)
   Literary Analysis 9(A), 10(E), 12(A)
   Reading Strategy 11(C), 13(E)

Vocabulary 14(A), 15(A), 18(A)
Grammar 16(A), 17(A), 19(E), 20(E)
E = Easy, A = Average, C = Challenging

Essay Questions

21. (Easy) *Guidelines for student response:* Students' essays should reflect a number of different examples of Frost's thematic use of regret. For example, students may cite the example of the boy who is killed by the saw in " 'Out, Out—.' " ("Then the boy saw all—/since he was old enough to know, big boy/Doing a man's work, though a child at heart—/He saw all spoiled.") They may point out the mournful refrain at the end of "Stopping by Woods on a Snowy Evening" or the speaker's wish to return to childhood and simple joy in "Birches." Students may mention that such longings are a part of human nature that is instantly recognizable and familiar. They may note that even at their relatively young age, they have a sense of lost childhood or regret about times gone by.

22. (Average) *Guidelines for student response:* Students' essays should reflect that while the story told in the poem seems a simple one, it actually reflects complicated ideas about the human condition and the American sensibility. The reasons for not wanting walls might include unspoiled natural beauty, easier access to the countryside, a stronger bonding with neighbors, and so on. Reasons for building and keeping walls might include such ideas as maintaining privacy and land rights, avoiding legal battles, and a desire to keep family affairs within the family. The poem points up the American ideas of open spaces and pioneering on the one hand, and rugged individualism and ownership on the other.

23. (Challenging) *Guidelines for student response:* Students should explore "Stopping by Woods on a Snowy Evening" in terms of the three parts Frost considered essential: the point or idea, the details that develop it, and the technique. For example, they might state the main idea as the conflict between desire for rest and duty; the details in the attractiveness of the woods and the little horse's eagerness to keep going; and the rhythm and rhyme scheme that sound like a moving sleigh.

"The Night the Ghost Got In"
by James Thurber
from *Here Is New York*
by E. B. White

Selection Test (p. 230)

Critical Reading/Vocabulary and Grammar

1. c 2. d 3. b 4. b 5. c 6. d 7. a 8. d 9. b
10. c 11. c 12. b 13. b 14. c 15. d 16. c
17. c 18. a 19. b 20. c

Questions are classified in these categories:
   Comprehension 5(E), 7(A), 10(A)
   Interpretation 1(A), 4(C), 6(A), 11(C), 14(E)
   Literary Analysis 2(C), 9(A), 13(C), 15(E)
   Reading Strategy 3(A), 8(A), 12(A)
   Vocabulary 18(A), 19(A), 20(E)
   Grammar 16(E), 17(A)
   E = Easy, A = Average, C = Challenging

Essay Questions

21. (Easy) *Guidelines for student response:* Students' responses should give a clear idea of the eccentricities of these characters through specific examples of their personalities and actions. For example, students might cite the mother's urge to throw another shoe and her belief that the wounded policeman really was a deserter as eccentric features, which come close to crossing the line of credibility. They might find the grandfather's reception of the police eccentric, but somewhat believable, given the implication that the old man is not in his right mind.

22. (Average) *Guidelines for student response:* Students should show White's wide-ranging interests and feeling for humanity through specific examples. For example, they might cite his sympathetic admiration for New Yorkers living under pressure, as an example that nothing human is alien to him. They could see evidence of his keen eye in such vivid examples as the young man writing to his girl or the overwhelmed newlywed visitors eating a dispirited meal. As evidence of White's intelligence, they might mention his clear analysis of New York's neighborhood pattern.

23. (Challenging) *Guidelines for student response:* Students should give some general criteria for where they draw the line between humor and unkindness and illustrate it with specific examples. For example, they might state that when Thurber calls attention to things people can't help, such as the grandfather's mental problems or the police's speech patterns, and exaggerates them, he crosses the line. In contrast, they might decide that White's depiction of tourists doesn't cross the line because he is more descriptive than critical.

from *Dust Tracks on a Road*
by Zora Neale Hurston

Selection Test (p. 233)

Critical Reading/Vocabulary and Grammar

1. a 2. b 3. c 4. b 5. a 6. c 7. b 8. d 9. b
10. b 11. c 12. b 13. d 14. a 15. a 16. d
17. c 18. d 19. b 20. c

Questions are classified in these categories:
   Comprehension 1(E), 6(A), 7(A)
   Interpretation 2(A), 3(C), 4(C), 5(A), 8(E)
   Literary Analysis 11(A), 14(A)
   Reading Strategy 9(A), 10(C), 12(A), 13(C)
   Vocabulary 15(A), 16(A), 17(E)
   Grammar 18(E), 19(E), 20(A)
   E = Easy, A = Average, C = Challenging

Essay Questions

21. (Easy) *Guidelines for student response:* Student responses should include several character traits revealed by specific information in the text. For example, they might mention Zora's self-confidence, eagerness to learn, sense of responsibility, and love of action. They might cite her hailing of white people from her gatepost as an example of self-confidence. Her sense of responsibility can be seen in her admiration for Heracles, who chose a life of duty over pleasure.

22. (Average) *Guidelines for student response:* Students should mention attitudes and give examples that illustrate them. As an example of an attitude to which Zora refers directly, students may cite the amusement white people probably felt when she asked to ride with them. On the other hand, it can be inferred from the fuss the white ladies make over Zora's reading ability that they had low expectations of African American schooling or intelligence. Students may suggest that the

women wanted to help Zora out of a life they considered impoverished and inadequate and that it made them feel good.

23. (Challenging) *Guidelines for student response:* Students should cite specific examples in discussing both how the critic's view is supported by the selection and how it is not. For example, they may say that Zora's descriptions of white people are generally positive enough to support the critic's view: she is curious about differences, but not critical; her view of the white women's hands arouses wonder, not distaste. In contrast, students might suggest that Zora implies criticism when she mentions white curiosity about a "Negro school." The fact that the ladies had Zora read from a magazine at the hotel implies that they had suspicions about her performance at school.

"Refugee in America," "Ardella," "The Negro Speaks of Rivers," and "Dream Variations"
by Langston Hughes
"The Tropics in New York"
by Claude McKay

Selection Test (p. 236)

Critical Reading/Vocabulary and Grammar

1. c 2. a 3. a 4. c 5. d 6. a 7. c 8. c 9. a 10. b 11. c 12. d 13. d 14. b 15. a 16. a 17. b 18. a 19. b 20. d

Questions are classified in these categories:
  Comprehension 3(A), 8(A), 12(A)
  Interpretation 1(C), 6(C), 9(A), 13(C), 15(E)
  Literary Analysis 2(E), 10(A), 14(A)
  Reading Strategy 4(E), 5(C), 7(A), 11(C)
  Vocabulary 16(E), 17(A)
  Grammar 18(E), 19(A), 20(A)
  E = Easy, A = Average, C = Challenging

Essay Questions

21. (Easy) *Guidelines for student response:* Students should mention some specific ways in which the poem is effective in contributing to African American awareness and pride. For example, they might cite how the association with ancient rivers from the earliest times reminds African Americans of their roots. Students might also suggest that the use of the pronoun *I* enables African American readers to identify with the history of their people. The connection of the Nile and Pyramids, representing one of the world's greatest civilizations, to African Americans provides a source of pride.

22. (Average) *Guidelines for student response:* In their essays, students should compare and contrast the speakers in the three poems, telling whom the *I* represents and what effect the use of this pronoun has on the reader. For example, in "Refugee in America" students might decide that the speaker is the poet who has experienced a lack of liberty, although a reader who shared these experiences might see the *I* as representing the African American race. In "The Tropics in New York," they might suggest that *I* is the poet, and any reader might identify with his feelings of homesickness. In "The Negro Speaks of Rivers," they might recognize that speaker as the whole African American race throughout time. The use of *I* invites the reader to become part of the narration and to identify with the race.

23. (Challenging) *Guidelines for student response:* Students should discuss words and images of darkness in "Ardella," "The Negro Speaks of Rivers," and "Dream Variations," using supporting details. For example, they might note that the word "dusky" connotes a physical trait Africans share with rivers and emphasizes the identification of the two. Students might point out that in "Dream Variations" the African American speaker identifies with evening and night in their darkness, which are represented positively as cool, gentle, and tender. They might note that although the darkness of Ardella is a physical fact and is presented as something mysterious and closed, it is not the point of what she is. Students could suggest that Hughes uses such words and images in positive ways to make African Americans take pride in their "blackness."

"From the Dark Tower"
by Countee Cullen
"A Black Man Talks of Reaping"
by Arna Bontemps
"Storm Ending" by Jean Toomer

Selection Test (p. 239)

Critical Reading/Vocabulary and Grammar

1. a 2. c 3. c 4. c 5. d 6. a 7. b 8. b 9. c
10. a 11. c 12. d 13. a 14. d 15. b 16. b
17. d 18. d 19. c 20. a

Questions are classified in these categories:
   Comprehension 7(C), 12(E)
   Interpretation 1(A), 2(A), 6(C), 8(E), 13(A)
   Literary Analysis 9(C), 10(A), 11(A), 14(C)
   Reading Strategy 3(A), 4(C), 5(A)
   Vocabulary 15(E), 16(E), 17(A)
   Grammar 18(A), 19(A), 20(A)
   E = Easy, A = Average, C = Challenging

Essay Questions

21. (Easy) *Guidelines for student response:*
   Students' essays should give a word or
   phrase describing the mood of the poem
   and cite details that show how it captures the mood of the poem. For example, students may choose the word "bitter" or a synonym, citing references to
   sowing much but reaping little and the
   detail of the speaker's children eating
   "bitter fruit."

22. (Average) *Guidelines for student response:*
   Students may select any one of the
   poems as long as they explain how it
   uses metaphors. For example, students
   might choose "From the Dark Tower" or
   "A Black Man Talks of Reaping," citing
   the comparison of African American life
   to planting without reaping, which reminds readers of the agricultural slavery
   of that life and evokes feelings of anger
   and despair. If they select "Storm Ending," they might mention that thunder is
   compared to bell-like flowers, which convey the noise and beauty of the storm
   and evoke a sense of awe.

23. (Challenging) *Guidelines for student response:* Students may agree or disagree
   with the statement but should support
   their position with examples. For example, students agreeing that Toomer intended to write about the African American experience might assert the thunder
   represents the trials of African Americans
   and, like other writers of the Harlem Renaissance, his purpose was to call attention to their life. Students who disagree
   might reason that the images of the
   storm give no hint of any further meaning and that the poem was written to
   show that African American writers could
   produce literature equal in quality to that
   of white writers.

"i yearn" by Ricardo Sanchez

Selection Test (p. 242)

Critical Reading/Vocabulary and Grammar

1. c 2. b 3. a 4. d 5. c 6. c 7. d 8. b 9. b
10. d

Questions are classified in these categories:
   Comprehension 2(A), 3(A), 4(E), 5(A), 7(A),
      8(A)
   Interpretation 1(E), 6(C), 9(C), 10(C)
   E = Easy, A = Average, C = Challenging

Essay Questions

11. (Easy) *Guidelines for student response:*
   Students should identify one of two
   themes: homesickness (the poet's yearn-
   ing for the food, customs, and fellowship
   of the people he has left behind), or love
   of life (the celebration of all that is good
   about the poet's people). Students should
   make an extended comparison of
   Sanchez's treatment of either theme with
   a similar work of their own choosing.

12. (Average) *Guidelines for student response:* Students should suggest that
   Sanchez in part paraphrases Mitchell's
   line, in the sense that he is celebrating
   his "home" only after having left it. Students might suggest further, however,
   that Sanchez nonetheless values his culture while that culture is still alive, finding its manifestations in places far from
   its place of origin. Students may suggest
   that Sanchez should never have left
   home, or, alternately, that Sanchez finds
   his culture in many places, and thus his
   love of his people is not tied down to a
   particular place.

13. (Challenging) *Guidelines for student response:* Students should cite several difficulties in maintaining an ethnic identity in a "melting pot" culture, such as the unfamiliarity of food, clothing, language, and personal manners. On the other hand, students should note that America is a land of immigrants and in many cases (such as the cities Sanchez mentions) has adopted "foreign" cultures, or become a sort of "home away from home" for peoples of other lands. In this sense, students might suggest that modern America is not homogeneous but incredibly diverse.

Part Test, Unit 5, Part 3: From Every Corner of the Land
(p. 244)

Critical Reading/Vocabulary and Grammar

1. d 2. b 3. b 4. d 5. c 6. d 7. c 8. a 9. c
10. b 11. c 12. a 13. c 14. a 15. c 16. b
17. d 18. b 19. a 20. b

Questions are classified in these categories:
- Comprehension 7(A), 10(A)
- Interpretation 8(E), 9(A)
- Literary Analysis 4(C), 5(C), 6(A)
- Reading Strategy 1(A), 2(E), 3(A), 7(A)
- Vocabulary 11(C), 12(A), 13(E), 14(C), 15(A)
- Grammar and Style 16(A), 17(E), 18(A), 19(A), 20(C)
- E = Easy, A = Average, C = Challenging

Essay Questions

21. (Easy) *Guidelines for student response:* Students' essays should reflect the fact that Porter shows us Granny Weatherall's death "from the inside," through her confused minglings of memory and reality, where Frost shows us the boy's death from the viewpoint of an almost neutral outside observer. Students should also draw conclusions about the nature of death and life as they appear in these works. Superior essays may note that, for Granny Weatherall, death is a kind of summing up of a life. In Frost's poem, death is an accident, a surprising disruption in the routine of life and work. It stands outside life, which closes over behind it ("life goes on").

22. (Average) *Guidelines for student response:* Students' essays should explain why the images of reaping and of night are important in works from the Harlem Renaissance. They should note that the poets of this movement had a special concern with their moment in history, when slavery was a relatively recent memory, discrimination a real part of the present, and a new cultural and political dignity for African Americans was a hope and an ambition for the future. The image of reaping allows these poets to show a strong, moral connection between what happened in the past and what the future holds. The image of night allows them to change the value that prejudiced people had assigned to darkness (the dark skin of African Americans). Superior essays will note that *reaping* has Biblical overtones, while *night* is such a basic image (like *dawn* and *spring*) that it helps these poems link up with the larger tradition of serious poetry.

23. (Average) *Guidelines for student response:* Students' essays will classify four of the poets from this part as either "the poets of the cloister" or the poets of "streets and struggles." Sandburg's description of Chicago places him in the "streets and struggles" group. Frost's concerns with traditional rural life and man's relation with nature may seem to put him in the "cloister," but students may also argue that his concern with the unforgivingness of rural life, and with the opposition of life and death, show him to be a poet of "streets and struggles." Hughes writes poems (such as "Refugee in America") that come from "streets and struggles," but poems such as "Ardella" come from the "cloister." Toomer's "Storm Ending" is also a poem of the "cloister" because of its focus on beautiful language and imagery.

24. (Challenging) *Guidelines for student response:* Students' essays should consider the role played by tradition or history in two of the works (or in the works of two of the authors) in this part. They

should reach a conclusion about whether the writer emphasizes the way in which the past defines the present, or whether the author is concerned with timeless truths. Of special note: Sandburg's "Grass," while making specific allusions to historical events, affirms the eternal power of grass to return history to oblivion; while Theodora in "April Showers" seems to pass through an experience that anyone might have; it makes an important difference to her that her father has had the same experience (history helps define the present).

25. (Challenging) *Guidelines for student response:* Students' essays should consider the role played by place in the works of two of the authors in this part. They should work toward a definition of how place functions in these pieces. For instance, students may note that rural Florida defines Zora Neale Hurston's early experiences, but that it is very important to her to hear from "beyond" (the visit of the Minnesotans); place would become a confinement otherwise. Even more strongly, Faulkner's Mississippi defines the identity of the narrator of "Race at Morning"; but Mister Ernest knows that the boy must move out of that life. Frost's Vermont is a test of truths and a source of revelations. The hard quality of life there, and the traditional thinking of its people, help him to achieve insights that might be lost in a city. Hughes's "dusky rivers" are not just places, but the stored-up experiences of a people's history.

Unit 6: Prosperity and Protest (1946–Present)

"The Life You Save May Be Your Own" by Flannery O'Connor

Selection Test (p. 248)

Critical Reading/Vocabulary and Grammar

1. d 2. b 3. c 4. a 5. a 6. c 7. b 8. d 9. d
10. b 11. c 12. d 13. a 14. a 15. a 16. b
17. c 18. a 19. d 20. c

Questions are classified in these categories:
   Comprehension 1(A), 3(C), 5(A), 12(A)
   Interpretation 2(A), 4(C), 6(A), 13(E), 14(C), 15(A)
   Literary Analysis 9(E), 10(A), 11(C)
   Reading Strategy 7(A), 8(E)
   Vocabulary 16(A), 17(E), 18(E)
   Grammar 19(C), 20(A)
   E = Easy, A = Average, C = Challenging

Essay Questions

21. (Easy) *Guidelines for student response:* Students should recognize that the only detail about the woman's physical appearance—the absence of teeth—creates a grotesque effect. The old woman lives in a desolate spot, though readers are not given any information as to exactly why or how it is desolate. This undesirable, slightly bizarre setting contributes to the woman's grotesque profile. Students must recognize that the woman is obsessed with her daughter—she believes that young Lucynell would be a "prize" for a husband. We are also told she is "ravenous for a son-in-law." This is really all we know about the old woman. She assumes that anyone who would marry Lucynell would stay at the farm because she, herself, cannot imagine being parted from Lucynell. That Mr. Shiftlet gains the old woman's trust so easily is a sign that the old woman's obsession has affected her judgment.

22. (Average) *Guidelines for student response:* Students may characterize Mr. Shiftlet as selfish and so absorbed in his own presentation of himself that he does not see that he is hypocritical. Students may conclude that he is sincere both in his helpfulness and in his "using" of the two women. He certainly is aware of what he is doing, and works toward his own goal—the car—systematically and carefully. Students may state that they almost

liked Mr. Shiftlet when he was chatting on the porch with the women, or when he was fixing up the farm. At those points he seems harmless enough, though he does, in the former situation, express some definite opinions.

23. (Challenging) *Guidelines for student response:* Students may choose any three symbols. The "crooked cross" is a reference to the Christian image of Christ being crucified on a cross. The symbolic nature of this reference is ironic. Shiftlet is anything but similar to the traditional concept of Christ. The human heart that doctors have cut out of a man's chest is a symbol for Shiftlet himself, who, it turns out, has no heart. Shiftlet spies the car's bumper almost immediately upon arriving at the farm. The car represents to him freedom and mobility. It may also symbolize his youth. He speculates that it's a 1928 or 1929 model, and we are told it has been sitting there for fifteen years, so it would be from a time when Shiftlet was young and innocent and still had his arm. The hitchhiker is a symbol for the truth. He speaks what he thinks is the truth, though it may be ugly. What he speaks is what Shiftlet claims to abhor. But what Shiftlet speaks is not the truth.

"The First Seven Years"
by Bernard Malamud

Selection Test (p. 251)

Critical Reading/Vocabulary and Grammar

1. d 2. b 3. d 4. b 5. c 6. b 7. d 8. a 9. a 10. b 11. c 12. d 13. c 14. b 15. d 16. d 17. c 18. a 19. b 20. a

Questions are classified in these categories:
Comprehension 3(E), 5(E), 9(A), 14(A)
Interpretation 1(A), 4(E), 6(C), 8(C), 11(A), 13(E), 15(C)
Literary Analysis 10(C), 12(A)
Reading Strategy 2(C), 7(A)
Vocabulary 17(E), 19(C), 20(A)
Grammar 16(A), 18(E)
E = Easy, A = Average, C = Challenging

Essay Questions

21. (Easy) *Guidelines for student response:* Students should note that Miriam's choice to take a job gives her some financial freedom as well as the freedom to continue to pursue her own interests, such as the books Sobel supplies to her. Her choice does give her independence, though some would say it is limited by the type of job she can get without any further education. Feld's plan for college would open up doors of knowledge and opportunity. Miriam is opening some of those doors on her own through her reading, it seems. As to Miriam's decision, students may side with Miriam or Feld but must explain their reasons. Those who support Miriam's decision may say it was the right decision for her simply because it was hers. Others may feel that she threw away an opportunity because her father was *offering* to send her to college, and it would be a good idea to go and see what it's all about.

22. (Average) *Guidelines for student response:* Students should acknowledge that Feld is absorbed by thoughts of his daughter's future right at the beginning of the story. He admires the diligence of Max, whom he sees trudging to school regularly. He wishes his daughter had that same diligence and desire for education. Feld runs his business as best he can, given his health. He tries not to meddle too much in Miriam's business, though he can't resist asking questions. Feld does admit that his least hope for Miriam is that she marry an educated man. This admission on Feld's part helps build to his epiphany. The second step on the way to the epiphany is Feld's thought about why Sobel reads so much. Feld resists the notion that "reading to know" is acceptable and is all that Miriam really wants from an "education" as well. When Sobel finally blurts out his reason for working for Feld for so long, Feld is both stunned and unsurprised. He had known and rejected the idea. Seeing Sobel's sincerity and earnestness, Feld gives up his notions of a "better" material life for Miriam and settles for the life that he assumes she

"The First Seven Years"
by Bernard Malamud
(continued)

will choose with Sobel. He leaves in silence, but then walks with a "stronger stride." It seems he is relieved that the issue has been settled, and is perhaps less disappointed than one might have thought.

23. (Challenging) *Guidelines for student response:* Students should recognize that Feld starts out thinking that education and the resultant material benefits are the only road to "a better life," or success and happiness. His views change, of course, as he sees that Sobel really loves Miriam, and he is saddened yet satisfied with the outcome of the whole situation. Sobel, who has fallen in love and sacrificed material gain just to be near Miriam, obviously has no use for material wealth. His riches come from the books he reads and shares with Miriam. Miriam accuses Max of being a materialist. It seems he is only interested in "things." This is in keeping with his relentless pursuit of his education. Max will not agree to call Miriam for a date until he verifies her age and sees a picture of her. He is not satisfied with her father's assurances about her positive qualities. Finally, Miriam appears at one level to pursue material comfort because she chooses a job over the deprivation of going to college. Where she really lives, though, is in her books. Max, in his pursuit of accountancy, values things, and this bores Miriam. She prefers to consider ideas and feelings—the ones she finds in her books and in Sobel. Students may agree with any one character's notions, or a combination of several.

"The Brown Chest" by John Updike

Selection Test (p. 254)

Critical Reading/Vocabulary and Grammar
1. c 2. b 3. a 4. b 5. c 6. a 7. c 8. d 9. b 10. d 11. d 12. b 13. d 14. c 15. b 16. a 17. b 18. d 19. a 20. c

Questions are classified in these categories:
Comprehension 2(E), 5(A), 6(C), 12(A)
Interpretation 1(A), 3(C), 8(C), 11(A), 14(E)
Literary Analysis 7(C), 10(A), 13(A)
Reading Strategy 4(A), 9(E), 15(E)
Vocabulary 16(A), 17(C), 18(E)
Grammar 19(E), 20(A)
E = Easy, A = Average, C = Challenging

Essay Questions

21. (Easy) *Guidelines for student response:* Students should acknowledge that as a young boy, he is somewhat fearful of the chest and its contents. He doesn't open it without an adult nearby. He saw "old" things inside that "disgusted" him. He is uninterested in the contents, even when his mother is explaining them to him. In the second house, the chest recedes somewhat in the boy's consciousness. It is in the attic, out of sight, and only occasionally does his mother open it to find something. When he must move the chest out of this house, he can't bring himself to go through the contents thoroughly. In his own barn, he avoids the chest. When Morna inquires, he claims he has forgotten what is in it. At the end, he is no longer disgusted by the contents. He sees the chest as an extension of his family, and of Gordon's family.

22. (Average) *Guidelines for student response:* Students should characterize the atmosphere of Gordon's first appearance as somewhat awkward. The two men have hard work to do under naturally difficult circumstances. Updike compares their motion from cellar to attic to sick men changing positions in bed. They occasionally "flee" the house and its contents and decisions. In addition, their packing and moving is thwarted by a too-small van, by getting lost, and by arriving late and unloading in the rain. Gordon's second appearance is a pleasant surprise to the main character, though partly just because Gordon wants to take away some of the furniture that his father "avoids" but can't bear to throw away. The addition of Morna to this scene brightens it further. The father and son do not seem awkward, as in the earlier scene. The barn is not represented as "haunted" but full of interesting things for Gordon and Morna. The circumstances are pleasant as Gordon announces his intention to marry Morna.

23. (Challenging) *Guidelines for student response:* Students should remember that the young boy seems to have a gentle relationship with his mother. She tries to explain items in the chest to him. He lies on the bed while she writes at her desk. Upon her death, he takes home many of her possessions. They bother him, but he cannot bear to throw them away. He respects her belongings, even though she is no longer living. He assumes her role as owner of the chest, and, in the end, perhaps sees its value as she did. With respect to the father-son relationship, students should recall the awkwardness between them. Some of this is due to Gordon's not having a job. His father does not approve, but those thoughts are revealed most gently. Nevertheless, there is respect between the two men, in spite of the awkwardness. One gets the feeling that they might genuinely like each other if they could relax a bit. On the whole, Updike creates feelings about relationships through subtle description of events and characters' thoughts and actions.

"Hawthorne" by Robert Lowell
"Gold Glade" by Robert Penn Warren
"The Light Comes Brighter" and "Traveling Through the Dark" by William Stafford
"The Adamant" by Theodore Roethke

Selection Test (p. 257)

Critical Reading/Vocabulary and Grammar

1. b 2. d 3. c 4. a 5. b 6. c 7. d 8. a 9. d
10. c 11. b 12. b 13. a 14. c 15. c 16. d
17. a 18. b 19. d 20. c

Questions are classified in these categories:
   Comprehension 4(E), 10(E), 12(E)
   Interpretation 1(A), 3(A), 8(A), 13(A)
   Literary Analysis 2(C), 5(A), 9(C), 14(A)
   Reading Strategy 6(A), 7(C), 11(A)
   Vocabulary 15(C), 16(E), 17(C)
   Grammar 18(E), 19(A), 20(A)
   E = Easy, A = Average, C = Challenging

Essay Questions

21. (Easy) *Guidelines for student response:* Students must identify one of the selections and indicate their response to it. Examples of inspiration or meditation might include the following: researching Hawthorne or Salem after reading "Hawthorne"; recalling a formative and inspiring childhood moment in nature after reading "Gold Glade"; considering the effect of modern society on nature after reading Stafford's poem.

22. (Average) *Guidelines for student response:* Students should state what the poet seems to discover about himself through the poem. For instance, Lowell expresses his admiration for Hawthorne and, in doing so, reveals dissatisfaction with the New England temperament that is his heritage as well as Hawthorne's. Students might note that Warren regains vitality from his youth by recalling the memory of the gold glade or that Stafford grapples with his complicity in nature's destruction.

23. (Challenging) *Guidelines for student response:* Students might select "Traveling Through the Dark" and "The Adamant." Students should point out clear differences in style, such as formal versus informal diction, traditional line and stanza structure versus free verse, and intimate versus formal tone.

"Average Waves in Unprotected Waters" by Anne Tyler

Selection Test (p. 260)

Critical Reading/Vocabulary and Grammar

1. a 2. d 3. b 4. b 5. a 6. b 7. c 8. d 9. c
10. c 11. d 12. b 13. c 14. a 15. b 16. d
17. a 18. c 19. b 20. d

Questions are classified in these categories:
   Comprehension 3(A), 9(A), 10(A)
   Interpretation 2(A), 7(C), 11(A), 14(E)
   Literary Analysis 1(E), 4(A), 5(C), 12(A)
   Reading Strategy 6(E), 8(C), 13(E)
   Vocabulary 15(A), 17(E), 20(A)
   Grammar 16(A), 18(C), 19(C)
   E = Easy, A = Average, C = Challenging

Essay Questions

21. (Easy) *Guidelines for student response:* Students should understand that foreshadowing is a suggestion of events to come. Students must provide valid exam-

"Average Waves in Unprotected Waters"
by Anne Tyler
(continued)

ples of foreshadowing with lines such as "She felt too slight and frail, too wispy for all she had to do today" and "But her voice was all wrong. He would pick it up, for sure." Students should make connections between these examples of foreshadowing and subsequent events. Students might explain that the first quotation hints at Bet leaving Arnold at the institution and that the second hints that Arnold is unaware of what awaits him.

22. (Average) *Guidelines for student response:* Students should recognize that the flashback confirms that Arnold has a disability and explains how Bet has come to care for Arnold without the help of her husband or family. Moreover, students should recognize that the recollections of Bet's childhood, her relationship with her parents, and her marriage and its aftermath all reveal Bet's coping mechanisms. She has always "stood staunch" in the face of calamity "as if standing staunch were a virtue, really." The details of the flashback also underscore Bet's isolation.

23. (Challenging) *Guidelines for student response:* Students must make reasonable predictions, based on story events and characterizations. Students might use the story's final line—"From now on, all the world was going to be like that—just something on a stage, for her to sit back and watch"—as the basis of their predictions. Students might predict that Bet does not remarry, that she goes through life alone with a quiet resignation, never realizing that she is no longer participating in life or allowing herself to feel emotions, either good or bad.

from *The Names* by N. Scott Momaday
"Mint Snowball" by Naomi Shihab Nye
"Suspended" by Joy Harjo

Selection Test (p. 263)

Critical Reading/Vocabulary and Grammar

1. b 2. d 3. c 4. c 5. a 6. b 7. d 8. c 9. b
10. a 11. d 12. a 13. c 14. a 15. d 16. b
17. d 18. b 19. c 20. a

Questions are classified in these categories:
Comprehension 1(A), 5(E), 7(E), 11(E)
Interpretation 2(A), 6(C), 9(A), 14(C)
Literary Analysis 4(A), 8(C), 13(E)
Reading Strategy 3(C), 10(A), 12(A)
Vocabulary 15(C), 17(A), 18(E)
Grammar 16(C), 19(A), 20(A)
E = Easy, A = Average, C = Challenging

Essay Questions

21. (Easy) *Guidelines for student response:* Students should state the writer's experience and name an experience of their own that relates to it. For example, students might relate Harjo's revelatory experience with jazz to an experience in which they first realized that their parents were human and capable of making mistakes. The best response will make the connection between an anecdotal experience and the reason for recalling it.

22. (Average) *Guidelines for student response:* Students should restate the anecdote and then analyze its meaning and effectiveness. For instance, students might point out that Momaday's anecdote about practicing the running mount with Pecos entertains as well as supports Momaday's themes of the importance of racial identity and of the journey of self-discovery.

23. (Challenging) *Guidelines for student response:* Students should choose one anecdote and clearly state the mood it creates. For example, Nye's anecdote about her great-grandfather selling the family recipe quickly introduces a sense of loss and sadness into an essay that had been fondly reminiscent. Students should also note that this anecdote underscores the purpose of Nye's essay—to convey a sense of displacement in the modern world.

"Everyday Use" by Alice Walker

Selection Test (p. 266)

Critical Reading/Vocabulary and Grammar

1. a 2. d 3. a 4. d 5. b 6. c 7. c 8. b 9. c
10. c 11. d 12. b 13. a 14. c 15. b 16. c
17. d 18. d 19. c 20. d

Questions are classified in these categories:
  Comprehension 1(A), 2(E), 3(E)
  Interpretation 4(A), 6(A), 7(A), 8(C), 9(C)
  Literary Analysis 5(A), 10(C), 14(E)
  Reading Strategy 11(C), 12(A), 13(C)
  Vocabulary 15(A), 16(E), 17(A)
  Grammar 18(E), 19(A), 20(A)
  E = Easy, A = Average, C = Challenging

Essay Questions

21. (Easy) *Guidelines for student response:* Students should note that the narrator is a strong, practical, hard-working woman. Students should support this analysis with details such as her "rough, man-working hands" and her ability to "kill and clean a hog as mercilessly as a man." The narrator is uneducated but intelligent and capable of insights such as, "in 1927 colored asked fewer questions than they do now." Dee is brash, spoiled, ashamed of her family's poverty, and insensitive toward her mother and sister. She wears "a dress so loud" it hurts the narrator's eyes. Supportive details of Dee's brashness include her uninformed reasons for changing her name; she thinks Dee is the name of her oppressors, when in fact, Dee was the name of her Aunt Dicie, Grandma Dee, and other relatives. In contrast with her large mother and thin sister, Dee has a "fuller figure" as well as a light complexion and "nicer hair." Dee has received an education, which opened her to reading, just as it closed her from her family: "She washed us in a river of make-believe, burned us with a lot of knowledge we didn't necessarily need to know. Pressed us to her with the serious way she read, to shove us away at just the moment, like dimwits, we seemed about to understand." Dee's insensitivity is also illustrated in the way she "rifles" through her mother's belongings looking for the quilts. Maggie, thin and scarred from a fire, walks with her "chin on chest, eyes on ground, feet in shuffle." She is not the beauty Dee is, and she has not had the benefit of education. Yet she is very insightful: "Mama, when did Dee ever *have* any friends?" Maggie does not expect anything and is, therefore, astounded ("Maggie just sat there on my bed with her mouth open") when the narrator takes the quilts out of Dee's arms and gives them to Maggie.

22. (Average) *Guidelines for student response:* Most students will probably disagree with Dee's statement, citing examples of Maggie's insight and her knowledge of quilting, which was taught to her by Grandma Dee. Dee does not see the practical value of the quilts—or the churn top and dasher. In other words, Dee is not capable of "appreciating" the real life value of these objects. Maggie does put these objects "to everyday use," which means that they are an intrinsic part of her daily life. Dee, in contrast, sees the objects as heirlooms, objects of her heritage which should be kept from use and preserved in ways foreign to their use: "I can use the churn top as a centerpiece for the alcove table, and I'll think of something artistic to do with the dasher."

23. (Challenging) *Guidelines for student response:* Most students will state that Dee's interest in her heritage seems motivated by her educated name change, which, ironically, through her uninformed knowledge of her own heritage, means she is throwing away a name handed down to her from her Aunt Dicie and Grandma Dee. Furthermore, at the sight of specific objects, such as the butter dish ("That's it! I knew there was something I wanted to ask you if I could have"), Dee is motivated to possess objects that symbolize her heritage—the butter dish, the churn top, the dasher, and Grandma Dee's quilts. In contrast, Maggie lives and works with these objects. To Maggie they are not symbols but real things, made by real people and put to real use. For Dee's professed interest in her heritage, she has removed herself from her family's life, does not know details pertaining to her heritage (her name, who whittled or made what), and does not know the crafts of her heritage. It is Maggie, however, who knows how to quilt, who knows who made what, and who lives a daily life in acceptance of that heritage.

from *The Woman Warrior*
by Maxine Hong Kingston

Selection Test (p. 269)

Critical Reading/Vocabulary and Grammar

1. c 2. a 3. c 4. b 5. c 6. d 7. c 8. b 9. b
10. d 11. a 12. b 13. a 14. b 15. a 16. c
17. d 18. b 19. a 20. b

Questions are classified in these categories:
   Comprehension 3(E), 5(A), 7(A), 9(A)
   Interpretation 2(A), 4(A), 8(E), 11(A), 12(A),
     15(A), 16(C)
   Literary Analysis 1(E), 14(A)
   Reading Strategy 6(C), 10(E), 13(A)
   Vocabulary 17(A), 19(A)
   Grammar 18(A), 20(A)
   E = Easy, A = Average, C = Challenging

Essay Questions

21. (Easy) *Guidelines for student response:*
Students should say that this selection
focuses on the feelings and impressions of
Brave Orchid. Examples include her negative feelings toward the war in Vietnam; her
belief that her children are restless, wasteful, disrespectful, and ashamed of her; and
her feelings toward the immigration experience. From these impressions the reader
learns about Brave Orchid's character—
that she is conservative, put off by aspects
of American culture, and afraid her children
don't respect her values or their culture.

22. (Average) *Guidelines for student response:*
Brave Orchid is a quiet woman who
values the traditions of her culture. Her
character is shaped by her Chinese ances-
try and her immigrant experience. She is
disapproving of many aspects of American
culture, especially those aspects that have
made her children difficult to understand.
Brave Orchid's values are revealed by her
thoughts on the Vietnam war; her determination to wait at the airport for as long
as she does; her belief that she can keep
her sister and her son safe by concentrating on them; and her disapproval of the
fact that her children cannot sit still or
cannot save their money.

23. (Challenging) *Guidelines for student response:* Brave Orchid often feels upset by
the actions of her children because she

feels they do not understand her or respect her values. At the airport, she becomes angry when they cannot sit still or
when she believes they are wasting their
money on foolish items. She feels annoyed
and hurt that her children do not seem to
understand the importance of her sister's
arrival or the importance of sitting still
and anticipating her arrival. She also becomes angry when she thinks the children
will not call their aunt at the airport because of their "American politeness."
These incidents illustrate a conflict faced
by immigrants and their children—the
children wanting to adopt new American
customs, the immigrants feeling that their
culture will be completely forgotten and
disregarded. Brave Orchid is defensive because she anticipates her children are
breaking away from their Chinese roots.

"Antojos" by Julia Alvarez

Selection Test (p. 272)

Critical Reading/Vocabulary and Grammar

1. b 2. a 3. b 4. d 5. b 6. c 7. b 8. d 9. a
10. c 11. b 12. b 13. b 14. b 15. c 16. b
17. c 18. a 19. d 20. b

Questions are classified in these categories:
   Comprehension 1(E), 2(E), 7(E), 12(A)
   Interpretation 4(A), 9(A), 10(C), 13(A), 14(C),
     15(C)
   Literary Analysis 3(A), 5(A)
   Reading Strategy 6(A), 8(A), 11(C)
   Vocabulary 16(A), 18(A), 20(A)
   Grammar 17(A), 19(A)
   E = Easy, A = Average, C = Challenging

Essay Questions

21. (Easy) *Guidelines for student response:*
Students should understand that the
flashback scene plays an important role in
this story. In the scene, Yolanda talks
with her family, telling them that she
wants to go for a drive to get guavas. They
respond by telling her that she should not
drive through the countryside by herself.
This scene gives readers the following information: that Yolanda comes from a
wealthy, sheltered family; that she has
been living in the United States; and that

her family wishes she were home. Also, the family's reaction to the fact that she wants to take a drive through the countryside indicates that the country is experiencing political problems that make parts of it unsafe. This scene also reveals that Yolanda is slightly different from her family, in that she is outgoing and unwilling to give up her independence out of fear.

22. (Average) *Guidelines for student response:* The title "Antojos" relates both to Yolanda's craving for guavas and to her craving to reconnect herself to the country of her birth. The word is first introduced in the story's flashback scene, when Yolanda is having a conversation with her aunts. Happy to have her home after she has been in the United States for many years, her aunts tell Yolanda they want to indulge "any little *antojo*" she might have. She reveals to them that she has been away so long, she no longer remembers what the word means. This shows Yolanda's separation from her country and her language. Yolanda then decides what her *antojo* is—fresh guavas. To find the fruit, she is forced to go on a trip out into the countryside. Once there, she meets people and sees parts of her country that help her to realize her true *antojo*—getting back in touch with her homeland which has been wounded by war.

23. (Challenging) *Guidelines for student response:* Students should understand that Yolanda's experiences in the countryside highlight the sincerity and kindness of strangers and make her feel a deeper connection to her country. At first, she is on a journey to find guavas in an area considered dangerous by her family. Although Yolanda feels her family is overreacting, when her car breaks down and she is alone in the dark country, she feels fear. Jose, a little boy who helps her pick guavas, offers to go for help. As she waits, two men approach, and she is paralyzed by fear and suspicion. She even allows them to believe that she is an American, out of concern that being a native might make her a threat to them. She is surprised to find that they help her out of pure kindness. She feels guilt for having suspected

the worst of them and lying to them. Then she learns that Jose is treated with the same suspicion by the people to whom he goes for help. Yolanda is moved by these experiences, and they help her to grow in the knowlege of her country and its people.

"Freeway 280" by Lorna Dee Cervantes
"Who Burns for the Perfection of Paper" by Martín Espada
"Hunger in New York City" by Simon Ortiz
"Most Satisfied by Snow" by Diana Chang
"What For" by Garrett Hongo

Selection Test (p. 275)

Critical Reading/Vocabulary and Grammar

1. a 2. d 3. c 4. c 5. b 6. c 7. b 8. d 9. a
10. d 11. c 12. b 13. a 14. d 15. c 16. b
17. c 18. a 19. d 20. b

Questions are classified in these categories:
   Comprehension 4(E), 7(E), 13(E)
   Interpretation 2(C), 3(A), 5(A), 6(C), 8(C), 10(A), 15(A)
   Literary Analysis 9(A), 11(E), 14(A)
   Reading Strategy 1(A), 12(C)
   Vocabulary 16(A), 18(A), 19(A)
   Grammar 17(A), 20(A)
   E = Easy, A = Average, C = Challenging

Essay Questions

21. (Easy) *Guidelines for student response:* In "Who Burns for the Perfection of Paper," the speaker describes his high-school job, at which he made legal pads. He describes cutting his hands on paper and feeling the sting of glue in his wounds. His hard and often painful work shaped his character and forever changed the way he viewed work and what one must go through to accomplish a task. Ten years later, as he uses legal pads and lawbooks, he is reminded of his high-school job and what went into every legal pad. In "What For," the speaker describes the years of hard work and sore muscles that filled the life of his father. He admired his father's hard work and dedication, but often wanted to lift his father from the everyday duties of life and help him to enjoy more peace and relaxation. He saw

"Freeway 280" by Lorna Dee Cervantes

"Who Burns for the Perfection of Paper" by Martín Espada

"Hunger in New York City" by Simon Ortiz

"Most Satisfied by Snow" by Diana Chang

"What For" by Garrett Hongo
(continued)

his father's physical labor as admirable but draining to the spirit and wanted to use magic to lift him away from it.

22. (Average) *Guidelines for student response:* In "Freeway 280," the speaker is describing how her neighborhood was replaced by a highway. She thinks about the small houses, gardens, and community spirit that was destroyed, and feels that a part of herself has also been destroyed. She decides that her heritage is an important part of her identity, and she needs to reconnect to it. When she visits the area of her old neighborhood, she finds signs of sprouting vegetation and feels a sense of hope and connection to her former home. In "Hunger in New York," the speaker talks about living in an unfamiliar city, apart from the values of his own people. In order to live peacefully and satisfy his emotional hunger in New York City, the speaker tries to turn to people and the natural world, drawing on traditional beliefs from his own heritage. In "What For," the speaker describes his childhood experiences, which include playing cards and listening to his grandfather's stories, listening to his grandmother's singing as she cooked meals, and witnessing the hard work of his father. These people clearly shaped his life as a writer and his attitudes toward work and family.

23. (Challenging) *Guidelines for student response:* Students might describe some of the following voice qualities in the poems: The voice of "Freeway 280" is contemplative and sad as the poet reveals her attachment to her old neighborhood. The presence of Spanish words shows the speaker's wish to reconnect with her heritage. "Who Burns for the Perfection of Paper" has a straightforward style, and the poet uses many concrete details. The poem is conversational, written almost as a story. "Hunger in New York City" has a tone of

desperation and longing, emphasized by the repetition of the word *hunger*. The poem is also more distant and less conversational than some of the others. "Most Satisfied by Snow" has a spare and abrupt style. The poet conveys her message using simple images of fog and snow and few words, and this makes the work stand apart in style from the other selections. "What For" has a peaceful, nostalgic tone, and it focuses on the activities and feelings of the speaker's youth. The poem illustrates the speaker's respect for his grandparents and his father. Images of music, chanting, and spells give the piece a magical, childlike quality.

Part Test, Unit 6, Part 1: Literature Confronts the Everyday (p. 278)

Critical Reading/Grammar and Style

1. a 2. c 3. a 4. b 5. a 6. a 7. b 8. d 9. b 10. b 11. b 12. d 13. c 14. a 15. d 16. a 17. c 18. d 19. a 20. b

Questions are classified in these categories:
Comprehension 1(E), 4(A)
Interpretation 3(A), 10(C)
Literary Analysis 5(A), 6(A), 7(C), 9(E)
Reading Strategy 2(A), 8(A)
Vocabulary 13(A), 14(E), 15(A), 16(A)
Grammar 11(A), 12(A), 17(A), 18(C), 19(A), 20(E)
E = Easy, A = Average, C = Challenging

Essay Questions

21. (Easy) *Guidelines for student response:* Students' essays should summarize one character's personality and behavioral traits, as well as compare and contrast this character with themselves. For example, students might focus on how their personalities and backgrounds compare and contrast with Joy Harjo's inclination to filter the world through the sense of hearing.

22. (Average) *Guidelines for student response:* Students' essays should accurately and thoroughly describe a selection's atmosphere, as well as explain how it contributes to the total effect of the work. For instance, Robert Penn Warren uses images, meter, and rhyme to create an atmosphere of breathtaking wonder and exuberance about the natural world. This atmosphere

imbues the speaker's recollection of his youth, and it causes him to determine to find this world once again.

23. (Average) *Guidelines for student response:* Students' essays should explicate the motivation for a character's actions. For example, one might suggest that the speaker of William Stafford's poem pushes the dead doe (holding the living unborn fawn) into the canyon because he feels that the fawn's quick death will be better than a slow death by starvation.

24. (Average) *Guidelines for student response:* Students' essays should paraphrase each sentence contained in a poem and then summarize the poem in one final sentence. For example, they might paraphrase "The Adamant" as follows: Ideas cannot be destroyed. No matter what attacks it, the truth can always bear the weight of the assault. The center of the truth is so strong and well-protected that it is invulnerable.

25. (Challenging) *Guidelines for student response:* Students' essays should compare and contrast the styles of two poets. For example, Theodore Roethke's style in "The Light Comes Brighter" is marked by simple, clear language, imagery from the natural world, and regular gentle rhythm and rhyme. In contrast, Robert Lowell's style features free verse, arresting diction, vivid imagery—often involving decay ("aged by yellow drain" and "their fungus of ice") or violence ("blazing roof," "flashes/that char")—and several historical references (to early photography, for instance).

from *The Mortgaged Heart*
by Carson McCullers
"Onomatopoeia" by William Safire
"Coyote v. Acme" by Ian Frazier

Selection Test (p. 282)

Critical Reading/Vocabulary and Grammar
1. b 2. c 3. a 4. c 5. d 6. c 7. b 8. a 9. d 10. c 11. a 12. b 13. b 14. d 15. d 16. c 17. a 18. b 19. d 20. a

Questions are classified in these categories:
   Comprehension 1(E), 7(A), 8(E)
   Interpretation 2(A), 4(C), 6(A), 10(C), 13(C)
   Literary Analysis 5(A), 9(E), 11(C)

Reading Strategy 3(A), 12(A), 14(A)
Vocabulary 15(A), 16(E), 17(E)
Grammar 18(A), 19(C), 20(A)
E = Easy, A = Average, C = Challenging

Essay Questions
21. (Easy) *Guidelines for student response:* Students must correctly identify the main point and provide two or three examples that demonstrate the line of reasoning. For example, students should note that the main point of McCullers's essay is that Americans' sense of loneliness stems from a search for identity. McCullers's line of reasoning is that when all people recognize their separateness from the world, they then search to make connections and find love; however, a peculiar maverick attitude in Americans makes this search difficult and leads to moral isolation.

22. (Average) *Guidelines for student response:* Students must correctly identify the essay as analytical, expository, or satirical and correctly state the writer's main point. As students analyze an essay's effectiveness, they should point to the use of elements specific to that type of essay. For example, students might admire Frazier's satirical essay for its use of humor and irony to criticize the growing numbers of product liability lawsuits. Students might praise Safire's use of the onomatopoeic *zap* in the first sentence of his essay, noting that this use illustrates the essay's topic as well as adds humor.

23. (Challenging) *Guidelines for student response:* Students should note that Wile E. Coyote is a popular icon, one that readers will readily identify. As Frazier details Mr. Coyote's complaints against Acme, the reader recognizes the incidents described and juxtaposes them with the lawsuit's formal language. This absurd juxtaposition is the basis of Frazier's satire. Students should acknowledge that the essay is a critique of persons who deny personal responsibility, preferring to blame their misjudgments or character flaws on others.

"Straw Into Gold" by Sandra Cisneros
"For the Love of Books" by Rita Dove
"Mother Tongue" by Amy Tan

Selection Test (p. 285)

Critical Reading/Vocabulary and Grammar

1. b 2. a 3. d 4. d 5. c 6. b 7. a 8. d 9. c
10. b 11. b 12. c 13. c 14. a 15. d 16. c
17. a 18. d 19. c 20. b

Questions are classified in these categories:
 Comprehension 1(A), 6(E), 11(E)
 Interpretation 4(C), 5(A), 9(A), 10(E),
   12(A), 15(A)
 Literary Analysis 3(A), 8(C), 13(A)
 Reading Strategy 2(C), 7(A), 14(A)
 Vocabulary 16(E), 17(E), 18(A)
 Grammar 19(A), 20(A)
 E = Easy, A = Average, C = Challenging

Essay Questions

21. (Easy) *Guidelines for student response:*
 Students might note that in detailing several instances in which she performs difficult tasks and "turns straw into gold," Cisneros comes to understand that she has overcome many obstacles in her life. This realization helps her understand her writing as well. Students might point out that Dove, in the course of her essay, moves from the question, "What made you want to be a writer?" to the realization that it wasn't just books but an inherent need for expression that sparked her love of books and writing.

22. (Average) *Guidelines for student response:*
 Students must use reasonable evidence to support their opinions. For example, students might believe that Cisneros reveals the most about herself because she details how she overcame obstacles as a child and continues to overcome them as an adult. Rather than simply describing a crucial moment or period in her childhood development, Cisneros demonstrates personal strengths that have defined her personality and helped her meet challenges.

23. (Challenging) *Guidelines for student response:* Students in agreement might cite Tan's interpretation of analogy questions and Cisneros's poor school performance but obvious intellect that was nurtured by her family. Students in disagreement

might point to Dove's consuming interest in reading, which seems largely uninfluenced by her family, and Cisneros's belief that her desire to write came from a "hunger" she felt, even with her family.

Part Test, Unit 6, Part 2: Focus on Literary Forms— Essay (p. 288)

Critical Reading/Vocabulary and Grammar

1. c 2. a 3. d 4. b 5. c 6. a 7. c 8. b 9. d
10. d 11. b 12. c 13. a 14. a 15. d

Questions are classified in these categories:
 Comprehension 1(A), 5(C), 9(A)
 Interpretation 2(E), 6(A), 10(C)
 Literary Analysis 3(E), 7(C)
 Reading Strategy 4(E), 8(A)
 Vocabulary 11(A), 12(C), 13(E)
 Grammar 14(E), 15(A)
 E = Easy, A = Average, C = Challenging

Essay Questions

16. (Easy) *Guidelines for student response:*
 Students' essays should deal with a single, well-focused subject. In their essays, students should express their own ideas, experiences, and reactions to their chosen topic. For example, Rita Dove uses recollections from her childhood—involving many sensory details, as well as anecdotes—in an involving discussion of her early attraction to the written word.

17. (Average) *Guidelines for student response:*
 Students' essays should clearly and fairly evaluate the idea of an essayist in this part of Unit 6. For instance, they might explain why they agree with Carson McCullers's idea that "loneliness is the great American malady." In support of this judgment, they might note Americans' tendency to move from place to place, to live some distance from their extended families, and similar characteristics.

18. (Challenging) *Guidelines for student response:* Students' essays should analyze the literary techniques of a single essayist. First, they should identify the kind of essay it is (reflective, analytical, expository, or satirical). Then they should identify the essay's main purpose and the techniques the author uses to achieve it. For example, Ian Frazier creates humor by using exact,

dry, legal language to describe outrageous actions derived from a celebrated cartoon. His masterful use of point-of-view—a first-person monologue by a defense lawyer—is the foundation for the essay. At once, he uses techniques of persuasion (to accurately portray the attorney's words and thinking) and imaginative literature.

"The Rockpile" by James Baldwin

Selection Test (p. 291)

Critical Reading/Vocabulary and Grammar

1. b 2. c 3. b 4. b 5. d 6. a 7. a 8. c 9. d
10. b 11. d 12. c 13. c 14. a 15. a 16. d
17. b 18. c 19. d 20. a

Questions are classified in these categories:
Comprehension 1(A), 8(A), 11(E)
Interpretation 2(E), 7(A), 9(E), 13(C), 14(A)
Literary Analysis 3(C), 4(A), 10(C)
Reading Strategy 5(A), 6(E), 12(A)
Vocabulary 15(A), 16(A), 17(C)
Grammar 18(A), 19(E), 20(A)
E = Easy, A = Average, C = Challenging

Essay Questions

21. (Easy) *Guidelines for student response:* Students should clearly identify a cause and effect relationship, such as the series of events that begins with Roy disobeying his mother and ends with his injury, the effects of Gabriel's favoring Roy, or the causes of Elizabeth's protectiveness of John. Students should draw logical conclusions about cause and effect. For instance, students might conclude that Elizabeth is protective of John because he is her first child, she feels guilty about her former "days in sin," or she identifies with John because Gabriel shuns her as he does John.

22. (Average) *Guidelines for student response:* Students might suggest that the rockpile, a real physical threat in the neighborhood, symbolizes the evil and danger lurking in the characters' home. For instance, the rockpile symbolizes the danger that Gabriel poses to his family. Elizabeth tries to protect John from Gabriel's anger and blame; as he does with the rockpile, John avoids contact with a possible danger. On the other hand, Roy ignores his mother's warnings; he believes that no real harm

can come to him, either from the rockpile or from Gabriel.

23. (Challenging) *Guidelines for student response:* Students should conclude that the dramatic tension in "The Rockpile" arises more from conflict among humans than between humans and nature. Students might explain that while the rockpile is a physical and natural threat, it serves only as a catalyst for the story's true tension—family conflict. For example, dramatic tension heightens as Elizabeth and John worry how Gabriel will react to Roy's injury. Tension increases as Gabriel's prejudice against John is revealed and Elizabeth confronts Gabriel.

from *Hiroshima* by John Hersey
"Losses" and "The Death of the Ball Turret Gunner" by Randall Jarrell

Selection Test (p. 294)

Critical Reading/Vocabulary and Grammar

1. b 2. d 3. b 4. c 5. b 6. b 7. b 8. b 9. d
10. b 11. c 12. a 13. c 14. b 15. c 16. d
17. c 18. a 19. d 20. b

Questions are classified in these categories:
Comprehension 1(A), 2(E), 6(E), 12(E)
Interpretation 3(A), 8(A), 10(A), 11(A), 13(A)
Literary Analysis 5(A), 7(C), 15(A)
Reading Strategy 4(C), 9(A), 14(C)
Vocabulary 16(A), 18(A), 20(A)
Grammar 17(A), 19(A)
E = Easy, A = Average, C = Challenging

Essay Questions

21. (Easy) *Guidelines for student response:* Students should understand that both poems reveal the inhumanity that the poet associates with war. Both lines present images of death being treated quite casually and indifferently, and soldiers being treated as if they were machines rather than human beings. Both lines express the theme that war encourages cold and cruel behavior.

22. (Average) *Guidelines for student response:* Students should understand that John Hersey has a negative attitude toward war and the bombing of Hiroshima. His images of people living in constant fear—waiting

from *Hiroshima* by John Hersey

"Losses" and **"The Death of the Ball Turret Gunner"** by Randall Jarrell
(continued)

for some kind of attack—and his images of the destruction caused by the bomb and its impact on survivors reveal this attitude. He includes detailed descriptions because often, during times of war, humanity is pushed aside. He wants readers to see that people killed by the dropping of the bomb were not just casualties of war, but they were living, breathing people with families, fears, and personalities.

23. (Challenging) *Guidelines for student response:* Students should say that *Hiroshima* focuses on the effects of war on civilians. Hersey tries to emphasize the tragedy of the bombing, which killed many innocent people. His piece is critical of the war and the ways in which the lives of everyday people were affected. In "Losses," young soldiers talk about the activities of war and about death. The soldiers describe how they must burn cities, kill, and regularly put their own lives in jeopardy. "The Death of the Ball Turret Gunner" focuses on the experience of a lonely gunner who is experiencing his last moments of life aboard his plane. The last line of the poem, in which the gunner's body is being washed out of the turret, is particularly effective in expressing Jarrell's negative attitude toward the cruelty and violence of war. Both poems end with similar lines, which comment on how people become indifferent to death. All three pieces are critical of the attitudes and behaviors associated with war.

"Mirror" by Sylvia Plath
"In a Classroom" by Adrienne Rich
"The Explorer" by Gwendolyn Brooks
"Frederick Douglass" and
"Runagate Runagate"
by Robert Hayden

Selection Test (p. 297)

Critical Reading/Vocabulary and Grammar

1. b 2. a 3. d 4. d 5. c 6. a 7. b 8. d 9. c

10. b 11. b 12. a 13. c 14. b 15. a 16. d
17. a 18. c 19. b 20. d

Questions are classified in these categories:
Comprehension 1(E), 5(E), 11(A), 15(E)
Interpretation 2(A), 3(A), 4(C), 6(A), 8(E), 12(A), 14(A)
Literary Analysis 10(A), 13(C), 16(C)
Reading Strategy 7(A), 9(C)
Vocabulary 17(A), 19(A)
Grammar 18(A), 20(A)
E = Easy, A = Average, C = Challenging

Essay Questions

21. (Easy) *Guidelines for student response:* Students should understand that both poems deal with themes related to African American slavery. "Frederick Douglass" focuses on the beliefs of abolitionist and former slave Frederick Douglass. "Runagate Runagate" deals with the experiences of slaves traveling the Underground Railroad to freedom. The poem "Frederick Douglass" reveals that Douglass wrote and spoke of freedom and liberty for all. The poem enhances factual accounts of the abolitionist movement because it shows how Douglass's work and teachings affect one individual, the speaker of the poem, who is living many years later. The poem illustrates the ways in which Douglass's message is still relevant and necessary in a modern world. In "Runagate Runagate," a reader's knowledge of slavery and the Underground Railroad is enhanced by detailed images of the struggles faced by slaves trying to escape. The poem also illustrates the risks people were willing to take to escape the brutality and indignity of slavery. The poems' themes are similar in that they both stress the importance of freedom and liberty.

22. (Average) *Guidelines for student response:* Students should understand that this passage reveals the frustration and struggle felt by the speaker, who is searching for a quiet place and some type of inner peace. The subject is unhappy with his surroundings, which are noisy and without hope. Words and phrases such as "frayed inner want," "frayed hope," "tatters," and "din" reveal

the depth of his unhappiness, frustration, and desire. Words and phrases such as "satin peace" and "wily hush" reveal what that speaker wants, in contrast to what he has. This passage relates to the poem's central message—that the speaker will most likely not be able to leave his surroundings to find the peace he craves because the prospect of choice is frightening.

23. (Challenging) *Guidelines for student response:* Students should say that the woman described in the poem "Mirror" faces a struggle both within herself and between herself and traditional, limited standards of beauty and worth. She looks in the mirror, which is supposed to be a truthful reflection of reality, and is continually unhappy with what she sees. She sees the drowning of her young face and the appearance of old age. This struggle reflects her fears of growing older and losing the young, beautiful woman inside herself. The mirror also reflects the struggle she faces in dealing with her own limited view of herself and the world. In the poem "In a Classroom," the speaker struggles with the question Why, which is what drives her to read poetry and examine her life. Other people are concerned with surface questions, while she and her subject Jude strive for deeper meaning. In the poem "The Explorer," the speaker struggles with loud and hopeless surroundings that keep him from finding the inner peace and quiet he craves. The speaker also reveals an internal struggle—his fear of facing choices. The poems "Frederick Douglass" and "Runagate Runagate" both deal with struggles for freedom. The speaker in "Frederick Douglass" wonders when freedom and liberty for all will be a natural part of life. He reflects on the struggles Douglass faced as an abolitionist and on the struggles for equality that continue in his own world. "Runagate Runagate" focuses on the Underground Railroad and the risks people were willing to take to find freedom.

"For My Children" by Colleen McElroy
"Bidwell Ghost" by Louise Erdrich

Selection Test (p. 300)

Critical Reading/Vocabulary and Grammar

1. a 2. c 3. b 4. d 5. d 6. b 7. c 8. a 9. c
10. d 11. d 12. b 13. a 14. c 15. b 16. d
17. c 18. a 19. c 20. c

Questions are classified in these categories:
  Comprehension 1(A), 7(E), 9(E)
  Interpretation 2(C), 6(A), 8(A), 11(C), 14(C)
  Literary Analysis 3(A), 4(C), 10(C)
  Reading Strategy 5(E), 12(A), 13(A)
  Vocabulary 15(E), 16(A), 17(A)
  Grammar 18(A), 19(C), 20(E)
  E = Easy, A = Average, C = Challenging

Essay Questions

21. (Easy) *Guidelines for student response:* Students should recognize that "the link between the Mississippi and the Congo" represents the connection between the cultural heritage of the speaker's past and present. In her memories of ancestors' stories, the speaker expresses her deep appreciation of the struggles her ancestors have endured throughout history. In her recognition of those physical characteristics that she and her children have inherited, the speaker expresses joy and celebration.

22. (Average) *Guidelines for student response:* Students should describe a lyric poem as musical or melodic verse that conveys the observations, thoughts, and feelings of a single speaker. Students should also note that a lyric poem produces a single, unified effect, such as the vital, life-affirming effect of "For My Children" and the sorrowful effect of "Bidwell Ghost." In "For My Children," the single speaker tells of her search for her heritage. In "Bidwell Ghost," the single speaker shares her observations of a ghost who revisits the scene of a tragedy. The opening lines of "For My Children" are highly musical, creating rhythm through repetition: "I have stored up tales for you, my children/My favorite children, my only children." The three-lined stanzas of "Bidwell Ghost" create a slow, quiet rhythm, befitting and enhancing its sorrowful effect.

"For My Children" by Colleen McElroy
"Bidwell Ghost" by Louise Erdrich
(continued)

23. (Challenging) *Guidelines for student response:* Students should recognize that each poem focuses on individuals and events central to each speaker's sense of heritage. For the speaker in "For My Children," those individuals and events embrace the diverse cultural heritage of the Watusi, Bantu, Ashanti, Seminole, and so on. For the speaker in "Bidwell Ghost," her sense of heritage is haunted, so to speak, by a tragic event, which is vividly realized through the character of the Bidwell ghost, who reaches out to the living speaker.

"The Writer in the Family"
by E. L. Doctorow

Selection Test (p. 303)

Critical Reading/Vocabulary and Grammar
1. b 2. d 3. c 4. a 5. d 6. b 7. c 8. d 9. d
10. b 11. c 12. a 13. b 14. b 15. c 16. a
17. c 18. b 19. c 20. d

Questions are classified in these categories:
Comprehension 1(E), 2(E), 3(A)
Interpretation 4(A), 7(C), 8(E), 13(A), 14(C)
Literary Analysis 6(A), 9(A), 10(C)
Reading Strategy 5(C), 11(E), 12(A)
Vocabulary 16(E), 17(A)
Grammar 15(E), 18(C), 19(A), 20(A)
E = Easy, A = Average, C = Challenging

Essay Questions
21. (Easy) *Guidelines for student response:* Students should note that Jonathan's final letter is an expression of personal protest for himself as well as for his dead father, who cannot defend himself against Aunt Frances's plan. Students might note that in belatedly stating the truth, "I am dying," Jonathan grants his father's life respect. By stating "I am simply dying of the wrong life," Jonathan acknowledges his father's unfulfilled dreams.

22. (Average) *Guidelines for student response:* Students should recognize that Jonathan is a dynamic character because he is changed by the events of the story. Most

specifically, Jonathan's feelings toward his father change. Furthermore, as Jonathan takes a more understanding and empathetic view of his father, Jonathan's maturity and depth of feeling can be seen. Students should recognize that it is not the death of his father that affects Jonathan so much as his later discovery/recognition of his father's youthful dreams and aspirations. The photo of handsome, young Jack standing with his shipmates sparks this recognition, which deepens when Jonathan connects this image of his father with the set of Great Sea Novels.

23. (Challenging) *Guidelines for student response:* Students may characterize Aunt Frances's words and actions in a number of ways: manipulative, haughty, arrogant, unfeeling, and so on. Students should also recognize that her point of view, therefore, is closed, not open to any family reconciliation. Furthermore, Aunt Frances's stinging words about Ruth have very little support in the story. The family's tight economic circumstances refute Aunt Frances's claim that Ruth thought only of "keeping up with the Joneses." Students must recognize that Jonathan has the more accurate understanding of Ruth. Not only does he see the complexities of the family situation, and Ruth's place in it, but he sees his mother without sentiment, noting that "she wasn't as pretty" as Aunt Frances. Jonathan's clear eye makes him the more accurate observer.

"Camouflaging the Chimera"
by Yusef Komunyakaa
"Ambush" by Tim O'Brien

Selection Test (p. 306)

Critical Reading/Vocabulary and Grammar
1. a 2. a 3. c 4. a 5. b 6. d 7. b 8. a 9. a
10. b 11. c 12. d 13. b 14. a 15 .c 16. d
17. c 18. c 19. d 20. b

Questions are classified in these categories:
Comprehension 1(E), 5(E), 8(E), 12(E)
Interpretation 3(A), 6(C), 10(A), 13(C), 14(A), 15(C)
Literary Analysis 2(A), 7(A), 9(A)
Reading Strategy 4(A), 11(A)

Vocabulary 16(A), 18(A), 20(A)
Grammar 17(A), 19(A)
E = Easy, A = Average, C = Challenging

Essay Questions

21. (Easy) *Guidelines for student response:*
For "Camouflaging the Chimera," students might describe soldiers painting their faces with mud, tieing branches to their helmets, and stuffing their coats with grass; soldiers hiding near bamboo; and soldiers waiting and observing the sunset and enemy soldiers from their positions near the bamboo. These images help readers envision soldiers anxiously preparing for an attack. They show the intensity of the situations in which soldiers find themselves. For "Ambush," students might mention the approach of the enemy soldier through the fog, the narrator's tossing of the grenade, and the descriptions of his victim just before and during his death. These images help the reader envision the frightening situation which prompts the soldier to toss the grenade, and then the horror of watching a man die. Envisioning these incidents helps the reader understand the plight of the frightened soldier who must accept killing as part of his job.

22. (Average) *Guidelines for student response:*
Students should understand that the narrator is devastated by the killing because he views his victim as a human being with value. The soldier who describes the death as "a good kill" sees the victim only as "the enemy" who must be destroyed. This soldier fails to understand the narrator's perception of the victim and even reprimands him for his reaction. This piece conveys the idea that in order to fight a war aggressively and effectively, one cannot identify with the enemy.

23. (Challenging) *Guidelines for student response:* Students should understand that both writers describe being on an ambush in a hot, unfamiliar jungle. In both selections, the reader gets a sense of the intensity of the soldiers' experiences. In "Camouflaging the Chimera," the poet describes an ambush, using the pronoun *we.* The soldiers are in camouflage, hiding in trees, waiting to attack. From their positions,

they are able to see the sunset and VC soldiers at a distance, struggling up a hillside. In "Ambush," the speaker describes a similar experience in that he, too, is keeping guard, watching out for any potential threats. Rather than view his enemy only from a distance, however, the speaker encounters a VC soldier at close range. He throws a hand grenade in a moment of panic but is overcome with regret after watching the man die. Seeing his enemy alone, at close range, gives him the chance to notice the man's humanity. Both pieces reveal the tension, terrors, and life and death situations that soldiers involved in war face.

The Crucible, Act I, by Arthur Miller

Selection Test (p. 309)

Critical Reading/Vocabulary and Grammar
1. c 2. a 3. c 4. b 5. d 6. a 7. d 8. a 9. c 10. b 11. b 12. c 13. a 14. b 15. d 16. c 17. d 18. b 19. c 20. b

Questions are classified in these categories:
Comprehension 1(E), 7(A), 14(C)
Interpretation 4(A), 5(E), 9(C), 10(A), 11(A), 12(E)
Literary Analysis 6(A), 15(C)
Reading Strategy 2(A), 3(C), 8(A), 13(A)
Vocabulary 16(E), 17(A), 18(C)
Grammar 19(E), 20(A)
E = Easy, A = Average, C = Challenging

Essay Questions

21. (Easy) *Guidelines for student response:*
Students should note that Miller indicates that there wasn't much good about Parris. He was formerly a merchant and apparently used to material wealth. He complains about his salary in an argument with Proctor and Putnam. He is apparently a devout minister who believes he is persecuted wherever he goes. This idea of persecution is obvious in discussions with both Abigail and Putnam. Parris worries that Betty's condition and the activities of the girls in the woods will be the undoing of him and will cause him to lose his post, his status, and so on. The confirmation of witchcraft, he tells Putnam, will "topple"

The Crucible, Act I, by Arthur Miller
(continued)

him in the community. He is a widower who has no interest in or "talent with" children. This leads to Parris's inability to understand that the girls might have been up to utterly harmless mischief just because that's what children do.

22. (Average) *Guidelines for student response:* Students should recognize that the first information about the woods comes in a conversation between Parris and Abigail. Parris discovered the girls "dancing like heathen in the forest." Abigail maintains they only danced. Parris speaks of witchcraft and conjuring; Abigail denies such charges. Then Parris says he saw Tituba waving her arms over a fire and screeching and that he saw someone naked. Later, Mrs. Putnam admits to having sent her Ruth to Tituba to conjure the spirits of her dead babies. Abigail offers that just Tituba and Ruth were conjuring. A conversation between Abigail, Mercy, and Mary reveals that Mercy was, indeed, naked. Finally, in the course of Mr. Hale's "inquisition," Abigail admits that Tituba called the Devil, then that Tituba made them drink chicken blood. Then Tituba says that Abigail begged her to conjure. Tituba, under pressure, begins naming names. Abigail joins in, and finally Betty rises up and joins in as well. Miller's development of these details through dialogue, rather than through background information, allows meting it out a little at a time. This builds suspense in such a way that readers as well as characters are led to the crying out at the end of the act.

23. (Challenging) *Guidelines for student response:* Students should acknowledge that the Salemites are described as parochial, snobby, hard-working, devout, strict, and interested in one another's business. The community is wedged between the sea and the forest, and the residents have to work hard just to survive, much less to thrive. Their success as a settlement is credited to working together and establishing a junta to govern the settlement. They believe in a strict, forbidding God who allows few pleasures in life. Virtue comes through hard work and prayer. Hard judgments were made against neighbors who did not attend meeting or who frittered away their time at idle pursuits. Neighbors frequently brought suits against another, which were settled by decision of a governing body. The play mentions one such instance between Proctor and Giles Corey. Miller suggests that the very hard-working, repressive nature of the Salemites' lives lent itself to the crying out. In such a society, there is little if any room for individuality. So how could individuals survive but by accusing others of being individuals? Miller's background information is nearly invaluable to a reader of the play in terms of adding meaning to the relationships among characters, to characters' actions and attitudes, and to the situation as a whole. Without the background information, many of the characters' motives, in particular, would not be apparent.

The Crucible, Act II, by Arthur Miller

Selection Test (p. 312)

Critical Reading/Vocabulary and Grammar

1. c 2. c 3. a 4. b 5. d 6. c 7. b 8. a 9. b
10. c 11. a 12. d 13. d 14. d 15. b 16. a
17. c 18. d 19. a 20. b

Questions are classified in these categories:
   Comprehension 2(C), 6(E), 10(A), 15(A)
   Interpretation 3(E), 4(A), 5(A), 11(C), 14(A)
   Literary Analysis 7(A), 12(C), 13(A)
   Reading Strategy 1(E), 8(A), 9(A)
   Vocabulary 16(E), 17(A), 18(C)
   Grammar 19(E), 20(E)
   E = Easy, A = Average, C = Challenging

Essay Questions

21. (Easy) *Guidelines for student response:* Responses should indicate that students understand these things about Abigail's effect on Act II: Her relationship with John Proctor has alienated Proctor from Elizabeth; his guilt over the relationship silences him about Abigail's character until too late; and she is sufficiently daring to attempt an overt move (the poppet plot) against Elizabeth. Although Abigail does not appear in Act II, her effects dominate it. The initial alienation between John and Elizabeth, which Miller dramatizes both in direction and dialogue, is a result of the relationship

between Abigail and John, which she still desires and with which he still struggles. Abigail has begun in Act II to lead the testifiers and has won awe for her performance, for "the crowd will part like the sea for Israel." She seizes on the doll to fabricate a false sorcery, and it is from guilt over his affair with her that John is reluctant to tell all he knows of her character. Although Mary finally admits she put the needle in, Abby has faked her own stabbing with a needle, and Hale has been sufficiently impressed with her performance to believe that claims against Abigail must be the result of witchcraft as well.

22. (Average) *Guidelines for student response:* Responses should indicate that students recognize that in the climate of fear, even so trivial a thing as a doll is seized upon as evidence of witchcraft. Mary has made the doll and given it to Elizabeth. Abigail, seeing the needle in the doll, fakes an attack of pain and somehow produces a needle. When Cheever discovers the needle in the doll, he takes it as a form of witchcraft perpetrated against Abigail by Elizabeth. Mary, though, is forced to admit that she made the doll, gave it to Elizabeth, and put the needle in. Rather than dismissing it all then, Hale, because he believes that there must be a fire to go with so much smoke, reasons backward to conclude that the witchcraft is not the doll itself, but in someone's compelling Mary to make the doll, store the needle, and blame no one. Hale, the most educated man in the play, employs a false theological analysis to justify a conclusion already made, all hinging on a ludicrous homemade doll and the transparent plot of a jealous lover.

23. (Challenging) *Guidelines for student response:* Mary Warren is a weak person, striving for status, easily used by people more clever than she. Mary wants to seem important, and when she has a chance to do so by joining in with the accusers, her imagination takes flight. She makes up an account about Sarah Good's mumbling. She enjoys being an "official of the court," using it to rise above her status as a servant. She defends her actions to the Proctors, "striving for her authority," but

when pressured, she collapses. Abigail easily uses her in her plot with the poppet. She is probably the most passive character in the play, and Hale's misinterpretation of her leads to disaster for the Proctors. Thus Miller illustrates that when fear and unreason substitute for logic, no amount of sanity may prevent horrible events from following.

The Crucible, Act III, by Arthur Miller

Selection Test (p. 315)

Critical Reading/Vocabulary and Grammar
1. c 2. a 3. b 4. c 5. d 6. d 7. a 8. c 9. b 10. b 11. d 12. a 13. b 14. a 15. a 16. c 17. d 18. c 19. c 20. b

Questions are classified in these categories:
Comprehension 5(A), 11(A), 13(A)
Interpretation 1(A), 2(A), 4(E), 6(C), 8(C), 9(C), 10(E), 14(C)
Literary Analysis 3(A), 7(A), 12(A)
Reading Strategy 15(E), 16(A)
Vocabulary 17(E), 18(C)
Grammar 19(E), 20(A)
E = Easy, A = Average, C = Challenging

Essay Questions
21. (Easy) *Guidelines for student response:* Students may choose any number of examples from Act III. Their explanations should focus on how the statement or situation represents something contrary to readers' expectations or knowledge. Here are a few examples from Act III: (1) Elizabeth Proctor's lie is ironic because her husband has sworn that she does not lie. Further, she thinks she is *saving* her husband with the lie, when she ends up condemning him by it. (2) Abigail reaches out to comfort the hysterical Mary "out of her infinite charity," say the stage directions. This is ironic because Abigail, in her condemnation of dozens of neighbors, is anything but charitable. (3) Early in the act, Herrick and the judges threaten Francis Nurse, Giles Corey, and John Proctor that they will be condemned for lying in the court. This is ironic because they are the only ones who *are* telling the truth. Abigail and the girls are lying and are certainly not being condemned for it.

The Crucible, Act III, by Arthur Miller
(continued)

22. (Average) *Guidelines for student response:* Students should be able to cite at least several incidents when Hale speaks up for Giles Corey, Francis Nurse, John Proctor, and Mary Warren as reasonable, reliable people. Hale feels strongly that the accused deserve to be defended, and that such defense is *not* an attack on the court, as Parris asserts. At the same time, he counsels the husbands to be calm and to follow the rules of the court, and not to be overwrought. Hale even challenges Danforth on at least one occasion, suggesting that he *must* hear or accept evidence, even if it is contrary to the direction in which the proceedings are going. Students may cite Hale's "differences" as follows: He is not a resident of Salem; he does not have any family members involved in the trial; he does not have a long history of acquaintance with the Salemites; he approaches the whole situation from an intellectual viewpoint and, some might say, a more objective one than the Salemites'. Students should recall that in Act I, Hale is eager to provide his services, confident that if there is evidence of the Devil's work, it will be tangible and he will find it. In Act II, Hale arrives at the Proctor home to let them know that Elizabeth has been "mentioned" in court. He quizzes the Proctors some on their beliefs, trying to find out for himself whether there is any cause for suspicion. Though Hale still believes that the Devil exists as an active force in the world, his opinion of the situation in Salem alters during Act III. He sees the girls for the frauds they are, he sees the vindictive nature of the accusations, and he denounces the court. This is in keeping with his intellectual approach to the subject, which would require hard evidence for proof. He recognizes that there is no hard evidence for anything that has been charged.

23. (Challenging) *Guidelines for student response:* Students should acknowledge that Danforth appears at the surface to be fair-minded and certainly that he adheres to general rules of the court. At the same time, he is powerful and he knows it. He has a high profile; his importance has brought him all the way from Boston. He understands that people all over the colonies are hearing or will hear of the proceedings in Salem and his role in them. Students should note that when presented with evidence that is contradictory to the general direction of the accusations, he accepts the evidence with reluctance. The "calculating" stage direction implies that he is quickly figuring the possible consequences of Mary's confession *and how those consequences reflect on him.* Similarly, when Danforth accepts Mary's deposition, he has misgivings because the whole situation could land on his shoulders. Evidence of Danforth's thoughts comes mostly from stage directions. He is variously described as "astonished," "horrified," and "dumbfounded" as new bits of information come to light. Students should be able to conclude that if Danforth accepts Mary's deposition and if Abigail and the girls are exposed as frauds, Danforth will have been responsible for putting to death dozens of innocent people. It is vital to Danforth's reputation as well as to his own peace of mind to continue to believe that Heaven *is* speaking through Abigail and the girls and that the community is being purged of its evil elements.

The Crucible, Act IV, by Arthur Miller

Selection Test (p. 318)

Critical Reading/Vocabulary and Grammar

1. b 2. c 3. c 4. d 5. a 6. b 7. c 8. a 9. a
10. d 11. a 12. d 13. b 14. b 15. d 16. d
17. b 18. c 19. a 20. c

Questions are classified in these categories:
  Comprehension 1(E), 8(E), 10(A), 14(A)
  Interpretation 2(A), 3(C), 5(A), 6(C), 9(E)
  Literary Analysis 7(A), 11(C), 13(A)
  Reading Strategy 4(E), 12(A), 15 (C)
  Vocabulary 16(E), 17(A), 18(C)
  Grammar 19(E), 20(A)
  E = Easy, A = Average, C = Challenging

Essay Questions

21. (Easy) *Guidelines for student response:* Student responses should indicate that they understand Abigail's action in run-

ning away as consistent with her character. She is introduced as capable of "endless dissembling" from the very beginning. She takes revenge on Proctor, whom she claims to love, and makes up lies that are fatal to Sarah, Tituba, and others. No strength of character is revealed here, so it is not surprising that she would steal. Additionally, her plans to win Proctor have gone awry. Finally shaken, Parris would reject her, and more and more people would eventually find out she lied. Her prospects for a future in Salem are not good, and it is reasonable she would take the easy way out. She will escape responsibility for her actions, while others will die, heightening the tragedy.

22. (Average) *Guidelines for student response:* Student essays should reflect an understanding that the trials reveal the true nature of the various characters. Parris's weakness and smallness are exposed. Abigail steals from her uncle and runs away. Hale abandons his intellectual vanity, and his fundamental decency appears. Elizabeth learns to forgive. Giles Corey never gives in. Danforth's leadership is mere bureaucratic cowardice. Proctor's essential core remains unchanged, but he dies for his honesty. The heat of the experience reduces the complicated trappings of personality and circumstance to an essential test of character: The Proctors and Reverend Hale, though their lives are destroyed, are genuine. Danforth, Parris, Abigail, and others are essentially cowards. Other lives melt away.

23. (Challenging) *Guidelines for student response:* The central reason that Salem is an ideal setting for Miller's explorations in *The Crucible* is that it is an American setting. Miller's themes about justice, law, the role of religion in society, individual rights, and due process are fundamental issues in American life and history. The play begins in familiar territory, for we all know the story of the Pilgrims, but goes beyond to explore the conflict between prevailing belief and civil liberties. The founding idea of the American nation is civil liberty, and the idea of freedom is part of the progression

of colonial history. Miller also shows that America has not been free of some of the things it tries to escape, both in that time and this, and although the setting of the play predates the founding of the United States, the parallels point out that we have not fully succeeded in establishing the rule of reason and the protection of the individual.

Part Test, Unit 6, Part 3: The Emerging American Identity— Social Protest (p. 321)

Critical Reading/Vocabulary and Grammar

1. c 2. a 3. b 4. a 5. b 6. c 7. d 8. d 9. c
10. d 11. b 12. b 13. c 14. d 15. b 16. a
17. b 18. a 19. c 20. b

Questions are classified in these categories:
Comprehension 1(A), 7(C)
Interpretation 2(E), 8(A)
Literary Analysis 3(C), 6(E), 9(A)
Reading Strategy 4(C), 5(C), 10(E)
Vocabulary 11(A), 12(A), 13(C), 14(E), 15(A)
Grammar 16(E), 17(A), 18(C), 19(A), 20(A)
E = Easy, A = Average, C = Challenging

Essay Questions

21. (Easy) *Guidelines for student response:* Students' essays should contain explanations of how they judge the actions of some character, as well as clear explanations of the criteria they used to evaluate these actions. For instance, one might assert that the narrator of "Ambush" was justified in throwing the grenade that caused the death of an unknown young man in Vietnam; at the same time, one might feel that he was not justified in lying to his daughter when she asked if he had ever killed anyone. The criteria for these judgments might be based on some kind of understanding about the "rules" of war—and on personal experiences involving the importance of telling the truth about one's actions.

22. (Average) *Guidelines for student response:* Students' essays should contain clear, thorough explanations of how setting shapes one or more characters in a literary work. For example, in John Hersey's work, all of the characters (and all of the other individuals living in Hiroshima in August 1945) have their lives profoundly, directly,

and violently shaped by the destruction of their city. The setting (i.e., the fact that they were present when and where the bomb exploded) caused them injury, disease, or the loss of loved ones, acquaintances, and property.

23. (Average) *Guidelines for student response:* Students' essays should clearly and concisely analyze a lyric poem and explain its appeal. For instance, Louise Erdrich employs personification ("orchard bowed low"), highly charged imagery involving fire and other aspects of the natural world, and second-person pronouns that draw the reader in (in stanzas 4 and 5) as she tells about the haunted, vivid behavior of a woman who perished twenty years ago—and yet seems to remain nearby.

24. (Average) *Guidelines for student response:* Students' essays should provide clear and thoughtful analyses of two works, using each work to help understand the other. For example, "Mirror" is a passionate, personal poem featuring a mirror as a first-person narrator. The work—which contains a cool, dispassionate tone and vivid imagery—sheds much light on the vanity and vulnerability of human beings in the face of aging and death. "Frederick Douglass" also features a first-person narrator, yet this poem concerns the enduring political influence of a man. Hayden uses repetitions and other rhythmic devices to develop an oratorical momentum. Both poems concern universal themes of an individual's "image," yet whereas Plath's work is personal, Hayden's is political.

25. (Challenging) *Guidelines for student response:* Students' essays should clearly identify one author's message of social protest and explain the reasons for its effectiveness. For example, toward the goal of registering a protest against war, Tim O'Brien uses an unflinchingly frank, uncannily perceptive first-person narrator to report—rather dryly—on some of the disturbing actions that occurred on battlefields in Vietnam.